# Strategies for Reading Assessment and Instruction

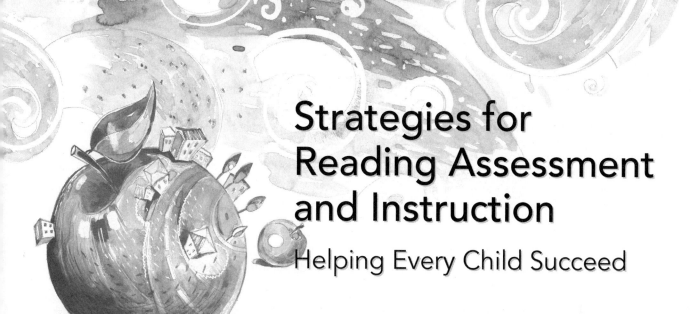

# Strategies for Reading Assessment and Instruction

## Helping Every Child Succeed

**FOURTH EDITION**

D. Ray Reutzel
*Utah State University*

Robert B. Cooter, Jr.
*Bellarmine University*

Boston   Columbus   Indianapolis   New York   San Francisco   Upper Saddle River
Amsterdam   Cape Town   Dubai   London   Madrid   Milan   Munich   Paris   Montreal   Toronto
Delhi   Mexico City   Sao Paulo   Sydney   Hong Kong   Seoul   Singapore   Taipei   Tokyo

*Editor-in-Chief:* Aurora Martínez Ramos
*Series Editorial Assistant:* Meagan French
*Vice President, Director of Marketing:* Quinn Perkson
*Executive Marketing Manager:* Krista Clark
*Production Editor:* Janet Domingo
*Editorial Production Service:* Omegatype Typography, Inc.
*Composition Buyer:* Linda Cox
*Manufacturing Buyer:* Megan Cochran
*Electronic Composition:* Omegatype Typography, Inc.
*Interior Design:* Omegatype Typography, Inc.
*Cover Designer:* Linda Knowles

Credits and acknowledgments borrowed from other sources and reproduced, with permission, in this textbook appear on appropriate page within text.

**Library of Congress Cataloging-in-Publication Data**

Reutzel, D. Ray (Douglas Ray)
  Strategies for reading assessment and instruction : helping every child succeed / D. Ray Reutzel, Robert B. Cooter, Jr.—4th ed.
        p. cm.
  Includes bibliographical references and index.
  ISBN-13: 978-0-13-704838-0 (pbk.)
  ISBN-10: 0-13-704838-6 (pbk.)
 1. Reading.  2. Reading—Remedial teaching.  3. Child development.
I. Cooter, Robert B.  II. Title.
  LB1050.R477  2011
  372.43—dc22

                                              2009041360

Printed in the United States of America

10  9  8  7  6  5  4  3  2     HAM     13  12  11  10

www.pearsonhighered.com

ISBN-10:  0-13-704838-6
ISBN-13:  978-0-13-704838-0

*For the many teachers, reading coaches, young children, and professional colleagues who have given me far more than I have given them.*

*—DRR*

*For Linda Bishop. Master editor, steadfast friend, amicus humani generis.*

*—RBC*

# ABOUT THE AUTHORS

**D. Ray Reutzel** is the Emma Eccles Jones Distinguished Professor and Endowed Chair of Early Childhood Education at Utah State University. Ray is a former provost and vice president for academic affairs at Southern Utah University, associate dean of teacher education in the David O. McKay School of Education, and former chair of the Department of Elementary Education at Brigham Young University. Several years ago, he took a leave from his university faculty position to return to full-time, first-grade classroom teaching in Sage Creek Elementary School. Ray has taught in kindergarten, first grade, third grade, and sixth grade.

Ray served as vice president and president of the College Reading Association from 2005 to 2007. He served as a member of the board of directors of the International Reading Association from 2007 to 2010. He has also served as technical assistant to the Reading Excellence Act and the Reading First federal reading reform projects in the state of Utah.

Dr. Reutzel is the author of more than 175 refereed research reports, articles, books, book chapters, and monographs. He is the past editor of *Reading Research and Instruction.* He was the coeditor of *The Reading Teacher* from 2002 to 2007. He is or has been a reviewer for various journals. He is coauthor, with Robert B. Cooter, Jr., of *The Essentials for Teaching Children to Read* (3rd ed.), *Teaching Children to Read: The Teacher Makes the Difference* (5th ed.), and *Strategies for Reading Assessment and Instruction: Helping Every Child Succeed* (4th ed.), published by Merrill/Prentice Hall and Allyn and Bacon. He has written a professional book with Parker C. Fawson entitled *Your Classroom Library: How to Give It More Teaching Power,* published by Scholastic. He is author or coauthor of several chapters published in *Handbook of Classroom Management, Handbook of Research on Literacy and Diversity,* and *Handbook of Reading Research* (Vol. IV). He was an author of Scholastic's *Literacy Place* (school reading program ed.). He is also a consultant on the 2009 edition of *Sadlier Phonics.*

While at Brigham Young University, he was the recipient of the 1992 Karl G. Maeser Distinguished Research and Creative Arts Professor Award. Dr. Reutzel received the 1999 A. B. Herr Award from the College Reading Association for Outstanding Research and Published Contributions to Reading Education. He was awarded the Researcher/Scholar of the Year Award by the College of Education and Human Services at Utah State University in 2004. Dr. Reutzel was recognized as a recipient of the College of Education's 2006 Distinguished Alumni Award at the University of Wyoming in Laramie, Wyoming, and is the D. Wynne Thorne Outstanding Career University Researcher Award recipient from Utah State University in April 2007. Dr. Reutzel was given the John C. Manning Public School Service Award from the International Reading Association in 2007.

**Robert B. Cooter, Jr.,** is the Ursuline Endowed Chair and professor of teacher education at Bellarmine University in Louisville, Kentucky. Cooter currently serves as editor of *The Reading Teacher,* a peer-reviewed journal for literacy educators published by the International Reading Association and the largest circulation literacy education journal in the world. His research focuses on the improvement of reading instruction for children living at the poverty level.

In the public schools, Dr. Cooter served as the first "Reading Czar" (associate superintendent) for the Dallas Independent School District (Texas) and was named a Texas State Champion for Reading for development of the Dallas Reading Plan. In 2007 Robert Cooter and colleagues J. Helen Perkins and Kathleen Spencer Cooter received the Urban Impact Award from the Council of Great City Schools for their work designing and implementing the Memphis Literacy Academy for teacher capacity building in high poverty elementary schools. Professor Cooter later designed and served as university principal investigator of the Memphis Striving Readers Program (grades 6–8 content areas), a $16 million middle school literacy research project in Memphis City Schools funded by the U.S. Department of Education.

He has authored or coauthored 20 books in reading education and more than 60 journal articles. Cooter's books include the best-selling *Teaching Children to Read: The Teacher Makes the Difference* (5th ed.), used at over 200 universities; *Perspectives on Rescuing Urban Literacy Education: Spies, Saboteurs, & Saints;* and *The Comprehensive Reading Inventory,* a norm-referenced reading assessment for classroom use. He is currently completing work on a new book with his wife and colleague, Professor Kathleen Spencer Cooter, entitled *Urban Literacy Education: Helping City Kids in Regular and Special Education Classrooms.*

In 2008 Cooter received the A. B. Herr Award for contributions to the field of literacy given by the Association of Literacy Educators and Researchers and was recently elected to serve as that organization's president (2011–2012).

Bob lives in Louisville, Kentucky, and enjoys family time on their houseboat, *Our Last Child,* with his bride, grandchildren, and golden retrievers.

# CONTENTS

CHAPTER *10*   Reading Comprehension: Focus on the Text   323

CHAPTER *11*   Academic Literacy and New Literacy Studies   370

Teaching reading effectively in today's schools is arguably as much science as it is art. To meet the literacy needs of increasingly diverse learners, teachers are obliged to first understand the indispensable knowledge and skills to be learned at each stage of development, then measure student abilities and progress quickly and efficiently, and finally provide evidence-based instruction. All of this and more must be delivered in real time, with real children in real classroom situations.

## NEW TO THIS EDITION

*Strategies for Reading Assessment and Instruction* has gained popularity as a quick and effective reference tool for teachers of reading analogous to the *Physicians' Desk Reference* that doctors use in patient treatment. The fourth edition of *Strategies for Reading Assessment and Instruction* is a "point-of-teaching" resource that offers teachers the following new and updated content.

- **A new chapter** (Chapter 2) containing the most up-to-date information available about how to implement **Response to Intervention (RtI)** three-tiered instruction in your classroom
- **A compact 12 chapters** reflect the streamlining of content in this edition, as shown in the Contents
- Updated **Background Briefings for Teachers** on important literacy research and trends in specific reading areas such as oral language development, phonemic awareness, concepts about print, phonics, vocabulary, comprehension, new literacies, and fluency
- New **assessment strategies** are discussed throughout for use in regular classrooms to determine individual reading instructional needs
- **Updated versions of our exclusive and time-saving If-Then Strategy Guides** rapidly match student needs to evidence-based teaching strategies (i.e., *IF students need to learn X, THEN these are the teaching strategies I could use to help them*)
- **Nearly 20% new evidence-based teaching strategies** designed to meet your students' needs
- **Updated useful and realistic suggestions** for offering differentiated instruction to meet the needs of **English learners** and **learners having special needs** are integrated in Chapters 3 through 12.

## RESOURCES BEHIND THIS EDITION

The scholarly and practical resources behind the strategies in this book are many. We mined the contents of this book from our direct experiences as project designers on federally and state-funded reading reform projects, most especially in high-poverty schools associated with the Reading First and Striving Readers projects funded by the U.S. Department of Education (USDOE); from practices shared by incredibly talented literacy coaches in the Dallas, Memphis, Ogden, Granite, and San Juan school districts, to name just a few; from ideas published in *The Reading Teacher* (International Reading Association) during our respective tenures as editors of that journal; and from our own direct experiences in the classroom. For contemporary trends in assessment, we drew on what has been learned using such resources as DIBELS (Dynamic Indicators of Basic Early Literacy Skills) along with the landmark reports *Preventing Reading Difficulties in Young Children* (1998), the *Report of the National Reading Panel* (2000), and the *Voices of Evidence in Reading Research* (2004).

## FOR THE PRACTICING EDUCATOR

Classroom reading teachers will also discover that *Strategies for Reading Assessment and Instruction* provides an extensive and recently updated selection of evidence-based instructional practices and assessment tools to (1) inform instruction, (2) meet the needs of individual learners, and (3) develop an understanding of the essentials of evidence-based reading instruction in a **Response to Intervention (RtI)** instructional environment. Because of our emphasis on an RtI model for meeting student needs, those who teach in special education resource rooms, Title 1 reading programs, and university reading clinics will find that this fourth edition is particularly useful for teaching a diverse group of students with special needs.

## ADVANTAGES FOR PRESERVICE TEACHERS

For preservice teachers, this fourth edition of *Strategies for Reading Assessment and Instruction* offers a practical resource for understanding past and present issues in reading instruction and assessment. It also provides an introduction to assessment purposes, types, and evidence as well as access to information about Response to Intervention (RtI) instructional models and practices. Teachers in training will also find the updated, ready-to-use instructional strategies useful in teacher education practicum experiences, classroom observations, clinical experiences, and in student teaching.

## USING THIS EDITION AS A TOOL FOR PROFESSIONAL DEVELOPMENT WORKSHOPS

Co-distributed and published with the endorsement of the International Reading Association (IRA), *Strategies for Reading Assessment and Instruction* is a proven tool for ongoing professional development in this age of evidence-based reading assessment and instruction. Widely used in such states as Ohio and Pennsylvania as an approved inservice reference, this book contains the latest in research on assessment purposes, types, and tools along with new information about Response to Intervention (RtI) models of classroom instruction for more effectively meeting the needs of students within the regular education classroom setting. In addition, the updated and newly revised Chapters 3 through 12 provide practicing teachers access to highly effective, reliable, valid, and classroom-proven assessments and teaching strategies, and presenting this information in an easy-to-use format that makes the implementation of effective reading assessment and appropriately selected instruction strategies in the classroom quick and easy. In fact, each previous edition of *Strategies for Reading Assessment and Instruction* has been used as the primary resource in literally thousands of workshop sessions on evidence-based reading instruction across the United States.

## SUPPLEMENTS FOR INSTRUCTORS AND STUDENTS

The following supplements provide an outstanding array of resources that facilitate learning about reading assessment. For more information, ask your local Pearson representative or contact the Pearson Faculty Field Support Department at 1-800-526-0485. For technology support, please contact technical support directly at 1-800-677-6337 or http://247 .pearsoned.com. Many of the supplements are available for download from the Instructor Resource Center at www.pearsonhighered.com/irc.

### Instructor's Manual and Test Bank

For each chapter, the Instructor's Manual features a Chapter Overview; Learner Objectives; Key Terms; suggestions for Before, During, and After Reading; and a list of suggested activities. The Test Bank has nearly 200 questions and includes multiple-choice and essay questions. Page references to the main text and suggested answers have been added to each question to help instructors create and evaluate student tests. It is available for download from the Instructor Resource Center at www.pearsonhighered.com/irc.

### MyEducationLab

Teacher educators who are developing pedagogies for the analysis of teaching and learning contend that analyzing teaching artifacts has three advantages: it enables new teachers time for reflection while still using the real materials of practice; it provides new teachers with experience thinking about and approaching the complexity of the classroom; and in some cases, it can help new teachers and teacher educators develop a shared understanding and common language about teaching. . . .*

As Linda Darling-Hammond and her colleagues point out, grounding teacher education in real classrooms—among real teachers and students and among actual examples of students' and teachers' work—is an important and perhaps even an essential part of training teachers for the complexities of teaching in today's classrooms. For this reason, we have created MyEducationLab, a valuable, time-saving website that provides the context of real classrooms

*Darling-Hammond, L., & Bransford, J. (Eds.). (2005). *Preparing teachers for a changing world.* San Francisco: John Wiley & Sons.

and artifacts that research on teacher education tells us is so important. The authentic in-class video footage, interactive skill-building exercises, and other resources available on MyEducationLab offer a uniquely valuable teacher education tool.

MyEducationLab is easy to use and integrate into assignments and courses. Whenever the MyEducationLab logo appears in the text, follow the simple instructions to access the interactive assignments, activities, and learning units on MyEducationLab. For each topic covered in the course you will find most or all of the following resources.

### Connection to National Standards

Now it is easier than ever to see how coursework is connected to national standards. Each topic on MyEducationLab lists intended learning outcomes connected to the appropriate national standards. And all of the Assignments and Activities and all of the Building Teaching Skills and Dispositions in MyEducationLab are mapped to the appropriate national standards and learning outcomes as well.

### Assignments and Activities

Designed to save instructors preparation time and enhance student understanding, these assignable exercises show concepts in action through video, cases, and/or student and teacher artifacts. They help students synthesize and apply concepts and strategies they read about in the book.

### Building Teaching Skills and Dispositions

These learning units help students practice and strengthen skills that are essential to quality teaching. They are presented with the core skill or concept and then given an opportunity to practice their understanding of this concept multiple times by watching video footage or interacting with other media, and then critically analyzing the strategy or skill presented.

### IRIS Center Resources

Funded by the U.S. Department of Education's Office of Special Education Programs (OSEP), the IRIS Center at Vanderbilt University (http://iris.peabody.vanderbilt.edu) develops training enhancement materials for preservice and inservice teachers. The center works with experts from across the country to create challenge-based interactive modules, case study units, and podcasts that provide research-validated information about working with students in inclusive settings. In your MyEducationLab course we have integrated this content where appropriate.

### Teacher Talk

This feature links to videos of Teachers of the Year across the country discussing their personal stories of why they teach. This National Teacher of the Year Program is sponsored by the Council of Chief State School Officers (CCSSO) and focuses public attention on teaching excellence.

### General Resources on Your MyEducationLab Course

The Resources section on MyEducationLab is designed to help students pass their licensure exams, put together effective portfolios and lesson plans, prepare for and navigate the first year of their teaching careers, and understand key educational standards, policies, and laws. This section includes

- *Licensure Exams.* Contains guidelines for passing the Praxis exam. The *Practice Test Exam* includes practice multiple-choice questions, case study questions, and video case studies with sample questions.
- *Lesson Plan Builder.* Helps students create and share lesson plans.
- *Licensure and Standards.* Provides links to state licensure standards and national standards.
- *Beginning Your Career.* Offers tips, advice, and valuable information on
    - Resume Writing and Interviewing. Expert advice on how to write impressive resumes and prepare for job interviews.
    - Your First Year of Teaching. Practical tips on setting up a classroom, managing student behavior, and planning for instruction and assessment.
    - Law and Public Policies. Includes specific directives and requirements educators need to understand under the No Child Left Behind Act and the Individuals with Disabilities Education Improvement Act of 2004.

Visit www.myeducationlab.com for a demonstration of this exciting new online teaching resource.

## ACKNOWLEDGMENTS

Our most sincere thanks goes out to Linda Bishop, who was our inspiration in the earliest editions of this book.

Thank you for choosing to purchase and use this fourth edition of *Strategies for Reading Assessment and Instruction.* We know from long experience and many thousands of comments from previous readers that it will assist you in your efforts to develop effective, efficient reading assessment and instruction plans. Please send us your comments and observations about whether we have achieved our aim.

Best wishes as you work to help every child become a successful reader and realize his or her full potential as an individual.

D. Ray Reutzel
ray.reutzel@usu.edu

Robert B. Cooter, Jr.
rcooter@bellarmine.edu

# Strategies for Reading Assessment and Instruction

# INTRODUCTION

# Quality Reading Instruction

## Literacy as a National Priority

Helping children achieve reading success has never been a higher priority in our nation. Given that literacy is the "gateway to social justice for all of our children" (Reutzel & Cooter, 2008), we feel this goal is the right one. We have witnessed literacy acquisition elevated to the highest level as a political issue over the past decade. Barack Obama (2005), in a speech titled "Literacy and Education in a 21st-Century Economy" given well before being elected president, summarized our current status in literacy education, and the need to do better:

> Literacy is the most basic currency of the knowledge economy we're living in today. . . . Nothing is more basic; no ability more fundamental. Reading is the gateway skill that makes all other learning possible, from complex word problems and the meaning of our history to scientific discovery and technological proficiency.

Then Senator Obama (2005) went on to describe the depths of our illiteracy epidemic over the past decade:

> In 2000, only 32% of all fourth graders tested as reading proficient. And the story gets worse when you take race and income into consideration. Children from low-income families score 27 points below the average reading level, while students from wealthy families score 15 points above the average. And while only one in twelve white 17-year-olds has the ability to pick up the newspaper and understand the science section, for Hispanics the number jumps to one in fifty; for African Americans it's one in one hundred.
>
> Over the last ten years, the average literacy required for all American occupations is projected to rise by 14%. It's not enough just to recognize the words on the page anymore—the kind of literacy necessary for 21st century employment requires detailed understanding and complex comprehension. But too many kids simply aren't learning at that level. . . .
>
> At the dawn of the 21st century, in a world where knowledge truly is power and literacy is the skill that unlocks the gates of opportunity and success, we all have a responsibility as parents and librarians, educators and citizens, to instill in our children a love of reading so that we can give them the chance to fulfill their dreams.

# *L*ITERACY AND ECONOMICS

Notice that the senator and future president was indicating that improved literacy attainment in our schools is an economic imperative at least as much as it is a social issue. This sentiment has been echoed in the most recent research of Nobel Prize–winning economist James Heckman (2006), who concluded,

> The most economically efficient way to remediate the disadvantage caused by adverse family environments is to invest in children when they are young. Neglecting the early years creates an underclass that is arguably growing in the United States. (p. 814)

William Tate (2007), past president of the American Educational Research Association (AERA), described in a speech titled "Literacy and Democracy: A Cost-Benefit Perspective" recent research on the earning advantages of literate students who stay in school. As you can see in Figure I.1 people who graduate from high school can expect to earn well over a quarter million dollars more than those who drop out of school. Persons having *any* college training earn over a half million dollars more than dropouts, and those having a bachelor's degree can expect to earn more than $1.2 million in their lifetimes over high school dropouts. Not only do people benefit personally by succeeding in school, the benefit to our society likewise increases through greater tax revenues for social programs. In a very literal sense, we cannot afford illiteracy in America.

*Strategies for Reading Assessment and Instruction: Helping Every Child Succeed* (4th ed.) has been developed and refined over many years as a practical classroom tool for teachers in need of practical assessment and teaching ideas to complement their existing reading instruction. We have tested these strategies ourselves to make sure they are useful for teachers in real-world classrooms.

**FIGURE I.1** Educational Attainment and Lifetime Earnings

|  | Lifetime Earning Estimate | Annual Average Earnings | Lifetime Impact |
|---|---|---|---|
| Not a high school graduate | $950,100 | $23,752 | — |
| High school graduate | $1,226,570 | $30,664 | $276,470 |
| Some college | $1,494,990 | $37,374 | $544,890 |
| Associate | $1,563,705 | $39,039 | $613,605 |
| Bachelor | $2,140,860 | $53,521 | $1,190,760 |

*Source:* From Day & Newberger (2002); Tate (2007).

# *H*OW THIS BOOK IS STRUCTURED

In Chapter 1 we introduce the fundamentals of classroom reading assessment. Chapter 2 continues this discussion, explaining how classroom reading assessment is used to assist struggling readers within a **Response to Intervention (RtI)** framework. Beginning in Chapter 3 and for the remaining chapters of the book, we provide a section called **Background Briefing for Teachers,** which is a crisp overview of theory and scientific research on the chapter's focus area (i.e., phonics, comprehension, fluency, etc.). Next, we recommend in each chapter a variety of quick and efficient **classroom assessment strategies** applicable to that area of reading development. For your convenience, we explain how each assessment idea may be used as a screening, diagnostic, progress-monitoring, and/or outcome assessment according to federal guidelines. In Chapter 1, we describe these four assessment types for you.

In this fourth edition, we have continued and improved our immensely popular **If-Then Charts,** which show how to directly link your assessment findings to specific teaching strategies according to each student's need. These If-Then guides make the sometimes complicated task of analyzing student data and deciding which teaching strategies to use a quick and easy process! The idea behind these guides is *if* you discover through assessment strategies that a child needs to learn a certain reading skill or strategy, *then* here are some effective tactics for teaching that skill, concept, or strategy. Following each If-Then Chart in Chapters 3 through 12 we offer you a collection of practical **teaching strategies** that have been validated in research or classroom practice.

# *A* VERSATILE RESOURCE

*Strategies for Reading Assessment and Instruction: Helping Every Child Succeed* is intended to serve as an advanced **professional development resource** for practicing teachers providing comprehensive, evidence-based reading assessment and instruction. It is also useful as a core reading assessment text for those preparing to teach reading in school classrooms through alternative licensure or certification routes (e.g., M.A.T. programs) that result in the awarding of a teaching credential. In summary, with *Strategies for Reading Assessment and Instruction: Helping Every Child Succeed,* teachers can quickly turn to an appropriate chapter that presents current information on a topic of concern to find clear and practical strategies to assess, teach, and organize for effective and comprehensive reading instruction.

It occurs to us that it may be useful for you, our reader, to know what this book is *not* as much as what it is. For instance, this book is not intended to serve as an introductory text on reading instruction. Rather, it is a supplemental text for both new and experienced teachers who need an extensive collection of classroom-proven assessment and teaching strategies that really work!

*Note:* For those who are just beginning the study of reading/literacy education and require a more complete orientation to the field, we suggest our companion text, *Teaching Children to Read: The Teacher Makes the Difference* (5th ed.) (Reutzel & Cooter, 2008), as a starting point, or one of the other major textbooks used in reading methods courses.

# *A*N INVITATION . . .

We know that your time is precious and that it is difficult to examine all the books and journals on reading instruction to find the "just right" ideas for your students. We, too, have experienced this time crunch dilemma and know how frustrating it can sometimes be when a teacher looks into the eyes of a child who is struggling with reading. Our goal has been to fill these pages with current, practical, immediately useful strategies for experienced and novice teachers alike. Along the way, we have tried out most of these ideas ourselves with children. As you use the ideas in this book with your students in coming years, we hope that you will find our goal was largely met and, if time permits, you will take time to write us and suggest ways that the next edition can be even better. We are a community of learners. Welcome!

## SELECTED REFERENCES

Day, J. C., & Newberger, E. C. (2002). *The big payoff: Educational attainment and synthetic estimates of work life earnings.* Washington, DC: U.S. Dept. of Commerce, Census Bureau.

Heckman, J. J. (2006, January 10). Catch 'em young. *Wall Street Journal*, p. 814.

IES. (2009). Assisting students struggling with reading: Response to intervention and multi-tiered intervention in the primary grades. Washington, DC: Institute of Education Sciences (IES): National Center for Educational Evaluation and Regional Assistance, U.S. Department of Education (NCEE 2009-4045).

Obama, B. (2005, June 25). Literacy and education in a 21st-century economy. Retrieved on April 4, 2009, from www.obamaspeeches.com.

Reutzel, D. R., & Cooter, R. B. (2008). *Teaching children to read: The teacher makes the difference* (5th ed.). Upper Saddle River, NJ: Merrill/Prentice-Hall.

Tate, W. F. (2007, August 9). *Literacy and democracy: A cost-benefit perspective.* Keynote address given for the Memphis Striving Readers Project Annual Conference. Memphis, TN: University of Memphis.

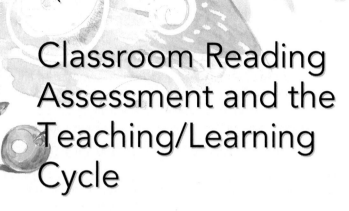

# 1

# Classroom Reading Assessment and the Teaching/Learning Cycle

*J*ason transferred into the classroom of Ms. Catlin Spears in mid-October from a distant state. Unfortunately, his mother was not permitted to bring along his cumulative assessment file from his previous school (they must be mailed by the central office), so Ms. Spears decided she had better gather some preliminary information on Jason's reading, writing, and mathematics abilities. But where to begin?

Ms. Spears was a first-year teacher and felt a bit unsure of herself. And to make the situation a little more dicey, Jason's mom had informed the principal that he had attention-deficit disorder (ADD) and it seemed to affect his learning, especially in reading. With that information in mind, she decided to focus first on reading because it is the most fundamental skill.

Ms. Spears thought to herself, "Okay, let's stay calm. I know I can pull something together that will let me know where to begin teaching Jason. I'll just pull out that strategies book and notes from my college class on reading assessment and go from there."

After perusing her study notes and readings from college classes, the mental haze started to lift along with Catlin's spirits. "I'll just put together a little battery of assessments that will help me find out just where ole Jason is in his reading. For his phonics and decoding, I'll go with a running record. For comprehension, I'll use a retelling assessment form. Ahhh, here's a good observation checklist that'll help me gather some informal data on his reading during class. Maybe I should also do an interest inventory—that would help me choose some books and other texts that he would enjoy reading . . ."

Soon Ms. Spears had enough information to begin making some judgments about where Jason was in his reading development, as well as discovering his "learning frontiers."

Expertise in reading assessment begins with an understanding of the learning fundamentals. The fundamentals—it seems to us, anyway—may be summed up in the answers to three questions, what we refer to as the *how* and *what* questions:

> *How* do children learn?
>
> *What* should good readers be able to do?
>
> *How* do we assess students' response to instructional interventions?

Answer these three questions and you are ready to delve into the principles of effective classroom assessment!

# *L*EARNING FUNDAMENTALS: HOW DO CHILDREN LEARN?

Certainly, volumes have been written on the subject of how children learn to read, so we will limit our conversation here to the bare essentials. For us, there are two primary beliefs as to how children learn that are indispensable in reading instruction: *zone of proximal development* (Vygotsky, 1986, 1990) and *gradual release of responsibility* (Pearson & Gallagher, 1983).

## Teaching in the "Zone"

Lev Vygotsky (1986, 1990), a Russian psychologist, teacher, and medical doctor, has had a tremendous effect on the field of education since the publication of his works in the West. According to Vygotsky, at any particular point in time, a child has a range in which he or she can learn. Applied to reading, at one end of the range are reading skills the child can do alone and at the other end are reading skills he or she could not do even with assistance. In the middle is what Vygotsky termed the **zone of proximal development.**

Vygotsky is well known for his maxim: *What the child can do in cooperation today he can do alone tomorrow.* He further explained: "Therefore the only good kind of teaching is that which marches ahead of development and leads it; it must be aimed not so much at the ripe as at the ripening functions. . . . Instruction must be oriented toward the future, not the past" (Vygotsky, 1986, pp. 188–189).

You may think of the zone of proximal development in this way: A child who has been riding his new bicycle using training wheels for some time asks that they be taken off so he can ride "like a big boy." The attentive parent, after removing the training wheels, runs along with the child with a hand firmly grasping the seat as he pedals his bike. Without the support of the parent, the child would not (in the beginning) have the confidence or skill to ride the bike without training wheels. This is the child's zone of proximal development for bike riding. After more practice that allows his skills to develop, the boy will one day ride without support.

For Vygotsky, therefore, the teacher has a significant role to play in a child's learning. The effective reading teacher (a) knows *what* skills one must learn and in what order, (b) is able to figure out *where* a student is in his or her reading development (i.e., via *classroom assessment*), and (c) knows which skills he or she is able to learn next (i.e., his or her zone of proximal development).

One reason classroom assessment is so important is that it helps the teacher know where the "frontier of learning" is for each student.

## The Gradual Release of Responsibility

Go to the Building Teaching Skills and Dispositions section of Topic 1: "Reading Instruction" in the MyEducationLab for your course and complete the activity entitled "Identifying Effective Reading Instruction." As you work through the learning unit, notice how children from diverse backgrounds are engaged (on task) using art and drama.

There is a way of putting Vygotsky's notion of the zone of proximal development into practice called the **gradual release of responsibility** (Pearson & Gallagher, 1983). Once you have correctly identified through classroom assessment the next reading skill a student is ready to learn, instruction begins with the teacher *modeling* the new skill to be learned for the student. This part of instruction and learning is *all teacher*—the student watches as you model the skill and may ask questions to clarify his or her understanding. When you believe the student understands the new skill you have modeled, you then urge him or her to personally "try out" the skill with your support, much like the parent in our story firmly grasping the bicycle seat when the child first attempts riding without training wheels. This first *gradual release of responsibility* for using the skill is known as **guided practice.** It is important here to include a good bit of practice, more than just one or two activities, while also gradually decreasing the amount of teacher support along the way. When we believe the student has mastered the skill, we let them try it again without teacher assistance and verify through assessment that permanent learning has occurred. We call this last step **independent practice.**

Figure 1.1 represents the shifting balance in the teaching and learning process as the gradual release of responsibility is applied to instruction. In this figure you see that teaching a new skill moves from "all teacher" modeling for the student to observe, through guided practice and application activities performed by the student with teacher support, and eventually arrives at "all student" individual practice where the skill is finally mastered. Note the three phases of development—modeling, guided practice, and independent practice—indicating that there is indeed a gradual release of responsibility from teacher to student for using the new reading skill to be learned.

Before moving on, let us be clear about what is meant by *teacher* in the gradual release of responsibility model. The "teacher" can actually be anyone who is more competent in using the targeted reading skill to be learned. Thus, learners can be helped by the teacher,

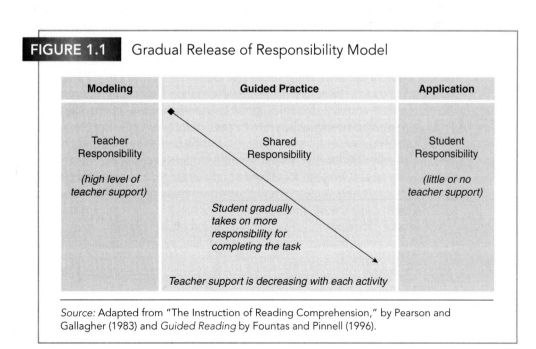

**FIGURE 1.1**   Gradual Release of Responsibility Model

| Modeling | Guided Practice | Application |
|---|---|---|
| Teacher Responsibility *(high level of teacher support)* | Shared Responsibility<br><br>*Student gradually takes on more responsibility for completing the task*<br><br>*Teacher support is decreasing with each activity* | Student Responsibility *(little or no teacher support)* |

*Source:* Adapted from "The Instruction of Reading Comprehension," by Pearson and Gallagher (1983) and *Guided Reading* by Fountas and Pinnell (1996).

yes, but they can also learn from more competent classmates, family members, or caring adults (May & Rizzardi, 2002). In Chapter 2 we will revisit the notion of gradual release of responsibility in our discussion of *explicit instruction*.

# WHAT SHOULD GOOD READERS BE ABLE TO DO?

## Every Journey Begins with a Map

Go to the Building Teaching Skills and Dispositions section of Topic 12: "Progress Monitoring" in the MyEducationLab for your course and complete the activity entitled "Developing a System for Progress Monitoring." As you work through the learning unit, identify ways students' progress in reading can be measured on a regular basis.

Classroom assessment, more than anything else, is the ongoing process of learning just where a student is in his or her journey to becoming a fluent reader. Gauging one's position in any journey is judged by using a kind of "map" to locate the starting point and the destination. Without a map we run the risk of losing our way, whether in a cross-country trip or in classroom instruction.

So what map should we use for students in their reading development? It should include the most essential **benchmark skills** students should master by the end of kindergarten, first grade, second grade, and so on that show us they are on course. In other words, this map should help us determine what students in our care should be able to do in reading at each level if they are progressing normally and do not have significant learning problems. It stands to reason that if we understand the reading skills students normally learn, and in what order, then we can set out to find the best research-proven strategies for assessing growth in each of these reading benchmark skills. In Figure 1.2 we present research-based *readinbenchmark skills* that serve as our "reading roadmap."

## Supplementing the Reading Benchmark Skills with State/National Standards

The reading benchmark skills provide an excellent starting point for assessment and instructional decisions, but they may not be entirely sufficient. Virtually all state departments of education have their own learning standards documents for reading and other literacy skills teachers are obliged to consider. These documents are helpful in rounding out your own version of the reading benchmark skills.

A teacher in California will note in their *California Reading Standards K–12* (available online at www.cde.ca.gov) the following skills to be learned by the end of first grade in the area of decoding and word recognition:*

### Decoding and Word Recognition

1.10 Generate the sounds from all the letters and letter patterns, including consonant blends and long- and short-vowel patterns (i.e., phonograms), and blend those sounds into recognizable words.

1.11 Read common, irregular sight words (e.g., *the, have, said, come, give, of*).

1.12 Use knowledge of vowel digraphs and *r*-controlled letter-sound associations to read words.

1.13 Read compound words and contractions.

*Reprinted with permission of the California Department of Education, CDE Press, 1430 N Street, Suite 3207, Sacramento, CA 95814.

**FIGURE 1.2**　Reading Benchmark Skills

**Kindergarten Accomplishments**

- Knows the parts of a book and their functions.
- Begins to track print when listening to a familiar text being read or when rereading own writing.
- "Reads" familiar texts emergently, i.e., not necessarily verbatim from the print alone.
- Recognizes and can name all uppercase and lowercase letters.
- Understands that the sequence of letters in a written word represents the sequence of sounds (phonemes) in a spoken word (alphabetic principle).
- Learns many, though not all, one-to-one letter–sound correspondences.
- Recognizes some words by sight, including a few very common ones (the, I, my, you, is, are).
- Uses new vocabulary and grammatical constructions in own speech.
- Makes appropriate switches from oral to written language styles.
- Notices when simple sentences fail to make sense.
- Connects information and events in texts to life and life experiences to text.
- Retells, reenacts, or dramatizes stories or parts of stories.
- Listens attentively to books the teacher reads to class.
- Can name some book titles and authors.
- Demonstrates familiarity with a number of types or genres of text (e.g., storybooks, expository texts, poems, newspapers, and everyday print such as signs, notices, labels).
- Correctly answers questions about stories read aloud.
- Makes predictions based on illustrations or portions of stories.
- Demonstrates understanding that spoken words consist of sequences of phonemes.
- Given spoken sets like dan, dan, den, can identify the first two as the same and the third as different.
- Given spoken sets like dak, pat, zen, can identify the first two as sharing one same sound.
- Given spoken segments, can merge them into a meaningful target word.
- Given a spoken word, can produce another word that rhymes with it.
- Independently writes many uppercase and lowercase letters.
- Uses phonemic awareness and letter knowledge to spell independently (invented or creative spelling).

- Writes (unconventionally) to express own meaning.
- Builds a repertoire of some conventionally spelled words.
- Shows awareness of distinction between "kid writing" and conventional orthography.
- Writes own name (first and last) and the first names of some friends or classmates.
- Can write most letters and some words when they are dictated.

**First-Grade Accomplishments**

- Makes a transition from emergent to "real" reading.
- Reads aloud with accuracy and comprehension any text that is appropriately designed for the first half of grade one.
- Accurately decodes orthographically regular, one-syllable words and nonsense words (e.g., sit, zot), using print–sound mappings to sound out unknown words.
- Uses letter–sound correspondence knowledge to sound out unknown words when reading text.
- Recognizes common, irregularly spelled words by sight (have, said, where, two).
- Has a reading vocabulary of 300 to 500 sight words and easily sounded-out words.
- Monitors own reading and self-corrects when an incorrectly identified word does not fit with cues provided by the letters in the word or the context surrounding the word.
- Reads and comprehends both fiction and nonfiction that is appropriately designed for the grade level.
- Shows evidence of expanding language repertoire, including increasing appropriate use of standard, more formal language.
- Creates own written texts for others to read.
- Notices when difficulties are encountered in understanding text.
- Reads and understands simple written instructions.
- Predicts and justifies what will happen next in stories.
- Discusses prior knowledge of topics in expository texts.
- Uses how, why, and what-if questions to discuss nonfiction texts.
- Describes new information gained from texts in own words.

(continued)

**FIGURE 1.2**   *Continued*

- Distinguishes whether simple sentences are incomplete or fail to make sense; notices when simple texts fail to make sense.
- Can answer simple written comprehension questions based on the material read.
- Can count the number of syllables in a word.
- Can blend or segment the phonemes of most one-syllable words.
- Spells correctly three- and four-letter short vowel words.
- Composes fairly readable first drafts using appropriate parts of the writing process (some attention to planning, drafting, rereading for meaning, and some self-correction).
- Uses invented spelling or phonics-based knowledge to spell independently, when necessary.
- Shows spelling consciousness or sensitivity to conventional spelling.
- Uses basic punctuation and capitalization.
- Produces a variety of types of compositions (e.g., stories, descriptions, journal entries) showing appropriate relationships between printed text, illustrations, and other graphics.
- Engages in a variety of literacy activities voluntarily (e.g., choosing books and stories to read, writing a note to a friend).

**Second-Grade Accomplishments**

- Reads and comprehends both fiction and nonfiction that is appropriately designed for grade level.
- Accurately decodes orthographically regular multisyllable words and nonsense words (e.g., *capital, Kalamazoo*).
- Uses knowledge of print–sound mappings to sound out unknown words.
- Accurately reads many irregularly spelled words and such spelling patterns as diphthongs, special vowel spellings, and common word endings.
- Reads and comprehends both fiction and nonfiction that is appropriately designed for the grade.
- Shows evidence of expanding language repertory, including increasing use of more formal language registers.
- Reads voluntarily for interest and own purposes.
- Rereads sentences when meaning is not clear.
- Interprets information from diagrams, charts, and graphs.
- Recalls facts and details of texts.
- Reads nonfiction materials for answers to specific questions or for specific purposes.

- Takes part in creative responses to texts such as dramatizations, oral presentations, fantasy play, and so on.
- Discusses similarities in characters and events across stories.
- Connects and compares information across nonfiction selections.
- Poses possible answers to how, why, and what-if questions.
- Correctly spells previously studied words and spelling patterns in own writing.
- Represents the complete sound of a word when spelling independently.
- Shows sensitivity to using formal language patterns in place of oral language patterns at appropriate spots in own writing (e.g., decontextualizing sentences, conventions for quoted speech, literary language forms, proper verb forms).
- Makes reasonable judgments about what to include in written products.
- Productively discusses ways to clarify and refine own writing and that of others.
- With assistance, adds use of conferencing, revision, and editing processes to clarify and refine own writing to the steps of the expected parts of the writing process.
- Given organizational help, writes informative, well-structured reports.
- Attends to spelling, mechanics, and presentation for final products.
- Produces a variety of types of compositions (e.g., stories, reports, correspondence).

**Third-Grade Accomplishments**

- Reads aloud with fluency and comprehension any text that is appropriately designed for grade level.
- Uses letter–sound correspondence knowledge and structural analysis to decode words.
- Reads and comprehends both fiction and nonfiction that is appropriately designed for grade level.
- Reads longer fictional selections and chapter books independently.
- Takes part in creative responses to texts such as dramatizations, oral presentations, fantasy play, and so on.
- Can point to or clearly identify specific words or wordings that are causing comprehension difficulties.

---

**FIGURE 1.2**   *Continued*

- Summarizes major points from fiction and non-fiction texts.
- In interpreting fiction, discusses underlying theme or message.
- Asks how, why, and what-if questions in interpreting nonfiction texts.
- In interpreting nonfiction, distinguishes cause and effect, fact and opinion, main idea, and supporting details.
- Uses information and reasoning to examine bases of hypotheses and opinions.
- Infers word meaning from taught roots, prefixes, and suffixes.
- Correctly spells previously studied words and spelling patterns in own writing.
- Begins to incorporate literacy words and language patterns in own writing (e.g., elaborates descriptions; uses figurative wording).

- With some guidance, uses all aspects of the writing process in producing own compositions and reports.
- Combines information from multiple sources in writing reports.
- With assistance, suggests and implements editing and revision to clarify and refine own writing.
- Presents and discusses own writing with other students and responds helpfully to other students' compositions.
- Independently reviews work for spelling, mechanics, and presentation.
- Produces a variety of written work (e.g., literature response, reports, "published" books, semantic maps) in a variety of formats including multimedia forms.

---

*Source:* Adapted from Burns, M. S., Griffin, P., & Snow, C. E. (Eds.). (1999). *Starting Out Right: A Guide to Promoting Children's Reading Success.* Committee on the Prevention of Reading Difficulties In Young Children, Commission on Behavioral and Social Sciences and Education. National Research Council. Washington, DC: National Academy Press. Available online at www.nap.edu. Reprinted with permission of the National Academy Press via Copyright Clearance Center.

---

1.14 Read inflectional forms (e.g., *-s, -ed, -ing*) and root words (e.g., *look, looked, looking*).

1.15 Read common word families (e.g., *-ite, -ate*).

1.16 Read aloud with fluency in a manner that sounds like natural speech.

So in this instance, where the reading benchmark skills provide us with an important end-of-year *goal* for instruction, the *California Reading Standards K–12* provide us with the specific *learning objectives* for instruction. Thus the combined information might look like the following for a California teacher working with English and Spanish speakers:

**First Grade End-of-Year Goals and Objectives: Decoding and Word Recognition**

| | |
|---|---|
| **Goal 1 (English/Spanish):** | Decodes phonetically regular one-syllable words and nonsense words accurately |
| **Goal 2 (Spanish only):** | Decodes two-syllable words, using knowledge of sounds, letters, and syllables including consonants, vowels, blends, and stress |
| **Objectives:** | 1.10 Generate the sounds from all the letters and letter patterns, including consonant blends and long- and short-vowel patterns (i.e., phonograms), and blend those sounds into recognizable words. |

1.11 Read common, irregular sight words (e.g., *the, have, said, come, give, of*).

1.12 Use knowledge of vowel digraphs and *r*-controlled letter–sound associations to read words.

1.13 Read compound words and contractions.

1.14 Read inflectional forms (e.g., *-s, -ed, -ing*) and root words (e.g., *look, looked, looking*).

1.15 Read common word families (e.g., *-ite, -ate*).

1.16 Read aloud with fluency in a manner that sounds like natural speech.

# PRINCIPLES OF CLASSROOM READING ASSESSMENT

Go to the Building Teaching Skills and Dispositions section of Topic 2: "Reading Assessment" in the MyEducationLab for your course and complete the activity entitled "Understanding Formal and Informal Assessment." As you work through the learning unit, notice that the teacher is trying to identify what students *can* do as a bridge for teaching those skills they cannot do *yet*.

Several basic assumptions govern good classroom reading assessment. Abiding by these principles helps teachers remain focused, systematic, and purposeful in their teaching.

## Principle 1: The Teacher's Goal Is to Find Out What Children *Can* Do

In reviewing our "roadmap," the reading benchmark skills, we see that the development of reading follows a certain path with clear markers along the way. Your job as a teacher is to locate where each child is on the path of development so that you can offer appropriate instruction to continue his or her growth. By carefully charting what children *can* do in reading (not what they cannot do) beginning with early reading benchmark skills and moving systematically toward the more complex, this will tell you where each child is in his or her reading development as well as what should come next.

## Principle 2: Assessment Informs Instruction

There has been a kind of "chicken versus the egg" debate in past years about which comes first—teaching or assessment. Principle 1 resolves that debate for us; effective teaching cannot possibly begin until we first discover where children are in their reading development. To do otherwise could result in "random acts of teaching"! Therefore, gathering assessment information that shows us what a student can do, charting those data using the reading benchmark skills, and then seeing which skills come next in the student's development help us know the appropriate "next steps" for students—their zone of proximal development. In short, this process avoids wasting class time teaching reading skills students already "own" or skills that are too advanced and beyond their grasp at this time.

### The Trouble with Letting Your State Test Drive Instruction

Reading instruction in many schools and school districts mirrors their state's mandated curriculum and reading tests—sometimes referred to as *high-stakes tests*—because whether a child is retained can be decided using these tests. In this situation, it is clear that reading tests—rather than an assessment of student needs—do indeed drive instruction. Thus, it is important to make sure that the state tests are measuring appropriate reading skills at each grade level as determined through scientific research. If some of the reading benchmark skills at your grade level are not being addressed by mandated tests, then we *must* use the kinds of supplemental assessments offered in this book if *every* child's needs are to be met.

## Principle 3: Be Prepared—Gather Your Assessment "Tools" in Advance

If you decide to repaint your living room at home, after deciding the color you want you would then go to your local DIY store and purchase all the necessary supplies before starting the job: a how-to book (a "roadmap" for painting), paint, brushes, rollers, ladder, drop cloth, and so forth. With your tools assembled you could begin work. In assessing reading development we also have some essential "tools of the trade." The tools of assessment include the reading benchmark skills for use as student and class profiling documents (Reutzel & Cooter, 2008), leveled books in the language of instruction (i.e., English and/or Spanish in many classrooms), an audio recorder to document student readings, carefully prepared observation checklists, and perhaps an informal reading inventory for quick assessments at the beginning and midpoint of the school year, such as *The Comprehensive Reading Inventory* (Cooter, Flynt, & Cooter, 2007). Later in this chapter (and in Chapters 3 through 12) we provide you with some of the most basic tools you will need for classroom reading assessment.

## Principle 4: Analyze Students' Assessment Results Using If-Then Thinking

One of the more difficult tasks for many teachers is to analyze assessment data they have gathered for each student, form needs-based small groups for instruction, and choose appropriate teaching strategies for instruction. Put another way, we sometimes get to be pretty good at *gathering* assessment evidence but then have difficulty *analyzing* our findings and converting them into classroom action plans.

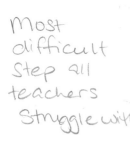

**Analysis** involves what we call *if-then thinking*. This is a way of analyzing assessment data and translating them into potent lesson plans. The basic philosophy goes something like this: *If* you know that a child is able to do X in reading, *then* he or she is now ready to learn Y. Put another way, *if* you know the highest level reading skills a student can do alone (the *independent* reading level—see Principles 1 and 2), *then* you can accurately predict which reading skill(s) the student should learn next with your assistance (the *zone of proximal development*). In each chapter, we provide you an **If-Then Chart** located for your convenience between the sections on assessment and teaching strategies. For example, Figure 1.3 shows an excerpt from Chapter 4, "Children's Concepts about Print."

## Principle 5: Document Students' Growth in Reading Over Time

Reading assessment is not just a one-shot activity done at the beginning of the year, but an ongoing and integral part of teaching and learning. Indeed, assessment and good teaching are virtually seamless. It is critical that we carry a veritable arsenal of assessment ideas in our teaching battery. It is equally critical that we devise ways to document what we learn about each student's reading development for instructional decision making.

# *F*INDING OUT WHAT KIDS CAN DO: BASIC ASSESSMENT STRATEGIES

In the development of readers, particularly in the early grades, teachers often focus on two very basic areas in their assessments: **decoding,** or the translation of letters and words into language (also called *word identification*), and **comprehension** of what has been read (comprehension

| Oral Reading Accuracy | Text Level Difficulty | Level of Support Needed by the Reader |
| --- | --- | --- |
| Below 90% | *Frustration level* or "too difficult" | This level of text is out of the students' *zone of proximal development* and should not be used for instruction. |
| 90 to 94% | *Instructional Level* or "adequate ability" | This level of text is within the student's *zone of proximal development* and is appropriate for reading instruction supported by a teacher or more capable reader. |
| 95% and above | *Independent Level* or "easy reading level" | This level of text requires little or no assistance and is appropriate for recreational or other independent reading activities. |

Running records are taken without a prepared script and may be recorded on a sheet of paper, requiring about 10 minutes to transcribe, as shown in the following guidelines for administration.

1. Prepare a reading sample from a book or story that is 100 to 200 words in length. For early readers, the text may fall below 100 words. Allow the student to read the passage one or two times without assistance before you take the running record.

2. Sit alongside while the student reads so that you can both see the page. It is not really necessary to have your own photocopy of the text; a blank sheet of paper will do. Record all accurate reading by making a check mark (sometimes called a tick mark) on a sheet of blank paper for each word said correctly. Errors (miscues) should be indicated using the notations listed in Figure 1.4. Figure 1.5 shows an example of a running record taken from the book Martha Speaks (Meddaugh, 1992, pp. 1–4) using the marking system. In the figure, the text on the left is a copy of the passage the student is reading. The box on the right is a running record taken by the teacher with each of the miscue types noted. Once the running record is taken, you then need to analyze the miscues so that you will know what the reader can do.

## Determining Oral Reading Accuracy Rate

The first level of running record analysis is to determine whether the level of reading passage used is appropriate for instruction (White, 2008). In order to decide whether the level of text is on the student's **independent, instructional,** or **frustration** level, we must determine the percentage of words read correctly in the passage used for the running record.

Let's return to Figure 1.5 for a moment as an example. As you can see, Paco had several oral reading miscues. Our first task is to decide which miscues are countable errors. For example, the following quick summary shows the miscues that are countable errors (refer back to Figure 1.4 to review a listing of miscues and their notations).

**Countable Errors**
- Omissions
- Insertions
- Student Appeal with Assistance
- Substitutions
- Teacher Assistance

**Not Countable Errors**
- Self-Correction
- Repetition

| FIGURE 1.4 | Notations for a Running Record |

| Reading Behavior | Notation | Explanation |
| --- | --- | --- |
| Accurate Reading | ✓✓✓✓✓ | *Notation:* A check is noted for each word pronounced correctly. |
| Self-Correction | ✓✓✓ Attempt \| SC <br> —————— <br> Word in Text | The child corrects an error himself or herself. This is not counted as a miscue. *Notation:* SC is the notation used for self-corrections. |
| Omission | —————— <br> Word in Text | A word or words are left out during the reading. <br> *Notation:* A dash mark is written over a line above the word(s) from the text that has/have been omitted. |
| Insertion | Word Inserted <br> —————— | The child adds a word that is not in the text. <br> *Notation:* The word inserted by the reader is placed above a line and a dash placed below it. |
| Student Appeal and Assistance | —————— \| A <br> Word from Text \| T | The child is "stuck" on a word he or she cannot call and asks (verbal or nonverbal) the teacher for help. <br> *Notation:* A is written above a line for "assisted," and the problem word from the text is written below the line. |
| Repetition | ✓✓✓ R ✓✓✓ | Sometimes children will repeat words or phrases. These repetitions are not scored as errors, but *are* recorded. <br> *Notation:* Write an R after the word repeated and draw a line back to the point where the reader returned. |
| Substitution | Substituted Word <br> —————— <br> Word from Text | The child says a word that is different from the word in the text. <br> *Notation:* The student's substitution word is written above a line under which the correct word from text is written. |
| Teacher Assistance | —————— \| <br> Word from Text \| T | The student pauses on a word for 5 seconds or more, so the teacher tells him or her the word. <br> *Notation:* The letter T is written to the right of a line that follows the word from text. A blank is placed above a cross-line to indicate that the student did not know the word. |

In Paco's running record (Figure 1.5) we see the following miscues noted: one self-correction (not a countable error), one omission, one insertion, one student appeal with assistance, one repetition (not a countable error), one substitution, and one teacher assistance. Of the seven miscues recorded, five are countable as oral reading errors. To determine whether this passage was on Paco's independent, instructional, or frustration level, we will use a two-step formula:

**Step 1:** Total words in running record passage – Number of miscues = Number of words read correctly

**Step 2:** Number of words read correctly ÷ Total words in running record passage = Accuracy rate percentage

## FIGURE 1.5    Running Record Example

Student: _____Paco, Grade 2_____

Title: **The Pig and the Snake**

| One day Mr. Pig was walking to | ✓ ✓ ✓ ✓ ✓ ✓ |
| town. He saw a big hole in the | ✓ ✓ sam\|sc over saw ✓ ✓ ✓ ✓ ✓ |
| road. A big snake was in the | ✓ ✓ ⎺ big ✓ ✓ ✓ ✓ |
| hole. "Help me," said the snake, | ✓ ✓ ✓ out ✓ ✓ ✓ |
| "and I will be your friend." "No, no," | ✓ ✓ ✓ ✓ ✓ − friend \|A ✓ ✓ |
| said Mr. Pig. "If I help you get | ✓ ✓ ✓ ✓ ✓ ✓ ✓ |
| out you will bite me. You're | ✓ ✓ ✓ R ✓ ✓ ✓ |
| a snake!" The snake cried and | ✓ ✓ ✓ ✓ ✓ ✓ |
| cried. So Mr. Pig pulled the | ✓ ✓ ✓ ✓ popped over pulled ✓ |
| snake out of the hole. | ✓ ✓ ✓ ✓ ✓ |
| Then the snake said, "Now I am | ✓ ✓ ✓ ✓ ✓ ✓ ✓ |
| going to bite you, Mr. Pig." | ✓ ✓ ✓ ✓ ✓ ✓ |
| "How can you bite me after | ✓ ✓ ✓ ✓ ✓ − after \| T |
| I helped you out of the hole?" | ✓ ✓ ✓ ✓ ✓ ✓ ✓ |
| said Mr. Pig. The snake said,// | ✓ ✓ ✓ ✓ ✓ ✓ |
| "You knew I was a snake | ✓ ✓ ✓ ✓ ✓ ✓ |
| when you pulled me out!" | ✓ ✓ ✓ ✓ ✓ |

*Source:* From *The Flynt/Cooter Reading Inventory for the Classroom* (5th ed.), by E. S. Flynt and R. B. Cooter, Jr., 2004. Upper Saddle River, NJ: Merrill/Prentice Hall. Copyright © 2004. Used with permission of Pearson Education.

In Paco's example, there were a total of 111 words. Applying the two-step formula gives the following result:

**Step 1:**  111 − 5 miscues = 106 words read correctly

**Step 2:**  106 ÷ 111 = 95% oral reading accuracy

Therefore because Paco is able to read this passage with 95% accuracy, this level of passage would be at his *independent* reading level.

### A Simple Alternative for Determining Words Read Correctly

In busy real-world classrooms it is important to "work smart." Cooter, Flynt, and Cooter (2007) have suggested a shortcut for determining words read correctly in a much quicker but still, we think, valid manner. Count the number of words in the passage used for the running record and note the one-hundredth word. After completing the running record only count miscues up to the 100th word and subtract the countable miscues from 100 and you will have the percentage of words read correctly in one step. If you will look again at Figure 1.5, you will note that the 100th word is indicated using two backslashes (//) immediately following the words "The snake said." Subtracting the number of countable miscues in Paco's example yields the same percentage of words read correctly (95%).

## Understanding Miscues Using MSV Analysis

Marie Clay (1985) also developed a way of interpreting miscues for use in her widely acclaimed Reading Recovery program. This method of analysis enables you to determine the extent to which the student uses three primary **cuing strategies** when he or she encounters a new word in print and an oral reading miscue occurs: meaning cues (M), syntax cues (S), and visual cues (V). The following summary is based on the work of Cooter, Flynt, and Cooter (2007).

- *M = Meaning (Semantic Cues—Does it make sense?)* In reviewing each miscue, consider whether the student is using meaning cues in her attempt to identify the unknown word in print. Context clues, picture cues, and information from the passage are examples of meaning cues used by the reader.

- *S = Syntax (Structure Cues—Does it sound right?)* A rule system or *grammar* governs the English language, as with all other languages. For example, English is essentially based on a "subject-verb" grammar system. **Syntax** is the application of this subject-verb grammar system in creating sentences. The goal in studying syntax cues as part of your miscue analysis is to try and determine the extent to which the student unconsciously uses rules of grammar in attempting to identify unknown words in print. For example, if a word in a passage causing a miscue for the reader is a verb, ask yourself whether the student's miscue is also a verb. Consistent use of the appropriate part of speech in miscues (i.e., a noun for a noun, a verb for a verb, articles for articles, etc.) is an indication that the student has internalized the rule system of English grammar and is applying that knowledge in attacking unknown words.

- *V = Visual (Graphophonic—Does it look right?)* Sometimes a miscue looks a good bit like the correct word appearing in the text. The miscue may begin with the same letter or letters, for example, saying *top* for *toy* or *sit* for *seat*. Another possibility is that the letters of the miscue may look very similar to the word appearing in text (e.g., *introduction* for *introspection*). Use of visual cues is essentially the student's ability or inability to apply phonics skills to decode words in print. The extent to which readers use visual cues is an important factor to consider when trying to better understand the skills employed by developing readers when attacking unknown words in print.

Applying MSV thinking is fairly simple once you get the hang of it. In Figure 1.6, we return to the miscues previously noted in Figure 1.5 and conduct an MSV analysis on each. Do you see why each interpretation was made?

## The Miscue Grid: An Alternative Running Records Scheme

As useful as the running record can be for teachers in planning instruction, many feel that the time required for administering and analyzing running records can be prohibitive in public school classes of 20 or more students. To make the process go more quickly and reliably, Cooter, Flynt, and Cooter (2007) developed a simplified process for completing running

| FIGURE 1.6 | Running Record with MSV Analysis |
|---|---|

Student: _____ Paco, Grade 2 _____

| Title: **The Pig and the Snake** | | E MSV | SC MSV |
|---|---|---|---|
| One day Mr. Pig was walking to | ✓ ✓ ✓ ✓ ✓ ✓ | | |
| town. He saw a big hole in the | ✓ ✓ sam\|sc / saw \| ✓ ✓ ✓ ✓ | | Ⓜ Ⓢ Ⓥ |
| road. A big snake was in the | ✓ ✓ —/big ✓ ✓ ✓ | M S V | |
| hole. "Help me," said the snake, | ✓ ✓ ✓ out/— ✓ ✓ ✓ | Ⓜ Ⓢ V | |
| "and I will be your friend." "No, no," | ✓ ✓ ✓ ✓ ✓ —/friend \|A ✓ ✓ | M S V | |
| said Mr. Pig. "If I help you get | ✓ ✓ ✓ ✓ ✓ ✓ ✓ ✓ | | |
| out you will bite me. You're | ⌒✓ ✓ ✓ R ✓ ✓ ✓ | | Ⓜ Ⓢ Ⓥ |
| a snake!" The snake cried and | ✓ ✓ ✓ ✓ ✓ ✓ | | |
| cried. So Mr. Pig pulled the | ✓ ✓ ✓ ✓ popped/pulled ✓ | Ⓜ Ⓢ Ⓥ | |
| snake out of the hole. | ✓ ✓ ✓ ✓ ✓ | | |
| Then the snake said, "Now I am | ✓ ✓ ✓ ✓ ✓ ✓ ✓ | | |
| going to bite you, Mr. Pig." | ✓ ✓ ✓ ✓ ✓ ✓ | | |
| "How can you bite me after | ✓ ✓ ✓ ✓ ✓ —/after \|T | M S V | |
| I helped you out of the hole?" | ✓ ✓ ✓ ✓ ✓ ✓ ✓ | | |
| said Mr. Pig. The snake said,// | ✓ ✓ ✓ ✓ ✓ ✓ | | |
| *"You knew I was a snake* | ✓ ✓ ✓ ✓ ✓ ✓ | | |
| *when you pulled me out!"* | ✓ ✓ ✓ ✓ ✓ | | |

*Source:* From *The Flynt/Cooter Reading Inventory for the Classroom* (5th ed.), by E. S. Flynt and R. B. Cooter, Jr., 2004. Upper Saddle River, NJ: Merrill/Prentice Hall. Copyright © 2004. Used with permission of Pearson Education.

records called the **miscue grid** that makes running records more practical for classroom use. In their informal reading inventory called the Comprehensive Reading Inventory (Cooter, Flynt, & Cooter, 2007) teachers learn how to follow along during oral reading, noting miscues on a special miscue grid. Teachers mark the miscue grid according to the kind of reading miscues the student has made. By totaling the number of oral reading errors in each miscue category (i.e., mispronunciations, substitutions, etc.), as well as completing an MSV analysis for each miscue, the teacher is then able to quickly determine "miscue patterns" and begin to plan instruction accordingly. Field-tested with thousands of teachers, the miscue grid has proven to be an extremely effective and efficient classroom tool. Figure 1.7 shows an example of a completed miscue grid for a student named Grace using an excerpt from *Martha*

## FIGURE 1.7 Grace's Miscue Grid Analysis Using an Excerpt from *Martha Speaks* (Meddaugh, 1992)

| | Error Types | | | | | | | Error Analysis | | |
|---|---|---|---|---|---|---|---|---|---|---|
| | Mis-pronounce | Substitute | Insertions | Teacher Assist | Omissions | Error Totals | Self-Correct | (M) Meaning | (S) Syntax | (V) Visual |
| The day Helen gave her dog Martha | | | | | | | | | | |
| *understood*<br>alphabet soup something ~~unusual~~ | | 1 | | | | 1 | | | | 1 |
| *I . . . let . . . letters (SC)*<br>happened. The ~~letters~~ in the soup went | | | | | | | 1 | | | |
| *Brin . . . brain (SC)*   *in* ^<br>up to Martha's ~~brain~~ instead of down | | | 1 | | | 1 | 1 | 1 | 1 | |
| to her stomach. That evening, Martha | | | | | | | | | | |
| *Rep.*<br>spoke. "<u>Isn't it</u> time for my dinner?" | | | | | | | | | | |
| *TA*<br>Martha's family had many ~~questions~~ to | | | | 1 | | 1 | | | | |
| ask her. Of course, she had a lot | | | | | | | | | | |
| *Rep.*<br>to tell them. "<u>Have you always</u> understood | | | | | | | | | | |
| *are*<br>what we ~~were~~ saying?" "You bet! Do | | 1 | | | | 1 | | 1 | 1 | |
| *Betty*<br>you want to know what ~~Benji~~ is really | | 1 | | | | 1 | | 1 | 1 | |
| saying?" "Why don't you come when we | | | | | | | | | | |
| *always*<br>call?" "You people are ^ so bossy. Come! | | | 1 | | | 1 | | 1 | 1 | |
| Sit! Stay! You never say please." | | | | | | | | | | |
| "Do dogs dream?" "Day and (!00) | | | | | | | | | | |
| night." Last night I dreamed I was chasing | | | | | | | | | | |
| a giant meatloaf!" | | | | | | | | | | |
| **TOTALS** | | 3 | 2 | 1 | | 6 | 2 | 4 | 4 | 1 |

Receptions – II (2) M S V is not applicable here.

*Speaks* (Meddaugh, 1992) as the text. In the next section, we show you how a miscue grid can be analyzed using the If-Then method described earlier.

## Analyzing Running Record Findings Using If-Then Thinking

In the example shown in Figure 1.7 we note that Grace had some difficulty reading a text sample from *Martha Speaks*. Notice that for each miscue, a tick mark " I " was recorded under the appropriate column heading, thus classifying each miscue as a mispronunciation, repetition, or other reading error. After all miscues have been studied and their "error type" identified, the tick marks in each column are totaled, which helps the teacher discern where consistent problems are occurring. This process revealed that, at least with this passage, most of Grace's miscues were substitutions (3), repetitions (2), and insertions (2). She also had one teacher assist and a total of six miscues.

When doing an MSV analysis on the six countable errors (repetitions are not considered countable errors nor are they analyzed, because the use of all three MSV cuing systems is assumed with repetitions), we can conclude that

1. Meaning (M) was used with four out of six miscues.
2. Syntax (S) was also used with four of six miscues.
3. A visual (V) cue such as phonics was only used one out of six times.

With a total of six miscues when reading this 100-word selection (note that we do not count any miscues after the 100th word), simple subtraction tells us that Grace read with 94% accuracy, placing her within the "instructional" reading level for this text sample according to Clay's system mentioned earlier. *Remember:* Conclusions about students' strengths and needs should *not* be drawn from only one running record—we are doing so here simply as an illustration of the process. As already noted, a minimum of three running records should be taken and comparisons made across all three to determine whether a pattern of reading behavior exists (Fawson, Ludlow, Reutzel, Sudweeks, & Smith, 2006).

Finally, let us summarize what we know about Grace's reading according to this sample running record and a careful study of her miscues. Remember, the goal here is to identify what Grace *can* do in reading to help the teacher decide what should come next in her learning program (see Principle 1 earlier in this chapter).

### Grace Is Able to Do the Following in Reading
- Use *context clues* most of the time to help identify unknown words in print
- Use *syntax clues* most of the time to help identify unknown words in print
- Use *beginning sounds* in words as a phonics skill in decoding
- Use *ending sounds* in words as a phonics skill in decoding
- Accurately *decode one- and two-syllable words*
- Recognize common *irregularly spelled words* (e.g., *have, questions*)
- Use *print-sound mappings* to sound out unknown words

The next step would be for the teacher to refer to the *reading benchmark skills* chart (see Figure 1.2) and use Figure 1.7 to chart Grace's growth. *If,* in Grace's case, she has advanced up through most of the required grade 2 accomplishments, *then* the teacher may reasonably conclude that some sort of classroom intervention may be needed using grade 3 accomplishments as a guide, as well as tips from our If-Then Charts in relevant chapters. After reviewing grade 3 and higher accomplishments in the reading benchmark skills, Grace's zone of proximal development with regard to (a) phonics/word attack skills and (b) reading fluency seems to include the following:

| Grace's "Next Steps" for Reading Instruction | |
| --- | --- |
| **Skills Needed** | **Teaching Strategies** |
| Morphemic/structural analysis (see Chapter 6) | Explicit instruction*; Nonsense words*; Making words*; Wide reading* |
| Syllabication (see Chapter 6) | Explicit instruction*; Letter–sound cards; Sound swirl; Tongue twisters; Nonsense words*; Making words*; Wide reading* |
| Accuracy of decoding/fluency (see Chapter 7) | Oral recitation lesson; Fluency development lesson; Repeated readings; Assisted reading |

*Note: These strategies aid both morphemic/structural analysis and syllabication.

For the sake of efficiency, most teachers form short-term groups for children having the same needs. In this example, a small group of students would be formed to help students (including Grace) needing help with morphemic/structural analysis, syllabication, and accuracy of decoding.

Running records, when analyzed using the grid system, can be a most informative addition to one's reading assessment program, and make if-then analyses go much more quickly.

## Implementing Running Records: A Self-Evaluation Rubric

As with most important teaching strategies, becoming an expert in administering running records comes in stages over time; it is a continuum of learning. A team of urban literacy researchers (Cooter, Mathews, Thompson, & Cooter, 2004) developed a rubric for use in coaching teachers learning to use running records in their classrooms. It was later published as a self-assessment instrument (see Figure 1.8). In this rubric, running records are divided into conventions (marking system), analysis, and frequency of use. There are six levels of implementation for each category. We recommend that you determine your own levels of implementation monthly as you begin using running records.

Are running records the *only* way to assess decoding skills? Certainly not. In Chapter 6, "Phonics and Decoding Skills," we offer a plethora of ideas for quickly and efficiently assessing decoding skills. In addition, we provide information on one of the most widely used tools in today's classrooms, known as the Dynamic Indicators of Basic Early Literacy Skills (DIBELS), available online at https://dibels.uoregon.edu.

# $\mathcal{C}$OMPREHENSION ASSESSMENT USING RETELLING

**Comprehension** is the heart and soul of reading because it involves understanding the author's message. In later chapters, we offer many specialized ways of assessing reading comprehension that you will find quite helpful. In this section, however, we want to share with you one of the most fundamental and versatile ways of assessing reader comprehension with almost any sort of passage, a procedure called *retelling*.

**Retelling** is one of the efficient strategies for finding out whether a child understands what he or she has read (Benson & Cummins, 2000; Cooter, Flynt, & Cooter, 2007; Gambrell, Pfeiffer, & Wilson, 1985; Hoyt, 1998; Morrow, 1985), especially when compared to the seemingly endless and tedious question/answer sessions that so often characterize basal or core reading programs and their myriad workbook pages (what we sometimes call the

## FIGURE 1.8 Running Records Self-Assessment Rubric

*Directions:* Using a red marker, draw a vertical line after the description on each row that best describes your current implementation of each aspect of graphic organizers. Using a yellow marker, indicate your end of the year goal for each aspect.

| Conventions: Marking System | I have never received training on a universal marking system | I created my own marking system. | I use markings that can be interpreted by my grade level. | I use markings that can be interpreted by my school. Some markings can be universally read. | I use markings that can be interpreted by district teachers. Most markings can be universally read. | I use markings that can be interpreted universally by teachers. |
|---|---|---|---|---|---|---|
| Scoring<br>• Accuracy Rate<br>• Error Rate<br>• Self-Correction | I do not score running records | I score for accuracy rate percentage. | I use the convention chart to score for accuracy rate percentage to group my students. | I use the conversion chart to score for accuracy rate percentage and error rate to group my students. | I use the conversion chart to calculate accuracy rate percentage, error rate, and self-correction rate for grouping. | I use the conversion chart to calculate accuracy, error rate, and self-correction rates daily to inform my instruction. |
| Analysis: Cuing Systems (MSV)<br>• Meaning<br>• Structure<br>• Visual | I do not analyze my running records. | I sometimes analyze errors on running records. | I analyze all errors on each running record. | I analyze all errors and self-corrections on each running record. | I analyze all errors and self-corrections for meaning structure, and visual on each running record to guide and inform instruction. | I analyze all errors and self-corrections for meaning, structure, and visual on each running record. In addition, I look for patterns over time to further guide instruction. |
| Frequency | I do not use running records | I use running records two times a year, at the beginning and end of school. | I do running records occasionally throughout the year. | I do one running record on my struggling students once per 6 weeks. | I do one running record on all my students once per 6 weeks. | I perform running records daily so that each student is assessed each 6 weeks. My struggling students are done twice each 6 weeks. |

*Source:* From "Searching for Lessons of Mass Instruction? Try Reading Strategy Continuums," by R. B. Cooter, B. Mathews, S. Thompson, and K. S. Cooter, 2004, *The Reading Teacher, 58*(4), 388–393. Copyright © 2004 by the International Reading Association (www.reading.org). Reproduced with permission of the International Reading Association via Copyright Clearance Center.

*reading inquisition*). Teachers who routinely use retellings for comprehension assessment find that they can monitor student progress effectively and can do so in a fraction of the time required by traditional questioning methods.

## Two Phases of Retelling

We recommend two phases in conducting a retelling with students. In the first phase, **unaided recall,** students simply retell what they recall from the passage they have just read *without* being questioned or prompted by the teacher. While each student retells a story (narrative), the teacher notes important information that has been retold such as characters, setting, central problem or challenge, conclusion, and theme/moral for story retellings. These elements of a narrative selection are called *story grammar.* It is critical that the teacher keep careful notes in student retellings. Thus, a **story grammar retelling record** for narrative texts can be quite helpful. Figure 1.9 is one example. A teacher is not limited to using a specific format for making notes, but it is essential that careful and thorough notes be made for each retelling.

We have found that after students conclude the unaided recall portion of a retelling, it is often helpful to then ask, "What else can you remember about the passage?" Students will typically offer more information. You can usually use this "What else" strategy each time the student seems to be finished and up to three times before exhausting the student's ability to recall information in the unaided recall segment.

Once the student has seemingly recalled all the information he or she can without assistance, your assessment progresses to the second phase, **aided recall.** This is the act of selectively questioning students about important elements of the passage that were not remembered

---

**FIGURE 1.9**   Story Grammar Retelling Record Sheet

Student's name: _____     Date: _____

Story: _____

Source/Book: _____

| *Category* | *Prompt Questions (after retelling)* | *Student's Retelling* |
|---|---|---|
| SETTING | Where did this story take place? <br> When did this story happen? | |
| CHARACTERS | Who were the characters in this story? <br> Who was the main character(s) in the story? <br> Describe _____ in the story | |
| CHALLENGE | What is the main challenge or problem in the story? <br> What were the characters trying to do? | |
| EVENTS | What were the most important things that happened in the story? <br> What did _____ do in the story? | |
| SOLUTION | How was the challenge/problem solved? <br> What did _____ do to solve the problem? <br> How did the other characters solve their problems? | |
| THEME | What was this author trying to tell us? <br> What did _____ learn at the end of the story? | |

during the unaided recall portion of retelling. When using the story grammar retelling record sheet, for example, it is relatively simple for the teacher to quickly survey the sheet for missing information and then use the generic questions provided to draw out additional story memories by the student. For example, if a student retold most of a story during unaided recall but neglected to describe the setting, the teacher may use the first question under "SETTING" (see Figure 1.9) on the story grammar retelling record, asking "Where did this story take place?" As in the first phase with unaided recall, the teacher records all memories the student has of the story and notes any story elements the student is unable to recall. If it appears that the student is consistently unable to remember certain story elements, then a minilesson should be offered to help him or her learn appropriate comprehension strategies.

## Three Levels of Retelling

Retelling has long been recognized as an effective method for assessing reading comprehension of both narrative and expository texts (e.g., Armbruster, Anderson, & Ostertag, 1987; Rinehart, Stahl, & Erickson, 1986; Taylor, 1982). Benson and Cummins (2000) described an effective scheme for assessing and boosting comprehension development to higher levels via a three-level retelling process.

The first retelling level involves **guided oral retelling.** At this level, the goal is for students to retell the text selection using *spoken* language. The term *guided* implies a structure that is first modeled *to* learners by the teacher, then practiced *with* learners, and eventually demonstrated *by* learners.

The second level of retelling is called **graphic organizer retelling** and is based on research showing that graphic organizers can be a powerful tool for improving comprehension in expository materials (e.g., Armbruster, Anderson, & Meyer, 1992; Simmons, Griffin, & Kameenui, 1988). This level of retelling builds on the oral retelling process by having students use (a) *written words* and (b) a *graphic organizer.* In this way, students learn to use written words as part of their retelling while also developing an organizational map to connect ideas and concepts. Flynt and Cooter (2005) explained that

> this helps learners move new vocabulary and concept knowledge from short-term memory to permanent learning. Teachers should limit themselves, preferably, to just one or two graphic organizers per semester so that students are *marinated* in their use . . . and can begin using [graphic organizers] automatically in new learning situations. (p. 778)

The highest level is **written retelling.** Here students use their completed graphic organizers as a prewriting tool to construct written summaries of the text selections. Having students construct written summaries of content readings has been shown to boost comprehension and retention of new concepts (Bean & Steenwyk, 1984). As with the prior two levels, extensive teacher modeling is required. It is also recommended that a writing structure be used to help students construct their first drafts.

# OBSERVATION AND COLLECTION STRATEGIES

Observation and collection are your primary assessment tools for gathering information for understanding where students are in their reading development. **Observation** is the part of assessment in which you document students' reading behaviors using indirect methods. We find it best, at least from our own classroom experiences, for teachers to focus on just

Go to the Assignments and Activities section of Topic 12: "Progress Monitoring" in the MyEducationLab for your course and complete the activity entitled "Monitoring Reading Progress." As you read the article and answer the accompanying questions, note the importance of measuring student growth in reading at regular time intervals to monitor progress and/or make adjustments to your teaching.

two or three students daily (without the students' knowledge, if possible) for observation assessments. Here are a few examples of observation tools and processes commonly used by teachers (many more are provided throughout this book beginning in Chapter 3):

- *Anecdotal notes.* Very structured observations taken while observing a student reading, focused on major reading milestones in the student's reading development or reading skills the teacher may be emphasizing or about to emphasize in class. Many teachers like to record their **anecdotal notes** on self-adhesive labels such as those used to print addresses. These notes can then be dated and easily attached inside students' reading folders at the end of the day.

- *Reading logs.* Daily records of student reading habits and interests, usually kept during independent reading periods or practice reading times (Cambourne & Turbill, 1990). Students keep these **reading logs** by completing simple forms from a reading log folder stored in students' desks or other appropriate locations.

- *Observation checklist.* Teachers often find it helpful to use **observation checklists** as a quick reference classroom tool that incorporates what we know about reading development. Some teachers find that checklists that include a kind of Likert scale can be useful in student portfolios, because many reading behaviors become more fluent over time. Diffily (1994), while teaching kindergarten and first grade, developed the checklist shown in Figure 1.10 for use with her students. While the reading behaviors listed in any scale or checklist naturally vary according to the grade level, these formats have proven to be quite helpful.

- *Literature response projects.* There are many ways students can demonstrate their reading comprehension. In the past and in many classrooms today, workbook pages and skill sheets have been used in great numbers as a postreading assessment activity. Unfortunately, these kinds of activities are a poor substitute for actual demonstrations of competence (Sizer, 1994). As an alternative, a growing number of classroom teachers are having students complete **literature response projects** to demonstrate their understanding of what they have read.

    Literature response projects can take many forms and may be completed by individual students or in literature response groups. The idea is for the students to choose a creative way to demonstrate their competence. As we explore many aspects of reading comprehension, you will find numerous literature response ideas described in this book. For example, one group of sixth graders (Cooter & Griffith, 1989) decided to develop a board game in the form of Trivial Pursuit based on their reading of *The Lion, the Witch and the Wardrobe* (Lewis, 1961). In an Ohio classroom, a student working independently decided to create a kind of comic strip that retold the book he had just completed. And a second-grade teacher in south Texas had her class make a "character report card" in which students graded a villain in a book on such character traits as honesty, trustworthiness, and so forth using inference skills and examples from the story to justify their opinions.

- *Writing samples.* Reading and writing are reciprocal processes (Reutzel & Cooter, 2008); that is, as one skill is developed, it tends to help the student to develop the other. A **writing sample** is often a marvelous window for viewing students' understanding of phonics elements, context clues, and story elements, for example. Later in this book, we directly address reading and writing connections and ways that writing samples can be used to assess reading development.

| FIGURE 1.10 | Diffily's Literacy Development Checklist |

**Literacy Development Checklist**

Student's name: _____ Date: _____

|  | Seldom |  |  |  | Often |
|---|---|---|---|---|---|
| Chooses books for personal enjoyment | 1 | 2 | 3 | 4 | 5 |
| Knows print/picture difference | 1 | 2 | 3 | 4 | 5 |
| Knows print is read from left to right | 1 | 2 | 3 | 4 | 5 |
| Asks to be read to | 1 | 2 | 3 | 4 | 5 |
| Asks that story be read again | 1 | 2 | 3 | 4 | 5 |
| Listens attentively during story time | 1 | 2 | 3 | 4 | 5 |
| Knows what a title is | 1 | 2 | 3 | 4 | 5 |
| Knows what an author is | 1 | 2 | 3 | 4 | 5 |
| Knows what an illustrator is | 1 | 2 | 3 | 4 | 5 |
| In retellings, repeats 2+ details | 1 | 2 | 3 | 4 | 5 |
| Tells beginning, middle, end | 1 | 2 | 3 | 4 | 5 |
| Can read logos | 1 | 2 | 3 | 4 | 5 |
| Uses text in functional ways | 1 | 2 | 3 | 4 | 5 |
| "Reads" familiar books to self/others | 1 | 2 | 3 | 4 | 5 |
| Can read personal words | 1 | 2 | 3 | 4 | 5 |
| Can read sight words from books | 1 | 2 | 3 | 4 | 5 |
| Willing to "write" | 1 | 2 | 3 | 4 | 5 |
| Willing to "read" personal story | 1 | 2 | 3 | 4 | 5 |
| Willing to dictate story to adult | 1 | 2 | 3 | 4 | 5 |

*Source:* Gratefully used by the authors with the permission of Deborah Diffily, Ph.D., Southern Methodist University.

**Collection** involves direct assessment of student reading abilities, often in small groups or one-on-one situations. Throughout this book, we provide you with collection tools that will assist you in gathering myriad data for charting students' reading development. Following are a few fundamental observation strategies for reading assessment.

- *Interest inventories.* One of the most important and elusive aspects of reading assessment is affect, which deals with a student's feelings about the reading act (Mathewson, 1994). Attitude, motivation, interest, beliefs, and values are all aspects of affect that have profound effects on reading development.

  Teachers building balanced literacy programs require information in student portfolios that provide insights not only into reading materials and teaching strategies that may be employed but also into positive affective aspects that drive the reading process. Ultimately, selection of materials and strategies should be based at least in part on affective considerations. A starting point for many teachers is the **interest inventory.**

Students are asked to complete or verbally respond to items on a questionnaire such as that shown in Figure 1.11. Responses give teachers a starting point for choosing reading materials that may interest the student and elicit the best reading possible, according to his or her abilities.

- *Teacher-made tests.* Though often overused in many classrooms, paper-and-pencil tests do sometimes serve a purpose. However, we favor **teacher-made tests** that are taken from the books, songs, poetry, and other text forms used in the classroom. Note that the tests should always follow the same format as any other teacher modeling examples presented to students to ensure transfer of learning. For instance, suppose that a teacher has chosen to use a cloze passage drawn from an old favorite classroom book such as *The Napping House* (Wood, 1984) to teach how context clues may be used to choose appropriate rhyming words. The teacher-made test developed to assess an individual student's understanding of this skill should then be in the form of a cloze passage (as opposed to a multiple-choice test). Consistency

- *Family surveys.* When one is attempting to develop a clear understanding of a student's reading development, his or her reading behavior at home is obviously of great importance. **Family surveys** are brief questionnaires (too long, and they will never be answered!) sent to the student's parents or primary caregivers periodically to provide the teacher with insights into the student's home reading behaviors. Teachers can then combine the family survey response with other assessment evidence from the classroom to develop a reliable profile of the student's reading ability. An example of a family survey is provided in Figure 1.12.

- *Story maps.* **Story maps** (Beck, Omanson, & McKeown, 1982; Routman, 1988) are used to determine whether a student understands the basic elements of a narrative text or passage: setting, characters, challenge, events, solution, and theme. After reading the story, a student completes a story map. A generic format for the story map, such as the one shown in Figure 1.13, may be applied to almost any narrative text. Reading comprehension assessment and teaching procedures are discussed in more detail in Chapters 9 and 10 of this book.

---

**FIGURE 1.11**   Interest Inventory

Student's Name: _____     Date: _____

*Instructions:* Please answer the following questions on a separate sheet of paper.

1. If you could have three wishes, what would they be?
2. What would you do with $50,000?
3. What things in life bother you most?
4. What kind of person would you like to be when you are older?
5. What are your favorite classes at school, and why?
6. Who do you think is the greatest person? Why do you think so?
7. Who is your favorite person? Why?
8. What do you like to do in your free time?
9. Do you read any parts of the newspaper? Which parts?
10. How much TV do you watch each day? What are your favorite shows, and why?
11. What magazines do you like to read?
12. Name three of your favorite movies.
13. What do you like best about your home?
14. What books have you enjoyed reading?
15. What kind of books would you like to read in the future?

---

**FIGURE 1.12**   Family Survey

September 6, 20_ _

Dear Parent:

As we begin the new school year, I would like to know a little more about your child's reading habits at home. This information will help me provide the best possible learning plan for your child this year. Please take a few minutes to answer the questions below and return this survey in the self-addressed stamped envelope provided. Should you have any questions, feel free to phone me at the school between 3:00 and 5:00 P.M. at xxx-xxxx.

Cordially,

Mrs. Spencer

1. **My child likes to read the following at least once a week (check all that apply):**

   comic books _____ sports page _____

   magazines (example: *Highlights*) _____ library books _____

   cereal boxes _____ cooking recipes _____

   *TV Guide* _____ comics page _____ others (please name): _____

2. **Have you noticed your child having any reading problems? If so, please explain briefly.**
3. **What are some of your child's favorite books?**
4. **If you would like a conference to discuss your child's reading ability, please indicate which days and times (after school) would be most convenient.**

---

- *Audio and video.* Using audio and/or video to record oral reading and retelling and video to record students performing a variety of reading activities is a great way to periodically map reading growth. Recordings made at regular intervals, such as monthly, can be played back for careful analysis by the teacher and during parent–teacher conferences to demonstrate growth over time.

- *Self-rating scales.* It is often true that no one knows better how he or she is doing at reading than the reader. In the process of assessment, a teacher should never fail to ask students how they feel about their reading ability. Although this may be best achieved in a one-on-one reading conference, large public school class sizes frequently make this impractical. A good alternative to one-on-one interviews for older elementary children, however, is a student **self-rating scale.** Students complete a questionnaire that is tailored to obtain specific information about the reader—from the reader's point of view.

- *Rubrics.* As scoring guides or rating systems used in performance-based assessment (Farr & Tone, 1997; Reutzel & Cooter, 2008; Webb & Willoughby, 1993), **rubrics** assist teachers in two ways. First, rubrics make the analysis of student exhibits in the portfolio simpler. Second, rubrics make the rating process more consistent and objective. Because any assessment process is rarely objective, value free, or theoretically neutral (Bintz, 1991), rubrics clearly have an important role. Webb and Willoughby (1993) explain that "the same rubric may be used for many tasks [once established] as long as the tasks require the same skills" (p. 14).

  While there may be any number of ways to establish a rubric, Farr and Tone (1997) suggested a seven-step process of developing rubrics that may be adapted to reading as-

---

| FIGURE 1.13 | Story Map |

Name: _____     Date: _____

Title: _____     Author: _____

**SETTING** (Where and when did this story take place?)

**CHARACTERS** (Who were the main characters in this story?)

**CHALLENGE** (What is the main challenge or problem in the story?)

**EVENTS** (What were the events that happened in the story to solve the problem/challenge?)

Event 1:

Event 2:

Event 3:

(List all the important events that happened.)

**SOLUTION** (How was the challenge/problem solved or not solved?)

**THEME** (What was this author trying to tell the reader?)

---

*Source:* Adapted from Routman (1988).

---

sessment. Reutzel and Cooter (2009) modified the method slightly to conform to reading assessment needs and shortened the process to five relatively easy steps:

**Step 1:** Identify "anchor papers." Begin by collecting and sorting into several stacks reading exhibits from the portfolio (e.g., reading response activities, student self-analysis papers, content reading responses, etc.) according to quality. These are known as anchor papers. Try to analyze objectively why you feel that certain exhibits represent more advanced development in reading than others and also why some exhibits cannot be characterized as belonging in the more "advanced" categories.

**Step 2:** Choose a scoring scale for the rubric. Usually a three-, four-, or five-point scoring system is used. A three-point scale may be more reliable, meaning that if other teachers were to examine the same reading exhibits, they would be likely to arrive at the same rubric score (1, 2, or 3). However, when multiple criteria are being considered, a five-point scale or greater may be easier to apply. However, a major problem with reading rubrics is that they imply a hierarchy of skills that does not really seem to exist in many cases. For example, in the upper grades, is the ability to skim text for information a higher- or lower-level skill than scanning text for information? Probably neither label applies in this instance.

**Step 3:** Choose scoring criteria that reflect what you believe about reading development. Two points relative to reading rubrics need to be considered in Step 3: scoring and learning milestones. A rubric is usually scored in a hierarchical fashion. That is, using a five-point scale, if a student fulfills requirements for a 1, 2, and 3 score but not the criteria for a 4, then despite also fulfilling the criteria for a 5 he or she would be ranked as a 3. In disciplines such as mathematics, certain skills can be ranked hierarchically in a developmental sense. However, many reading skills cannot be ranked so clearly; thus, we recommend a procedure slightly different from that typically used to rank reading skills: If a five-point rubric is being used, survey all five reading skills or strategies identified in the rubric when reviewing exhibits found in the portfolio. If the student has the ability to do four of them, for example, then rank the student as a 4 regardless of where those skills are situated in the rubric. We hasten to add that this modification may not always be appropriate, however, especially with emergent readers for whom clearer developmental milestones are evident.

**Step 4:** Select sample reading development exhibits for each level of the rubric as exemplars and write descriptive annotations. It is important for teachers to have samples of each performance criterion in mind when attempting to use a rubric. From the Step 1 process in which anchor papers or other kinds of exhibits (e.g., running records, literature response activities, story grammar maps, etc.) have been identified, the teacher will have in his or her possession good examples, or exemplars, of each reading skill or strategy being surveyed. After a careful review of these anchor papers, it will be possible to write short descriptive statements, or annotations, that summarize what the teacher is searching for in the assessment for each level of the rubric. Figure 1.14 shows a sample rubric developed for a fifth-grade class wherein students were to de-

---

**FIGURE 1.14**   Sample Rubric for a Fifth-Grade Reading Class

**Cause–Effect Relationships: Scale for Oral and Written Response**

**Level 4:** **Student clearly describes a cause and effect of water pollution and provides concrete examples of each.**
**Student can provide an example not found in the readings.**
"We read about how sometimes toxic wastes are dumped into rivers by factories and most of the fish die. I remember hearing about how there was an oil spill in Alaska that did the same thing to fish and birds living in the area."

**Level 3:** **Student describes a cause and effect of water pollution found in the readings.**
**Student can define *pollution.***
"I remember reading about how factories sometimes dump poisonous chemicals into rivers and all the fish die. *Pollution* means that someone makes a place so dirty that animals can't live there anymore."

**Level 2:** **Student can provide examples found in the readings of water pollution or effects that pollution had on the environment.**
"I remember reading that having enough clean water to drink is a problem in some places because of garbage being dumped into the rivers."

**Level 1:** **Student is not able to voluntarily offer information found in the readings about the cause and effects of pollution.**

scribe (orally and through written response) cause–effect relationships based on in-class readings about water pollution.

**Step 5:**   Modify the rubric criteria as necessary. In any assessment, the teacher should feel free to modify the rubric's criteria as new information emerges.

- *Standardized test data.* **Standardized test data** are usually included in teacher portfolios and are sometimes discussed in parent–teacher conferences. These data do not really inform instruction—our prime motive for classroom assessment—but they do present a limited view of how the student compares to other students nationally who have also taken that particular test. Many times parents or guardians want to know how their child compares to others. Standardized tests are somewhat useful for that purpose. They may also help teachers who work mainly with students having learning problems to maintain perspective. It is sometimes easy to lose sight of what "normal reading development" is when you work only with students having learning problems. While we feel that standardized tests are not useful for making instructional decisions, they may be helpful in the situations we have mentioned.

# $\mathcal{U}$SING ASSESSMENT DATA TO INFORM INSTRUCTION

## Assessment and the Teaching/Learning Cycle

Effective instruction begins with assessment. As assessment data are gathered, the teacher is able to plan instruction that responds to learners' specific literacy learning needs. Assessment is an integral and ongoing part of the instructional cycle. Without assessment informing our instructional decisions, we are left with little more than random acts of teaching that do not address specific learning needs.

The **teaching/learning cycle** in literacy education is a logical structure for high-quality developmental instruction, also known as **Tier 1 instruction.** The teaching/learning cycle shows us how to structure daily instruction. Figure 1.15 is a flowchart representing the teaching/learning cycle (Tier 1 instruction).

### Begin with "Reading Roadmap" Data

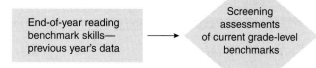

Earlier in this chapter we talked about the necessity of having a kind of "reading roadmap" for charting the progress of your learners and planning future instruction. One reading roadmap we recommended as a starting point was the reading benchmark skills. As mentioned earlier in this chapter, you may also want to supplement the reading benchmark skills with your state's learning standards (available online for most states).

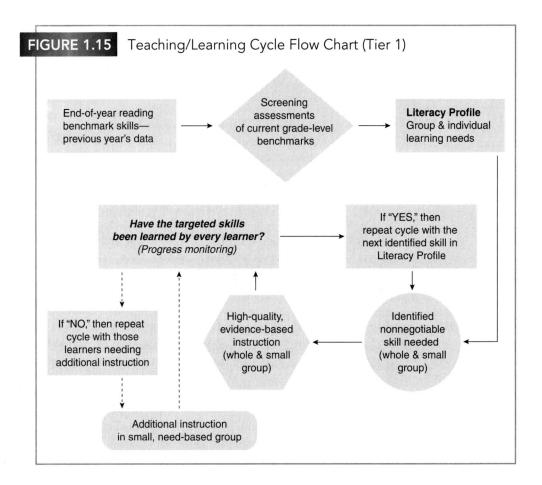

**FIGURE 1.15** Teaching/Learning Cycle Flow Chart (Tier 1)

The teaching/learning cycle begins with an analysis of our students' records regarding mastery of the previous year's end-of-year reading benchmark skills or state standards for reading. For example, if you have been assigned to teach second grade, then you would want to review your new students' data regarding first-grade end-of-year reading benchmark skills. This step helps you to better understand your new class's common abilities as well as individual needs.

Next in the teaching/learning cycle, done at the beginning of the new school year, is to assess what your students have already learned with regard to the *current* grade's end-of-year reading benchmark skills. For example, as a second-grade teacher you would administer **screening assessments** focused on the second-grade end-of-year reading benchmark skills.

### Construct a Literacy Profile

**Literacy Profile**
Group & individual
learning needs

Armed with data from the previous year's records, as well as from your beginning-of-year screening assessments, you are now able to construct a **literacy profile** for your entire class. A literacy profile reveals precisely which skills *all* your students have previously learned, as well as individual learner needs. Figure 1.16 provides an example of a first-grade literacy profile pertaining to decoding and word recognition. This literacy profile is for about one-half of a normal class for illustrative purposes. In this example we have used the reading benchmark skills for grade 1, "decoding and word recognition," as our end-of-year goals and the California Reading Standards as objectives, a good way to use the reading benchmark skills in tandem with state reading standards. We have also taken the liberty of inserting fundamental decoding skills for first grade based on our own practice with 6-year-olds (designated as "R&C").

### Forming Groups for Instruction

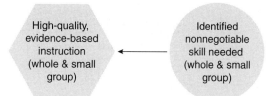

One of the things that jumps out in Figure 1.16 is that no two children are exactly the same in reading development. Thus, the old aphorism—"one size fits all"—is a poor fit in reading education! Yes, we can offer *some* instruction for the class as a whole, but clearly *some* small-group instruction is needed if we are to meet every child's needs.

For planning whole-group and small-group instruction, ask yourself three questions:

1. Based on the assessment data, what are the skills every student in my class needs to learn?
2. Which skills should I teach in small groups according to individual learner needs?
3. Understanding that reading skills are not of equal importance, which skills should be taught first according to their value to the developing reader?

Having a literacy profile makes answers to these questions easier to decide. Let's return to the literacy profile in Figure 1.16 of our partial first-grade class to see how this is done.

- *Planning whole-group instruction.* In planning for whole-group reading instruction, we want to identify the skills that *most* of our students need to learn. Why not skills that *all* students need? Frankly, it rarely happens that all students will need to learn a skill; usually, one to three will have reached proficiency with any given skill, but revisiting a skill for those students will do no harm—like good oral hygiene, brushing one's teeth an extra time per day will not harm anyone. With that in mind, here is what we see in our literacy profile in Figure 1.16 as possible skills to teach in whole-group instruction, remembering that we will select skills that *most* students need to learn. It appears that there are four reading skills with which all but two learners have not reached proficiency.

  - Decoding: Uses context clues (CC) plus beginning sounds
  - Uses CC plus beginning sounds and ending sounds
  - Uses CC plus beginning sounds, ending sounds, and medial sounds
  - Word families (onset and rime)

  It happens that all of these decoding skills in reading are of high importance. So the next question relates to the order in which they should be taught. Note that the first three skills to be taught (and really all four) as part of a decoding strategy depend on context clues, the first skill in the literacy profile.

**FIGURE 1.16** Example: Grade 1 (Partial Class) Literacy Profile—Decoding and Word Recognition

Reading Benchmark Skills: Decoding and Word Recognition: 1st grade
Decodes phonetically regular one-syllable words and nonsense words accurately

| | Cody | Tomeka | LeeRoy | Robert | Hope | Bailey | Kate | James | Eva | Natalie | Ana Grace | Danny |
|---|---|---|---|---|---|---|---|---|---|---|---|---|
| **R&C Decoding** | | | | | | | | | | | | |
| Uses context clues (CC) | P | P | P | D | E | P | P | P | D | D | E | P |
| Uses CC plus beginning sounds | D | D | P | D | E | E | P | D | D | D | E | D |
| Uses CC plus beginning sounds & ending sounds | E | D | P | E | E | E | P | E | E | E | E | E |
| Uses CC plus beginning sounds, ending sounds, & medial sounds | E | E | P | E | E | E | P | E | E | E | E | E |
| **California Standards** | | | | | | | | | | | | |
| Consonant blends | P | D | D | D | E | E | P | P | D | P | D | P |
| Long & short vowel sounds | P | P | D | E | E | E | P | P | E | P | E | P |
| Common, irregular sight words | D | D | D | D | D | P | P | P | D | P | D | P |
| Compound words | P | P | P | P | D | D | P | P | D | P | D | D |
| Word families (onset & rimes) | D | D | D | D | E | E | P | D | E | P | E | E |

Key:
**P = Proficient** (Skill Mastered—5/5 attempts)
**D = Developing** (Needs more development—3–4/5 attempts)
**E = Emergent** (Not Sufficiently Developed—less than 3/5 attempts)

Even though seven of the students have reached proficiency in the skill "Decoding: Uses context clues," this is the first skill we would recommend teaching in a whole-group setting. It is a worthy skill for review even for those who have already reached proficiency. Indeed, the students proficient in decoding with context clues can be helpful "teaching assistants" to the other learners during guided practice activities. Therefore, in planning whole-group instruction, the sequence of reading skills to be taught all learners are

1. Decoding: Uses context clues
2. Decoding: Uses context clues (CC) plus beginning sounds
3. Uses CC plus beginning sounds and ending sounds
4. Uses CC plus beginning sounds, ending sounds, and medial sounds
5. Word families (onset and rime)

• *Planning small-group instruction.* Now that we have identified skills to be taught in the whole group, we turn our attention to planning small-group instruction. Small-group instruction is by nature fluid and ever-changing in terms of learners. The purpose of small-group instruction is to meet the needs of learners *as identified by assessment.*

At the beginning of the year, small groups are formed based on screening assessments. As whole-class and small-group instruction is offered, learner needs are also identified through **progress-monitoring assessments,** which are used to help us determine whether learning has been achieved (i.e., proficiency) or, conversely, if more modeling and guided practice are indicated.

Returning to Figure 1.16 we see that for the four important decoding skills just mentioned, some students are at the emergent or developing levels. **Emergent level** means that the student has little to no ability in using the reading skill as yet and requires direct, explicit instruction. The rule of thumb we use for the emergent level is less than three out of five successful attempts at using the target skill. **Developing level** means that the students have partially learned the target skill but need further instruction (e.g., teacher modeling, guided practice, independent practice). The rule of thumb we use for the developing level is three to four out of five successful attempts at using the target skill. **Proficient level** means that the reading skill has been learned to the point of mastery and no further instruction is indicated. The rule of thumb we use for the developing level is five out of five successful attempts at using the target skill.

It is fine to have both emergent and developing learners in a needs-based group, but it is usually better to have these learners in separate groups, if possible. With that in mind, a review of Figure 1.16 suggests the following small groups:

**Skill 1: Consonant Blends** (CA Standard 1.10—Generate the sounds from all the letters and letter patterns, including consonant blends)*

**Small Group 1 (Emergent Students):** Hope, Bailey

**Small Group 2 (Developing-Level Students):** Tomeka, LeeRoy, Robert, Eva, Ana Grace

**Skill 2: Long and Short Vowel Sounds** (CA Standard 1.10—Generate the sounds from all the letters and letter patterns, including long- and short-vowel patterns [i.e., phonograms])

*Reprinted with permission of the California Department of Education, CDE Press, 1430 N Street, Suite 3707, Sacramento, CA 95814.

**Small Group 1 (Emergent Students):** Robert, Hope, Bailey, Eva, Ana Grace

**Small Group 2 (Developing-Level Students):** LeeRoy

Note that because LeeRoy was the only developing-level student in our example, we would elect to include him with the emergent-level students, though he could be taught one-on-one either by the teacher or possibly with a more proficient student in structured activities (e.g., Cody, Tomeka, Kate, James, etc.).

**Skill 3: Common, Irregular Sight Words** (CA Standard 1.11)

**Small Group 1 (Emergent Students):** None

**Small Group 2 (Developing-Level Students):** Cody, Tomeka, LeeRoy, Robert, Hope, Eva, Ana Grace

**Skill 4: Compound Words** (CA Standard 1.13)

**Small Group 1 (Emergent Students):** None

**Small Group 2 (Developing-Level Students):** Hope, Bailey, Eva, Ana Grace, Danny

- *Grouping options.* We have described above how one goes about forming groups, small and whole, for reading instruction. Though these are the main staples of group instruction, there are other alternatives to consider. In Figure 1.17 we present five options: the two shared earlier and three others, along with their relative advantages, disadvantages, and appropriate uses.

**Decision Point: Following High-Quality Instruction, Has the Skill(s) Been Learned?**

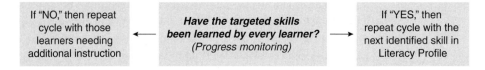

If "NO," then repeat cycle with those learners needing additional instruction ← *Have the targeted skills been learned by every learner? (Progress monitoring)* → If "YES," then repeat cycle with the next identified skill in Literacy Profile

Once decisions have been made about how you will deliver high-quality instruction on the targeted skill (i.e., grouping strategies) and you have completed learning activities, a progress-monitoring assessment is given. The question now is, *Has every student learned the targeted skill to the point of proficiency?* If the answer is yes, then those students can now move on to the next skill in the literacy profile and the learning cycle begins anew. For students who have not reached proficiency level with the skill, then the learning cycle is repeated for that same skill but with alternative teaching/learning strategies.

In the chapters that follow we offer a plethora of assessment and learning activities that will help you put the teaching/learning cycle into operation in your classroom.

# *O*NLY THE BEGINNING . . .

The purpose of this book is to provide you with myriad classroom assessment strategies that help you with your daily planning and teaching. This chapter, while providing a few of the mainstays of classroom assessment, only scratches the surface.

In Chapter 2 you will learn the basics of Response to Intervention (RtI), a teaching/learning model that describes what we should do when students do not respond well to basic developmental instruction as we have outlined in the teaching/learning cycle.

| FIGURE 1.17 | Grouping Options for Reading Instruction |
|---|---|

| Group Type | What It Is | Advantages | Disadvantages | When It Is Best to Use |
|---|---|---|---|---|
| **Whole Group** | The teacher works with all learners participating. | An efficient use of teacher contact to address a common need. | Limits student interaction and is more difficult for the teacher to assess understanding. | When there is a common need for most students. |
| **Small Group** | Two or more students work together to learn a skill or complete a task. This may be with the teacher guiding instruction or an independent task. | Provides instruction to meet the specific needs of learners; a form of needs-based differentiated instruction. Also allows other students not in the group to work independently to practice literacy skills. | Groups may become stagnant in terms of student members that leads to stigmatizing and negative perception if not addressed (i.e., Eagles, Bluebirds, Buzzards phenomenon). Also requires skillful class management skills (learning centers, seat work) for those not working with the teacher. | When a portion of the class have a common learning need in reading. |
| **Joint Productive Activity (JPA)** (Information online at http://crede.berkeley.edu) | Learners of varying ability work together using their literacy skills to solve a common problem and present a product that demonstrates their understanding. | By working together to solve a problem learners are motivated to assist one another. Promotes language and discussion while students learn. | Students must be taught how to interact with peers because collaboration skills may not come naturally. Tasks must have very clear outcome expectations. | When students have some knowledge of a new concept and need opportunities to apply it, and will benefit from language interaction. |
| **Individual (1:1)** | Students work one-on-one with the teacher or a more able peer to complete a literacy-learning task. | Provides focused instruction or practice with needed skills in a structured setting. | Requires skillful class management (learning centers, seat work) for those not working with the teacher. | When a single student has a unique learning need or requires additional instruction after others have become proficient. |
| **Buddy/Partners** | Students are paired to complete a structured literacy task. Usually a more able student is assisting the other learner. | Provides focused instruction or practice for both learners needed skills in a structured setting. | Some training is required for each structured task. | When students needs additional structured practice. |

*Source:* Based on Opitz & Ford (2008).

Chapters 3 and beyond each contain a section on assessment strategies that can help you determine each student's zone of proximal development for each major reading milestone. Each has been carefully researched, and we have used most of them in our own classrooms. So we invite you to keep reading along with us about classroom assessment. This is only the beginning!

## SELECTED REFERENCES

Armbruster, B. B., Anderson, T. H., & Meyer, J. L. (1992). Improving content-area reading using instructional graphics. *Reading Research Quarterly, 26*(4), 393–416.

Armbruster, B. B., Anderson, T. H., & Ostertag, J. (1987). Does text structure/summarization instruction facilitate learning from expository text? *Reading Research Quarterly, 22,* 331–346.

Bean, T. W., & Steenwyk, F. L. (1984). The effect of three forms of summarization instruction on sixth graders' summary writing and comprehension. *Journal of Reading Behavior, 16*(4), 297–306.

Beck, I. L., Omanson, R. C., & McKeown, M. G. (1982). An instructional redesign of reading lessons: Effects on comprehension. *Reading Research Quarterly, 17,* 462–481.

Benson, V., & Cummins, C. (2000). *The power of retelling.* New York: The Wright Group.

Betts, E. (1946). *Foundations of reading instruction.* New York: American Book.

Bintz, W. P. (1991). Staying connected—Exploring new functions for assessment. *Contemporary Education, 62*(4), 307–312.

Cambourne, B., & Turbill, J. (1990). Assessment in whole language classrooms: Theory into practice. *Elementary School Journal, 90,* 337–349.

Clay, M. (1966). *Emergent reading behaviour.* Unpublished doctoral dissertation, University of Auckland, New Zealand.

Clay, M. (1972). *The early detection of reading difficulties.* Portsmouth, NH: Heinemann Educational Books.

Clay, M. (1985). *The early detection of reading difficulties* (3rd ed.). Portsmouth, NH: Heinemann Educational Books.

Clay, M. (1997). *An observation survey of early literacy achievement.* Portsmouth, NH: Heinemann Educational Books.

Cooter, R. B., Flynt, E. S., & Cooter, K. S. (2007). *The Comprehensive Reading Inventory.* Upper Saddle River, NJ: Pearson/Merrill/Prentice Hall.

Cooter, R. B., Mathews, B., Thompson, S., & Cooter, K. S. (2004). Searching for lessons of mass instruction? Try reading strategy continuums. *The Reading Teacher, 58*(4), 388–393.

Cooter, R. B., Jr., & Griffith, R. (1989). Thematic units for middle school: An honorable seduction. *Journal of Reading, 32*(8), 676–681.

Diffily, D. (1994, April). *Portfolio assessment in early literacy settings.* Paper presented in a Professional Development Schools workshop at Texas Christian University, Fort Worth, TX.

Durrell, D. D. (1940). *Improvement of basic reading abilities.* New York: World Book.

Farr, R., & Tone, B. (1997). *Portfolio and performance assessments.* Fort Worth, TX: Harcourt Brace College.

Fawson, P. C., Ludlow, B., Reutzel, D. R., Sudweeks, R., & Smith, J. A. (2006). Examining the reliability of running records: Attaining generalizable results. *Journal of Educational Research, 100*(2), 113–126.

Flynt, E. S., & Cooter, R. B. (2005). Improving middle-grades reading in urban schools: The Memphis Comprehension Framework. *The Reading Teacher, 58*(8), 774–780.

Gambrell, L. B., Pfeiffer, W., & Wilson, R. (1985). The effects of retelling upon reading comprehension and recall of text information. *Journal of Educational Research, 78,* 216–220.

Goodman, Y. M. (1967). *A psycholinguistic description of observed oral reading phenomena in selected young beginning readers.* Unpublished doctoral dissertation, Wayne State University.

Goodman, Y. M., & Burke, C. L. (1972). *Reading miscue inventory manual: Procedures for diagnosis and evaluation.* New York: Macmillan.

Hoyt, L. (1998). *Revisit, reflect, retell.* Portsmouth, NH: Heinemann Educational Books.

Lewis, C. S. (1961). *The lion, the witch, and the wardrobe.* New York: Macmillan.

Mathewson, G. (1994). Toward a comprehensive model of affect in the reading process. In H. Singer & R. B. Ruddell (Eds.), *Theoretical models and processes of reading* (4th ed.). Newark, DE: International Reading Association.

May, F. B., & Rizzardi, L. (2002). *Reading as communication* (6th ed.). Upper Saddle River, NJ: Merrill/Prentice Hall.

Meddaugh, S. (1992). *Martha speaks.* New York: Houghton Mifflin.

Morrow, L. M. (1985). Retelling stories: A strategy for improving children's comprehension, concept of story structure and oral language complexity. *Elementary School Journal, 85,* 647–661.

Opitz, M. F., & Ford, M. P. (2008). *Do-able differentiation: Varying groups, texts, and supports to readers.* Portsmouth, NH: Heinemann.

Pearson, P. D., & Gallagher, M. C. (1983). The instruction of reading comprehension. *Contemporary Educational Psychology, 8*(3), 317–344.

Reutzel, D. R., & Cooter, R. B. (2008). *Teaching children to read: The teacher makes the difference* (5th ed.). Upper Saddle River, NJ: Merrill/Prentice Hall.

Reutzel, D. R., & Cooter, R. B. (2009). *The essentials of teaching children to read* (2nd ed.). Upper Saddle River, NJ: Merrill/Prentice Hall.

Rinehart, S. D., Stahl, S. A., & Erickson, L. G. (1986). Some effects of summarization training on reading and studying. *Reading Research Quarterly, 21*(4), 422–438.

Routman, R. (1988). *Transitions: From literature to literacy.* Portsmouth, NH: Heinemann Educational Books.

Simmons, D. C., Griffin, C. C., & Kameenui, E. J. (1988). Effects of teacher-constructed pre- and post-graphic organizer instruction on sixth-grade science students' comprehension and recall. *Journal of Educational Research, 82*(1), 15–21.

Sizer, T. (1994). *Reinventing our schools.* Bloomington, IN: Phi Delta Kappa.

Taylor, B. M. (1982). Text structure and children's comprehension and memory for expository material. *Journal of Educational Psychology, 74*(3), 323–340.

Vygotsky, L. S. (1986). *Thought and language.* Cambridge, MA: MIT Press.

Vygotsky, L. S. (1990). *Mind in society.* Boston: Harvard University Press.

Webb, K., & Willoughby, N. (1993). An analytic rubric for scoring graphs. *The Texas School Teacher, 22*(3), 14–15.

White, D. (2008). *Assessment first: Using just-right assessments to plan and carry out effective reading instruction.* New York: Scholastic.

Wiener, R. B., & Cohen, J. H. (1997). *Literacy portfolios: Using assessment to guide instruction.* Columbus, OH: Merrill/Prentice Hall.

Wood, A. (1984). *The napping house.* New York: Harcourt.

**PEARSON**
**myeducationlab**
**The Power of Classroom Practice**
www.myeducationlab.com

Now go to Topic 1: "Reading Instruction," Topic 2: "Reading Assessment," and Topic 12: "Progress Monitoring" in the MyEducationLab (www.myeducationlab.com) for your course, where you can:

- Find learning outcomes for "Reading Instruction," "Reading Assessment," and "Progress Monitoring," along with the national standards that connect to these outcomes.
- Complete the tasks in the Assignments and Activities to help you more deeply understand the chapter content.
- Examine challenging situations and cases presented in the IRIS Center Resources.
- Apply and practice your understanding of the core teaching skills identified in the chapter with the Building Teaching Skills and Dispositions learning units.

# 2

# Response to Intervention (RtI)

## Differentiating Instruction for Struggling Readers

$M$rs. Bachio, a third-grade teacher in an inner-city school, had just finished up administering the DIBELS Oral Reading Fluency (ORF) subtest to her student, Alfonso. After scoring the ORF, Mrs. Bachio determined that Alfonso was reading 67 words correct per minute (wcpm). This placed Alfonso well below accuracy and rate norms established for a third-grade student at the middle of the year.

Alfonso was a cheerful, willing student who tried hard to please Mrs. Bachio. He was attentive during core reading instruction lessons delivered to the whole class, but could not read the third-grade level core reading program selections without someone to buddy-read with him. Also, Alfonso usually was not able to independently use strategies or skills taught him during core reading instruction, nor did he easily pick up on new concepts taught during vocabulary instruction. Mrs. Bachio was becoming increasingly frustrated with her inability to accelerate Alfonso's reading development. She was faithfully teaching the core reading program lessons and presented well-planned and explicit strategy, skill, and concept lessons to her class. What more could she do?

Mrs. Bachio approached her school reading coach, Ms. George, for assistance. "What can I do to help Alfonso? I just don't seem to be reaching him with my core reading instruction," lamented Mrs. Bachio.

"I was just in a workshop two days ago and I learned about a new way to meet the needs of all students in a classroom called Response to Intervention, or RtI," said Ms. George. "It provides a structure for regularly monitoring the progress of your students and then placing them into small groups for intensive instruction targeted to their particular learning needs. After you try out an intervention intended to meet your students' learning needs for a brief period, their progress is monitored regularly to determine if the intervention selected to meet their needs is helping them to make the desired growth. If not, you select another intervention to try and continue to monitor the effect of the new intervention on the students' progress. If students do not respond positively after several attempts to alter the intervention, you can then enlist the help of other specialized teachers, such as the Title I reading specialist or the special education teacher in the school."

"Sounds interesting! When will we learn more about this?" asked Mrs. Bachio. "We can begin to read and discuss how RtI could be used in our school at our next grade-level study group meeting. What do you think?" "I think I could use the help," Mrs. Bachio replied. "What can I start reading now to get ready for our discussion?" "I'll email you an article they gave us at the workshop," Ms. George said with a smile. "Great!" said Mrs. Bachio. "Maybe RtI is just the help I need to reach Alfonso," she thought to herself as she headed back to her classroom.

Differentiating instruction is essential if we are to help *every* child succeed. In Chapter 1 we saw in the teaching/learning cycle how high-quality instruction is offered to all students. We also saw that small-group instruction is offered selectively to some students according to their particular learning needs as identified through the assessment-driven literacy profile. Thus, high-quality developmental reading instruction is offered to all learners, sometimes in differentiated small-group instruction. But what happens when our best efforts do not work for some learners, even after we have offered second or even third rounds of explicit instruction as shown in the teaching/learning cycle?

In recent years a model for addressing the needs of struggling readers has emerged called Response to Intervention, or RtI. In this chapter we see how RtI is used in reading/literacy instruction in assisting struggling readers to fill in learning gaps as quickly as possible and return them to core (i.e., developmental) literacy instruction.

# WHAT IS RtI?

## RtI: Three-Tiered Instruction

With the emergence of frequent progress-monitoring assessment and instructional differentiation as central features of effective literacy instruction, so too has the acceptance and use of **Response to Intervention** (RtI) models grown in popularity. In RtI, all students are initially screened to determine if they are making adequate progress in developing established literacy benchmark skills, objectives, and standards. Students who are shown in initial screening assessment to be on track in their literacy development continue to receive core reading instruction, or Tier 1–level developmental instruction. In Chapter 1, the teaching/learning cycle we discussed *is* Tier 1 instruction. Students discovered to be lagging substantially behind in literacy development, or at risk of failure, receive specially selected evidence-based interventions in reading and writing, or Tier 2–level instruction.

Tier 2 interventions are intended to fill in learning gaps as quickly as possible and return students to core (i.e., developmental) literacy instruction. Tier 2 interventions are delivered at least three times per week in small-group settings *in addition* to regular classroom instruction. Frequent and regular progress-monitoring assessment is used to determine the success of Tier 2 interventions with students. All instructional interventions must be documented and must be offered for a substantial amount of time (e.g., a minimum of eight weeks). If Tier 2 instructional intervention fails to accelerate or positively impact a student's literacy learning, then Tier 3 evidence-based interventions are attempted with greater frequency and delivered in even smaller groups or individually until the student shows a positive response. Figure 2.1

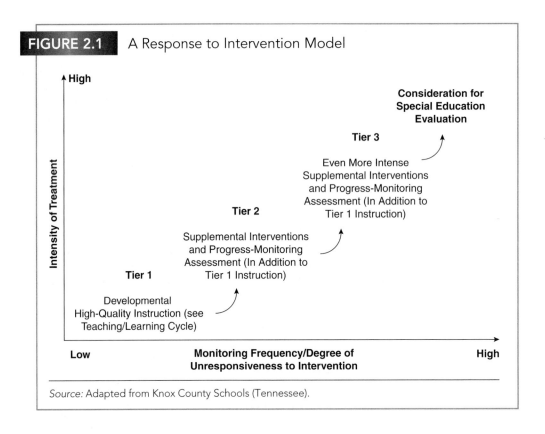

**FIGURE 2.1**  A Response to Intervention Model

*Source:* Adapted from Knox County Schools (Tennessee).

places the teaching/learning (Tier 1) model from Chapter 1 into the context of Response to Intervention (RtI).

In summary, RtI integrates high-quality evidence-based instruction and frequent use of reliable and valid assessments in a systematic way. In this way struggling learners can be quickly given the chance to succeed using alternative instructional interventions. One online tool we recommend for those just learning about RtI are the training modules offered by the IRIS Center at Vanderbilt University at http://iris.peabody.vanderbilt.edu/index.html.

Response to Intervention, though not an entirely new concept, represents a major theoretical and practical shift in federal policy and law that affects both regular and special education classrooms. RtI is intended to increase student access to rapid instructional intervention when they *begin* to struggle in literacy instead of the "wait to fail" discrepancy model that was in effect for so many years. There are several concepts central to Response to Intervention models (see Figure 2.2; McCook, 2007).

One of the concepts central to the use of RtI models is the systematic and planned use of valid and reliable assessments (Fuchs, Fuchs, & Vaughn, 2008). These assessments have undergone extensive evaluation to be certain that the scores obtained actually measure what is supposed to be measured in stable, consistent, and dependable ways. Another concept central to the use of RtI models is making instructional decisions based on systematically collected assessment data rather than on impressions, hunches, or incidental observations such as what some once called *kid watching* (Haager, Klinger, & Vaughn, 2007).

The use of scientifically-based or evidence-based core literacy instructional programs and practices are usually a part of RtI models. Teachers implement core literacy instructional programs and practices that have been shown in multiple studies to endow students with consistent, replicable learning advantages over other tested interventions (Brown-Chidsey & Steege, 2005). To discover which of these programs have been found effective, we recom-

Go to the Assignments and Activities section of Topic 11: "Reading Difficulties and Intervention Strategies" in the MyEducationLab for your course and complete the activity entitled "Early Intervention." As you watch the video and answer the accompanying questions, note how early reading achievement predicts later reading performance. Why do you think that early reading achievement has such a profound lasting effect on later academic achievement in school?

| FIGURE 2.2 | Concepts Typically Associated with Response to Intervention (RtI) Models |
| --- | --- |

- *Universal screening.* All students are evaluated according to benchmark norms for literacy development. Benchmark data are collected three times per year in the fall, winter, and spring. Data from these benchmark assessments must be "user friendly" and shared with teachers, principals, parents, and school district staff.

- *Measurable definition of the problem area.* If a problem in reading and/or writing development is thought to exist, then a specific definition of the problem must be stated. The problem area description must be specific and lend itself to objective measurement. It cannot be anecdotal or opinion data.

- *Baseline data prior to an intervention.* Once a learning problem has been tentatively identified, the teacher will use a curriculum-based measurement (CBM) to identify specifically the performance of an individual child on a specific measure (e.g. words read correctly in one minute). The CBM must have the capacity to compare the child's performance to that of the class, school, or performance nationally by other children.

- *Establishment of a written plan that details who is accountable.* Once a student (or group of students) having a learning deficit is identified, an intervention plan is created. This plan cannot simply include the same teaching strategies and materials as were used before and expect a different result. In the written plan the teacher must describe which learning strategies are to be used, who will provide the instruction, when and where it will be provided, and for how long before the next progress-monitoring assessment is conducted.

- *Intervention is delivered.* Teachers use an "evidence-based" instructional intervention, either a commercially published program having substantial evidence as to its effectiveness (What Works Clearinghouse [online at http://ies.ed.gov/ncee/wwc] is a good source to identify these), or locally developed core literacy instruction program with a clearly articulated scope and sequence of instruction.

- *Progress monitoring.* These assessments are meant to be formative in nature (occur while instruction is being provided so that adjustments can be made). There should be a variety of data-collection methods that measure a student's development over time so as to evaluate the student's response to the intervention.

- *Comparison of pre-intervention data to post-intervention data to determine effectiveness.* The purpose at this stage is to find out if the intervention worked. A decision-making rubric should be used to make that determination.

*Source:* Adapted from McCook (2007).

mend you consult the website for the What Works Clearinghouse online at http://ies.ed.gov/ncee/wwc.

As noted earlier, RtI models envision the prevention of student reading failure through the systematic implementation of a series of "tiered" or cascading instructional safety nets in which identified students receive timely, targeted, high-quality, intensive, evidence-based core and supplemental instructional interventions (Brown-Chidsey & Steege, 2005).

## "Outsourcing" Is Out

Although research on the effectiveness of various literacy instructional interventions has been in place for many years, the findings of this research have not always been consistently consulted or used by classroom teachers to inform their classroom instructional decisions. Furthermore, when students in the past failed to make adequate progress in becoming readers and writers, they were often required to be referred for out-of-the-classroom special services. This "outsourcing" of teaching interventions was no doubt owing to the many federal

*grouping happens
on Tier 1*

---

*Tier 2 extra dose
of instruction*

---

*T3 non-responders
Add. 30 min. +
30 min.*

ıggling students were to have access to such special programs
n under Public Law 94-142. A kind of silo effect has resulted
ıded to place special service providers (i.e., Title I and special
regular classroom instead of working as a team.
working harder than ever to differentiate their literacy instruc-
ıre also able to work with other educators as a team to offer
possible within the context of the regular classroom. School
e viewed shifts in practice associated with the use of RtI models
case that the use of RtI models has been made part of the law
federal educational programs: the Elementary and Secondary
Child Left Behind (NCLB) and the Individuals with Disabilities
ping, educational leaders and policymakers at the federal level
hat RtI methods will become an essential feature of effective
ment in today's classrooms. However, at this juncture RtI is not
es.

## Connecting the Use of RtI Models to Assessment

There are four major assessment purposes: (1) screening assessment, (2) diagnostic assessment, (3) progress-monitoring assessment, and (4) outcomes assessment. **Screening assessments** are administered at the beginning of the academic year to *all* students to determine whether there are preexisting deficits in any given student's literacy development and growth that may put him or her at risk for making inadequate progress in classroom literacy instruction. If students perform as expected according to grade-level benchmarks on screening assessments, then there is no need for additional assessment beyond progress monitoring; these students are likely to be well served with a high-quality evidence-based classroom core literacy program (Tier 1). On the other hand, if students perform below expectations on literacy screening assessments, then this may signal the need for additional **diagnostic assessment** to pinpoint the source of the problem. Diagnostic assessment will help you design interventions that address potential problems.

During the school year students' progress is monitored at least three times at predetermined intervals using **progress-monitoring assessment.** However, students identified as making inadequate progress in literacy will be assessed or "progress-monitored" once or preferably twice weekly (McCook, 2007) to determine if they are making desired progress. If progress monitoring shows acceptable literacy growth for these at-risk learners, then one can conclude that the literacy intervention in use is effective and can be continued. If progress monitoring demonstrates little or no student progress, then the intervention selected is not having the desired effect and another or additional literacy instructional intervention may be needed.

At or near the end of the school year, state and federal mandates often require that **outcomes assessments** be used to determine the overall effectiveness of the literacy program for all students. Typically outcome assessments are one of two types: norm-referenced tests (NRT), in which students' literacy progress is compared with other students nationally, or criterion-referenced tests (CRT), in which students' progress is judged against established literacy benchmarks or standards.

All students are entitled to receive high-quality, evidence-based, grade-level literacy instruction regardless of their performance on screening, diagnostic, or progress-monitoring assessments. The literacy instruction or core classroom literacy program offered to all grade-level students within classrooms is referred to as **Tier 1** intervention (see Figure 2.3).

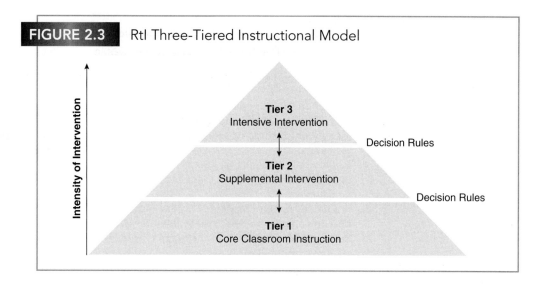

**FIGURE 2.3**   RtI Three-Tiered Instructional Model

Decisions about **Tier 2** literacy interventions are determined initially from the results of screening assessments. Tier 2 literacy interventions often occur in small (1:5, 1:4, or 1:3) differentiated instructional groups in the regular education classroom (McCook, 2007; Walpole & McKenna, 2007). It is recommended that Tier 2 students receive, for a minimum of 30 minutes per day three times per week or daily if possible, evidence-based instruction designed to supplement the core literacy program in a small-group format in addition to 90 minutes of core instruction. The professional delivering Tier 2 services may be the classroom teacher and/or a specialized teacher (e.g., Title I or special education teacher) or an external interventionist. Supplemental Tier 2 instruction may be delivered in the regular classroom or outside the classroom. The duration of Tier 2 instruction is usually at least eight weeks. If Tier 2 interventions are found to be insufficiently effective over time and students have not responded, they then move into **Tier 3** interventions.

Tier 3 interventions provide the last layer of instructional safety netting intended to address the needs of struggling literacy learners. Tier 3 interventions, as with Tier 2 interventions, can be provided within the classroom, through what is called a *push in* approach, or outside the classroom, in what is referred to as a *pull out* approach. At Tier 3 students receive even more intensive and sustained instruction in addition to the core literacy program. It has been recommended that Tier 3 students receive a minimum of three 30-minute periods daily of supplemental instruction (i.e., in addition to the core reading program other children also receive) using evidence-based practices (McCook, 2007). In terms of assessment, Tier 3 students receive progress monitoring twice a week or at a minimum weekly on target skills to ensure adequate progress and learning. In cases where a student has not made sufficient progress after Tier 3 interventions have been tried and documented over time (at least eight weeks), she is then assessed further by a certified diagnostician to determine whether the student qualifies for special education services.

## RtI and Problem Solving

Response to Intervention models are intended to provide teachers and other educational service providers with a model for an integrated approach to problem solving. Based on the work of Brown-Chidsey and Steege (2005, pp. 64–87), we list a sequence of 10 steps for problem-solving students' literacy progress as found in typical RtI models (see Figure 2.4).

| FIGURE 2.4 | Ten Steps to Problem-Solving Students' Literacy Progress in RtI Models |
| --- | --- |

1. Implement evidence-based core literacy instruction programs and practices in Tier 1 instruction.
2. Collect progress-monitoring assessment data on all students at three equally spaced "benchmark" intervals during the academic year.
3. Identify which students scored below established literacy benchmark targets or indicators.
4. Provide daily doses of additional evidence-based and targeted literacy instruction in small groups (Tier 2) for identified students scoring below established benchmarks.
5. Frequently monitor student progress in daily small group literacy instruction to determine students' response to the intervention.
6. Review small-group literacy instruction for revision or discontinuation based on results of frequent progress monitoring of students.
7. If revisions are needed consider increasing the intensity, duration, or frequency of small-group literacy instruction groups to meet students' literacy instructional needs.
8. After making revisions, continue to review the use of small-group literacy instruction based on frequent progress-monitoring data for further revision or discontinuation.
9. If after additional revisions to small-group literacy instruction students evidence the need on progress-monitoring assessments for additional instructional support, recommend such students for comprehensive literacy diagnostic evaluation.
10. Determine eligibility and need of the student for supplemental literacy instructional support services (Tier 3), including special education, Title I, tutoring, and speech-language or English language learning programs.

## Alternative RtI Models

Although scholars continue to debate RtI models with more than three tiers (Shanahan, 2008), most school districts typically use a three-tiered model. For example, preliminary research on the use of a three-tiered RtI model showed that students' receiving Tier 1 + SS (traditional school services) outperformed a historical control group on end-of-year Letter Naming, Phonemic Segmentation, and Oral Reading Fluency DIBELS subtests (Good & Kaminski, 2002) and on two subtests of the Woodcock-Johnson Reading Mastery Test (Woodcock, 1987). Students in a Tier 1 + 2 instruction treatment group outperformed the students receiving Tier 1 + SS (traditional school services) and the historical control group (Vaughn, Linan-Thompson, Elbaum, et al., 2004). These results indicate greater effectiveness for using RtI models to increase at-risk students' literacy progress compared to a historical control group and a comparison group receiving only the Tier 1 + SS (core reading instruction plus traditional school services) offered in most schools (Vaughn, Wanzek, Woodruff, & Linan-Thompson, 2007).

Because RtI models of instruction are intended to provide *every* student equitable access to effective literacy instruction, we now turn our attention in this chapter to how classroom teachers can provide effective Tier 1 and 2 literacy instruction that is responsive to the needs of each student. In the following sections of this chapter, we discuss the elements of effective evidence-based core literacy instruction programs and practices (Tier 1) and differentiated small-group literacy instruction (Tier 2) in the regular education classroom.

# RESPONSE TO INTERVENTION (RtI): EFFECTIVE TIER 1 READING INSTRUCTION

Effective Tier 1 literacy instruction is anchored in the findings of scientific research evidence. Scientific research evidence is derived from studies that report the results of experiments in which one or more instructional interventions are tested against a control or comparison instructional intervention (Stanovich & Stanovich, 2003). Scientific research reports are published in "blind" peer-reviewed research journals. Blind peer review means that the reviewers do not know the identity of the authors submitting the report for potential publication, thus protecting against studies being selected for publication based on an author's reputation and not on the quality of the study. For an instructional intervention to be considered evidence based, findings or results from multiple studies must come to the same conclusion about its effectiveness. Findings from a single study or even several studies (less than a dozen or so) are insufficient to qualify an instructional intervention as evidence based. Thus, the bar for claiming an instructional intervention to be evidence based is extremely high, and classroom teachers are well advised to use these practices and programs. Teachers can familiarize themselves with evidence-based literacy instructional practices by consulting the following websites: www.nationalreadingpanel.org and www.reading.org.

## Essential Components of Evidence-Based Literacy Instruction

In the past two decades, a series of reports has been commissioned to determine the essential evidence-based components of literacy programs and practices that students of all ages need to be taught in order to become successful readers and writers. In one of these reports, sponsored by the National Academy of Sciences and National Research Council, prominent reading and education experts convened to review existing research studies to determine which skills, concepts, and strategies must be taught to prevent students from falling into early reading difficulties or eventual reading failure. This panel issued a report entitled *Preventing Reading Difficulties in Young Children* (Snow, Burns, & Griffin, 1998). A companion document intended to make the findings of this research report more accessible to parents and teachers was published in 1999 entitled *Starting Out Right: A Guide to Promoting Children's Reading Success* (Burns, Griffin, & Snow, 1999). In these reports, the National Research Council spelled out several essential evidence-based literacy instruction components that need to be taught to prevent students from encountering early reading difficulties and failure.

Two years later, in direct response to a U.S. congressional mandate to examine the status of scientific research on teaching young children to read, the *Report of the National Reading Panel: Teaching Children to Read* was jointly published by the National Institute of Child Health and Human Development (2000), the National Institutes of Health, and the U.S. Department of Education. A companion document entitled *Put Reading First: The Research Building Blocks for Teaching Children to Read* (Armbruster, Lehr, & Osborn, 2001) was distributed with the intent to widely disseminate the findings of the National Reading Panel report to parents and educators.

We now know that high-quality evidence-based literacy instruction programs and practices focus instruction on the following essential components of effective literacy instruction:

- Oral language development
- Concepts of print
- Letter name knowledge

Go to the Assignments and Activities section of Topic 11: "Reading Difficulties and Intervention Strategies" in the MyEducationLab for your course and complete the activity entitled "Causes of Reading Failure." As you watch the video and answer the accompanying questions, make a list of the major causes of reading failure and what the indicators are of the causes.

Go to the Building Teaching Skills and Dispositions section of Topic 13: "Struggling Readers and Others with Special Needs" in the MyEducationLab for your course and complete the activity entitled "Explicitly Instructing Struggling Readers." As you work through the learning unit, consider how by using student data teachers can group, progress-monitor instructional effectiveness, and adjust the instruction each student receives to differentiate instruction to meet each student's need.

Go to the Building Teaching Skills and Dispositions section of Topic 11: "Reading Difficulties and Intervention Strategies" in the MyEducationLab for your course and complete the activity entitled "Understanding How to Use Various Strategies to Accommodate the Factors That Affect Reading Development." As you work through the learning unit, consider the importance that knowing individual word meanings has for understanding what one reads. Think about how comprehension is built one word meaning at a time and why knowing and teaching oral and reading vocabulary should assume such a central role in literacy instruction.

- Sight word recognition
- Phonemic awareness
- Phonics
- Fluency
- Vocabulary
- Comprehension
- Writing/spelling
- Volume reading and writing

Rather than elaborate on each of the foregoing essential evidence-based literacy instruction components here, we provide detailed treatment of each in the remaining chapters of this book. In these subsequent chapters, we describe the background knowledge needed, the assessment tools and procedures required, and the instructional strategies associated with the use of each of the evidence-based components of effective literacy instruction listed above.

An equally important component of evidence-based reading instruction includes students' access to appropriately challenging and volume reading and writing of a variety of text types such as books, poetry, graphic novels, and so on (Neuman, 1999; Neuman & Celano, 2001, 2006). Access to printed texts and printmaking supplies or materials may include but are not limited to

- A variety of interesting and appropriately challenging reading and writing materials to include both good literature and information books
- Supportive and assistive technologies for learning to read and write
- Socio-dramatic, literacy-enriched play in kindergarten
- A variety of paper, writing media, binding materials, stencils, etc.
- A computer with word processing software and a printer

## Characteristics of High-Quality Literacy Instruction

The quality of literacy instruction provided by the classroom teacher is the single greatest determiner of a student's later literacy achievement (Sanders & Rivers, 1996). Several studies have described the practices, beliefs, and knowledge of exemplary elementary classroom literacy teachers (Au, 2006; Block, Oakar, & Hurt, 2002; Morrow, Tracey, Woo, & Pressley, 1999; Pressley, Allington, Wharton-McDonald, Collins Block, & Morrow, 2001; Rogg, 2001; Taylor, Pearson, Clark, & Walpole, 1999; Taylor, Pearson, Peterson, & Rodriguez, 2005). Taken together these research reports reveal identifiable characteristics of teachers whose classroom instructional practices lead to exceptional reading achievement for their students. Highly effective literacy teachers who make a difference in their students' literacy achievement share the characteristics shown in Figure 2.5.

## Grouping Students for Tier 1 Literacy Instruction

Tier 1 literacy instruction typically makes use of multiple grouping formats to meet each student's needs. Although the exclusive use of whole-group literacy instruction is not significantly associated with strong gains in students' literacy growth, conversely, too much small-group instruction time results in students spending large amounts of time in independent seatwork or in centers engaged in relatively low-level literacy learning activities with little or no accountability. Exemplary classroom teachers seek a balance between using both whole-class and small-group instruction when offering Tier 1 and 2 literacy instruction in classrooms (Taylor, 2008).

Because literacy instruction and learning is a social as well as a cognitive endeavor, whole-class instruction can engage teachers and students in a classroom community of socially

*Student engagement Response*

---

**FIGURE 2.5** Characteristics of High Quality Literacy Instruction

- *Instructional balance.* Teachers integrate explicit instruction into authentic reading and writing experience within connected text.
- *Instructional density.* Teachers instruct a large quantity of skills/concepts/strategies per hour of instruction. Every moment in the classroom is oriented toward promoting literacy learning—even lining up for lunch or recess!
- *Instructional scaffolding.* Teachers support students as they develop the ability to independently perform literacy processes and tasks.
- *Work in the zone.* Teachers determine each child's zone of proximal development (ZPD) through assessment prior to providing instruction.
- *Encourage self regulation.* Teachers structure the classroom environment and learning activities so that students understand expectations, behaviors, and outcomes to promote independence, cooperation, and task completion.
- *Integrate reading and writing.* Teachers use reading and writing in mutually supportive ways. Children learned to "read what they write" and "write what they read."
- *High expectations.* Teachers expect all children to learn and meet high standards of literacy performance.
- *Effective classroom management.* Teachers painstakingly organize classroom spaces and provide students procedural training about purposes and expectations. Routines and procedures are clearly defined, well understood, conspicuously displayed, and consistently applied.
- *Skills/concepts/strategies explicitly taught.* Teachers teach literacy strategies, skills, and concepts through explanations, modeling, and a gradual release of responsibility over time to independence. Teachers believe that reading and writing skills, strategies, processes, and concepts are "taught" not "caught."

- *Quick transitions among literacy instruction activities.* Teachers strive to maximize instructional time by minimizing transitions between literacy learning activities in the classroom. Procedures for making transitions should be smooth, orderly, and quick—typically around 1 minute.
- *Volume reading and writing.* Teachers provide abundant daily opportunities to read and write texts.
- *Match the task difficulty to student competence.* Teachers ensure that the tasks assigned in reading and writing are sufficiently challenging to promote engagement and progress but not so challenging as to induce frustration and failure.
- *Connect literacy across the curriculum.* Teachers teach and encourage students to use reading and writing skills, strategies, and concept when learning in other curriculum content areas.
- *Positive, personally reinforcing classroom environment.* Teachers maintain a classroom atmosphere of respect, support, collaboration, and clear expectations.
- *Multidimensional word recognition instruction.* Teachers teach children to use letter–sound information, word parts and patterns, and contextual information to identify unknown words.
- *Printed prompts prominently displayed.* Teachers recognize the human tendency to forget rules, routines, and procedures and ensure that such critical information is conspicuously displayed.
- *Sufficient daily allocated literacy instruction time.* Teachers set aside between 120 and 180 minutes per day for high-quality evidence-based literacy instruction.
- *Culturally responsive instruction.* Teachers build on their students' varied cultural, linguistic, and personal background experiences and knowledge. They teach with books and text materials in which children can see others similar to themselves.

---

shared literacy activities, demonstrations, lessons, and discussions. Shared literacy learning activities generally provided in whole-class instruction ought to be a regular and integral part of daily literacy instruction (Cunningham, Hall, & Defee, 1998; Flood, Lapp, Flood, & Nagel, 1992; Wilkinson & Townsend, 2000). A few examples of shared literacy learning activities during whole-class instruction include telling stories; teacher demonstrations of strategy use; dramatizing stories; reading books aloud; discussing books; sharing student-authored stories, poems, and songs; reading enlarged texts of stories, songs, poems, raps, and jingles; and participating in experiments or other active-learning experiences.

## Establishing a Routine in Tier 1 Literacy Instruction

Children develop a sense of security when the events of the school day revolve around a predictable sequence of literacy learning events and activities. Students find comfort in familiar instructional routines and daily classroom schedules in a well-organized and managed classroom (Morrow, Reutzel, & Casey, 2006). There are any number of ways to organize activities and instruction for Tier 1 literacy instruction. However, one of the most critical considerations for the teacher is time allocation and scheduling.

There seems to be a fairly wide range as to how long literacy instruction should be in elementary school classrooms, but many schools require 120 to 180 minutes of instruction each day in reading and writing. Shanahan (2004) also recommends the allocation of at least 120 minutes per day for Tier 1 literacy instruction. As shown in Figure 2.6, this total time allocation of 120 minutes of Tier 1 literacy instruction is further subdivided into four 30-minute literacy instructional blocks focused on the essential elements of evidence-based literacy instruction, namely word work, fluency, writing, and comprehension strategies.

The purpose of the 30-minute **word work** instructional block is to develop students' phonological and phonemic awareness, concepts about print, letter name knowledge, decoding and word recognition, and spelling concepts, skills, and strategies. During these 30 minutes, the effective literacy teacher provides the whole class with explicit instruction on each of these word-related skills, strategies, and concepts. Students receive clear verbal explanations or "think alouds" coupled with expert modeling of reading and writing concepts, skills, and strategies. Having clearly modeled reading and writing word work concepts, skills and strategies, teachers then provide students guided or supervised practice.

The purpose of the daily 30-minute **fluency** instructional block is two-fold. First, students are given brief explicit lessons that help them understand the elements of fluent reading: accuracy, rate, and expression. Students also see and hear the teacher model the elements of fluent reading as well. This is followed by the teacher involving students in reading practice to develop fluency. Effective Tier 1 literacy teachers use various formats for reading fluency practice, such as choral reading, including such variations as echoic (echo chamber), unison (all together), antiphonal (one group of students reading against another), mumble reading (whisper), line-a-child, and so on. For those who are unfamiliar with these choral reading variations, we recommend Opitz and Rasinski's (2008) *Good-Bye Round Robin* or Rasinski's (2003) *The Fluent Reader*. Students can also read in pairs, with same-age peers or older peers from higher grade-level classrooms. Each pair alternates the roles of reader and listener. After each oral reading, the listener provides feedback. Students can also prepare oral reading performances, for which effective Tier 1 literacy teachers can select one of three well-known oral reading performance approaches: readers' theater, radio reading, or recitation.

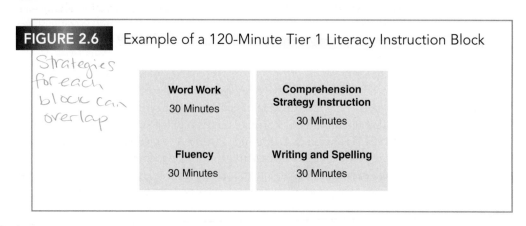

Strategies for each block can overlap

**FIGURE 2.6** Example of a 120-Minute Tier 1 Literacy Instruction Block

**Word Work**
30 Minutes

**Comprehension Strategy Instruction**
30 Minutes

**Fluency**
30 Minutes

**Writing and Spelling**
30 Minutes

*[handwritten margin note: Comprehension reading program - what should be included]*

The purpose of the **writing** instructional block in Tier 1 literacy instruction is to develop students' composition skills, spelling, writing mechanics, and grammatical understandings. Effective instructional practices used within this time allocation include modeled writing by the teacher; a writer's workshop, including drafting, conferencing, revising, editing, publishing, and disseminating; and direct explicit whole-class instruction on each of these writing skills, strategies, and concepts. We also strongly recommend that daily lessons provide a time allocation for sharing children's writing in an "author's chair" or some other method of disseminating and sharing children's writing products.

The purpose of the **comprehension strategies** 30-minute instructional block is to develop students' vocabulary and comprehension strategies. Effective instructional practices used within this time segment include explicit instruction of vocabulary concepts, using a variety of methods and requiring a variety of responses such as word play and word awareness (Beck, McKeown, & Kucan, 2002; Johnson, 2001; McKenna, 2002). As for comprehension instruction, effective Tier 1 literacy teachers focus attention on explicitly teaching evidence-based reading comprehension strategies, including question answering, question asking, story and text structure, graphic organizers, monitoring, summarizing, and activating/building background knowledge. At some point in time, effective Tier 1 literacy teachers teach students to use a set or family of multiple comprehension strategies such as reciprocal teaching (Palincsar, 2003), concept-oriented reading instruction (Guthrie, 2003; Swan, 2003), and transactional strategies (Brown, Pressley, Van Meter, & Schuder, 1996) to be used strategically while interacting with a variety of texts over long periods of time (National Institute of Child Health and Human Development, 2000; Reutzel, Smith, & Fawson, 2005).

## Systematic and Explicit Tier 1 Literacy Instruction

**Systematic instruction** means that classroom teachers teach each grade level's identified scope or range of literacy concepts, skills, and strategies found in the school's adopted core literacy program. Systematic instruction is also interpreted to mean that teachers teach this range of concepts, skills, and strategies in the sequence or order spelled out in the core literacy program. The range *and* order of literacy concepts, skills, or strategies to be taught in core literacy programs are typically found in the "scope and sequence" chart usually located in each grade-level program's teachers' manual or edition. It is important to note that *systematic* does not mean that teachers must pace the instruction as found in many teachers' manuals. Appropriate instructional pacing requires that teachers observe student responses to the pace of instruction and make needed adjustments.

*[handwritten margin note: blending sounds individually, scope + sequence]*

**Explicit instruction** means that classroom teachers state a clear, concise instructional objective to be taught. A clear, concise instructional objective identifies a specific literacy concept, skill, or strategy to be taught along with the cognitive thinking processes and assigned tasks to be completed. An example might be, *Students will learn to blend letter sounds in consonant-vowel-consonant words (CVC words) to pronounce words with a short /a/ vowel sound.* Next, teachers provide students explanations about why it is important to learn the identified literacy concept, skill, or strategy, as well as when and where it will be useful in literacy (Duffy, 2003). This is followed by the teacher modeling and "thinking aloud" how to understand a literacy concept or consciously performing or demonstrating the thinking process steps needed to effectively use a literacy strategy (Duffy, 2003; Hancock, 1999). After modeling, the teacher "scaffolds" by guiding and coaching students' use of the concept or strategy, gradually releasing responsibility (see Figure 2.7) to students for using the associated thinking processes during subsequent lessons over many days, weeks, or months (Duffy, 2003; Hancock, 1999; Raphael, George, Weber, & Nies, 2009).

*[handwritten margin notes: To with by, Model it first]*

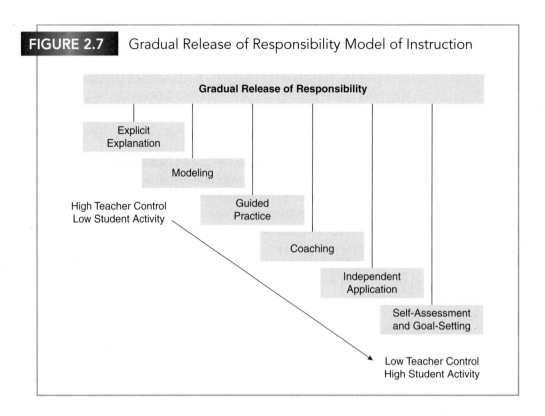

**FIGURE 2.7** Gradual Release of Responsibility Model of Instruction

Tier 1 instruction also includes **differentiated instruction.** Differentiated literacy instruction implies a movement away from a "one-size-fits-all" literacy curriculum and is intended to meet the needs of the diverse learners in our classrooms today. For example, many children from high-poverty circumstances need a much greater infusion of vocabulary instruction than do children from more affluent families (Johnson, 2001; Snow, Burns, & Griffin, 1998). Tier 1 literacy instruction is focused on responding to individual, specific literacy learning needs identified by studying the data obtained from the use of screening, diagnostic, or progress-monitoring assessments.

Optiz (1998) describes flexible groups as allowing "students to work in differently mixed ability groups depending upon the learning task at hand" (p. 10). Small differentiated literacy instruction groups vary in size from two to eight depending on the number of students with similar instructional needs. Group membership is never fixed and varies according to students' response to the interventions offered to them in Tier 1 literacy instruction.

As teachers work with students in differentiated small literacy instruction groups, they provide targeted, explicit lessons and teacher guided practice to help students understand and use effective literacy strategies embedded in the reading and writing of texts. Students in differentiated small instruction groups are placed in appropriately challenging text levels, typically the instructional-level text. Instructional-level text typically represents a difficulty level where students can read the text with 90 to 95% accuracy.

To achieve full differentiation within these small instruction groups, classroom teachers pursue the teaching of dissimilar literacy learning objectives in each group. In other words, differentiation requires teachers to identify objectives within each group of students that meet their specific literacy learning needs. Teachers engage each small instruction group in different learning routines, objectives, tasks, and activities. For example one small instruction group might focus on activities and tasks that help students to recognize high-frequency sight words fluently, while yet another small instruction group might be focused on a lesson in which students are focused on writing a summary of a text to demonstrate comprehension. We point out these features of differentiation because in many schools teachers form small groups for "guided reading instruction" in which the only difference is the level of text used in the group. The objectives, format, routines, and activities in many such groups are the same—introduce the book, take a picture walk, read the book, retell, revisit the text, and so forth.

We repeat with emphasis, Tier 1 literacy instruction provides all students with increased, targeted, intense instruction and practice to meet individual literacy learning needs. For some students Tier 1 literacy instruction offers much needed time for "double doses" of teacher-directed explicit instruction and guided practice to learn a previously taught but not yet mastered literacy skill, concept, or strategy. For other students, Tier 1 literacy instruction offers students the opportunity to extend and accelerate the acquisition of advanced literacy skills, strategies, and concepts in literature circle groups or book club discussions beyond those typically taught at grade level.

In summary, Tier 1 literacy instruction is not intended to address individual or specific literacy learning needs but rather to provide all students equal opportunity to receive grade-level evidence-based literacy instruction. High-quality Tier 1 literacy instruction is systematically and explicitly taught to the whole class of students and in small groups using either a commercially published or locally developed literacy instructional program. Evidence-based Tier 1 literacy instruction requires that teachers allocate sufficient time for instruction of at least 120 minutes daily. As previously noted, this allocated instructional time is often distributed across four essential components of effective literacy instruction—word work, fluency work, comprehension strategy instruction, and writing. Shanahan (2003) has reported increased student achievement when high-quality evidence-based Tier 1 literacy instruction is provided to all students as described here.

## TIER 2 INSTRUCTION: TRIAGE IN CLASSROOMS

Tier 2 reading instruction is typically taught by the classroom teacher, although other educators and service providers, such as reading specialists, tutors, or aides, can be asked to assist in providing Tier 2 literacy instruction in *push in* or *pull out* programs. Nevertheless, the responsibility for designing, documenting, and coordinating effective Tier 2 literacy instruction rests with the classroom teacher. In many effective schools, classroom teachers work together as teams, often with the assistance of other specialized teachers (e.g., literacy coaches, special education teachers, Title I teachers) to analyze student needs and develop written plans of action.

According to the RtI Network (2009) and others, Tier 2 literacy instruction is intended to assist students not making adequate progress in the regular classroom in Tier 1. Struggling students are provided with increasingly intensive instruction matched to their needs on the basis of levels of performance and rates of progress. Intensity of instruction varies across group size, frequency and duration of intervention, and level of training of the professionals providing instruction or intervention. These services and interventions are provided in small-group settings in addition to instruction in the core literacy curriculum (Gregory & Chapman, 2002; Tyner, 2004; Wilkinson & Townsend, 2000). Students who continue to struggle at this level of intervention are then considered for more intensive Tier 3 interventions.

Go to the Assignments and Activities section of Topic 11: "Reading Difficulties and Intervention Strategies" in the MyEducationLab for your course and complete the activity entitled "Successful Tutoring." As you watch the video and answer the accompanying questions, note that the use of tutors can offer individual students encouragement, support, and feedback about their reading. Tutors can provide students with additional guided oral reading practice that helps to build their fluency.

Another concept central to the success of Tier 2 literacy instruction is "curricular alignment." Teacher-directed Tier 2 literacy instruction, especially when other providers are involved such as reading specialists or classroom aides, can ensure that students receive instruction in literacy strategies, concepts, and skills that align with the scope and sequence of skills, concepts, and strategies, as well as the academic language that is used in Tier 1 core classroom literacy instruction. The failure of supplementary literacy instruction provided to students has often been attributed to a lack of alignment between classroom literacy instruction and the instruction provided in addition to or beyond the classroom (Allington, 1994; Davis & Wilson, 1999). Alignment of Tier 1 and 2 literacy instructional programs has been shown recently to significantly and positively affect literacy growth among at-risk students (Wonder-McDowell, Reutzel, & Smith, in preparation).

## Providing Independent Practice during Tier 2 Differentiated Small-Group Instruction

Teachers must also plan productive work for those students who are not participating in differentiated small-group literacy instruction under the direct supervision of the classroom teacher. The question teachers ask often ask us goes something like this: "What do I do with the other 20 children who are not in my differentiated small literacy instructional group?" Many elementary classroom teachers use learning centers, stations, or activities. When planning such formats to support or accompany Tier 2 small-group differentiated literacy instruction, there are several important decisions to be made before doing so.

Teachers need to consider how many learning centers they can reasonably manage while simultaneously providing a small group of students with Tier 2 supplemental literacy instruction. For an inexperienced teacher, managing the complexities of multiple literacy learning centers may seem too much! Literacy learning centers are not the only effective way to give students meaningful practice in reading and writing. Pairing students with peers or buddies can provide students with effective reading practice when they are not participating in a small differentiated literacy instruction group under the direct guidance of the classroom teacher. Involving other educators in Tier 2 classroom literacy instruction—such as Reading Recovery teachers with differentiated assignments, aides, tutors, or reading specialists—can provide additional personnel and supervision for other small groups in a classroom.

For other more experienced teachers, the question is not whether to use literacy learning centers or stations but rather how to design effective centers that promote the learning of essential literacy skills, concepts, or strategies. Several key features are associated with effectively designed literacy learning centers. Unsupervised literacy learning centers are established primarily to give students independent or peer-assisted practice in applying literacy concepts, skills, or strategies previously taught by the classroom teacher. Therefore, if learning centers are not staffed by another educator, materials and tasks to be independently practiced in literacy learning centers should never represent new or novel learning experiences.

Literacy learning centers should provide students with practice in the essential components of evidence-based reading instruction—fluency, comprehension, vocabulary, and word recognition. Literacy learning centers that focus on low-level completion of seatwork activities or participation in easy, repetitious games to keep students occupied are not useful and do not represent the most effective use of classroom or practice time. Engaging students in applying their literacy learning in the reading and writing of texts or interaction and discussion around texts in a variety of formats is clearly preferred. Students must also have well-defined and structured assignments, tasks, or activities that require them to demonstrate completion, performance, and accountability. Teachers who fail to state expectations, give clear directions and assignments, and hold students accountable for the time spent in literacy learning centers will find that students do not consistently make good use of independent practice opportunities, wasting valuable instruction time.

Procedures for using literacy learning centers need to be explicitly taught, modeled, and practiced under the guidance of the teacher prior to allowing students to engage in the independent use of literacy learning centers. Likewise procedures for transitioning among a variety of literacy learning centers need to be explicitly taught, modeled, and practiced to reduce transition times. Teachers who design effective literacy learning centers clearly display the literacy learning objectives, standards, or benchmarks as well as the rules or behavior to be expected in literacy learning centers and the directions for completing assignments, tasks, or work in the centers.

## Training Students to Effectively Use Literacy Centers

Reutzel and Morrow (2007) have developed a 6-week procedural training process for successfully engaging students in independent or guided practice activities found in classroom literacy learning centers. At the beginning of the school year, literacy learning centers should be ready to be used by the students, but teachers should not be tempted to let students use them right away. Allowing students to enter and use a variety of literacy centers or stations and the accompanying print/literacy tools at the very beginning of the school year without adequate procedural training is an invitation for a classroom management disaster. Cordon off the literacy learning centers for a few weeks, usually 5 to 6 weeks. We've actually seen classrooms in which teachers use yellow plastic crime scene tape for this purpose! During this time, students will be trained to successfully enter, move among, and engage in tasks found in the centers. A daily schedule of literacy routines and a literacy learning center rotation chart need to be posted in the classroom and reviewed each day (see Figure 2.8).

During the first week of the school year, ignore the literacy centers around the room. Focus attention on whole-group instruction. Spend small amounts of time collecting informal assessment data on children's behavioral abilities to follow directions, listen, and remain on task and focused in whole-group settings. Administer literacy screening tests to all students in the classroom during this first week if possible. Finally, spend a bit of time learning about students' interests, attitudes, and motivations generally and those specific to reading and writing.

By the second week, tell students that in a few weeks they will be working more often in small groups and in the literacy learning centers set up around the classroom. But before they can do so, there is much they need to learn. Doing this heightens students' curiosity

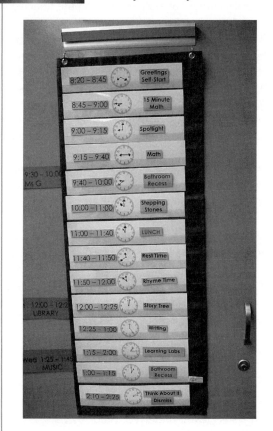

**FIGURE 2.8**   A Daily Literacy Schedule

and motivation to learn literacy learning center expectations and procedures. Also during the second week, briefly in 2 minutes or less explain what each literacy space of the classroom is for, such as paired reading, word work, and writing centers. Take about 5 minutes each day to explain one or two literacy learning centers until all have been described.

In the third week, select one or two centers to more fully explain and model how students are to enter, use, clean up, and rotate or move to other small-group and literacy learning centers in the classroom. On the first day of the third week model how students should move from their seats to the selected centers in the classroom. On the second day of the third week, explain that a team leader will be appointed to lead their group in a quick review of the rules and directions each day through a quiet oral reading of the posted rules and directions for working in the literacy center.

On the third day of the third week, the teacher models how and where students are to seat themselves in the selected literacy centers and how, once seated, students should wait for the team leader to distribute materials necessary for completing the displayed task in each center. On this same day, the teacher discusses expectations for completing assigned literacy center tasks. On the fourth day, the teacher explicitly explains the consequences for failure to follow center directions and obey the rules, directing attention to posted consequences displayed in each literacy center. On the last day of the third week, the teacher models the literacy center clean-up process.

The training of these selected literacy or content-area learning spaces will likely require approximately 10 minutes per day for the entire third week of the school year. This training process is repeated at a slightly accelerated pace over the next 2 weeks, weeks 4 and 5, within each of the remaining classroom literacy centers or stations. During the final week of training, teachers form small groups with assigned team leaders to role-play movement to, use of, and clean-up of literacy centers. The wise teacher realizes that students must be able to role-play and practice these procedures to fully internalize them. During role play, anyone who fails to follow directions precisely causes the entire group to stop and repractice the expected procedures. Remaining firm about meeting expectations as students role-play their use of literacy centers will save many potential management problems later.

## Making Efficient Transitions among Literacy Centers

Training students to make efficient movements between literacy centers and into and out of various classroom activities is essential for minimizing transition times and maximizing literacy practice and instructional time. Experience has taught us the value of using timers or

---

**FIGURE 2.9**   Making Efficient Transitions When Using Literacy Centers

1. Signal students to freeze and listen for directions using a hotel registration bell, turning off the lights, or similar method.
2. Provide brief, well-sequenced, and repetitive oral directions coupled with displayed written directions. For example, say and display something like: (1) put materials away and (2) line-up. Children must listen or read to get the directions for what is to be done.
3. Signal using your hotel bell, lights, or similar method for students to follow the oral and written displayed directions.
4. Signal students to move to the next classroom literacy center or return to their regularly assigned classroom seats.

stop watches to motivate students to accomplish transitions briskly and without dallying. A worthwhile goal is to reduce transition times to a single minute. We recommend a quick four-step process to make this happen, as shown in Figure 2.9. An excellent resource for more information about designing and implementing effective literacy centers is found in Morrow's *The Literacy Center: Contexts for Reading and Writing* (2nd ed., 2002).

## TIER 3 INSTRUCTION: INTENSIVE LITERACY INTERVENTIONS BEYOND THE CLASSROOM

As classroom teachers continue to monitor students' progress and responses to Tier 2 small-group differentiated literacy instruction, they systematically determine whether students are making adequate progress toward established literacy learning benchmarks, standards, or objectives. Students who are not responsive to Tier 1 and 2 classroom literacy instruction require diagnostic assessment and more specific and intensive literacy interventions. Tier 3 literacy instruction and assessment is provided by the classroom teacher and/or other special-ized educational providers such as reading specialists, Title I teachers, or special education teachers as consultants (McCook, 2007). Supplemental Tier 3 instruction should be offered at a minimum in three 30-minute sessions per week, daily if possible, in small groups (1:1, 1:2, or 1:3) or individually *in addition* to core literacy instruction. Progress-monitoring as-sessment should occur as often as twice a week or, at a minimum, weekly on targeted literacy skills to ensure adequate progress and learning (McCook, 2007).

In the rare cases where Tier 3 supplemental instruction is not successful, the student may then be referred for further diagnostic testing to determine whether the student may qualify for special education services, as illustrated previously in Figure 2.1, which shows a model for three-tier RtI instruction along with a fourth step, consideration for special education evaluation and services.

Special educators are becoming more and more informed about how to use RtI pro-cedures in making eligibility decisions for students requiring special education services. For those special educators seeking more information about how to use RtI processes to provide effective Tier 3 assessment and instructional services, we recommend *Response to Interven-tion: Principles and Strategies for Effective Practice* (Brown-Chidsey & Steege, 2005).

## AN RtI CAVEAT: "TIERS TO TEARS"

The final regulations for the reauthorized Individuals with Disabilities Education Act (IDEA) were published in the Federal Register on August 14, 2006, and became effective on Oc-tober 13, 2006. Because the RtI section of the legislation *still* allows for the discrepancy formula to continue in use, children could *still* be denied needed services if they have cogni-tive limitations (Cooter & Cooter, 2009). For example, a fourth-grade child with a tested IQ of 75 reading on a first-grade level may be working toward their potential according to a discrepancy formula and, thus, not be eligible for extra services. Even for these students, we believe that RtI is an idea whose time has come.

# SUMMARY

Response to Intervention (RtI) is not a program! RtI is a systematic way of viewing multitiered literacy instruction and intervention in the regular classroom. Shanahan (2008) summarizes three generally agreed-on elements of RtI models that classroom teachers should know. First, the classroom teacher bears the major responsibility for providing a high-quality and differentiated program of core literacy instruction in Tier 1. Second, the middle tier describes targeted instruction that can be provided by the classroom teacher or other team members in addition to the core literacy program. As students with learning difficulties progress from tier to tier, they should receive further assessment and supplemental literacy instruction with increasing intensity.

RtI is firmly rooted in the collection and analysis of student data to make decisions about how to plan the most effective literacy instruction that meets individual students' learning needs. A key to success in using RtI models is a team approach involving committed educators who work together to address the literacy learning needs of each and every student. In conclusion, the use of RtI models provides struggling students with a rich and varied menu of literacy assessments, interventions, and instructional providers.

## SELECTED REFERENCES

Allington, R. L. (1994). What's special about special programs for children who find learning to read difficult? *Journal of Reading Behavior, 26*(1), 95–115.

Armbruster, B. B., Lehr, F., & Osborn, J. (2001). *Put reading first: The research building blocks for teaching children to read.* Washington, DC: U.S. Department of Education.

Au, K. H. (2006). Diversity, technology, and the literacy achievement gap. In M. McKenna, L. Labbo, R. Kieffer, & D. Reinking (Eds.), *International handbook of literacy and technology* (Vol. II, pp. 363–368). Mahwah, NJ: Lawrence Erlbaum.

Beck, I. L., McKeown, M. G., & Kucan, L. (2002). *Bringing words to life: Robust vocabulary instruction.* New York: Guilford Press.

Block, C. C., Oakar, M., & Hurt, N. (2002). The expertise of literacy teachers: A continuum from preschool to grade 5. *Reading Research Quarterly, 37*(2), 178–206.

Brown, R., Pressley, M., Van Meter, P., & Schuder, T. (1996). A quasi-experimental validation of transactional strategies instruction with previously low-achieving second-grade readers. *Journal of Educational Psychology, 88,* 18–37.

Brown-Chidsey, R., & Steege, M. W. (2005). *Response to intervention: Principles and strategies for effective practice.* New York: Guilford Press.

Burns, M. S., Griffin, P., & Snow, C. E. (Eds.). (1999). *Starting out right: A guide to promoting children's reading suc-*

*cess.* Committee on the Prevention of Reading Difficulties in Young Children, Commission on Behavioral and Social Sciences and Education, National Research Council. Washington, DC: National Academy Press.

Cooter, K. S., & Cooter, R. B. (2009). *Response to Intervention (RTI): A roadmap for classroom teachers.* Keynote address for the dean's lecture series on multicultural education, Murray State University. Murray, KY.

Cunningham, P. M., Hall, D. P., & Defee, M. (1998). Non-ability-grouped, multilevel instruction: Eight years later. *The Reading Teacher, 51*(8), 652–664.

Davis, M. M., & Wilson, E. K. (1999). A Title I teacher's beliefs, decisions-making, and instruction at the third and seventh grade levels. *Reading Research and Instruction, 38*(4), 289–300.

Duffy, G. G. (2003). *Explaining reading: A resource for teaching concepts, skills, and strategies.* New York: Guilford Press.

Flood, J., Lapp, D., Flood, S., & Nagel, G. (1992). Am I allowed to group? Using flexible patterns for effective instruction. *The Reading Teacher, 45*(8), 608–616.

Fuchs, D., Fuchs, L. S., & Vaughn, S. (2008). *Response to intervention: A framework for reading educators.* Newark, DE: International Reading Association.

Good, R. H., & Kaminski, R. A. (2002). DIBELS oral reading fluency passages for first through third grades (Technical Report No. 10). Eugene: University of Oregon.

Gregory, G. H., & Chapman, C. (2002). *Differentiated instructional strategies: One size doesn't fit all.* Thousand Oaks, CA: Corwin Press.

Guthrie, J. T. (2003). Concept-oriented reading instruction. In C. E. Snow & A. P. Sweet (Eds.), *Rethinking reading comprehension* (pp. 115–140). New York: Guilford Press.

Haager, D., Klinger, J., & Vaughn, S. (2007). *Evidence-based reading practices for response to intervention.* Baltimore: Paul H. Brookes Publishing Company.

Hancock, J. (1999). *The explicit teaching of reading.* Newark, DE: International Reading Association.

Johnson, D. D. (2001). *Vocabulary in the elementary and middle school.* Boston: Allyn & Bacon.

McCook, J. E. (2007). *Implementing a response to intervention (RtI) model.* Striving Readers Grantee Annual Conference. Washington, DC: United States Department of Education.

McKenna, M. C. (2002). *Help for struggling readers: Strategies for grades 3–8.* New York: Guilford Press.

Morrow, L. M. (2002). *The literacy center: Contexts for reading and writing* (2nd ed.). Portland, ME: Stenhouse.

Morrow, L. M., Reutzel, D. R., & Casey, H. (2006). Organization and management of language arts teaching: Classroom environments, grouping practices, and exemplary instruction. In C. Evertson (Ed.), *Handbook of classroom management* (pp. 559–582). Mahwah, NJ: Lawrence Erlbaum.

Morrow, L. M., Tracey, D. H., Woo, D. G., & Pressley, M. (1999). Characteristics of exemplary first-grade literacy instruction. *The Reading Teacher, 52*(5), 462–476.

National Institute of Child Health and Human Development. (2000). *Report of the National Reading Panel: Teaching children to read.* Washington, DC: Author.

Neuman, S. B. (1999). Books make a difference: A study of access to literacy. *Reading Research Quarterly, 34,* 286–311.

Neuman, S. B., & Celano, D. (2001). Access to print in low-income and middle-income communities: An ecological study of four neighborhoods. *Reading Research Quarterly, 36*(1), 8–26.

Neuman, S. B., & Celano, D. (2006). The knowledge gap: Implications of leveling the playing field for low-income and middle-income children. *Reading Research Quarterly, 42*(2), 176–201.

Opitz, M. F. (1998). *Flexible grouping in reading: Practical ways to help all students become better readers.* New York: Scholastic.

Opitz, M. F., & Rasinski, T. V. (2008). *Good-bye round robin: 25 effective oral reading strategies.* Portsmouth, NH: Heinemann.

Palincsar, A. S. (2003). Collaborative approaches to comprehension instruction. In C. E. Snow & A. P. Sweet (Eds.), *Rethinking reading comprehension* (pp. 99–114). New York: Guilford Press.

Pressley, M., Allington, R. L., Wharton-McDonald, R., Collins Block, C., & Morrow, L. M. (2001). *Learning to read: Lessons from exemplary first-grade classrooms.* New York: Guilford Press.

Raphael, T. E., George, M. A., Weber, C. M., & Nies, A. (2009). Approaches to teaching reading comprehension. In G. G. Duffy & S. E. Israel (Eds.), *Handbook of research on reading comprehension* (pp. 449–469). New York: Routledge.

Rasinski, T. V. (2003). *The fluent reader: Oral reading strategies for building word recognition, fluency, and comprehension.* New York: Scholastic.

Reutzel, D. R., & Morrow, L. M. (2007). Promoting and assessing effective literacy learning classroom environments. In R. McCormick & J. Paratore (Eds.), *Classroom literacy assessment: Making sense of what students know and do* (pp. 33–49). New York: Guilford Press.

Reutzel, D. R., Smith, J. A., & Fawson, P. C. (2005). An evaluation of two approaches for teaching reading comprehension strategies in the primary years using science information texts. *Early Childhood Research Quarterly, 20*(3), pp. 276–305.

Rogg, L. J. (2001). *Early literacy instruction in kindergarten.* Newark, DE: International Reading Association.

RTI Network. (2009). *What is RTI?* Retrieved March 29, 2009, from www.rtinetwork.org/Learn/What/ar/WhatIsRTI.

Shanahan, T. (2003). *A framework for improving reading achievement.* Paper presented at the National Conference on Family Literacy and the California Family Literacy Conference. Long Beach, CA, March 16, 2003.

Shanahan, T. (2004, November). *How do you raise reading achievement?* Paper presented at the Utah Council of the International Reading Association, Salt Lake City.

Shanahan, T. (2008). Implications of RTI for the reading teacher. In D. Fuchs, L. S. Fuchs, & S. Vaughn (Eds.), *Response to intervention: A framework for reading educators* (pp. 105–122). Newark, DE: International Reading Association.

Snow, C. E., Burns, M. N., & Griffin, P. (1998). *Preventing reading difficulties in young children.* Washington, DC: National Academy Press.

Stanovich, P. J., & Stanovich, K. E. (2003). *Using research and reason in education: How teachers can use scientifically-based research to make curricular and instructional decisions.* Washington, DC: National Institute for Literacy.

Swan, E. A. (2003). *Concept-oriented reading instruction: Engaging classrooms, lifelong learners.* New York: Guilford Press.

Taylor, B. M. (2008). Tier 1: Effective classroom reading instruction in the elementary grades. In D. Fuchs, L. S. Fuchs, & S. Vaughn (Eds.), *Response to intervention: A framework for reading educators* (pp. 5–25). Newark, DE: International Reading Association.

Taylor, B. M., Pearson, P. D., Clark, K. E., & Walpole, S. (1999). *Beating the odds in teaching all children to read* (Ciera Report No. 2-006). Ann Arbor, MI: Center for the Improvement of Early Reading Achievement.

Taylor, B. M., Pearson, P. D., Peterson, D. S., & Rodriguez, M. C. (2005). The CIERA School Change Framework: An evidence-based approach to professional development and school reading improvement. *Reading Research Quarterly, 40*(1), 40–69.

Tyner, B. (2004). *Small-group reading instruction: A differentiated teaching model for beginning and struggling readers.* Newark, DE: International Reading Association.

Vaughn, S., Linan-Thompson, S., Elbaum, B., Wanzek, J., & Rodriguez, K. T. (2004). Centers for implementing K–3 behavior and reading intervention models preventing reading difficulties: A three-tiered intervention model. Unpublished report, University of Texas Center for Reading and Language Arts.

Vaughn, S., Wanzek, J., Woodruff, A. L., & Linan-Thompson, S. (2007). Prevention and early identification of students with reading disabilities. In D. Haager, J. Klinger, & S. Vaughn (Eds.), *Evidence-based reading practices for response to intervention* (pp. 11–28). Baltimore: Paul H. Brookes Publishing Company.

Walpole, S., & McKenna, M. C. (2007). *Differentiated reading instruction: Strategies for the primary grades.* New York: Guilford Press.

Wilkinson, I. A., & Townsend, M. A. R. (2000). From Rata to Rimu: Grouping for instruction in best practice New Zealand classrooms. *The Reading Teacher, 53*(6), 460–471.

Wonder-McDowell, C., Reutzel, D. R., & Smith, J. A. (in preparation). *Aligning supplemental and core reading instruction: Effects on second-grade students' reading achievement.* Unpublished report, Utah State University's Emma Eccles Jones Center for Early Childhood Education.

Woodcock, R. W. (1987). *Woodcock reading mastery test–revised.* Circle Pines, MN: AGS Publications.

## RECOMMENDED READINGS

Fuchs, D., Fuchs, L., Vaughn, S. (Eds.). (2009). *Response to intervention: A framework for reading educators.* Newark, DE: International Reading Association.

Walpole, S., & McKenna, M. C. (2007). *Differentiated reading instruction: Strategies for the primary grades.* New York: Guilford Press.

PEARSON
**myeducationlab**
The Power of Classroom Practice
www.myeducationlab.com

Now go to Topic 11: "Reading Difficulties and Intervention Strategies" and Topic 13 "Struggling Readers and Others with Special Needs" in the MyEducationLab (www.myeducationlab.com) for your course, where you can:

- Find learning outcomes for "Reading Difficulties and Intervention Strategies" and "Struggling Readers and Others with Special Needs," along with the national standards that connect to these outcomes.
- Complete the tasks in the Assignments and Activities to help you more deeply understand the chapter content.
- Apply and practice your understanding of the core teaching skills identified in the chapter with the Building Teaching Skills and Dispositions learning units.

# 3

# Oral Language Assessment and Development

*L*ife is good this year in fifth grade. Janet was able to move into a vacant classroom on the corner of the school with lots of windows, and her students seem eager to learn. So far, so good! The first challenges on Janet's horizon are Molly and Roberto. They both seem to have limited abilities in speaking English, but for very different reasons.

Molly is one of four children born to a single mother. Molly's mom, Theresa, works hard as a waitress but simply does not earn enough to make ends meet. Molly's family moves around a lot for financial reasons, which has taken its toll on her language learning. When Janet asked Theresa how things were going, her eyes welled up as she explained their situation. Here's the pattern: The rent comes due and Theresa rarely has sufficient resources to pay the bill. After 2 or 3 months of nonpayment, eviction is threatened, so she gathers up her children and moves to another apartment complex offering a $99 move-in special. This state of affairs is repeated time and again because Theresa's income remains in the poverty range. In the end, she is working two minimum wage jobs and has very little time to spend with Molly, who stays at home tending her younger siblings while her mom is working.

Roberto's situation is quite different. His family recently immigrated to the United States from Chile when his father, a civil engineer, was transferred with his company. Roberto studied English at his private Catholic school in Chile and can read and understand the language fairly well. His main problem seems to be oral communication.

It seems obvious that both Molly and Roberto need to build their English vocabulary and develop oral speaking fluency. The questions in Janet's mind are (a) *How can I find out what they already know?* and (b) *When I know that, where should I begin oral language instruction for each of these students?*

# *B*ACKGROUND BRIEFING FOR TEACHERS

A rich and extensive oral language foundation is critical to the development of reading and writing (Dickinson & Tabors, 2001; Hart & Risley, 1995, 2002; Honig, 2007; Kirkland & Patterson, 2005). Children must be relatively fluent with their oral language to communicate effectively with the teacher and other students in "learning networks" (Pinnell, 1998). Oral language also paves the way for learning such reading skills as phonemic awareness, alphabetic principles, phonics, decoding abilities, fluency, vocabulary, and reading comprehension. In fact, oral language ability is the bedrock foundation on which all future literacy learning is built. There are essentially four major views of how children acquire oral language: (1) *behaviorist,* (2) *innatist,* (3) *constructivist,* and (4) *social interactionist.* We have found that each of these views helps to explain one or more aspects of how children acquire and use oral language.

# *T*HE BEHAVIORIST VIEW OF ORAL LANGUAGE DEVELOPMENT

Go to the Assignments and Activities section of Topic 4: "Oral Language" in the MyEducationLab for your course and complete the activity entitled "Literacy." As you watch the video and answer the accompanying questions, note characteristics of building children's oral language as a foundation for early reading. Make a quick list of ways in which teachers and parents support young children's oral language development.

Behaviorists believe that oral language is learned through a process of conditioning and shaping—based on response to stimulus, reward, or punishment. Human role models in an infant's social and cultural environment provide the stimuli, rewards, or punishments that shape or condition the acquisition of certain features of oral language.

The speech of parents or other caregivers acts as the stimulus in a sociocultural speech environment. When a baby imitates the sounds or speech of the adult models, praise and affection are given as rewards for the infant's attempts to learn language. Thus, the **behaviorist theory** of language acquisition states that infants learn oral language from other human role models through a process involving stimulation, imitation, rewards, punishment, and practice. However, behaviorist theories of language development fail to explain a number of important questions associated with children's language acquisition.

For example, if a parent is hurried, inattentive, or not present when the child attempts speech, then rewards for the desired speech responses are not always provided. Thus, if a baby's language learning were only motivated by rewards, speech attempts would cease when regular and systematic rewards are absent.

One weakness of the behaviorist theory of oral language acquisition is that young children do not simply imitate other human speech. Imitation implies certain behaviors. For example, when mother says, "Baby, say Mama," a baby would imitate or *echo* the mother by saying, "Baby, say Mama." Anyone who has raised children knows this is not the case. In fact, the baby may not say anything at all! But one thing is clear—children are not mere echo chambers. They are processing language meaning and sorting out the relevant from the irrelevant. Behaviorist language acquisition theories fail to account for this kind of selective or strategic cognitive processing.

Behaviorist language acquisition theories also do not account for speech terms invented by infants. For example, one girl we know used to call a sandwich a *weechie* even though no one in her home called a sandwich by any such name. Another failure of behaviorist theories to fully explain oral language development is the "jargon" language that is often developed between identical twins and no one else. Although behaviorist theories may explain to some extent the role of the social environment and the importance of role models in shaping chil-

---

| FIGURE 3.4 | Student Oral Language Observation Matrix | | | | |
|---|---|---|---|---|---|
| | **1** | **2** | **3** | **4** | **5** |
| **Comprehension** | Cannot understand simple conversation | Only understands conversational language spoken slowly | Can understand most conversations if the speech is slow and includes repetitions | Understands almost everything at normal speed, but may require some repetitions | Understands class conversations and discussions without difficulty |
| **Fluency** | Speech is halting and fragmentary; makes it extremely difficult to initiate a conversation | Usually silent or hesitant due to language limitations | Often speech is interrupted while the student searches for the right word or expression | Generally fluent in class discussions, but may lapse sometimes into word searches | Fluent and effortless conversation |
| **Vocabulary** | Very little vocabulary makes conversation nearly impossible | Limited vocabulary and often misuses words | Frequently uses incorrect words, and speech is limited by insufficient vocabulary | Sometimes uses inappropriate terms or must rephrase due to limited vocabulary | Fully capable in using vocabulary and idioms |
| **Pronunciation** | Difficult to understand due to severe pronunciation problems | Pronunciation problems make it necessary to repeat a great deal | Pronunciation problems cause listeners to have to listen closely; some misunderstandings | Always intelligible, but may have heavy accent or inappropriate intonation patterns | Normal pronunciation and intonation |
| **Grammar** | Acute problems with grammar and syntax making speech nearly unintelligible | Grammar and syntax problems often force repetition or overreliance on simple or familiar patterns | Frequent errors with grammar and syntax that sometimes alters meanings | Sometimes makes grammar or syntax errors | Appropriate grammar and syntax usage |

Stages of Development
Stage I: Score of 5–11 = Not Proficient in English
Stage II: Score of 12–18 = Limited English Proficiency (Emergent)
Stage III: Score of 19–24 = Limited English Proficient (Developing)
Stage IV: Score of 25 = Fully English Proficient

---

*Source:* Adapted from an instrument developed by the California State Department of Education.

but be sure to make multiple observations to ensure greater reliability and generalizabilty of your conclusions.

For each trait, place an *X* in the box that best describes what the student is able to do and note the point value (1 to 5). For example, a student who understands nearly everything spoken at normal speed would receive a score of 4 for Comprehension. After you have marked the box that best describes the student's language use in each trait category, add up the point values to determine his or her stage of development in English proficiency

A key for scoring your observations is found at the bottom of the SOLOM in Figure 3.4. As an example, say that you have rated Jaime's oral language performance using the SOLOM traits and come up with the following rating:

| | |
|---|---|
| Comprehension | 4 |
| Fluency | 4 |
| Vocabulary | 4 |
| Pronunciation | 3 |
| Grammar | 4 |
| Total | 19 |

A score of 19 would indicate that Jaime's oral language development is at Stage III or "Limited English Proficient."

## Teacher Rating of Oral Language and Literacy

### Purpose

To be able to read and write effectively, children must develop strong oral language skills. According to Dickinson, McCabe, and Sprague (2003), the Teacher Rating of Oral Language and Literacy (TROLL) system measures speaking and listening skills critical to meeting new standards in today's classrooms. The TROLL can be used to track children's progress in language and literacy development, to inform curriculum, and to stimulate focused communication between parents and teachers.

Oral language skills relevant to later literacy development include the development of the ability to tell stories, use of talk while pretending in play, and varied vocabulary usage (Dickinson & Tabors, 2001). Although oral language skills flourish during the preschool years, they are also very susceptible to stimulation and intervention in the early years of preschool, kindergarten, and primary-grade education. Examination of the TROLL assessment has shown Cronbach's alpha estimates of internal consistency ranging from .77 to .92 for separate subscales. For the total TROLL scores, alphas exceeded .89 for each age (Dickinson et al., 2003). The TROLL has also been shown to compare favorably to formal assessments such as the well-established Peabody Picture Vocabulary Test (PPVT-III), which is a measure of receptive vocabulary (see the discussion later in this section). According to Dickinson et al. (2003), teacher ratings of children's language and literacy development on the TROLL show moderate associations with children's scores on all three areas (oral language, reading, and writing) of those direct assessments.

In about 5 minutes, and with no special training on the TROLL, according to Dickinson et al. (2003), teachers themselves can index what trained researchers would spend roughly 25 to 30 minutes per child assessing.

### Materials

- One copy of the TROLL for each student you observe (see Figure 3.5)

### Procedure

No formal training is required to use the TROLL instrument, according to its authors. However, the TROLL is most effective if teachers know a bit about language and literacy development. The TROLL requires only 5 to 10 minutes for each child you observe and it can be used without disrupting classroom activities.

FIGURE 3.5    Teacher Rating of Oral Language and Literacy (TROLL)

**Language Use**

1. How would you describe this child's willingness to start a conversation with adults and peers and continue trying to communicate when he or she is not understood on the first attempt? Select the statement that best describes how hard the child works to be understood by others.

| 1 | 2 | 3 | 4 |
|---|---|---|---|
| Child almost never begins a conversation with peers or the teacher and never keeps trying if unsuccessful at first. | Child sometimes begins a conversation with either peers or the teacher. If initial efforts fail, he or she often gives up quickly. | Child begins conversations with both peers and teachers on occasion. If initial efforts fail, he or she will sometimes keep trying. | Child begins conversations with both peers and teachers. If initial efforts fail, he or she will work hard to be understood. |

2. How well does the child communicate personal experiences in a clear and logical way? Assign the score that best describes this child when he or she is attempting to tell an adult about events that happened at home or some other place where you were not present.

| 1 | 2 | 3 | 4 |
|---|---|---|---|
| Child is very tentative, only offers a few words, requires you to ask questions, has difficulty responding to questions you ask. | Child offers some information, but information needed to really understand the event is missing (e.g., where or when it happened, who was present, the sequence of what happened). | Child offers information and sometimes includes the necessary information to understand the event fully. | Child freely offers information and tells experiences in a way that is nearly always complete, well sequenced, and comprehensible. |

3. How would you describe this child's pattern of asking questions about topics that interest him or her (e.g., why things happen, why people act the way they do)? Assign the score that best describes the child's approach to displaying curiosity by asking adults questions.

| 1 | 2 | 3 | 4 |
|---|---|---|---|
| To your knowledge, the child has never asked an adult a question reflecting curiosity about why things happen or why people do things. | On a few occasions, the child has asked adults some questions. The discussion that resulted was brief and limited in depth. | On several occasions, the child has asked interesting questions. On occasion these have led to an interesting conversation. | Child often asks adults questions reflecting curiosity. These often lead to interesting, extended conversations. |

4. How would you describe this child's use of talk while pretending in the house area or when playing with blocks? Consider the child's use of talk with peers to start pretending and to carry it out. Assign the score that best applies.

| 1 | 2 | 3 | 4 |
|---|---|---|---|
| Child rarely or never engages in pretend play or else never talks while pretending. | On occasion the child engages in pretending that includes some talk. Talk is brief, may only be used when starting the play, and is of limited importance to the ongoing play activity. | Child engages in pretending often, and conversation are sometimes important to the play. On occasion child engages in some back-and-forth pretend dialogue with another child. | Child often talks in elaborate ways while pretending. Conversations that are carried out "in role" are common and are an important part of the play. Child sometimes steps out of pretend play to give directions to another. |

*(continued)*

**FIGURE 3.5**　*Continued*

**5.** How would you describe the child's ability to recognize and produce rhymes?

| 1 | 2 | 3 | 4 |
| --- | --- | --- | --- |
| Child cannot ever say if two words rhyme and cannot produce a rhyme when given examples (e.g., *rat, cat*). | Child occasionally produces or identifies rhymes when given help. | Child spontaneously produces rhymes and can sometimes tell when word pairs rhyme. | Child spontaneously rhymes words of more than one syllable and always identifies whether words rhyme. |

**6.** How often does child use a varied vocabulary or try out new words (e.g., heard in stories or from teacher)?

| 1 | 2 | 3 | 4 |
| --- | --- | --- | --- |
| Never | Rarely | Sometimes | Often |

**7.** When child speaks to adults other than you or the teaching assistant, is he or she understandable?

| 1 | 2 | 3 | 4 |
| --- | --- | --- | --- |
| Never | Rarely | Sometimes | Often |

**8.** How often does child express curiosity about how and why things happen?

| 1 | 2 | 3 | 4 |
| --- | --- | --- | --- |
| Never | Rarely | Sometimes | Often |

*Language Use Subtotal ( )*

**Reading**

**9.** How often does child like to hear books read in the full group?

| 1 | 2 | 3 | 4 |
| --- | --- | --- | --- |
| Never | Rarely | Sometimes | Often |

**10.** How often does child attend to stories read in the full group or small groups and react in a way that indicates comprehension?

| 1 | 2 | 3 | 4 |
| --- | --- | --- | --- |
| Never | Rarely | Sometimes | Often |

**11.** Is child able to read storybooks on his or her own?

| 1 | 2 | 3 | 4 |
| --- | --- | --- | --- |
| Does not pretend to read books | Pretends to read | Pretends to read and reads some words | Reads the written words |

**12.** How often does child remember the storyline or characters in books that he or she heard before either at home or in class?

| 1 | 2 | 3 | 4 |
|---|---|---|---|
| Never | Rarely | Sometimes | Often |

**13.** How often does child look at or read books alone or with friends?

| 1 | 2 | 3 | 4 |
|---|---|---|---|
| Never | Rarely | Sometimes | Often |

**14.** Can child recognize letters? (Choose one answer.)

| 1 | 2 | 3 | 4 |
|---|---|---|---|
| None of the letters of the alphabet | Some of them (up to 10) | Most of them (up to 20) | All of them |

**15.** Does child recognize his or her own first name in print?

| 1 | 2 |
|---|---|
| No | Yes |

**16.** Does child recognize other names?

| 1 | 2 | 3 | 4 |
|---|---|---|---|
| No | One or two | A few (up to four or five) | Several (six or more) |

**17.** Can child read any other words?

| 1 | 2 | 3 | 4 |
|---|---|---|---|
| No | One or two | A few (up to four or five) | Several (six or more) |

**18.** Does child have a beginning understanding of the relationship between sounds and letters (e.g., the letter *B* makes a "buh" sound)

| 1 | 2 | 3 | 4 |
|---|---|---|---|
| No | One or two | A few (up to four or five) | Several (six or more) |

**19.** Can child sound out words that he or she has not read before?

| 1 | 2 | 3 | 4 |
|---|---|---|---|
| No | One or two | One-syllable words often | Many words |

*Reading Subtotal ( )*

## Writing

**20.** What does child's writing look like?

| 1 | 2 | 3 | 4 |
|---|---|---|---|
| Only draws or scribbles | Some letterlike marks | Many conventional letters | Conventional letters and words |

*(continued)*

**FIGURE 3.5** *Continued*

**21.** How often does child like to write or pretend to write?

| 1 | 2 | 3 | 4 |
|---|---|---|---|
| Never | Rarely | Sometimes | Often |

**22.** Can child write his or her first name, even if some of the letters are backward?

| 1 | 2 | 3 | 4 |
|---|---|---|---|
| Never | Rarely | Sometimes | Often |

**23.** Does child write other names or real words?

| 1 | 2 | 3 | 4 |
|---|---|---|---|
| No | One or two | A few (up to four or five) | Several (six or more) |

**24.** How often does child write signs or labels?

| 1 | 2 | 3 | 4 |
|---|---|---|---|
| Never | Rarely | Sometimes | Often |

**25.** Does child write stories, songs, poems, or lists?

| 1 | 2 | 3 | 4 |
|---|---|---|---|
| Never | Rarely | Sometimes | Often |

***Writing Subtotal ( )***

| | | | |
|---|---|---|---|
| Writing Subtotal | ( ) (Out of 24 Possible) | Reading Subtotal | ( ) (Out of 42 Possible) |
| Oral Language Subtotal | ( ) (Out of 32 Possible) | Total TROLL Score | ( ) (Out of 98 Possible) |

*Source:* Copyright ©1997 Education Development Center, Inc. www.edc.org. Reprinted by permission.

You can use the TROLL to inform your teaching by identifying children who are displaying evidence of serious oral language developmental delays and may need formal assessment by speech professionals or children who are showing high levels of literacy development and may benefit from additional challenges. By completing the TROLL several times over the course of a year, you can track the progress of all your students' oral language development. Finally, you can combine results for all your students to determine whether the class needs additional oral language experiences or more systematic instruction. For example, if all of your students score relatively low on asking questions, you will want to begin providing numerous opportunities to listen to and ask questions during the daily routine in your classroom.

## The Dynamic Indicators of Basic Early Literacy Skills Word Use Fluency Test

### Purpose

The Dynamic Indicators of Basic Early Literacy Skills (DIBELS) is a set of several standardized, individually administered measures of early literacy development. The DIBELS was

| FIGURE 3.6 | Directions for Administration of the Word Use Fluency Test |
|---|---|

1. Place the examiner probe on clipboard and position so that student cannot see what you record.
2. Say these specific directions to the student:

   *Listen to me use a word in a sentence. "green" (Pause) The grass is green. Here is another word. "jump" (Pause) I like to jump rope. Your turn to use a word in a sentence. (Pause) "rabbit"*

   | Correct Response: | Incorrect Response: |
   |---|---|
   | If student uses the word correctly in a phrase, say<br><br>*Very good.* | If student gives any other response, say,<br><br>*Listen to me use the word "rabbit" in a sentence. (Pause) "The rabbit is eating a carrot." Your turn. "rabbit"* |

   *OK. Here is your first word.*

3. Give the student the first word and start your stopwatch. If the student does not begin to use the word after *5 seconds*, give him or her the second word and score the first word as 0.
4. Provide the next word when the student has used the word in a phrase, expression, or utterance or when the student hesitates or pauses for *5 seconds*. As soon as the student is finished using the word, present the next word promptly and clearly.
5. At the end of *1 minute*, stop presenting words and recording further responses. Count the number of words used correctly in phrases, expressions, and sentences, and record at the end of the row. Total these scores and record at the bottom of the scoring sheet.

---

*Source:* Copyright © 2002 Dynamic Measurement Group, Inc. http://dibels.uoregon.edu/measures/wuf_tutorial.pdf. Reprinted by permission. DIBELS® is a registered trademark of the Dynamic Measurement Group, Inc. Use of the DIBELS® trademark here does not indicate approval or endorsement by the Dynamic Measurement Group, Inc.

specifically designed to assess three of the National Reading Panel's (National Institute of Child Health and Human Development, 2000) five essential components of early literacy development: phonological awareness, alphabetic principle, and oral reading fluency (measured as a corrected reading rate) with connected text.

### Materials

- The Word Use Fluency Test and directions (available online for free, along with the examiner probe, at http://dibels.uoregon.edu/measures/wuf.php or from Sopris West Publishers at www.sopriswest.com; see Figure 3.6)
- Stopwatch or timer
- Examiner probe
- Pencil or pen
- Clipboard

### Procedure

The Word Use Fluency (WUF) Test assesses a child's oral language expression ability by asking him or her to use a list of words in sentences. The WUF test procedure involves instructing the child to listen to a word and use it in a sentence. For analysis a DIBELS data and reporting service is available on the Internet for a fee of $1 per year per child tested. Using this Internet-based system, teachers can enter assessment data directly into the DIBELS database on the Web and receive a nearly instantaneous report as often as desired. More recently, DIBELS measures have become available in Spanish; however, such measures have not yet been validated or proven reliable among Spanish-speaking populations.

| FIGURE 3.7 | Sample Picture Naming Stimulus |

**FIGURE 3.7** Sample Picture Naming Stimulus Card from the Picture Naming Test: Get It Got It Go!

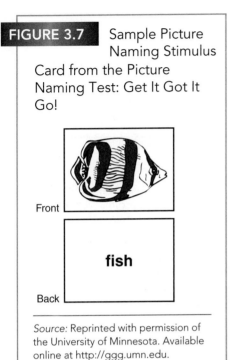

Front

**fish**

Back

*Source:* Reprinted with permission of the University of Minnesota. Available online at http://ggg.umn.edu.

## Get It Got It Go! Individual Growth and Development Indicators—Picture Naming Test

### Purpose

The Get It Got It Go! Individual Growth and Development Indicators (IGDI) are a set of several standardized, individually administered measures of early language and literacy development. The Picture Naming (PN) Test was specifically designed to assess language development for children ages 3 to 5. The measure assesses oral language expression ability by asking a child to look at picture cards drawn from typical home, classroom, and community environments, such as the one in Figure 3.7. Next, the child is asked to name the object(s) in the pictures.

The PN test, administration guidelines, and scoring forms, along with stimulus materials and the pictures to be named are available free on the Internet at http://ggg.umn.edu. A Get It Got It Go! data and reporting service is also available on the Internet for free, but users must enter their own data. By using this Internet-based system, teachers can enter assessment data directly into the Get It Got It Go! database on the Web and generate class-level reports as often as desired. The Picture Naming Test is now also available in Spanish. See Missal and McConnell (2004) for a report of reliability and validity data for the IGDI Picture Naming Test.

### Materials

- The Picture Naming Test
- Stopwatch or timer
- Pencil or pen
- Picture naming cards
- Form for recording scores
- Administration instructions
- Clipboard

### Procedure

The directions for administration of the Picture Naming test include preparation guidelines and standardized administration directions.

#### Preparation Guidelines for the Sample Administration

- You need a copy of the instructions to read from while administering tests.
- Be sure to do the Sample Administration first before conducting the Test Administration.
- Continue to the Picture Naming Test administration *only* if the child names *all four* sample cards correctly during the Sample Administration.
- Sit with the child in a quiet area; a distraction-free spot is best.
- Follow the scripted directions *exactly* as they are written.
- Read aloud all words in bold.
- Write down the number correct on the recording form *immediately* after completing each test administration. *Do not include* sample responses.

**Directions for the Sample Administration of the Picture Naming Test***

1. Select these four cards from the stack to use as sample items: baby, bear, car, cat. Do not choose different sample cards, even if you are readministering the test.
2. Say, **"I'm going to look at these cards and name these pictures. Watch what I do."**
3. Look at and clearly name the four sample cards while the child observes.
4. Say, **"Now you name these pictures."**
5. Show the four sample cards to the child in the same order as you named them, and give the child an opportunity to name each picture.
6. Praise the child for naming the picture correctly; otherwise, provide the correct picture name. If the child responds in a different language, say, **"This is a [picture name]. Call it a [picture name]."**
7. Continue on to Test Administration *only* if the child names *all four* pictures correctly.

Write *NA* on the recording form if you do not continue administration.

**Preparation Guidelines for the Test Administration**

- This is a timed 1-minute task. Be sure to watch your stopwatch!
- Shuffle cards prior to each administration.
- Separate correctly named pictures into one pile and incorrectly named or skipped pictures into another pile.
- Follow directions *exactly* as written.
- Read aloud all words in bold.

**Directions for the Test Administration of the Picture Naming Test**

1. Say, **"Now we are going to look at some other pictures. This time, name them as fast as you can!"**
2. Start the stopwatch and immediately show the first card to the child.
3. If the child does not respond within 3 seconds, point to the picture and say, **"Do you know what that is?"** or **"What is that?"**
4. If the child still does not respond within an additional 2 seconds, show the next card.
5. As soon as the child names a picture, show the next card.
6. After 1 minute, stop showing cards to the child. Record the total number of correctly named pictures on the recording form.

## The Peabody Picture Vocabulary Test/Expressive Vocabulary Test

### Purpose

The Peabody Picture Vocabulary Test (PPVT)-III was developed primarily to assess younger children's (ages 2 to 6) receptive oral language vocabulary using a series of word prompts and pictures (Dunn & Dunn, 2007). The PPVT-III takes about 10 to 15 minutes to administer to an individual student. It comes in two parallel forms (A and B) for testing and in a new Spanish language version called the Test de Vocabulario en Imagenes Peabody. Even though the test was developed originally for English-speaking children, more recently the PPVT has found renewed use among teachers who want to assess English language learners (ELLs) for understanding of oral English words as well. The PPVT has also been used in the past as one measure of a young child's verbal intelligence quotient (IQ) to determine

*Reprinted with permission of the University of Minnesota.

discrepancies between current and potential functioning that qualify for federally supported special services and has been approved for use in federally funded Early Reading First and Reading First projects.

Norms have been extended in the PPVT-III for ages 2.5 to 90 years. Test items have increased to 204 for each of the two forms, A and B. There are newer illustrations for better gender and ethnic balance.

Reliability for the PPVT-III has been measured as follows:

Internal alpha range .92 to .98

Split-half: alternate-form range .86 to .97

Test-retest range .88 to .96

Validity evidence includes a .91 correlation with verbal ability on the WISC-III VIQ, .89 on the KAIT Crystallized IQ, and .81 with the K-BIT Vocabulary test.

The Expressive Vocabulary Test (EVT) was developed primarily to assess younger children's (ages 2 to 6) expressive oral language vocabulary using a series of word prompts and pictures (AGS, 2005). The EVT is conormed with the PPVT-III. The test takes about 15 minutes to administer to an individual student.

For the labeling items (38), the examiner points to a picture or a part of the body and asks the child to respond to a question. On the 152 synonym items, the examiner presents a picture and stimulus word(s) within a phrase. The child responds to each item with a one-word answer. All pictures are in color and balanced for gender and ethnic representation.

The EVT reliability analyses indicate a high degree of internal consistency. Split-half reliabilities range from .83 to .97 with a median of .91. Alphas range from .90 to .98 with a median of .95. Test-retest studies with four separate age samples resulted in reliability coefficients ranging from .77 to .90, indicating a strong degree of test stability.

### Materials
- PPVT-III/EVT administration manual
- PPVT-III/EVT scoring records
- PPVT-III/EVT picture flip chart
- PPVT-III/EVT scoring software

(Materials needed for administering the PPVT-III or EVT available for purchase online at www.agsnet.com/Group.asp?nGroupInfoID=a12010)

### Procedure

Specific standardized procedures for administering the PPVT-III/EVT are found in the published administration manuals. A recent addition is a training video/DVD for the PPVT-III that can be purchased to prepare for administering, scoring, and interpreting the results of the PPVT-III. The PPVT-III and EVT are quick and easy to administer and score and are excellent screening assessments for examining children's receptive and expressive oral language development.

## Oral Language Checklist

### Purpose

Many times, teachers are able to learn a great deal by simply making anecdotal records of students they wish to observe and then transferring that information to a checklist (Figure 3.8). Johnson (1993) developed a research-based oral language checklist that is well suited to this type of assessment.

**FIGURE 3.8**  Oral Language Checklist

While interacting with the child you wish to study in your classroom, note any of the following:

1. Was there any indication that the child misperceived words?    Yes    No
   List examples:

2. Did the child have difficulty understanding directions for various tasks?    Yes    No
   Examples:

3. Did the child have difficulty understanding any specific vocabulary?    Yes    No
   Examples:

4. Did the child have difficulty comprehending complex/lengthy sentences?    Yes    No
   Examples:

5. Did the child have difficulty listening to and comprehending extended discourse?    Yes    No
   (e.g., stories)
   Examples:

6. Did the child have difficulty remembering series of instructions?    Yes    No
   How many?
   Give examples:

7. Did the child have difficulty retrieving (recalling) words?    Yes    No
   Under what conditions? Picture naming, spontaneous conversation?
   Other:

8. Did the child have difficulty pronouncing multisyllabic words?    Yes    No
   Give examples:

9. Did the child make grammatical mistakes when speaking?    Yes    No
   List examples:

10. Could the child convey thoughts clearly when relating an event or telling a story?    Yes    No
    Give examples of problems such as sequencing of events, lack of transition words,
    failure to include relevant information.

11. Did the child have good nonverbal communication?    Yes    No
    Give examples: (eye contact, gesture)

12. Did the child have any specific articulation problems?    Yes    No
    Give examples:

13. Were any of the preceding problems reflected in the child's *oral* reading or    Yes    No
    reading comprehension?
    Give examples:

14. Were any of the preceding *oral language* problems reflected in the child's    Yes    No
    *written language?*
    Give examples:

### Materials

- Copy of the oral language checklist found in Figure 3.8 for each student whose oral language development you wish to study
- A clipboard with a legal pad or peel-off sticky labels for making anecdotal notes during observations
- Folder for each child observed

### Procedure

First, carefully review the oral language checklist found in Figure 3.8 for key points to observe. Then, identify one or two children per day whose language development you wish to study. During the school day, keep your clipboard handy and make anecdotal notes on each child according to the criteria represented in the questions on the oral language checklist. At the end of each observation day, transfer your notes to a folder for each child and answer all questions that apply. Observations should be repeated about once every 6 weeks in order to identify growth trends and determine educational (i.e., language development) needs.

In Figure 3.9, we summarize the oral language assessment instruments we have discussed thus far and provide summary information about federally related assessment purposes (i.e., screening, diagnostic, progress-monitoring, or outcomes assessment), as well as type of test or procedure and psychometric evidence about the test scores (any available reliability and validity evidence).

## Connecting Assessment Findings to Teaching Strategies

Once you have determined who in your class may need further oral language development, as well as the areas of oral language to be developed, then you should select appropriate learning activities. Most oral language development activities tend to fall into certain types: conversations, discussions, description/comparison/evaluation, reporting, storytelling, and creative drama or choral reading. In the If-Then Strategy Guide for Oral Language Development we have listed the teaching strategies that appear in the next section and link them to key need areas your oral language assessments are likely to reveal (see Figure 3.10 on p. 87).

## TEACHING STRATEGIES FOR DEVELOPING ORAL LANGUAGE

Children's oral language is improved when teachers and family members provide high-quality language models and numerous opportunities to practice oral language in authentic situations and when students receive supportive feedback for their attempts at approximating proficient English usage (Morrow, 1999, 2005). Whether teaching English as a second language or working to shore up the language abilities of native speakers, learning activities selected by teachers should help children improve their receptive (listening/reading) and expressive (speaking/writing) language skills. In this section, we provide a menu of teaching strategies that have served many teachers well in the classroom.

### Rule of Five

### Purpose

There is a plethora of scientific research showing that helping children increase the length of spoken and added written sentences can have a very positive effect on learning to read

**FIGURE 3.9** Summary Matrix of Oral Language Assessments

| Name of Assessment Tool | Screening Assessment | Diagnostic Assessment | Progress-Monitoring Assessment | Outcomes Assessment | Norm-Referenced Test | Criterion-Referenced Test | Reliability Evidence | Validity Evidence |
|---|---|---|---|---|---|---|---|---|
| Informal Language Inventory (ILI) | + | – | + | – | – | + | Not Available | Not Available |
| Student Oral Language Observation Matrix (SOLOM) | + | + | + | – | – | + | Not Available | Not Available |
| Teacher Rating of Oral Language and Literacy (TROLL) | + | – | + | – | – | + | TROLL internal consistency (Cronbach's alpha) ranged from .77 to .92 for three separate subscales. For the total TROLL scores, alphas exceeded .89 for each age. | TROLL shows moderate associations with PPVT-III according to the TROLL's authors. |
| DIBELS Word Use Fluency Test (WUF) | + | – | + | – | – | + | As Word Use Fluency is a new DIBELS measure, its technical adequacy has not of yet been determined. | As Word Use Fluency is a new DIBELS measure, its technical adequacy has not of yet been determined. |

(continued)

**FIGURE 3.9** *Continued*

| Name of Assessment Tool | Screening Assessment | Diagnostic Assessment | Progress-Monitoring Assessment | Outcomes Assessment | Norm-Referenced Test | Criterion-Referenced Test | Reliability Evidence | Validity Evidence |
|---|---|---|---|---|---|---|---|---|
| Peabody Picture Vocabulary Test/Expressive Vocabulary Test (PPVT/EVT) | + | – | – | + | + | – | PPVT-III: Internal Alpha range .92 to .98; Split-half: Alternate-form range .86 to .97; Test-Retest range .88 to .96. | PPVT-III: .91 correlation with the WISC-III VIQ, .89 with the KAIT Crystallized IQ, and .81 with the K-BIT Vocabulary Test. |
| Get it Got it Go! Picture Naming Test | + | – | + | – | – | + | Alternate-form range .44 to .78; Test-Retest is .67. | .56 to .75 correlation with the PPVT-III |
| Oral Language Checklist | – | – | + | – | – | – | Not Available | Not Available |

Key: + can be used for
     – not appropriate for

**FIGURE 3.10** If-Then Strategy Guide for Oral Language Development

| "If" the student is ready to learn / "Then" try these teaching strategies → | Rule of Five | Let's talk | One Looks/One Doesn't | Poetry Potpourri: Teaching Modeling | Poetry Potpourri: Unison Reading | Poetry Potpourri: Repeated Lines and Refrains | Poetry Potpourri: Antiphonal Call and Response | Poetry Potpourri: Singing Poems | Poetry Potpourri: Poetry Response | Storytelling | Dialogic Reading | Critical Dialogues |
|---|---|---|---|---|---|---|---|---|---|---|---|---|
| Comprehensible expressive language | + | + | + | + | * | * | − | * | + | + | + | + |
| Fluent expressive language production | + | + | − | − | + | + | + | + | + | + | + | − |
| Word pronunciation | * | − | + | + | + | + | + | + | + | + | + | + |
| Word usage | + | − | + | + | + | + | + | + | + | + | + | + |
| Grammatical constructions | * | − | + | + | + | + | + | + | + | + | + | + |
| Comprehends received language | − | + | + | * | + | + | + | + | + | + | + | + |
| Organizes ideas logically and sequentially | * | * | + | + | − | − | − | − | + | + | + | + |
| Provides supporting details | * | − | − | + | − | − | − | − | + | + | + | + |
| Word meaning acquisition | − | * | + | + | * | * | * | * | + | * | + | + |

Key: + Excellent strategy
* Adaptable strategy
− Unsuitable strategy

87

(e.g., Dickinson & Tabors, 2001; Tharp & Gallimore, 1988). The Rule of Five strategy (Cooter, 2005) is an adaptation of research findings by Dickinson and Tabors (2001) intended to increase verbal sentence length, also known as *mean length of utterance* (MLU), by simply requiring students (and teachers) to always speak in complete sentences in their conversations using at least *five* words. These researchers concluded that children need opportunities to be part of conversations that use "extended discourse"—talk that requires students to develop complete sentences in explanations, narratives, or even "pretend" talk.

### Materials

- A laminated copy of a drawing of a small hand similar to the one shown in Figure 3.11
- A small self-adhesive magnet for each laminated copy so the children can put them on their refrigerator at home as a reminder to themselves and their parents that our goal is to speak in complete sentences
- A letter to parents explaining what the Rule of Five is, encouraging them to practice this strategy at home in their family interactions

### Procedure

Distribute the Rule of Five hands to each of your students. Explain that it is a fun strategy and easy to do and that both students and teachers must use at least *five* words in all talk. As ever, the best way to introduce this activity is with teacher modeling. You may begin by saying, for instance,

> *Girls and boys, instead of me saying something to you like "Line up!" I should say a complete sentence like "Students, it is time for us to line up for lunch."*

You should explain that you expect students to express themselves in at least five or more words. For instance,

> *If I should ask your classmate Molly a question like, "How was your weekend, Molly?" I would not accept an answer like "Good." No, the Rule of Five would require Molly to give me a complete sentence of five or more words such as "This weekend I played baseball and I had a great time."*

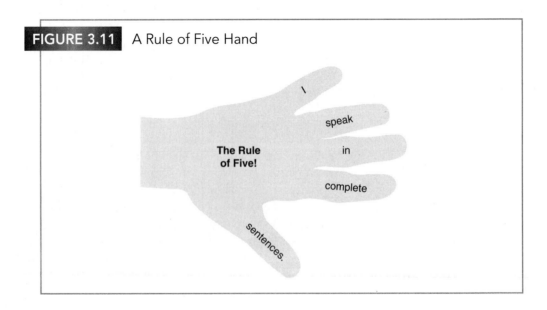

**FIGURE 3.11**   A Rule of Five Hand

For best results, introduce the Rule of Five idea to parents at your first open house of the year and ask for their support at home. You will be amazed at the positive results that will occur in reading and writing instruction as a result.

## Let's Talk!

### Purpose

As teachers of language, we must always have a wide range of exercises of varying complexity, interest level, and difficulty available to reach children where they are in their oral language development (Avery & Bryan, 2001). For young learners, this can be as simple and basic as describing familiar things in their environment. Recognizing that oral language is the starting point for later literacy growth and a key predictor in children's acquisition of early reading ability, Woodward, Haskins, Schaefer, and Smolen (2004) describe an oral language development project called Let's Talk! that was designed to address a "nearly two-year long lag in oral language development" (p. 92). Results from implementing the Let's Talk! project for just 10 weeks revealed statistically significant improvements in pre-K and kindergarten students' verbal fluency and grammatical complexity.

### Materials

- A Let's Talk! box for the dramatic toys in five different categories
- 10 family figures (representing diverse ethnicities)
- 12 pieces of furniture
- 2 trucks
- 11 farm animals
- A folding fence
- 11 wild animals

### Procedure

The idea of Let's Talk is to have pairs of students work at a "talk table" using the "talk box" for at least 15 minutes per week of uninterrupted talk and play. Pairs of students are selected such that in each pair a verbally fluent speaker is paired with a less verbally fluent speaker. The teacher introduces the Let's Talk! project by telling students that they need to be good talkers and listeners so that one day they can also be good readers and writers (Woodward, Haskins, Schaefer, & Smolen, 2004). Students are further instructed that the Let's Talk! table is designed to give them opportunities to talk more. At that table there is a "talk box" containing special toys. When it is their turn, each pair of students can go to the table and talk about what they are doing with the special toys in the box. Teachers in the Let's Talk! project established the following rules:

- Only two children at a time can work at the Let's Talk! table.
- Students at the table should not be interrupted.
- Table toys must stay at the table.
- The last pair of students at the table need to put the toys back into the "talk box."

The teacher's role each day is to schedule four pairs of students to have a daily turn at the Let's Talk! table. All of the toys are not placed into the box initially; rather, each category of toys is introduced as additions to the "talk box" over several weeks to avoid the distraction of too many new toys at once. The teacher shows students the new toys within a category while using new vocabulary to describe the new category of toys. Teachers also model how to use and talk about the toys. The teacher connects other events during the day in drawing and writing to the new category of toys. The Let's Talk! table can be used for a center in many classrooms at different levels depending on the "toys" or objects placed into the "talk box." Intermediate-grade classroom adaptations involve placing more sophisticated objects related to science, math, or social science content for students to use and discuss to develop their academic language proficiencies.

## One Looks, One Doesn't

### Purpose

It is important for us to help students expand their oral communications abilities because, as "producers" (speakers) of language, they will also become better "receivers" (readers) of language; these are reciprocal processes. In One Looks, One Doesn't (Peregoy & Boyle, 2001), students are able to take turns practicing their oral communications with a peer as they describe a picture or object selected by the teacher.

### Materials

- Stimulus objects for students to describe, which can include interesting pictures from magazines or books, pictures on transparencies shown at the overhead projector for all groups to see and describe, objects that can be held, and so forth
- A blindfold for each group (one only for each group) for adding a little spice to this activity (optional)
- An egg timer or other timing device

### Procedure

First, place students in groups of two for this activity (also called *dyads*). If possible, arrange it so that in each twosome you have a more capable speaker of English, such as pairing a native English speaker with an English language learner (ELL), or perhaps a sixth-grade student paired with a third grader.

If using a transparency of a picture, place the transparency on the overhead projector after explaining that one student will look at the transparency while the other turns away (or wears a blindfold). The student who looks at the picture describes it to his or her partner and the listener attempts to guess what the partner is describing.

A variation is for the listener to try to draw what his or her partner is describing. After about 5 minutes (use an egg timer to keep it fair for all), the one drawing the picture can turn around and compare his or her drawing with what his or her partner was describing.

Areas that could be stressed in teacher-led minilessons for this activity include

- Expressing ideas clearly and with variety
- Organizing ideas effectively before speaking
- Word usage appropriate for the situation
- Appropriate articulation
- Listening to questions carefully from your partner and asking for clarification as necessary
- Politely asking the speaker to repeat or explain

## Poetry Potpourri

### Purpose

Nancy Hadaway and her colleagues (Hadaway, Vardell, & Young, 2001) have assembled a wonderful collection of classroom activities that use poetry to stimulate oral language development, particularly for students learning English as a second language. They point out that reading and rereading poetry through read-aloud and choral reading activities promote fluency, develop concept knowledge and vocabulary, and serve as splendid springboards into writing. In this section, we highlight several of the poetry activities that Hadaway et al. have recommended.

## Materials

- A variety of poetry books for language-development activities—the following list shows the selections cited by Hadaway et al. (2001), many of which are found in school libraries:

Ada, A. F., Harris, V., & Hopkins, L. B. (1993). *A chorus of cultures anthology.* Carmel, CA: Hampton Brown.

Fleischman, P. (1985). *I am phoenix.* New York: HarperCollins.

Fleischman, P. (1988). *Joyful noise.* New York: HarperCollins.

Fleischman, P. (2000). *Big talk: Poems for four voices.* Cambridge, MA: Candlewick Press.

Florian, D. (1994). *Bing bang boing.* San Diego, CA: Harcourt Brace.

Greenfield, E. (1978). *Honey, I love.* New York: Harper & Row.

Herrera, J. F. (1998). *Laughing out loud, I fly: Poems in English and Spanish.* New York: HarperCollins.

Holbrook, S. (1996). *The dog ate my homework.* Honesdale, PA: Boyds Mills Press.

Holbrook, S. (1997). *Which way to the dragon!: Poems for the coming-on-strong.* Honesdale, PA: Boyds Mills Press.

Hughes, L. (1932/1994). *The dreamkeeper and other poems.* New York: Knopf.

Johnston, T. (1996). *My Mexico—Mexico mio.* New York: Penguin Putnam.

Kuskin, K. (1975). *Near the window tree.* New York: Harper & Row.

Kuskin, K. (1980). *Dogs and dragons, trees and dreams.* New York: HarperCollins.

Mora, P. (1999). *Confetti: Poems for children.* New York: Lee & Low.

Nye, N. S. (1995). *The tree is older than you are.* New York: Simon & Schuster.

Pappas, T. (1991). *Math talk: Mathematical ideas in poems for two voices.* San Carlos, CA: Wide World/Tetra.

Prelutsky, J. (1984). *The new kid on the block.* New York: Greenwillow.

Shields, C. D. (1995). *Lunch money.* New York: Dutton.

Silverstein, S. (1974). *Where the sidewalk ends.* New York: HarperCollins.

Silverstein, S. (1981). *A light in the attic.* New York: HarperCollins.

Soto, G. (1992). *Neighborhood odes.* San Diego, CA: Harcourt.

Soto, G. (1995). *Canto familiar.* San Diego, CA: Harcourt Brace.

Wong, J. (1996). *A suitcase of seaweed.* New York: Simon & Schuster.

## Procedure

Following are brief descriptions of oral language development activities that have been recommended using poetry as the primary catalyst. (Citations in this section are from the preceding "Materials" list.)

- *Teacher modeling.* It is hard to sell something you do not love yourself, so begin with poems that you particularly like. Introduce key words and phrases at the chalkboard so that students can see as well as hear new vocabulary and concepts. If you need help with this, try "Three Wishes" by Karla Kuskin (1975). All of us "kids" have made wishes and can relate to this poem. For those of us with, shall we say, wacky relatives, Gary Soto's (1992) "Ode to Family Photographs" can be great fun with older students.

- *Unison reading.*   After the previous activity, students will usually be loosened up a bit and ready to take on more of the performance role. Choose shorter poems with repeating lines, and read the poem aloud first yourself to help students get the feel. When we each taught first grade, we found that children could hardly be stopped from joining in on the second reading of a fun poem! "My Monster" (Florian, 1994) is very popular from grades 1 through 4, for example.

- *Repeated lines and refrains.*   Another great choral activity has students learn about timing and coming in just when their assigned line comes up or as a group when a refrain appears. Sometimes a key word is said extra loud for emphasis, such as with the poem "Louder" by Jack Prelutsky (1984).

- *Antiphonal: Call and response.*   Teachers divide the class into two groups, and one side repeats the lines first spoken by the other. This is a form of antiphonal reading, an ancient tradition begun by monks in monasteries during medieval times. Try out the "call and response" method using "Copycat" by Sara Holbrook (1997).

- *Singing poems.*   Children love to put poetry to song—matching poems and songs having the same meter. It works best when using tunes that are familiar to all such as "Row, Row, Row Your Boat" or "Mary Had a Little Lamb." If you give students a copy of the poem, they will end up reading and singing the poem over and over, providing them with needed repetition of high-frequency words and a chance to develop language fluency. Try "The Dog Ate My Homework" by Sara Holbrook (1996) sung to "On Top of Old Smokey" or the poem "School Cafeteria" (Florian, 1996) sung to the tune of "Ninety-Nine Bottles of 'Pop.'"

- *Poetry response.*   A good language development exercise should elicit a great deal of oral language in an authentic discussion situation for student practice and teacher coaching. Draw students into discussions about interesting poems using such questions as

  What did this poem make you think?

  What did you like about this poem?

  What do you think the poet was trying to say?

  Does this remind you of anything you know about?

  Let's talk about what is going on here . . .

  What is this poem about?

## Storytelling

### Purpose

Many cultures have strong oral traditions to describe their religious beliefs, politics, triumphs, and family stories (McHenry & Heath, 1994). As a tool for language development, storytelling can be powerful (Cooper, 2005; Strickland & Morrow, 1989). As an art form, storytelling has certain aspects that should be respected for the storyteller to be effective in his or her communications. The following teacher-directed method for bringing storytelling to the table can be a valuable tool in your teaching arsenal.

### Materials

- Several stories that would be appropriate for retelling from which students can choose one (what we term *limited choice*)
- A copy of The Storyteller's Planning Guide (Figure 3.12) for each student

### Procedure

Begin with a storytelling experience for the students in which you model telling one of your favorite stories from memory. Next, introduce the Storyteller's Planning Guide (Figure 3.12) and explain each of its key points. Walk through a planning session in which you model how you went about planning to share the story they witnessed you sharing earlier.

In some cases, it is best to start younger students into storytelling by using Vivian Paley's approach (Cooper, 2005). Paley (1981) invited young students to begin by dictating a story the teacher would write down. Next, they were invited to act out or dramatize their story. Finally, they were asked to retell their story. In the case of both younger and older students, the story to be told should be easy to read and in concert with the student's interests and background.

Be sure to include discussion about any props, voices, and other points that add drama to the telling. Place students into groups of two and have them select one of the stories you have available for them to use in storytelling. Have them account for each step in the planning process using the Storyteller's Planning Guide. When each group of two feels they are ready, have them take turns practicing storytelling with each other. The final "act" will be for each student to perform his or her favorite part of the story to you (or the entire group, if the student is not too nervous). Follow up the performance with questioning, such as "Why did you choose that part of the story to tell?" or "Why was that your favorite part of the story?" This draws students into even more dialogue.

## Dialogic Reading

### Purpose

Dialogic reading, originally described by Whitehurst et al. (1988), involves the shared reading of a book as teachers ask students to respond to strategic questions while reading the book. The dialogic reading technique involves multiple reading of the same book and multiple conversations about books with students in small groups. Over the course of the repeated readings, students are encouraged to become the storytellers. The teacher prompts students with questions and well-planned responses that encourage students to say more. Dialogic reading has been systematically studied for more than a decade in a variety of populations of children from 2 to 6 years old and has demonstrated uniformly positive effects on students' oral language development, the keystone of emergent literacy (Whitehurst et al., 1988). Although the relationships among phonemic awareness, emergent writing, concepts about print, letter name and sound knowledge, and phonics weakens during first and second grade, the importance of oral language facility reemerges in intermediate grades as a strong, direct influence on reading development (Storch & Whitehurst, 2002).

### Materials

- Engaging children's story or book
- Highlighter or highlighter tape
- Sticky notes of different sizes and colors

---

**FIGURE 3.12**  The Storyteller's Planning Guide

Storyteller: _____

Story: _____

Source: _____

**Motivation:** *I want to tell this story because . . .*

**Props:** *What kinds of props ("properties"), if any, would I need to tell this story? (Clothing, sound-making devices, other?)*

**Introduction:** *How will I begin the story? What are the exact words I should use?*

**Setting:** *How do I describe the setting? How can I make the listener feel like she is there? Is time and place important to the story?*

**Characters:** *How can I best describe each character? What makes the main character "tick"? How should I present each character to the audience? Should I use different voices for the different characters? If not, how can I make the audience understand who is talking?*

**Sequence of Events:** *What are the key events I will describe in my story? What is the correct order for each "scene"?*

**Conclusion:** *How will I bring my story to a successful end? What are my final words? (Exact words, please) How do I want my audience to feel at the conclusion?*

**Rehearsal:** *Have I practiced telling my story alone at least three times, and before a friend at least once?*

---

### Procedure

After carefully selecting an engaging children's story for dialogic reading, teachers study the story before reading to locate and highlight interesting vocabulary words that can be discussed during dialogic reading. They can also prepare carefully thought-out questions to promote students' thinking and encourage them to "say more" as they assume the role of storyteller. Some teachers have found it useful to write their questions on sticky notes and place them on the pages of the story to remind them when they should be asked.

Dialogic reading is best done in small groups (Doyle & Bramwell, 2006). The teacher begins by reading the interesting story she has previously selected and studied, such as *The Cat Who Wore a Pot on Her Head* (Slepian & Seidler, 1980), in which interesting vocabulary words have been highlighted and for which strategic questions have been written to promote dialogue among the teacher and students. The selected book is repeatedly read aloud several times to promote student questioning and dialogue. Repeatedly reading stories aloud has also been shown to promote elaborated interpretations of stories. During dialogic reading, teacher-selected vocabulary words are either explicitly taught or the context is used to help students develop a "student-friendly" definition of the words. For example, the teacher might ask, "What do the authors mean when they wrote that Bendemolena *raced* home?" Or, "Why was Bendemolena getting all of the directions from her mother mixed up?" Also during the reading, the teacher asks questions to get the conversation around the story started. For example, the teacher might show the first picture in the book and say, "Why do you think the cat is wearing a pot on her head?" We have found that asking questions, in order, about the elements of story structure (see Chapter 10), setting, characters, problems, goals, events, and resolution, helps students develop an internal framework for remembering, telling, and retelling stories. Story structure questions also help them to recall events of stories in the correct sequence and remember to use well-known phrases in their retellings, such as "once upon a time" or "they lived happily ever after." Examples of story structure questions might include "Where did the story of *The Cat Who Wore a Pot on Her Head* take place?" and "Who was the main character in this story?" In addition to story structure, we recommend that teachers write questions that probe complex relationships between and among the elements of the story, the vocabulary, and students' lives. For example, "What problems were caused by the cat wearing a pot on her head?" Dialogic reading provides a setting for rich concept, oral language, and listening comprehension to develop.

## Critical Dialogues

### Purpose

Critical dialogues are structured conversations between teachers and children around stories, information texts, and other media sources such as DVDs, videos, and websites. Students link their own experiences, feelings, and knowledge to learn content knowledge in science, social studies, mathematics, art, music, and so on. Gentile and McMillan (1992, 1995) based the critical dialogue strategy on the work of the Brazilian educator Paulo Freire, who used dialogues as a method to help free Brazilian peasants from the oppression of illiteracy and poverty. Gentile (2003) claims that using critical dialogues helps to create "a threshold level of language proficiency" necessary to build the higher order cognition children need to process information for academic purposes and become literate (p. 38).

### Materials

- Critical Dialogue Planning and Lesson Guide (see Figure 3.13)
- One narrative or story text
- One or more short information texts
- One or more media-related resources, for example, videos, websites, DVDs, CD-ROMs, audiotapes, and so on

### Procedure

A critical dialogue is planned and executed using a sequential four-stage approach.

- *Stage 1.* The teacher organizes and frames the dialogue. This is accomplished by setting the parameters for a successful conversation, that is, turn-taking, active listening, not interrupting a person speaking, participation, and so on. Next, the teacher introduces the

---

**FIGURE 3.13** Critical Dialogue Planning and Lesson Guide for Plants

**Stage 1: Organizing and Framing the Critical Dialogue**

*Selected Topic or Theme:* Plants

*Necessary Materials:*

Story Text: Krauss, R. (1945). *The Carrot Seed.* New York: Scholastic.
Information Texts: McEvoy, P. (2002). *Plants.* New York: Newbridge.
                 Roberts, C. (2004). *Where Plants Live.* Northborough, MA:
                 Sundance Publishing.
Video/DVD/CD: VHS (2004). *How Do Plants Grow and Change?* Questar, Inc.
Website: Plants for Kids—www.kathimitchell.com/plants.html

*Assessing/Activating Background Knowledge:*

- List of Key Vocabulary Concepts

**Stage 2: Guiding the Critical Dialogue**

*Purpose for Learning:*

- Ask children what they want to learn about the topic or theme.

*Active Processing:*

- Read the story text.
- Read the information texts.
- View the media selections.
- Visit the websites.
- Discuss what was read, viewed, or listened to.

**Stage 3: Developing and Expanding the Critical Dialogue**

- Ask children what they want to learn about the topic or theme.

*Active Processing:*

- Read the story text.
- Read the information texts.
- View the media selections.
- Visit the websites.
- Discuss what was read, viewed, or listened to.

**Stage 4: Closing the Dialogue**

- Invite children to write a response to several questions posed by the teacher; for example,
  - What is the most important thing you learned about plants from the selections and our dialogues?
  - What is the most important question you have about plants from the selections and our dialogues?
  - What difference does any of this make to you?

---

topic or theme of the text and media materials—say, for example, "plants"—by assessing, activating, and building students' background knowledge and previous life experiences.

- *Stage 2.* The teacher guides students to identify a significant purpose, formulate a set of questions, or engage in "I wonder" brainstorming for listening to, reading, or viewing the texts or media selected on a topic like "plants." Next the teacher highlights new vocabulary, concepts, or information and clearly identifies the main idea, important facts, problems, or story sequence and elements for the students, such as *stem, pistol, pollen, ovules, flowering,* and so on. At this point, children view, read, or listen to the story or information texts or the media resources selected by the teacher. Afterward, children are invited to talk about what they were thinking or feeling as they watched, read, or listened.

- *Stage 3.* The teacher develops and expands the dialogue. After their initial conversations about the materials read, listened to, or watched, the teacher asks the children to perform two tasks: (a) identify the most important thing they learned and (b) think of the most important question they could ask about the materials they have viewed, heard, or read. Next, the children and teachers summarize and clarify the major ideas of the selection and their dialogues. Finally, the teacher may model how to pose questions of differing types and how one goes about answering these questions.

- *Stage 4.* The teacher helps children to close the dialogue. This is accomplished by asking children to write a response to several questions posed by the teacher:
  - What is the most important thing you learned from the selections and our dialogues?
  - What is the most important question you have about the selections and our dialogues?
  - What difference does any of this make to you?

For younger children, the teacher can ask children to respond to these questions orally and write down what the children say on a large chart paper or wall display. This helps to validate the importance of what the children learned and said about what they learned. The questions the children dictate may very well lead to future dialogues, reading, listening, and viewing.

# ADAPTING INSTRUCTION FOR THOSE WHO STRUGGLE

How can teachers effectively respond to the variability of children's oral language development and usage in classrooms? Even with the plethora of previously recommended assessments and strategies, we want to offer a few parting suggestions about how oral language instruction can be differentiated to meet the needs of those students who struggle.

- Remember to be a high-quality model of conventional English usage.
- You can also help by partnering less capable children with more capable and supportive children.
- Pair pictures and objects with oral language use in the classroom.
- When asking questions or expecting a response, remember to extend the "wait time" before you rephrase or redirect your question or request. When questioning, ask open-ended questions so that children can express themselves more fully than just giving a correct response.
- Provide explicit instruction in oral language vocabulary development, how sentences work, and word pronunciations.
- Encourage language play, extended conversations, and telling and retelling stories with struggling learners. Do not be afraid to use rare words or engage in discussions of a wide range of topics.

## SELECTED REFERENCES

Avery, S., & Bryan, C. (2001). Improving spoken and written English: From research to practice. *Teaching in Higher Education, 6*(2), 169–183.

Bruner, J. (1978). The role of dialog in language acquisition. In A. Sinclair, R. J. Jarvella, & W. M. Levelt (Eds.), *The child's conception of language* (pp. 241–256). New York: Springer-Verlag.

Burns, P. C. (1980). *Assessment and correction of language arts difficulties.* Columbus, OH: Merrill.

Chomsky, N. (1965). *Aspects of the theory of syntax.* Cambridge, MA: MIT Press.

Cooper, P. M. (2005). Literacy learning and pedagogical purpose in Vivian Paley's "storytelling curriculum." *Journal of Early Childhood Literacy, 5*(3), 229–251.

Cooter, K. S. (2005, February). *The Principals' Fellowship: Strategies for improving oral language and reading abilities.* Paper presented at the meeting of The Principals' Fellowship, Memphis, TN.

Cox, C. (2002). *Teaching language arts* (4th ed.). Boston: Allyn & Bacon.

CREDE. (2009). *Indicators of language development.* Berkeley, CA: Center for Research on Education, Diversity, and Excellence. Retrieved from http://crede.berkeley.edu/research/crede/lang_dev.html.

Dickinson, D. K., McCabe, A., & Sprague, K. (2003). Teacher Rating of Oral Language and Literacy (TROLL): Individualizing early literacy instruction with a standards-based rating tool. *The Reading Teacher, 56*(6), 554–564.

Dickinson, D. K., & Tabors, P. O. (2001). *Beginning literacy with language.* Baltimore: Paul H. Brookes.

Doyle, B. G., & Bramwell, W. (2006). Promoting emergent literacy and social–emotional learning through dialogic reading. *The Reading Teacher, 59*(6), 554–564.

Dunn, L. M., & Dunn, D. M. (2005). *PPVT-III: Peabody Picture Vocabulary Test* (3rd ed.). Retrieved from www.agsnet.com/Group.asp?nGroup InfoID=a12010.

Dunn, L. M., & Dunn, D. M. (2007). *PPVT-IV: Peabody Picture Vocabulary Test* (4th ed.). San Antonio, TX: Pearson/Psychology Corporation.

Florian, D. (1994). *Bing bang boing.* San Diego, CA: Harcourt Brace.

Florian, D. (1996). *Bing bang boing: Poems and drawings.* New York: Puffin/Penguin.

Gentile, L. M. (2003). *The oracy instructional guide: Linking research and theory to assessment and instruction.* Carlsbad, CA: Dominie Press.

Gentile, L. M., & McMillan, M. (1992). Literacy for students at risk: Developing critical dialogues. *The Journal of Reading, 35*(8), 636–641.

Gentile, L. M., & McMillan, M. (1995). Critical dialogue: A literacy curriculum for students at risk in the middle grades. *Reading and Writing Quarterly, 11,* 123–126.

Greenhalgh, K. S., & Strong, C. J. (2001). Literate language features in spoken narratives of children with typical language and children with language impairments. *Language, Speech, & Hearing Services in Schools, 32*(2), 114–126.

Hadaway, N. L., Vardell, S. M., & Young, T. A. (2001). Scaffolding oral language development through poetry for students learning English. *The Reading Teacher, 54*(8), 796–807.

Halliday, M. A. K. (1975). *Learning how to mean: Explorations in the development of language.* London: Edward Arnold.

Hart, B., & Risley, T. R. (1995). *Meaningful differences in the everyday experience of young American children.* Baltimore: Paul H. Brookes.

Hart, B., & Risley, T. R. (2002). *The social world of children: Learning to talk.* Baltimore: Paul H. Brookes.

Holbrook, S. (1996). *The dog ate my homework.* Honesdale, PA: Boyds Mills Press.

Holbrook, S. (1997). *I never said I wasn't difficult.* Honesdale, PA: Boyds Mills Press.

Honig, A. S. (2007). Oral language development. *Early Child Development and Care, 177*(6 & 7), 581–613.

Johnson, D. J. (1993). Relationships between oral and written language. *School Psychology Review, 22*(4), 595–610.

Kirkland, L. D., & Patterson, J. (2005). Developing oral language in primary classrooms. *Early Childhood Education Journal, 32*(6), 391–395.

Kuskin, K. (1975). *Near the window tree.* New York: Harper & Row.

Lenneberg, E. H. (1964). *New directions in the study of language.* Cambridge, MA: MIT Press.

Lyon, G. R. (1999). Reading development, reading disorders, and reading instruction: Research-based findings. ASHA Special Interest Division I Newsletter. *Language Learning and Education, 6*(1), 8–16.

McHenry, E., & Heath, S. B. (1994). The literate and the literary. *Written Communication, 11*(4), 419–445.

Melear, J. D. (1974). An informal language inventory. *Elementary English, 41,* 508–511.

Menyuk, P. (1988). *Language development knowledge and use.* Glenview, IL: Scott, Foresman/Little, Brown College Division.

Missal, K. N., & McConnell, S. R. (2004). *Technical report: Psychometric characteristics of individual growth and development indicators: Picture naming, rhyming, and alliteration.* Minneapolis: University of Minnesota.

Morrow, L. M. (1999). Where do we go from here in early literacy research and practice? *Issues in Education, 5*(1), 117–125.

Morrow, L. M. (2005). *Literacy development in the early years: Helping children read and write* (5th ed.). Boston: Allyn & Bacon.

Morrow, L. M., Strickland, D. S., & Woo, D. G. (1998). *Literacy instruction in half- and whole-day kindergarten: Research to practice.* Newark, DE: International Reading Association.

National Institute of Child Health and Human Development. (2000). *Report of the National Reading Panel: Teaching children to read.* Washington, DC: Author.

Neuman, S. B. (1999). Books make a difference: A study of access to literacy. *Reading Research Quarterly, 34,* 286–311.

Neuman, S. B. (2006, October). N is for nonsensical: Low-income preschool children need content-rich instruction, not drill in procedural skills. *Educational Leadership,* 28–31.

Neuman, S. B., & Roskos, K. (1992). Literacy objects as cultural tools: Effects on children's literacy behaviors in play. *Reading Research Quarterly, 27,* 202–225.

Paley, V. G. (1981). *Wally's stories: Conversations in the kindergarten.* Cambridge, MA: Harvard University Press.

Pappas, C. C., Kiefer, B. Z., & Levstik, L. S. (1999). *An integrated language perspective in the elementary school* (3rd ed.). New York: Longman.

Paul, R. (2001). *Language disorders from infancy through adolescence* (2nd ed.). St. Louis: Mosby.

Payne, R. K. (1998). *A framework for understanding poverty.* Highlands, TX: RFT.

Peregoy, S. F., & Boyle, O. F. (2001). *Reading, writing, & learning in ESL* (3rd ed.). New York: Longman.

Piaget, J. (1959). *The language and thought of the child* (3rd ed.). London: Routledge & Kegan Paul.

Pinnell, G. S. (1998). *The language foundation of reading recovery.* Keynote address to the Third International Reading Recovery Institute. Third, Cairns, Australia.

Piper, T. (1998). *Language and learning: The home and school years* (2nd ed.). Upper Saddle River, NJ: Merrill/Prentice Hall.

Prelutsky, J. (1984). *The new kid on the block.* New York: Greenwillow/HarperCollins.

Ramey, C. T. (1999). *Right from birth: Building your child's foundation for life, birth to 18.* New York: Goddard Press.

Slepian, J., & Seidler, A. (1980). *The cat who wore a pot on her head.* New York: Scholastic.

Snow, C. E., Scarborough, H. S., & Burns, M. S. (1999). What speech-language pathologists need to know about early reading. *Topics in Language Disorders, 20*(1), 48–58.

Soto, G. (1992). *Neighborhood odes.* San Diego, CA: Harcourt.

Storch, S. A., & Whitehurst, G. J. (2002). Oral language and code-related precursors to reading: Evidence from a longitudinal structural model. *Developmental Psychology, 38,* 934–947.

Strickland, D. S., & Morrow, L. M. (1989). Oral language development: Children as storytellers (emerging readers and writers). *The Reading Teacher, 43*(3), 260–261.

Tharp, G., & Gallimore, R. (1988). *Rousing minds to life: Teaching, learning, and schooling in social context.* Cambridge, MA: Cambridge University Press.

Vygotsky, L. S. (1986). *Thought and language.* Boston: MIT Press.

Vygotsky, L. S. (1990). *Mind in society.* Boston: Harvard University Press.

Warren, S. F. (2001). The future of early communication and language intervention. *Topics in Early Childhood Special Education, 20*(1), 33–38.

Warren, S. F., & Yoder, P. J. (1997). Emerging model of communication and language intervention. *Mental Retardation and Development Disabilities Research Reviews, 3,* 358–362.

Watson, R. (2001). Literacy and oral language: Implications for early literacy acquisition. In S. B. Neuman & D. K. Dickinson (Eds.), *Handbook of early literacy* (pp. 43–65). New York: Guilford Press.

Whitehurst, G. J., Falco, F. L., Lonigan, C. J., Fischel, J. E., DeBaryshe, B. D., Valdez Menchaca, M. C., et al. (1988). Accelerating language development through picture book reading. *Developmental Psychology, 24,* 552–559.

Wiig, E. H., Becker-Redding, U., & Semel, E. M. (1983). A cross-cultural, cross-linguistic comparison of language abilities of 7- to 8- and 12- to 13-year-old children with learning disabilities. *Journal of Learning Disabilities, 16*(10), 576–585.

Woodward, C., Haskins, G., Schaefer, G., & Smolen, L. (2004). Let's Talk!: A different approach to oral language development. *Young Children, 59*(4), 92–95.

**The Power of Classroom Practice**
www.myeducationlab.com

Now go to Topic 4: "Oral Language" and Topic 14: "English Language Learners" in the MyEducationLab (www.myeducationlab.com) for your course, where you can:

- Find learning outcomes for "Oral Language" and "English Language Learners," along with the national standards that connect to these outcomes.
- Complete the tasks in the Assignments and Activities to help you more deeply understand the chapter content.
- Examine challenging situations and cases presented in the IRIS Center Resources.
- Access video clips of CCSSO National Teachers of the Year award winners responding to the question, "Why Do I Teach?" in the Teacher Talk section.
- Apply and practice your understanding of the core teaching skills identified in the chapter with the Building Teaching Skills and Dispositions learning units.

# 4

# Children's Concepts about Print

*M*s. Solomon's kindergarten class excitedly gathered around her on the carpet. She had a big book displayed on the easel entitled *On Market Street* (Lobel & Lobel, 1981) and was ready to start reading. As the children settled in, Ms. Solomon pointed to the cover of the book and asked, "What do you see here?"

"A girl carrying a bunch of stuff!" "Yes, she is. It's quite a stack of things. Where do you suppose she has been to get all that stuff?" Bobby responded somewhat quizically, "I guess she's been to a junkyard." "No, no, she's been shopping!" interrupted Brit. "Why do you say that, Brit?" "Because in the picture she is walking away from a town and some buildings." "Good observation! What do you think the words will tell us about the picture on the cover of this book?" "It's the title," Jana blurts out confidently. "Thank you, Jana. That is what the writing on the cover is called. So, let me ask my question another way. What do you think the writing in the title will tell us about the picture on the cover?" "Oh, I think it will say something about going shopping," answers Brit. "OK, shall we see? Listen to me read the title and watch as I point to the words with my pointer." Ms. Solomon points to the words one at a time while reading, "ON—MARKET—STREET."

Ms. Solomon continues into the book and comes to a picture of a girl covered with clocks. "What is the letter at the top of this page?" "C," says Mica. "Good; by looking at the picture on this page, what do you think the girl is going to buy on Market Street?" The children cry out as a group, "Clocks." "Good thinking. Let's look at this word, *clocks*. Does *clocks* start with the letter *c*? Look carefully and compare the first letter in *clocks* with the letter *c* at the top of the page." The teacher and children interactively share this book noting the pattern in the book—letter at the top of the page, a picture, and a word on each page that begins with the letter at the top of the page.

After the first reading of the big book *On Market Street*, Ms. Solomon talks with the children about making their own *On Market Street* big book. "Now, let's see if we can make our own big book of what we would buy on Market Street," she says. Ms. Solomon lays out a big pile of labels and print taken from the children's everyday environment. Labels from soda drinks, candy, cereal boxes, and canned goods are all over the floor. "So, we are going to Market Street and we are going to buy something that begins with a *B*. What will we buy?" One little boy, Jackson, pulls up a candy bar wrapper and says, "Let's buy Butterfinger or Baby Ruth candy bars." They all agree and Ms. Solomon pastes the two candy bar wrappers on the letter *B* page of the class's version of the big book *On Market Street*.

# $\mathcal{B}$ACKGROUND BRIEFING FOR TEACHERS

Many children enter school already knowing a great deal about how books work and how to carefully look at printed language, while others do not (McGee & Richgels, 2003; Yaden & Templeton, 1986). Some children know the difference between a word and a letter; others know where a story begins in a book; and others have had little access to books and guided experiences with print (Neuman, 1999; Neuman & Celano, 2001). Concepts associated with printed text, known as **print concepts** (also *concepts about print*), are a critical part of early literacy development and understanding among beginning readers (Clay, 2000a; Hiebert, Pearson, Taylor, Richardson, & Paris, 1998).

Assessing print concepts in the early years is important so that children who come to school without prior learning opportunities, access to books and print, or guided experiences with printed language can be helped to develop these necessary concepts to prevent possible reading problems later on (Clay, 2000a; Durkin, 1989; Nichols, Rupley, Rickelman, & Algozzine, 2004; Snow, Burns, & Griffin, 1998). Wren (2002) noted that teachers can

> observe how the child handles a book, and can assess the child's knowledge about how information is presented in the book . . . [and] determine the child's general knowledge of books. (Does the child know where the cover is? Does the child hold the book right-side up? Does the child turn the pages appropriately? Does the child know the message of the book is contained in the text?) (p. 12)

Research studies have shown that some children require direct, explicit instruction in learning print concepts (Hiebert et al., 1998; Nichols, Rupley, Rickelman & Algozzine, 2004; Snow et al., 1998). For example, Nichols, Rupley, Rickelman, and Algozzine (2004) found that low SES and Latino children lag behind the general population in acquiring concepts about printed language even after a full year in kindergarten. Yaden (1982) also found that even after a year of reading instruction some readers' concepts of letters, words, and punctuation marks had not yet developed to a level that was functionally useful. Johns (1980) also learned that end-of-first-grade reading achievement could be reliably predicted using entering kindergarten students' knowledge of print concepts. Further, Morrow (1993) found that mastery of certain characteristics, conventions, and details associated with printed language is necessary for successful literacy development. Several other researchers have shown that children's early learning of concepts about print influence language development, initial writing development, phonemic awareness, phonics learning, word reading, and reading development (Lomax & McGee, 1987; Morris, 1993; Roberts, 1992). Lomax and McGee (1987) found that 92% of the variance in letter name learning can be attributed to concepts about print. They also found that 98% of the variance in letter–sound learning is related to concepts about print knowledge.

Morris, Bloodgood, Lomax, and Perney (2003) found that roughly one-third of the variance in word reading and connected text reading as well as 38% of the variance in ability to spell beginning and ending consonants in words can be traced to knowledge of a **concept of word.** These same researchers also found that a concept of word precedes acquisition of phonemic segmentation. Hiebert et al. (1998), in a document disseminated through the Center for the Improvement of Early Reading Achievement (CIERA) titled *Every Child a Reader,* have called for teachers, administrators, curriculum developers, and publishers to focus on assessing and developing print concepts among all young learners. You can access *Every Child a Reader* by going online to www.ciera.org. We focus in this next section on defining and explaining print concepts to children.

# WHAT ARE CONCEPTS ABOUT PRINT?

Go to the Assignments and Activities section of Topic 10: "Reading and Writing" in the MyEducationLab for your course and complete the activity entitled "The Reading/ Writing Connection." As you watch the video and answer the accompanying questions, note how the teacher uses the word wall and classroom displays to help children write "Tiffany likes pink." How does this help students gain the sense that they are becoming writers?

Concepts about print can be divided into three distinct and different print aspects (Clay, 2000a; Taylor, 1986): (a) the functional aspects of print, (b) the mapping aspects of print, and (c) the technical aspects of print. We discuss each of these separately.

## Functions of Print

Children learn early that written language is useful for a variety of purposes. Halliday's (1975) landmark research describes how oral and written language functions in our daily lives. The purposes children and adults have for using language can be divided into three parts: (a) *ideational,* or expressing one's thoughts; (b) *interpersonal,* or intimate social language; and (c) *textual,* or informational language. Smith (1977) expanded Halliday's teachings to purposes for which language can be used. Each of the 10 purposes or **functions of language** (p. 640) is detailed here with related examples:*

- *Instrumental.* "I want." Language is used as a means of getting things and satisfying material needs.

  *Examples in written language: Classified advertisements, notes, sign-up sheets, applications, bills, invoices, and so on.*

- *Regulatory.* "Do as I tell you." Language is used to control the attitudes, behaviors, and feelings of others.

  *Examples in written language: Traffic signs, procedures, policies, traffic tickets, prompts, and so on.*

- *Interactional.* "Me and you." Language is used as a means of getting along with others and establishing relative status. Also, "Me against you." Language is used for establishing separateness.

  *Examples in written language: Love notes, invitations, dialogue journals, friendly letters, and so on.*

*From "The Uses of Language" by F. Smith, 1977, *Language Arts, 54*(6), 640. Reprinted with permission of the National Council of Teachers of English.

- *Personal.* "Here I come." Language is used to express individuality, awareness of self, and pride.

  *Examples in written language: Opinion papers, letters to the editor, and so on.*

- *Heuristic.* "Tell me why." Language is used to seek and test world knowledge.

  *Examples in written language: Letters of inquiry, requests, registration forms, and so on.*

- *Imaginative.* "Let's pretend." Language is used as a means of creating new worlds and making up stories and poems.

  *Examples in written language: Stories, tall tales and yarns, and so on.*

- *Representational.* "I have something to tell you." Language is used for communicating information, providing descriptions, and expressing propositions.

  *Examples in written language: Arguments, lists, problem solving, and so on.*

- *Divertive.* "Enjoy this." Language is used for humor and fun.

  *Examples in written language: Puns, jokes, and riddles.*

- *Authoritative/contractual.* "This is how it must be." Language is used to communicate rules.

  *Examples in written language: Statutes, laws and regulations, and so on.*

- *Perpetuating.* "How it was." (Records)

  *Examples in written language: Personal histories, diaries, journals, scrapbooks, and so on.*

Children make varied use of oral language in their own lives, at least in a subconscious way. As you help students become aware of these oral language functions, they will readily apply this knowledge in their written language use as well.

## Mapping Speech onto Print

The ability to match or **map** speech sounds onto printed symbols (letters) develops rather slowly. Some researchers believe that the ability to map speech sounds onto printed language and knowledge of the sound–symbol code, or phonics knowledge, may develop simultaneously (Lomax & McGee, 1987). Mapping involves several important skills that the student learns.

- Understanding that speech can be written down and read and that what is written down can be spoken
- Awareness of print in the environment and ability to read at least some signs and logos
- Understanding that the message of the text is constructed more from the print than the pictures
- Knowledge that written language uses different structures (Halliday, 1975; Smith, 1977) from spoken language
- Comprehension that the length of a spoken word is usually related to the length of the written word

- Insight that one written word equals one spoken word
- Identification of correspondences between spoken sounds and written symbols
- Ability to use context and other language-related clues to construct meaning and identify words

Mapping speech onto print helps students become successful readers and benefit from further experiences with written language (Johnston, 1992; Reutzel, Oda, & Moore, 1989). For some readers, failing to acquire an understanding of mapping principles can slow their progress in reading and writing development (Clay, 2000a; Ehri & Sweet, 1991; Johns, 1980).

## Technical Aspects of Print

*"Technical aspects of print"* refers to the rules, also called *conventions,* that govern written language. Examples include directionality (left-to-right/top-to-bottom progression on the page in reading), spatial orientation, and instructional terms used in classrooms to refer to written language elements. Because many of these technical concepts are commonsense matters for adults, it is little wonder that sometimes teachers and parents mistakenly assume that children already understand them. However, ample evidence exists that this knowledge of the technical aspects of written language shown in the following list develops slowly for many learners (Clay, 1979; Day & Day, 1979; Downing & Oliver, 1973; Johns, 1980; Meltzer & Himse, 1969).

### Levels of Language Concepts

*Ordinal*
- First, second, third, and so on
- Beginning
- Last
- Book
- Paragraph
- Sentence
- Word
- Letter

*Visual Clues Embedded in Books and Print*
- Cover, spine, pages
- Margins, indentations
- Spacing
- Print size
- Punctuation

*Location Concepts*
- Top
- Bottom
- Left
- Right
- Beginning (front, start, initial)

- Middle (center, medial, in between)
- End (back, final)

It is very important that teachers assess what young children know about the technical aspects of printed language. In the next section of this chapter, we describe five useful assessment tools for teachers to gain insights into children's understanding of concepts about print.

# ASSESSING CHILDREN'S CONCEPTS ABOUT PRINT

Go to the Assignments and Activities section of Topic 12: "Progress Monitoring" in the MyEducationLab for your course and complete the activity entitled "Emergent Literacy Progress Monitoring." As you read the article and answer the accompanying questions, note the behaviors young children evidence as they emerge into literacy. Knowing and recognizing these will help you to work in the zone of proximal development in helping young children pay attention to particular print behaviors and know where and how to look at a page of print.

The assessment strategies offered in this section provide you with a comprehensive approach for assessing all three aspects of concepts about print: (a) the functional aspects of print, (b) the mapping aspects of print, and (c) the technical aspects of print.

## Concepts about Print Test

### Purpose

The Concepts about Print (CAP) Test was designed by Marie Clay (1972a,b, 2000b,c) to assess children's mapping and technical aspects of print knowledge such as letter, word, sentence, story, directionality, text versus picture, and punctuation. The CAP test is based on four small booklets, also by Clay, two published in 1972, *Sand* and *Stones*, and two published in 2000, *No Shoes* and *Follow Me, Moon.* One set of booklets may be used as a pretest and posttest in the kindergarten year and the other two may be used as a pretest and a posttest during the first-grade year to measure concepts about print growth. More information about the Concepts about Print test booklets and the manual for administration, scoring, and interpretation can be found online at www.heinemann.com.

### Materials

- *Concepts about Print: What Have Children Learned about the Way We Print Language* (Clay, 2000a)
- The four actual test booklets: *Sand, Stones, No Shoes,* and *Follow Me, Moon* (Clay, 1972a,b, 2000b)

### Procedure

The test process involves the teacher and student together viewing and reading one or more of the test booklets. Procedures for administering, scoring, and interpreting the tests are found in *Concepts about Print: What Have Children Learned about the Way We Print Language* (pp. 8–15). Print concepts tested include front of book; proper book orientation to begin reading; beginning of book; print rather than pictures carrying the message; directional rules of left to right, top to bottom on a page; return sweep to the beginning of a line of print; matching spoken words with written words; concepts of first and last letters in a word; mapping spoken word and letter order onto the print; beginning and ending of a story; punctuation marks; sight words; identifying printed letters, words, and uppercase versus lowercase letters.

In order to adequately test children's print concepts, the *Sand, Stones, No Shoes,* and *Follow Me, Moon* booklets include some rather unusual features. At certain points, the print or pictures are upside down, letter and word order are changed or reversed (*saw* for *was*), line order is reversed, and paragraph indentions are removed or inverted. The CAP test has established a long and excellent record as a valid and reliable screening test to be used as part of a battery of screening tasks for young, inexperienced, or at-risk readers. A major limitation of this test, however, is that it is based on error-detection tasks that require the child to find problems and explain them. Because of the somewhat tedious nature of this test and its tasks, children need to be tested in a calm environment and also need to have a trusting relationship with the examiner in order to obtain reliable results.

## Reading Environmental Print

### Purpose

This task is designed to assess students' ability to read commonplace or "highly frequent" print accessible in their local and daily environment, such as signs in the school like STOP, EXIT, or NO SMOKING. Other examples of environmental print include signs on the outsides of businesses and stores and on products commonly available across the nation, such as McDonald's, Cheerios, Diet Coke, and so forth.

Environmental print information can be used to assess the access a child has had or the attention given to printed language in the environment (Reutzel et al., 2003). Further, teachers can discover ways that environmental print may be used to help each child develop successful reading and writing behaviors. An added advantage of environmental print is that it encourages beginning readers to develop an "I can read!" attitude. Researchers who have examined the value of teaching children using environmental print have consistently shown it to be useful (Kuby & Aldridge, 1994; Neuman & Roskos, 1993; Orellana & Hernandez, 1999; Proudfoot, 1992; Reutzel et al., 2003; Vukelich, 1994; West & Egley, 1998).

### Materials

- Three sets of 10 plain index cards (30 cards total) are needed to construct this task, the first set to display traffic signs or informational logos found on roads and in public buildings, the second set to display logos of restaurant chains, television shows, gasoline stations, and national chain stores such as Kmart, and the third set to display food product logos such as Diet Pepsi, Cheerios, and Butterfinger

### Procedure

Materials selected for this task are based on a survey of children's recognition and access to environmental print completed by Briggs and Richardson (1994). Classification procedures (see Figure 4.1, "Written Language Knowledge Taxonomy") are used to sort student responses to the set of 30 cards into pragmatic response, inclusion of part of the print response, meaning conversion response, and attention to graphic detail response (Harste, Burke, & Woodward, 1981; McGee, Lomax, & Head, 1988). This taxonomy has been used to help reading researchers determine how well children process print in their environment. The environmental print task helps teachers gain insights into students' growing understanding of print concepts using environmental language. Children who show little awareness of print in the environment are also likely to have had few experiences with printed text in other contexts, such as books and writing.

## Mow Motorcycle Task

### Purpose

As children begin to learn to read and write, some discover how spoken words or sounds are mapped onto letters and printed words in books and other written language sources. One

| FIGURE 4.1 | Written Language Knowledge Taxonomy |
| --- | --- |

| Response Category | Level | Examples |
| --- | --- | --- |
| Pragmatic perspective | Attempts to read | |
| | *Maintains communication contract* | |
| | single word or name (with no article) | "potato chips," "bread" |
| | phrases (not beginning with article "a") | "trouble with the football team" |
| | letters, numbers | "A" on telephone (index letter), on "7:30" in TV Guide |
| | *Renegotiates communication contract* | |
| | names print object (usually with article) | "a newspaper" |
| | describes something in picture of print item | "a man" |
| | describes what can be found on the print item | "words," "phone numbers," "pictures" |
| | describes what can be done with the print item | "take it to the store" |
| | *Refuses to respond* | no response or "I don't know" |
| Inclusion of text from print item | Attempt to read includes text of print item | "State Times" on newspaper |
| | Attempt partially includes text of print item (at least one word of response is included in text of print) | "Gulf State" for "State Times" on newspaper |
| | Attempt does not include text of print item | "gum, candy" not in text of grocery list |
| Meaning | *Meaningful* | |
| | Attempt includes print text central in meaning | "eggs" on grocery list |
| | Attempt does not include text but makes sense | "tomato" on grocery list (not in text) |
| | *Nonmeaningful* | |
| | Attempt includes print text not central in meaning | "by," "is" on newspaper |
| | Attempt does not include text and does not make sense | "redfish" in book (not in text) |
| | Naming letters embedded in words | "S" "T" for "State" text |
| Attention to graphic detail | *Evidence of attention to graphic detail* | |
| | Attempt includes print text for item with no picture | "dog food" on grocery list |
| | Attempt includes print text when child points to correct text | "potato chips" and points to text "potato chips" |
| | Attempt practically includes print text (one word plus one letter same) | "Sunday Times" for text "State Times" |
| | Attempt does not include text, but it's obvious child is referring to text | "the" and child points to "to" |
| | Attempt includes identification of letters in text | "S" "T" on newspaper |

*Source:* Adapted with permission from the National Reading Conference and Lea McGee, from "Young Children's Written Language Knowledge: What Environmental and Functional Print Reading Reveals" by L. McGee, R. Lomax, & M. Head, 1988, *Journal of Reading Behavior, 20*(2), 105. Copyright 1988 by the National Reading Conference.

concept students need to discover is that the length of a printed word is related to the length of the same spoken word. The Mow Motorcycle Task (Rozin, Bressman, & Taft, 1974) taps students' awareness of this basic mapping relationship between speech and print.

### Materials

- 10 pairs of teacher-prepared word cards (20 cards total), each pair containing two words beginning with the same letter and differing in written and spoken length, as shown in Figure 4.2, printed neatly either by hand in uppercase manuscript or from a computer printer in plain, block, or print style font rather than a calligraphic or stylized font

### Procedure

Seat the child comfortably next to you at an appropriately sized table or desk. Displaying only one pair at a time, show the child 10 pairs of cards bearing printed words beginning with the same letter. For example, tell the student, "One of these words is *mow* and the other is *motorcycle*. Which one is *mow*?" The child responds by pointing. The total score is the number of correct responses, with 0 to 10 points possible. Items should be varied so that the "target" word (the one you name) and the "foil" (the incorrect choice) are not always in the same position. This helps prevent the possibility that mere guessing on the student's part—always choosing the left-hand word, for example—will result in a high number of false correct responses.

## Metalinguistic Interview

### Purpose

The Metalinguistic Interview (MI) is a set of questions designed to assess children's understanding of academic or instructional language, that is, language teachers use in instruction as they talk about printed language in books and displayed elsewhere. For example, researchers (Clay, 1966; Denny & Weintraub, 1966; Downing, 1970, 1971–1972; Reid, 1966) interviewed young children and found that they often do not have a clear understanding about many of the common academic or instructional terms used in beginning reading instruction, such as *alphabet, letter, word,* and *sentence.* Obviously, knowledge of these terms is most likely linked to how well children understand and respond to early reading and writing instruction.

Academic or instructional language terms or concepts assessed in the Metalinguistic Interview include the following:

- That the term *alphabet* or *ABCs* refers to letters
- That the actual location on a page of a single letter, word, or sentence is an indication of directionality L → R (left to right), T → D (top/down), and so on

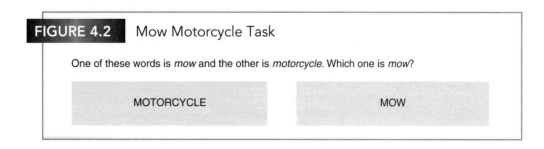

**FIGURE 4.2**    Mow Motorcycle Task

One of these words is *mow* and the other is *motorcycle*. Which one is *mow*?

| MOTORCYCLE | MOW |

- Punctuation
- How to differentiate uppercase and lowercase letters
- Terms such as the *front* and *back* of a book and an understanding of *page(s)*

### Materials

- Any children's trade book or literature book containing both pictures and print (use a book that has print on one page and a full-page picture on an adjoining page for best results)
- A scoring sheet easily constructed by duplicating Figure 4.3

### Procedure

Make a copy of the 20 tasks or questions in Figure 4.3. Seat the child comfortably next to you. Hand the student a picture book such as *The Gingerbread Man* (Schmidt, 1985) or *The Little Red Hen* (McQueen, 1985) upside down, with the spine of the book facing the child. Once the child takes the book, tell him that the two of you are going to read the book together. Then ask him to respond to the 20 tasks listed in Figure 4.3 and mark the responses on the question sheet.

Scores on the interview range from a low of 0 to a high of 20. Carefully examine which items were missed to determine areas of future instructional focus.

## The Burke Reading Interview

### Purpose

The Burke Reading Interview (Burke, 1980) is designed to help you discover what students understand about the reading process and the strategies students use to unlock unknown words and construct meaning. Children are asked to describe how they learned to read as well as what they can do to become better readers (Burke, 1980; DeFord & Harste, 1982).

---

**FIGURE 4.3**   The Metalinguistic Interview

1. "What are books for? What do books have in them?"
2. "Show me the front cover. Show me the back cover."
3. "Show me the title of the story."
4. "Show me the author's name."
5. "Open the book to where I should begin reading."
6. "Show me which way my eyes should go when I begin reading."
7. "Show me the last line on the page."
8. Begin reading. At the end of the page ask, "Now where do I go next?"
9. "Show me where to begin reading on this page. Will you point to the words with your finger as I say them?"
10. "Show me a sentence on this page."
11. "Show me the second word in a sentence."
12. "Show me a word."
13. "Show me the first letter in that word."
14. "Show me the last letter in that word."
15. "Show me a period on this page."
16. "Show me a question mark on this page."
17. Show the child a quotation mark and ask, "What is this?"
18. Ask the child to put his fingers around a word.
19. Ask the child to put his fingers around a letter.
20. Ask the child to show you an upper- and lowercase letter.

Correct responses are given a 1 and incorrect responses are scored 0.

You can determine whether students recognize that the goal of reading is to understand the author's message or if they mistakenly think that the only goal of reading is to recode letters into sounds.

## Materials

- The Burke Reading Interview (Burke, 1980)
- An audio recorder to document the child's responses to the interview questions

## Procedure

Seat the child comfortably near you and the microphone for effective recording purposes. Visit with the student for a moment to establish rapport. Tell the student that you will be asking a few questions and that you will be recording his or her answers. Then turn the recorder on and begin by asking the child's name. Next ask the questions found in the Burke Reading Interview in Figure 4.4. The audio recording can be used later to analyze student responses. Interpretation of the instrument is based on the response to each question. A total score is not useful to guide instructional decision making. Each response must be examined to reveal to the teacher the next steps necessary for the child to progress in his or her reading and writing development.

In Figure 4.5 we summarize the tools we have just discussed for assessing factors associated with children's concepts about print. In this Summary Matrix of Assessments we provide information about federally related assessment purposes (i.e., screening, diagnostic,

---

**FIGURE 4.4**   The Burke Reading Interview

Name: _____   Age: ____   Date: _____

Occupation: _____   Educational level: _____

Gender: _____   Interview setting: _____

1. When you are reading and come to something you don't know, what do you do? Do you ever do anything else?
2. Who is a good reader you know?
3. What makes _____ a good reader?
4. Do you think _____ ever comes to something he or she doesn't know?
5. "Yes" When _____ does come to something he or she doesn't know, what do you think he or she does?
   "No" Suppose _____ comes to something he or she doesn't know. What do you think he or she would do?
6. If you knew someone was having trouble reading, how would you help that person?
7. What would your teacher do to help that person?
8. How did you learn to read?
9. What would you like to do better as a reader?
10. Do you think you are a good reader? Why?

---

*Source:* Adapted from *Reading Miscue Inventory: Alternative Procedures* by Y. Goodman, D. Watson, and C. Burke, 1987. New York: Richard C. Owen, Publisher, Inc. Reprinted with permission.

**FIGURE 4.5** Summary Matrix of Assessments to Measure Children's Concepts about Print

| Name of Assessment Tool | Screening Assessment | Diagnostic Assessment | Progress-Monitoring Assessment | Outcomes Assessment | Norm-Referenced Test | Criterion-Referenced Test | Reliability Evidence | Validity Evidence |
|---|---|---|---|---|---|---|---|---|
| Concepts about Print Test | + | + | – | + | – | + | + | + |
| Reading Environmental Print | + | – | – | + | – | + | Not Available | Not Available |
| Mow Motorcycle Task | + | – | – | + | – | + | Not Available | Not Available |
| Metalinguistic Interview | + | – | – | + | – | + | Not Available | Not Available |
| Burke Reading Interview | + | – | – | + | – | + | Not Available | Not Available |

Key:  + can be used for
      – not appropriate for

progress-monitoring, or outcomes assessment), as well as type of test or procedure and psychometric evidence about the test or procedure scores (any available reliability and validity evidence).

## Connecting Assessment Findings to Teaching Strategies

Before discussing intervention strategies, consider the If-Then matrix connecting assessment to intervention and strategy choices (see Figure 4.6). It is our intention to help you, the teacher, select the most appropriate instructional inventions and strategies to meet students' needs based on assessment data. Teaching strategies discussed in the next section are listed across the top of the grid in Figure 4.6. Aspects of concepts about print are listed vertically in the left-hand column. The grid shows which strategies go with which concepts. In the next part of this chapter, we offer strategies for intervention based on the foregoing assessments.

# *I*NSTRUCTIONAL INTERVENTIONS AND STRATEGIES: HELPING EVERY STUDENT LEARN CONCEPTS ABOUT PRINT

After a careful assessment of a student's reading progress, one or more of the following strategies may be appropriately applied. Perhaps the most important thing to remember is that children with poorly developed print concepts must be immersed in a multitude of print-related activities in a "print-rich" classroom environment (Venn & Jahn, 2004). Authentic reading and writing experiences coupled with the informed guidance of a caring teacher or other literate individuals (e.g., parents, peers, and volunteers) can do much to help students learn necessary print concepts.

Go to the Assignments and Activities section of Topic 1: "Reading Instruction" in the MyEducationLab for your course and complete the activity entitled "Creating a Print-Rich Environment." As you watch the video and answer the accompanying questions, note several ways in which you can help children to learn more about print and how print works. Make a list of some of these ideas for your classroom.

## Environmental Print Reading

### Purpose

The purpose of reading environmental print is to give children an experience that allows them to read familiar print drawn from the world around them that they are likely to have seen. Such experiences not only bring the outside world of print closer to the classroom but also build children's confidence in their ultimate ability to learn to read (Reutzel et al., 2003).

### Materials

- Product labels and logos from a variety of items including cans, cups, wrappers, packaging, and so on
- Blank books or template books modeled after other children's books prepared for children to use in creating their own *I Can Read* environmental print books

### Procedure

Using environmental print commonly found in students' daily lives, teachers and children can learn about important print concepts. One application of using environmental print involves creating *I Can Read* books (see Figure 4.7).

Topics for environmental print *I Can Read* books may include *My Favorite Foods, Signs I See, A Trip to the Supermarket, My Favorite Things, My Favorite Toys,* and so on,

**FIGURE 4.6** If-Then Strategy Guide for Concepts about Print (CAP) Development

| "If" the student is ready to learn / "Then" try these teaching strategies | Read Environmental Print | Interactive Read Alouds | LEA | Voice Point | Frame | Masking/ Highlight | Context Transfer | Error Detect | Verbal Punctuation | Shared Reading | Letter Manipulatives |
|---|---|---|---|---|---|---|---|---|---|---|---|
| Book handling | – | + | – | – | – | – | – | – | – | + | – |
| Directionality | * | + | * | + | – | – | * | – | – | + | * |
| Print carries message | + | + | + | + | + | * | + | + | – | * | * |
| Voice-print matching | * | + | * | + | * | + | + | * | – | + | – |
| Punctuation | * | + | + | * | * | + | * | + | + | + | – |
| Concept of word/letter | + | + | + | * | + | + | * | + | – | + | * |
| Order—letters/words | + | + | * | * | + | + | * | + | – | + | + |
| Pragmatic response to environmental print | + | + | – | * | * | * | + | * | – | – | * |
| Reader relies on a single strategy to unlock unknown words | * | – | * | – | * | * | * | * | – | + | * |
| Academic or instructional language | – | – | * | * | * | + | * | * | – | + | * |

Key: + Excellent strategy
* Adaptable strategy
– Unsuitable strategy

**FIGURE 4.7** *I Can Read* Book Cover

Children begin by choosing a topic. Next, they can select to use a blank book or a template book. Following their choice of a blank or template book, they select from the environmental print collection of product labels to construct their own *I Can Read* books. Using a template book, based on the well-known children's book *On Market Street* (Lobel & Lobel, 1981), students innovate on the contents of the original book by selecting what they would have purchased "on Market Street" using the product labels to create their own *I Can Read* book. Because students select logos they can already read, they can easily read the environmental books while acquiring print concepts. Further, these books become a source of confidence building and enjoyment.

Teachers can create logo language displays in the classroom as well as placing labels on furniture and fixtures in the classroom. Using a pointer or flashlights, teachers and children can "read the room" together by reading the labels in the classroom environment or the logo on the logo language display. By using print familiar to children from their homes and out-of-school world experiences, they very quickly develop an "I can do this . . . I can read!" attitude.

## Interactive Read Alouds

### Purpose

**Interactive read alouds** using enlarged text help children develop valuable concepts about print underpinnings needed for later learning in such areas as phonemic awareness, phonics, and comprehension (Venn & Jahn, 2004). Children follow along as the teacher reads from enlarged text (i.e., big books, rhymes and songs written on large chart paper, etc.) and they respond to carefully posed questions. This draws the students' attention to key print concepts.

### Materials

- High-quality big books or other enlarged texts diverse in gender and multicultural points of view and from multiple genres, such as nonfiction, storybooks, poetry, songs, and popular rhymes, perhaps from the following is a sampling of big books or books that can be enlarged that we and other teachers have found very useful for interactive read alouds

### Stories

Brown, M. W. (1991). *Good night, moon.* New York: Harper.

Carle, E. (1994). *The very hungry caterpillar.* New York: Scholastic.

Carlstrom, N. (1988). *Better not get wet, Jesse Bear.* New York: Simon & Schuster.

Cowley, J. (1992). *Mrs. Wishy-Washy.* New York: Philomel.

dePaola, T. (1983). *The legend of the bluebonnet.* New York: Putnam.

dePaola, T. (1988). *The legend of the Indian paintbrush.* New York: Putnam.

Guarino, D. (1997). *Is your mama a llama?* New York: Scholastic.

Numeroff, L. (2000). *If you give a mouse a cookie.* New York: HarperCollins.

Westcott, N. (1998). *The lady with the alligator purse.* Boston: Little Brown.

### Poetry

Christelow, E. (1998). *Five little monkeys jumping on the bed.* Boston: Houghton Mifflin.

Collins, H. (2003). *Little Miss Muffet.* Toronto: Kids Can Press.

Martin, B. (1983). *Brown bear, brown bear, what do you see?* New York: Henry Holt.

Seuss, Dr. (1960). *Green eggs and ham.* New York: Random House.

Trapani, I. (1994). *Twinkle, twinkle, little star.* Watertown, MA: Charlesbridge.

Wood, A. (1992). *Silly Sally.* New York: Harcourt.

## Procedure

During interactive read alouds, children respond to the teacher and their classmates before, during, and after the reading. Careful decisions are made prior to teaching as to which print concepts will be highlighted in the before-, during-, and after-reading experiences to increase the enjoyment and engagement of the learners (Venn & Jahn, 2004). Enlarged text, such as in big books, enables students to see the teacher modeling such book-handling skills as reading the title, deciding where to start reading, gaining information from pictures, knowing how to proceed through the book, turning pages, and understanding that the message is coming from the text.

Some of the concepts about print that can be taught in an interactive read aloud include

- Locating the front of the book
- Finding information on the title page
- Learning that print contains the message
- Recognizing one-to-one correspondence of printed and spoken words
- Page turning
- Learning how to handle books properly
- Recognizing picture clues
- Reading from the left page before the right page
- Using a return sweep
- Understanding *first, next,* and *last*

## The Language Experience Approach

### Purpose

The **Language Experience Approach** (LEA) uses children's firsthand or vicarious experiences to create personalized reading materials. Children learn print conventions and concepts by seeing how their speech looks in printed form. They learn mapping of speech onto print and the technical aspects of print (i.e., directionality, punctuation marks, etc.) from LEA reading materials. Teachers have found that children's dictated LEA stories can be recorded in at least two different forms: the Group Experience Chart or the Individual Language Experience Story. The latter is tremendously motivating because children see their own story produced in a book format.

## The Group Experience Chart

### Materials

- Large chart paper displayed on an easel; the upper half of each page should be blank for a picture and the lower half of the pages should be one-inch lines for printing the students' dictated story
- Illustration or drawing supplies for illustrating the stories
- Cut-out pictures or magazines for cutting out pictures to illustrate the stories

### Procedure

The Group Experience Chart is a means for recording the experiences of a group of children. In all group LEA activities, it is essential that students have a shared experience about which they can talk and dictate lines, sentences, and stories. The following steps are typically associated with the creation of a Group Experience Chart:

- The children participate in a shared experience, such as a field trip, an experiment, or listening to a guest speaker.
- Teachers and children discuss the shared experience.
- Children dictate the story while the teacher transcribes the dictation onto chart paper.
- Teachers and children share in reading the chart story.
- The chart is used to teach about print concepts, words, and other important language concepts.

The selection of an interesting and stimulating experience or topic for children can spell the success or failure of an LEA group activity. Topics and experiences must capture the interest of children in order to provide the motivation necessary for learning, as demonstrated by the following examples of topics and themes that have been successfully used:

- How our classroom pet had babies last night
- A description of our field trip
- Writing a new version of a favorite book
- What we want for Christmas
- Planning our Valentine's Day party
- What we know about Martin Luther King
- Scary dreams we've had
- How I got into trouble one time
- Making a get well card from the class for a classmate who is ill

Be sure to discuss the experience or topic carefully. This helps children to self-assess what they know about the topic and to make personal connections. Also, it motivates them to share their knowledge, experiences, and personal connections with others. Be careful not to dominate the discussion, however. Asking too many focused questions can turn what would otherwise be an open and exciting discussion into an interrogation. Questions should invite discussion instead of encouraging short and unelaborated responses. Be careful not to make the mistake of beginning dictation too early in the discussion, as this may lead to a dull, even robotic, recounting of the experience or topic.

After plenty of discussion, ask children to dictate the ideas they wish to contribute to the chart. With learners in the early grades who have special needs, you may want to record each child's dictation in different colored markers to help the child identify his or her contribution to the chart. Later in the year, write the child's name by his or her dictation rather than using different marker colors. When the chart is complete, read the children's composition aloud in a natural rhythm, pointing to each word as you read. After the first reading, invite students to read along on the second reading. Next, ask volunteers to read aloud portions of the story. Other strategies for reading the composition include the following:

- Read aloud a selected dictation line from the chart and ask a child to come up to the chart and point to the line you just read aloud.
- Copy several lines of the chart onto sentence strips and have children pick a sentence strip and match it to the line in the chart.
- Copy the LEA story to make copies to go home with students for individual practice.
- Put copies of favorite words in the chart story onto cards for word banks and matching activities.

## The Individual Language Experience Story

### Materials

- Small booklets containing from 8 to 10 pages of $8\frac{1}{2} \times 11$-inch paper, with the upper halves of pages blank for pictures and the lower halves containing horizontal lines at half-inch vertical intervals for printing the students' dictated stories
- Illustration or drawing supplies for illustrating the stories
- Cut-out pictures or magazines for cutting out pictures to illustrate the stories
- An audio recorder
- Card pockets and cards
- Tools to cut books into shapes (optional)

### Procedure

For most young students, who are typically in an egocentric stage, no one is more important and exciting to talk or read about than themselves. The Individual Language Experience Story provides an excellent opportunity for learners to talk about their own experiences and to have these events recorded in print to learn about the concepts of print.

Ask the children to tell their stories into an audio recorder and then listen to them for editing. Listening and editing on audio can have a very positive transfer value for the writing process. This oral editing encourages children to retell or revise their stories until they are satisfied with the final product. We also suggest, where circumstances permit, that parent volunteers be invited to transcribe students' Individual Language Experience Stories from audio to paper.

Next, turn these Individual Language Experience Stories into books. Recognize the value of students' Individual Language Experience Stories by placing a card pocket and library card in each child's book. These books are added to the classroom library for other children to read. A story reader's chair can be established to encourage children to read their Individual Language Experience Stories aloud to peers in their own classroom and in other classrooms in the school.

One variation of Individual Language Experience Stories that children particularly like is shape books. As shown in Figure 4.8, the cover and pages of the dictated Individual Language Experience Story are drawn and cut into the shape of the book topic. For example, if a child has just created a story about a recent family trip to Disneyland, the book could be cut into the shape of Mickey Mouse's head; a trip to Texas may be recorded in a book cut into the shape of the state of Texas.

## Voice Pointing

### Purpose

Pointing to the print in an enlarged book, on a chart, or on a whiteboard while reading aloud interactively with a group of children draws the eyes of the readers into contact with the print (Clay, 1993). Otherwise, children in the earliest stages of reading acquisition will have a tendency to study the illustrations and listen to the story language without paying a great deal of attention to the print. Voice pointing shows children (a) how the print rather than the picture carries the message of reading; (b) the beginning, ending, and directionality of the print; (c) how the spoken language of the reader is represented or mapped onto print on the page or display; and (d) the technical concepts of print such as word, letter, or punctuation.

**FIGURE 4.8**   Examples of Shape Books

### Materials

- A pointer ranging from something as simple as an unsharpened pencil to a ruler, from a telescoping pen pointer to a laser pointer
- An enlarged copy of a story, poem, song lyrics, or book

### Procedure

Clay (1979) indicates that pointing to the print while reading, or *voice pointing,* is a critical strategy to develop during the early stages of learning to read. To help beginning readers make the connection that the print is guiding the speech of the reader, teachers point to the print as they interactively read aloud.

If the teacher wants to demonstrate the beginning point of print; the flow and directionality of print from top to bottom, left to right, and so on; and where the print ends on the page, then he or she can run the pointer smoothly under the print as he or she reads aloud. However, if the teacher wants to demonstrate how each word read aloud is represented by its corresponding word in print, then he or she can move the pointer in a broken, word-by-word method. To draw attention to letters, single words, or punctuation, the teacher should point using a circular motion around the print element to be given attention by the readers.

## Framing Print

### Purpose

Some young readers have not yet grasped the idea that a given word is the same every time it appears in print. For instance, the word *football* is always *football* whenever and wherever it appears in print, whether it is handwritten text or text appearing in a book. Understanding this basic concept is a major milestone in reading development. **Framing** is one strategy that can help students grasp this important print concept (Holdaway, 1979).

### Materials

- A framing tool made from oak tagboard or posterboard materials, either a simple frame as shown in Figure 4.9, which is constructed of white posterboard, or a more complicated shutter frame that allows teachers to not only frame words on the page but also expose words to students one letter at a time from left to right to encourage the use of verbal blending of letter sounds in temporal sequence, as shown in Figure 4.10, which is constructed of white posterboard with a white posterboard shutter
- A razor knife
- Stapler

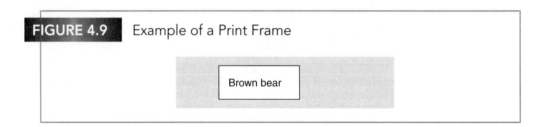

**FIGURE 4.9**   Example of a Print Frame

Brown bear

**FIGURE 4.10**    Example of a Sliding Print Frame

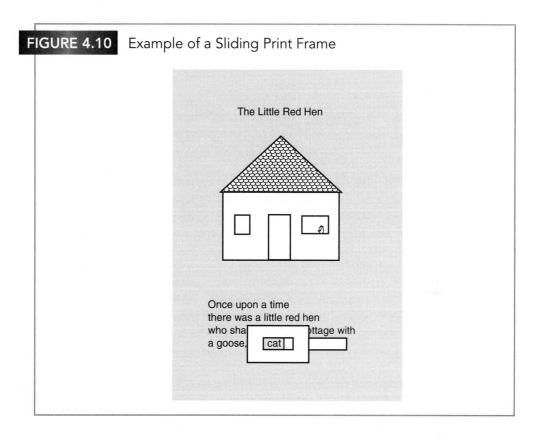

## Procedure

Begin by reading aloud an enlarged text several times without interruption or discussion about print features. This can be text from an LEA Group Experience Chart or a big book such as *Brown Bear, Brown Bear* (Martin, 1983). Remember to voice-point to the text as you read. Highlight aspects of written language by pointing and framing a word or words using the simple frame. For example, frame the text that asks "Brown Bear, Brown Bear, What do you see?" one word at a time. Frame each highlighted word (e.g., *brown, bear, what, do, you, see*) using the simple frame. After framing several words, ask children to look carefully at a word with only one letter exposed using the shutter frame. Ask children to notice the letters as you expose them. Once all letters are exposed, ask children to look carefully at the word. Talk with them about how words are made up of letters, demonstrating to them the difference between letters and words. Using the shutter frame, teachers can also frame punctuation marks for attention and discussion.

## Masking or Highlighting Print

### Purpose

Some young readers do not yet know how to look at print or what to look for on the printed page. Helping young children know where to look and what to look for on the printed page is the major purpose for using masking and highlighting techniques. Understanding the basics of how to look at print and knowing what to look at is a critical milestone in the development of young readers before they can profit from instruction about letters, words, and punctuation.

## Materials

- A big book or text with enlarged print on chart paper
- Semitransparent tape of differing colors to highlight selected print concepts
- Stick-on notes of differing sizes to mask selected print concepts

## Procedure

Select the print concept to be taught, such as attention to concept of word, concept of letters, punctuation, or figuring out an unknown word. To direct students' visual attention to spaces between words, to letters within words, to specific words, or to punctuation marks, use semitransparent highlighting tape. For example, use light blue tape to direct students' visual attention to the use of periods in text. Or use light pink tape to direct students' attention to the letter *w* in the big book *Mrs. Wishy-Washy* (Cowley, 1990).

Use stick-on notes to mask from students' view selected concepts about print such as words, letters, and punctuation. Once masked from view, point to the masked print feature and discuss with students what they think would be behind the stick-on note. Once discussion has led to a reasonable prediction, unmask the print feature by removing the stick-on note. Using stick-on notes in this manner to mask print features directs students' attention very specifically to the covered print feature.

Use stick-on notes and enlarged text or big books to also create cloze passages. Masking specific words or masking every fifth word in a pattern creates a cloze passage. Students use the surrounding text and pictures to decide which word would make sense for the masked text. When students determine the masked word and the stick-on notes are removed, this focus of attention to the masked words brings "closure" to the cloze passage. Masking emphasizes the differences between words and sentences as well as basic concepts about print, while also demonstrating the importance of context clues in understanding the author's message.

Two variations of cloze that can be used to focus young readers' attention on either content or structure words in predictable books are progressive and regressive cloze. In **progressive cloze,** the text is read aloud. Next, several words are masked using stick-on notes, as shown in Figure 4.11, and then the text is read aloud again. Each time a deleted word is encountered, children are asked to identify the missing word. When the deleted word is correctly identified, it is uncovered. For example, in the story *The Gingerbread Man* (Schmidt, 1985), the entire text of the book may be read and then several pages used for a progressive cloze procedure.

In **regressive cloze,** the process also begins by reading the entire text aloud. Next, the text is reduced to only its structure words by covering all content words with stick-on notes. Children are then asked to identify the missing words. As each content word is identified, it is uncovered. Regressive cloze focuses on deleting all content words until only structure words remain and then revealing these words. In comparison, progressive cloze does not cover as many words as regressive cloze; only selected words are covered, as opposed to covering all except structure words. By using these cloze variations, children begin to focus on identifying individual words within the context of familiar stories. Teachers can repeat these cloze variations in other contexts such as on charts, sentence strips, or a chalkboard, as shown in Figure 4.12.

section of this chapter. This game may focus children's attention on beginning, ending, or middle sounds in words. Once a list of beginning syllable words is created, a list of ending sounds and then medial sounds should be composed for this game as well.

## Materials

- One paper sack
- A list of 10 sets of three words (i.e., *hen, hammer,* and *pencil*)
- Objects for the "odd word out"

## Procedure

This game is played by comfortably seating a group of children on the floor or at a table. Begin by saying that you have a "grab bag" filled with objects while showing children the bag. Next, tell the children you will be saying three words and that they are to listen carefully for the word that does not fit. If they know the word, they are to raise their hand but not call it out. A child is selected to reach into the "grab bag" without looking and feel around to find the object. After finding it, the child can say the word and show the object to the group. When an object has been used, it is returned to the "grab bag" for use with the next set of words. This process continues until all the objects in the "grab bag" have been used.

## Picture Box Sound Counting ("Elkonin Boxes")

### Purpose

*How many sounds do you hear?*

Learning to hear sounds in words requires that students hear syllables and sounds (phonemes). Students need to develop the ability to hear these features of words in proper sequence. Counting the number of syllables and sounds in words helps children attend more carefully to these parts of words (Yopp & Troyer, 1992). A version of this activity (Elkonin, 1963) has been used successfully for a number of years in successful intervention programs such as Reading Recovery.

### Materials

- 5 to 10 teacher-prepared cards with pictures of words already familiar to the student, as shown in Figure 5.14
- Chips (markers)

### Procedure

This activity uses a card with a picture, such as the one shown in Figure 5.14 for the word *cat.* The teacher begins by pronouncing the word very slowly while placing a chip into a box below for each letter or sound heard, progressing sound by sound (*CCCCC–AAAAAAA–TTTTTT*). After an initial demonstration, the child is encouraged to join in the activity by saying the word for the picture on the next card while the teacher places a chip into a box for each letter or sound.

The teacher gradually releases responsibility to the child by exchanging roles. For example, the teacher can pronounce the word and the child can place chips into the boxes for each letter or sound. Finally, the child both says the word and places a chip into a box for each letter or sound entirely on his or her own. Eventually, children should be able to count the number of sounds in a word and be able to answer questions about the order of sounds in words (Griffith & Olson, 1992).

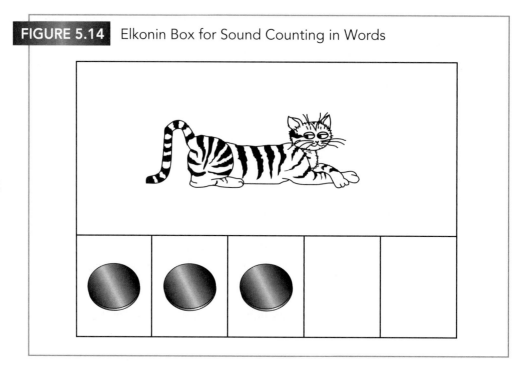

**FIGURE 5.14** Elkonin Box for Sound Counting in Words

Go to the Assignments and Activities section of Topic 5: "Phonemic Awareness and Phonics" in the MyEducationLab for your course and complete the activity entitled "Name Lotto." As you watch the video and answer the accompanying questions, note how Name Lotto is used as an activity. What criteria could be used to decide whether students are grasping the new information?

## Beginning with Children's Names

### Purpose

Children's names can be used to teach many phonemic awareness tasks (Kirk & Clark, 2005). By using children's (and classmates') own names, an inherently motivational activity, teachers can draw students' attention to specific sounds in words they wish to emphasize.

### Materials

- Your student roster of first names

### Procedure

Decide which phonemic awareness segmenting or blending task you should emphasize with a particular small group, or with the whole class, based on your prior assessments. This activity is appropriate for any of the phonemic awareness tasks. Follow your usual procedures—teacher modeling using selected student names, extensive guided practice with teacher coaching, and, when students are ready, students working independently. Picture sound boxes as previously described can be a great tool in this activity. Once students understand the phonemic awareness concept demonstrated using student names, *bridge* this new knowledge to other common words (nouns work best) that students know, such as locomotion words (e.g., *truck, car, airplane, jeep*).

## Add a Sound/Take a Sound

### Purpose

Go to the Assignments and Activities section of Topic 5: "Phonemic Awareness and Phonics" in the MyEducationLab for your course and complete the activity entitled "Building Phonemic Awareness." As you watch the video and answer the accompanying questions, identify ways children are helped to hear and become aware of individual sounds in spoken words (phonemic awareness).

Adding or substituting sounds in words in familiar songs, stories, or rhymes may help readers with special needs and younger readers attend to the sounds in their speech. The ability to add or substitute sounds in words in familiar language is easier than segmenting sounds and benefits students in many of the same ways.

### Materials

- Any song, rhyme, chant, or song

### Procedure

Two strategies add enjoyment to developing awareness of phonemes and the alphabetic principle. The first of these is called *consonant substitution.* When using this strategy, initial, final, or medial consonants in words found in a phrase or sentence can be exchanged. For example, in the Shel Silverstein (1976) poem "Jimmie Jet and His TV Set," change the consonants from /j/ to /n/ or /b/ to produce:

> "Nimmie Net and His TV Set"
> "Bimmie Bet and His TV Set"

Another approach is to delete the sound /j/ as follows:

> "Jimmie Jet and His TV Set"
> "immie et and His TV Set"

Young children find the nonsensical result to be both humorous and helpful in understanding how consonants work in connected text. Other consonants may be exchanged in the future to vary the number of consonants exchanged and the position of the consonants in the words.

A second strategy, called *vowel substitution,* involves selecting a single vowel (and sound) to be substituted in key words in the text. For example, in the poem, "Mary Had a Little Lamb," the vowel sounds can be changed to produce a completely nonsensical version, "Miry hid a little limb," by substituting the /i/ short vowel sound in place of the vowels in the original poem.

Children find that adding, changing, or substituting sounds in this way turns learning about letters and sounds into a game. One first-grade Chapter 1 student who had been working with his teacher late one afternoon using these strategies remarked on his way out the door to catch his bus, "Teacher, can we play some more games tomorrow?" This statement sums up the enthusiasm these two strategies generate among young children as they learn to focus their attention on phonemic awareness.

## Sing It Out

### Purpose

The purpose of "sounding it out" when one reads is to blend spoken sounds together to form words. Blending is a critical skill for learning to read successfully. Hearing individual sounds and then putting them together quickly to hear a word that is already known orally is the same process often encouraged by teachers when they say, "Sound it out!" Listening to spoken sounds and saying these sounds quickly to blend them together into words are what most teachers mean when they say to "sound it out."

### Materials

- One copy of the song "When You're Happy and You Know It"

### Procedure

Teacher modeling is needed in the beginning to help children understand the process. Sing the song "When You're Happy and You Know It" several times so that children learn the song and the words. Change the words at the end of the song from "clap your hands" to "say this word." Then give the letters of a word you want the children to blend together. For example, the sounds /b/-/r/-/d/ are spoken slowly for the children. When you clap, they are to say the word—*bird!* The song can go on for as long as you wish to engage children in auditory blending of the spoken sounds you offer to make words. By singing and saying words phoneme by phoneme students blend these sounds together to discover words.

## Word Rubber Banding

### Purpose

*Segmenting* refers to isolating individual sounds in a spoken word. Although it can be one of the more difficult phonemic awareness tasks for students, segmenting is nonetheless an important skill for children to develop if they are to profit from implicit or indirect instruction related to letter names, sounds, and the connections between the two. Segmenting sounds in words can be done by rubber banding or stretching a word into its sounds like a rubber band as described in the following procedure explanation.

### Materials

- Any song, poem, rhyme, chant, or story

### Procedure

Begin by singing a favorite song such as "Old MacDonald Had a Farm." Next, ask the children to repeat the first sounds of selected words as follows: "Old m-m-m-MacDonald had a f-f-f-farm, e i e i o, and on this f-f-f-farm he had a c-c-c-cow, e i e i o. With a m-m-m-moo here and a m-m-m-moo there, here a moo there a moo everywhere a moo moo . . ." Children's names can be used in this fashion such as "J-J-J-Jason" or "K-K-K-Kate." Still another variation involves drawing a sound out or exaggerating the sound, for example, "MMM-MMaaaaarrrryyyy had a little lllllllaaaaammmmm." Beyond this iterative technique, children can be asked to segment entire words. Yopp (1992) recommends a song set to the tune of "Twinkle, Twinkle, Little Star" for this purpose:

> "Listen, Listen,
>
> To my word,
>
> Tell me all the
>
> Sounds you heard.
>
> *race* [pronounce this word slowly]"
>
> "/r/ is one sound,
>
> /a/ is two,
>
> /s/ is last in *race,*
>
> It's true."

When working with the segmentation of entire words, it is best to use words of no more than three to four sounds because of the difficulty of these tasks for younger learners or learners with special needs. Children seem to enjoy these tasks and with careful guidance can enjoy high levels of success as they develop phonemic awareness through segmentation tasks.

# *I*NTERVENTION CATEGORY II: STRATEGY FOR LEARNING ABOUT LETTERS

## Using Environmental Print

### Purpose

The purpose of this strategy is to use familiar examples of writing from the students' environment (such as cereal boxes, signs, bumper stickers, and candy wrappers) to help them begin to understand how sounds and letters go together (the alphabetic principle). Hiebert and Ham (1981) have found in their research that children taught using environmental print learned significantly more letter names and sounds than did children who learned alphabet letters without using environmental print. Familiar print in the environment can be used in interesting ways to give children confidence in reading and writing and to help them understand how print works.

### Materials

* Collectibles from home and school such as can labels, empty cereal boxes, bumper stickers, advertisements from the local papers, or other old boxes or containers

### Procedure

Begin by setting aside a classroom display area, bulletin board, or wall that is designated as an Environmental Print wall. Children may be asked to bring environmental print or product logos from home to put on this display wall in random order. Next, the environmental print items can be taken down and rearranged in an alphabet display with 26 blocks or areas reserved for each alphabet letter, as shown in Figure 5.15. For example, specific print items such as *Butterfinger, Best Buy,* and *Batman* can be placed in a block for the letter *B*.

In some cases, children can be asked to bring environmental print to school for a specific letter name or sound. After discussing and displaying letter-specific environmental print, teachers and children can cut and paste environmental print items onto 5 × 7-inch plain index cards. These letter-specific environmental print collections are often bound together to be read in small groups or by individuals in an alphabet and letter play center, such as the example for the letter *C* shown in Figure 5.16. Other possibilities for using environmental print to produce letter knowledge include cutting up environmental print to compose or make new words or making letter collages for an art activity.

# *I*NTERVENTION CATEGORY III: TEACHING THE ALPHABETIC SYSTEM

## Playing with the Alphabet

### Purpose

Morrow (2001) has suggested that children can learn the alphabetic principle by enjoying playful activities centering on letter naming, letter sounds, and the connection between letter names and sounds. Providing relaxed and gamelike learning opportunities can often spark the desire to learn the letters and sounds.

**FIGURE 5.15** Environmental Print Chart

| Alphabet Wall | | Aa | Bb | Cc | Dd | Ee |
|---|---|---|---|---|---|---|
| Ff | Gg | Hh | Ii | Jj | Kk | Ll |
| Mm | Nn | Oo | Pp | Qq | Rr | Ss |
| Tt | Uu | Vv | Ww | Xx | Yy | Zz |

## Materials

- Alphabet puzzles
- Games, charts, logos, or commercially published alphabet books
- Magnetic or sandpaper letters
- Letter stencils or flash cards
- Dry-erase boards
- Clay trays
- Paper, pencils, or markers

**FIGURE 5.16** Environmental Print Ring

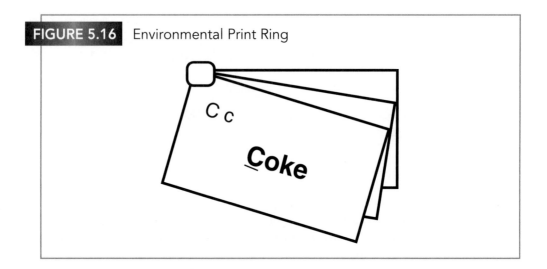

- Painting easels
- Alphabetic cereals and foods

## Procedure

An alphabet station or center stocked with alphabet puzzles, magnetic letters, sandpaper letters, alphabet games, stencils, flash cards, and alphabet charts can be a part of every kindergarten or first-grade classroom station or learning center. Children are invited to write, trace, or copy alphabet letters. Individual-size chalkboards, dry-erase boards, clay trays, tracing paper, and painting easels naturally draw children into copying, tracing, and experimenting with letters.

Delicious possibilities can be periodically added to this rich alphabet activity menu. Samples of alphabet soup, animal crackers, and alphabet cereal may be provided. Children may be encouraged to sort the letters or animals into alphabet letter categories prior to eating. Children can be encouraged to eat in pairs or small groups and talk about which letter they are eating. This playful interaction increases children's awareness of letters, sounds, and alphabetical order. Other playful experiences may be used as well. To emphasize specific letter sounds found in the course of language watching, activities involving a sip of Sprite, a bite of a Snickers candy bar, a long spaghetti noodle to munch on, and a handful of Skittles to taste may be used successfully to emphasize /s/. Art experiences can be designed in which children create pictures using an *S* as the beginning point. Collages of things that begin with /s/, such as a sack, screw, safety pin, salt, silver, or sand can be created and displayed.

Environmental print logos can be used to make *I Can Read* alphabet pattern books. These books are often patterned after well-known alphabet books such as *The Z Was Zapped* (Van Allsburg, 1987) and *On Market Street* (Lobel, 1981). Children select a product label to represent the /c/ sound from a group of alphabetized logos such as Coca-Cola, Cocoa Puffs, Cap'n Crunch, and so on. Other alphabetized product labels are selected to represent the remaining letters of the alphabet in child-produced *I Can Read* Alphabet pattern books. Because children select product logos they can already read, every child easily reads these pattern books. They become a source of confidence building and enjoyment.

## Reading Published Alphabet Books

### Purpose

The purpose of using alphabet books is to assist young readers and readers with special needs to discover the order and elements of the alphabet, both names and sounds. To do this, teachers may wish to acquire collections of quality alphabet trade books. *On Market Street* (Lobel, 1981), *Animalia* (Base, 1986), and *The Z Was Zapped* (Van Allsburg, 1987) are just a few of the many delightful books that can be used to teach children the alphabet.

### Materials

- Commercially published alphabet books

### Procedure

After multiple readings of commercially produced alphabet books, teachers and children can construct their own highly predictable alphabet books using the commercial books as patterns. In an established writing center, young students can create both reproductions and innovations of commercial alphabet books shared in class. A *reproduction* is a student-made copy of an original commercially produced alphabet book. Children copy the text of each page exactly and draw their own illustrations for a reproduction. *Innovations* borrow the basic pattern of commercially produced alphabet books but change the selected words. For instance, one group of first-grade students made innovations on *The Z Was Zapped* (Van Allsburg, 1987). Each child chose a letter and made a new illustration as an innovation. One child, Kevin, picked the letter *D* and drew a picture of the letter *D* in the shape of a doughnut being dunked into a cup of hot chocolate. The caption underneath the picture read, "THE D WAS DUNKED." Reproductions and innovations of alphabet books help students take ownership of familiar text and encourage them to learn about the alphabetic principle through experimentation. Reproductions and innovations of alphabet books also help children sense that they can learn to read successfully.

# ENGLISH LANGUAGE LEARNERS

## Song, Chant, and Poetry

### Purpose

The purpose of using songs, chants, and poetry is to explore and discover how letter sounds combine to create words, word parts, and, when combined, written and oral language. Weaver (1988, 1990) suggested that many teachers use songs, poetry, raps, and chants to convey the alphabetic principle as an alternative to the more tedious direct teaching and drill of phonic generalizations and letter sounds.

### Materials

- Suggested songs, chants, and poems organized by alphabet letter themes

### Procedure

When using poetry, songs, and chants, teachers can watch for specific letters that are repeated in texts to be used as examples for learning the alphabetic principle and developing phonemic awareness. For example, to emphasize the letter *S* for a day or so, teachers may select and enlarge onto chart paper the text of the chants "Sally Go Round the Sun" or "Squid Sauce" to be read aloud by the group. Songs such as "See Saw, Margery Daw" or "Sandy Land" may be selected and the lyrics enlarged onto charts for practice and group singing. Shel Silverstein's (1976) "Sister for Sale" or Jack Prelutsky's (1984) "Sneaky Sue" poems could be likewise enlarged and used to emphasize the name and sound of the letter *S* through repeated group readings.

## The Sounds Rhythm Band

### Purpose

The tapping task developed by Liberman et al. (1974) is the basis for the Sounds Rhythm Band activity. Using this activity, children learn to hear sounds in words in sequence. This is a critical prerequisite for blending sounds together to make words in reading and for segmenting words into sounds for writing and spelling words.

### Materials

- A list of 5 to 10 words containing two, three, or four sounds

the aid of a strong phonics program and a caring and skillful teacher (Blevins, 1996, NELP, 2008).

Phonics instruction is an essential part of comprehensive reading programs in the early grades and is one component of a larger constellation of word analysis skills students learn known as **decoding** (National Institute of Child Health and Human Development, 2000). Other decoding skills (besides phonics) include structural analysis, onset and rime, body and coda, and use of sight words. Each is discussed in this chapter. A comprehensive approach to reading instruction emphasizes both meaning and decoding cues and provides numerous opportunities to practice these cuing systems.

In this chapter we summarize some of the more recent research on decoding skills, particularly phonics, and suggest activities we have found useful in assessing and developing this important area.

## RESEARCH ON PHONICS

Go to the Building Teaching Skills and Dispositions section of Topic 5: "Phonemic Awareness and Phonics" in the MyEducationLab for your course and complete the activity entitled "Teaching Phonemic Awareness and Phonics." As you work through the learning unit, notice the importance of explicit, sequenced phonics instruction.

Surveys conducted by The International Reading Association (IRA) have indicated that phonics is one of the most talked about subjects in the field of reading education. In reviewing

---

**FIGURE 6.1**   Phonics Quick Test

1. The word *charkle* is divided between _____ and _____ . The *a* has an _____-controlled sound, and the *e* is _____ .
2. In the word *small*, *sm-* is known as the *onset* and *-all* is known as the _____ .
3. *Ch* in the word *chair* is known as a _____ .
4. The letter *c* in the word *city* has a _____ sound; in the word *cow*, the letter *c* has a _____ sound.
5. The letters *bl* in the word *blue* are referred to as a consonant _____ .
6. The underlined vowels in the words <u>*au*thor</u>, *spr<u>ea</u>d*, and *bl<u>ue</u>* are known as vowel _____ .
7. The words *tag, run, cot,* and *get* have which vowel pattern? _____
8. The words *glide, take,* and *use* have the _____ vowel pattern.
9. The single most powerful phonics skill we can teach to emergent readers for decoding unfamiliar words in print is _____ sounds in words. We introduce this skill using (*consonants* or *vowels*—choose one) _____ sounds first because they are the most _____ .
10. The word part *work* in the word *working* is known as a _____ .
11. The word part *-ing* in the word *working* is known as a _____ .
12. Cues to the meaning and pronunciation of unfamiliar words in print are often found in the print surrounding the unfamiliar, also known as _____ .

*Note:* Answer key on page 193.

the literature, we have concluded that there are two essential areas for you to know about: *which* phonics skills and generalizations are important for students to learn and *how* you might teach these skills in your classroom. Because teachers should be *the* phonics expert in the classroom, you may want to begin your study of phonics with a little self-assessment. We have included a Phonics Quick Test in Figure 6.1 on the previous page so that you can determine just how much you already know. (The results may surprise you!) Please complete the exercise before reading on.

What are some of the important early skills to develop for reading, writing, and spelling development? In recent research looking at numerous evidence-based studies, Lonigan, Schatschneider, and Westberg (2008) found that certain skill areas were strong predictors of later literacy success. These researchers concluded that there is "strong evidence for the importance of AK [alphabet knowledge], PA [phonological awareness], rapid naming tasks, 'writing or writing name,' and phonological STM [short-term memory] as predictors of later reading and writing skills" (pp. 77–78). In Table 6.1 we share with you their ten "best predictors" for later success in literacy (we focus in this table on the predictors that influence the learning of decoding skills). The researchers went on to add: "Of these 10 variables, six variables (AK, PA, rapid naming of letters and digits, rapid naming of objects and colors, 'writing or writing name,' phonological STM) were consistently related to later conventional literacy outcomes, and these six variables continued to be predictive when other variables were controlled in multivariate analyses" (p. 67).

# THE NEED FOR EXPLICIT AND SYSTEMATIC PHONICS INSTRUCTION

Research confirms that systematic and explicit phonics instruction is more effective than non-systematic instruction or programs that ignore phonics (Carnine et al., 2006; National Institute of Child Health and Human Development, 2000; Stahl, 1992). When delivered as part of a comprehensive reading program—one that includes expansive vocabulary instruction, com-

| TABLE 6.1    Best Predictors for Literacy Success: Decoding | |
|---|---|
| **Top Ten Skill Areas: Decoding** | **Predictive Value for Later Literacy Success** |
| Alphabet knowledge (AK) | Highest value |
| Phonological awareness (PA) | Valuable |
| Concepts about print | Valuable |
| Rapid naming: letters and digits | Valuable |
| Rapid naming: objects and colors | Valuable |
| Writing or writing name | Valuable |
| Oral language | Valuable |
| Phonological short-term memory (STM) | Modest value |
| Visual perception | Modest value |
| Print awareness | Modest value |

*Source:* Adapted from Lonigan, Schatschneider, and Westberg (2008).

prehension development, reading fluency practice in great books, and writing development, all delivered by a skillful teacher, phonics instruction can help children become enthusiastic lifelong readers. But if offered in isolation, it can stifle children's reading growth and create a dislike for reading, especially for children living at the poverty level (Kozol, 2005).

Marilyn Jager Adams (1990), in her exhaustive review of phonics and other factors essential to word identification, *Beginning to Read: Thinking and Learning about Print,* found that approaches in which systematic code instruction was included with the reading of meaningful connected text resulted in superior reading achievement overall, for both low-readiness and better-prepared students (p. 125). Adams also noted that these conclusions seem to hold true regardless of the instructional approach through which reading is taught.

# APPROACHES TO PHONICS INSTRUCTION

Go to the Assignments and Activities section of Topic 8: "Word Recognition" in the MyEducationLab for your course and complete the activity entitled "Characteristics of Good Phonics Instruction." As you watch the video and answer the accompanying questions, identify what you feel are the "non-negotiables" of good phonics instruction you want to include in your classroom.

Several approaches to phonics instruction have found support in the research (Armbruster & Osborn, 2001; National Institute of Child Health and Human Development, 2000; Reutzel & Cooter, 2008). These approaches are sometimes modified or combined in reading programs.

- *Synthetic phonics instruction.*   Traditional phonics instruction in which students learn how to change letters or letter combinations into speech sounds and then blend them together to form known words (*sounding out*).
- *Embedded phonics instruction.*   Teaching students phonics by embedding phonics instruction in text reading, a more implicit approach that relies to some extent on incidental learning (National Institute of Child Health and Human Development, 2000, p. 8).
- *Analogy-based phonics.*   A variation of onset and rime instruction that has students use their knowledge of word families to identify new words that have that same word part. For example, students learn to pronounce *light* by using their prior knowledge of the -*ight* rime from three words they already know: *right, might,* and *night.*
- *Analytic phonics instruction.*   In this variation of the previous two approaches, students study previously learned whole words to discover letter–sound relationships. For example, *Stan, steam,* and *story* all include the *st* word element (*st* is known as a *consonant blend*).
- *Phonics through spelling.*   Students segment spoken words into phonemes and write letters that represent those sounds to create the word in print. For example, *rat* can be sounded out and written phonetically. This approach is often used as part of a "process writing" program.

The question in building a comprehensive reading program is not whether one should teach phonics strategies. Rather, we need to ask, *Which phonics skills should be taught and how should we teach them?* The next section partially answers the "which phonics skills" question.

# PHONICS THEY WILL USE

We have compiled a little phonics primer for you that summarizes the main content of instruction, beginning with the most simple, individual sound–symbol relationships and proceeding to the more complex.

## Letter Names and Sounds

Though the English alphabet has only 26 letters, there are actually some 44 speech sounds. These 44 sounds can be represented in about 350 different ways; hence, English can become a formidable challenge for children when they try to "crack the code." Fortunately, there is a high degree of regularity in English that teachers can focus on to introduce phonics rules and relationships.

The place to begin is at the beginning: rapid letter naming/identification and knowing the sounds they represent (Lonigan et al., 2008). In Figure 6.2, we have compiled a list of the 44 speech sounds and the most common way they are represented by various alphabet letters. Note that in many cases we have listed the percentage of the time each sound is represented by a specific letter. For instance, speech sound /b/ (as in the beginning sound heard in *basket* and *bunk*) is represented by the letter *b* 97% of the time in written English.

## Common Rules Governing Letter Sounds

There are several rules governing letter sounds that have a high degree of reliability and are certainly worth teaching.

### The C Rule

The letter *c* is an irregular consonant letter that has no phoneme of its own. Instead, it assumes two other phonemes found in different words: /k/ and /s/. In general, when the letter *c* is followed by *a, o,* or *u*, it will represent the sound /k/ we usually associate with the letter *k*, also known as the "hard *c* sound." Some examples are the words *cake, cosmic,* and *cute.* On the other hand, the letter *c* can sometimes represent the sound /s/ commonly associated with the letter *s*, referred to as the "soft *c* sound." The soft *c* sound is usually produced when *c* is followed by *e, i,* or *y*. Examples of the soft *c* sound are in the words *celebrate, circus,* and *cycle.*

### The G Rule

The letter *g* is the key symbol for the phoneme /g/ we hear in the word *get* (Hull, 1989). It is also irregular, having a soft *g* and a hard *g* sound. The rules remain the same as they are for the letter *c*. When *g* is followed by the letters *e, i,* or *y*, it represents a soft *g* or /j/ sound, as in the words *gently, giraffe,* and *gym.* If *g* is followed by the letters *a, o,* or *u*, then it usually represents the hard (or regular) sound, as in the words *garden, go,* and *gust.*

### The CVC Generalization

When a vowel comes between two consonants, it usually has a short vowel sound. Examples of words following the CVC pattern include *sat, ran, let, pen, win, fit, hot, mop, sun,* and *cut.*

### Vowel Digraphs

When two vowels come together in a word, usually the first vowel is long and the second vowel is silent. This occurs especially often with the *oa, ee,* and *ay* combinations. Some examples are *toad, fleet,* and *day.* In the words of a common slogan used by teachers to help children remember this generalization, "When two vowels go walking, the first one does the talking."

### The VCE Final E Generalization

When two vowels appear in a word separated by a consonant *and* the final one is an *e* at the end of the word, the first vowel is generally long and the final *e* is silent. Examples include *cape, rope,* and *kite.*

Go to the Assignments and Activities section of Topic 5: "Phonemic Awareness and Phonics" in the MyEducationLab for your course and complete the activity entitled "Strategies for Teaching Phonics." As you watch the video and answer the accompanying questions, note how instruction emphasizes the connection of sounds (phonemes) with letters (graphemes). Without drawing attention regularly to this connection, phonics instruction is ineffective for many students.

| FIGURE 6.2 | The 44 Sounds of English and Their Most Common Spellings | |
|---|---|---|

| Sound | Spellings | Examples |
|---|---|---|
| **1.** /b/ | b (97%), bb | ball |
| **2.** /d/ | d (98%), dd, ed | dot |
| **3.** /f/ | f (78%), ff, ph, lf | fun |
| **4.** /g/ | g (88%), gg, gh | goat |
| **5.** /h/ | h (98%), wh | hall |
| **6.** /j/ | g (66%), j (22%), dg | jug |
| **7.** /k/ | c (73%), cc, k (13%), ck, lk, q | kite |
| **8.** /l/ | l (91%), ll | leap |
| **9.** /m/ | m (94%), mm | moat |
| **10.** /n/ | n (97%), nn, kn, gn | no |
| **11.** /p/ | p (96%), pp | pit |
| **12.** /r/ | r (97%), rr, wr | rubber |
| **13.** /s/ | s (73%), c (17%), ss | sat |
| **14.** /t/ | t (97%), tt, ed | tap |
| **15.** /v/ | v (99.5%), f | vast; of |
| **16.** /w/ | w (92%) | wood |
| **17.** /y/ | i (55%), y (44%) | onion; yell |
| **18.** /z/ | z (23%), zz, s (64%) | zip |
| **19.** /ch/ | ch (55%), t (31%) | chair |
| **20.** /sh/ | ti (53%), sh (26%), ssi, si, sci | shorts |
| **21.** /zh/ | si (49%), s, ss, z | Asia; azure |
| **22.** /th/ | th (100%) | (voiceless sound) bath |
| **23.** /th/ | th (100%) | (voiced) than, together |
| **24.** /hw/ | wh (100%) | what, wheat |
| **25.** /ng/ | ng (59%), n (41%) | rung, sing |
| **26.** /ā/ | ā (45%), ā_e (35%), āi, āy, eā | A; bake |
| **27.** /ē/ | ē (70%), y, ēā (10%), ēē (10%), īē | free |
| **28.** /ī/ | ī_e (37%), ī (37%), y (14%) | five |
| **29.** /ō/ | ō (73%), ō_e (14%), ōw, ōa, ōe | go |
| **30.** /yōō/ | u (69%), u_ē (22%), ēw, uē | cube |
| **31.** /ā/ | ā (96%) | cab |
| **32.** /ē/ | ē (91%), ē_ē (15%) | best |
| **33.** /ī/ | ī (66%), y (23%) | brick |
| **34.** /ō/ | ō (79%) | hot |
| **35.** /u/ | u (86%), ō, ōu | bug |
| **36.** /ə/ (schwa) | ā (24%),  ē (13%),  ī (22%),  ō (27%), u | America |

*(continued)*

| FIGURE 6.2 | *Continued* | | |
|---|---|---|---|

| Sound | Spellings | | Examples |
|---|---|---|---|
| **37.** /â/ | ā (29%), -āre (23%), -āɪr (21%) | | dare |
| **38.** /û/ | -ēr (40%), -īr (13%), -ur (26%) | | bird |
| **39.** /ä/ | ā (89%) | | b ar |
| **40.** /ô/ | ō, ā, āu, āw, ōugh, āugh | | for |
| **41.** /ōī/ | ōī (62%), ōy (32%) | | boil, boy |
| **42.** /ōu/ | ōu (56%), ōw (29%) | | trout |
| **43.** /ōō/ | ōō (38%), u (21%), ō, ōu, u_ē | | boom |
| **44.** /oo/ | oo (31%), u (54%), o (8%), ould, ou, o | | cook |

*Source:* Adapted from Blevins (1998).

### The CV Generalization

When a consonant is followed by a vowel, the vowel usually produces a long sound. This is especially easy to see in two-letter words such as *be, go,* and *so.*

### R-Controlled Vowels

Vowels that appear before the letter *r* are usually neither long nor short but tend to be overpowered or "swallowed up" by the /r/ sound. Examples include *person, player, neighborhood,* and *herself.*

## Special Consonant Rules

### Single Consonants

Single consonants nearly always make the same sound. We recommend that they be taught in the following order due to their frequency in our language:

*T, N, R, M, D, S (sat), L, C (cat), P, S, F, V, G (got), H, W, K, J, Z, Y*

### Consonant Digraphs

Two consonants together in a word producing only one speech sound (*th, sh, ng*) are known as a *consonant digraph.*

### Initial Consonant Blends or "Clusters"

Two or more consonants coming together in which the speech sounds of all the consonants may be heard are called *consonant blends* (*bl, fr, sk, spl*). Consonant blends that come at the beginning of words are the most consistent in the sounds they make. It is recommended that they be taught in the following order according to their frequency in English.

| Group 1 | Group 2 | Group 3 | Group 4 |
|---------|---------|---------|---------|
| *st* | *pl* | *sc* | *sm* |
| *pr* | *sp* | *bl* | *gl* |
| *tr* | *cr* | *fl* | *sn* |
| *gr* | *cl* | *sk* | *tw* |
| *br* | *dr* | *sl* | |
| | *fr* | *sw* | |

Go to the Assignments and Activities section of Topic 8: "Word Recognition" in the MyEducationLab for your course and complete the activity entitled "Structural Analysis." As you watch the video and answer the accompanying questions, notice the direct instruction methods used to teach multisyllabic words. Direct instruction is a highly structured method of instruction that can be used with most students but is especially effective with many struggling readers.

### Double Consonants

When two identical consonants come together in a word, they typically make the sound of a single consonant (*all, apple, arrow, attic*).

### PH and the /f/ Sound

*Ph* is always pronounced as /f/ (*phone, phoneme, philosophy, phobia, phenomenon*).

## Special Vowel Rules

### Schwa /ə/

A vowel letter that produces the "uh" sound (*A* in *America*) is known as a *schwa*. The schwa is represented by the upside-down *e* symbol (/ə/).

### Diphthongs

A *diphthong* consists of two vowels together in a word that produce a single glided sound (*oi* in *oil*, *oy* in *boy*).

### Y Rules

When the letter *y* comes at the end of a long word (or a word having at least one other vowel), it will have the sound of long *e* ( ē ) as in *baby*. When *y* comes at the end of a short word or in the middle of a word, it will make the sound of long *i* (/ī/) as in *cry* and *cycle*.

# $\mathcal{R}$ESEARCH ON OTHER DECODING SKILLS

## Syllabication

The ability to segment words into syllables is yet another form of "phonic awareness" that may be helpful to students when encountering unknown words in print. Though the research on syllabication has been somewhat inconclusive, we have found certain syllabication rules to be the most reliable for (a) dividing words and (b) pronouncing words, as presented in Figures 6.3 and 6.4 (Manzo & Manzo, 1993). (*Note:* We tend to favor teaching students to use common onset and rime knowledge whenever possible to segment words in print.)

## Onset and Rime: "Word Families"

We need to keep in mind that knowing letter names is not all there is in learning to decode. Learning to analyze a printed word into component sounds followed by blending of those sounds requires knowledge of other reliable letter–sound associations (Pressley, 1998).

---

**FIGURE 6.3**    Syllabication Rules for Dividing Words

1. When two identical consonants come together, they are divided to form two syllables. Examples: *ap / ple, but / ter, lit / tle.*
2. The number of vowel sounds that occur in a word usually indicate how many syllables there will be in the word. Examples: *slave* (one vowel sound/one syllable); *caboose* (four vowels, but only two vowel sounds, hence, two syllables—*ca / boose*).
3. Two adjoining unlike consonants are also usually divided to form syllables, unless they form a consonant digraph. Example: *car / pet.*
4. Small words within a compound word are syllables (as with onset/rimes). Examples: *book / store, fire / fly.*

*Source:* Adapted from *Literary Disorders: Holistic Diagnosis and Remediation* by A. V. Manzo and U. C. Manzo, 1993. Reprinted with permission of Wadsworth, a division of Cengage Learning, Inc. (www.cengage.com/permissions).

---

Significant research in recent years confirms that certain word elements known as *onset* and *rime* are extremely reliable sound–symbol patterns and can be very helpful to new decoders. Simply put, a **rime** is the vowel at the beginning of a syllable and the letters that go along with it, and the **onset** is the consonant or consonants that come just before the vowel. For example, in the word *tack, t* is the onset and *-ack* is the rime; in the word *snow, sn* is the onset and *-ow* is the rime. In Figure 6.5, we have provided a comprehensive list of rimes for your use. The rimes in bold should be taught first and, when combined with various onsets (i.e., beginning consonants, consonant blends, or consonant digraphs), produce some 500 primary-level words (Adams, 1990).

## Body and Coda

As mentioned earlier in Chapter 5, recent evidence suggests that children are able to blend word sounds most easily by using an approach called *body* and *coda*. **Body word chunks** include the onset plus the vowel sound in a syllable. **Coda word chunks** include all sounds following the vowel sound in a syllable. For example a student using this technique to blend

---

**FIGURE 6.4**    Syllabication Rules for Pronouncing Words

1. *le* is pronounced as *ul* when it appears at the end of a word. Examples: *shuttle, little, remarkable.*
2. Syllables that end with a vowel usually have a long vowel sound. Examples: *bi / lingual, re / read.*
3. When a vowel does not come at the end of a syllable, and it is followed by two consonants, it will usually have a short sound. Examples: *letter, all, attic.*

*Source:* Adapted from *Literary Disorders: Holistic Diagnosis and Remediation* by A. V. Manzo and U. C. Manzo, 1993. Reprinted with permission of Wadsworth, a division of Cengage Learning, Inc. (www.cengage.com/permissions).

---

### FIGURE 6.5 · Rimes (Word Families)

| -ab | -ang | -ear (short e) | **-ice** | **-ir** | -out |
|-----|------|----------------|----------|---------|------|
| -ace | **-ank** | **-eat** | **-ick** | -it | -ow (snow) |
| **-ack** | **-ap** | -ed | -id | -ob | -ow (sow) |
| -ad | -ar | -ee | **-ide** | **-ock** | -ub |
| -ade | -are | -eed | -ies | -od | **-uck** |
| -ag | -ark | -eek | -ig | -og | -uff |
| -ail | **-ash** | -eep | **-ight** | **-oke** | **-ug** |
| **-ain** | -at | -eet | -ile | -old | -um |
| **-ake** | **-ate** | **-ell** | **-ill** | -one | **-ump** |
| **-ale** | -ave | -em | -im | -ong | -ung |
| **-all** | **-aw** | -end | -ime | **-oop** | **-unk** |
| -am | **-ay** | -ent | **-in** | **-op** | -ush |
| **-ame** | -aze | -ess | **-ine** | -ope | -ust |
| -amp | -eak | **-est** | **-ing** | **-or** | -ut |
| **-an** | -eal | -et | **-ink** | **-ore** | -y |
| -ane | -eam | -ew | **-ip** | -ot | |

*Note:* Rimes in bold type have some of the most reliable sounds and, when adding an onset (consonant, consonant blends, or digraphs), create some 500 primary-level words.

*Source:* Adapted from Adams (1990); Fry, Kress, & Fountoukidis (1993); and Pressley (1998).

---

the word *hat* would say the *body* /ha/ and the *coda* /t/) (Murray, Brabham, Villaume, & Veal, 2008). This recent evidence demonstrates that blending word sounds using body and coda may be more effective than using onsets and rimes.

## Structural Analysis

**Structural analysis** refers to the study of words to identify their individual meaning elements (called *morphemes*). Words are made up of two classes or morphemes—*free* and *bound*. **Free morphemes** are word parts (words, really) that sometimes stand alone. They are also known as **root words.** For example, in the word *working, work* is the root word (free morpheme). In contrast, **bound morphemes** must be attached to a root word to carry meaning. Prefixes and suffixes (together referred to as *affixes*) are bound morphemes. Common prefixes, which come *before* a root word, include *intro-, pro-, post-, sub-,* and *dis-.* Some of the more common suffixes, which come *after* a root word, include *-ant, -ist, -ence, -ism, -s,* and *-ed.*

## Sight Words

Many reading experts and researchers feel that learning high-frequency vocabulary or **sight words** is an important component of decoding for beginning readers. These are words that occur frequently in print and are usually best learned through memorization, words like *is,* *are, the, was, this,* and so on. The rapid naming of words is likewise an important part of reading fluency. We agree that sight words are an element of decoding as well as reading fluency, but because sight words are also "vocabulary," we have chosen to include this information in Chapter 8, "Teaching and Assessing Vocabulary Development."

# WHEN TO TEACH SPECIFIC PHONICS AND OTHER DECODING SKILLS: THE SCOPE AND SEQUENCE OF INSTRUCTION

When should specific decoding skills be taught? Does research suggest a specific order? As with so many things in life, the answer is not entirely clear. For instance, there is no set rule about how quickly or how slowly to introduce letter–sound relationships (Chard & Osborn, 1999), but there is adequate scientific research data for us to set down a comprehensive listing of important skills.

In Figure 6.6, we suggest a scope and sequence of decoding instruction based on some of the most credible research (e.g., Bear, Templeton, Invernizzi, & Johnston, 1996; Blevins,

---

**FIGURE 6.6**　Recommended Scope and Sequence of Instruction: Decoding

*Kindergarten*
- Phonemic awareness
- Print awareness (concepts about print)
- Rapid letter naming (alphabet recognition)
- Alphabet knowledge (sounds matched to letters)
- Writing letters
- Writing name
- Familiarity with the basic purposes and mechanisms of reading and writing
- Sense of story
- Vocabulary development (oral language, some high-frequency words)

*First Grade*
- Explicit instruction on phonemic awareness (if not previously developed in kindergarten)
- Letter–sound correspondences and common spelling conventions and uses in identifying printed words
  1. Consonants: In beginning, ending, and medial positions as part of a decoding strategy. Letters pronounced the same regardless of context: (*d, f, l, n, r, v, z*)
  2. Short vowels: *a, e, i, o,* and *u*
  3. Consonant-vowel-consonant (CVC) pattern: Use simple words that begin with

consistent sounds to introduce simple blending, such as *fan, lad, ran.*
  4. Vowel-consonant-*e* (VCE) pattern
  5. Long vowel digraphs (*ai, ay, ea, ee, oa, ow*)
  6. Consonant blends (*tr, br, bl, cl, st,* etc.)
  7. Early structural analysis such as root words, prefixes, and suffixes
  8. Onset and rime (most frequent)
  9. Body and coda word chunks
- Sight recognition of frequent words
- Use of context clues
- Independent reading including reading aloud (a wide variety of well-written and engaging texts that are below the children's frustration level should be provided)

*Second Grade and Above*
- Sound out and identify visually unfamiliar words
- Recognize words primarily through attention to letter–sound relationships
- Context and pictures should be used only to monitor word recognition
- Accuracy in word recognition and fluency should be assessed regularly

1997; Eldredge, 1995; Lonigan, Schatschneider, & Westberg, 2008; Moustafa, 1997; National Research Council, 1999; Pressley, 1998). Instead of trying to enumerate each minute skill, in most cases we simply recommend major categories in sequence and leave decisions about the fine points to you. This knowledge of *what* and *when* to teach can be extremely helpful in (a) assessing phonics knowledge in students and (b) planning instruction and grouping effectively to meet their needs.

## English Learners

Go to the Assignments and Activities section of Topic 14: "English Language Learners" in the MyEducationLab for your course and complete the activity entitled "Helping ELL Students with Phonics." As you read the article and answer the accompanying questions, identify the common elements of phonics instruction between ELLs and English-first students. What are the differences that should be incorporated into the curriculum?

The *Report of the National Literacy Panel on Language Minority Children and Youth* (August & Shanahan, 2006) sheds new light on the reading instruction needs of **English learners (EL).** First, it was found that evidence-based reading research confirms that focusing instruction on key reading components, such as phonemic awareness, decoding, oral reading fluency, reading comprehension, vocabulary, and writing, has clear benefits. The researchers went on to say that differences due to children's second-language proficiency make it important to adjust instruction to meet the needs of second-language learners. This important study makes it clear that phonics instruction is critical to English learners and must be delivered by a knowledgeable teacher.

### English Learners (Spanish)

Native Spanish speakers are the most rapidly growing population of English learners in many states. There are some basic similarities and differences between English and Spanish languages that may cause problems in the learning of phonics. In Table 6.2 we present a few teaching points adapted from Honig, Diamond, and Gutlohn (2000) for you to consider in planning phonics instruction with EL students. Happily, most phonics generalizations in English and Spanish are the same. If anything, Spanish is far more consistent than English!

### TABLE 6.2   Planning Phonics Instruction for English Learners

| Sound | Explanation | Examples |
|---|---|---|
| /s/ | This sound is spelled with *s* in English and Spanish. | English: *seed, secret*<br>Spanish: *semilla, secreto* |
| /m/ | This sound is spelled with *m* in English and Spanish. | English: *map, many*<br>Spanish: *mapa, mucho* |
| Spanish *e* | The letter *e* in Spanish has the long-*a* sound, as with *eight*. | Spanish: *bueno, recibir* |
| /ch/ | In Spanish the digraph "ch" also make the /ch/ sound. However, *ch* only appears in the beginning or medial positions in Spanish | English: *church, each*<br>Spanish: *chico, ocho* |
| /sh/ | The *sh* digraph does not exist in Spanish! Sorting new words with *sh* and *ch* will be helpful. Be sure to also focus on the meaning of each word. | |

*Source:* Adapted from Honig, Diamond, and Gutlohn (2000).

## What Does a Good Phonics and Decoding Program Look Like?

Three main accomplishments characterize good readers: they understand the alphabetic system of English, they use background knowledge and strategies to obtain meaning from print, and they read fluently (National Research Council, 1999, p. 6). Similarly, successful phonics instruction has a number of common qualities (Stahl, 1992). First of all, it builds on children's knowledge about how print functions. In the early stages, phonics and decoding instruction also builds on students' phonological awareness when the alphabet is introduced.

Phonics is integrated into a comprehensive reading program and focuses, ultimately, on reading words, not memorizing rules. Research confirms that effective programs include onset and rime instruction, which can also be woven into writing instruction (for instance, using "temporary" or *phonemic* spellings). A prime objective of exemplary phonics instruction is to develop independent word-recognition strategies, focusing attention on the internal structure of words (structural analysis). All effective instruction is preceded by an assessment of student knowledge, our next topic.

## Assessing Phonics and Decoding Knowledge

The goal of phonics and decoding assessment is to discover what students understand about sound–symbol relationships. Knowing what a student can and cannot do makes it clear what your course of action should be in the classroom. There are a number of basic strategies that one can use to discover which skills have been learned and which need attention. In general, assessment should proceed developmentally according to the sequence in which skills are learned: phonemic awareness—to alphabet knowledge—to phonics and other decoding skills.

Assessment of early phonics and decoding knowledge often begins with a running record. Using words in context, running records permit teachers to observe how well a student's phonics skills are developing while reading real text. In Chapter 1, we discussed how to conduct running records, so we do not duplicate that information in this chapter; just know that we see running records as *the* way to assess phonics and decoding in context.

A good starting point for assessing novice decoding abilities is the Reutzel/Cooter Phonics and Decoding Record (Figure 6.7). The PDR is a comprehensive tool you can use to analyze students' development of decoding benchmark skills over the course of the school year. It is not an assessment instrument, but rather a tool to help you tally up areas of strength and needs based on your assessments and observations of students. Many of the assessment tools discussed in this chapter and throughout the book are basically summarized in the PDR.

One of the assessment tools explained in this section, the Early Names Test (Mather, Sammons, & Schwartz, 2006), is useful in assessing students' mastery of fundamental phonics patterns. Another assessment procedure we recommend is the Starpoint Phonics Assessment (Williams, Cooter, & Cooter, 2003), which uses nonsense words read in a list (without context). Together with running records (see Chapter 1), you will learn a great deal about students' phonics and decoding knowledge using these two assessment tools.

## The Early Names Test

### Purpose

Originally developed by Cunningham (1990) and refined later by Duffelmeyer and colleagues (1994), the names test was developed as quick and easy tool for teachers to use in gathering information about students' emerging decoding skills. More recently, Mather and colleagues

**FIGURE 6.7**   The Reutzel/Cooter Phonics and Decoding Record (PDR)

Student name: _____      Teacher/Grade level: _____

**Skill Areas: Phonics and Decoding**                                                    Survey Dates

| Alphabet | Aug./ Sept. | Nov./ Dec. | Feb./ Mar. | May/ June |
|---|---|---|---|---|
| Alphabet Knowledge [See "Letter Identification" in Chapter 5] | | | | |
| Rapid Letter Naming—Uppercase | | | | |
| Rapid Letter Naming—Lowercase | | | | |
| Letter Production Task [See Chapter 5] | | | | |
| Consonant Sounds (most stable): *R, T, N, L, S /s/, D, C /k/, M, P, B* | | | | |
| Vowel Sounds (long): *a, e, u* | | | | |

**Words and Word Elements**

| | | | | |
|---|---|---|---|---|
| Sight Words—First 25 (Dolch or Fry) [See Chapter 8] | | | | |
| Sight Words—First 50 (Dolch or Fry) [See Chapter 8] | | | | |
| Sight Words—First 100 (Dolch or Fry) [See Chapter 8] | | | | |
| Body Word Chunks (Onset plus first vowel in syllable) | | | | |
| Coda Word Chunks (all sounds in syllable following body word chunk) | | | | |
| Rimes (37 most frequent) | | | | |

**Word Attack (from Running Records*)**

| | | | | |
|---|---|---|---|---|
| Instructional Reading Level (90–94% Accuracy)—Fiction | | | | |
| Instructional Reading Level (90–94% Accuracy)—Nonfiction | | | | |
| Meaning (Use of meaning cues in decoding) | | | | |
| Syntax (Knowledge and use in decoding) | | | | |
| Reading and Decoding: Basic Phonics Applications (Early Names Test) | | | | |
| Strategic Decoding (unknown words in print)—Uses context clues plus beginning consonant sounds | | | | |
| Strategic Decoding (unknown words in print]—Uses context clues plus beginning consonant sounds and ending sounds | | | | |
| Strategic Decoding—Uses context clues plus beginning, medial, and ending sounds | | | | |

**Phonics Generalizations—One-Syllable Decoding Patterns**

| | | | | |
|---|---|---|---|---|
| Single Consonant Sounds: High Frequency and Reliability— *T, N, R, M, D, S* (e.g., *sat*), *L, C* (*cat*), *P, S, F, V, G* (*got*), *H, W, K, J, Z, Y* | | | | |
| Initial Consonant Blends (*pr, tr, gr, br, cr, dr, sm, sn, pl, cl, bl*) | | | | |
| Consonant Digraphs (*ch, th, sh, wh*) | | | | |
| "C" Rule | | | | |
| "G" Rule | | | | |

*(continued)*

FIGURE 6.7    *Continued*

| Phonics Generalizations—One-Syllable Decoding Patterns *(continued)* | Aug./ Sept. | Nov./ Dec. | Feb./ Mar. | May/ June |
|---|---|---|---|---|
| Consonant-Vowel-Consonant (CVC) | | | | |
| Vowel Digraphs (*ai, ea, ee, ie, oo, oi, ou, oa*) | | | | |
| Vowel-Consonant-*e* (VCE) | | | | |
| Consonant-Vowel (CV) | | | | |
| *R*-Controlled Vowels (*qr, er, ir, or, ur*) | | | | |
| Final Consonant Blends (*ld, lf, sk, st, nk*) | | | | |
| Double Consonants (e.g., *apple, all, arrow, attic*) | | | | |
| *ph* for /f/ sound (e.g., *phone, phobia, Phillip*) | | | | |
| **Phonics Generalizations—Multisyllabic Decoding Patterns** | | | | |
| Syllabication (Dividing Words/Rules) | | | | |
| Syllabication (Pronunciation Words/Rules) | | | | |
| Structural Analysis: Common Prefixes (e.g., *intro-, pro-, post-, sub-, dis-*) | | | | |
| Structural Analysis: Common Suffixes (e.g., *-s, -ed, -ing, -ant, -ist, -ence, -ism*) | | | | |

*Note:* *See Chapter 1 for a review of Running Records.

(2006) developed an enhanced validated and highly reliable version of this screening tool they call the **Early Names Test.** Administered to individual students, this tool will assist you in assessing learners' abilities to apply grapheme–phoneme knowledge to simple word patterns.

### Materials

- A copy of the Early Names Test (Figure 6.8)
- Administration Instructions and Scoring Sheet: Early Names Test (Figure 6.9)
- Scoring Matrix for Early Names Test (Table 6.3)

### Procedure

Seat the student, if possible, across from you at a small table. Provide the student with a copy of the Early Names Test. You should have in front of you a copy of the Administration Instructions and Scoring Sheet and a pencil for recording student responses. As indicated in the instructions say,

> I want you to pretend that you are a teacher and you are calling out your students' names to take attendance. You are trying to figure out who is at school and who is not. Some of these names may be hard, but just do the best you can.

Record a 1 for a correct response and a 0 for an incorrect response. Score both the first and last names. Write incorrect responses directly above the name. Once you have administered the test, you will be able to use the scoring matrix to identify any need areas for the student.

| FIGURE 6.8 | Early Names Test |
|---|---|

| Rob Hap | Pam Rack | Flip Mar | Frank Lug | Ross Quest |
|---|---|---|---|---|
| Jud Lem | Trish Mot | Jet Mit | Grace Nup | Dane Wong |
| Ray San | Fred Tig | Rand Lun | Beck Daw | Tom Zall |
| Pat Ling | Bab Fum | Jen Dut | Dell Smush | Gail Vog |
| Tim Bop | Kate Tide | Jake Bin | Gus Lang | Rod Blade |
| Brad Tash | Brent Lake | Sid Gold | Lex Yub | Tag Shick |

*Source:* From "Adaptations of the Names Test: Easy-to-Use Phonics Assessments," by N. Mather, J. Sammons, and J. Schwartz, 2006, *The Reading Teacher, 60*(2), 117. Copyright © 2006 by the International Reading Association (www.reading.org). Reproduced with permission of the International Reading Association via Copyright Clearance Center.

| FIGURE 6.9 | Administration Instructions and Scoring Sheet: Early Names Test |
|---|---|

Say: "I want you to pretend that you are a teacher and you are calling out your students' names to take attendance. You are trying to figure out who is at school and who is not. Some of these names may be hard, but just do the best you can." Record a 1 for a correct response and a 0 for an incorrect response. Score both the first and last names. Write incorrect responses directly above the name.

Name: _____   Grade: _____   Date: _____

| Rob | _____ | Hap | _____ | Jen | _____ | Dut | _____ |
|---|---|---|---|---|---|---|---|
| Jud | _____ | Lem | _____ | Jake | _____ | Bin | _____ |
| Ray | _____ | San | _____ | Sid | _____ | Gold | _____ |
| Pat | _____ | Ling | _____ | Frank | _____ | Lug | _____ |
| Tim | _____ | Bop | _____ | Grace | _____ | Nup | _____ |
| Brad | _____ | Tash | _____ | Beck | _____ | Daw | _____ |
| Pam | _____ | Rack | _____ | Dell | _____ | Smush | _____ |
| Trish | _____ | Mot | _____ | Gus | _____ | Lang | _____ |
| Fred | _____ | Tig | _____ | Lex | _____ | Yub | _____ |
| Bab | _____ | Fum | _____ | Ross | _____ | Quest | _____ |
| Kate | _____ | Tide | _____ | Dane | _____ | Wong | _____ |
| Brent | _____ | Lake | _____ | Tom | _____ | Zall | _____ |
| Flip | _____ | Mar | _____ | Gail | _____ | Vog | _____ |
| Jet | _____ | Mit | _____ | Rod | _____ | Blade | _____ |
| Rand | _____ | Lun | _____ | Tag | _____ | Shick | _____ |

Total first and last names read correctly _____

*Source:* From "Adaptations of the Names Test: Easy-to-Use Phonics Assessments," by N. Mather, J. Sammons, and J. Schwartz, 2006, *The Reading Teacher, 60*(2), 118. Copyright © 2006 by the International Reading Association (www.reading.org). Reproduced with permission of the International Reading Association via Copyright Clearance Center.

## TABLE 6.3 Scoring Matrix for the Early Names Test

| Name | Initial Consonant | Ending Consonant | Consonant Blend | Consonant Digraph | Short Vowel | Long Vowel/ Vowel-Consonant-Final e | Vowel Digraph | Rime |
|---|---|---|---|---|---|---|---|---|
| Bab | B | -b | | | a | | | -ab |
| Beck | B | | | -ck | e | | | -eck |
| Bin | B | -n | | | i | | | -in |
| Blade | | -d | Bl- | | | a-e | | -ade |
| Bop | B | -p | | | o | | | -op |
| Brad | | -d | Br- | | a | | | -ad |
| Brent | | | Br- | -nt | e | | | -ent |
| Dane | D | -n | | | | a-e | | -ane |
| Daw | D | | | | | | -aw | -aw |
| Dell | D | -ll | | | e | | | -ell |
| Dut | D | -t | | | u | | | -ut |
| Flip | | -p | Fl- | | i | | | -ip |
| Frank | | | Fr- | -nk | a | | | -ank |
| Fred | | -d | Fr- | | e | | | -ed |
| Gold | G | | | -ld | | | | -old |
| Grace | | | Gr- | | | a-e | | -ace |
| Gus | G | -s | | | u | | | -us |
| Hap | H | -p | | | a | | | -ap |
| Jake | J | -k | | | | a-e | | -ake |
| Jen | J | -n | | | e | | | -en |
| Jet | J | -t | | | e | | | -et |
| Jud | J | -d | | | u | | | -ud |
| Kate | K | -t | | | | a-e | | -ate |
| Lake | L | -k | | | | a-e | | -ake |
| Lang | L | | | -ng | a | | | -ang |
| Lem | L | -m | | | e | | | -em |
| Lex | L | -x | | | e | | | -ex |
| Ling | L | | | -ng | i | | | -ing |
| Lug | L | -g | | | u | | | -ug |
| Lun | L | -n | | | u | | | -un |
| Mar | M | | | | | | | -ar |
| Mit | M | -t | | | i | | | -it |
| Mot | M | -t | | | o | | | -ot |
| Nup | N | -p | | | u | | | -up |
| Pam | P | -m | | | a | | | -am |
| Pat | P | -t | | | a | | | -at |
| Quest | (Qu)* | | | -st | e | | | -est |
| Rack | R | | | -ck | a | | | -ack |

| | | | | | | Long vowel/ Vowel-Consonant-Final e | | |
|---|---|---|---|---|---|---|---|---|
| Name | Initial Consonant | Ending Consonant | Consonant Blend | Consonant Digraph | Short Vowel | | Vowel Digraph | Rime |
| Rand | R | | | -nd | a | | | -and |
| Ray | R | | | | | | -ay | -ay |
| Rob | R | -b | | | o | | | -ob |
| Rod | R | -d | | | o | | | -od |
| Ross | R | -ss | | | o | | | -oss |
| San | S | -n | | | a | | | -an |
| Shick | | | Sh- | -ck | i | | | -ick |
| Sid | S | -d | | | i | | | -id |
| Smush | | | Sm- | -sh | u | | | -ush |
| Tag | T | -g | | | a | | | -ag |
| Tash | T | | | -sh | a | | | -ash |
| Tide | T | -d | | | | i-e | | -ide |
| Tig | T | -g | | | i | | | -ig |
| Tim | T | -m | | | i | | | -im |
| Tom | T | -m | | | o | | | -om |
| Trish | | | Tr- | -sh | i | | | -ish |
| Vog | V | -g | | | o | | | -og |
| Wong | W | | | -ng | o | | | -ong |
| Yub | Y | -b | | | u | | | -ub |
| Zall | Z | -ll | | | | | | -all |

*Note:* Qu is sometimes referred to as a consonant oddity or a consonant blend.

*Source:* From "Adaptations of the Names Test: Easy-to-Use Phonics Assessments," by N. Mather, J. Sammons, and J. Schwartz, 2006, *The Reading Teacher, 60*(2), 120–121. Copyright © 2006 by the International Reading Association (www.reading.org). Reproduced with permission of the International Reading Association via Copyright Clearance Center.

## The Starpoint Phonics Assessment

### Purpose

For many years, nonsense words ("made-up words" having common phonics patterns) have been used in reading assessment to determine students' knowledge of English spelling patterns. These nonsense words are usually read in a list and the teacher records any miscues. Critics say that nonsense words, because they are not real words, do not permit students to use their prior knowledge—a primary reading tool used in decoding unfamiliar words in print. Advocates counter that nonsense words, because they preclude the use of background knowledge, force the student to use only those phonics skills that he or she has internalized. We support the limited use of nonsense words as simply one tool in a teacher's toolbox of assessment ideas that may shed some light on a student's phonics skills development.

The Starpoint Phonics Assessment (Williams, Cooter, & Cooter, 2003) was designed to provide a beginning-of-the-year phonics assessment for children attending the Starpoint

Go to the Assignments and Activities section of Topic 8: "Word Recognition" in the MyEducationLab for your course and complete the activity entitled "Assessing Phonics Knowledge." As you watch the video and answer the accompanying questions, note the possible ways the Starpoint Phonics Assessment (SPA) in our text could be used in similar situations.

Laboratory School at Texas Christian University. The SPA is also included as a subtest in *The Spanish and English Reading Inventory for the Classroom* (2nd ed.), by Flynt & Cooter (2003). Areas of special focus include initial consonant sounds (onsets), correct pronunciation of common rimes, syllabication, affixes (prefixes/suffixes), and *r*-controlled vowels. These phonics features are embedded within nonsense words that students are asked to read (see Figure 6.10). Analysis of children's phonics abilities focuses on these five areas.

## Materials

- Flash cards showing each row of nonsense words from Figure 6.10 (e.g., row 1 words on one card—*runk, mip, bor*)
- Copy of the SPA Analysis Grid Form (Figure 6.11) for each student to be assessed
- Audio recorder

## Procedure

Seat the student at a table directly across from where you are sitting. Turn on your audio recorder and say the student's name aloud and the date to mark the record. Beginning with the first flash card you have prepared from Figure 6.10, say to the student, "Please read the words on each card as I hold it up. The words are all *nonsense* words. That means they are not real words. Just pronounce them the way you think they would sound. For instance, this first word is *runk*. Go ahead and try to say the other words for me as I hold them up."

As the student reads each word, make a notation to the right of each grouping of words on the SPA Analysis Grid Form indicating whether the child said the word correctly. Words pronounced correctly should be noted with a checkmark (✓). Incorrect pronunciations should be written phonetically. For example, if a student pronounces the nonsense word *wabor* (line 18) as "way-bee," make a note to the right of the word cluster on line 18 that reflects the way the student said it. Continue having the student read each cluster of words and mark *every* **miscue** (a mispronounced word) in the blank area to the right of the relevant word cluster.

---

**FIGURE 6.10**  Starpoint Phonics Assessment Nonsense Words

| | | | | | | | |
|---|---|---|---|---|---|---|---|
| 1. | runk | mip | bor | 11. | dop | femmit | yadder |
| 2. | pight | caw | jor | 12. | gapple | sheal | telbis |
| 3. | wunk | lemmock | zatting | 13. | lome | ridnip | hade |
| 4. | nash | soug | zad | 14. | tade | chogging | vappel |
| 5. | battump | dapping | yod | 15. | minzif | kosh | waig |
| 6. | mur | hote | seg | 16. | tain | demsug | nater |
| 7. | lattum | yinter | poat | 17. | festrip | bowunk | thiping |
| 8. | telbin | vike | leat | 18. | wapir | polide | wabor |
| 9. | dar | mur | foat | 19. | polide | siler | jiper |
| 10. | pice | gar | whesp | 20. | atur | niping | quen |

| FIGURE 6.11 | Starpoint Phonics Assessment Analysis Grid Form |
|---|---|

| | | | Initial Sound | Rimes | Syllabication | Affixes | *R*-controlled |
|---|---|---|---|---|---|---|---|
| **1.** runk | mip | bor | | | | | |
| **2.** pight | caw | jor | | | | | |
| **3.** wunk | lemmock | zatting | | | | | |
| **4.** nash | soug | zad | | | | | |
| **5.** battump | dapping | yod | | | | | |
| **6.** mur | hote | seg | | | | | |
| **7.** lattum | yinter | poat | | | | | |
| **8.** telbin | vike | leat | | | | | |
| **9.** dar | mur | foat | | | | | |
| **10.** pice | gar | whesp | | | | | |
| **11.** dop | femmit | yadder | | | | | |
| **12.** gapple | sheal | telbis | | | | | |
| **13.** lome | ridnip | hade | | | | | |
| **14.** tade | chogging | vappel | | | | | |
| **15.** minzif | kosh | waig | | | | | |
| **16.** tain | demsug | nater | | | | | |
| **17.** festrip | bowunk | thiping | | | | | |
| **18.** wapir | polide | wabor | | | | | |
| **19.** polide | siler | jiper | | | | | |
| **20.** atur | niping | quen | | | | | |
| *Totals* | | | | | | | |

*Examiner's Notes:*

## Analyzing the Miscues

The Starpoint Phonics Assessment (SPA) is quick and easy to analyze. First, replay the recording to be sure that any miscues have been correctly recorded. Next, for each miscue noted, simply place a hash mark " | " in the box to the right indicating which phonics skill(s) the student seems to be lacking when trying to decode that particular nonsense word: beginning sounds (onset), rimes, syllabication, affixes (common prefixes and suffixes), and/or *r*-controlled vowels. You should have at least one box marked for each miscue. If none of the phonics categories seems to be appropriate, which is possible, then make a note of the miscue at the bottom of the sheet in the area marked "Examiner's Notes" along with your interpretation of what the student may need to learn (e.g., CVC rule, hard *g* sound, vowel digraphs, etc.).

Finally, add up the number of miscues in each column and record that number in the appropriate Totals box. If the student has had two or more miscues in one category (i.e., beginning sounds/onset, rimes, syllabication, affixes, or *r*-controlled vowels), you should consider developing explicit instruction plans to teach that skill.

## Assessing via Running Records

We just could not resist putting in one last reminder that you should use running records as your primary assessment tool for analyzing student decoding ability. Chapter 1 gives you the full picture on using this valuable diagnostic procedure.

In Figure 6.12 we summarize the procedures and instruments we have just discussed for assessing factors associated with phonics and decoding skills. In this Summary Matrix of Assessments we provide information about federally related assessment purposes (i.e., screening, diagnostic, progress-monitoring, or outcomes assessment), as well as the type of test or procedure and psychometric evidence about the test or procedure scores (any available reliability and validity evidence).

## Connecting Assessment Findings to Teaching Strategies

Before discussing phonics and decoding teaching strategies, we provide an If-Then chart connecting assessment findings to intervention and strategy choices (see Figure 6.13). It is our intention to help you select the most appropriate instructional interventions and strategies to meet your students' needs based on assessment data. In the next part of this chapter, we offer instruction strategies for interventions based on the foregoing assessments.

# TEACHING STRATEGIES: HELPING STUDENTS INCREASE PHONICS AND DECODING KNOWLEDGE

## Tips on Teaching Phonics

Go to the Building Teaching Skills and Dispositions section of Topic 8: "Word Recognition" in the MyEducationLab for your course and complete the activity entitled "Improving Word Recognition." As you work through the learning unit, consider how you could structure your teaching to help students become automatic in identifying and recognizing (comprehending) unfamiliar words in print. To what extent do you feel nonfiction texts should be used for these activities because they introduce students to many new "real world" words?

Research over the past decade or so has taught us much about the best ways to teach phonics (Blevins, 1998; Carnine et al., 2006; National Institute of Child Health and Human Development, 2000; Stahl, 1992). Here is our advice about what you should (and should not) do to establish solid phonics instruction.

### Ten Things to Do

1. *Sequence your instruction.* Earlier in the chapter, we provided you with a scope and sequence of instruction (see Figure 6.6).
2. *Be very direct (explicit and implicit) in your teaching.* Model each new skill thoroughly, offer students a good bit of practice under your guidance, and then assess to make sure they have it.
3. *Have daily lessons and review sessions.* Phonics instruction should be an everyday occurrence in the early grades (K–2) and include a great deal of repetition. Teachers sometimes forget that even our best students need as much as 30 days of repetition for a new phonics skill to become their own (Cooter, 2001). According to the National Research Council (1999), "[Children] need sufficient practice with a variety of texts to achieve fluency, so that both word recognition and reading comprehension become increasingly fast, accurate, and well coordinated" (p. 6).
4. *Focus on one skill at a time.* All too often, we try to do too much in introducing new skills and, consequently, teach few skills well. Phonics lessons should keep a tight focus and work on the target skill until the student becomes proficient.
5. *Keep lessons brief.* If, in fact, you are teaching within the student's "zone of proximal development," then you must limit instruction sessions to 10 to 15 minutes. Otherwise, the student's attention wanders and your teaching is ineffective.

FIGURE 6.12 Summary Matrix of Assessments to Measure Phonics and Decoding Skills

| Name of Assessment Tool | Screening Assessment | Diagnostic Assessment | Progress-Monitoring Assessment | Outcomes Assessment | Norm-Referenced Test | Criterion-Referenced Test | Reliability Evidence | Validity Evidence |
|---|---|---|---|---|---|---|---|---|
| Early Names Test | + | + | – | – | – | + | For 2nd graders the KR-20 reliability was .93, and .98 for 4th and 5th graders | Not Available |
| Starpoint Phonics Assessment | + | + | + | + | – | + | – | – |
| Running Records | + | + | + | + | – | + | * | + |

*Note:* Reliability evidence is not usually available for running records since it is an "informal" procedure used by teachers with passages they select. However, the new *Comprehensive Reading Inventory* (CRI), by R. Cooter, E. S. Flynt, and K. S. Cooter (Merrill/Prentice Hall Publishers) does provide reliability and validity data for all of its running records.

Key: + can be used for
   * adaptable for
   – not appropriate for

FIGURE 6.13 If-Then Strategy Guide for Phonics and Decoding

| "If" the student is ready to learn → "Then" try these teaching strategies | Explicit Phonics Instruction | Letter-Sound Cards | Phonics Fish | Spelling in Parts (SIP) | Sound Swirl | "Button Sounds" | Stomping, Clapping, Tapping, and Snapping Sounds | Tongue Twisters | Creating Nonsense Words | Making Words | Wide Reading | Word Boxes | Word Detectives |
|---|---|---|---|---|---|---|---|---|---|---|---|---|---|
| Alphabet knowledge | + | + | - | + | - | + | - | - | - | + | - | - | - |
| Rapid naming: letters | + | + | - | + | - | + | - | - | - | - | - | - | - |
| Letter sounds | + | + | * | + | + | + | + | + | + | + | + | + | + |
| Sight words | + | - | - | - | - | + | - | - | + | + | + | - | + |
| Onset and rime | + | + | + | + | + | * | + | + | + | + | + | + | + |
| Syllabication | + | + | - | + | - | - | + | * | + | + | + | - | + |
| Structural analysis | + | * | * | + | * | - | - | - | + | + | + | * | + |
| "C" rule | + | + | * | + | * | - | - | - | + | + | + | + | + |
| "G" rule | + | + | * | + | * | - | - | - | + | + | + | + | + |
| CVC generalization | + | + | + | + | - | - | - | - | + | + | + | - | + |
| Vowel digraphs | + | + | + | + | - | - | - | - | + | + | + | - | + |
| VCE pattern | + | + | + | + | - | - | - | - | + | + | + | - | + |
| CV pattern | + | + | + | + | - | - | - | - | + | + | + | - | + |
| R-controlled vowels | + | + | + | + | - | - | - | - | + | + | + | - | + |
| Consonant digraphs | + | + | * | + | - | + | - | - | + | + | + | * | + |
| Consonant blends | + | + | * | + | - | + | - | - | + | + | + | * | + |
| Double consonants | + | + | * | + | - | * | - | - | + | + | + | * | + |

Key: + Excellent strategy
* Adaptable strategy
– Unsuitable strategy

6. *When practicing a new phonics skill, use easy reading materials.* Many times, the very best way to introduce new phonics skills is through the use of great books, poems, songs, chants, or raps. Be sure that reading materials are predominantly at students' independent reading level with the "target" words (i.e., words unknown to the students in print that you will use to introduce a new phonics skill) woven into the text. That way, students can use what they already know, as well as some context information, to aid them in practicing the new skill.

7. *Help kids become "wordsmiths."* We have noticed that great readers and writers are also word watchers; they seem to always notice new and interesting words in their text encounters. We must do whatever we can each day to model this attitude of fascination with words and how they are put together. This makes word study far more interesting to students—"A spoonful of sugar helps the medicine go down."

8. *Adjust the pace of instruction to meet the individual needs of students.* This can only be done consistently in small-group instruction in which students come together based on a common need to know.

9. *Link phonics instruction to spelling.* Enough said on this one!

10. *Make clear what you want kids to do.* Be sure to say in clear terms (i.e., the words of a 7-year-old instead of college-level jargon) what the skill is, why it is worth knowing, and what you will expect students to do as a result of this lesson.

### What Not to Do

1. *Avoid round-robin teaching.* Do not have kids waiting continually for their turn. Small-group instruction usually makes this problem go away.

2. *Try not to direct students too quickly.* Let kids have an opportunity to self-correct before intervening.

3. *Avoid drill-and-kill teaching.* There is no question that phonics knowledge is important. However, we need to avoid militaristic teaching that drums information into young readers' heads at the cost of killing their interest in reading. Some things must be learned by rote, but be sure to include ample practice in rich and interesting texts.

In this section, we recommend several activities that may be useful for many of the phonics skills enumerated earlier. Therefore, please note that if we recommend an activity that is useful in teaching, say, consonant sounds, it may be just as useful in teaching consonant digraphs, rimes, or vowel generalizations.

## A Format for Explicit Phonics Instruction

### Purpose

Glazer (1998) has developed a step-by-step procedure for teaching phonics skills. Try it as one way to provide explicit instruction for your students.

### Materials

- Tongue twisters, riddles, jokes, songs, poems, or stories specially selected for the phonics pattern you wish to teach

### Procedure

- *Bombard students with correct models.* New phonics knowledge is heavily dependent on students having already internalized in their listening and speaking vocabularies correct pronunciations and usages of thousands of words. After deciding which phonics element you wish to teach, select reading materials that use the element. Read, retell, and organize simple plays or raps involving students, or use other means to build in many encounters with the words you want to emphasize. As you use the target words in your readings or retellings, write the words on your easel chart paper or highlight them when using a big book. Say, "Read these words with me as I say them." Then ask, "What is the same about these words we just read?" to guide them to the phonics element you want to emphasize. Always provide the correct answer if the students are in doubt.

- *Provide structured practice.* With students gathered in a small group, write the letter(s) being emphasized at the top of your easel chart. If, for instance, we are emphasizing the consonant digraph *ch,* the following words can be written and said aloud slowly by the teacher: *cheese, church, cherry.* Then students are encouraged to contribute others having that same beginning sound (perhaps *chain, change, charm, child*).

- *Assess learning using a phonics game.* The object of this game is to assess student learning by matching the letter or letter combination being emphasized with pictures representing words beginning with that sound.

  - Cut a sheet of tagboard into several pieces about flash card size.
  - Create cards for each student showing the letter or sound being studied.
  - Collect several pictures of objects or creatures from magazines whose names begin with that letter or sound.
  - Place students into pairs. Then demonstrate to students how to cut and paste pictures from magazines onto the tagboard cards showing the beginning sound you are emphasizing. Repeat the exercise, except this time students are doing the task with you in their groups of two (i.e., finding pictures of objects or creatures whose names begin with the specified sound).
  - Check the products from each group with the students. Ask them to name the picture that begins with that sound.

- *Sharing what they have learned.* Children love to share (and brag about) their accomplishments. Help them create word banks, pocket dictionaries, or word charts showing off how many words they can find containing the phonics element you have been studying together. These may include the names of animals, foods, toys, friends, family members, or objects from their environment having the target letter–sound combination. Have students share their accomplishments in small groups or with the whole class in a kind of author's chair format. They will love showing off their new knowledge!

## Letter–Sound Cards

### Purpose

Letter–sound cards are intended as prompts to help students remember individual and combination (i.e., digraphs and blends) letter sounds that have been introduced during minilessons or other teachable moments.

### Materials

- A word bank for each child (children's shoe boxes, recipe boxes, or other small containers in which index cards can be filed)
- Alphabetic divider cards to separate words in the word bank
- Index cards
- Colored markers

### Procedure

This is essentially the same idea as the word bank activity shown in Chapter 8 on vocabulary instruction. The idea is to provide students with their own word cards on which you (or they) have written a key letter sound or sounds on one side and a word that uses that sound on the other. Whenever possible, it is best to use nouns or other words that can be depicted with a picture, so that, for emergent readers, a drawing can be added to the side having the word (as needed). Two examples are shown in Figure 6.14.

## Phonics Fish (or Foniks Phish?) Card Game

### Purpose

Remember the age-old children's card game Fish (sometimes called "Go Fish")? This review activity helps students use their growing visual awareness of phonics sounds and patterns to construct word families (i.e., groups of words having the same phonetic pattern). It can be played in small groups, at a learning center with two to four children, or during reading groups with the teacher.

### Materials

- A deck of word cards with words selected either from the students' word banks or chosen by the teacher or parent/teaching assistant from among those familiar to all students; the word cards should contain ample examples of at least three or four phonetic patterns that you wish to review (e.g., beginning consonant sounds, *r*-controlled vowels, clusters, digraphs, rime families, etc.)

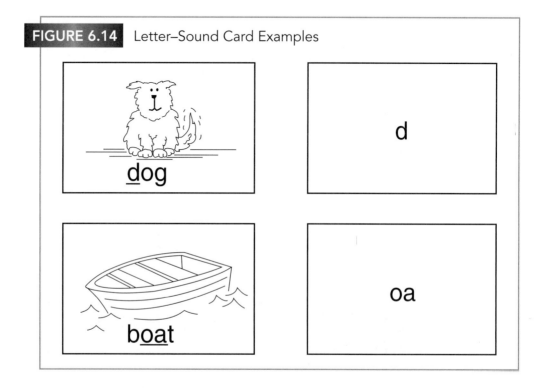

**FIGURE 6.14**    Letter–Sound Card Examples

**Procedure**

Before beginning the game, explain which word families or sound patterns are to be used in this game of "Phonics Fish." Next, explain the rules of the game:

1. Each child will be dealt five cards.
2. The remaining cards (deck of about 50) are placed face down in the middle of the group.
3. Taking turns in a round-robin fashion, each child can ask any other if he or she is holding a word having a particular sound or pattern. For example, if one of the patterns included is the /sh/ sound, then the first student may say something like, "Juanita, do you have any words with the /sh/ sound?" If Juanita does not have any word cards with that pattern, she says "Go Fish!" The student asking the question then draws a card from the deck.
4. Cards having matching patterns (two or more) are placed face up in front of the student asking the question.
5. The first student to get rid of all his or her cards wins the game.

## Spelling in Parts (SIP)

The **spelling in parts (SIP)** strategy (Powell & Aram, 2008) gives learners an opportunity to discover new spelling patterns and also allows readers who may be intimidated by large words to break them down into small chunks. This strategy can be helpful in improving both spelling and reading skills through the teaching of onset and rime, as well as vowel patterns, such as VCE (vowel-consonant-e), CVC (closed-syllable) words, or CV (open-syllable) words. This would be a great word wall activity, but can also be used with sight words, free reading books, and core subject area materials in science, social studies, mathematics, and English/ language arts. The procedure we describe are the steps recommended by Powell and Aram (2008).

### Materials

- Ordinary writing materials

### Procedure

The teacher models examples first and provides other demonstrations as required. The children do the following:

1. Say and clap the word in syllables.
2. Divide the word into syllables while pronouncing each syllable. (The teacher may check that it is a reasonable division without teaching the explicit syllabication rule(s). For example, the division for the word *bucket* is *buck-et; buc-ket* would be acceptable for this exercise, but *bu-cket* would not be.)
3. Say a syllable and then spell it. (The teacher checks that students are saying each phoneme within the syllable as they have written it.)
4. Circle any syllable with an unusual [irregular] or difficult pattern.
5. Study the circled syllable and think of a mnemonic or analogy to recall the spelling pattern (e.g., the mnemonic "to-get-her" might be used for *together* even though it requires the child to divide the word in an unconventional way).
6. Cover the syllable and then write it.
7. Check the syllable spelling and repeat as necessary.

## Sound Swirl

### Purpose

Sound Swirl is a simple activity that is used (a) to help students think of "words in their head" that have a certain sound element and (b) then to use invented or "temporary" spellings to construct the words they have recalled. This helps students learn to sound out words and to notice particular word sounds as their phonics awareness grows. This activity is usually best applied as a guided practice exercise or for review.

### Materials

- Chart paper
- Markers in different colors

### Procedure

Gather a group of children around you with whom you wish to review a phonics sound pattern (for our example here, we will use the beginning sound represented by /ch/ as in *church*). Write the letters representing the sound you wish to emphasize (*ch* in our example) on the chart paper using a colorful marker. Say, "Boys and girls, I want us to see just how many words we can think of that begin with the sound made by the letters *ch,* which make the /ch/ sound. So get your mouth ready to make the /ch/ sound, swirl around all the letters in your head (making a grand gesture of a swirling motion above his or her head), and say the first words that come to your mind, right now!" At this point, the students will call out such words as *church, chump, change, child, chirp,* and so on. Select a few of the words they have called out and, in whole-group fashion (using volunteers), have them sound out the written words (as you write them, each time with *ch* in a different color from the rest of the word) so they can recognize visually how words can be sounded out and written.

## "Button" Sounds

### Purpose

Children often enjoy wearing buttons that are unique. Similarly, many schools have button-making machines that can inexpensively produce buttons for special projects (inexpensive button labels can also be produced on a personal computer). "Button sounds," as we call them, take advantage of children's attraction to buttons to help cement their understanding of introductory sounds in words. (*Note:* This is recommended only as an adjunct to other more comprehensive minilessons.)

### Materials

- A button-making machine and materials (or a local vendor who can make the buttons for you inexpensively)

### Procedure

Identify the phonics sounds or symbols you wish to emphasize. For example, we first used this activity with first-grade students to help them learn alphabet letters as initial sounds in words (e.g., *Bb* together with a picture of a butterfly, *Cc* with a picture of a cat, *Gg* with a picture of a goat, etc.). However, any sound or symbol relationship can be used that can be illustrated with a picture. Once you have introduced the "sound for the day" and linked it to a key illustration (e.g., a witch for the letters *Ww* or a ship for the digraph *sh*), distribute the buttons to all students in the group or class. You should instruct the children that whenever they are asked by anyone about their button, they should respond with a statement such as "This is my *sh* and *ship* button." An example of a button is shown in Figure 6.15.

## Stomping, Clapping, Tapping, and Snapping Sounds

### Purposes

Helping children hear syllables in words enables them to segment sounds. This knowledge can be used in myriad ways to improve writing and spelling, increase awareness of letter combinations used to produce speech sounds, and apply knowledge of onsets and rimes. All these skills and more enable students to sound out words in print more effectively. For ages, teachers have found success in helping children hear syllables by clapping them out when reading nursery rhymes, such as "Mar-y had a lit-tle lamb, lit-tle lamb, lit-tle lamb . . . "

### Materials

- Rhyming poetry, songs, chants, or raps
- A document camera/projector (e.g., Elmo)
- An overhead projector for showing enlarged text
- A big book version, or simply text rewritten on large chart paper using a colored ink marker

### Procedure

First, model reading the enlarged text aloud in a normal cadence for your students. Then re-read the selection at a normal cadence, inviting students to join in as they wish. Next, explain

**FIGURE 6.15** Button from "Button Sounds" Activity

wh

wheelchair

that you will reread the selection but that this time you will clap (or snap, or stomp, etc.) the syllables in the words. (*Note:* If you have not already explained the concept of syllables, you will need to do so at this point.) Finally, invite students to clap (or make whatever gesture or sound that you have chosen), as you reread the passage.

## Tongue Twisters

### Purpose

Many students enjoy word play. Tongue twisters can be a wonderful way of reviewing consonants (Cunningham, 1995) in a way that is fun for students. We have found that tongue twister activities can combine reading and creative writing processes to help children deepen their understanding of phonics elements. All you need to do is decide which sounds or letter pattern families are to be used.

### Materials

- Traditional tongue twisters from published children's literature or student-created examples (which children enjoy perhaps even more)
- Chart paper and markers

### Procedure

Cunningham (1995) suggests that you begin by simply reciting some tongue twisters aloud and inviting students to join in. We recommend that you produce two or three examples on chart paper and post them on the wall as you introduce the concept of tongue twisters. For example, you may use the following:

> Silly Sally sat in strawberries.
>
> Peter Piper picked a peck of pickled peppers.
> If Peter Piper picked a peck of pickled peppers,
> Then how many peppers did Peter Piper pick?
>
> Peter Piper panhandles pepperoni pizza,
> With his pint-sized pick-up he packs a peck of pepperoni pizzas,
> For Patti his portly patron.
>
> Simple Simon met a pieman going to the fair,
> Said Simple Simon to the pieman,
> "Let me taste your wares!"
> Said the pieman to Simple Simon,
> "Show me first your penny!"
> Said Simple Simon to the pieman,
> "I'm afraid I haven't any."

Children especially love it when teachers create tongue twisters using names of children in the class, such as the following example:

> Pretty Pam picked pink peonies for Patty's party.

Last, challenge students to create their own tongue twisters to "stump the class." It may be fun to award students coupons that can be used to purchase take-home books for coming up with clever tongue twisters.

## Creating Nonsense Words

### Purpose

Many of the most popular children's poets, such as Shel Silverstein and Jack Prelutsky, have tapped into children's fascination with word play in their very creative poetry. For instance, when Silverstein (1974) speaks of "gloppy glumps of cold oatmeal," we all understand what he means, even though *glumps* is really a nonsense word. Getting students to create nonsense words and apply them to popular poetry is a motivating way to help students practice phonics patterns.

### Materials

- Books of poetry or songs with rhyming phrases
- Chart paper or overhead transparencies
- Markers

### Procedure

First decide which phonics sound or letter pattern families you wish to emphasize. For instance, it may be appropriate to review the letter or sound families represented by *-ack, -ide, -ing,* and *-ore.* As with all activities, begin by modeling what you expect students to do. On a large sheet of chart paper or at the overhead projector, write the word family parts that you wish to emphasize (for this example, *-ack, -ide, -ing,* and *-ore*). Illustrate how you can convert the word parts into nonsense words by adding a consonant, consonant blend, or consonant digraph before each one, such as shown by the following:

| **-ack** | **-ide** | **-ing** | **-ore** |
|---|---|---|---|
| gack | spide | gacking | zore |
| clack | mide | zwing | glore |
| chack | plide | kaching | jore |

In the next phase of the demonstration, select a poem or song that rhymes and review it with students (use enlarged text for all of your modeling). Next, show students a revised copy of the song or poem in which you have substituted nonsense words, as in the following example we have used with the song "I Know an Old Lady Who Swallowed a Fly."* We show only the first verse here, but you could use the entire song, substituting a nonsense word in each stanza. Compare the original version on the left with the nonsense word version on the right.

| | |
|---|---|
| I know an old lady who swallowed a fly, | I know an old lady who swallowed a *bly*, |
| I don't know why, | I don't know why, |
| she swallowed the fly, | she swallowed the *bly*, |
| Perhaps she'll die. | Perhaps she'll die. |

## Making Words

Cunningham and Cunningham (1992) describe making words as a hands-on manipulative activity in which students look for patterns in words. Students also learn how new words can be created by simply changing one letter or letter combination. Making words can be useful for either vocabulary building or for developing phonetic understanding. For a complete explanation of making words, please see the discussion of this activity in Chapter 8.

*"I Know an Old Lady Who Swallowed a Fly" by Rose Bonne and Alan Mills © 1952 by Peer International LTD. Reprinted with permission.

## Wide Reading

John J. Pikulski (1998), a recent president of the International Reading Association, has noted the importance of massive amounts of reading in high-quality texts as a tool for developing decoding fluency. Specifically, he points out that children can benefit from three main types of practice: wide reading, independent-level reading, and multiple rereadings of texts.

**Wide reading** simply refers to the notion of encouraging children to read about a variety of topics in different genres. Teachers can encourage wide reading by regularly conducting "book talks," in which the teacher reads aloud a particularly interesting portion of a great book or other text form but leaves the students "hanging" at a particularly suspenseful point in the narrative. This often makes students mad with desire to finish reading the selection!

**Independent-level reading** refers to helping children find many and varied books of interest that are easy for them to read. In this case, "easy" reading refers to books in which students will be able to read about 98% or more of the words without difficulty. In addition to improving phonics fluency, research shows that independent-level reading for at least 20 minutes each day also greatly improves reading rate.

**Multiple rereadings of texts** means just what the words imply—rereading favorite books, poems, or other text forms. Multiple rereadings will essentially provide the same benefits as independent-level reading. To make wide reading, independent-level reading, and multiple rereadings happen every day, we recommend that you institute *DEAR* time (*Drop Everything And Read*) in your classroom. For about 20 to 30 minutes each day, have students stop at a designated time and read a book of their choosing. DEAR can be broken into two shorter time segments just as effectively, if you wish. The teacher may participate and read a book for fun or work with a small group of struggling readers rereading familiar texts in choral fashion. You will love the results.

## Word Boxes

### Purpose

**Word boxes** (Clay, 1993) are "designed to help children make letter–sound correspondences and note letter–sound sequence patterns in words" (Devault & Joseph, 2004, p. 22). On a drawn rectangle divided into sections according to the number of sounds in a word, magnetic or tile letters are placed below the divided boxes, and the children slide the letters into the respective sections of the rectangle as each sound is articulated. This technique has been found to be effective for helping first graders and elementary children with disabilities achieve phonemic awareness, word identification, and spelling skills, as well as for high school students with severe reading difficulties.

### Materials

- Word boxes like the one shown in Figure 6.16 for each focus word
- Magnetic letters, letter tiles from a Scrabble game, or laminated cutout letters
- Large teacher's word box with pockets or clips to attach index cards
- Index cards with printed letters for teacher's word box

### Procedure

Repeated readings coupled with word boxes can be practiced with your students, depending on age and attention span, for 5 to 10 minutes for approximately 5 days per week. Begin (in small groups of four or so) with a modeling exercise involving a read aloud of a favorite book at the group's instructional (i.e., zone of proximal development) reading level. Using a preselected target word displayed below a large word box with letters on index cards, say the sound represented by each letter while sliding it into place in its section of the word box.

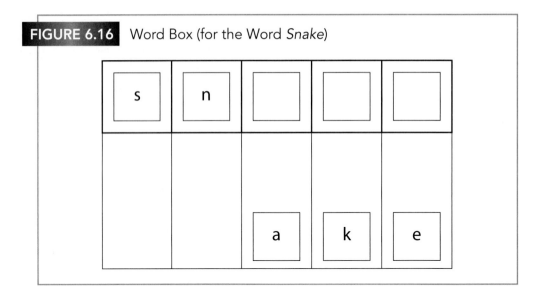

**FIGURE 6.16**   Word Box (for the Word *Snake*)

After modeling this activity to the point of overlearning for students, have students begin trying it themselves, providing feedback and correction as needed. At the completion of each word box lesson, present the same passage and provide students with appropriate time to read it orally. During the following session, a different passage should be presented using the same procedures as previously described.

## Word Detectives

### Purpose

Word detectives (Gaskins, 2004) is an approach to phonics awareness that asks students to segment words in print into sounds, compare sounds to the letters they see, and decide which letter or letters match each sound. The job of a "word detective" is to discover letter–sound matches.

### Materials

- One or more books on the student's instructional level
- Paper or small whiteboard
- Pencil or markers

### Procedure

We believe strongly in lessons that proceed from whole text to text elements (words) to reapplication of the new skill in a new text. We also believe that direct instruction should progress from teacher modeling to guided practice with teacher input as needed, then to independent practice, and finally to conclusion with reapplication of the new knowledge in other texts. Thus, you should begin with a read aloud from an interesting book on the student's instructional level and then repeatedly model word detective examples drawn from the text just read. In modeling begin by choosing a word from the text you wish to target for learning. Instruct your students to use "word rubber banding" to stretch the word and then model this step for them holding up a finger for each sound you say. Ask students to repeat the word rubber-banding technique in unison with the target word while holding up a finger for each sound they hear as it is spoken. Next, using a word box and letter cards (as described in the previous activity), ask students to tell you which letter should go in each box to represent the sounds of the target word. In this way, you can help students proceed from decoding letter–sound relationships to blending these same sounds to again create whole words as well as focus on unusual spellings. This procedure has been shown to be very effective in a longitudinal study by Gaskins (2004).

### A PHONICS QUICK TEST (ANSWER KEY)

1. The word *charkle* is divided between *r* and *k*. The *a* has an *r-* controlled sound, and the *e* is *silent*.
2. In the word *small, sm-* is known as the *onset* and *-all* is known as the *rime*.
3. *Ch* in the word *chair* is known as a *consonant digraph*.
4. The letter *c* in the word *city* has a *soft* sound; in the word *cow,* the letter *c* has a *hard* sound.
5. The letters *bl* in the word *blue* are referred to as a consonant *blend*.
6. The underlined vowels in the words <u>au</u>thor, spr<u>ea</u>d, and bl<u>ue</u> are known as vowel digraphs.
7. The words *tag, run, cot,* and *get* have which vowel pattern? *consonant-vowel-consonant (CVC)*
8. The words *glide, take,* and *use* have the *vowel-consonant-e* vowel pattern.
9. The single most powerful phonics skill we can teach to emergent readers for decoding unfamiliar words in print is *beginning* sounds in words. We introduce this skill using *consonant* sounds first because they are the most *constant* (or "dependable" or "reliable").
10. The word part *work* in the word *working* is known as a *root* (or "base" or "unbound morpheme") word.
11. The word part *-ing* in the word *working* is known as a *suffix* (or "bound morpheme").
12. Cues to the meaning and pronunciation of unfamiliar words in print are often found in the print surrounding the unfamiliar, also known as *context.*

### GRADING KEY FOR TEACHERS

| Number Correct | Evaluation |
| --- | --- |
| 12 | Wow, you're good! (You must have had no social life in college.) |
| 10–11 | Not too bad, but you may need a brush-up. (Read this chapter.) |
| 7–9 | Emergency! Take a refresher course, quick! (Read this chapter.) |
| 0–6 | Have you ever considered a career in telemarketing?! (Just kidding, but read this chapter . . . right away!) |

## SELECTED REFERENCES

Adams, M. J. (1990). *Beginning to read: Thinking and learning about print.* Cambridge, MA: MIT Press.

Armbruster, B. B., & Osborn, J. (2001). *Put reading first: The research building blocks for teaching children to read.* Washington, DC: National Institute for Literacy. Available free online at www.nifl.gov.

August, D., & Shanahan, T. (2006). *Developing literacy in second-language learners: Report of the National Literacy Panel on language-minority children and youth.* Mahwah, NJ: Lawrence Erlbaum.

Bear, D. R., Templeton, S., Invernizzi, M., & Johnston, F. (1996). *Words their way: Word study for phonics, vocabulary, and spelling instruction.* Columbus, OH: Merrill/Prentice Hall.

Blevins, W. (1996). *Phonics: Quick-and-easy learning games.* New York: Scholastic Professional Books.

Blevins, W. (1997). *Phonemic awareness activities for early reading success.* New York: Scholastic Professional Books.

Blevins, W. (1998). *Phonics from A to Z: A practical guide.* New York: Scholastic Professional Books.

Carnine, D. W., Silbert, J., Kameenui, E. J., Tarver, S. G., & Jongjohann, K. (2006). *Teaching struggling and at-risk readers: A direct instruction approach.* Upper Saddle River, NJ: Prentice Hall.

Chard, D. J., & Osborn, J. (1999). Phonics and word recognition instruction in early reading programs: Guidelines for accessibility. *Learning Disabilities Research & Practice, 14*(2), 107–125.

Clay, M. M. (1993). *An observation survey for early literacy achievement.* Portsmouth, NH: Heinemann Educational Books.

Cooter, K. S. (2001, November). *Teaching phonics skills to urban student populations.* Unpublished manuscript, Texas Christian University, Fort Worth, TX.

Cooter, R. B., Flynt, E. S., & Cooter, K. S. (2007). *The comprehensive reading inventory.* Upper Saddle River, NJ: Prentice Hall.

Cunningham, P. (1990). The Names Test: A quick assessment of decoding ability. *The Reading Teacher, 44,* 124–129.

Cunningham, P. M. (1995). *Phonics they use* (2nd ed.). New York: HarperCollins.

Cunningham, P. M., & Cunningham, J. W. (1992). Making words: Enhancing the invented spelling-decoding connection. *The Reading Teacher, 46,* 106–107.

Devault, R., & Joseph, L. M. (2004). Repeated readings combined with word boxes phonics technique increases fluency levels of high school students with severe reading delays. *Preventing School Failure, 49*(1), 22–27.

Duffelmeyer, F. A., Kruse, A. E., Merkley, D. J., & Fyfe, S. A. (1994). Further validation and enhancement of the names test. *The Reading Teacher, 48,* 118–128.

Eldredge, J. L. (1995). *Teaching decoding in holistic classrooms.* Columbus, OH: Merrill/Prentice Hall.

Flynt, E. S., & Cooter, R. B. (2003). *The Spanish & English reading inventory for the classroom* (2nd ed.). Upper Saddle River, NJ: Merrill/Prentice Hall.

Gaskins, I. W. (2004). Word detectives. *Educational Leadership, 61*(6), 70–73.

Glazer, S. M. (1998). A format for explicit phonics instruction. *Teaching PreK–8, 28*(4), 102–105.

Honig, B., Diamond, L., & Gutlohn, L. (2000). *Teaching reading: Sourcebook for kindergarten through eighth grade.* Novato, CA: Arena Press.

Hull, M. A. (1989). *Phonics for the teacher of reading.* Upper Saddle River, NJ: Merrill/Prentice Hall.

Kozol, J. (2005). *The shame of the nation: The restoration of apartheid schooling in America.* New York: Crown.

Lonigan, C. J., Schatschneider, C., & Westberg, L. (2008). Identification of children's skills and abilities linked to later outcomes in reading, writing, and spelling. In *Developing early literacy: Report of the National Early Literacy Panel.* Jessup, MD: National Institute for Literacy.

Manzo, A. V., & Manzo, U. C. (1993). *Literacy disorders: Holistic diagnosis and remediation.* Fort Worth, TX: Harcourt Brace Jovanovich College Publishers.

Mather, N., Sammons, J., & Schwartz, J. (2006). Adaptations of the names test: Easy-to-use phonics assessments. *The Reading Teacher, 60*(2), 114–122.

McKee, D. (1968). *Elmer.* New York: McGraw-Hill.

Moustafa, M. (1997). *Beyond traditional phonics: Research discoveries and reading instruction.* Portsmouth, NH: Heinemann Educational Books.

Murray, B. A., Brabham, E. G., Villaume, S. K., & Veal, M. (2008). The Cluella study: Optimal segmentation and voicing for oral blending. *Journal of Literacy Research, 4*(4), 395–421.

National Institute for Literacy. (2008). *Developing early literacy: Report of the National Early Literacy Panel.* Jessup, MD: Author.

National Institute of Child Health and Human Development. (2000). *Report of the National Reading Panel: Teaching children to read* (NIH Pub. No. 00-4769). Washington, DC: U.S. Government Printing Office.

National Research Council. (1999). *Starting out right: A guide for promoting children's reading success.* Washington, DC: National Academy Press.

Pikulski, J. J. (1998, February). *Improving reading achievement: Major instructional considerations for the primary grades.* Commissioner's Reading Day Statewide Conference, Austin, TX.

Powell, D. A., & Aram, R. (2008). Spelling in parts: A strategy for spelling and decoding polysyllabic words. *The Reading Teacher, 61*(7), 567–570.

Pressley, M. (1998). *Reading instruction that works: The case for balanced teaching.* New York: Guilford Press.

Rasinski, T., & Padak, N. (1996). *Holistic reading strategies: Teaching children who find reading difficult.* Columbus, OH: Merrill/Prentice Hall.

Reutzel, D. R., & Cooter, R. B. (2008). *The essentials of teaching children to read,* (2nd ed.). Upper Saddle River, NJ: Merrill/Prentice Hall.

Silverstein, S. (1974). *Where the sidewalk ends.* New York: HarperCollins.

Stahl, S. (1992). Saying the "p" word: Nine guidelines for exemplary phonics instruction. *The Reading Teacher, 45*(8), 618–625.

Williams, S. G., Cooter, K. S., & Cooter, R. B. (2003). *The Starpoint Phonics Quick Test.* Unpublished manuscript.

**The Power of Classroom Practice**
www.myeducationlab.com

Now go to Topic 5: "Phonemic Awareness and Phonics," Topic 8: "Word Recognition," and Topic 14: "English Language Learners" in the MyEducationLab (www.myeducationlab.com) for your course, where you can:

- Find learning outcomes for "Phonemic Awareness and Phonics," "Word Recognition," and "English Language Learners," along with the national standards that connect to these outcomes.
- Complete the tasks in the Assignments and Activities to help you more deeply understand the chapter content.
- Examine challenging situations and cases presented in the IRIS Center Resources.
- Access video clips of CCSSO National Teachers of the Year award winners responding to the question, "Why Do I Teach?" in the Teacher Talk section.
- Apply and practice your understanding of the core teaching skills identified in the chapter with the Building Teaching Skills and Dispositions learning units.

# 7

# Reading Fluency

Mikhal, a third grader, walked reluctantly toward the chair placed next to his teacher, Mrs. Smith. He carried a tattered copy of his favorite book. He had practiced reading several pages in preparation for his regularly scheduled individual reading conference.

"Mikhal, I'm so glad I get to spend some time today listening to you read. Are you ready?" queried Mrs. Smith.

"Yah, I think so," answered Mikhal.

"So, what story are you going to read for me today?"

"I have a book called *The Boy Who Owned the School* I'd like to share," answered Mikhal.

"Great! I have your audiocassette tape here. I need to load it into the recorder, and then we can begin," remarked Mrs. Smith. "OK, I'm ready for you to read now, Mikhal. Where are you going to start reading?"

"I'm going to start on page 7, Chapter 2. It's called 'The Joys of Home Life.'"

"OK then, start when you are ready."

Mrs. Smith pushed the record button on the cassette tape recorder. Mikhal began reading. "His father was a mechanical engineer who designed or invented a new drill bit for oil drilling, a self-cleaning, self-sharpening bit."

When Mikhal finished his reading, Mrs. Smith praised him on how well he had done. "Mikhal, you are reading very fluently. You sound just like you are speaking!"

Mikhal beamed with pride. "Thanks," he said quietly.

"Can you tell me what you remember from the pages you read?"

"I think so," responded Mikhal.

Mrs. Smith turned the recorder back on. When Mikhal finished, Mrs. Smith praised him again and then asked, "Would you like to hear what you said and add anything to it?"

"Uh-huh."

Mrs. Smith played the tape for Mikhal, and he added one more detail he had remembered as he listened to his oral retelling of his own reading.

That afternoon, Mrs. Smith looked at the record she had made from Mikhal's earlier oral reading. He had read the text with 97% accuracy, so she knew that decoding this text was not a problem for Mikhal. Next, she timed his reading and figured out Mikhal's reading rate in words read correctly per minute and compared this against a chart showing expected reading rate ranges by grade level. Mikhal was on the upper end of the range for his grade level. Next, Mrs. Smith listened to Mikhal's reading tape recording again, noting any problems with expression, pacing, smoothness, and phrasing. Again, Mikhal had performed well. Finally, Mrs. Smith listened to Mikhal's oral retelling of the pages he had read aloud. He had remembered the major ideas and a good number of the details, evidencing his comprehension of the text. There was no doubt in Mrs. Smith's mind; Mikhal was progressing well toward the goal of becoming a fluent reader!

# BACKGROUND BRIEFING FOR TEACHERS

In recent decades **reading fluency,** the ability to read aloud smoothly at a reasonable rate and with expression, has been acknowledged as an important goal in becoming a proficient and strategic reader (Allington, 1983, 1984, 2001; Blevins, 2001; Dowhower, 1991; Klenk & Kibby, 2000; National Institute of Child Health and Human Development, 2000; Optiz & Rasinski, 1998; Osborn, Lehr, & Hiebert, 2002; Pikulski & Chard, 2005; Prescott-Griffin & Witherell, 2004; Rasinski, 2000, 2003; Rasinski, Blachowicz, & Lems, 2006; Rasinski & Padak, 1996; Reutzel, 1996; Reutzel & Cooter, 2004; Reutzel, Hollingsworth, & Eldredge, 1994; Stahl, 2004). Prior to the 1980s, however, there had been a gradual shift in emphasis away from proficient oral reading. Beginning in the early 1900s there developed a trend toward silent reading for private and personal purposes and the goal of developing fluent oral readers all but disappeared from the reading curriculum (Kameenui & Simmons, 2001; Rasinski, 2003; Reutzel et al., 1994). This was so much the case that it prompted Allington (1983, 1984) to declare reading fluency to be a neglected goal of reading instruction. However, a visit to many elementary school classrooms today would reveal that fluency development has become an integral part of contemporary reading instruction and assessment.

How can teachers assess and assist all students in becoming fluent readers? First, they must understand *how* children develop fluency in reading. Second, they must be able to assess fluency to determine which aspects of fluent reading require instruction and practice. Finally, teachers should know about successful and proven ways to provide fluency instruction and practice so that all children develop fluent reading behaviors. This chapter is intended to boost teacher knowledge in the area of reading fluency, share fluency assessment strategies, and connect assessment results to selected teaching and practice interventions that help all students develop fluent reading.

# WHAT IS FLUENCY?

What is fluent reading? Although teachers and reading researchers have yet to agree on every minor element of reading fluency, significant consensus has been achieved in recent years

Go to the Assignments and Activities section of Topic 7: "Fluency" in the MyEducationLab for your course and complete the activity entitled "Definition of Fluency." As you watch the video and answer the accompanying questions, note the three major elements of fluent reading and be able to explain why fluency is considered a bridge in the middle of the five essential elements of reading.

as to the major components of reading fluency (Allington, 2001; Deeney, in press; National Institute of Child Health and Human Development, 2000; Pikulski & Chard, 2005; Richards, 2000). Typically, fluency is described as (a) accuracy and ease of decoding *(automaticity)*; (b) an age- or grade-level appropriate reading speed or *rate;* (c) appropriate use of volume, pitch, juncture, and stress *(prosody)* in one's voice; and (d) appropriate text phrasing or *chunking*. Thus, a fluent reader can decode words smoothly at an appropriate speed and do so with appropriate voice intonation. Figure 7.1 shows a flowchart (Cooter, 2005) used currently in one large urban school district to describe reading fluency and its connection to improved comprehension.

In 1995, Harris and Hodges characterized reading fluency as reading smoothly, without hesitation, and with good comprehension. More recently, others (Kuhn and Stahl, 2004; Paige, 2008; Rasinski, 1989; Reutzel & Hollingsworth, 1993; Samuels, 2007) have also underscored the point that comprehension is an important result of good reading fluency. It is indeed hard to imagine that one would regard a reader as fluent if he or she didn't simultaneously understand what had been read! On the other hand, Paris (Paris, Carpenter, Paris, &

---

**FIGURE 7.1**   Reading Fluency Flow Chart

**Automaticity**

Automaticity is a quick and accurate level of word recognition with little conscious attention.

↓

**Fluency**

Fluency is the flow of a reader's delivery in an oral reading. It involves a combination of rate, accuracy, and prosody.

↓

**Prosody**

Prosody includes expression, appropriate phrasing, and attention to punctuation.

- The teacher accurately adjusts the tone, inflection, speed, and fluency to match the intended message of a passage.
- The reader reads aloud with appropriate pauses, stops, and starts.
- The rate and speed are well-coordinated and enable the oral reading to sound natural.

↓

**Comprehension**

Fluent readers are able to focus attention on understanding the text.

Hamilton, 2005) has questioned whether fluency, or the lack thereof, can predict how well students will comprehend what they read. He has shown that in some cases the relationship between fluency and comprehension decreases over time as children develop reading skill.

How do readers achieve oral reading fluency? This is a popular subject of contemporary research (Jenkins, Fuchs, Van den Broek, Espin, & Deno, 2003; Kameenui & Simons, 2001; Kuhn & Schwanenflugel, 2008; National Institute of Child Health and Human Development, 2000; Paige, 2008; Rasinski, Blachowicz, & Lems, 2006; Samuels & Farstrup, 2006; Snow, Burns, & Griffin, 1998; Stahl, 2004; Wolf & Katzir-Cohen, 2001). We offer seven insights into how readers develop fluent oral reading over time with teacher instruction and support, as well as abundant amounts of reading practice.

1. *Modeling.* Exposure to rich and varied models of fluent oral reading helps *some* children. For other students, modeling of nonfluent oral reading seems to alert attention to the specific characteristics of fluent reading that are sometimes transparent or taken for granted when teachers only model fluent oral reading. In other words, some students need to know what fluency *is* and is *not* to achieve clarity on the concept of fluency and its attendant characteristics (Reutzel, 2006). In this case, parents, teachers, or siblings spend significant amounts of time reading aloud to children while modeling fluent oral reading. Through this process of modeling fluent (and sometimes nonfluent) oral reading, children learn the behaviors of fluent readers as well as the elements of fluent oral reading. Many researchers have documented the significant impact of modeling on the attainment of fluent reading (Kuhn & Schwanenflugel, 2008; Rasinski, 2003; Rasinski, Padak, McKeon, Wilfong, Friedauer, & Heim, 2005; Reutzel, 2006; Stahl, 2004).

2. *Quality of instruction.* For fluency instruction to be effective and of high quality, elementary students need explicit instruction about what constitutes fluent reading and how to self-regulate and improve their own fluency (Pressley, Gaskins, & Fingeret, 2006; Rasinski, Blachowicz, & Lems, 2006; Reutzel, 2006; Worthy & Broaddus, 2002).

3. *Reading practice.* Good readers are given more opportunities to read connected text and for longer periods of time than are students having reading problems. This dilemma led Allington (1977) to muse, "If they don't read much, how they ever gonna get good?" The National Reading Panel (Allington, 2006, 2007; Altwerger, Jordan, & Shelton, 2007; National Institute of Child Health and Human Development, 2000) has emphasized the need for children to experience regular, daily reading practice.

4. *Access to appropriately challenging reading materials.* Proficient readers spend more time reading appropriately challenging texts than students having reading problems (Gambrell, Wilson, & Gnatt, 1981; Stahl & Heubach, 2006). Reading appropriately challenging books with instruction and feedback may help proficient readers make the transition from word-by-word reading to fluent reading, whereas poorer readers often spend more time in reading materials that are too difficult. Doing so denies those students who are having reading problems access to reading materials that could help them develop fluent reading abilities. For the most part, children need to be reading in instructional-level texts with instruction, modeling, support, monitoring, and feedback (Bryan, Fawson, & Reutzel, 2003; Kuhn, 2005; Kuhn & Stahl, 2003; Stahl, 2004).

5. *Oral and silent reading.* The *Report of the National Reading Panel* (National Institute of Child Health and Human Development, 2000) indicated there was ample scientific evidence to support reading practice for fluency that included (a) oral reading, (b) repeated reading of the same text, and (c) feedback and guidance during and after the reading of a

Go to the Assignments and Activities section of Topic 7: "Fluency" in the MyEducationLab for your course and complete the activity entitled "Strategies for Fluency Building." As you watch the video and answer the accompanying questions, note the major components of providing students with effective fluency practice.

text. On the other hand, sustained silent reading (SSR) of self-chosen books without monitoring or feedback did not have substantial scientific evidence to support its near exclusive use across the grades of the elementary school without regard to the reading fluency developmental levels of students. Recent experimental research suggests that silent, wide reading (across genre or text types, e.g., stories, poems, information books) with monitoring seemed to produce equivalent or better fluency gains in second- and third-grade students (Kuhn, 2005; Pikulski & Chard, 2005; Reutzel, Jones, Fawson, & Smith, 2008; Stahl, 2004). There is mounting evidence that the old practice of SSR, in which the teacher also read as a model for children while they read silently, is giving way to a new model of using silent reading practice, one that incorporates book selection instruction, student monitoring and accountability, and reading widely (Bryan, Fawson, & Reutzel, 2003; Kuhn, 2005; Marzano, 2004; Reutzel, Fawson, & Smith, 2008; Stahl, 2004).

6. *Monitoring and accountability are key.* For many years, teachers thought that sitting and reading a book silently were modeling sufficient to promote students' desires and abilities to read. This, of course, has never been proven to be the case. In recent years, Bryan et al. (2003) have reported that monitoring disengaged readers with quick stop-in visits to listen to oral reading and discuss a piece of literature during silent reading has a salutary effect on their engagement during silent reading. Furthermore, asking that children account for their fluency practice time by reading onto a tape or for a teacher has positive impact on their fluency engagement and growth (Reutzel, Jones, Fawson, & Smith, 2008).

7. *Wide and repeated reading.* There is considerable evidence that repeated readings of the same text lead to automaticity—fast, accurate, effortless word recognition (Dowhower, 1991; National Institute of Child Health and Human Development, 2000). However, once automaticity is achieved, reading widely seems to provide the necessary ingredients to move a student's fluency from automaticity to comprehension. Thus, it is important that at the point a student has achieved grade-level automaticity this student receive encouragement to read widely as well as repeatedly to develop connected text comprehension (Kuhn, 2005; Pikulski & Chard, 2005; Reutzel, Fawson, & Smith, 2008; Reutzel, Jones, Fawson, & Smith, 2008; Stahl, 2004). From the currently available evidence (Wright, Sherman, & Jones, 2004), this occurs in second grade or third grade for some children while others may need to continue to read texts repeatedly until they achieve automaticity at grade level into the intermediate years.

An awareness of these seven insights into fluency development can help teachers create optimal conditions for students to become fluent readers.

Rasinski (1989), Rasinski and Padak (1996), Reutzel (2006), Richards (2000), and Worthy and Broaddus (2002) have described six effective instructional principles to guide teachers in providing effective fluency instruction: (1) repetition, (2) modeling, (3) explicit instruction and feedback, (4) support or assistance, (5) phrasing practice, and (6) appropriately challenging materials. When students who lack decoding automaticity practice a single text repeatedly (three to five times), oral reading becomes increasingly automatic. Observing, listening to, and imitating fluent reading models also help students learn how to become fluent readers themselves. Modeling fluent reading for students and pointing out specific behaviors as texts are read aloud, as well as providing informative feedback, can also help students become fluent. Teaching children explicitly what constitutes the chief characteristics of fluent reading, coupled with instruction on how to detect and fix up fluency problems, is also critical in helping students become self-regulating readers (Reutzel, 2006). Supporting students with strategies like choral reading, buddy reading, and technology-assisted reading can be most effective in a well-conceived reading fluency program. Finally, providing readers with appropriately challenging reading materials for reading practice is essential for developing fluency. Understanding the nature, quantity, and quality of teacher feedback during oral reading is a crucial part of helping students become fluent readers (Shake, 1986). Self-assessment questions for teachers who provide students oral reading feedback are provided in Figure 7.2 to assist in this process.

Recent research on English learners' (ELs) development of reading fluency suggests these students develop reading fluency (accuracy and rate) similarly to children who speak English as their first language (August & Shanahan, 2006; Fitzgerald, Amendum, & Guthrie, 2008). This same research indicates the need for much more research on how ELs develop prosody and comprehension as a part of developing reading fluency.

Armed with an understanding of the problems, obstacles, and possibilities for helping students become fluent readers, we now turn our attention toward assessing students' reading fluency to inform and direct our selection of instructional strategies.

# ASSESSING CHILDREN'S READING FLUENCY

Assessing fluency has for many years focused somewhat exclusively on how quickly students could read a given text. This is known as "reading rate" or reading speed. Reading teachers have historically used words per minute (wpm) to indicate reading rate. Although wpm is one

---

**FIGURE 7.2** Teacher Verbal Feedback Think Questions

1. Am I more often telling the word than providing a clue?
2. What is the average self-correction rate of my students?
3. Do I assist poor readers with unknown words more often than good readers? If so, why?
4. Am I correcting miscues even when they do not alter the meaning of the text? If so, why?
5. Does one reader group tend to engage in more self-correction than other groups? If so, why?
6. Does one reading group have more miscues that go unaddressed than other groups?
7. What types of cues for oral reading errors do I provide and why?
8. What is *my* ultimate goal in reading instruction?
9. How do I handle interruptions from other students during oral reading? Do I practice what I preach?
10. How does my feedback influence the self-correction behavior of students?
11. Does my feedback differ across reader groups? If so, *how* and *why*?
12. Would students benefit more from a form of feedback different from that which I normally offer?
13. Am I allowing students time to self-correct (3 to 5 seconds)?
14. Am I further confusing students with my feedback?
15. Do I digress into "minilessons" midsentence when students make a mistake? If so, why?
16. Do I analyze miscues to gain information about the reading strategies students employ?
17. Does the feedback I offer aid students in becoming independent, self-monitoring readers? If so, how?
18. Do I encourage students to ask themselves, "Did that make sense?" when they are reading both orally and silently? If not, why not?
19. Do students need the kind of feedback I am offering them?

*Source:* Adapted from "Teacher Interruptions during Oral Reading Instruction: Self-Monitoring as an Impetus for Change in Corrective Feedback," by M. Shake, 1986, *Remedial and Special Education,* 7(5), 18–24. Copyright © 1986 by Sage Publications Inc. Journals. Reproduced with permission of Sage Publications Inc. Journals via Copyright Clearance Center.

Go to the Assignments and Activities section of Topic 7: "Fluency" in the MyEducationLab for your course and complete the activity entitled "Assessing Fluency." As you watch the video and answer the accompanying questions, note the student's reading behaviors in relation to the definition of fluency. How is she doing on all three fluency components? How would you describe this student's reading performance to a parent?

indicator of fluent oral reading, it is only one. To adequately assess fluent oral reading, one should consider at least four different components: (1) accurate decoding of text; (2) reading rate or speed; (3) use of volume, stress, pitch, and juncture (prosodic markers); and (4) mature phrasing or chunking of text.

Educators have in recent years begun to discuss how one may more efficiently and authentically assess the ability to read fluently (Kuhn & Stahl, 2000). Most teachers feel that paper-and-pencil assessment tools appear to be inadequate or at least incomplete measures of fluency. One issue for many teachers today is accessing valid and reliable estimates of reading rates appropriate for children of differing ages and grades. In 1990, Harris and Sipay (see Figure 7.3) presented information about reading rates associated with several norm-referenced or standardized reading rate measures in the past.

We offer a word of caution in strictly applying these ranges as the only assessment of fluency because other factors such as decoding accuracy, expression, and phrasing are also important. Furthermore, we do not believe that words per minute (wpm) is the best measure of reading rate as we shall explain later in this section on fluency assessment. Several approaches to assessing readers' fluency are described in this section. None of these approaches is sufficient alone, but, taken together, they offer a fairly complete picture of the fluency assessment.

## One-Minute Reading Sample (Age/Grade Appropriate: Grades 1.5 and Up)

### Purpose

One of the simplest and most useful means of collecting reading fluency data is the one-minute reading sample (Rasinski, 2003). A one-minute reading sample is typical of that used in the Oral Reading Fluency (ORF) test drawn from the Dynamic Indicators of Basic Early Literacy Skills (DIBELS) battery (Good & Kaminski, 2002). The passages and procedures in the DIBELS ORF measure are based on the research and development of Curriculum-Based Measurement (CBM) of reading by Stan Deno and his colleagues at the University of Minnesota and use procedures described by Shinn (1989). Reading rate norms using CBM procedures have been established by Hasbrouck and Tindal (2005).

According to the DIBELS Administration and Scoring Guide (Good & Kaminski, 2002), evidence of technical adequacy (reliability and validity) of this measure is drawn from a series of

---

**FIGURE 7.3**  Reading Rate Chart

**Reading Rates by Grade Levels Expressed as Ranges of Words per Minute (WPM)**

| Grades | WPM | Grades | WPM |
|--------|---------|--------|---------|
| 1 | 60–90 | 6 | 195–220 |
| 2 | 85–120 | 7 | 215–245 |
| 3 | 115–140 | 8 | 235–270 |
| 4 | 140–170 | 9 | 250–270 |
| 5 | 170–195 | 12 | 250–300 |

*Source:* From *How to Increase Reading Ability* (9th ed.), by T. L. Harris and E. R. Sipay, 1990. New York: Longman. Copyright © 1990. Reprinted with permission of Pearson Education.

studies based on the CBM reading procedures in general. Test-retest reliabilities for elementary students ranged from .92 to .97, and alternate-form reliability of different reading passages drawn from the same level ranged from .89 to .94 (Tindal, Marston, & Deno, 1983). In addition, criterion-related validity studied in eight separate studies in the past two decades ranged from .52 to .91 (Good & Jefferson, 1988; Good, Simmons, & Kameenui, 2001).

It should be noted that the question of reading endurance, or the ability to read orally at a particular rate for periods of time exceeding one minute, is largely unknown at this time (Deeney, in press; Rasinski, Reutzel, Chard, & Linan-Thompson, in press). Similarly almost nothing is known about students' silent reading rates. There is considerable debate currently around the unintended instructional consequences of assessing students' reading fluency using one-minute samples, particularly as found in the DIBELS test battery (Altwerger, Jordan, & Shelton, 2007; Goodman, 2006). Many express concern that the one-minute reading assessments have led teachers to focus reading fluency instruction almost exclusively on increasing reading rates without attention to expression or comprehension. As Deeney (in press) explains, measures such as AIMSweb and DIBELS are valid and reliable for their stated purposes—as surface level screening tools to identify students who may be having reading issues and to assist teachers in planning and monitoring instruction. However, two elements are missing in one-minute measures: capturing students' reading endurance (i.e., the ability to continue reading with appropriate accuracy, rate, prosody, and comprehension over an extended period of time) and reading processes (e.g., comprehension).

## Materials

- One blank audiocassette tape per student (120-minute length strongly suggested)
- A portable audiocassette recorder with an internal microphone
- An audiocassette tape storage case for the class set
- DIBELS grade-level passage
- DIBELS administration and scoring directions
- One-minute cooking timer (which should count down backward from 60 seconds to zero with an alarm sounding at zero)
- Pencil for marking the DIBELS passage

## Procedure

To administer the ORF measure, children are asked to read aloud three passages (one passage only for progress-monitoring purposes) that are at their grade level for one minute. Words omitted, words substituted, or hesitations of more than 3 seconds are scored as errors. Words self-corrected within 3 seconds are scored as accurate. The number of words read correctly in one minute is the reading rate. By using this metric words correct per minute (wcpm), reading rate is corrected for the accuracy of the reading. If a student is unable to read correctly any of the words in the first line of print of the grade-level passage or if the student reads less than 10 words correctly in a passage, the student ORF test is discontinued. Full directions for using the ORF measurement can be obtained by going to the DIBELS website (http://dibels.uoregon.edu), registering as a user (registration is free), and downloading the grade-level passages and the administration and scoring procedures.

To minimize time spent by the teacher monitoring progress using DIBELS grade-level passages, many teachers have found the use of an audiocassette recording tape for each child to be quite handy. The grade-level DIBELS passage to be read, with a line for the student's name at the top, is made available in a quiet section of the classroom where each student's personal cassette is stored and the recorder is placed on a table or desk along with the cooking timer and a pencil for marking on the copy of the DIBELS passage where the student finishes reading at the end of one minute. Students go to this area by assignment of the teacher on a regularly scheduled basis, roughly three or four students per day. They put their personal audiocassette tape into the recorder, set the time for one minute, turn on the record button, and start the cooking timer. At this point they begin reading the DIBELS passage into the recorder and record on their personal audiocassette tape the one-minute reading sample (DIBELS passage). When the one-minute timer rings, the student rewinds his or her personal audiocassette tape and marks the point where he or she stopped reading onto the DIBELS passage using the pencil. This paper copy of the DIBELS passage and the audiocassette tape is turned into the teacher for analysis and feedback. The teacher's job is to listen to four taped one-minute samples per day making note of each student's wcpm rate and accuracy rates. Feedback from this analysis by the teacher can be given to students in written form when they are in the intermediate grades and orally during a very brief individual reading conference for the primary-grade students. Teachers who have done this find the requirements of monitoring oral reading fluency growth to be much easier and a normal part of the daily routine in a classroom.

## Curriculum-Based Oral Reading Fluency Norms (Age/Grade Appropriate: Grades 1–8)

One of the most common measures of oral reading fluency is that of reading rate or reading speed. A words correct per minute (wcpm) measure has been used extensively to research a new set of Oral Reading Fluency Curriculum-Based Norms for Grades 1–8 (Hasbrouck & Tindal, 2005b). Hasbrouck and Tindal compiled their new ORF norms from a far larger number of scores, ranging from a low of 3,496 in the winter assessment period of eighth graders to a high of 20,128 scores in the spring assessment of second graders. They collected data from schools and districts in 23 states and were able to compile more detailed norms, reporting percentiles from the 90th through the 10th percentile levels. To ensure that these new norms represented reasonably current student performance, they used only ORF data collected between the fall of 2000 through the 2004 school year. (A more complete summary of the data files used to compile the norms table in this article is available at the website of Behavioral Research and Teaching at the University of Oregon: http://brt.uoregon.edu/techreports/TR_33_NCORF_DescStats.pdf [Hasbrouck & Tindal, 2005a].) The new ORF norms align closely with those published in 1992 and also closely match the widely used DIBELS norms (http://dibels.uoregon.edu) and those developed by Edformation with their AIMSweb system (www.edformation.com).

### Purpose

The purposes for assessing oral reading fluency are varied. Some reasons include the following:

- Screening students for special program eligibility
- Setting instructional goals and objectives
- Assigning students to specific groups for instruction
- Monitoring academic progress toward established goals
- Diagnosing special needs for assistance or instruction

### Materials

- A teacher-selected passage of 200 to 300 words
- Curriculum-based measurement procedures for assessing and scoring oral reading fluency

- Audio recorder
- Curriculum-Based Norms in Oral Reading Fluency for Grades 1–8 as shown in Figure 7.4

## Procedure

A student reads aloud for one minute from an unpracticed DIBELS passage. For screening decisions, the DIBELS passage is at the student's grade level. For diagnostic or progress-monitoring decisions, the difficulty level of the passage may need to be at either the student's instructional or goal levels. As the student reads, the teacher records errors as follows:

- A word that is mispronounced or substituted for another word or an omitted word is counted as an error.
- Words transposed in a phrase count as two errors (reading "jumped and ran" instead of "ran and jumped").
- A word read incorrectly more than once is counted as an error each time.
- Words read correctly repeated more than once, errors self-corrected by the student, and words mispronounced due to dialect or speech impairments are not counted as errors.
- An inserted word (one that does not appear in the text) is not counted as an error because the final score is an indication of the number of words that were in the text that were read correctly by the student within the one-minute time period.

After one minute, the student stops reading. The teacher subtracts the total number of errors from the number of words read by the student to obtain a score of "words correct per minute" (wcpm). Using more than one passage to assess fluency rates helps to control for any text-based or genre-type differences or variations. If standardized passages are used such as those from published sources of CBM materials (e.g., DIBELS, Reading Fluency Monitor, AIMSweb), a score from a single passage can be used (Hintze & Christ, 2004). The final wcpm score can then be compared to the ORF norms for making screening, diagnostic, or progress-monitoring decisions.

## Multidimensional Fluency Scale (Age/Grade Appropriate: Grades 1.5 and Up)

### Purpose

The purpose of Rasinski's (2003) Multidimensional Fluency Scale (MFS) is to provide a practical measurement of students' oral reading fluency that provides clear and valid information about four components of fluent reading: (a) volume and expression, (b) phrasing, (c) smoothness, and (d) pace. Rasinski's (2003) recent revision of Zutell and Rasinski's original 1991 Multidimensional Fluency Scale (MFS) adds assessment of a student's reading volume and expression. In the 1991 version, the MFS comprised three subscales: (1) phrasing, (2) smoothness, and (3) pace. In the revised version, Rasinski has added a fourth and fifth subscale: (4) accuracy and (5) volume and expression. Zutell and Rasinski (1991) report a .99 test-retest reliability coefficient for the original MFS. Although no audio recording is necessary to use this instrument, it is highly recommended for accurate documentation.

### Materials

- A teacher-selected grade-level or instructional-level passage for a one-minute sample (depending on decision-making purpose—diagnosis, screening, or progress monitoring)
- A paper copy of the Multidimensional Fluency Scale (MFS) as provided in Figure 7.5
- Audio recorder

**FIGURE 7.4**    Oral Reading Fluency Norms, Grades 1–8, 2005

| Grade | Percentile | Fall WCPM | Winter WCPM | Spring WCPM |
|-------|------------|-----------|-------------|-------------|
| 1 | 90 | XX | 81 | 111 |
|   | 75 | XX | 47 | 82 |
|   | 50 | XX | 23 | 56 |
|   | 25 | XX | 12 | 28 |
|   | 10 | XX | 6 | 15 |
| 2 | 90 | 106 | 125 | 142 |
|   | 75 | 79 | 100 | 117 |
|   | 50 | 51 | 72 | 89 |
|   | 25 | 25 | 42 | 61 |
|   | 10 | 11 | 18 | 31 |
| 3 | 90 | 128 | 146 | 162 |
|   | 75 | 99 | 120 | 137 |
|   | 50 | 71 | 92 | 107 |
|   | 25 | 44 | 62 | 78 |
|   | 10 | 21 | 36 | 48 |
| 4 | 90 | 145 | 166 | 180 |
|   | 75 | 119 | 139 | 152 |
|   | 50 | 94 | 112 | 123 |
|   | 25 | 68 | 87 | 98 |
|   | 10 | 45 | 61 | 72 |
| 5 | 90 | 166 | 182 | 194 |
|   | 75 | 139 | 156 | 168 |
|   | 50 | 110 | 127 | 139 |
|   | 25 | 85 | 99 | 109 |
|   | 10 | 61 | 74 | 83 |
| 6 | 90 | 177 | 195 | 204 |
|   | 75 | 153 | 167 | 177 |
|   | 50 | 127 | 140 | 150 |
|   | 25 | 98 | 111 | 122 |
|   | 10 | 68 | 82 | 93 |
| 7 | 90 | 180 | 192 | 202 |
|   | 75 | 156 | 165 | 177 |
|   | 50 | 128 | 136 | 150 |
|   | 25 | 102 | 109 | 123 |
|   | 10 | 79 | 88 | 98 |
| 8 | 90 | 185 | 199 | 199 |
|   | 75 | 161 | 173 | 177 |
|   | 50 | 133 | 146 | 151 |
|   | 25 | 106 | 115 | 124 |
|   | 10 | 77 | 84 | 97 |

*Source:* Compiled by Jan Hasbrouck, Ph.D, & Gerald Tindal, Ph.D. From "Oral Reading Fluency Norms: A valuable assessment tool for reading teachers," by Jan Hasbrouck, 2006, *The Reading Teacher, 59*(7), 636–644. Copyright © 2006 by the International Reading Association (www.reading.org). Reproduced with permission of the International Reading Association via Copyright Clearance Center.

---

**FIGURE 7.5**   Multidimensional Fluency Scale

Use the following scale to rate reader fluency on the five dimensions of accuracy, volume and expression, phrasing, smoothness, and pace.

**A. Accuracy**

1. Word recognition accuracy is poor: generally below 85%. Reader clearly struggles in decoding words. Makes multiple decoding attempts for many words, usually without success.
2. Word recognition accuracy is marginal: 86%–90%. Reader struggles on many words. Many unsuccessful attempts at self-correction.
3. Word recognition accuracy is good: 91%–95%. Self-corrects successfully.
4. Word recognition accuracy is excellent: 96%–100%. Self-corrections are few but successful as nearly all words are read correctly on initial attempt.

**B. Volume and Expression**

1. Reads with little expression or enthusiasm in voice. Reads words as if simply to get them out. Little sense of trying to make text sound like natural language. Tends to read in a quiet voice.
2. Some expression. Begins to use voice to make text sound like natural language in some areas of the text but not others. Focus remains largely on saying the words. Still reads in a voice that is quiet.
3. Sounds like natural language throughout the better part of the passage. Occasionally slips into expressionless reading. Voice volume is generally appropriate throughout the text.
4. Reads with good expression and enthusiasm throughout the text. Sounds like natural language. Reader is able to vary expression and volume to match his or her interpretation of the passage.

**C. Phrasing**

1. Monotonic with little sense of phrase boundaries, frequent word-by-word reading.
2. Frequent two- and three-word phrases giving the impression of choppy reading; improper stress and intonation that fails to mark ends of sentences and clauses.
3. Mixture of run-ons, mid-sentence pauses for breath, and possibly some choppiness; reasonable stress/intonation.
4. Generally well-phrased, mostly in clause and sentence units, with adequate attention to expression.

**D. Smoothness**

1. Frequent extended pauses, hesitations, false starts, sound-outs, repetitions, and/or multiple attempts.
2. Several "rough spots" in text where extended pauses, hesitations, and so on are more frequent and disruptive.
3. Occasional breaks in smoothness caused by difficulties with specific words and/or structures.
4. Generally smooth reading with some breaks, but word and structure difficulties are resolved quickly, usually through self-correction.

**E. Pace (during Sections of Minimal Disruption)**

1. Slow and laborious.
2. Moderately slow.
3. Uneven mixture of fast and slow reading.
4. Consistently conversational.

---

*Source:* From *The Fluent Reader: Oral Reading Strategies for Building Word Recognition, Fluency, and Comprehension* by T. Rasinski. Copyright 2003 by Timothy V. Rasinski. Reprinted by permission of Scholastic, Inc.

### Procedure

We recommend that students read a one-minute sample passage (see previous discussion of the one-minute sample in this chapter) using the Multidimensional Fluency Scale shown in Figure 7.5 to assess each student's reading fluency. Teachers can rate fluency using the MFS either immediately following a student's reading or rate the student's fluency later if the one-minute sample reading has been recorded. The MFS can also be used to rate group performances such as plays, readers' theater, and radio readings (Reutzel & Cooter, 2004). For radio readings, students can also prepare a text for reading and recording, complete with sound effects if they wish. After recording, the teacher can analyze the performance of individual students and provide helpful modeling and feedback for future improvement.

In Figure 7.6, we summarize the fluency assessment procedures and instruments we have discussed thus far and provide summary information about federally related assessment purposes (i.e., screening, diagnostic, progress-monitoring, or outcomes assessment), as well as type of test or procedure and psychometric evidence of test or procedure scores (any available reliability and validity evidence).

## Connecting Assessment Findings to Teaching Strategies

Before discussing fluency intervention strategies, we provide an If-Then matrix connecting assessment to intervention and strategy choices. It is our intention to help you select the most appropriate instructional interventions and strategies to meet your students' fluency development needs based on assessment data. Most fluency development activities tend to fall into differing types of practice strategies. In the If-Then chart we have listed the teaching strategies that appear in the next section and link them to key areas of need that your fluency assessments are likely to reveal (see Figure 7.7).

# DEVELOPING READING FLUENCY FOR ALL CHILDREN

After a careful assessment of a student's reading fluency as outlined previously, one or more of the following fluency development strategies or integrated fluency lesson frameworks may be appropriately applied. Perhaps the most important thing to remember is that children with poorly developed fluency must receive regular opportunities to read and reread for authentic and motivating reasons, such as to gather information, to present a dramatization, or simply to reread a favorite story. The strategies described in this section offer effective and varied means to help learners become more fluent readers in authentic, effective, and motivating ways.

## Oral Recitation Lesson

### Purpose

The oral recitation lesson format is drawn from the one-room schoolhouse period of American education (Hoffman, 1987). During these early years of American education, teachers modeled reading aloud and students were then assigned all or part of the text for practice, which they later read aloud to the class using a practice called *recitation*. The oral recitation lesson (ORL) shares many important theoretical and practical characteristics with the shared book approach strategy described in Chapter 4. According to Rasinski (1990a), the shared book approach and the oral recitation lesson are similar in respect to teacher modeling, repeated readings of text, independent reading, and the use of predictable and meaningful materials. Thus, the shared book approach may be seen in many respects as a less formalized approach to developing fluency with children (Nelson & Morris, 1986). However, for some readers (and teachers), the oral recitation lesson (ORL) offers a degree of security through providing a predictable lesson structure for planning.

### Materials

- Student self-selected books appropriate for reading aloud

**FIGURE 7.6** Summary Matrix of Fluency Assessment Procedures or Tests

| Name of Assessment Tool | Screening Assessment | Diagnostic Assessment | Progress-Monitoring Assessment | Outcomes Assessment | Norm-Referenced Test | Criterion-Referenced Test | Reliability Evidence | Validity Evidence |
|---|---|---|---|---|---|---|---|---|
| One-Minute Reading Sample (Oral Reading Fluency—ORF) | + | + | + | – | + | – | Test-retest reliabilities for elementary students ranged from .92 to 97; alternate-form reliability of different reading passages drawn from the same level ranged from .89 to .94 | Criterion-related validity studied in eight separate studies in the past two decades ranged from .51 to .91 |
| Oral Reading Fluency Norms CBM Scoring Procedures | + | + | + | – | + | – | Not Applicable | Not Applicable |
| Multidimensional Fluency Scale (MFS) | + | – | + | – | – | + | MFS has a .99 test-retest stability coefficient according to the MFS's authors | Criterion validity with the definition of fluency components |

Key:  + can be used for
  – not appropriate for

# FIGURE 7.7    If-Then Intervention Strategy Guide for Reading Fluency Development

| "If" the student is ready to learn / "Then" try these teaching strategies | Oral Recitation Lesson (ORL) | Fluency-Oriented Reading Instruction (FORI) | Wide Reading | Repeated Readings | Assisted and Partner Reading | Readers' Theater | Radio Reading | Scaffolded Silent Reading (ScSR) | Explicit Fluency Instruction | Neurological Impress | Closed Caption TV | Choral Reading |
|---|---|---|---|---|---|---|---|---|---|---|---|---|
| Accuracy of decoding | + | + | + | + | + | + | + | + | + | + | * | + |
| Reading rate or speed | + | + | + | + | + | + | + | + | + | + | + | + |
| Expressive reading | + | + | + | + | + | + | + | + | + | + | * | + |
| Appropriate volume | + | + | * | + | + | + | + | – | + | + | * | + |
| Smoothness of reading | + | + | + | + | + | + | + | + | + | + | + | + |
| Phrasing of the text | + | + | + | + | + | + | + | + | + | + | + | + |
| Monitoring and self-regulation of fluency | * | * | * | * | * | * | * | * | + | * | * | – |

Key: + Excellent Strategy
      * Adaptable Strategy
      – Unsuitable Strategy

### Procedure

The oral recitation lesson incorporates two basic components, with each made up of several subroutines as delineated in the following outline.

I. Direct Instruction
   A. Comprehension
   B. Practice
   C. Performance
II. Indirect Instruction
   A. Fluency practice
   B. Demonstrate expert reading

Direct instruction consists of three subroutines: a comprehension phase, a practice phase, and a performance phase. The teacher begins an oral recitation lesson by reading a story aloud and then leading the students through an analysis of the story's content with the aid of a story grammar map to help frame a discussion of the major elements of the story, such as setting, characters, goals, plans, events, and resolution. Students are asked to tell what they remember about these parts of the story, and the teacher records their responses on the story grammar map. At the conclusion of this discussion, the story grammar map is used as an outline for students to write a story summary.

During the second subroutine, practice, the teacher works with students to improve their oral reading expression. The teacher models fluent reading aloud with parts of the text and then the students individually or chorally practice imitating the teacher's oral expressions. Choral readings of texts can be accomplished in a number of ways (for example, see the discussion of 4-way oral reading later in this chapter in "Choral Reading"). Text segments modeled by the teacher during the practice phase may begin with only one or two sentences and gradually move toward modeling and practicing whole pages of text.

The third subroutine is the performance phase. Students select and perform a part of the text for others in the group. Then listeners are encouraged to comment positively on the performance by asking them to state what they liked about the oral reading by their peers. Next we ask questions about parts of the reading they liked less. Teacher modeling is very important with this latter activity. For instance, the teacher may model a question about a strange rendition of the Big Bad Wolf in the Three Pigs story by saying, "I noticed that your voice had a nice and friendly tone when you read the Big Bad Wolf's part. I'm curious. Why did you choose to read his part that way when so many other readers choose to use a mean-sounding voice for that character?" Many times the student has a perfectly logical reason for irregular intonation or other anomalies. Sometimes it is simply a matter of not enough practice time. If so, this regular format helps students be aware that there is some accountability for these lessons.

The second major component of the Oral Recitation Lesson is an indirect instruction phase. During this part of the lesson, students practice a single story until they become expert readers. Hoffman (1987) defined *expert reader* as one who reads with 98% accuracy and 75-words-per-minute fluency. For 10 minutes each day, students practice reading a story or text segment in a soft or mumble reading fashion. Teachers use this time to check students individually—what we term "house calls"—for story mastery before moving on to another story. The direct instruction component creates a pool of stories from which the students can select a story for expert reading activities in the indirect instruction phase. In summary, the ORL provides teachers with a workable strategy to break away from the traditional practice of round-robin oral reading.

## Fluency-Oriented Reading Instruction

### Purpose

Fluency-Oriented Reading Instruction (FORI), based on repeated reading research, is an integrated lesson framework for providing comprehensive instruction and practice in fluency in the elementary school (Stahl, 2004; Stahl, Heubach, & Cramond, 1997). FORI consists of three interlocking aspects, according to its authors: (1) a redesigned basal or core reading program lesson, (2) a free-reading period at school, and (3) a home reading program. Recent research on the effects of FORI showed that children receiving FORI instruction significantly outperformed a control group comparison (Kuhn & Schwanenflugel, 2008; Stahl, 2004; Stahl, Bradley, Smith, Kuhn, Schwanenflugel, Meisinger, et al., 2003; Stahl & Heubach, 2006).

### Materials

- Core reading or basal reading program text
- Richly appointed classroom library for free reading at school and home
- Extension activities drawn from the core or basal reading program text
- Teacher-prepared graphic organizer of the text in the core or basal program
- Teacher-prepared audio for assisted reading practice

### Procedure

On the first day of a FORI lesson, the teacher begins by reading the core reading program story or text aloud to the class. Following the reading by the teacher, the students and teacher interactively discuss the text to place reading comprehension up-front as an important goal to be achieved in reading any text. Following this discussion, the teacher teaches vocabulary words and uses graphic organizers and other comprehension activities focused around the story or text the teacher has read aloud.

On the second day of a FORI lesson, teachers can choose to have children echo read the core reading program text with the teacher *or* have children read only a part of the story repeatedly for practice with a partner or with the teacher. Following this practice session on the second day, the story or text is sent home for the child to read with parents, older siblings, or other caregivers. On the third and fourth days of a FORI lesson, children receive additional practice as well as participate in vocabulary and comprehension exercises around the story. On these two days, children are also given decoding instruction on difficult words in the core reading story or text. Finally, on the fifth and final day of the FORI lesson, children are asked to give a written response to the story to cement their comprehension of the text.

In addition to the basal or core reading program instruction to develop fluency found in the FORI framework, the teachers provide additional in-school free-reading practice with easy books that students read alone or with partners for between 15 and 30 minutes per day.

At the beginning of the year, the time allocated to this portion of a FORI lesson is closer to 15 minutes; the time increases throughout the year to 30 minutes. As a part of their homework assignment in the FORI framework, children are expected to read at home 15 minutes a day at least 4 days per week. This outside reading is monitored through the use of reading logs (Stahl, 2004).

## Wide Reading

### Purpose

Wide reading involves reading a range of new books for fewer repetitions than is found in traditional implementations of repeated reading practice. In repeated reading practice, a single text may be read and reread three to five times or more over multiple days. In wide reading, any repeated reading of text is usually confined to a single day, lesson, or sitting before moving on to a new book the next day. Wide reading, like repeated reading, also incorporates assisted reading facilitated by teachers and peers into the lesson structure (Kuhn, 2004, 2005).

Kuhn (2004, 2005) investigated the effect of using wide reading compared to repeated reading with 24 struggling second-grade readers in three randomly assigned classrooms. Long-term use of Wide Reading significantly increased second-grade students' sight word reading, oral reading rates, and reading comprehension over controls and was roughly equivalent to the effects of using FORI (Kuhn & Woo, 2008).

### Materials

- A classroom collection of at least 300 books organized in tubs containing different genres (e.g., fairy tales, information books, realistic fiction, biographies, etc.), with a variety of differing levels of challenging books placed into each genre tub
- One or more genre wheels for each student

### Procedures

Although one key characteristic of wide reading is student choice, this is not to suggest that students are left entirely to make unguided or unconstrained choices. In fact, faced with a wall full of books, many young readers experience something called "browser overload" (Reutzel & Gali, 1998). To guide students toward wide reading across a variety of genres, Reutzel and Fawson (2002) propose the use of a genre wheel, as shown in Figure 7.8.

Students are instructed that they can choose to read a book on their independent reading level from any one of the genres represented on the wheel. After reading their choice, they are instructed to color in that genre slice on the wheel. They then must choose from another genre on the wheel that is not colored in. They continue making choices on the genre wheel until all the slices are colored in. Once the genre wheel is completed, another is begun and students can once again select a genre that they have previously read. Some teachers allow students to read up to three books from each genre wheel slice before students must choose a book from another slice. This approach accommodates students who develop a liking for a particular genre featuring favorite authors or a series of sequel books to be read.

Wide reading must involve teachers in oversight, monitoring, and requiring student accountability such as described in FORI or in "Scaffolded Silent Reading" (ScSR) in this chapter. When used as described in these instructional frameworks, wide reading has been shown to be effective for improving students' reading fluency and comprehension (Kuhn & Woo, 2008; Reutzel, Jones, Fawson, & Smith, 2008).

## Repeated Readings

### Purpose

Repeated readings engage students in reading short (100- to 200-word) passages orally over and over again. The essential purpose (and benefit) of repeated readings is to enhance students' reading automaticity—rate and accuracy (Dowhower, 1989; Rasinski, 2003; Rasinski et al., 2005; Samuels, 1979). Although it may seem that reading a text again and again could lead to boredom, it can actually have just the opposite effect, especially for younger readers.

In the beginning, texts selected for repeated readings should be short, predictable, and easy. Examples of poetry we recommend for repeated readings with at-risk readers include

**FIGURE 7.8** Wide Reading Genre Wheel

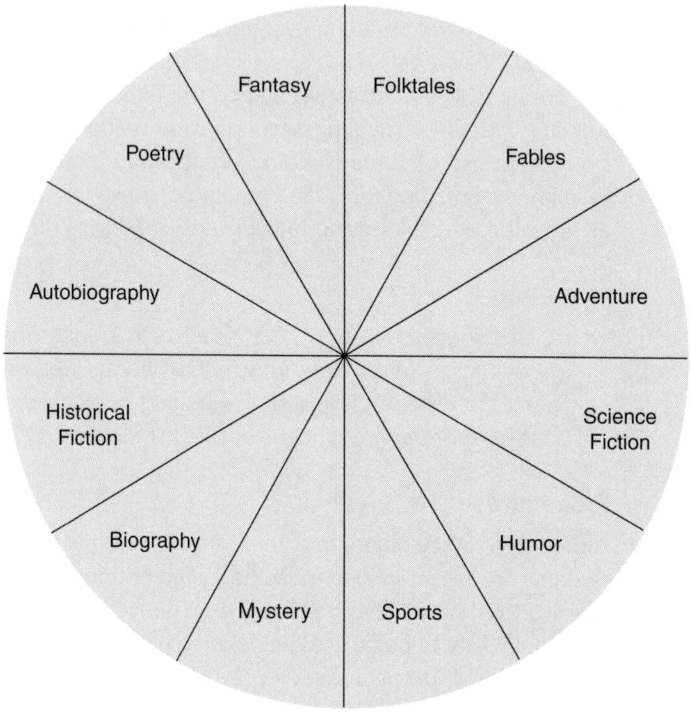


*Source:* From *Your Classroom Library: Ways to Give it More Teaching Power* by D. R. Reutzel & P. C. Fawson. Copyright © 2002 by D. R. Reutzel and P. C. Fawson. Reprinted by permission of Scholastic, Inc.

those authored by Shel Silverstein and Jack Prelutsky. Stories by Bill Martin, such as *Brown Bear, Brown Bear,* or Eric Carle's *The Very Hungry Caterpillar* are also wonderful places to start this activity. When students attain adequate speed and accuracy with easy texts, the length and difficulty of the stories and poems can gradually be increased.

### Materials

- Short texts of varying difficulty
- Tracking graph for each student (Figure 7.9)
- One or more audiocassette recorders (or other audio recording devices)

### Procedure

In this exercise, each reading is timed and recorded on a chart or graph. Students compete with themselves, trying to better their own reading rate and cut down on errors with each successive attempt. With each attempt, students' comprehension and prosody (vocal inflections) improve (Dowhower, 1987; Reutzel & Hollingsworth, 1993). Students with reading problems find it reinforcing to see visible evidence of improvement. Figure 7.9 illustrates a tracking graph of student progress in repeated readings. To increase reading rate, all students must learn to recognize words without having to sound them out. In Figure 7.9, both the

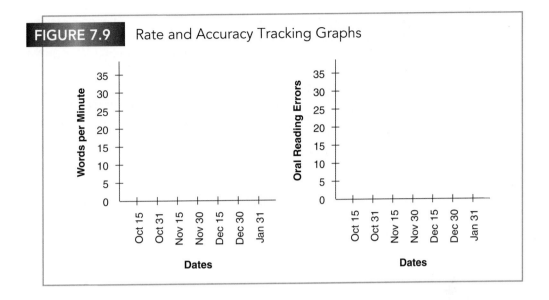

**FIGURE 7.9** Rate and Accuracy Tracking Graphs

amount of time it took to read the selection and the number of oral reading errors that occurred during each trial day can be graphed.

Repeated readings help students by expanding the total number of words they can recognize instantaneously and, as previously mentioned, help improve students' comprehension and oral elocution (performance) with each succeeding attempt. Improved performance quickly leads students to improved confidence regarding reading aloud and positive attitudes toward the act of reading. Additionally, because high-frequency words (*the, and, but, was,* and so on) occur in literally all reading situations, the increase in automatic sight word knowledge developed through repeated readings transfers far beyond the practiced texts.

One way of supporting readers during repeated readings is to use a tape-recorded version of the story or poem. Students can read along with an audiocassette tape to develop fluency similar to the model on the tape. Also, students can tape-record their oral reading performance as a source of immediate feedback. If two audiocassette tape players/recorders are available, ask students to listen and read along with the taped version of the text using headphones. At the same time, use the second recorder for recording the student's oral reading. The child can then either replay his or her version simultaneously with the teacher-recorded version to compare or simply listen to his or her own rendition alone. Either way, the feedback can be both instant and effective.

You may use taped recordings of repeated readings for further analysis of each reader's improvement in fluency and comprehension. Also, using a tape recorder frees the teacher to work with other students, thereby conserving precious instructional time and leaving behind an audit trail of student readings for later assessment and documentation. On occasion, teachers should listen to the tape with the reader present. During this time, the teacher and student can discuss effective ways of reducing word-recognition errors and increasing reading rate.

## Assisted and Partner Reading

### Purpose

Assisted reading can be accomplished in one of two ways: (a) with human support or (b) with technology support. When human support is provided, this is usually called *partner reading* (also called *buddy, dyad, peer,* or *paired reading*). Partner reading involves two students reading the same text aloud in unison for mutual support or one listening and one reading for informative feedback and guidance (Eldredge & Quinn, 1988; Greene, 1970; Lefever-Davis & Pearman, 2005; Osborn et al., 2002; Rasinski, Reutzel, Chard, & Linan-Thompson, in press; Topping, 2006; Topping & Ehly, 1998).

When technology support is provided this is usually called *tape- or computer-assisted reading*. Two excellent but somewhat expensive computer-assisted programs are Read Naturally (Ihnot, 1997) and Insights: Reading Fluency (Adams, 2002). You can learn more about these two programs by going to their websites: www.readnaturally.com and www .charlesbridge-fluency.com.

### Materials

- Appropriately challenging practice passages typically on the student's instructional level; for partner reading sessions, materials that are equally familiar and motivating for both students

### Procedure

Tape-assisted reading involves students listening to a recording of a passage or book multiple times for practice. Computer-assisted reading can be complex or simple depending on the software employed. In most cases, computer-assisted reading is much like tape-assisted reading with the exception that the text is presented on the computer screen. As children read the words, the computer program often backlights or highlights the words with a color. If students do not know a word after a predetermined period of time, the computer will say the word. Some more expensive and complex computer-assisted programs even have voice-recognition software and maintain an individual student record of each student's fluency development over multiple rereadings.

In partner reading, students are paired according to their general reading level; just as important, they should be paired according to their ability to work well with one another. A spirit of teamwork and cooperation must be present so that when one reader stumbles, the other lends assistance. The partner reading practice sessions can be recorded and played back for the students and teachers to evaluate. Discussions of replays should center not just on word recognition accuracy but also on reading rate, pausing, volume, intonation, expressive oral interpretation, and comprehension of the text.

## Readers' Theater

### Purpose

Readers' theater is a strategy whereby students practice reading from a script and then share their oral reading with classmates and selected audiences (Allington, 2001; Opitz & Rasinski, 2008; Sloyer, 1982). Unlike a play, students do not memorize lines or use elaborate stage sets to make their presentation. Emphasis is placed on presenting an interpretation of literature read in a dramatic style for an audience who imagines setting and actions. Readers' theater has been widely used, and reports indicate that it is an effective practice strategy for increasing students' reading fluency at a variety of ages (Flynn, 2005; Griffith & Rasinski, 2004; Martinez, Roser, & Strecker, 1999).

### Materials

- Readers' theater scripts
- Minimal props (masks, hats, simple costumes)

## Procedure

We strongly recommend that scripts obtained for readers' theater be drawn from tales originating from the oral tradition, poetry, or quality picture books designed to be read aloud by children. Selections should be packed with action and have an element of suspense; they should also comprise an entire, meaningful story or episode. Moreover, texts selected for use in readers' theater should contain sufficient dialogue to make reading and preparing the text a challenge, as well as involving several children as characters. A few examples of such texts include Martin and Archambault's *Knots on a Counting Rope* (1987), Viorst's *Alexander and the Terrible, Horrible, No Good, Very Bad Day* (1972), and Barbara Robinson's *The Best Christmas Pageant Ever* (1972). Several excellent websites make many excellent readers' theater scripts readily available to classroom teachers: www.aaronshep.com/rt/index .html, www.readinglady.com, and http://readers-theatre.com. Commercially published readers' theater scripts are now available for the same script at differing levels of difficulty, allowing all children to participate in a readers' theater performance at their own level. Sundance Publishing Company is one of the first groups to publish leveled readers' theater scripts (Flynn, 2005; Griffith & Rasinski, 2004; Martinez et al., 1999).

If a story is selected for reading, students are assigned to read characters' parts. If poems are selected, students may read alternating lines or groups of lines. Readers' theater in the round, in which readers stand around the perimeter of the room and the audience is in the center surrounded by the readers, is a fun and interesting variation for both the performers and audience. Students often benefit from a discussion prior to reading a readers' theater script. The purpose of this discussion is to help students make connections between their own background experiences and the text to be read. Also, struggling students benefit from listening to a previously recorded performance of the text as a model prior to the initial reading of the script.

Hennings (1974) described a simplified procedure for preparing readers' theater scripts for classroom performance. First the text to be performed is read silently by the individual students. Second, the text is read again orally, sometimes using choral reading in a group. After the second reading, children choose their parts or the teacher assigns parts to the children. We suggest that students be allowed to write their three most desired parts on a slip of paper submitted to the teacher and that teachers do everything possible to assign one of these three choices to the requesting student. The third reading is also an oral reading with students reading their parts with scripts in hand. There may be several rehearsal readings as students prepare for the final reading or performance in front of the class or a selected audience.

Readers' theater offers students a unique opportunity to participate in reading along with other, perhaps more skilled readers. Participating in the mainstream classroom with better readers helps students having reading problems feel a part of their peer group while providing them with ready models of good reading and demonstrating how good readers, through practice, become even better readers. Working together with other readers fosters a sense of teamwork, support, and pride in personal and group accomplishment.

## Radio Reading

### Purpose

A variation on repeated reading and readers' theater, radio reading (Greene, 1979; Opitz & Rasinski, 1998; Rasinski, 2003; Searfoss, 1975) is a procedure for developing oral reading fluency in a group setting intended to provide an alternative to the old and now discredited approach to oral reading called "round robin," in which students were assigned by the teacher to take turns reading aloud while all of the other students in the circle or small group listened and presumably followed along in the text (Eldredge, Reutzel, & Hollingsworth, 1996). We have found radio reading to be most effectively used with short selections from information texts threaded together to make a news broadcast performance.

### Materials

- News story "scripts" for each student drawn from any print media, such as newspapers, magazines, or any print source that can be converted into a news story, such as short selections from articles or sections in information books

### Procedure

One student acts as a broadcast news anchor, and other students act in the roles of various reporters reporting on the weather, sports, breaking news, and so on. Only the radio readers and the teacher have copies of the scripts. Because other students have no script to follow, minor word-recognition errors will go unnoticed if the text is well presented. Struggling students enjoy radio reading from *Know Your World Extra,* a publication well suited for use in radio reading activities because the content and level of difficulty make it possible for older readers with fluency problems to read with ease and enjoyment. Short selections from information books on weather, volcanoes, spiders, sports figures, and so on can be presented as short reports by various reporters during the news broadcast.

A script for the anchor may need to be written by the children with help from the teacher to thread the various news reports together in a cohesive fashion. Before performing a radio reading for an audience, students should rehearse the selections repeatedly with a partner or the teacher until they gain confidence and can read the script with proper volume, accuracy, rate, phrasing, and expression. Emphasis is first placed on the meaning of the text segments so that the students can paraphrase any difficult portions of the text if needed during the presentation. Students are encouraged to keep the ideas flowing in the same way as a reporter or anchor news broadcaster.

## Scaffolded Silent Reading (ScSR)

### Purpose

Scaffolded Silent Reading (ScSR) is silent reading practice that redesigns practice conditions to deal affirmatively with past concerns and criticisms surrounding traditionally implemented Silent Sustained Reading (SSR). ScSR is intended to provide students with necessary support, guidance, structure, accountability, and monitoring that will assist them in transferring their oral reading skills to successful and effective silent reading practice (Hiebert, 2006; Reutzel, Jones, Fawson, & Smith, 2008).

### Materials

- A classroom book collection arranged in tubs or crates containing different genres
- Genre wheel
- Overhead projector and water marker pens

### Procedure

To begin, teachers carefully arrange the classroom library to support and guide children's book reading choices toward appropriately challenging books at the independent reading level. Color-coded cloth tape on the book bindings or stickers in the upper-right-hand corners of the covers are used to show the difficulty levels of books within the classroom library. The opportunity to choose their reading materials increases students' motivation to read (Gambrell, 1996; Guthrie & Wigfield, 1997; Turner & Paris, 1995). Unguided choice on the other hand can often lead to selections of inappropriately difficult books for reading practice (Donovan, Smolkin, & Lomax, 2000; Fresch, 1995). Because recent research suggests that wide reading is effective in promoting children's reading choices as well as fluency and comprehension development (Kuhn, 2005), books are organized into tubs or crates of different genres.

Students choose books using a reading genre wheel as shown in Figure 7.8 in the section "Wide Reading" earlier in this chapter. Students are given brief lessons about book selection strategies including (1) orienting students to the classroom library, (2) book talks and getting children excited about books, (3) selecting a book in the classroom library, (4) selecting a "just right" or appropriately leveled book from the classroom library, and (5) checking the reading levels of books. Students are taught the "three finger" rule, which, as described by Allington (2006), involves indicating with a finger each word they don't recognize on a page of print. If there are three or more fingers extended for a page of print, the text is considered to be too difficult.

Each day, ScSR practice time begins with a short (usually about 5 to 8 minutes) explanation and modeling of an aspect or element of fluent reading or how to use a comprehension strategy with a teacher-selected text. For example, a teacher wanting to help students become more expressive through effective phrasing might provide a lesson on observing the punctuation in the text. Displaying a text on the overhead projector and using water marker pens, she might color code the commas with yellow and the terminal punctuation marks with red. The teacher then would model how to use the punctuation marks to phrase the text appropriately. She might also demonstrate how the same text would sound if the punctuation marks were ignored while reading. The teacher might also invite students to join with her in a quick rereading of the overhead displayed text in a choral reading.

As students silently read appropriately challenging books from different genres, the teacher makes monitoring visits called individual teacher–student reading conferences. During each individual reading conference, the teacher asks the student to read aloud from his or her book while making a running record analysis of the reading. After the student reads aloud for 1 to 2 minutes, the teacher initiates a discussion about the book the student is reading. To monitor comprehension, the teacher can ask, "Please tell me about what you just read." A follow-up might involve asking students to answer general story structure questions if the book is narrative. For informational books, students can answer questions about facts related to the topics. This is a brief discussion of about 2 minutes. Finally, during each individual reading conference, the teacher asks the student to set a goal for a date to finish the book. Students are also asked to think about how they might share what the book is about from a displayed menu of "book response projects," such as drawing and labeling a character wanted poster, making a story map, or filling in a blank graphic organizer. After each individual reading conference, the teacher records the running record score, comprehension retell and question answers, the goal for book completion, and the selected book response project to be completed after finishing the book.

## Explicit Fluency Instruction

### Purpose

The primary purposes of explicit fluency instruction are twofold: (a) to teach students to clearly understand what is meant by *fluency* and (b) to teach students how to self-monitor, evaluate, self-regulate, and otherwise "fix up" their own fluency problems over time. "Some students struggle with reading because they lack information about what they are trying to do and how to do it. They look around at their fellow students who are learning to read [fluently and well] and say to themselves, 'How are they doing that?' In short they are mystified about how to do what other students seem to do with ease" (Duffy, 2004, p. 9).

It is typically very difficult for teachers to provide explicit explanations for how to read fluently. To do so, they must become aware of the processes they use. However, because teachers are already fluent readers, they do not think deeply about the processes they use to read text fluently (Duffy, 2004; Reutzel, 2006; Reutzel, Jones, Fawson, & Smith, 2008).

### Materials

- Template lesson plan (Figure 7.10)
- Selections from among several sources representing at least the genres of information, story, and poem, segmented into practice texts of 100 to 300 words at grade level for whole-class lessons and practice
- Means to enlarge text (board, charts, computer projector, or overhead projector)
- Assessment rubric (Figure 7.11)
- Fluency fix-up strategies document (Figure 7.12)

### Procedure

Teaching an explicit fluency lesson requires a framework and template lesson plan. Reutzel (2006) has developed an explicit lesson framework called **EMS**—explanation, model, scaffold, based on the expectation that teachers will explicitly explain what fluency is composed of—accuracy, rate, and expression—as well as what each of these three concepts entails. For example, explicit fluency lessons are taught on accurate reading, reading at the proper rate, and expression that includes smoothness, volume, expression, and phrasing. Explanations include what is to be learned, where and when it is to be used, and why it is important. Modeling demonstrates how an aspect of fluency, like expression, is to be done (and, for some students, *not* done). Finally, teachers gradually release through a series of guided practice experiences the reading of the class text to individual application through a process we call *You* (teacher model), *You and Me* (teacher and student share fluency reading in whole class and with partners), *and Me* (student reads independently). A template explicit fluency lesson is found in Figure 7.10 to demonstrate each part of the EMS explicit fluency lesson.

Finally, students are also taught how to monitor, assess, and "fix up" their fluency through the use of a simple assessment rubric of the elements of oral reading fluency found in Figure 7.11 and through explicit fluency lessons on using the fluency fix-up strategies found in Figure 7.12.

## Neurological Impress

### Purpose

The neurological impress method (NIM) involves the student and the teacher in reading the same text aloud simultaneously (Heckleman, 1966, 1969; Hollingsworth, 1970, 1978). The use of multiple sensory systems is thought to "impress" upon the student the fluid reading patterns of the teacher through direct modeling. It is assumed that exposing students to numerous examples of texts (read in a more sophisticated way than the at-risk students could achieve on their own) will enable them to learn the patterns of letter–sound correspondence in the language more naturally. This assumption stands to reason when viewed in light of well-established advances in learning theory, especially those espoused by Vygotsky (1978).

| **FIGURE 7.10** | Explicit Fluency Lesson Plan Template |

**Objective:** *Children will pay attention to punctuation to help them read expressively.*

**Supplies**

- Book—*In a Tree*, pp. 18–19
- Overhead transparency
- Overhead projector
- Three colored pens (overhead)
- Text Types: Narrative ( ) Information Books (x) Poetry ( )

**Explain**

- **What**

  Today, boys and girls, we are going to be learning about how to read expressively. Important parts of reading expressively are pausing, stopping, or raising or lowering our pitch as we read. Pitch is how high or low the sounds are that we make with our voices (demonstrate high and low pitch). Stopping means we quit reading for a moment like this . . . Pausing means we take a breath and keep reading. Marks on the page called punctuation marks (point to) help us to know when we need to pause, stop, or raise or lower our pitch.

- **Why**

  We need to read expressively with pauses or stops so that we can show that we understand what we are reading. Punctuation tells us what we need to know about how to express the words, phrases, and sentences with the right pauses, stops, and pitch.

- **When/Where**

  Whenever we read, we should pay attention to the punctuation so that we know where to pause, stop, and raise or lower our pitch.

**Modeling**

- **Example**

  First, I am going to read this page with good expression paying attention to what the punctuation tells me to do, such as pause, stop, or raise or lower my pitch. Please look at the page on the overhead. Notice that I have colored each punctuation mark with a different color to help you see them more clearly. Follow what I read

  with your eyes. Listen very carefully to see if I stop, pause, or change my pitch where I should.

- **Non-Example**

  Next, I am going to read this page with poor expression paying no or little attention to what the punctuation tells me to do. I won't pause, stop, or raise or lower my pitch. Please look at the page on the overhead. Notice that I have colored each punctuation mark with a different color to help you see them more clearly. Follow what I read with your eyes. Listen very carefully to see where I should have changed my reading to stop, pause, or raise or lower my pitch.

**Scaffolding: (Me, You and Me, You)**

- **Whole Group (Me and You)**

  Now that I have shown you how and how not to read this page, let's practice it together! We will begin reading this page all together. (Point) Watch my pen so that we can all stay together. Next, we will read this again using echo reading. How many of you have ever heard an echo? So if I say, *Hello,* the echo will say *Hello.* So now I will read and you will echo me. Let's begin.

- **Small Group/Partners/Teams (Me and You)**

  Now turn to your neighbor. One person will read and the other will echo.

- **Individual (You)**

  Next, take the fluency phone and read this again to yourself listening carefully to see where you are stopping, pausing, or raising or lowering your pitch.

Now, take your fluency phone and read this again to yourself listening carefully to see where you are stopping, pausing, or raising or lowering your pitch.

**Assess**

- Rubric for assessment
- Set personal goals
- Graph progress

**Reflect**

- What went well?
- How would you change the lesson?

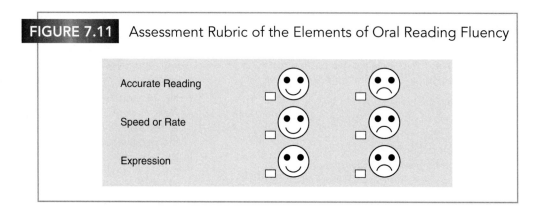

**FIGURE 7.11** Assessment Rubric of the Elements of Oral Reading Fluency

## Materials

- Easy and predictable reading material that makes sense for the reader (for the first few sessions); more challenging materials for later sessions
- Audio recording equipment

## Procedure

Each NIM session is aimed at reading as much material as is possible in 10 minutes. The student sits slightly in front of and to one side of the teacher as they hold the text. The teacher moves his or her finger beneath the words as they are spoken in near-unison fashion. Both try to maintain a comfortably brisk, continuous rate of oral reading. The teacher's role is to keep the pace when the student starts to slow down. Pausing for analyzing unknown words is not permitted. The teacher's voice is directed at the student's ear so that the words are seen, heard, and said simultaneously.

**FIGURE 7.12** Fluency Fix-Up Strategies for Major Fluency Elements

### Accuracy

1. Slow your reading speed down.
2. Look carefully at the words and the letters in the words you didn't read correctly on the page.
3. Think about if you know this word or parts of this word. Try saying the word or word parts.
4. Make the sound of each letter from left to right and blend the sounds together quickly to say the word.
5. Listen carefully to see if the word you said makes sense.
6. Try reading the word in the sentence again.
7. After saying the word, you may use pictures to help you make sure you have the right word.
8. If the word still doesn't make sense, then ask someone to help you.

### Rate

1. Adjust your reading speed to go slower when the text is difficult or unfamiliar or if you need to read to get detailed information.
2. Adjust your reading speed to go faster when the text is easy, familiar, or you are reading to just enjoy this book.

### Expression

1. Try to read three or more words together before pausing, stopping, or taking a breath.
2. Take a big breath and try to read to the comma or end punctuation without stopping for another breath.
3. Be sure to raise or lower your pitch when you see punctuation marks at the ends of sentences.

In the first few NIM sessions, students should become acquainted with the process by practicing on short, familiar texts. Most students with reading problems typically take some time to adjust to the NIM, and, because most of them have not read at an accelerated pace before, their first efforts often have a mumbling quality. However, within a few sessions they start to feel at ease. Many students with reading problems say they enjoy the NIM because it allows them to read more challenging and interesting material like "good readers."

At first, the teacher's voice will dominate the oral reading, but in later sessions it should be reduced gradually. This will eventually allow the student to assume the vocal lead naturally. Usually three sessions per week are sufficient to obtain noticeable results. The routine should be followed for a minimum of 10 consecutive weeks (Henk, 1983).

The NIM can also be adapted for group use (Hollingsworth, 1970, 1978). The teacher records 10 minutes of his or her own oral reading in advance. Individual students can read along with the recording while following the text independently, or the recording can be used in a listening center to permit the teacher to spend individual time with each student as others participate in reading with the recording. Despite the advantages of the prerecorded format, teachers' one-to-one interactions with individual students result in a better instructional experience.

# ENGLISH LANGUAGE LEARNERS

## Closed-Caption Television

### Purpose

Several researchers (Koskinen, Wilson, & Jensema, 1985; Neuman & Koskinen, 1992) have found that closed-caption television is a particularly effective tool for motivating students who are learning English as a second language to improve fluency and comprehension. Closed-caption television, which uses written subtitles, provides students with meaningful and motivating reading material.

### Materials

- Carefully selected high-interest television programs

### Procedure

Teachers should record and preview programs before making final selections and then introduce the programs to students with attention to vocabulary and prior knowledge factors (Koskinen et al., 1985). Three elements should be considered in a successful closed-caption lesson. First, watch a part of the captioned television program together as a group (5 to 10 minutes). Stop the recording and ask students to predict what will happen next in the program. Then, continue showing the program so that students can check their predictions. Second, watch a segment of the program that has examples of certain kinds of phonics patterns, word uses, or punctuation. For example, students can be alerted to the use of quotation marks and the fact that these marks signal dialogue. Students can then watch the remainder of the tape to identify the dialogue using their knowledge of quotation marks. Third, after watching a closed-caption television program, students can practice reading aloud along with the captions. If necessary, both the auditory portion and the closed captioning can be played simultaneously to provide students with fluency problems support through their initial attempts to read. At some later point, students can be allowed to practice reading the captioning without the auditory portion of the program. Koskinen et al. (1985) added that they "do not recommend that the sound be turned off if this, in effect, turns off the children. The major advantage of captioned television is the multisensory stimulation of viewing the drama, hearing the sound, and seeing the captions" (p. 6).

# *I*NCLUDING ALL STUDENTS

## Choral Reading

Go to the Assignments and Activities section of Topic 7: "Fluency" in the MyEducationLab for your course and complete the activity entitled "Shared Reading for Fluency." As you watch the video and answer the accompanying questions, note how the students develop an almost singsong prosodic pattern. How would you model and encourage these students to improve their expression when reading? How well did these students remain together in this unison choral reading? Could the teacher or students use different types of choral reading to add variety to the oral reading? What other choral reading strategies might you suggest?

### Purpose

**Choral reading** is one of the most commonly used research-based fluency development strategies. In many classrooms, students are asked to read aloud in a solo, barbershop, or round-robin fashion. However, note that round-robin oral reading carries with it significant instructional, emotional, and psychological risks for all children, but most especially for struggling readers (Eldredge, Reutzel, & Hollingsworth, 1996; Opitz & Rasinski, 2008). Homan, Klesius, and Hite (1993) found that choral reading practice yields excellent gains in fluency and comprehension for all children. All choral reading strategies may be done in whole groups, small groups, and with students working in pairs. The same text may be used each time for four or five sessions in repeated reading, or you may decide to use a variety of texts. There are actually three choral reading strategies for teachers to choose from: unison, echo, and antiphonal.

- *Unison.* The teacher and students read the same text passage together.
- *Echo.* The teacher reads a passage aloud and then students "echo" by repeating it.
- *Antiphonal.* Derived from ancient monastic traditions, antiphonal reading involves two groups. The first reading group, or person if they are reading in pairs, reads a section of a passage aloud (usually a sentence or two), and the second group reads the next section. The groups continue alternating passages in this way.

### Materials

- One copy of a passage from any text genre, including poetry, nonfiction (e.g., science, social studies), fiction, or even songs

### Procedure

For teachers who are new to using choral reading, Cooter (2009) has developed an implementation plan that may be used over the course of a week and only takes 5 to 10 minutes per day. This particular example is for use with core-content texts (e.g., science, social studies). This plan begins with unison reading and then expands into echo and antiphonal reading to provide variety. You will see that this plan uses explicit instruction elements as well as the gradual release of responsibility.

#### Preteaching Preparations

**A.** *Identify a unit of study* (at least 1 to 2 weeks ahead in your curriculum).

**B.** *Identify an important text selection of about 250 words you will use for whole class choral reading.* (Planning Tip: Try using a chapter introduction or summary for this activity.)

**Teaching Students How To Participate In Whole-Class Choral Reading**

*Strategy Steps: Monday*

1. *Introducing new words.* Briefly review the correct pronunciations and meanings of words that may be unfamiliar to students.
2. *Teacher modeling and first reading.* Ask students to pay attention to how the teacher uses punctuation and phrasing (commas, question marks, etc.) for correct prosody or voice intonation while reading the selected passage aloud. Students are asked to read along silently from their copy of the text selection while the teacher is reading aloud.
3. *Second reading.* After completing Step 2, inform students that they will begin reading aloud and in unison (the whole class together) and that they should start after the teacher counts down from 3.

   - Teacher then says "Begin reading at 3–2–1."
   - Teacher leads the students by reading aloud in a strong voice, being careful to read at a moderate rate (speed) so that everyone can keep up.
   - While reading aloud, the teacher should walk about the room to ensure that everyone is reading and should also listen for any words or phrases that students have difficulty with for possible reteaching (as we did in Step 1).

4. *New word review.* After the first whole-class reading the teacher should review any words or phrases with which students are having difficulty.
5. *Third reading.* The teacher explains to students that we will be reading the same text another time and that they should read a little louder this time as the teacher will be reading a little softer. The teacher begins the class reading with a 3–2–1 countdown and monitors class reading while walking the room.

*Strategy Steps: Tuesday through Friday*

- The same passage is to be read once each day by the whole class.
- You may use echo or antiphonal reading on Wednesday through Friday, if desired.

## Teacher Evaluation Continuum: Choral Reading

Teachers, like students, go through stages of expertise development in the implementation of new teaching strategies. Cooter (2009) has developed a kind of rubric, or *continuum,* for implementing choral reading to help you monitor your own use of choral reading and discover ways to deepen its use in your classroom (see Figure 7.13).

To add additional variety to choral reading, Karen Wood (1983) has suggested an approach for reading a story orally in a group. In four-way oral reading, the reading of a text should be varied by using four different types of oral reading: (a) unison choral reading, (b) echoic or imitative reading, (c) paired reading, and (d) mumble reading (Wood, 1983). All of these approaches to oral reading, except mumble reading, are described elsewhere in this chapter. Mumble reading, or reading quietly aloud, is typically heard among young readers as they are initially told to read silently. These young readers tend to "mumble" as they attempt to read silently. Teachers should model this approach to oral reading before asking students to mumble read.

To use four-way oral reading, Wood (1983) suggests that the teacher introduce the story content and the varied methods to be used in reading it. The teacher should pause briefly during the oral reading of the story to help students reflect on the story and predict ahead to focus and improve comprehension. During four-way oral reading, students are called on in random order to read but none of them are put on the spot because none of the four-way

**FIGURE 7.13** Whole-Class Choral Reading Implementation Continuum

Text materials to be used in Choral Reading:
- Passages of about 250 worlds are selected from the adopted textbook.
- The passage selected should be at least 1 to 3 weeks ahead of the teacher's curriculum.
- The *same* passage is used each time for five consecutive days.

| Exemplary A | Above Average B | Acceptable C | Early Implementation D | Traditional Instruction E |
|---|---|---|---|---|
| Teacher conducts a preassessment to gain some understanding of the range of students' reading abilities with on-level textbook readings (e.g., timed reading, cloze passages, maze passages). Data used to decide whether supplemental readings may be needed for some students (i.e., differentiating instruction). | Teacher conducts a preassessment to gain some understanding of the range of students' reading abilities with on-level textbook readings. | Teacher introduces and explains the purpose of choral reading. | Teacher introduces one of the choral reading activities (unison, echo, or antiphonal). | Uses "round robin" or "popcorn reading" for oral reading practice. |
| Puts the text selection in context and explains the purpose of choral reading. | Models the reading, attending to punctuation and using appropriate prosody (voice, intonation), volume, and reading speed). | New or unfamiliar academic words from the text are pronounced. | Teacher and students practice reading a passage from their textbook together. | When students read aloud, they do so without previewing the text or having it modeled. |
| New academic and other challenging words from the text are pronounced. | Teacher uses a "countdown" queuing system (e.g., 3–2–1) so that students begin together. | Models the choral reading strategy with a reasonably loud voice. | Teacher has 5-minute choral reading practice one to three times per week using the current unit of study. | Teacher remains in one place during oral reading practice. |
| Models the reading, attending to punctuation and using appropriate prosody (voice, intonation, volume, and reading speed). Students are given an opportunity for further vocabulary decoding or pronunciation. | Teacher travels about the room during the reading to attend to reading difficulties and makes mental notes for reteaching or clarifying. | Teacher uses a "countdown" queuing system (e.g., 3–2–1) so that students began together. Teacher travels about the room during the reading. | | |
| | | Teacher uses the same passage from the textbook for each choral reading session during the week. | | |

| | | |
|---|---|---|
| Teacher uses a "countdown" queuing system (e.g., 3–2–1) so that students begin together. Teacher travels about the room during the reading to attend to reading miscues or other difficulties, and makes mental notes for reteaching or clarifying. Teacher reviews difficult words and phrases after each subsequent reading. On the second and third day using choral reading, teacher uses the same passage from the textbook as before. Each day, the teacher's voice becomes less loud/dominant as students become familiar with the passage. Teacher uses the same passage as before, but may now use either antiphonal reading or echo reading. The passage selected is at least 1 to 3 weeks ahead of the teacher's curriculum. | Teacher reviews difficult words and phrases after one of the readings. Teacher has a 5-minute choral reading practice each day using the same text selection. The passage selected is at least 1 to 3 weeks ahead of the teacher's curriculum. | Teacher has 5-minute choral reading practice for at least four days during the week using the same text selection. The passage selected is at least 1 to 3 weeks ahead of the teacher's curriculum. |

oral reading strategies require that students read solo. Because of this, all students participate repeatedly throughout the oral reading of the story, thus helping them remain actively involved and keep their place in the story. Also, students read together, often providing many minutes of reading aloud for pleasure and practice to support readers with special needs in becoming more fluent.

## SELECTED REFERENCES

Adams, M. J. (2002). *Insights: Reading fluency.* Watertown, MA: Charlesbridge.

Allington, R. L. (1977). If they don't read much, how they ever gonna get good? *Journal of Reading, 21,* 57–61.

Allington, R. L. (1983). Fluency: The neglected reading goal. *The Reading Teacher, 36*(6), 556–561.

Allington, R. L. (1984). Oral reading. In R. Barr, M. Kamil, & P. Mosenthal (Eds.), *Handbook of reading research.* New York: Longman.

Allington, R. L. (2001). *What really matters for struggling readers: Designing research-based programs.* New York: Addison-Wesley/Longman.

Allington, R. L. (2006). *What really matters for struggling readers: Designing research-based programs* (2nd ed.). Boston: Allyn & Bacon.

Allington, R. L. (2007). Forward. In B. Altwerger, N. Jordan, & N. R. Shelton (Eds.), *Reading fluency: Process, practice, and policy* (pp. vii–xi). Portsmouth, NH: Heinemann.

Altwerger, B., Jordan, N., & Shelton, N. R. (2007). *Reading fluency: Process, practice, and policy.* Portsmouth, NH: Heinemann.

August, D., & Shanahan, T. (2006). *Developing literacy in second-language learners: Report of the national literacy panel on language-minority children and youth.* Mahwah, NJ: Lawrence Erlbaum.

Blevins, W. (2001). *Building fluency: Lessons and strategies for reading success.* New York: Scholastic.

Bryan, G., Fawson, P. C., & Reutzel, D. R. (2003). Sustained silent reading: Exploring the value of literature discussion with three non-engaged readers. *Reading Research and Instruction, 43*(1), 47–73.

Cooter, R. (2005). *Fluency flow chart: The Memphis Literacy Academy.* Unpublished manuscript. Bellarmine University, Kentucky.

Cooter, R. (2009). *Choral reading: An implementation continnum.* Unpublished manuscript, Bellarmine University, Kentucky.

Deeney, T. (in press). One-minute fluency measures: Mixed messages in assessment and instruction. *The Reading Teacher.*

Donovan, C. A., Smolkin, L. B., & Lomax, R. G. (2000). Beyond the independent-level text: Considering the reader-text match in first-graders' self-selections during recreational reading. *Reading Psychology: An International Quarterly, 21*(4), 309–333.

Dowhower, S. (1987). Effects of repeated readings on second-grade transitional readers' fluency and comprehension. *Reading Research Quarterly, 22,* 389–406.

Dowhower, S. (1989). Repeated reading: Research into practice. *The Reading Teacher, 42*(7), 502–507.

Dowhower, S. (1991). Speaking of prosody: Fluency's unattended bedfellow. *Theory into Practice, 30*(3), 158–164.

Duffy, G. G. (2004). *Explaining reading: A resource for teaching concepts, skills, and strategies.* New York: Guilford Press.

Eldredge, J. L., & Quinn, D. W. (1988). Increasing reading performance of low-achieving second graders with dyad reading groups. *Journal of Educational Research, 82,* 40–46.

Eldredge, J. L., Reutzel, D. R., & Hollingsworth, P. M. (1996). Comparing the effectiveness of two oral reading practices: Round-robin reading and the shared book experience. *Journal of Literacy Research, 28*(2), 201–225.

Fitzgerald, J., Amendum, S. J., & Guthrie, K. M. (2008). Young Latino students' English-reading growth in all-English classrooms. *Journal of Literacy Research, 40*(3), 59–94.

Flynn, R. M. (2005). Curriculum-based readers theatre: Setting the stage for reading and retention. *The Reading Teacher, 58*(4), 360–365.

Fresch, M. J. (1995). Self selection of early literacy learners. *The Reading Teacher, 49*(5), 220–227.

Gambrell, L. B. (1996). Creating classroom cultures that foster reading motivation. *The Reading Teacher, 50*(1), 14–25.

Gambrell, L. B., Wilson, R. M., & Gnatt, W. N. (1981). Classroom observations of task-attending behaviors of good and poor readers. *Journal of Educational Research, 74,* 400–404.

Good, R. H., & Jefferson, G. (1988). Contemporary perspectives on curriculum-based measurement validity. In

M. R. Shinn (Ed.), *Advanced applications of curriculum-based measurement* (pp. 61–88). New York: Guilford Press.

Good, R. H., & Kaminski, R. A. (Eds.). (2002). *Dynamic indicators of basic early literacy skills* (6th ed.). Eugene, OR: Institute for the Development of Educational Achievement. Available online: http://dibels.uoregon.edu.

Good, R. H., Simmons, D. C., & Kameenui, E. J. (2001). The importance and decision-making utility of a continuum of fluency-based indicators of foundational reading skills for third-grade high-stakes outcomes. *Scientific Studies of Reading, 5*(3), 257–288.

Goodman, K. S. (2006). *The truth about DIBELS: What it is, what it does.* Portsmouth, NH: Heinemann.

Greene, F. (1979). Radio reading. In C. Pennock (Ed.), *Reading comprehension at four linguistic levels* (pp. 104–107). Newark, DE: International Reading Association.

Greene, F. P. (1970). *Paired reading.* Unpublished manuscript, Syracuse University, New York.

Griffith, L. W., & Rasinski, T. V. (2004). A focus on fluency: How one teacher incorporated fluency with her reading curriculum. *The Reading Teacher, 58*(2), 126–137.

Guthrie, J. T., & Wigfield, A. (1997). *Reading engagement: Motivating readers through integrated instruction.* Newark, DE: International Reading Association.

Harris, T. L., & Hodges, R. E. (1995). *The literacy dictionary: The vocabulary of reading and writing.* Newark, DE: International Reading Association.

Harris, T. L., & Sipay, E. R. (1990). *How to increase reading ability* (9th ed.). New York: Longman.

Hasbrouck, J. E., & Tindal, G. (2005a). *Oral reading fluency: 90 years of assessment.* BRT Technical Report No. 33. Eugene, OR: Behavioral Research and Teaching. Data available at: www.brtprojects.org/publications/tech_reports/ORF_90Yrs_Intro_TechRpt33.pdf.

Hasbrouck, J. E., & Tindal, G. (2005b). Oral Reading Fluency Norms: A valuable tool for reading teachers. *The Reading Teacher* (in submission).

Heckleman, R. G. (1966). Using the neurological impress remedial reading technique. *Academic Therapy, 1,* 235–239, 250.

Heckleman, R. G. (1969). A neurological impress method of remedial reading instruction. *Academic Therapy, 4,* 277, 282.

Henk, W. A. (1983). Adapting the NIM to improve comprehension. *Academic Therapy, 19,* 97–101.

Hennings, K. (1974). Drama reading, an ongoing classroom activity at the elementary school level. *Elementary English, 51,* 48–51.

Hiebert, E. H. (2006). Becoming fluent: Repeated reading with scaffolded texts. In S. J. Samuels & A. E. Farstrup

(Eds.), *What research has to say about fluency instruction* (pp. 204–226). Newark, DE: International Reading Association.

Hintze, J. M., & Christ, T. J. (2004). An examination of variability as a function of passage variance in CBM progress monitoring. *School Psychology Review, 33*(2), 204–217.

Hoffman, J. V. (1987). Rethinking the role of oral reading in basal instruction. *The Elementary School Journal, 87*(3), 367–374.

Hollingsworth, P. M. (1970). An experiment with the impress method of teaching reading. *The Reading Teacher, 24,* 112–114.

Hollingsworth, P. M. (1978). An experimental approach to the impress method of teaching reading. *The Reading Teacher, 31,* 624–626.

Homan, S. P., Klesius, J. P., & Hite, C. (1993). Effects of repeated readings and nonrepetitive strategies on students' fluency and comprehension. *The Journal of Educational Research, 87*(2), 94–99.

Ihnot, C. (1997). *Read naturally.* St. Paul, MN: Reading Naturally: The Fluency Company.

Jenkins, J. R., Fuchs, L. S., Van den Broek, P., Espin, C., & Deno, S. L. (2003). Accuracy and fluency in list and context reading of skilled and RD groups: Absolute and relative performance levels. *Learning Disabilities Research and Practice, 18*(4), 237–245.

Kameenui, E. J., & Simmons, D. C. (2001). The DNA of reading fluency. *Scientific Studies of Reading, 5*(3), 203–210.

Klenk, L., & Kibby, M. W. (2000). Re-mediating reading difficulties: Appraising the past, reconciling the present, constructing the future. In M. L. Kamil, P. B. Mosenthal, P. D. Pearson, & R. Barr (Eds.), *Handbook of reading research* (Vol. 3). Mahwah, NJ: Lawrence Erlbaum.

Koskinen, P., Wilson, R., & Jensema, C. (1985). Closed captioned television: A new tool for reading instruction. *Reading World, 24,* 1–7.

Kuhn, M. (2005). Helping students become accurate, expressive readers: Fluency instruction for small groups. *The Reading Teacher, 58*(4), 338–345.

Kuhn, M. R. (2004). Helping students become accurate, expressive readers: Fluency instruction for small groups. *The Reading Teacher, 58*(4), 338–344.

Kuhn, M. R., & Schwanenflugel, P. J. (2008). *Fluency in the classroom.* New York: Guilford Press.

Kuhn, M. R., & Stahl, S. A. (2000). *Fluency: A review of developmental and remedial practices.* Ann Arbor, MI: Center for the Improvement of Early Reading Achievement.

Kuhn, M. R., & Stahl, S. A. (2003). Fluency: A review of developmental and remedial practices. *Journal of Educational Psychology, 95,* 3–21.

Kuhn, M. R., & Stahl, S. A. (2004). Fluency: A review of developmental and remedial practices. In R. B. Ruddell and N. J. Unrau (Eds.), *Theoretical models and processes of reading* (5th ed., pp. 412–452). Newark, DE: International Reading Association.

Kuhn, M. R., & Woo, D. G. (2008). Fluency oriented reading: Two whole-class approaches. In M. R. Kuhn & P. J. Schwanenflugel (Eds.), *Fluency in the classroom* (pp. 17–35). New York: Guilford Press.

Lefever-Davis, S., & Pearman, C. (2005). Early readers and electronic texts: CD-ROM storybook features that influence reading behavior. *The Reading Teacher, 58*(5), 446–454.

Martin, B., & Archambault, J. (1987). *Knots on a counting rope.* New York: Henry Holt.

Martinez, M., Roser, N., & Strecker, S. (1999). "I never thought I could be a star": A reader's theatre ticket to reading fluency. *The Reading Teacher, 52,* 326–334.

Marzano, R. J. (2004). *Building background knowledge for academic achievement: Research on what works in schools.* Alexandria, VA: Association for Supervision and Curriculum Development.

National Institute of Child Health and Human Development. (2000). *Report of the National Reading Panel: Teaching children to read.* Washington, DC: U.S. Government Printing Office.

Nelson, L., & Morris, D. (1986). *Supported oral reading: A year-long intervention study in two inner-city primary grade classrooms.* Paper presented at the annual meeting of the National Reading Conference, Austin, TX.

Neuman, S. B., & Koskinen, P. (1992). Captioned television as comprehensible input: Effects of incidental word learning from context for language minority students. *Reading Research Quarterly, 27*(1), 94–106.

Opitz, M. F., & Rasinski, T. V. (1998). *Good-bye round robin: 25 effective oral reading strategies.* Portsmouth, NH: Heinemann Educational Books.

Opitz, M. F., & Rasinski, T. V. (2008). *Good-bye round robin: 25 effective oral reading strategies* (updated edition). Portsmouth, NH: Heinemann.

Osborn, J., Lehr, F., & Hiebert, E. H. (2002). *A focus on fluency: Research-based practices in early reading series.* Honolulu, HI: Pacific Resources for Education and Learning (PREL). Available online: http://www.prel.org.

Paige, D. D. (2008). *An evaluation of choral reading using science text on oral reading fluency in struggling adolescents.* Unpublished doctoral dissertation, University of Memphis, Tennessee.

Paris, S. G., Carpenter, R. D., Paris, A. H., & Hamilton, E. E. (2005). Spurious and genuine correlates of children's reading comprehension. In S. G. Paris & S. A. Stahl (Eds.), *Children's reading: Comprehension and assessment* (pp. 131–160). Mahwah, NJ: Lawrence Erlbaum.

Pikulski, J. J., & Chard, D. J. (2005). Fluency: Bridge between decoding and reading comprehension. *The Reading Teacher, 58*(6), 510–519.

Prescott-Griffin, M. L., & Witherell, N. L. (2004). *Fluency in focus: Comprehension strategies for all young readers.* Portsmouth, NH: Heinemann Educational Books.

Pressley, M., Gaskins, I. W., & Fingeret, L. (2006). Instruction and development of reading fluency in struggling readers. In S. J. Samuels & A. E. Farstrup (Eds.), *What research has to say about fluency instruction* (pp. 47–69). Newark, DE: International Reading Association.

Rasinski, T. (1989). Fluency for everyone: Incorporating fluency instruction in the classroom. *The Reading Teacher, 42*(9), 690–693.

Rasinski, T. (1990a). Effects of repeated reading and listening-while-reading on reading fluency. *The Journal of Educational Research, 83*(3), 147–150.

Rasinski, T. (1990b). Investigating measure of reading fluency. *Educational Research Quarterly, 14*(3), 37–44.

Rasinski, T. (2000). Speed does matter. *The Reading Teacher, 54*(2), 146–151.

Rasinski, T. V. (2003). *The fluent reader: Oral reading strategies for building word recognition, fluency, and comprehension.* New York: Scholastic.

Rasinski, T. V., Blachowicz, C., & Lems, K. (2006). *Fluency instruction: Research-based best practices.* New York: Guilford Press.

Rasinski, T. V., & Padak, N. (1996). Five lessons to increase reading fluency. In L. R. Putnam (Ed.), *How to become a better reading teacher: Strategies for assessment and intervention.* Columbus, OH: Merrill/Prentice Hall.

Rasinski, T. V., Padak, N., Linek, W., & Sturtevant, E. (1994). Effects of fluency development on urban second-grade readers. *The Journal of Educational Research, 74,* 400–404.

Rasinski, T. V., Padak, N. D., McKeon, C. A., Wilfong, L. G., Friedauer, J. A., & Heim, P. (2005). Is reading fluency a key for successful high school reading? *Journal of Adolescent and Adult Literacy, 49*(1), 22–27.

Rasinski, T. V, Reutzel, D. R., Chard, D., & Linan-Thompson, S. (in press). Reading Fluency. In P. Afflerbach, M. L. Kamil, E. Moje, & P. D. Pearson (Eds.), *Handbook of Reading Research, Vol. IV.* Mahwah, NJ: Lawrence Erlbaum.

Reutzel, D. R. (1996). Developing special needs readers' oral reading fluency. In L. R. Putnam (Ed.), *How to become a better reading teacher: Strategies for assessment and intervention.* Columbus, OH: Merrill/Prentice Hall.

Reutzel, D. R. (2006). Hey teacher, when you say fluency, what do you mean: Developing fluency and meta-fluency in elementary classrooms. In T. V. Rasinski, C. Blachowicz, & K. Lems (Eds.), *Fluency instruction: Research-based best practices* (pp. 62–85). New York: Guilford Press.

Reutzel, D. R., & Cooter, R. B. (2004). *Teaching children to read: Putting the pieces together* (4th ed.). Upper Saddle River, NJ: Merrill/Prentice Hall.

Reutzel, D. R., & Fawson, P. C. (2002). *Your classroom library: New ways to give it more teaching power.* New York: Scholastic Professional Books.

Reutzel, D. R., Fawson, P. C., & Smith, J. A. (2008). Reconsidering silent sustained reading: An exploratory study of scaffolded silent reading (ScSR). *Journal of Educational Research, 102*(1), 37–50.

Reutzel, D. R., & Gali, K. (1998). The art of children's book selection: A labyrinth unexplored. *Reading Psychology, 19*(1), 3–50.

Reutzel, D. R., & Hollingsworth, P. M. (1993). Effects of fluency training on second grade students' reading comprehension. *The Journal of Educational Research, 86*(6), 325–331.

Reutzel, D. R., Hollingsworth, P. M., & Eldredge, J. L. (1994). Oral reading instruction: The impact on student reading development. *Reading Research Quarterly, 29*(1), 40–62.

Reutzel, D. R., Jones, C. D., Fawson, P. C., & Smith, J. A. (2008). Scaffolded silent reading (ScSR): An alternative to guided oral repeated reading that works! *The Reading Teacher, 62*(3), 194–207.

Richards, M. (2000). Be a good detective: Solve the case of oral reading fluency. *The Reading Teacher, 53*(7), 534–539.

Robinson, B. (1972). *The best Christmas pageant ever.* New York: Harper & Row.

Samuels, S. J. (1979). The method of repeated reading. *The Reading Teacher, 32,* 403–408.

Samuels, S. J. (2007). The DIBELS tests: Is speed of barking at print what we mean by fluency? *Reading Research Quarterly, 42,* 563–566.

Samuels, S. J., & Farstrup, A. E. (2006). *What research has to say about fluency instruction.* Newark, DE: International Reading Association.

Searfoss, L. W. (1975). Radio reading. *The Reading Teacher, 29,* 295–296.

Shake, M. (1986). Teacher interruptions during oral reading instruction: Self-monitoring as an impetus for change in corrective feedback. *Remedial and Special Education, 7*(5), 18–24.

Shinn, M. R. (Ed.). (1989). *Curriculum-based measurement: Assessing special children.* New York: Guilford Press.

Silverstein, S. (1974). *Where the sidewalk ends.* New York: HarperCollins.

Sloyer, S. (1982). *Reader's theater: Story dramatization in the classroom.* Urbana, IL: National Council of Teachers of English.

Snow, C. E., Burns, M. N., & Griffin, P. (1998). *Preventing reading difficulties in young children.* Washington, DC: National Academy Press.

Stahl, S. (2004). What do we know about fluency? In P. McCardle & V. Chhabra (Eds.), *The voice of evidence in reading research* (pp. 187–211). Baltimore: Paul H. Brookes.

Stahl, S. A., Bradley, B., Smith, C. H., Kuhn, M. R., Schwanenflugel, P., Meisinger, E., et al. (2003). *Teaching children to become fluent and automatic readers.* Paper presented at the annual meeting of the American Educational Research Association, Chicago.

Stahl, S. A., & Heubach, K. (2006). Fluency-oriented reading instruction. In K. A. Dougherty Stahl & M. C. McKenna (Eds.), *Reading research at work: Foundations of effective practice* (pp. 177–204). New York: Guilford Press.

Stahl, S. A., Heubach, K., & Cramond, B. (1997). *Fluency-oriented reading instruction.* Washington, DC: National Reading Research Center and U.S. Department of Education, Office of Educational Research and Improvement, Educational Resources Information Center.

Tindal, G., Marston, D., & Deno, S. L. (1983). *The reliability of direct and repeated measurement* (Research Rep. No. 109). Minneapolis: University of Minnesota Institute for Research on Learning Disabilities.

Topping, K. J. (2006). Building reading fluency: Cognitive, behavioral, and socioemotional factors and the role of peer-mediated learning. In S. J. Samuels & A. E. Farstrup (Eds.), *What research has to say about fluency instruction* (pp. 106–129). Newark, DE: International Reading Association.

Topping, K., & Ehly, S. (1998). *Peer-assisted learning.* Mahwah, NJ: Lawrence Erlbaum.

Turner, J., & Paris, S. G. (1995). How literacy tasks influence children's motivation for literacy. *The Reading Teacher, 48*(8), 662–673.

Viorst, J. (1972). *Alexander and the terrible, horrible, no good, very bad day.* New York: Atheneum.

Vygotsky, L. S. (1978). *Mind in society.* Cambridge, MA: Harvard University Press.

Wolf, M., & Katzir-Cohen, T. (2001). Reading fluency and its intervention. *Scientific Studies of Reading, 5*(3), 211–229.

Wood, K. D. (1983). A variation on an old theme: 4-way oral reading. *The Reading Teacher, 37*(1), 38–41.

Worthy, J., & Broaddus, K. (2002). Fluency beyond the primary grades: From group performance to silent, independent reading. *The Reading Teacher, 55*(4), 334–343.

Wright, G., Sherman, R., & Jones, T. B. (2004). Are silent reading behaviors really silent? *The Reading Teacher, 57*(6), 546–553.

Zutell, J., & Rasinski, T. (1991). Training teachers to attend to their students' oral reading fluency. *Theory into Practice, 30*(3), 211–217.

**PEARSON**
# myeducationlab
**The Power of Classroom Practice**
www.myeducationlab.com

Now go to Topic 7: "Fluency" in the MyEducationLab (www.myeducationlab.com) for your course, where you can:

- Find learning outcomes for "Fluency," along with the national standards that connect to these outcomes.
- Complete the tasks in the Assignments and Activities to help you more deeply understand the chapter content.
- Apply and practice your understanding of the core teaching skills identified in the chapter with the Building Teaching Skills and Dispositions learning units.

# 8

# Teaching and Assessing Vocabulary Development

$\mathcal{T}$he sun was streaming into the classroom on a crisp October morning as Mr. Roberts sat with a group of fifth-grade students. They were about to begin studying the rainforests of the Amazon. Tomorrow they would embark on an interactive online exploration at a site called passporttoknowledge.com, so Mr. Roberts thought a vocabulary lesson would help the kids get the most out of the experience. Because they lived in an urban setting in a desert region of the West, he knew there would be some fairly alien notions for his students.

Mr. Roberts wrote the following words on the easel chart—*Amazon River, South America, biodiversity, canopy, Brazil, photosynthesis, species,* and then said, "As I mentioned this morning, we're going to begin an exciting unit of study on the rainforests of the Amazon. These are a few of the words from the lesson guide that will be coming up in our Internet experiences, so I thought we should talk about them a little. Let's begin with the basics—who can tell me where South America is?"

James eagerly responded, "I think it's near Orlando."

LaJean retorted, "I don't think so. It's where Chile is, isn't it?"

Mr. Roberts said, "Very good, LaJean. Let's all take a look at the map and see exactly where South America is. Now let's all gather round the television screen and I'll use Google Earth on the Internet so we can take an even better look at South America from space!" He then proceeded with a short geography lesson using the Google Earth map, moving around the continent and finally ending up tracing the Amazon River. Regularly, Mr. Roberts would cross-reference images the children were seeing on Google Earth with the large map so they could see how the two matched and yet served different purposes, such as the map showing boundaries.

Roberts then returned to the vocabulary words he had written on the easel chart. "Okay, then, can anyone tell me something about the word *biodiversity*? I'll give you a hint: If you break away the first part of the word, *bio*, which means 'life,' that leaves you with a pretty familiar word—*diversity*. What does *diversity* mean?"

After a long silence and a few blank stares, Mr. Roberts tried another tack. "OK, forget that one for now. What about the word *canopy?*"

Again, no takers.

Finally, Julio took a chance, "Isn't canopy the stuff they make tents out of?"

"Well, a tent is a kind of canopy, but some kinds of canopy aren't necessarily tents. I think Julio may have given us a kind of riddle we will need to solve!"

Clearly, most of his students did not have the slightest notion what these words meant, so some serious vocabulary development was in order. Fortunately, Mr. Roberts had prepared for this possibility.

"Well, it *just so happens* that I have a few games we can play [teacher talk for "learning activities"] that will help us solve the canopy riddle and also get us ready to explore the rainforests. So let's go."

Go to the Assignments and Activities section of Topic 6: "Vocabulary" in the MyEducationLab for your course and complete the activity entitled "Student Vocabularies." As you read the article and answer the accompanying questions, note the multiple types of vocabularies.

Words are the symbols we use to express ideas—*captions,* you might say, that describe life experiences. Vocabulary learning is a process that goes on throughout life and can be enhanced in the classroom through enticing learning experiences. Except for children who are economically deprived or have a learning disability, most acquire a vocabulary of over 10,000 words during the first 5 years of their lives (Smith, 1987). Most schoolchildren learn between 2,000 and 3,600 words per year, though estimates vary from 1,500 to more than 8,000 (Clark, 1993; Johnson, 2001; Nagy, Herman, & Anderson, 1985). Clearly, vocabulary development is a critical aspect of learning to read (Rupley, Logan, & Nichols, 1999).

There seems to be a cyclical effect between vocabulary knowledge and reading. As Johnson and Rasmussen (1998) have stated, "Word knowledge affects reading comprehension, which in turn helps students expand their knowledge bases, which in turn facilitates vocabulary growth and reading comprehension" (p. 204). As students move forward in their schooling, vocabulary becomes even more important. In content-area instruction (e.g., science, social studies, etc.), new vocabulary constitutes both information students must learn and concepts they need to understand to function within the subject (Rekrut, 1996).

Since the latter part of the 19th century in America, there has been a great deal of investigation and debate about the role of vocabulary knowledge in learning to read. In 1885 James M. Cattell argued that children should learn entire words as a method of beginning reading. Though learning "sight words" alone is no longer recommended as an effective beginning reading approach, most teachers and researchers still believe that the acquisition of a large number of sight words should be part of *every* child's beginning reading program.

There are actually several different "vocabularies" housed in one's mind and usable for language transactions. The largest of these is known as the **listening vocabulary.** These are words you are able to hear and understand but not necessarily use in your own speech. For example, when the famous Hale-Bopp Comet visited our solar system in 1997, most children in the middle and upper elementary grades were quite capable of watching news telecasts about the comet and understanding most of what was reported. However, if you were to ask many of these same children to explain what they had just learned, many of the technical words and factual bits of information would not have been included in their description. It is not that the children somehow forgot everything they had just learned; rather, they did not "own" the words for speech purposes quite yet. Although they were able to hear and understand the technical words, the words were in their listening vocabulary only.

Words that students can hear, understand, and use in their speech are known as **speaking vocabulary.** It is a subset of the listening vocabulary and, thus, is smaller. The gap between people's listening and speaking vocabularies is greatest in youth. The gap tends to narrow as adulthood approaches, though the two vocabularies are never equal. The next largest vocabulary is the **reading vocabulary.** As you may guess, it is a subset of one's listening and speaking vocabularies and consists of words one can read and understand. The smallest vocabulary that one learns is the **writing vocabulary**—words that one can understand when listening, speaking, and reading, and can reproduce when writing.

Cooter and Flynt (1996) group listening and reading vocabularies into a collective category known as the **receptive vocabulary,** and they group writing and speaking vocabularies into a category known as the **expressive vocabulary.** These descriptors reflect the broader language functions of these vocabularies for the student as either information receiver or spoken or written language producer.

# $\mathcal{B}$ACKGROUND BRIEFING FOR TEACHERS

For students to be able to read and understand a word, they must have first acquired it at the listening and speaking levels. Teachers, then, must somehow find out which words are already "owned" by their students as listening and speaking vocabulary and then teach the unknown words that may be critical in their assigned reading. Without this kind of knowledge, adequate context for word identification will be missing and can threaten further reading development and, of course, hinder comprehension.

## Research Findings on Vocabulary Learning

To determine how vocabulary can best be taught and related to the reading comprehension process, the National Reading Panel (National Institute of Child Health and Human Development, 2000) examined more than 20,000 research citations identified through electronic and manual literature searches. From this set, citations were removed if they did not meet predetermined scientific criteria. Fifty studies dating from 1979 to 2000 were reviewed in detail. In the next sections, we briefly summarize key research-supported findings by the National Reading Panel, as well as other important research.

### Three Levels of Vocabulary Learning

The truth is, words are not either "known" or "unknown." As with most new learning, new vocabulary words and concepts are learned by degree. The Partnership for Reading (2001), in summarizing conclusions drawn by the National Reading Panel, described three levels of vocabulary learning: *unknown, acquainted,* and *established.* Definitions for each of these three levels are presented in Figure 8.1. Keep in mind that these levels or "degrees" of learning apply to each of the four vocabulary types—listening, speaking, reading, and writing, so helping children build strong reading and writing vocabularies can sometimes be a formidable task indeed.

Sometimes we learn new meanings of words that are already known to us. The word *race,* for example, has many different meanings (a running competition, a classification of human beings, etc.). One of the most challenging tasks for students can be learning the meaning of a new word representing an unknown concept. According to the research, much of learning in the content areas involves this type of word learning. As students learn about deserts, hurricanes, and immigrants, they may be learning both new concepts and new words. Learning words and concepts in science, social studies, and mathematics is even more challenging

---

### FIGURE 8.1 Levels of Vocabulary Learning

**Defining Levels of Word Knowledge**

| | |
|---|---|
| *Unknown* | The word is completely unfamiliar and its meaning is unknown. |
| *Acquainted* | The word is somewhat familiar; the student has some idea of its basic meaning. |
| *Established* | The word is very familiar; the student can immediately recognize its meaning and use the word correctly. |

*Source:* From Partnership for Reading (2001).

---

because each major concept often is associated with many other new concepts. For example, the concept *desert* is often associated with other concepts that may be unfamiliar, such as *cactus, plateau,* and *mesa* (Partnership for Reading, 2001, p. 43).

## Building a Robust Vocabulary: Which Words Should We Teach?

Not all words are created equal, at least in terms of how common or useful they are in English. Beck, McKeown, and Kucan (2002) suggest that words may be put into one of three "tiers" in terms of frequency of occurrence and usage. **Tier one words** consists of the most basic words that occur frequently in life and rarely require direct instruction. *Clock, baby, ball, happy, walk,* and *run* are a few examples of tier one words. Beck and her colleagues (2002) suggest that there are about 8,000 tier one words that do not need instruction.

Tier two words are high frequency in terms of use by mature English language users and are found across a variety of knowledge domains: *coincidence, absurd, industrious,* and *fortunate* are examples. Tier two words are not exclusive to one event, a single content area, or one context. Tier two words play an enormous role in the language user's inventory of words. They tend to be transposable in a wide variety of settings or contents. Instruction directed at tier two words can be most fruitful and have a major impact on verbal functioning, reading, and writing development. Beck and colleagues (2002) estimate that there are about 7,000 tier two words to be learned, and indicate teaching 200 to 400 words per year in grades K through 12 can have significant impact.

Tier three words are low-frequency terms that tend to be limited to certain domains and areas of study (e.g., mathematics, science, the social studies). Examples of tier three words include *carburetor, isotope, lathe,* and *pentathlon.*

### Developing Robust Vocabularies

Beck and her colleagues (2002) recommend "student-friendly" explanations when teaching tiers two and three words, using the following procedure.

1. Describe the word and how it is generally used.
2. Explain how the word is used in everyday language.
3. Invite students to help you explain the word.

Once instruction is completed, a formative assessment may be given to check for understanding. For example, one first-grade teacher* uses the book *Antarctic Ice* (Mastro & Wu,

---

*Note:* We discovered and adapted these classroom examples on the website www.trussvillecityschools.com. Teacher Donna Reynolds from Florida is credited with creating these splendid examples.

2003) as inspiration to introduce these tier two words: *nuzzled, pranced, raging, adapt, intriguing, inhabit.*

To describe the word *nuzzled* the following example was offered along with a matching picture:

> *If an animal* nuzzled *against you, it would be rubbing you with its face or nose.*

To explain the word *nuzzled* in a variety of contexts, the following examples were offered and discussed:

> *When the weather was stormy, the mother horse* nuzzled *her colt with her soft face to comfort him and keep him warm.*
>
> *The colt must have felt very safe when his mother* nuzzled *her face against him.*
>
> *Have you ever had a pet* nuzzle *against you? How did it make you feel?*

Then, to extend the conversation about *nuzzled* and *invite* students to help explain the new word, the teacher and children discussed these questions:

> *Name an animal that you would like to* nuzzle *you.*
>
> *Do you think a person can* nuzzle? *How?*
>
> *Would an animal who* nuzzled *you be friendly or not friendly? Why do you think so?*

Later, once all new words had been introduced, they reviewed the words in a testlike format, demonstrated in the following excerpt.

> *Fill in the blanks with the correct word.*
>
> ### nuzzled   pranced   inhabit
>
> *My sister* _____ *around the room as she showed us her new shoes.*
>
> *Last night, my puppy and I* _____ *close to each other while we relaxed on the couch watching TV.*

In this chapter, as you will see, we offer assessment and teaching strategies focused almost entirely on tier two and tier three words. You will note that each of the instructional activities in this chapter are marked *Robust Vocabulary Tier Two, Robust Vocabulary Tier Three,* or *Robust Vocabulary Tiers Two & Three* as appropriate.

## What Research Tells Us about Teaching Vocabulary

Go to the Building Teaching Skills and Dispositions section of Topic 6: "Vocabulary" in the MyEducationLab for your course and complete the activity entitled "Building Vocabulary Knowledge." As you work through the learning unit, consider ways the teacher is offering direct instruction and multiple exposures to new words for depth of learning.

Most vocabulary is learned indirectly, but some vocabulary *must* be taught directly. The following conclusions about indirect vocabulary learning and direct vocabulary instruction are of particular importance to classroom teachers (National Institute of Child Health and Human Development, 2000):

- *Children learn the meanings of most words indirectly through everyday experiences with oral and written language.* There are typically three ways children learn vocabulary indirectly. First, they participate in oral language every day. Children learn word meanings through conversations with other people; as they participate in conversations, they often hear words repeated several times. The more conversations children have, the more words they learn!

   Another indirect way children learn words is by being read to. Reading aloud is especially powerful when the reader pauses during reading to define an unfamiliar word and, after reading, engages the child in a conversation about the book. Conversations about books help children learn new words and concepts and relate them to their prior knowledge and experience (Partnership for Reading, 2001)

words in reading groups or literature circles—are far more effective in cementing new knowledge and improving comprehension.

- *Students require a good bit of repetition to learn new words and integrate them into existing knowledge (schemas).* In some cases, students may require as many as 40 encounters to fully learn new vocabulary. To know a word well means knowing what it means, how to pronounce it, and how its meaning changes in different contexts. Repeated exposure to the word in different contexts is the key to successful learning.
- *Students should be helped to develop their own strategies for word learning from written and oral contexts.* This includes the use of context clues, structural analysis (root words, prefixes, suffixes), and research skills (use of the dictionary, thesaurus, etc.).

# 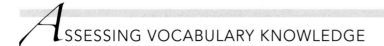SSESSING VOCABULARY KNOWLEDGE

Most vocabulary assessment done by master teachers is through careful classroom observations of student reading behaviors. As teachers work with their pupils each day in needs-based group instruction, they discover high-utility words that seem to cause trouble for one or more students. Teachers can work these words into vocabulary instruction activities like those featured later in this chapter. But this is not to suggest that more cannot be done early in the school year to discover which words most of your students need to learn. Following are a few classroom-proven ideas to help with that process.

## Oral Reading Assessment

### Purpose

Oral reading assessment is a method by which problem vocabulary words in print can be identified by the teacher in a quick and efficient manner. It is drawn from the running record style of assessment frequently used to note reading miscues. Ideally, the passages used should be sufficiently challenging so that students will have trouble with about 5 to 10% of the words. It will be necessary for you to do a quick word count to determine if the passages are appropriate once the student has read them. It is also essential that you have a range of passages, in terms of difficulty, to account for the vast differences among students' reading abilities. (*Note:* A student who pronounces fewer than 10% of the words correctly may not be getting enough context from the passages for adequate comprehension.)

### Materials

- Photocopies (two copies each) of three or four passages drawn from reading materials commonly used in your classroom curriculum that you believe to be at the student's instructional or frustration reading level

### Procedure

Give the student a copy of the first passage to be read and keep one for yourself. Ask the student to read the passage aloud. Note any words that the student either does not know or mispronounces. Repeat the procedure until the student has read all of the passages. We recommend that you discontinue a passage if the student consistently has trouble with more than one or two words in any one sentence.

After the student has finished, tally the number of miscalled words and determine if the passage is acceptable for analysis (no more than about 10% miscalled or unknown words).

List any words that seem to be problematic for the student. Repeat this procedure with all of your students during the first week or so of the new school year and then create a master list of words that seem to be problematic and determine the number or percentage of the class who seem to find each word difficult or unknown. Use the more frequent problem words as part of your vocabulary instruction program.

## Cloze Tests

### Purpose

Cloze tests are short (250 words) screening assessment passages drawn from reading materials found in your instructional program. Though they are often used with fiction texts, we feel their best use is with adopted subject-area textbooks that all students are required to read because of the relatively high frequency of unusual words.

Cloze tests have key words deleted and replaced with a blank line (Johnson, 2001). Students are asked to read the teacher-constructed cloze passages and fill in missing words based on what they believe makes sense using context clues. Students guess the missing words based on knowledge of a subject, understanding of basic syntax (word order relationships), and word or sentence meaning (semantics).

Cloze tests have distinct advantages and disadvantages. Perhaps the major advantage is that they can be administered to a group of students rather than to one individual at a time. Another advantage is the emphasis on context and therefore comprehension. On the other hand, cloze tests can be pretty frustrating to kids. However, you can soften the frustration problem, especially with struggling readers, by using a maze test as an alternative (discussed in the next section).

### Materials

- Cloze tests based on nonfiction/core subject-area textbooks

### Procedure

Begin by identifying three passages of about 250 words each from the book you plan to use for instruction (e.g., science, social studies, supplemental texts, etc.). One passage should be selected near the beginning of the textbook, a second from around the middle, and the third from the end of the book. Using a word processing program, type each of the three selections using the Arial font (or similar font) as this tends to be easier for students to read, especially those who may have minor visual discrimination issues. Once you have created your three text documents, edit them as follows:

1. Leave the first sentence intact (no changes).
2. Beginning with the second sentence, delete one of the first five words and replace it with an underlined blank space large enough for students to write in the word they think is missing.
3. Continue to delete and replace every fifth word thereafter with an underlined blank space until you have 50 blanks. After the 50th blank has been reached, simply leave the remaining part of that sentence intact (no deletions).
4. Include another sentence or two at the end of the cloze passage. Your cloze passage is now ready.

Follow the same steps to compose your other two cloze passages. Refer to Figure 8.2 for an example of a partial cloze passage.

---

| FIGURE 8.2 | Cloze Passage (Partial Extract) |

**Diamonds**

A diamond is one of the most beautiful treasures that nature ever created, and one of the rarest. It takes thousands _____ years for nature to _____ a chunk of carbon _____ a rough diamond. Only _____ important diamond fields have _____ found in the world—_____ India, South America, and Africa.

_____ first diamonds were found _____ the sand and gravel _____ stream beds. These types _____ diamonds are called alluvial _____. Later, diamonds were found _____ in the earth in _____ formations called pipes. These _____ resemble extinct volcanoes. The _____ in which diamonds are _____ is called blue ground. _____ even where diamonds are _____, it takes digging and _____ through tons of rock _____ gravel to find enough _____ for a one-carat _____.

Gem diamonds' quality is _____ on weight, purity, color, _____ cut. The weight of a diamond is measured by the carat. Its purity is determined by the presence or absence of impurities, such as foreign minerals and uncrystallized carbon.

*Source:* From *Comprehensive Reading Inventory,* by R. B. Cooter, E. S. Flynt, and K. S. Cooter, 2007. Upper Saddle River, NJ: Pearson/Merrill/Prentice Hall. Copyright © 2007. Used with permission of Pearson Education.

### Scoring Cloze Passages

With cloze passages, students must guess the *exact* missing word to get the response correct. However, misspellings are not counted as errors. Students tend to make many errors on cloze passages so do not be alarmed. The scoring criteria reflect this requirement:

- **Independent Level** = 50% or more correct (25 or more correct out of 50)
- **Instructional Level** = 33–49% (17–24 correct)
- **Frustration Level** = 0–32% (0–16 correct)

If you administer three cloze passages from each textbook as recommended, average the results to determine each student's overall reading level for the screening assessment.

## Maze Test

### Purpose

The maze test (Guthrie et al., 1974) is essentially the same in purpose and format as the cloze test with one exception. Children are given passages constructed in the same way as the cloze test but there are three choices for students to choose from for each blank. This reduces student stress but also requires a different scoring scale.

### Materials

- Maze tests primarily based on nonfiction/core subject-area textbooks because of the relatively high frequency of unusual words

### Procedure

Follow the same steps in creating maze passages as described for creating cloze passages. The one exception is that three choices are given to the reader for replacing the deleted word (Alexander & Heathington, 1988):

1. The correct word
2. An incorrect word that is the same part of speech
3. An incorrect word that is a different part of speech

**Maze Sample Sentence**

Gem diamonds' quality is _____ on weight, purity, color, and cut.
(based, stored, seem)

The criteria for assessing maze tests is as follows (Bradley et al., 1978):

*Independent Level* = 85% or more correct (43 or more correct out of 50)
*Instructional Level* = 50–84% (25–42 correct)
*Frustration Level* = 0–49% (0–24 correct)

If you administer three maze passages from each textbook as recommended, average the results to determine each student's overall reading level.

## Vocabulary Flash Cards

### Purpose

One of the most traditional ways to do a quick assessment of a student's vocabulary knowledge is the flash card technique. High-frequency words, as well as other high-utility words for specific grade levels, are printed individually on flash cards and shown to students for them to identify. Though some reading researchers argue that flash cards are not a valid assessment tool because the words are presented in isolation instead of in complete sentences and paragraphs, flash cards continue to be used by many master teachers as one way to determine the direction of classroom instruction.

### Materials

- List of high-frequency sight words (*Note:* We provide a copy of the Fry [1980] word list later in the chapter)
- Index cards with words printed using a bold marker (or printed on a computer printer in a large font size onto heavy paper stock and then cut into uniform flash cards)
- A photocopy/master list of the words for each student in your class for recording purposes

### Procedure

"Flash" each card to the student one at a time and ask him or her to name the word. Allow approximately 5 seconds for each word to be identified. Circle any unknown or mispronounced words on a copy of the master sheet you are using for that student (simply note the student's name at the top of the photocopy along with the date of testing). After you have shown the flash cards to all students, compile a master list of troublesome words for whole-class or small-group instruction. We highly recommend the "Word Banks" activity found later in this chapter as one way to use this information. The flash cards can be reused periodically to determine whether students have learned the words being taught.

In Figure 8.3 we summarize the procedures and instruments we have just discussed for assessing factors associated with vocabulary development. In this Summary Matrix of Assessments we provide information about federally related assessment purposes (i.e., screening, diagnostic, progress-monitoring, or outcomes assessment) as well as type of test or procedure

---

**FIGURE 8.3**   Summary Matrix of Assessments to Measure Vocabulary Development

| Name of Assessment Tool | Screening Assessment | Diagnostic Assessment | Progress-Monitoring Assessment | Outcomes Assessment | Norm-Referenced Test | Criterion-Referenced Test | Reliability Evidence | Validity Evidence |
|---|---|---|---|---|---|---|---|---|
| Oral Reading Assessment | + | − | − | + | − | + | − | − |
| Cloze Test | + | − | + | − | − | + | + | + |
| Maze Test | + | − | + | − | − | + | + | + |
| Vocabulary Flash Cards | + | − | + | + | − | + | − | − |

Key:  + can be used for      − not appropriate for

---

and psychometric evidence about the test or procedure scores (any available reliability and validity evidence).

## Connecting Assessment Findings to Teaching Strategies

Before discussing phonics and word attack teaching strategies, we provide an If-Then chart connecting assessment findings to intervention and strategy choices (see Figure 8.4). It is our

---

**FIGURE 8.4**   If-Then Strategy Guide for Vocabulary Instruction

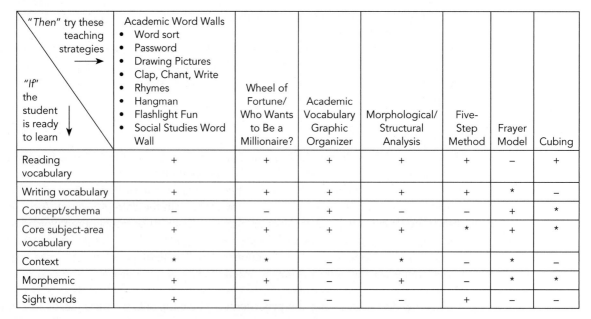

| *"If"* the student is ready to learn / *"Then"* try these teaching strategies → | Academic Word Walls • Word sort • Password • Drawing Pictures • Clap, Chant, Write • Rhymes • Hangman • Flashlight Fun • Social Studies Word Wall | Wheel of Fortune/ Who Wants to Be a Millionaire? | Academic Vocabulary Graphic Organizer | Morphological/ Structural Analysis | Five-Step Method | Frayer Model | Cubing |
|---|---|---|---|---|---|---|---|
| Reading vocabulary | + | + | + | + | + | − | + |
| Writing vocabulary | + | + | + | + | + | * | − |
| Concept/schema | − | − | + | − | − | + | * |
| Core subject-area vocabulary | + | + | + | + | * | + | * |
| Context | * | * | − | * | − | * | − |
| Morphemic | + | + | − | + | − | * | * |
| Sight words | + | − | − | − | + | − | − |

Key:  + Excellent strategy     * Adaptable strategy     − Unsuitable strategy

intention to help you select the most appropriate instructional interventions and strategies to meet your students' needs based on assessment data. The following list briefly describes each vocabulary instruction area found in the If-Then strategy guide.

- *Reading vocabulary.* Describes words in the student's listening and speaking vocabularies that are not yet recognized in print.
- *Writing vocabulary.* Describes words in the student's listening, speaking, and reading vocabularies that are not yet known well enough to be used when writing compositions.
- *Concept/schema.* Describes inability to comprehend a new word because of a lack of conceptual knowledge related to the word.
- *Technical vocabulary.* Describes new words that are unknown to the student and directly related to a content area (i.e., science, social studies, mathematics, etc.).
- *Context.* Describes inability to use context clues to figure out the meaning of an unknown word.
- *Morphemic analysis.* Describes lack of knowledge about word parts such as prefixes, suffixes, and root words—also known as *structural analysis.*
- *Sight words.* Describes difficulty with common words in print that should be recognized instantly.

In the next part of this chapter, we offer vocabulary instruction strategies for intervention based on the foregoing assessments.

| Vocabulary Bingo! | SAVOR | Peer Teaching | Personal Word List | Semantic Maps | Making Words | Word Banks | Comparison Grid | Vocabulary Cluster | Contextual Redefinition |
|---|---|---|---|---|---|---|---|---|---|
| + | * | * | + | + | + | + | − | + | + |
| + | * | + | + | + | + | + | * | + | + |
| * | + | + | − | + | * | − | + | + | + |
| * | + | + | + | + | − | + | + | + | + |
| * | + | * | − | − | − | − | − | − | + |
| − | − | + | * | − | * | * | − | − | − |
| + | − | * | + | − | * | + | − | − | − |

# TEACHING STRATEGIES: HELPING STUDENTS INCREASE THEIR READING VOCABULARIES

Susan Watts (1995) has described five attributes of effective vocabulary instruction. These criteria, delineated in the following list, have guided our selection of teaching activities in this chapter.

Go to the Assignments and Activities section of Topic 6: "Vocabulary" in the MyEducationLab for your course and complete the activity entitled "Strategic Vocabulary Instruction." As you watch the video and answer the accompanying questions, consider ways the strategies presented help students connect new information with what is already known by learners.

- Students should be provided with *multiple exposures* to new words in a *variety of contexts* over *time.* This will help students move new vocabulary from short-term to long-term (permanent) memory.
- Words should be taught within the *context* of a *content-area* unit or topic, theme, or story. This helps the new vocabulary to find the right "schema home."
- Teachers should help students *activate prior knowledge* (i.e., what they already know) when learning new words.
- *Relationships* should be emphasized in your lesson between *known* words and concepts and the *new* vocabulary you are introducing. This provides the all-important *scaffolding* for learning.
- Students should be taught to *use context clues* and *reference tools* in their reading and writing (i.e., dictionary, thesaurus, online aids) for building word knowledge.

## Academic Word Walls

Appropriate for *Robust Vocabulary Tiers Two & Three Words*

Patricia Cunningham (2000) provides us with a wonderful description of a **word wall** as a place where teachers can direct students' attention to high-frequency words, important words in a content unit of study, or useful words for books they are reading. There are many possible types of word walls. In essence, you simply post important words on a section of wall, usually on butcher paper or a pocket chart, and categorize them according to your purpose.

**Academic word walls** or **AW$^2$** (Cooter, 2009) is a new research-based procedure created especially for schools serving large numbers of children from poverty circumstances. Based on the work of Cunningham (2000), AW$^2$ is a method to focus students' attention on new and important words in core subject areas (e.g., science, social studies, mathematics), while providing them with *multiple exposures* to new vocabulary. AW$^2$ can help teachers increase students' retention of new words, improve their comprehension of assigned readings, and boost writing performance on state tests and other measures. Note that materials for AW$^2$ need not be expensive or elaborate—function is everything. It is very important that any word wall allow for target words to be easily moved, grouped, or removed.

### Materials

- A blank section of the classroom wall, a blank bulletin board, a large whiteboard, or large sheets of butcher paper
- Card stock (approximately 5 × 8 inches each) for writing individual academic words or longer pieces for sentence strips
- Colored markers (dry-erase markers for whiteboards)
- Text and supplemental readings for your required unit of study
- Your state's "academic vocabulary lists" for your subject/grade level (usually accessible online at your state department of education website)

## Procedure

Based on several years of experimentation in schools serving large numbers of poverty-level children, the following procedure is a good way to begin using academic word walls.

- *Choosing academic words.* It is important that academic word walls are *group generated* (i.e., teachers and students work *together* in selecting academic words to go on the wall). Begin with students working in small groups provided with the text chapter and/or supplemental texts you plan to use in a new unit of study. Ask them to identify in their groups three to five academic words in the text selection that are

  1. Known Words
  2. Familiar Words (i.e., words I have heard before, but don't know very well)
  3. Unknown Words (i.e., words I have never heard before or don't know what they mean)

  Ask each group to write these three academic word types on a sheet of chart paper and be prepared to share their findings with the class. (*Note:* If students should come across new or interesting *general vocabulary* as they preview the text materials, they can include these in their list, too.)

- *Academic words "Gallery Walk."* Ask each group to take turns sharing and discussing their words with the class. If general vocabulary words are mentioned, they may be discussed and linked to other words and concepts about which students are aware.

- *Creating a group-generated AW². After the groups have finished their presentations, ask the class to help you identify words that should go onto a master list or the group-generated academic word wall. Help students notice the words they had in common by underlining or circling them. The first words to go onto the AW² should be ones that two or more groups had in common. Write these words on card stock large enough for all students to see and post on a section of wall or a large bulletin board.*

## Tips for Using AW² in Your Classroom

The key to success with AW² is to provide students with multiple exposures to new academic words and lots of discussion about their meanings. As a rule of thumb, students usually need from 20 to 40 *meaningful exposures* for academic words to be truly learned. Having students sort academic words on your AW² in different ways on a daily basis for just 5 to 10 minutes, and talking about *why* these new arrangements of words make sense, will help your students learn and succeed.

There are many ways academic words can be sorted and talked about with your students, and you may be able to invent some of your own in the different subject areas. The purpose of doing word sorts with your academic word walls is to get students to group, discuss, regroup, and further discuss important vocabulary in your field of study.

Following are three of the most basic *word sort* strategies that may be used with your students in AW² activities. Word sort activities are appropriate for *Robust Vocabulary Tiers Two & Three Words.*

*Note: The teacher retains the right to add academic words she or he feels should be included. You must be sure to have enough words for your academic word wall for vocabulary activities. How many? Twenty or more is a good target. Remember, you can always introduce words from prior units that are related to the new unit. It is also permissible to include general vocabulary words that are new to students, but not necessarily specific to content subject area, such as adjectives, adverbs, and so on.

- *Closed word sorts.* With closed word sorts, students are told in advance the categories in which they must arrange their vocabulary cards.
- *Open word sorts.* With open word sorts, students are required to group words from the academic word wall according to how they think they are related and then provide their own label for each group of words. The label may be an important concept in your unit of study, a relationship, or a common characteristic the words share.
- *Speed sorts.* Open or closed sorts are used (teacher's choice) and students have to complete them within a certain amount of time (e.g., 1-minute sort, 2-minute sort). This is a great review or assessment activity.

It is important in each word sort activity that students should be expected to explain or justify *why* they think specific academic words belong under a label or category. This creates an opportunity for students to talk about the words, explore their meanings, and retell what they have learned. Word sort activities using academic word walls are *ideal* for either whole-class discussions or small-group instruction.

## Popular AW² Activities

Activities already mentioned in this chapter may be adaptable for AW². We now share a few more found to be popular in urban schools participating in our research.

- *Password* (Appropriate for *Robust Vocabulary Tiers Two & Three Words*). Divide the class into two teams. One person from each team sits in a chair in front of the class. Those two people receive a card with a vocabulary word from the AW². The first person gives a one-word clue to his or her team. If no one from the team can guess the word, the second person gives a clue to his or her team. This alternates back and forth until someone from one of the teams guesses the word, or until a specified number of clues have been given.

- *Drawing pictures* (Appropriate for *Robust Vocabulary Tier Three Words*). The students draw pictures—but no words—on the board so that the students in the other group can guess the word or expressions they're trying to represent. This is a fun way to review some vocabulary and break up the class routine.

- *Clap, Chant, Write—Introduction of new words* (Appropriate for *Robust Vocabulary Tiers Two & Three Words*). Adapted from Sigmon (1997), the teacher introduces five new words per week by having students
  - See the words
  - Say the words
  - Chant the words (snap, clap, stomp, cheer)
  - Write the words and check them together with the teacher
  - Trace around the words and check together with the teacher

  1. Have the students number a sheet of paper 1 to 5.
  2. Place one of the five new academic word cards on the academic word wall. Say the word, use the word in a sentence, provide a picture clue if appropriate, and then have students write the word on their paper. Continue in this way with your four new additional words.
  3. When all five words have been written, point to the words and have the students clap and chant the spellings of the words.
  4. Students use a red pen, marker, or crayon to trace around the word.
  5. On the following days of the week, the teacher practices the new word wall words and reviews previous words with practice activities.

- *Word wall rhymes* (Appropriate for *Robust Vocabulary Tiers Two & Three Words*). Recommended by Cunningham (1999), the teacher says a sentence that contains a word that rhymes with one of the target words on the AW$^2$ and is spelled with the same pattern. Children must decide which AW$^2$ word rhymes and how to spell it as demonstrated in the following simple AW$^2$ example where students are learning about alternative verbs for the word *said*.

  1. Students number their paper from 1 to 5.
  2. The teacher gives the following clues for the AW$^2$ words.

     Number one begins with *cr* and rhymes with *stowed*

     Student writes *crowed* on paper

     Number two begins with an *m* and rhymes with *stumbled*

     Student writes *mumbled* on paper

     Number three begins with an *f* and rhymes with *melt*

     Student writes *felt* on paper

  3. To check the answers, teacher says the rhyming word and students then say the word they wrote and chant its spelling.

- *Hangman* (Appropriate for *Robust Vocabulary Tiers Two & Three Words*). An old favorite game, hangman is a simple (though perhaps gruesome) vocabulary review activity. Proceed according to the following easy steps substituting words and details as needed for those used in this example from a unit on the moon for the target word *crater*:

  1. On a whiteboard or chart paper, draw a "gallows" and the number of spaces below it representing each letter of the target word (see illustration below).

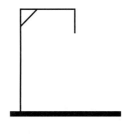

  2. Say, "I'm thinking of a word on our academic word wall that has six letters and has something to do with an *impact.*"
  3. The student(s) guess one letter at a time. As a correct letter is guessed, write the letter in the corresponding blank. For each incorrect guess, draw one part of a stickman in this order—head, body, one arm, then the next, and ending with each leg. If the whole body is drawn due to incorrect responses, the man is hanged (see below) and

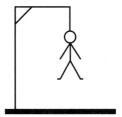

the teacher/partner supplies the correct answer. (*Note:* You can also play hangman on the Internet by going to this fun website: www.hangmangame.net.)

- *Flashlight Fun* (Appropriate for many *Robust Vocabulary Tier Two Words*). Flashlight Fun is a simple activity suggested by Gruber (1998) that students through middle school enjoy. (*Note:* Students enjoy taking turns using the flashlight.)

   1. Turn out the lights in your classroom.
   2. Say this poem together with the class: *Flashlight, flashlight, oh so bright, Shine on a word with your light.*
   3. Shine the flashlight on individual AW$^2$ words placed around the room for the class to read and chant.

- *Social studies academic word wall* (Appropriate for *Robust Vocabulary Tier Three Words*). This AW$^2$ activity works well with any core subject-area vocabulary or current events. The following example focuses on issues in the Middle East.

   1. Put up a map showing countries of the Middle East.
   2. Using yarn, target the areas or countries of interest and attach a string of yarn to the map.
   3. Create a card for your AW$^2$ with the name of the country and a number and attach to the yarn.
   4. Cover the label with a sticky note and have the children guess which country is which with a worksheet numbered 1 to 10 or with the number of yarn cards you have placed on the wall.

### Teacher Self-Evaluation Continuum: AW$^2$

Teachers, like students, go through zones of proximal development (from novice to expert) in the implementation of new teaching strategies. As part of a large-scale federal project in urban schools, Cooter (2009) developed a kind of rubric or *continuum* for implementing AW$^2$ to help you monitor your own use of this strategy and discover ways to deepen its use in your classroom (see Figure 8.5).

## Wheel of Fortune

Appropriate for most *Robust Vocabulary Tiers Two & Three Words*

### Purpose

Based on the popular television program, Wheel of Fortune is an exhilarating game for vocabulary review in small-group settings. This game can be played with eight students as described below with minimal materials or, if you want to create your own computer version, there are many free sites online (for example, http://jc-schools.net/tutorials/PPT-games).

### Materials
- A number wheel with the numbers 1 through 8 as pictured in Figure 8.6
- Index cards
- Markers

| FIGURE 8.5 | Teacher Self-Evaluation Continuum: AW² |
|---|---|

| Exemplary A | Above Average B | Acceptable C | Early Implementation D | Traditional Instruction E |
|---|---|---|---|---|
| Teacher explicitly describes the AW² vocabulary activity, provides a purpose, and explains why it is helpful. | Teacher explicitly describes the AW² vocabulary activity and provides a purpose for learning it. | Teacher introduces the AW² activity and explains its purpose. | Teacher gives directions for activities that provide some meaningful interaction with new academic words (e.g., using words in a crossword puzzle, writing sentences using new words). | Teacher identifies or distributes a list of new academic vocabulary to be learned. |
| New words are introduced, explained, and connected to students' prior learning (e.g., using graphic organizers like semantic maps). | Teacher models the strategy, sometimes using a "think aloud" strategy to clarify. | Teacher models/ demonstrates the strategy in a step-by-step manner. | | Teacher assigns independent activities (e.g., looking up dictionary definitions, fill-in-the-blank activities, matching, other worksheets). |
| Involves students in word selection (i.e., new words to be learned). | After modeling the AW² strategy, the teacher engages students in discussion to determine whether more modeling is required. | Teacher reads aloud texts containing new academic words. | Teacher provides some modeling of vocabulary activities, but engages students in dialogue while also modeling. | |
| Teacher models the strategy using a "think aloud" strategy to clarify. | | Teacher explains expectations for students for each AW² activity. | Teacher reviews new vocabulary as needed according to observations. | Homework is assigned (e.g., worksheets, activities from textbook) for vocabulary learning. |
| Teacher and students have meaningful dialogues about all new words to be learned. | | Teacher invites student input and questions in order to check their understanding at each phase of the activity. | A summative assessment is given at the end of the academic unit of study to check for new academic vocabulary knowledge. | An end-of-unit test is given to check for new academic vocabulary knowledge. |
| Students compile list of new academic vocabulary for future use. | | Teacher observes students while they are working to assess learning. | | |
| Students create their own tests or other products using new academic vocabulary to demonstrate their understanding. | | Teacher reassesses students' understanding and reteaches or reviews as needed. | | |
| Teacher disaggregates formative and summative assessment data to inform instruction and determine which students may need additional instruction. | | | | |

## Procedure

Give each student an index card with a number already printed on it (i.e., from 1 to 8) and one of the target vocabulary words to be reviewed. Instruct students to write a review question that goes with their vocabulary word on their card (allow students to use their word banks or other text resources as necessary). Next, spin the arrow on the wheel. The student whose index card is chosen by the wheel selects who will receive the question on their card.

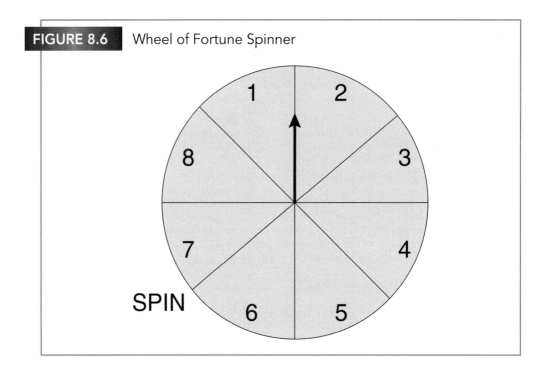

FIGURE 8.6 Wheel of Fortune Spinner

## Who Wants to Be a Millionaire?

Appropriate for most *Robust Vocabulary Tiers Two & Three Words*

### Purpose

Another popular television game show adapted for vocabulary review is "Who Wants to Be a Millionaire?" As with Wheel of Fortune, this game can be constructed by using a free download from the Internet (usually a PowerPoint program). This game can be played in a learning center, in small-group sessions with the teacher, or as a whole class. *Warning:* Students get very excited playing this game! *Note:* It is easy and cost effective to download the game from the Internet to a classroom computer and create your own program, which can be reused year after year; one site we often use for this and other vocabulary review games is found at http://jc-schools.net/tutorials/PPT-games.

### Materials

- Index cards
- Markers
- Academic word wall

### Procedure

Who Wants to Be a Millionaire? is a game that features a series of questions in ascending levels of difficulty (easiest to most difficult) with four possible answers from which contestants may choose. In other words, it is a 15-item multiple-choice test. Thus, simply prepare a 15-item multiple-choice test with the questions arranged from easiest to most difficult using the following categories for the questions:

| Question | Dollar Value of Question |
|:---:|:---:|
| 15 | $1 Million |
| 14 | $500,000 |
| 13 | $250,000 |
| 12 | $125,000 |
| 11 | $64,000 |
| 10 | $32,000 |
| 9 | $16,000 |
| 8 | $8,000 |
| 7 | $4,000 |
| 6 | $2,000 |
| 5 | $1,000 |
| 4 | $500 |
| 3 | $300 |
| 2 | $200 |
| 1 | $100 |

The game may be played with students in pairs (one as the host, one as the contestant) in a learning center, in small groups with the teacher as host and students working as a team, or the whole class. As each question and four choices are posed, students decide on the correct answer. If they get the answer correct, they advance to the next question. If they answer incorrectly, then the game ends and another contestant can play the game (requiring one set of questions and answers for each contestant).

As with the television version, a contestant who is unsure of an answer has three options: phone a friend (i.e., ask a classmate), use the 50–50 option (two of the multiple choices are eliminated, leaving the correct answer and one incorrect answer from which to choose), or ask the audience (classmates write the answer they would choose and then totals for each choice are announced to help the contestant make an informed choice).

Go to the Assignments and Activities section of Topic 6: "Vocabulary" in the MyEducationLab for your course and complete the activity entitled "Content Vocabulary Instruction." As you watch the video and answer the accompanying questions, notice the way these strategies increase student engagement and thoughtful reflection about new content vocabulary.

## Academic Vocabulary Graphic Organizer

Appropriate for *Robust Vocabulary Tier Three Words*

### Purpose

An academic vocabulary graphic organizer helps students see relationships in known and new vocabulary while also helping to give students the necessary multiple exposures to new words so they are permanently learned. Cooter, Flynt, and Cooter (2005) developed and field-tested a graphic organizer to assist in the learning of new content vocabulary (see Figure 8.7). This example in the figure relates to the science topic of fiber optic communications. The column headings are selected to fit the teacher's instructional goals.

## Morphemic Analysis (Structural Analysis)

Appropriate for *Robust Vocabulary Tier Two Words*

| FIGURE 8.7 | Graphic Organizer for Content Vocabulary |
|---|---|

| Key Words | Page | Example Sentence from Text | Definition Found in the Article | Definition Using Context Clues | The Word Used Correctly in a Sentence |
|---|---|---|---|---|---|
| advent | | | | | |
| fiber optics | | | | | |
| Rayleigh scattering | | | | | |
| diffused | | | | | |
| Fresnel reflection | | | | | |
| regen | | | | | |
| OTDR | | | | | |

Go to the Assignments and Activities section of Topic 6: "Vocabulary" in the MyEducationLab for your course and complete the activity entitled "Word Parts." As you watch the video and answer the accompanying questions, consider the various ways we can draw students' attention to affixes in known words and deductively determine new word meanings

## Purpose

**Morphemic analysis,** also referred to as *structural analysis,* is the process of using one's knowledge of word parts to deduce meanings of unknown words. A **morpheme** is the smallest unit of meaning in a word. There are two types of morphemes: free and bound. A **free morpheme** is a freestanding root or base of any word that cannot be further divided and still have meaning. In the word *farmer, farm* is the root word or free morpheme. The *-er* portion of the word *farmer* is considered to be a bound morpheme. **Bound morphemes** carry meaning but only when attached to a free morpheme. The most common bound morphemes are **prefixes** (*in-, pre-, mono-*), **suffixes** (*-er, -ous, -ology*), and **inflectional endings** (*-s, -es, -ing, -ed, -est*).

There are several ways teachers commonly introduce morphemic analysis to students as a way of learning the meanings of new words. Sometimes we use students' knowledge of morphemes to analyze the meaning of a new word by showing a list of similar words having the same morpheme (e.g., words ending in the morpheme *-phobia* or *-er* to decipher meaning). Other times, teachers simply tell students the meanings of new morphemes and let them figure out word meanings on their own or in small groups.

The essential activity for teachers is to research the meanings of morphemes and, in the case of activities involving word family lists, examples of other words having the morphemes to be used. A resource we have found helpful in planning many vocabulary activities is *The Reading Teacher's Book of Lists* (Fry, Kress, & Fountoukidis, 2000).

## Materials

- A list of words taken from a reading selection
- Words with similar morphemes for some of the words
- Individual morphemes defined for some of the words

## Procedure

Preselect words to be learned from the reading selection; then do the necessary background research and planning about the morphemes found in the new words. One activity is to construct word family lists that help students determine morpheme meanings. For example, a middle school teacher may decide to focus on the word *claustrophobia.* Her research into the morpheme -*phobia* may lead to the construction of the following list:

claustrophobia

cardiophobia

olfactophobia

telephonophobia

verbaphobia

This activity leads students to use compare-and-contrast methods of morphemic analysis. That is, they must look at the unfamiliar word and use their prior knowledge of other words that look like parts of the unfamiliar word to figure out what each word probably means. For example, *cardio-* probably reminds you of *cardiac,* which deals with the heart, and -*phobia* means "fear of." Therefore, *cardiophobia* must mean a fear of heart disease. To use this compare-and-contrast technique with students, first select words that have morphemes that can be compared to other words students are likely to know; then present both the new word and other words that begin or end like the unfamiliar word. Look at the following example from Cooter and Flynt (1996):

*Because of my expansive vocabulary, my teacher called me a verbivore.*

*verbi- vore*
*verbal carnivore*
*verbose herbivore*
*verbalize omnivore*

The teacher would write the sentence on the chalkboard and list below it examples of words that begin and end like the unfamiliar word. Then, through questioning, the teacher would lead students to specify the word's meaning by comparing and contrasting the known words to the unfamiliar one, concluding in this case that a verbivore is a person who loves (eats) words.

Another way of using morphemic analysis to help students deduce meaning is to present unfamiliar terms along with explanations of the morphemes that make up the terms. The following procedure may be used as part of an introduction to a new text containing the words listed.

**Step 1:**  Identify the terms that need preteaching.

pro-life

illegal

pro-choice

rearrest

unable

forewarn

**Step 2:**  Along with these terms, write on the board a list of appropriate morphemes and their meanings.

*pro*      in favor of

*il*        not

*fore*    earlier

> *re*     to do again
>
> *un*     not

**Step 3:** Engage students in a discussion of what each term means and how the terms are interrelated. When there is confusion or disagreement, direct students to the terms in the text or the glossary for verification.

As useful as morphemic analysis can be, Cooter and Flynt (1996) offer a word of caution:

> Although we encourage the teaching of how to use context and morphemic analysis, we in no way advocate the overuse of these two techniques nor the memorization of lists of morphemes or types of context clues. Teachers who make students memorize common prefixes and suffixes run the risk of having students view the task as an end and not a means to help them become better readers. The story is told of a student who memorized the prefix *trans-* as meaning *across*. Later the same week, the student was reading a science text and was asked what the word *transparent* meant. He replied confidently "a cross mother or father." The point being that all vocabulary instruction in the upper grades should be meaning-oriented, connected to text, functional, and capable of being used in the future. (p. 154)

## Five-Step Method

Appropriate for *Robust Vocabulary Tiers Two & Three Words*

### Purpose

Smith and Johnson (1980) suggested a five-step direct method of teaching new vocabulary for instant recognition. It uses multiple modalities to help students bring new words into the four vocabularies: listening, speaking, reading, and writing.

### Materials

- A dry-erase board, chalkboard, or an overhead projector
- Flash cards
- Different color markers

### Procedure

1. *Seeing.* The new vocabulary word is shown on the overhead projector, chalkboard, or dry-erase board in the context of a sentence or (better) a short paragraph.
2. *Listening.* The teacher next discusses the word with students and verifies that they understand its meaning.
3. *Discussing.* Students are asked to create their own sentences using the new word or, perhaps, to think of a synonym or antonym for the word. This is done orally.
4. *Defining.* Students try to create their own definitions for the new word. This is often much more difficult than using it in a sentence and may not even be possible for some words (i.e., *is, the, if,* etc.). Sometimes it is helpful to ask students questions such as "What does this word mean?" or "What does this word do in the sentence?"
5. *Writing.* We advocate using word banks or similar strategies in grades K to 3. Students, sometimes requiring help, add each new word to their word bank and file it in alphabetical order. Each word is listed in isolation on one side of an index card and in the context of a sentence on the reverse side. Emergent readers may want to draw a picture clue on the word bank card to remind them of the word's meaning.

## Frayer Model

Appropriate for *Robust Vocabulary Tiers Two & Three Words*

### Purpose

The Frayer Model (Frayer, Frederick, & Klausmeir, 1969) is a classic strategy that helps students understand new vocabulary and concepts in relation to what is already known. Frayer is especially useful for nonfiction terms—especially in the sciences—because it presents essential and nonessential information related to the term, as well as examples and nonexamples.

### Materials

- A blank Frayer Model form on a transparency
- An overhead projector for demonstration purposes
- Paper and pencils for student notetaking

### Procedure

The teacher presents or helps students determine essential and nonessential information along with examples and non-examples of a concept and identify coordinate and subordinate relationships of the concept. This classification procedure can be done as a group, in dyads, or individually. Figure 8.8 shows an example for the concept of mammals.

## Cubing: The Die Is Cast!

Appropriate for *Robust Vocabulary Tier Three Words*

### Purpose

Cubing (Cowan & Cowan, 1980) is a postreading activity requiring students to analyze, discuss, and write about important new terms. The process helps activate prior knowledge or schemata that relate to the new term, which in turn helps the new information to become part of long-term memory.

---

**FIGURE 8.8** Frayer Model: Mammals

**Concept: MAMMALS**

| **Essential Information or Attributes:** | **Examples:** |
|---|---|
| 1. higher-order vertebrates | 1. dogs |
| 2. nourish young with milk from mammary glands | 2. humans |
| 3. warm blooded | 3. monkeys |
| 4. have skin covered with hair | 4. whales |
| **Nonessential Information or Attributes:** | **Non-examples:** |
| 1. size of the mammal | 1. spiders |
| 2. number of young born | 2. fish |
| 3. where the mammal lives (i.e., water, land, etc.) | 3. reptiles |

### Materials

- A large foam or wooden cube covered with contact paper.

### Procedure

On each side of the cube write a different direction or question related to the new term. The following examples show questions for the term *wheelchair*:

1. What does it look like?
2. What is it similar to or different from?
3. What else does it make you think of?
4. What is it made of?
5. How can it be used?
6. Where are you likely to find one?

Once the cube is rolled and the question or direction facing the class or group is seen, each student is given a set number of minutes to record his or her answer. All six sides of the cube can be used in the activity or, if you prefer, only a few. Once the cubing has ended, students can share their responses with the class or in small groups.

## Vocabulary Bingo!

Appropriate for *Robust Vocabulary Tiers Two & Three Words*

### Purpose

Vocabulary Bingo! (Spencer, 1997) is a whole-group word review activity in the format of the popular game Bingo. This activity is an especially useful review for students learning English as a second language (ESL) and students in language enrichment programs, as well as for students whose first language is English.

### Materials

- Vocabulary Bingo! boards on which you have printed new words learned in reading and writing activities during the year or chosen from a classroom word bank
- Definitions for each word found on the cards written on slips of paper for the caller to read aloud during the game

### Procedure

Unlike traditional Bingo games in which participants cover spaces on their boards when a number such as "B23" is called, students playing Vocabulary Bingo! cover board spaces showing review vocabulary words matching the definitions that are read aloud by a caller. Boards can all be the same or can differ from one another, depending on the size of the group and the abilities of the learners. When all spaces in a row are covered, the student calls out "Bingo!" An example of a Vocabulary Bingo! card is shown in Figure 8.9.

## SAVOR: Subject Area Vocabulary Reinforcement Activity

Appropriate for *Robust Vocabulary Tiers Two & Three Words*

### Purpose

The **Subject Area Vocabulary Reinforcement Activity** (SAVOR; Stieglitz & Stieglitz, 1981) is an excellent postreading vocabulary learning procedure. As its name implies, SAVOR

---

**FIGURE 8.9**  Vocabulary Bingo! Card

**VOCABULARY BINGO!**

| silo | desert | umpire | dromedary | elevator |
|------|--------|--------|-----------|----------|
| aviatrix | conifer | photography | precious | caravan |
| financier | meteoric | flank | declaration | cleats |
| maladjusted | payee | odoriferous | seizure | oasis |
| biannual | proceed | semicircle | humorous | proverb |

---

is intended for use with factual readings. Students combine research and rereading skills to identify similarities and differences among new terms taken from topics being studied in science, social studies, mathematics, health, history, or another content area. Make a content analysis of the unit of study and list selected new terms in the left-hand column of the SAVOR grid and list characteristics related to the terms across the top row. An example is shown in Figure 8.10.

### Materials
- A SAVOR grid constructed on a bulletin board or worksheet to be photocopied

### Procedure
SAVOR is intended to be used as a postreading activity to reinforce learning of new vocabulary. After students have completed their initial reading of the subject-matter text, introduce the SAVOR grid bulletin board or photocopied worksheet. Discuss how to complete each grid space with either a plus (+) or minus (–), based on whether the term has the trait listed across the top of the grid. As with all minilessons, the teacher should first model the thinking process he or she is using to determine whether to put a plus or minus in the space provided. In Figure 8.10, we show an example of a SAVOR grid completed by children in a southern Texas school as they studied the solar system.

## Peer Teaching

Appropriate for *Robust Vocabulary Tiers Two & Three Words*

### Purpose
An activity that has been proven to be effective with ESL students is called **peer teaching** (Johnson & Steele, 1996). It is considered to be a **generative strategy,** or one that is student initiated and monitored and can be used in different situations. In peer teaching, a student chooses from the reading selection a word he or she feels is new and important and then teaches that term to another student, after which the roles are reversed.

### Materials
- A reading selection to be shared with the whole group
- Typical supplies usually found in a writing center for students to use as they wish
- A list showing several ways of teaching new vocabulary words to others, like those techniques found in this chapter that you commonly use with the students in your class

| FIGURE 8.10 | SAVOR Grid: Solar System |
|---|---|

| Planets | Inner Planet | Outer Planet | Made Up of Gas | Has More Than One Moon | Longer Revolution Than Earth's 365 days | Has Rings | Has Been Visited by a Space Probe | Stronger Gravity Than Earth's |
|---|---|---|---|---|---|---|---|---|
| Venus | + | − | − | − | − | − | + | − |
| Neptune | − | + | + | + | + | ? | + | + |
| Saturn | − | + | + | + | + | + | + | + |
| Mercury | + | − | − | − | − | − | + | − |

### Procedure

First, conduct a one- or two-session minilesson in which you model choosing a word from the reading selection that seems to be important to understanding what the author is saying. As an example, in Betsy Byars's Newberry Award–winning book *The Summer of the Swans* (1970), the main character, Sara, has a "grudging tolerance" of her Aunt Willie. Because this is important to understanding Sara and her feelings, you may select "grudging tolerance" as a term to teach someone reading the book. Next, model how you would choose one of the common strategies you use in class (on a list you post for all to see) and demonstrate how you would plan to teach your term to another. Finally, ask someone to role-play with you as you teach "grudging tolerance."

## Personal Word Lists

Appropriate for *Robust Vocabulary Tiers Two & Three Words*

### Purpose

Most words are learned through repeated encounters in a meaningful context in spoken and written forms. All too often, however, when students come to a word they do not know, they simply run to the dictionary or to someone else for a quick definition instead of using sentence or passage context to figure out for themselves the word's meaning. While we certainly want students to develop dictionary skills, the first line of attack for gaining word meaning should be sentence or passage context. **Personal word lists,** as described in this section, have been around elementary and secondary classrooms for a very long time and have recently found success with ESL learners (Johnson & Steele, 1996). A personal word list is a structured way of helping students develop the habit of using context to determine vocabulary meaning and to permanently fix the vocabulary in long-term memory.

### Materials

- Multiple blank copies of the personal word list, as shown in Figure 8.11
- A transparency version for demonstrations
- Overhead projector

---

**FIGURE 8.11**  Personal Word List: *Lincoln* (Donald, 1995)

| New Word | What I Think It Means . . . | Clues from the Book or Passage | Dictionary Definition (Only When I Needed to Look) |
|---|---|---|---|
| 1. abolitionists | people against slavery | John Brown was called one and was the leader of the Harper's Ferry raid. | |
| 2. Republican | the party that Lincoln joined and ran for President | Lincoln went to the first meeting in 1855 (page 187) and later became its candidate in 1860. | |
| 3. dispatches | a telegraph | Lincoln and Lee sent dispatches to people during the Civil War. | a message sent with speed |

---

## Procedure

Distribute blank copies of the personal word list sheet for students to review as you explain its function. Using a passage read recently by the class, model two or three examples of how you would complete the form for words you found in the passage that seemed important. Next, do a guided practice exercise with the whole group in which you provide several more words from the passage. Ask students to complete the form for each word, and have volunteers share what they found with the class. Once students seem secure with the personal word list form, ask them to make several new entries with words of their own choosing in the next reading assignment. This will serve as a kind of individual practice exercise. Further use of the personal word list will depend on your class needs and how well you feel it works with your students. An example of a personal word list for the book *Lincoln* (Donald, 1995) is shown in Figure 8.11.

## Semantic Maps

Appropriate for *Robust Vocabulary Tiers Two & Three Words*

## Purpose

**Semantic maps** are useful in tying together new vocabulary with prior knowledge and related terms (Johnson & Pearson, 1984; Monroe, 1998). They are essentially a kind of "schema blueprint" in which students map what is stored in their brain about a topic and related concepts. Semantic maps help students relate new information to schemata already in the brain, integrate new information, and restructure existing information for greater clarity (Yopp & Yopp, 1996). Further, for students having learning problems, using semantic maps prior to reading a selection has also proven to promote better story recall than traditional methods (Sinatra, Stahl-Gemake, & Berg, 1984).

## Materials

- Writing materials

### Procedure

There are many ways to introduce semantic mapping to students, but the first time around you will likely want to use a structured approach. One way is to introduce semantic maps through something we call "wacky webbing." The idea is to take a topic familiar to all, such as the name of one's home state, and portray it in the center of the web, inside an oval. Major categories related to the theme are connected to the central concept using either bold lines or double lines. Details that relate to the major categories are connected using single lines. Figure 8.12 shows a semantic web for the topic "Tennessee."

Semantic webs can also be constructed that relate to a story or chapter book the students are reading. In Figure 8.13, we share one example of a semantic web from a story in the book *Golden Tales: Myths, Legends, and Folktales From Latin America* (Delacre, 1996).

## Making Words

Appropriate for *Robust Vocabulary Tier Two Words*

### Purpose

**Making Words** (Cunningham & Cunningham, 1992) is a word-learning strategy that may fit just as well in our chapter on phonics. It is a strategy that helps children improve their phonetic understanding of words through invented or "temporary" spellings (Reutzel & Cooter, 2000) while also increasing their repertoire of vocabulary words they can recognize in print. Making Words will be a familiar strategy for anyone who has ever played the crossword board game Scrabble.

### Materials

- A pocket chart
- Large index cards
- Markers

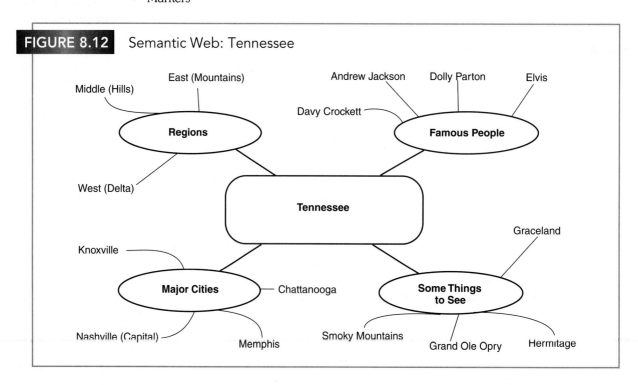

**FIGURE 8.12**  Semantic Web: Tennessee

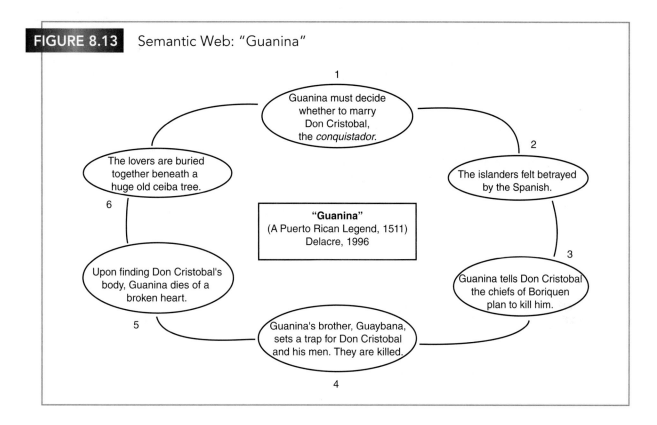

**FIGURE 8.13**   Semantic Web: "Guanina"

1 — Guanina must decide whether to marry Don Cristobal, the *conquistador.*

"Guanina" (A Puerto Rican Legend, 1511) Delacre, 1996

2 — The islanders felt betrayed by the Spanish.

3 — Guanina tells Don Cristobal the chiefs of Boriquen plan to kill him.

4 — Guanina's brother, Guaybana, sets a trap for Don Cristobal and his men. They are killed.

5 — Upon finding Don Cristobal's body, Guanina dies of a broken heart.

6 — The lovers are buried together beneath a huge old ceiba tree.

## Procedure

Students are given a number of letters with which to make words. They begin by making two- or three-letter words with the letters during a set amount of time, progressing to words having more letters until they finally arrive at the teacher's target word that uses all of the letters. This final word can be the main word to be taught for the day, but the other words discovered during the activity may also be new for some students. By manipulating the letters to make words of two, three, four, and more letters using temporary spellings, students have an opportunity to practice their phonemic awareness skills. Making words is recommended as a 15-minute activity when used with first and second graders. In Figures 8.14 and 8.15, we summarize and adapt the steps in planning and teaching a Making Words lesson as suggested by Cunningham and Cunningham (1992). Figure 8.16 provides details necessary for making two more Making Words lessons suggested by Cunningham and Cunningham (1992) that may be useful in helping your students learn the procedure.

## Word Banks

Appropriate for *Robust Vocabulary Tiers Two & Three Words*

### Purpose

It is important for students to learn to recognize a number of words on sight to facilitate the decoding process. Many sight words carry little meaning *(the, of,* and *a)* but provide the "glue" of language that helps us represent thoughts. One question for teachers is how to go about helping students increase the numbers of words they can recognize immediately on sight. **Word banks** are one method to help students collect and review sight words. Word

---

**FIGURE 8.14**   Planning a "Making Words" Lesson

1. Choose the final word to be emphasized in the lesson. It should be a key word from a reading selection, fiction or nonfiction, to be read by the class, or it may be of particular interest to the group. Be sure to select a word that has enough vowels and/or one that fits letter–sound patterns useful for most children at their developmental stage in reading and writing. For illustrative purposes, in these instructions we will use the word *thunder* that was suggested by Cunningham and Cunningham (1992).

2. Make a list of shorter words that can be spelled using the main word to be learned. For the word *thunder*, one could derive the following words: *red, Ted, Ned/den/end* (Note: these all use the same letters), *her, hut, herd, turn, hunt, hurt, under, hunted, turned, thunder.*

   From the You Were Able To list, select 12 to 15 words that include such aspects of written language as a) words that can be used to emphasize a certain kind of pattern, b) big and little words, c) words that can be made with the same letters in different positions (as with *Ned, end, den*), d) a proper noun, if possible, to remind students about using capital letters, and especially e) words that students already have in their listening vocabularies.

3. Write all of these words on large index cards and order them from the shortest to the longest words. Also, write each of the individual letters found in the key word for the day on large index cards (make two sets of these).

4. Reorder the words one more time to group them according to letter patterns and/or to demonstrate how shifting around letters can form new words. Store the two sets of large single-letter cards in two envelopes—one for the teacher and one for children participating during the modeling activity.

5. Store the word stacks in envelopes and note on the outside of each the words/patterns to be emphasized during the lesson. Also, note definitions you can use with the children to help them discover the words you desire. For example, "*Den* is a three-letter word that is the name of the room in some people's homes where they like to watch television."

*Source:* Based on "Making Words: Enhancing the Invented Spelling-Decoding Connection" by P. M. Cunningham and J. Cunningham, 1992, *The Reading Teacher, 46*(2), 106–115. Copyright © 1992 by the International Reading Association (www.reading.org). Reproduced with permission of the International Reading Association via Copyright Clearance Center.

---

banks also can be used as personal dictionaries. A word bank is simply a student-constructed box, file, or notebook in which newly discovered words are stored and reviewed.

### Materials

- Small shoe boxes (early grades)
- Notebooks or recipe boxes (upper grades)
- Alphabetic dividers

### Procedure

In the early grades, teachers often collect small shoe boxes from local stores to serve as word banks. The children are asked at the beginning of the year to decorate the boxes in order to make them their own. In the upper grades, more formal-looking word banks are used. Notebooks or recipe boxes are generally selected. Alphabetic dividers can also be used at all levels to facilitate the quick location of word bank words. In addition, use of alphabetic dividers in the early grades helps students rehearse and reinforce knowledge of alphabetical order. Figure 8.17 shows an example of a word bank.

---

**FIGURE 8.15** Teaching a "Making Words" Lesson

1. Place the large single letters from the key word in the pocket chart or along the chalkboard ledge.
2. For modeling purposes, the first time you use Making Words, select one of the students to be the "passer" and ask that child to pass the large single letters to other designated children.
3. Hold up and name each of the letter cards and instruct students selected to participate in the modeling exercise to respond by holding up their matching card.
4. Write the numeral 2 (or 3, if there are no two-letter words in this lesson) on the board. Next, tell the student "volunteers" the desired word and its definition. Then, tell the student

volunteers to put together two (or three) of their letters to form the desired word.
5. Continue directing the students to make more words using the letter cards until you have helped them discover all but the final key word (the one that uses all the letters). Ask the student volunteers if they can guess the key word. If not, ask the remainder of the class if anyone can guess it. If no one is able to do so, offer students a meaning clue (e.g., "I am thinking of a word with _____ letters that means . . .").
6. As a guided practice activity, repeat these steps the next day with the whole group using a new word.

---

*Source:* Based on "Making Words: Enhancing the Invented Spelling-Decoding Connection" by P. M. Cunningham and J. Cunningham, 1992, *The Reading Teacher, 46*(2), 106–115. Copyright © 1992 by the International Reading Association (www.reading.org). Reproduced with permission of the International Reading Association via Copyright Clearance Center.

---

Go to the Assignments and Activities section of Topic 6: "Vocabulary" in the MyEducationLab for your course and complete the activity entitled "Sight Words." As you watch the video and answer the accompanying questions, discover why it is important to teach some vocabulary as sight words and how we can teach them very systematically for "deep learning."

Once students have constructed word banks, the next issue for the teacher is helping students decide which words should be included and from what sources. At least four sources can be considered for sight word selection and inclusion in word banks (Reutzel & Cooter, 2000): basal reader sight word lists; "key vocabulary" words that students have self-selected for learning (Ashton-Warner, 1963); "discovery" words (i.e., words that are discovered during

---

**FIGURE 8.16** Making Words: Additional Examples

**Lesson Using One Vowel:**

Letter cards: u k n r s t

Words to make: us, nut, rut, sun, sunk, runs, ruts/rust, tusk, stun, stunk, trunk, *trunks* (the key word)

You can sort for . . . rhymes, "s" pairs (run, runs; rut, ruts; trunk, trunks)

**Lesson Using Big Words:**

Letter cards: a a a e i b c h l l p t

Words to make: itch, able, cable, table, batch, patch, pitch, petal, label, chapel, capital, capable, alphabet, *alphabetical* (the key word)

You can sort for . . . el, le, al, -itch, -atch

---

*Source:* Based on "Making Words: Enhancing the Invented Spelling-Decoding Connection" by P. M. Cunningham and J. Cunningham, 1992, *The Reading Teacher, 46*(2), 106–115. Copyright © 1992 by the International Reading Association (www.reading.org). Reproduced with permission of the International Reading Association via Copyright Clearance Center.

---

**FIGURE 8.17**   A Word Bank

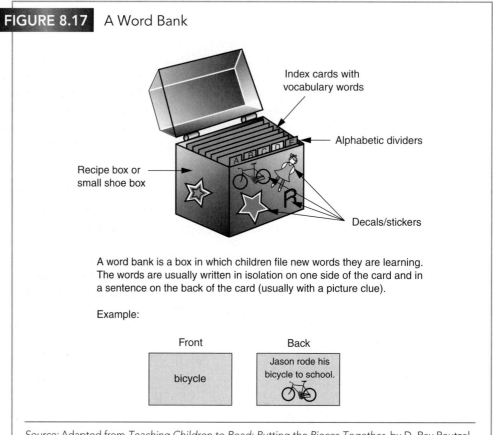

A word bank is a box in which children file new words they are learning. The words are usually written in isolation on one side of the card and in a sentence on the back of the card (usually with a picture clue).

Example:

| Front | Back |
|-------|------|
| bicycle | Jason rode his bicycle to school. |

*Source:* Adapted from *Teaching Children to Read: Putting the Pieces Together,* by D. Ray Reutzel and Robert B. Cooter, Jr., 2004. Upper Saddle River, NJ: Merrill/Prentice Hall. Copyright © 2004. Reprinted with permission of Pearson Education.

---

class discussions); and "function words" (words that supply structure to sentences but carry little or no meaning, such as *with, were, what, is, of*). A list of high-frequency sight words is supplied in Figure 8.18.

## Comparison Grids for Content-Area Vocabulary

Appropriate for *Robust Vocabulary Tier Three Words*

### Purpose

In content-area instruction, it is important to create conceptual bridges between new vocabulary and their meanings and their relationships to other concepts (Harmon, Hedrick, & Fox, 2000). **Comparison grids** can create a kind of two-dimensional framework for students that greatly simplifies abstract thinking. See Figure 8.19 for an example adapted from Harmon and others (2000) for the new vocabulary terms *executive, legislative,* and *judicial.*

### Materials

- A simple grid that has one set of terms along the left-hand column and the vocabulary you want students to compare and contrast along the top row

FIGURE 8.18 Instant Words

Teach these words any way you can. Teaching suggestions might include (1) flashcards for flashing and sorting, (2) word walls, (3) pocket charts for short sentences or stories using instant words, (4) teacher-written cooperative stories shown on the chalkboard, (5) spelling lessons, (6) games such as Bingo or board games, (7) lots of easy reading, and (8) a copy of this sheet given to the student for home study.

Test these words by asking the students to read them instantly. Test each student at the beginning, middle, and end of the year.

| First Hundred | | | | | Second Hundred | | | | | Third Hundred | | | |
|---|---|---|---|---|---|---|---|---|---|---|---|---|---|
| 1–25 | 26–50 | 51–75 | 76–100 | 101–125 | 126–150 | 151–175 | 176–200 | 201–225 | 226–250 | 251–275 | 276–300 |
| the | or | will | number | over | say | set | try | high | saw | important | miss |
| of | one | up | no | new | great | put | kind | every | left | until | idea |
| and | had | other | way | sound | where | end | hand | near | don't | children | enough |
| a | by | about | could | take | help | does | picture | add | few | side | eat |
| to | words | out | people | only | through | another | again | food | while | feet | face |
| in | but | many | my | little | much | well | change | between | along | car | watch |
| is | not | then | than | work | before | large | off | own | might | mile | far |
| you | what | them | first | know | line | must | play | below | close | night | Indian |
| that | all | these | water | place | right | big | spell | country | something | walk | really |
| it | were | so | been | year | too | even | air | plant | seem | white | almost |
| he | we | some | call | live | mean | such | away | last | next | sea | let |
| was | when | her | who | me | old | because | animal | school | hard | began | above |
| for | your | would | am | back | any | turn | house | father | open | grow | girl |
| on | can | make | its | give | same | here | point | keep | example | took | sometimes |
| are | said | like | now | most | tell | why | page | tree | begin | river | mountain |
| as | there | him | find | very | boy | ask | letter | never | life | four | cut |
| with | use | into | long | after | follow | went | mother | start | always | carry | young |
| his | an | time | down | thing | came | men | answer | city | those | state | talk |
| they | each | has | day | our | want | read | found | earth | both | once | soon |
| I | which | look | did | just | show | need | study | eye | paper | book | list |
| at | she | two | get | name | also | land | still | light | together | hear | song |
| be | do | more | come | good | around | different | learn | thought | got | stop | being |
| this | how | write | made | sentence | farm | home | should | head | group | without | leave |
| have | their | go | may | man | three | us | America | under | often | second | family |
| from | if | see | part | think | small | move | world | story | run | later | it's |

Source: From "The New Instant Word List," by Edward Fry, 1980, The Reading Teacher, 34, 284–289. Copyright © 1980 by the International Reading Association (www.reading.org). Reproduced with permission of the International Reading Association via Copyright Clearance Center.

---

**FIGURE 8.19**   Comparison Grid: Branches of Government

*Directions:* Decide which of the words or phrases in the left-hand column can be used to describe each of the three branches of government. Write "yes" or "no" in each block, and be prepared to share your ideas with a partner.

|  | Executive | Legislative | Judicial |
|---|---|---|---|
| Elected |  |  |  |
| Veto power |  |  |  |
| President |  |  |  |
| Judges |  |  |  |
| Representatives |  |  |  |
| Senators |  |  |  |
| Commander-in-chief |  |  |  |
| Constitutional authority |  |  |  |
| Checks and balances |  |  |  |
| Amendment |  |  |  |
| Declares war |  |  |  |
| Protects and defends the Constitution |  |  |  |

*Source:* Adapted from Harmon, Hedrick, and Fox (2000).

---

## Vocabulary Cluster

Appropriate for *Robust Vocabulary Tiers Two & Three Words*

### Purpose

It is especially important that students who struggle with reading use the context of a passage with vocabulary they know to understand new words in print. English language learners (ELLs) and students who have language deficiencies due to poverty are two large groups of students who benefit from direct instruction of this kind (Peregoy & Boyle, 2001). With the **vocabulary cluster strategy,** students are helped to read a passage, gather context clues, and then predict the meaning of a new word you have targeted for learning.

### Materials

- Multiple copies of a text students are to read
- An overhead transparency and projector
- Erasable marking pens for transparencies

### Procedure

First, select vocabulary you want to teach from a text the students will be reading. This could be a poem, a song, a novel, a nonfiction textbook, or other appropriate reading. Next, gather the students around the overhead projector and draw their attention to the transparency you

Go to the Assignments and Activities section of Topic 6: "Vocabulary" in the MyEducationLab for your course and complete the activity entitled "Using Context Clues." As you watch the video and answer the accompanying questions, note the importance of this strategy for students who have challenges with organization and study skills.

have prepared. The transparency should contain an excerpt from the text with sufficient context to help students predict what the unknown word may be.

The target word should have been deleted and replaced with a blank line, much the same as with a cloze passage (discussed earlier in this chapter). In Figure 8.20 you find a passage prepared in this way along with a vocabulary cluster supporting the new word to be learned. This example is based on the book *Honey Baby Sugar Child* by Alice Faye Duncan (2005) written as a read-aloud book for young children. Through discussion, you will lead students into predicting what the unknown word may be. If the word is not already in students' listening vocabulary, as with ELL students or those with otherwise limited vocabularies, then you will be able to introduce the new word quite well using the context and synonyms provided in the vocabulary cluster.

**FIGURE 8.20**    Vocabulary Cluster Based on *Honey Baby Sugar Child* (Duncan, 2005) for Target Word *Twirl*

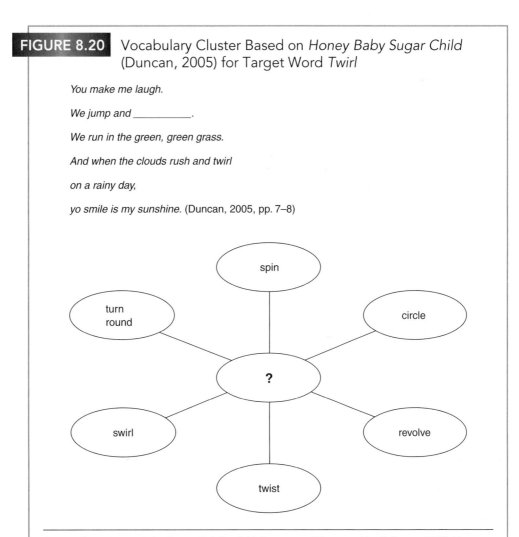

*You make me laugh.*

*We jump and _____.*

*We run in the green, green grass.*

*And when the clouds rush and twirl*

*on a rainy day,*

*yo smile is my sunshine.* (Duncan, 2005, pp. 7–8)

*Source:* From *Honey Baby Sugar Child* by A. F. Duncan and illustrated by S. Keeter, 2005. New York: Simon & Schuster Children's Publishing. Used with permission of Simon & Schuster Books for Young Readers, an imprint of Simon & Schuster Children's Publishing Division. Text copyright © 2005 by Alice Faye Duncan.

## Contextual Redefinition for Technical Vocabulary

Appropriate for *Robust Vocabulary Tier Three Words*

### Purpose

While there has been some debate over the years about the extent to which context should be emphasized, it is clear that learning from context is a very important component of vocabulary acquisition (Adams, 1990, p. 150). An excellent method of introducing terminology in context, such as that found in informational readings, as well as demonstrating to students why they should use context whenever possible to figure out unfamiliar words, is a strategy called **contextual redefinition** (Cunningham, Cunningham, & Arthur, 1981).

### Materials

- Chalkboard, overhead projector, and/or teacher-constructed activity sheets

### Procedure

The steps in this procedure have been adapted from Cooter and Flynt (1996). Begin by selecting five or six terms that are unfamiliar or probably known by only a few students in the class. Introduce the topic and display the new terms on the chalkboard or overhead. Ask each student or pair of students to predict a brief definition for each term, encouraging them to guess at word meanings and reminding them that the goal is to try to come up with logical ideas and not to worry about being "right." After the students have had an opportunity to discuss probable definitions, call for individuals to share their ideas and write them on the chalkboard or overhead projector transparency. Briefly discuss why the students were unable to do much more than guess at the word's meanings.

Next, tell the students that you have written these same words in sentences or short paragraphs and that you want them to read each passage to see if they want to revise their original guesses. Be sure to present each word in a contextually rich sentence. During the ensuing discussion, encourage students to explain why they think the word means what they now think it means. Record varying responses next to each term as they occur.

Finally, if there are differences, have students find the word in either the text or the glossary and read its definition. Then have students copy the finalized sentences in their notebooks or journals.

Contextual redefinition provides students with opportunities to share their skills in using context and can be helpful in promoting independent use of context clues. Teachers find it an invigorating means for preteaching terms and showing that the glossary is not the first tool readers can use in figuring out the meanings of new words; context usually is.

## SELECTED REFERENCES

Adams, M. J. (1990). *Beginning to read: Thinking and learning about print.* Cambridge, MA: MIT Press.

Alexander, J. E., & Heathington, B. S. (1988). *Assessing and correcting classroom reading problems.* Boston: Scott Foresman.

Allington, R., & Cunningham, P. (1996). *Schools that work: Where all children read and write.* New York: Longman.

Ashton-Warner, S. (1963). *Teacher.* New York: Simon & Schuster.

Beck, I. L., McCaslin, E. S., & McKeown, M. G. (1980). *The rationale and design of a program to teach vocabulary to fourth grade students* (LRDC No. 1980-25). Pittsburgh: University of Pittsburgh, Learning Research and Development Center.

Beck, I. L., McKeown, M. G., & Kucan, L., (2002). *Bringing words to life: Robust vocabulary instruction.* New York: Guilford.

Bradley, J. M., Ackerson, G., & Ames, W. S. (1978). The reliability of maze procedures. *Journal of Reading Behavior, 10*(Fall), 291–296.

Brett, A., Rothlein, L., & Hurley, M. (1996). Vocabulary acquisition from listening to stories and explanations of target words. *Elementary School Journal, 96*(4), 415–422.

Byars, B. (1970). *The summer of the swans.* New York: Puffin Books.

Cattell, J. M. (1885). Veber die zeit der erkennung und bennenung von schriftzeichen, bildem und farben. *Philosophische Studien, 2,* 635–650.

Clark, E. (1993). *The lexicon in acquisition.* Cambridge, UK: Cambridge University Press.

Cooter, R. B. (2009). *Academic word walls (AW²): A research-based strategy for core subject area instruction.* Louisville, KY: Unpublished manuscript.

Cooter, R. B., & Flynt, E. S. (1996). *Teaching reading in the content areas: Developing content literacy for all students.* Columbus, OH: Merrill/Prentice Hall.

Cooter, R. B., Flynt, E. S., & Cooter, K. S. (2005). Teaching academic vocabulary. *Proceedings from the Memphis Literacy Academy Annual Conference.* Memphis, TN: Memphis Literacy Academy.

Cowan, E., & Cowan, G. (1980). *Writing.* New York: John Wiley & Sons.

Cox, C., & Boyd-Batstone, P. (1997). *Crossroads: Literature and language in culturally and linguistically diverse classrooms.* Columbus, OH: Merrill/Prentice Hall.

Cunningham, J., Cunningham, P., & Arthur, S. V. (1981). *Middle and secondary school reading.* New York: Longman.

Cunningham, P. M. (1999). *The teacher's guide to the four blocks.* Greensboro, NC: Carson-Dellosa.

Cunningham, P. M. (2000). *Phonics they use* (3rd ed.). New York: Addison-Wesley.

Cunningham, P. M., & Cunningham, J. (1992). Making words: Enhancing the invented spelling-decoding connection. *Reading Teacher, 46*(2), 106–115.

Delacre, L. (1996). *Golden tales: Myths, legends, and folktales from Latin America.* New York: Scholastic.

Donald, D. H. (1995). *Lincoln.* New York: Simon & Schuster.

Duncan, A. F. (2005). *Honey baby sugar child.* New York: Simon & Schuster.

Flynt, E. S., & Cooter, R. B., Jr. (2001). *The Flynt/Cooter Reading Inventory for the Classroom* (4th ed.). Columbus, OH: Merrill/Prentice Hall.

Frayer, D., Frederick, W. C., & Klausmeir, H. J. (1969). *A schema for testing the level of concept mastery* (Working Paper No. 16). Madison: University of Wisconsin, Wisconsin Research and Development Center for Cognitive Learning.

Fry, E. B. (1980). The new instant word list. *The Reading Teacher, 34,* 284–289.

Fry, E. B., Kress, J. E., & Fountoukidis, D .L. (2000). *The reading teacher's book of lists* (4th ed.). San Francisco: Jossey-Bass.

Gruber, B. (1998). *Instant word wall high frequency words.* Chino Hills, CA: Practice & LearnRight Publications.

Guthrie, J. T., Seifert, M., Burnham, N. A., & Caplan, R. I. (1974). The maze technique to assess, monitor reading comprehension. *The Reading Teacher, 28*(3), 161–168.

Harmon, J. M., Hedrick, W. B., & Fox, E. A. (2000). A content analysis of vocabulary instruction in social studies textbooks for grades K–8. *The Elementary School Journal, 100*(3), 253–271.

Hart, B., & Risley, T. R. (1995). *Meaningful differences in the everyday experience of young American children.* Baltimore: Paul H. Brookes.

Hoff-Ginsburg, E. (1998). The relation of birth order and socioeconomic status to children's language experience and language development. *Applied Psycholinguistics, 19*(4), 603–629.

Johnson, A. P., & Rasmussen, J. B. (1998). Classifying and super word web: Two strategies to improve productive vocabulary. *Journal of Adolescent & Adult Literacy, 42*(3), 204–209.

Johnson, D. D. (2001). *Vocabulary in the elementary and middle school.* Boston: Allyn & Bacon.

Johnson, D. D., & Pearson, P. D. (1984). *Teaching reading vocabulary.* New York: Holt, Rinehart & Winston.

Johnson, D., & Steele, V. (1996). So many words, so little time: Helping college ESL learners acquire vocabulary strategies. *Journal of Adolescent & Adult Literacy, 39*(5), 348–357.

Krashen, S. (1993). *The power of reading: Insights from the research.* Englewood, CO: Libraries Unlimited.

Mastro, J, & Wu, N. (2003). *Antarctic ice.* New York: Henry Holt.

May, F. B., & Rizzardi, L. (2002). *Reading as communication* (6th ed.). Upper Saddle River, NJ: Merrill/Prentice Hall.

Monroe, E. E. (1998). Using graphic organizers to teach vocabulary: Does available research inform mathematics instruction? *Education, 118*(4), 538–542.

Nagy, W. E., Herman, P. A., & Anderson, R. C. (1985). Learning words from context. *Reading Research Quarterly, 20*(2), 233–253.

National Center for Educational Statistics. (1999, September). *NAEP 1998: Writing report card for the nation and the states.* Washington, DC: U.S. Department of Education.

National Institute of Child Health and Human Development. (2000). *The Report of the National Reading Panel: Teaching children to read: An evidence-based assessment of the scientific research literature on reading and its implications for reading instruction: Reports of the subgroups.* Washington, DC: U.S. Government Printing Office.

National Research Council. (1998). *Preventing reading difficulties in young children.* Washington, DC: U.S. Department of Education.

Partnership for Reading. (2001). *Put reading first: Helping your child learn to read.* Washington, DC: The Partnership for Reading.

Paulsen, G. (1987). *Hatchet.* New York: Bradbury Press.

Peregoy, S. F., & Boyle, O. F. (2001). *Reading, writing, & learning in ESL.* New York: Longman.

Rekrut, M. D. (1996). Effective vocabulary instruction. *High School Journal, 80*(1), 66–78.

Reutzel, D. R., & Cooter, R. B. (2000). *Teaching children to read: Putting the pieces together.* Upper Saddle River, NJ: Merrill/Prentice Hall.

Rowling, J. K. (1997). *Harry Potter and the sorcerer's stone.* New York: Scholastic.

Rupley, W. H., Logan, J. W., & Nichols, W. D. (1999). Vocabulary instruction in a balanced reading program. *The Reading Teacher, 52*(4), 336–347.

Sigmon, C. (1997). *4-blocks literacy model.* Greensboro, NC: Carson-Dellosa.

Silverstein, S. (1974). *Where the sidewalk ends.* New York: HarperCollins.

Sinatra, R., Stahl-Gemake, J., & Berg, D. (1984). Improving reading comprehension of disabled readers through semantic mapping. *The Reading Teacher, 38,* 22–29.

Smith, F. (1987). *Insult to intelligence.* Portsmouth, NH: Heinemann Educational Books.

Smith, R. J., & Johnson, D. D. (1980). *Teaching children to read.* Reading, MA: Addison-Wesley.

Spencer, K. M. (1997). *Vocabulary bingo!: A language review activity.* Unpublished manuscript, Texas Christian University.

Stahl, S. (1986). Three principles of effective vocabulary instruction. *Journal of Reading, 29*(7), 662–668.

Stieglitz, E. L., & Stieglitz, V. S. (1981). SAVOR the word to reinforce vocabulary in the content areas. *Journal of Reading, 25,* 46–51.

Watts, S. (1995). Vocabulary instruction during reading lessons in six classrooms. *Journal of Reading Behavior, 27,* 399–424.

Wixson, K. K. (1986). Vocabulary instruction and children's comprehension of basal stories. *Reading Research Quarterly, 21*(3), 317–329.

Yopp, H. K., & Yopp, R. H. (1996). *Literature-based reading activities.* Boston: Allyn & Bacon.

Now go to Topic 6: "Vocabulary" in the MyEducationLab (www.myeducationlab.com) for your course, where you can:

- Find learning outcomes for "Vocabulary," along with the national standards that connect to these outcomes.
- Complete the tasks in the Assignments and Activities to help you more deeply understand the chapter content.
- Apply and practice your understanding of the core teaching skills identified in the chapter with the Building Teaching Skills and Dispositions learning units.

# 9

# Reading Comprehension: Focus on the Reader

"Gather around, boys and girls," Mrs. Jensen spoke gently. "I have a new book to read to you today. How many of you know the story of Peter Cottontail?" "Teacher, I know what a cottontail is, it's a tiny bunny with a tail that looks like a cotton ball," exclaims Julianna.

"Very good thinking, Julianna, but this story isn't really so much about a bunny. It is a story about something that all little boys and girls need to learn. Have any of you ever disobeyed your parents? Can you share with us what it was you did and what happened when you disobeyed?"

"Oh, once my Mom told me not to ride my scooter off jumps or I would wreck and hurt myself. I didn't listen and did it anyway. One day I made a big jump off a wooden ramp at Georgio's house and landed sideways and fell over. I put my hand out to stop from falling and broke my wrist real bad. It had to be in a cast for 6 weeks," explained José.

"Well, that is a very good example, José. Our story today tells us about a little rabbit named Peter, who always liked to stop in the best garden in the country for a snack on the way home from school—Mr. McGregor's garden. And Mr. McGregor didn't like having bunnies in his garden patch eating his prize vegetables. Peter's mom bought him some nice new clothes and reminded him *not* to go into Mr. McGregor's garden. What do you think might have happened?"

"Before we read, boys and girls," intones Mrs. Jensen, "let's think of some questions we might ask about Peter's adventure in Mr. McGregor's garden. Turn to your neighbor on the rug and talk about one question you might want to have answered as we read the story of Peter Cottontail. I will give you 2 minutes to think of a question. Then, when you are ready, fold your arms so that I know you have a question to ask. When everyone is ready, I will call on one person in your pair to tell me your question. I will write the questions on this large piece of chart paper. I'll leave a space for filling in the answers as we read," said Mrs. Jensen.

Mrs. Jensen skillfully introduced this age-old tale, helping the children connect to experiences they or others have had when disobeying their parents' instructions. By asking the right questions, Mrs. Jensen helped her students activate the appropriate prior knowledge related to the message of the story—disobedience—rather than activating knowledge related to the topic—rabbits—to help guide their comprehension of the text. To motivate children to read with a purpose, Mrs. Jensen invited the children in collaboration with a partner to choose questions they would like to have answered by reading the story. As they read, they will discuss the answers to the questions that are displayed on the chart paper. This is an excellent way to help children begin to monitor their understanding of a text.

They soon realize that reading should result in getting answers to their own questions and that they should monitor whether they are getting the answers to their questions as they go along in reading. Mrs. Jensen is one of those rare primary-grade teachers who help students understand from the outset of reading instruction that comprehension is the ultimate goal!

# BACKGROUND BRIEFING FOR TEACHERS

Go to the Assignments and Activities section of Topic 9: "Reading Comprehension" in the MyEducationLab for your course and complete the activity entitled "Dimensions of Comprehension." As you watch the video and answer the accompanying questions, take note of the four dimensions of reading comprehension in this video. Be able to describe each to someone else.

Reading comprehension has been well defined by two major national review panels: the National Reading Panel (National Institute of Child Health and Human Development, 2000) and the RAND Reading Study Group (2001). The National Reading Panel (2000) defined reading comprehension as follows:

Comprehension is a complex process . . . often viewed as "the essence of reading." Reading comprehension is . . . intentional thinking during which meaning is constructed through interactions between text and reader. Meaning resides in the intentional, problem-solving, thinking processes of the reader that occur during an interchange with a text. The content of meaning is influenced by the text and by the reader's prior knowledge and experience that are brought to bear on it. Reading comprehension is the construction of the meaning of a written text through a reciprocal interchange of ideas between the reader and the message in a particular text. (pp. 4–5)

By way of comparison, the RAND Reading Study Group (2002) defined reading comprehension (Pardo, 2004; Sweet & Snow, 2003, p. 1) "as the process of simultaneously extracting and constructing meaning." Within this definition, the dual challenges of "figuring out how print represents words (the text)" and "how to integrate new meanings with old information (prior and new knowledge)" are acknowledged. The act of comprehending entails four essential elements: (a) the reader, (b) the text, (c) the activity, and (d) the sociocultural context. The first three essential elements of reading comprehension occur within the fourth essential element of reading comprehension—the sociocultural context of the school classroom, the home, and other social and cultural situations.

Because reading comprehension is a complex process and because it is also the ultimate goal of reading instruction, we devote two full chapters in this edition of our strategies book to the study of reading comprehension. In this chapter, we discuss the first essential element of reading comprehension—the reader or the one doing the comprehending. In Chapter 10, we discuss the second essential element of reading comprehension—the text or the object to be comprehended. Within the discussion of the **reader** and the **text** in these two chapters, we simultaneously discuss cognitive comprehension strategies and sociocultural contexts that are supported by scientific research evidence for improving children's reading comprehension of texts.

## The Reader

Go to the Building Teaching Skills and Dispositions section of Topic 9: "Reading Comprehension" in the MyEducationLab for your course and complete the activity entitled "Building Reading Comprehension." As you work through the learning unit, consider the purposes and process of reading comprehension. What elements are needed to enhance or render useful comprehension processes noted in this chapter?

The first essential element of reading comprehension in the RAND Reading Study Group's (2001) definition of reading comprehension is the reader. In 1978–1979, Durkin made what was at the time a startling discovery—U.S. elementary schoolchildren were not receiving much instruction from their teachers on how to comprehend what they read. The National Reading Panel (National Institute of Child Health and Human Development, 2000; Pressley, 2006), in its extensive review of research on teaching reading comprehension, found a paucity of research focused on comprehension instruction in the early grades (K–2). Taylor, Pearson, Clark, and Walpole (1999) reported that only 16% of teachers emphasized comprehension as a part of primary-grade reading instruction.

Neuman similarly observed in 2001 that there is "little" comprehension instruction occurring in early childhood classrooms (K–3) across the nation. Pearson and Duke in 2002 commented that the terms *comprehension instruction* and *primary grades* do not often appear in the same sentence. In fact, many primary-grade educators do not consider comprehension instruction to be an important part of primary-grade education (Pearson & Duke, 2002). From this long line of research, we can conclude that children are not getting sufficient instruction in reading comprehension nor is the little comprehension instruction children do receive appropriately focused on effective tasks, strategies, and so on, and promoted with effective instructional and classroom contexts. Consequently, there is considerable variation among young children's abilities to comprehend what they read.

Add to this the fact that when teachers do provide comprehension instruction, the scope and sequence of strategies in core reading programs often recommend the teaching of too many comprehension strategies (Collins-Block & Lacina, 2009; Dewitz, Jones, & Leahy, 2009; Stahl, 2009). The teaching of too many comprehension strategies may dilute focus on critical evidence-based comprehension strategies (e.g., question answering and asking, graphic organizers, story and text structure, comprehension monitoring, and summarizing). The teaching of too many comprehension strategies might also dilute practice time with evidence-based comprehension strategies favored over teaching and practicing other comprehension strategies with less well-established evidence (Stahl, 2004, 2008).

Why do children differ in their abilities to comprehend what they have read? The RAND Reading Study Group (2002) describes four factors that explain the variability we often see among students with differing abilities in reading comprehension: (a) oral language development; (b) word recognition fluency; (c) world and domain knowledge and experiences; and (d) motivation, purposes, goals, and strategies. Because we have previously discussed oral language development in Chapter 3 and fluency development in Chapter 7, we focus our attention in this chapter on understanding how the reader's background knowledge and motivations, purposes, goals, and strategies influence reading comprehension.

## The Influence of Readers' Prior Knowledge and Experience on Reading Comprehension

Research in the past 25 to 30 years has contributed greatly to our collective understanding of the cognitive or thinking processes involved in reading comprehension (Collins Block &

Lacina, 2009; Collins-Block & Parris, 2008). Reading comprehension instruction has been profoundly influenced in the past by **schema theory,** a theory that explains how information we have stored in our minds and what we already know help us gain new knowledge. A **schema** (plural is *schemata* or *schemas*) can be thought of as a kind of file cabinet of information in our brains containing related (a) concepts (chairs, birds, ships), (b) events (weddings, birthdays, school experiences), (c) emotions (anger, frustration, joy, pleasure), and (d) roles (parent, judge, teacher) drawn from our life experiences (Rumelhart, 1981).

Researchers have represented the total collection of our schemata as neural networks of connected associated meanings (Collins & Quillian, 1969; Lindsay & Norman, 1977). Each schema is connected to other related schemata, forming our own unique, vast, interconnected network of knowledge and experiences. The size and content of each schema are influenced by past opportunities to learn. Thus, younger children typically possess fewer, less well-developed schemata than do mature adults.

One of the most important findings from the past two to three decades of comprehension research, from our point of view, is that *readers can remember a text without learning from it and they can learn from a text without remembering much about it* (Kintsch, 1998)! When readers successfully comprehend what they read, the levels of meaning constructed are interrelated to form a coherent, integrated representation of meaning in memory that readers draw on in other circumstances to help themselves understand and learn from new experiences and from reading other texts.

Kintsch (1998) developed construction-integration theory to explain the complex cognitive processes employed by readers to comprehend a text. Let us briefly illustrate how this construction-integration process works using the example of the story, *The Frog Prince Continued,* by Jon Scieszka (1991).\* We begin by reading a familiar series of statements in the text:

> The Princess kissed the frog.
> He turned into a prince.
> And they lived happily ever after . . .

To understand these three lines, we draw from our previous experiences reading or having been read to from the fairy tale genre in general. The familiar ending in fairy tales is that everyone lives happily ever after. We also call up our specific situational recollections for this particular fairy tale; the princess kissed a frog, and the frog turned into a prince. This, of course, would make sense because princesses and princes "living together happily" makes more sense than "frogs living happily with princesses." Next we read:

> Well, let's just say they lived sort of happily for a long time.

At this point, we focus in on the meaning of "sort of," which means not really, not so, and so forth. This alerts our curiosity and motivates us to keep reading because we are now alerted to something that is not normally the case. Next we read:

> Okay, so they weren't so happy.
> In fact, they were miserable.

\* From *The Frog Prince Continued* by Jon Scieszka, copyright 1991 by John Scieszka. Used by permission of Viking Penguin, A Division of Penguin Young Readers Group. A member of Penguin Group (USA) Inc., 345 Hudson Street, New York, NY 10014. All rights reserved.

These two clauses lead us to the conclusion that this fairy tale is going to be different from most. Our motivation is engaged to find out why, in this fairy tale, the traditional "happily ever after" situation does not apply.

The surface code or written text as shown in the preceding excerpts preserves for an extremely short period of time the exact letters, words, and grammatical organization or syntax of the text in our iconic memory. This memory is like the image you see quickly fading in your eyes after turning off your television set in a dark room. Once the surface information is moved from iconic memory and processed through short-term or working memory, it is transformed into a text base that preserves the meaning of the text and represents details in the text. This may include connective inferences, for example, the inference that a kiss from a princess has a transformative effect on frogs (the microstructure). This also includes important or "gist" ideas such as the fact that princesses and princes always live happily ever after (the macrostructure). Once the text base is placed into long-term memory, it is usually retained for several hours but may also be forgotten in a few days. As the text base is formed and placed into long-term memory, these same memory processes integrate the details of the text base to form what is called a *situation model,* which according to Kintsch (1998) is what the text is about—ideas, people, objects, processes, or world events. The situation model is remembered longest—lasting days, months, or even years. Processing of a text by a reader occurs in cycles, usually clause by clause, just as we discussed in the story of the frog prince, and it involves multiple, simultaneous cognitive processes. The cognitive processes involved in creating a situation model are influenced by (a) the reader's knowledge about the topic or message; (b) the reader's goals, motivations, and strategy selection and use; (c) the reader's ability to function in the sociocultural context (group, classroom) in which the text is processed; (d) the genre, type, and difficulty of the text; and (e) the processing constraints of the reader's memory (Kintsch, 1998; van Dijk, 1999).

Two phases of processing occur for each clause the reader encounters: a construction phase and an integration phase. In the construction phase, lower-level processes, such as activating prior knowledge and experiences, retrieving word meanings, examining the surface and grammatical structure of the printed text, and analyzing each clause into idea units called *propositions* occur. Propositions include text elements, connecting inferences, and generalizations, which are formed into a coherent network of connected meanings. For example, a sentence like "The student placed a tack on the teacher's chair" would be reduced in memory to a generalization that the student played a prank on his teacher (Zwann, 1999). In the **construction phase** of processing, other closely associated ideas also are activated, including irrelevant and even contradictory ideas. If, for example, a reader encounters the phrase " 'Stop sticking your tongue out like that,' nagged the Princess" in *The Frog Prince Continued* (Scieszka, 1991), this particular clause may activate associated concepts such as frogs, eating, and inappropriate facial expressions. All of these activated elements are initially part of the coherence network of meaning under construction.

During the second phase of processing meaning, the **integration phase,** the ideas from the text that are strongly interconnected with our prior knowledge are strengthened; those associated concepts that do not fit with the meaning context of the story or text are deactivated and deleted from the network. From this two-phase process, one first constructs meaning from text and then integrates it with prior knowledge to make what Kintsch (1998) calls the *situational model* that is stored in and retrieved from long-term memory. In the case of Scieszka's (1991) *The Frog Prince Continued,* the situational model categorizes this story as a "fractured fairy tale" and stores this particular instance with other such instances in long-term memory.

As important as prior knowledge is, it only partly explains how readers comprehend texts and create a situational memory model for later recall and use. Motivation, social situation, selection, and orchestration of cognitive comprehension strategies also influence readers' ability to comprehend what they read.

## The Influence of Readers' Motivations, Sociocultural Contexts, and Strategies on Reading Comprehension

Researchers in the past decade have added substantially to our understanding of how reading comprehension is considerably influenced by readers' motivations to engage a text and to take intentional control of their thinking processes while reading a text (Malloy & Gambrell, 2008; Miller & Fairchild, 2009). Wigfield (1997) describes various facets of motivation that influence children's engagement in reading:

- *Efficacy.* The sense that "I can do this"
- *Challenge.* Easy and more difficult tasks
- *Curiosity.* The desire to know or find out
- *Involvement.* Active, intentional control of one's thinking
- *Importance.* Personal value or worth
- *Recognition.* Praise, certificates, awards, and so on.
- *Grades.* A specific form of recognition in schools
- *Social.* Working cooperatively with others
- *Competition.* Working to win or be the best
- *Compliance.* Working to avoid punishment or negative recognition
- *Work avoidance.* Seeking the pleasurable and avoiding the difficult

Other researchers, Turner and Paris (1995), have reduced the foregoing complex web of motivations to six *C*s: (1) choice, (2) challenge, (3) control, (4) collaboration, (5) constructing meaning, and (6) consequences. We briefly discuss each of these six motivational factors that influence readers' comprehension of text.

*Choice* is the first factor, which of course does not mean that students are free to choose to comprehend any text in the world or to choose to remember what is in the text or make up what they have read. Choices are never unlimited; instead, they are bounded or limited. To offer choice may mean choosing to read from two different information books on rocks and rock formations. To offer students choice also means to encourage them to make connections between the text and their own knowledge and experiences. It does not mean they should just say words and make up what they have read when discussing it with others or when answering questions you have posed. But when children have some sense that they can make *some* choices, they are more willing to persist and remain intellectually engaged while reading.

*Challenge* is the second way in which we can encourage increased reading motivation and engagement to increase reading comprehension. Turner and Paris (1995) suggested that the common wisdom that children like "easy" reading texts and tasks more than more difficult or challenging reading texts or tasks is not supported in research. In fact, children enjoy a sense of being challenged. Of course, here again, the level of challenge associated with the text or task must not become excessive to the point of frustration. But giving children appropriately challenging texts and tasks has been shown to positively affect readers' motivations to read for comprehension.

*Control* is the third motivational factor associated with increasing students' reading comprehension. Sharing the control of texts and tasks in the classroom with the teacher or other

Go to the Assignments and Activities section of Topic 9: "Reading Comprehension" in the MyEducationLab for your course and complete the activity entitled "Research on Reading Comprehension." As you watch the video and answer the accompanying questions, note what and how teaching reading comprehension strategies can help readers achieve better recall and understanding of text. Can you describe the difference between a comprehension skill and strategy?

students is associated with greater engagement while reading. Children need to feel and sense that they have an integral role to play while reading a text in order to take sufficient control of their own thinking processes to be successful in reading for comprehension.

*Collaboration* has been shown to be a comprehension strategy for which there is sufficient scientific evidence that the National Reading Panel (National Institute of Child Health and Human Development, 2000) has recommended this as valid for immediate implementation into classroom practice to improve students' reading comprehension. As students discuss, interact, and work together with each other and their teachers to construct the meaning of texts to improve reading comprehension, collaboration results in students obtaining greater insights into the thinking processes of others around a text. Collaborative discussions and interactions also elaborate the outcomes of the reading comprehension process by adding to one another's memories for and meanings constructed from the reading of a text.

*Constructing meaning* is the very essence of reading comprehension instruction, requiring the conscious selection, control, and use of various cognitive comprehension strategies while engaged in reading a text. Again, the National Reading Panel (National Institute of Child Health and Human Development, 2000) found that there was sufficient scientific evidence to warrant the immediate implementation of six cognitive comprehension strategies in classrooms to aid in the construction of meaning from text: (1) using graphic organizers, (2) monitoring comprehension, (3) answering questions, (4) self-posing of questions, (5) story or text structure, and (6) summarizing. When these are used as a group or as a set, comprehension strategies have even more power to impact students' abilities to construct meaning (National Institute of Child Health and Human Development, 2000; Reutzel, Jones, Fawson, & Smith, 2008).

*Consequences* represent the final factor that leads students to increased motivation and reading comprehension. This concept refers to the nature of the outcomes expected when comprehending. If the outcome expected is completing or participating in an open- rather than a closed-ended task, such as contributing to a discussion rather than getting the "right" answers to questions on a worksheet, then students interpret their failures in comprehension differently. When seeking correct or "right" answers, they often feel that they just do not have enough ability (Turner & Paris, 1995). On the other hand, if through discussion they detect that they have failed to pick up on some element in the text, they often view this failure as the result of insufficiently or improperly selecting or applying effective comprehension strategies rather than just that they are not "smart enough" or "do not have the ability."

In conclusion, when preparing to teach reading comprehension, teachers must carefully prepare the reader, the one who is doing the reading, by assessing, activating, building, or modifying prior knowledge in relation to the theme (narratives) or topic (expository) of the text. Also, teachers need to consider how they can increase students' motivation to actively engage in and take control of their own thinking processes while reading texts, such as using the six Cs we have discussed: choice, challenge, control, collaboration, constructing meaning, and consequences.

# *A*SSESSING FACTORS WITHIN THE READER THAT INFLUENCE READING COMPREHENSION

How can students' background knowledge, strategy selection and use, and motivations be assessed? How can students be helped to activate their background knowledge, appropriately select strategies, and be motivated to increase their reading enjoyment and comprehension? Teachers need to have a repertoire of successful and proven assessment and instructional alternatives available to assist children in activating their prior knowledge, select effective comprehension strategies, and increase their engagement and motivation. The assessment strategies outlined in this section provide you with the means to assess these factors that influence children's comprehension.

## Assessing Readers' Prior Knowledge: Langer's Background Knowledge Assessment Procedure

### Purpose

Children's background information and experiences are among the most important contributors or inhibitors of comprehension. Researchers have determined that students who possess a great deal of background information about a subject tend to recall greater amounts of information more accurately from reading than do students with little or no background knowledge (Carr & Thompson, 1996; Pearson, Hansen, & Gordon, 1979; Pressley, 2000). It is also a well-known fact that well-developed background information can inhibit the comprehension of new information that conflicts with or refutes prior knowledge and assumptions about a specific topic. Thus, knowing how much knowledge a reader has about a concept or topic can help teachers better prepare students to read and comprehend successfully. One way that teachers can assess background knowledge and experience is to use a procedure developed by Langer (1982) for assessing the amount and content of students' background knowledge about selected topics, themes, concepts, and events.

### Materials

- The checklist and materials represented in Figure 9.1

### Procedure

Select a story for children to read. Construct a list of specific vocabulary terms or story concepts related to the topic, message, theme, or events to be experienced in reading the story. For example, students may read *Stone Fox* by John R. Gardiner (1980) about a boy named Willy who saves his grandfather's farm from the tax collector. Construct a list of 5 to 10 specific vocabulary terms or concepts related to the story. Use this list to probe background knowledge and experiences of the students about the story's message and plot. Such a list may include the following:

- broke
- taxes
- tax collector
- dogsled race
- Samoyeds

Students are asked to respond to each of these terms in writing or through discussion by using one of several stem statements, as shown in Figure 9.1, such as, "What comes to mind when you think of paying bills and you hear the term *broke?*" Once students have responded to each of the specific terms, the teacher can score the responses using the information in Figure 9.1 to survey the class or individual's knowledge and experience. Awarding the number of points that most closely represents the level of prior knowledge in the response is used to score each item. Divide the total score by the number of terms or concepts in the list (five

---

**FIGURE 9.1**  Checklist of Levels of Prior Knowledge

Phrase 1   What comes to mind when . . . ?
Phrase 2   What made you think of . . . ?
Phrase 3   Have you any new ideas about . . . ?

_____

Stimulus used to elicit student background knowledge _____
(Picture, word, or phrase, etc.)

|  | Much (3)<br>category labels<br>definitions<br>analogies<br>relationships | Some (2)<br>examples<br>attributes<br>defining characteristics | Little (1)<br>personal associations<br>morphemes<br>sound alikes<br>personal experiences |
|---|---|---|---|
| **Student** | | | |
| *Maria* | _____ | ___X____ | _____ |
| *Jawan* | ___X____ | _____ | _____ |
| _____ | _____ | _____ | _____ |
| _____ | _____ | _____ | _____ |
| _____ | _____ | _____ | _____ |

---

in our example) to determine the average knowledge level of individual students. These average scores are compared against the Checklist of Levels of Prior Knowledge in Figure 9.1 for each student. By scanning the Xs in the checklist, a teacher can get a sense of the entire class's overall level of prior knowledge. Information thus gathered can be used to inform both the content and nature of whole-group comprehension instruction.

# ASSESSING READERS' USE OF COMPREHENSION STRATEGIES

## A Classroom-Modified Version of the Reading Strategy Use Scale

### Purpose

*Metacognition* refers to two important concepts related to reading comprehension: (a) a reader's knowledge of the status of his or her own thinking and the appropriate strategies to facilitate ongoing comprehension and (b) the executive control one has over one's own thinking, including the use of comprehension strategies to facilitate or repair failing comprehension while reading (Paris, Wasik, & Turner, 1991). For many readers, problems in comprehension result from failures related to one or both of these two important concepts. The purpose of metacognitive assessment is to gain insight into how students select strategies to use in comprehending text and how well they regulate the status of their own comprehension as they read. We have modified the Reading Strategy Use (RSU) scale developed by Pereira-Laird and Deane (1997) for classroom application. Scores obtained

---

**FIGURE 9.2**  A Classroom-Modified Reading Strategy Use Table

Name:_____ Grade: _____

Teacher: _____ School: _____

**Directions:** Read each item and the number of the word that best describes how often you do what is stated. Let's do number 1 together to make sure you understand how you are to respond to each item.

1. I read quickly through the story to get the general idea before I read the story closely.

   | Always | Sometimes | Never |
   |--------|-----------|-------|
   | 3 | 2 | 1 |

2. When I come to a part of the story that is hard to read, I slow my reading down.

   | Always | Sometimes | Never |
   |--------|-----------|-------|
   | 3 | 2 | 1 |

3. I am able to tell the difference between important story parts and less important details.

   | Always | Sometimes | Never |
   |--------|-----------|-------|
   | 3 | 2 | 1 |

4. When I read, I stop once in a while to go over in my head what I have been reading to see if it is making sense.

   | Always | Sometimes | Never |
   |--------|-----------|-------|
   | 3 | 2 | 1 |

5. I adjust the speed of my reading by deciding how difficult the story is to read.

   | Always | Sometimes | Never |
   |--------|-----------|-------|
   | 3 | 2 | 1 |

6. I stop once in a while and ask myself questions about the story to see how well I understand what I am reading.

   | Always | Sometimes | Never |
   |--------|-----------|-------|
   | 3 | 2 | 1 |

7. After reading a story, I sit and think about it for a while to check my memory of the story parts and the order of the story parts.

   | Always | Sometimes | Never |
   |--------|-----------|-------|
   | 3 | 2 | 1 |

8. When I get lost while reading, I go back to the place in the story where I first had trouble and reread.

   | Always | Sometimes | Never |
   |--------|-----------|-------|
   | 3 | 2 | 1 |

9. When I find I do not understand something when reading, I read it again and try to figure it out.

   | Always | Sometimes | Never |
   |--------|-----------|-------|
   | 3 | 2 | 1 |

10. When reading, I check how well I understand the meaning of the story by asking myself whether the ideas fit with the other information in the story.

    | Always | Sometimes | Never |
    |--------|-----------|-------|
    | 3 | 2 | 1 |

11. I find it hard to pay attention when I read.

    | Always | Sometimes | Never |
    |--------|-----------|-------|
    | 3 | 2 | 1 |

12. To help me remember what I read, I sometimes draw a map or outline the story.

    | Always | Sometimes | Never |
    |--------|-----------|-------|
    | 3 | 2 | 1 |

13. To help me understand what I have read in a story, I try to retell it in my own words.

    | Always | Sometimes | Never |
    |--------|-----------|-------|
    | 3 | 2 | 1 |

14. I learn new words by trying to make a picture of the words in my mind.

    | Always | Sometimes | Never |
    |--------|-----------|-------|
    | 3 | 2 | 1 |

15. When reading about something, I try to relate it to my own experiences.

    | Always | Sometimes | Never |
    |--------|-----------|-------|
    | 3 | 2 | 1 |

from administering the Classroom-Modified Reading Strategy Use (CMRSU) scale provide insights into how well students select, apply, and regulate their use of comprehension strategies.

## Materials

- The Classroom-Modified Reading Strategy Use scale shown in Figure 9.2

## Procedure

The CMRSU scale is group administered. Tell students that the CMRSU scale is not a test and there are no right or wrong answers. Ask students to fill in the personal information at the top of the CMRSU scale. Read the directions aloud and ask children if they have any questions about the nature of the responses to be given to each statement. Once you are sure that the students understand, instruct them to read each item and circle the number under the response that best represents their behavior in relation to each statement. When children finish the CMRSU scale, ask them to remain in their seats. They should quietly take out a book, write, or draw so as not to disturb others who are still completing the scale.

Scoring is accomplished by summing the response numbers circled and dividing by the total of the 15 items in the CMRSU scale: Sum of individual responses/15 items = Mean score.

A mean score near 3 demonstrates the strong selection, use, and self-regulation of comprehension-monitoring strategies. A mean score near 2 indicates occasional selection and use of comprehension-monitoring strategies. The pattern of responses should be carefully studied to see which of the comprehension-monitoring strategies are in use and which are not to inform instructional planning for the future. A mean score near 1 indicates poorly developed selection, use, and self-regulation of comprehension-monitoring strategies. These students need explicit teacher explanation of (a) comprehension-monitoring strategies; (b) how, when, and why to use comprehension-monitoring strategies; (c) teacher modeling of comprehension-monitoring strategy use; and (d) guided practice applying selected comprehension-monitoring strategies during the reading and discussion of stories in the classroom.

## Metacomprehension Strategy Index

### Purpose

The Metacomprehension Strategy Index (MSI) developed by M. C. Schmitt (1988, 1990, 2005) is a valuable tool for assessing students' awareness of a variety of reading comprehension strategies that are appropriate for use before, during, and after the reading of a text. The individual items in the MSI are correlated with six categories of reading comprehension strategies: (1) predicting and verifying, (2) previewing, (3) purpose setting, (4) self-questioning, (5) drawing from prior knowledge, and (6) summarizing and using fix-up strategies. Schmitt (2005) asserts that the MSI is "a valid means for measuring learners' metacognition or metacomprehension for the purpose of designing instructional programs [interventions]" (Schmitt, 2005, p. 106). She has also shown that the MSI correlates with other measures of strategy use and metacognition such as the Index of Reading Awareness (Paris & Jacobs, 1984).

### Materials

- The MSI scale shown in Figure 9.3

---

| FIGURE 9.3 | Metacomprehension Strategy Index |

**Directions**

Think about what kinds of things you can do to help you understand a story better before, during, and after you read it. Read each set of four statements and decide which one of them would help you the most. *There are no right or wrong answers.* It is just what *you* think would help the most. Circle the letter of the statement you choose.

**Questionnaire Items**

**In each set of four, choose the one statement that tells a good thing to do to help you understand a story better before you read it.**

1. *Before* I begin reading, it is a good idea to
   A. see how many pages are in the story.
   B. look up all of the big words in the dictionary.
   C. make some guesses about what I think will happen in the story.
   D. think about what has happened so far in the story.

2. *Before* I begin reading, it is a good idea to
   A. look at the pictures to see what the story is about.
   B. decide how long it will take me to read the story.
   C. sound out the words I do not know.
   D. check to see if the story is making sense.

3. *Before* I begin reading, it's a good idea to
   A. ask someone to read the story to me.
   B. read the title to see what the story is about.
   C. check to see if most of the words have long or short vowels in them.
   D. check to see if the pictures are in order and make sense.

4. *Before* I begin reading, it is a good idea to
   A. check to see that no pages are missing.
   B. make a list of the words I am not sure about.
   C. use the title and pictures to help me make guesses about what will happen in the story.
   D. read the last sentence so I will know how the story ends.

5. *Before* I begin reading, it is a good idea to
   A. decide on why I am going to read the story.
   B. use the difficult words to help me make guesses about what will happen in the story.
   C. reread some parts to see if I can figure out what is happening if things are not making sense.
   D. ask for help with the difficult words.

6. *Before* I begin reading, it is a good idea to
   A. retell all of the main points that have happened so far.
   B. ask myself questions that I will like to have answered in the story.
   C. think about the meanings of the words that have more than one meaning.
   D. look through the story to find all of the words with three or more syllables.

7. *Before* I begin reading, it is a good idea to
   A. check to see if I have read this story before.
   B. use my questions and guesses as a reason for reading the story.
   C. make sure I can pronounce all of the words before I start.
   D. think of a better title for the story.

8. *Before* I begin reading, it is a good idea to
   A. think of what I already know about the things I see in the pictures.

    B.  see how may pages are in the story.
    C.  choose the best part of the story to read again.
    D.  read the story aloud to someone.

9.  *Before I b*egin reading, it is a good idea to
    A.  practice reading the story aloud.
    B.  retell all of the main points to make sure I can remember the story.
    C.  think of what the people in the story might be like.
    D.  decide if I have enough time to read the story.

10. *Before* I begin reading, it is a good idea to
    A.  check to see if I am understanding the story so far.
    B.  check to see if the words have more than one meaning.
    C.  think about where the story might be taking place.
    D.  list all of the important details.

**In each set of four, choose the one statement that tells a good thing to do to help you understand a story better *while you are reading it.***

11. *While* I am reading, it is a good idea to
    A.  read the story very slowly so that I will not miss any important parts.
    B.  read the title to see what the story is about.
    C.  check to see if the pictures have anything missing.
    D.  check to see if the story is making sense by seeing if I can tell what has happened so far.

12. *While* I am reading, it is a good idea to
    A.  stop to retell the main points to see if I am understanding what has happened so far.
    B.  read the story quickly so that I can find out what happened.
    C.  read only the beginning and the end of the story to find out what it is about.
    D.  skip the parts that are too difficult for me.

13. *While* I am reading, it is a good idea to
    A.  look all of the big words up in the dictionary.
    B.  put the book away and find another one if things are not making sense.
    C.  keep thinking about the title and the pictures to help me decide what is going to happen next.
    D.  keep track of how many pages I have left to read.

14. *While* I am reading, it is a good idea to
    A.  keep track of how long it is taking me to read the story.
    B.  check to see if I can answer any of the questions I asked before I started reading.
    C.  read the title to see what the story is going to be about.
    D.  add the missing details to the pictures.

15. *While* I am reading, it is a good idea to
    A.  have someone read the story aloud to me.
    B.  keep track of how many pages I have read.
    C.  list the story's main characters.
    D.  check to see if my guesses are right or wrong.

16. *While* I am reading, it is a good idea to
    A.  check to see that the characters are real.
    B.  make a lot of guesses about what is going to happen next.
    C.  not look at the pictures because they might confuse me.
    D.  read the story aloud to someone.

*(continued)*

| FIGURE 9.3 | *Continued* |
|---|---|

17. *While* I am reading, it is a good idea to
    A. try to answer the questions I asked myself.
    B. try not to confuse what I already know with what I am reading about.
    C. read the story silently.
    D. check to see if I am saying the new vocabulary words correctly.

18. *While* I am reading, it is a good idea to
    A. try to see if my guesses are going to be right or wrong.
    B. reread to be sure I have not missed any of the words.
    C. decide on why I am reading the story.
    D. list what happened first, second, third, and so on.

19. *While* I am reading, it is a good idea to
    A. see if I can recognize the new vocabulary words.
    B. be careful not to skip any parts of the story.
    C. check to see how many of the words I already know.
    D. keep thinking of what I already know about the things and ideas in the story to help me decide what is going to happen.

20. *While* I am reading, it is a good idea to
    A. reread some parts or read ahead to see if I can figure out what is happening if things are not making sense.
    B. take my time reading so that I can be sure I understand what is happening.
    C. change the ending so that it makes sense.
    D. check to see if there are enough pictures to help make the story ideas clear.

**In each set of four, choose the one statement that tells a good thing to do to help you understand the story better after you have read it.**

21. *After* I have read a story, it is a good idea to
    A. count how many pages I read with no mistakes.
    B. check to see if there were enough pictures to go with the story to make it interesting.
    C. check to see if I met my purpose for reading the story.
    D. underline the causes and effects.

22. *After* I have read a story, it is a good idea to
    A. underline the main idea.
    B. retell the main points of the whole story so that I can check to see if I understood it.
    C. read the story again to be sure I said all of the words right.
    D. practice reading the story aloud.

23. *After* I have read a story, it is a good idea to
    A. read the title and look over the story to see what it is about.
    B. check to see if I skipped any of the vocabulary words.
    C. think about what made me make good or bad predictions.
    D. make a guess about what will happen next in the story.

24. *After* I have read a story, it is a good idea to
    A. look up all of the big words in the dictionary.
    B. read the best parts aloud.
    C. have someone read the story aloud to me.
    D. think about how the story was like things I already knew about before I started reading.

**25.** *After* I have read a story, it is a good idea to
   A. think about how I would have acted if I were the main character in the story.
   B. practice reading the story silently for practice of good reading.
   C. look over the story title and picture to see what will happen.
   D. make a list of the things I understood the most.

*Source:* From "A Questionnaire to Measure Children's Awareness of Strategic Reading Processes" by M. C. Schmitt, 1990, *The Reading Teacher, 43,* 454–461. Copyright © 1990 by the International Reading Association (www.reading.org). Reproduced with permission of the International Reading Association via Copyright Clearance Center.

## Procedure

The MSI can be given to students as a group if they are able to read it without undue difficulty. If there is any doubt, the MSI should be read aloud to the students during administration. To begin, children are instructed: "Think about what kinds of things you can do to help you understand a story [text] better before, during, and after you read it." Next, read each item in the MSI aloud. Tell children that they are to be thinking about which of the four responses underneath each item they believe would "help them the most." Children are also told that there are no right or wrong answers. Then children are told to circle one of the four responses underneath each of the 25 total MSI items.

Schmitt (2005) indicates that the scores on the MSI can be used to assess students' individual weaknesses in strategy selection and use or the MSI can be used to determine general patterns of strengths and weaknesses in an entire class's selection and use of comprehension strategies. Schmitt recommends that teachers begin by examining the performance of the entire class. To help with the analysis process, she recommends contemplating the following three questions:

1. Which strategies were the most well known?
2. Were there differences among the before, during, and after stages that might signal specific areas of concern?
3. Were there patterns indicating difficulty with understanding the items on the MSI? For example, did several students select a nonsensical distracter underneath a specific item?

# ASSESSING READERS' SOCIAL COLLABORATIONS IN READING COMPREHENSION

## Social Collaboration Performance Outcome Evaluation

### Purpose

Although process is important during cooperative and collaborative learning activities, a quality process should frequently result in a quality product. Assessment of the collaborative performance outcome is necessary to ensure that a spirit of accountability and consequence is maintained. As discussed previously, an essential element of quality cooperative learning groups is to ensure an element of accountability and consequence for task completion whether it is an open- or closed-ended test. The Performance Outcome Team Evaluation tool is a means of helping teachers assess the products of collaboration and discussion around texts to promote reading comprehension.

### Materials

- A Performance Outcome Team Evaluation form as shown in Figure 9.4 (a type of assessment that is usually and preferably ungraded, although you will note a column provided for grading if that is required)

### Procedure

Teachers collect student or group projects, papers, or other products for evaluation. We suggest that students be provided the form shown in Figure 9.4 as a guide for their own understanding of teacher expectations. The completed evaluation form should accompany feedback to the group or team about the quality of the team's product.

---

**FIGURE 9.4**   Performance Outcome Team Evaluation Form

Team name: _____     Date: _____

Teacher's name: _____     Class: _____

| Outcomes | Points | Grade |
| --- | --- | --- |
| Completes assigned tasks (assignments, quizzes, reports, work units, homework) | | |
| Applies skills taught in task completion (work units, use in problem-solving situations, homework) | | |
| Understands concepts and principles (team scores, reports, homework, observations) | | |
| Communication<br>1. Communicates ideas and feelings effectively (observations, direct discussion)<br>2. Participates actively in problem-solving groups | | |
| Writing work (homework, reports) | | |
| Cooperation (observations, team products) | | |
| Competitive ability (observations, performances in competitions) | | |
| Independent work (observations, performances in individualized activities) | | |
| Affective learning | | |
| Appreciation of subject areas | | |
| Appreciates learning (receives enjoyment and satisfaction from learning) | | |
| Aware of and appreciates own abilities, achievements, talents, and resources | | |
| When appropriate, helps others, shares resources, etc. | | |
| Accepts and appreciates cultural, ethnic, linguistic, and individual differences | | |
| Values free and open inquiry into all problems | | |
| | **Total** | |

## Self-Assessment of Collaboration: Individual and Group Accountability

### Purpose

The purpose of self-assessment centers on developing each student's ability to judge the quality of his or her own contributions to a cooperative team effort (Ellis & Whalen, 1990; Johnson & Johnson, 1999). Students of any age and ability can engage in self-assessment. This is important to cooperative learning because it helps students take responsibility for their own behavior and learning.

### Materials

- Group and individual assessment forms, as shown in Figures 9.5 and 9.6, that can be duplicated and distributed to teams or individuals to be completed at the conclusion of daily cooperative group activities

### Procedure

For group assessment, students can fill out the form shown in Figure 9.5 individually. Then students can be encouraged to share their responses with the group and compare how they perceived the group functioning with their teammates. At the conclusion of the discussion, the group fills out a single form representing the consensus of the group. Dissenting opinions should be given space at the bottom of the form to express differences from the group.

---

**FIGURE 9.5**    Group Self-Assessment

**Group:** _____     **Date:** _____

**Today:**

1. **We offered our ideas to each other.**
   Usually _____        Sometimes _____        Seldom _____

2. **We listened carefully to each other.**
   Usually _____        Sometimes _____        Seldom _____

3. **We offered encouragement to each other.**
   Usually _____        Sometimes _____        Seldom _____

4. **We helped each other with building ideas or solving problems.**
   Usually _____        Sometimes _____        Seldom _____

5. **We completed the assigned tasks well.**
   Usually _____        Sometimes _____        Seldom _____

Signatures

_____        _____

_____        _____

_____        _____

---

**FIGURE 9.6**    Individual Self-Assessment

**Name:** _____    **Date:** _____

**Today:**

1. **I offered my ideas.**

   Usually _____    Sometimes _____    Seldom _____

2. **I listened carefully to others.**

   Usually _____    Sometimes _____    Seldom _____

3. **I offered encouragement to others.**

   Usually _____    Sometimes _____    Seldom _____

4. **I helped others with building ideas or solving problems.**

   Usually _____    Sometimes _____    Seldom _____

5. **I completed the assigned tasks well.**

   Usually _____    Sometimes _____    Seldom _____

Signature

_____

---

For individual assessment, students simply fill out the form shown in Figure 9.6 independently and turn it in to the teacher, who places it in the student's self-assessment file. Teachers create this file for each child to keep a running account of how the child rates his or her own learning and involvement.

## Assessing Student Motivation for Reading: Motivation for Reading Questionnaire, Revised Version

### Purpose

The Motivation for Reading Questionnaire (MRQ), Revised Version, was designed to assess eight different possible dimensions of reading motivations (Wigfield, Guthrie, & McGough, 1996): (1) curiosity, (2) involvement, (3) preference for challenge, (4) recognition, (5) grades, (6) social status, (7) competition, and (8) compliance. These eight dimensions of reading motivation tap into both extrinsic and intrinsic motivational factors. The MRQ has been used as a measure of reading motivation in many reported and published research studies in recent years because of the extensive validation and reliability work surrounding the development and application of this easy-to-use instrument. Changing the classroom environment and the dimensions of classroom literacy instructional practices can only occur when teachers have access to data that help them to understand how their practices, programs, and environments are affecting the development of students' reading motivations. Promoting lifelong engagement in reading is a primary goal for all literacy educators; the MRQ instrument allows teachers to measure the efficacy and effects of their in-school and out-of-school literacy programs on children's ongoing literacy motivation and engagement (Wigfield, 1997).

### Materials

- Multiple copies of the Motivation for Reading Questionnaire, Revised Version, for recording individual student responses (see Figure 9.7)
- One form for recording categories of class responses

### Procedure

Distribute individual paper copies of the MRQ, Revised Version, for each student in your classroom. Instruct the children to put their names in the upper right-hand corner of the first page of the MRQ, Revised Version. If the children are capable of reading the MRQ items independently, then they may do so. Otherwise, each item is read aloud by the teacher and each student is asked to mark independently his or her response on the 4-point scale beneath the item. Once all 44 items have been read aloud by the teacher and responded to by the students, the MRQs are picked up.

A class copy of the MRQ can then be used to tally the number of responses underneath each item for the four points of the scale. Once the tally is complete, the teacher should carefully note which students have low motivation across or within motivational categories. Also, the teacher can make note of which reading motivation dimensions are low in the whole class of students. By doing this, the teacher has a way to screen for problems in an individual child's reading motivations as well as to monitor the reading motivation of the whole class. Furthermore, the MRQ, Revised Version, can be used to individually diagnose areas of motivation that are strengths or weaknesses for individual students. As a result, the teacher can select individual or small-group reading motivation strategies to address these measured weaknesses. The teacher can also measure the motivation of the whole class and determine interventions that may be used to promote increased motivation at the whole-class level.

## The Reader Self-Perception Scale

### Purpose

A sense of personal self-efficacy in learning and using comprehension strategies plays a key role in every reader's development of competence and confidence. Self-efficacy denotes one's beliefs about his or her own capabilities to learn or to perform a given task at specified or designated levels of proficiency (Bandura, 1986; Paris & Winograd, 2001; Schunk & Zimmerman, 1997). Previous research has clearly demonstrated a strong link between learners' sense of self-efficacy, motivation, and self-regulatory processes (Schunk, 1996). Self-efficacy has been shown to influence task choice, effort, persistence, and ultimate achievement. Effective comprehension strategy instruction requires that students develop a sense of self-efficacy as well as self-regulating behaviors and dispositions. Henk and Melnick (1995) developed an instrument for measuring how children feel about themselves as readers, an indicator of self-efficacy, called the Reader Self-Perception Scale (RSPS). See a description of the scale and instructions for use in Figure 9.8.

### Materials

- One copy for each student of the Reader Self-Perception Scale (RSPS) shown in Figure 9.9 on page 295
- One copy for each student of the RSPS scoring sheet shown in Figure 9.10 on page 296

**FIGURE 9.7**    The Motivation for Reading Questionnaire, Revised Version

| | Very different from me | A little different from me | A little like me | A lot like me |
|---|---|---|---|---|
| **Curiosity** | | | | |
| 1. I like to read because I always feel happy when I read things that are of interest to me. | 1 | 2 | 3 | 4 |
| 2. If the teacher discusses something interesting, I might read more about it. | 1 | 2 | 3 | 4 |
| 3. I have favorite subjects that I like to read about. | 1 | 2 | 3 | 4 |
| 4. I read to learn new information about topics that interest me. | 1 | 2 | 3 | 4 |
| 5. I read about my hobbies to learn more about them. | 1 | 2 | 3 | 4 |
| 6. I like to read about new things. | 1 | 2 | 3 | 4 |
| 7. I enjoy reading books about people in different countries. | 1 | 2 | 3 | 4 |
| **Involvement** | | | | |
| 8. If I am reading about an interesting topic, I sometimes lose track of time. | 1 | 2 | 3 | 4 |
| 9. I read stories about fantasy and make believe. | 1 | 2 | 3 | 4 |
| 10. I like mysteries. | 1 | 2 | 3 | 4 |
| 11. I make pictures in my mind when I read. | 1 | 2 | 3 | 4 |
| 12. I feel like I made friends with people in good books. | 1 | 2 | 3 | 4 |
| 13. I like to read a lot of adventure stories. | 1 | 2 | 3 | 4 |
| 14. I enjoy a long, involved story or fiction book. | 1 | 2 | 3 | 4 |
| **Preference for Challenge** | | | | |
| 15. I like hard, challenging books. | 1 | 2 | 3 | 4 |
| 16. If the project is interesting, I can read difficult material. | 1 | 2 | 3 | 4 |
| 17. I like it when the questions in books make me think. | 1 | 2 | 3 | 4 |
| 18. I usually learn difficult things by reading. | 1 | 2 | 3 | 4 |
| 19. If a book is interesting, I do not care how hard it is to read. | 1 | 2 | 3 | 4 |
| **Recognition** | | | | |
| 20. I like having the teacher say I read well. | 1 | 2 | 3 | 4 |
| 21. I like having my friends sometimes tell me I am a good reader. | 1 | 2 | 3 | 4 |
| 22. I like to get compliments for my reading. | 1 | 2 | 3 | 4 |
| 23. I am happy when someone recognizes my reading. | 1 | 2 | 3 | 4 |

| | Very different from me 1 | A little different from me 2 | A little like me 3 | A lot like me 4 |
|---|:---:|:---:|:---:|:---:|
| 24. I like having my parents often tell me what a good job I am doing in reading. | 1 | 2 | 3 | 4 |

**Grades**

| | | | | |
|---|:---:|:---:|:---:|:---:|
| 25. Grades are a good way to see how well you are doing in reading. | 1 | 2 | 3 | 4 |
| 26. I look forward to finding out my grade in reading on my report card. | 1 | 2 | 3 | 4 |
| 27. I like to read to improve my grades. | 1 | 2 | 3 | 4 |
| 28. I like my parents to ask me about my reading grade. | 1 | 2 | 3 | 4 |

**Social**

| | | | | |
|---|:---:|:---:|:---:|:---:|
| 29. I like to visit the library often with my family. | 1 | 2 | 3 | 4 |
| 30. I often like to read to my brother or sister. | 1 | 2 | 3 | 4 |
| 31. My friends and I like to trade things to read. | 1 | 2 | 3 | 4 |
| 32. I sometimes read to my parents. | 1 | 2 | 3 | 4 |
| 33. I like to talk to my friends about what I am reading. | 1 | 2 | 3 | 4 |
| 34. I like to help my friends with their schoolwork in reading. | 1 | 2 | 3 | 4 |
| 35. I like to tell my family about what I am reading. | 1 | 2 | 3 | 4 |

**Competition**

| | | | | |
|---|:---:|:---:|:---:|:---:|
| 36. I try to get more answers right than my friends. | 1 | 2 | 3 | 4 |
| 37. I like being the best at reading. | 1 | 2 | 3 | 4 |
| 38. I like to finish my reading before other students. | 1 | 2 | 3 | 4 |
| 39. I like being the only one who knows an answer in something we read. | 1 | 2 | 3 | 4 |
| 40. I am willing to work hard to read better than my friends. | 1 | 2 | 3 | 4 |

**Compliance**

| | | | | |
|---|:---:|:---:|:---:|:---:|
| 41. I always do my reading work exactly as the teacher wants it. | 1 | 2 | 3 | 4 |
| 42. Finishing every reading assignment is very important to me. | 1 | 2 | 3 | 4 |
| 43. I read because I have to read. | 1 | 2 | 3 | 4 |
| 44. I always try to finish my reading on time. | 1 | 2 | 3 | 4 |

---

**FIGURE 9.8** Directions for Administration, Scoring, and Interpretation of the Reader Self-Perception Scale

The Reader Self-Perception Scale (RSPS) is intended to provide an assessment of how children feel about themselves as readers. The scale consists of 33 items that assess self-perceptions along four dimensions of self-efficacy (Progress, Observational Comparison, Social Feedback, and Physiological States). Children are asked to indicate how strongly they agree or disagree with each statement on a 5-point scale (5 = Strongly Agree, 1 = Strongly Disagree). The information gained from this scale can be used to devise ways to enhance children's self-esteem in reading and, ideally, to increase their motivation to read. The following directions explain specifically what you are to do.

**Administration**
For the results to be of any use, the children must (a) understand exactly what they are to do, (b) have sufficient time to complete all items, and (c) respond honestly and thoughtfully. Briefly explain to the children that they are being asked to complete a questionnaire about reading. Emphasize that this is not a test and that there are no *right* answers. Tell them that they should be as honest as possible because their responses will be confidential. Ask the children to fill in their names, grade levels, and classrooms as appropriate. Read the directions aloud and work through the example with the students as a group. Discuss the response options and make sure that all children understand the rating scale before moving on. It is important that children know that they may raise their hands to ask questions about any words or ideas they do not understand.

The children should then read each item and circle their response for the item. They should work at their own pace. Remind the children that they should be sure to respond to all items. When all items are completed, the children should stop, put their pencils down, and wait for further instructions. Care should be taken that children who work more slowly are not disturbed by children who have already finished.

**Scoring**
To score the RSPS, enter the following point values for each response on the RSPS scoring sheet (Strongly Agree = 5, Agree = 4, Undecided = 3, Disagree = 2, Strongly Disagree = 1) for each item number under the appropriate scale. Sum each column to obtain a raw score for each of the four specific scales.

**Interpretation**
Each scale is interpreted in relation to its total possible score. For example, because the RSPS uses a 5-point scale and the Progress scale consists of 9 items, the highest total score for Progress is 45 (9 x 5 = 45). Therefore, a score that would fall approximately in the middle of the range (22–23) would indicate a child's somewhat indifferent perception of herself or himself as a reader with respect to Progress. Note that each scale has a different possible total raw score (Progress = 45, Observational Comparison = 30, Social Feedback = 45, and Physiological States = 40) and should be interpreted accordingly.

*Source:* From "The Reader Self-Perception Scale (RSPS): A New Tool for Measuring How Children Feel about Themselves as Readers," by W. A. Henk and S. A. Melnick, 1995, *The Reading Teacher, 48*(6), 480. Copyright © 1995 by the International Reading Association (www.reading.org). Reproduced with permission of the International Reading Association via Copyright Clearance Center.

**Procedure**
The RSPS assessment tool is group rather than individually administered. In order to obtain valid results, it is imperative that students clearly understand the nature of the task and be given sufficient time to thoughtfully and honestly respond to each item. Tell children that this is not a test and that there are no right or wrong answers. Also tell them that responses will be kept strictly confidential. Ask children to fill in the personal information at the top of the RSPS. Read the directions aloud to the group and guide them through the completion of the example item. Make sure children understand the response categories and understand the task. Then have

---

**FIGURE 9.9**　The Reader Self-Perception Scale

Listed below are statements about reading. Please read each statement carefully. Then circle the letters that show how much you agree or disagree with the statement. Use the following:

　　　　SA = Strongly Agree
　　　　A = Agree
　　　　U = Undecided
　　　　D = Disagree
　　　　SD = Strongly Disagree

Example: **I think pizza with pepperoni is the best.**　SA　　A　　U　　D　　SD

　　　If you are *really positive* that pepperoni pizza is best, circle SA (Strongly Agree).
　　　If you *think* that it is good but maybe not great, circle A (Agree).
　　　If you *can't decide* whether or not it is best, circle U (undecided).
　　　If you *think* that pepperoni pizza is not all that good, circle D (Disagree).
　　　If you are *really positive* that pepperoni pizza is not very good, circle SD (Strongly Disagree).

| | | | | | | | |
|---|---|---|---|---|---|---|---|
| [GP] | 1. | I think I am a good reader. | SA | A | U | D | SD |
| [SF] | 2. | I can tell that my teacher likes to listen to me read. | SA | A | U | D | SD |
| [SF] | 3. | My teacher thinks that my reading is fine. | SA | A | U | D | SD |
| [OC] | 4. | I read faster than other kids. | SA | A | U | D | SD |
| [PS] | 5. | I like to read aloud. | SA | A | U | D | SD |
| [OC] | 6. | When I read, I can figure out words better than other kids. | SA | A | U | D | SD |
| [SF] | 7. | My classmates like to listen to me read. | SA | A | U | D | SD |
| [PS] | 8. | I feel good inside when I read. | SA | A | U | D | SD |
| [SF] | 9. | My classmates think that I read pretty well. | SA | A | U | D | SD |
| [PR] | 10. | When I read, I don't have to try as hard as I used to. | SA | A | U | D | SD |
| [OC] | 11. | I seem to know more words than other kids when I read. | SA | A | U | D | SD |
| [SF] | 12. | People in my family think I am a good reader. | SA | A | U | D | SD |
| [PR] | 13. | I am getting better at reading. | SA | A | U | D | SD |
| [OC] | 14. | I understand what I read as well as other kids do. | SA | A | U | D | SD |
| [PR] | 15. | When I read, I need less help than I used to. | SA | A | U | D | SD |
| [PS] | 16. | Reading makes me feel happy inside. | SA | A | U | D | SD |
| [SF] | 17. | My teacher thinks I am a good reader. | SA | A | U | D | SD |
| [PR] | 18. | Reading is easier for me than it used to be. | SA | A | U | D | SD |
| [PR] | 19. | I read faster than I could before. | SA | A | U | D | SD |
| [OC] | 20. | I read better than other kids in my class. | SA | A | U | D | SD |
| [PS] | 21. | I feel calm when I read. | SA | A | U | D | SD |
| [OC] | 22. | I read more than other kids. | SA | A | U | D | SD |
| [PR] | 23. | I understand what I read better than I could before. | SA | A | U | D | SD |
| [PR] | 24. | I can figure out words better than I could before. | SA | A | U | D | SD |
| [PS] | 25. | I feel comfortable when I read. | SA | A | U | D | SD |
| [PS] | 26. | I think reading is relaxing. | SA | A | U | D | SD |
| [PR] | 27. | I read better now than I could before. | SA | A | U | D | SD |
| [PR] | 28. | When I read, I recognize more words than I used to. | SA | A | U | D | SD |
| [PS] | 29. | Reading makes me feel good. | SA | A | U | D | SD |
| [SF] | 30. | Other kids think I'm a good reader. | SA | A | U | D | SD |
| [SF] | 31. | People in my family think I read pretty well. | SA | A | U | D | SD |
| [PS] | 32. | I enjoy reading. | SA | A | U | D | SD |
| [SF] | 33. | People in my family like to listen to me read. | SA | A | U | D | SD |

*Source:* From "The Reader Self-Perception Scale (RSPS): A New Tool for Measuring How Children Feel about Themselves as Readers," by W. A. Henk and S. A. Melnick, 1995, *The Reading Teacher, 48*(6), 478–479. Copyright © 1995 by the International Reading Association (www.reading.org). Reproduced with permission of the International Reading Association via Copyright Clearance Center.

| FIGURE 9.10 | The Reader Self-Perception Scale Scoring Sheet |
| --- | --- |

Student name: _____

Teacher: _____

Grade: _____ Date: _____

Scoring key:    5 = Strongly Agree (SA)
                    4 = Agree (A)
                    3 = Undecided (U)
                    2 = Disagree (D)
                    1 = Strongly Disagree (SD)

**Scales**

| General Perception | Progress | Observational Comparison | Social Feedback | Physiological States |
| --- | --- | --- | --- | --- |
| 1. ____ | 10. ____ | 4. ____ | 2. ____ | 5. ____ |
| | 13. ____ | 6. ____ | 3. ____ | 8. ____ |
| | 15. ____ | 11. ____ | 7. ____ | 16. ____ |
| | 18. ____ | 14. ____ | 9. ____ | 21. ____ |
| | 19. ____ | 20. ____ | 12. ____ | 25. ____ |
| | 23. ____ | 22. ____ | 17. ____ | 26. ____ |
| | 24. ____ | | 30. ____ | 29. ____ |
| | 27. ____ | | 31. ____ | 32. ____ |
| | 28. ____ | | 33. ____ | |
| Raw score | ____ of 45 | ____ of 30 | ____ of 45 | ____ of 40 |

Score interpretation

| | | | | |
| --- | --- | --- | --- | --- |
| High | 44+ | 26+ | 38+ | 37+ |
| Average | 39 | 21 | 33 | 31 |
| Low | 34 | 16 | 27 | 25 |

them complete their responses for each item of the RSPS. When children finish, ask them to quietly take out a book, write, or draw at their seats so as not to disturb others who are still completing the scale.

Scoring is accomplished by using the RSPS scoring sheet. Sum the numerical rating for each RSPS item within the categories listed on the RSPS scoring sheet. Interpretation of scores is found at the bottom of the scoring sheet.

## Student Reading Interest Survey

### Purpose

For many years, researchers have found that reading comprehension is positively affected when children are interested in the reading materials (Asher, 1980; Corno & Randi, 1997).

This is so much the case that interest in reading materials has been shown also to compensate for children's problems with strategy use and ability in comprehension specifically and reading generally (Sweet, 1997). Knowing how important interests are in shaping and influencing students' reading comprehension, the Student Reading Interest Survey (see Figure 9.11) provides teachers with an efficient and effective tool to gain insights into student interests.

### Materials

- One laminated copy of the questions found in the Student Reading Interest Survey (SRIS)
- Form for recording individual student responses
- Form for recording categories of class responses

### Procedure

Once the necessary materials are in place, schedule a time during the day to meet with students individually. Using the laminated copy of the SRIS, seat the child comfortably next to you at a table in a quiet corner of the classroom. (This survey may also be given by an aide or volunteer who has been trained to completely record answers.) Ask each question and record the answers given. Be sure to tell each child several times to return to earlier questions if he or she remembers anything else to tell you or to even share it at a later time.

After the entire class has been surveyed, compile the individual responses into a class survey response profile (see Figure 9.12) in which you record abbreviated answers to each question for each student. Noting variances in the responses to specific questions helps indicate categories of interests to guide your teaching and reading materials acquisition plan.

During the year, particularly if children's writing skills are well developed, distribute the SRIS to the entire group of children. Ask them to write their answers to the SRIS questions on their own copy and turn it in. Make any changes you discover throughout the year on the

---

**FIGURE 9.11**   Student Reading Interest Survey

*In-School Interests*

1. What is the title of your favorite book that you have read?
2. Do you have a favorite book title that someone has read to you?
3. What kinds of books do you like to read on your own?
4. Do you have favorite books, magazines, or comic books at home?
5. Do you ever read the newspaper at home? If so, what parts of the newspaper do you read?
6. What is your favorite school subject (other than recess and lunch)?
7. Have you ever done a special research project? What was the topic?

*Out-of-School Interests*

1. What do you do for fun on weekends or after school?
2. Do you have a hobby? If so, what?
3. What is your favorite TV show?
4. What is your favorite movie?
5. Do you play sports? If so, what?
6. Do you like animals or have a pet?
7. Do you have favorite video or computer games?
8. If you surf the Internet, what do you generally look for as you surf?
9. Have you ever collected something like coins, stamps, and so on? If you have, what?

| FIGURE 9.12 | Class Student Reading Interest Survey Profile Recording Table |
|---|---|

In-School Interests

| Student | Q1 | Q2 | Q3 | Q4 | Q5 | Q6 | Q7 |
|---|---|---|---|---|---|---|---|
|  |  |  |  |  |  |  |  |
|  |  |  |  |  |  |  |  |
|  |  |  |  |  |  |  |  |
|  |  |  |  |  |  |  |  |
|  |  |  |  |  |  |  |  |

*Note:* Extend the form for as many students as needed. Use a similar form with 9 question spaces for out-of-school interests.

class profile sheet. This updated information about your students' reading interests will help you adjust your selection of topics and reading materials as the year progresses.

In Figure 9.13, we summarize the procedures and instruments we have just discussed for assessing factors associated with the reader that affect reading comprehension. In this Summary Matrix of Assessments to Measure Comprehension Factors Associated with the Reader, we provide information about federally related assessment purposes (i.e., screening, diagnostic, progress-monitoring, *or* outcomes assessment), as well as the type of test or procedure and any available psychometric evidence of test or procedure scores (reliability and validity evidence).

### Connecting Assessment Findings to Teaching Strategies

Before discussing intervention strategies, we provide a guide connecting assessment to intervention and strategy choices (see Figure 9.14). It is our intention to help you select the most appropriate instructional interventions and strategies to meet students' needs based on assessment data. In the next part of this chapter, we offer strategies for intervention based on the foregoing assessments.

# INSTRUCTIONAL INTERVENTIONS AND STRATEGIES: HELPING THE READER IMPROVE READING COMPREHENSION

After a careful assessment of a student's comprehension, one or more of the following strategies may be appropriately applied. Perhaps the most important thing to remember is that children with poor background knowledge, motivation, and strategy selection or use can be helped to improve their comprehension by teachers who are sensitive to the need to assess these components of reading comprehension and take affirmative steps to address student needs. If students lack background, then teachers need to build it. If they have incorrect or incomplete background knowledge, then teachers need to activate this knowledge and add

**FIGURE 9.13** Summary Matrix of Assessments to Measure Comprehension Factors Associated with the Reader

| Name of Assessment Tool | Screening Assessment | Diagnostic Assessment | Progress-Monitoring Assessment | Outcomes Assessment | Norm-Referenced Test | Criterion-Referenced Test | Reliability Evidence | Validity Evidence |
|---|---|---|---|---|---|---|---|---|
| Langer's Background Knowledge Assessment Procedure | – | – | + | – | – | + | Not Available | Not Available |
| A Classroom-Modified Version of the Reading Strategy Use Scale | + | – | – | + | – | + | Cronbach's Alpha for Subscales Ranged from .70–.72 | Factor Analysis Intercorrelation Ranged from .65–.78 with the Three-Factor Model at .97 |
| Metacomprehension Strategy Index (MSI) | + | – | – | + | – | + | Kuder Richardson Formula .20–.87 Coefficient | Concurrent Validity with Index of Reading Awareness .48; .49 with Cloze Task; .50 with Error Detection Task |
| Social Collaboration Performance Outcome Evaluation | – | – | + | + | – | + | Not Available | Not Available |
| Self-Assessment of Collaboration: Group Accountability | + | – | – | + | – | + | Not Available | Not Available |
| Self-Assessment of Collaboration: Individual Accountability | + | – | – | + | – | + | Not Available | Not Available |
| Motivation for Reading Questionnaire (MRQ), Revised Version | + | + | + | + | – | + | Cronbach's Alpha Reliability on Eight Subscales of .43–.83 | Principal Components Factor Analysis All But Two Items Loaded at Greater Than .40 on Primary Factor Motivation |
| The Reader Self-Perception Scale (RSPS) | + | – | + | + | – | + | Cronbach's Alpha Ranges .81–.84 | Construct Validity Drawn From Theoretical Literature on Self-Efficacy |
| Student Reading Interest Survey | + | – | + | – | – | + | Not Available | Not Available |

Key: + can be used for   – not appropriate for

**FIGURE 9.14**  If-Then Intervention Strategy Guide for Improving Readers' Comprehension

| *"If"* the student is ready to learn ↓ / *"Then"* try these teaching strategies → | Students and Teachers Actively Reading Text (START) | Picture Walk | Online Reading Comprehension | Comprehension Process Motions (CPMs) | Think-Pair-Share | Explicit Cognitive Comprehension Strategy Instruction | Click or Clunk and Fix-Up | Elaborative Interrogation | Comprehension Strategy Framework | Reciprocal Teaching |
|---|---|---|---|---|---|---|---|---|---|---|
| Cognitive strategies | + | + | + | + | + | + | + | + | + | + |
| Background knowledge | * | + | * | * | * | + | * | – | * | * |
| Choice | * | * | * | * | * | + | – | – | * | * |
| Challenge | * | * | * | * | * | * | * | * | * | * |
| Consequences | – | – | * | + | * | + | + | – | * | * |
| Control | – | * | * | + | * | – | + | * | * | * |
| Collaboration | * | * | * | * | + | * | * | * | * | * |

Key: + Excellent strategy
     * Adaptable strategy
     – Unsuitable strategy

to it or modify or correct it. If students lack motivation, then teachers need to know what is lacking and why. Then they can select strategies that socially involve students actively in comprehension to increase motivation. Finally, if students lack strategies, then teachers can take steps to teach these cognitive comprehension strategies explicitly and scaffold their use to student independence. Our first comprehension instructional strategy—the interactive read-aloud method—is valuable for activating and building students' prior or background knowledge while motivating students to comprehend what they read and giving them comprehension strategies to accomplish it. Following the discussion of this general strategy, we present applications for each of these three strategic purposes: (a) activating and building prior or background knowledge, (b) increasing motivation to comprehend text, and (c) explicitly teaching cognitive comprehension strategies.

## Teaching Young Children Listening Comprehension through Read Aloud: Students and Teachers Actively Reading Text (START)

### Purpose

Go to the Assignments and Activities section of Topic 9: "Reading Comprehension" in the MyEducationLab for your course and complete the activity entitled "Reading Strategies Before Reading." As you watch the video and answer the accompanying questions, make a list of the before and during reading comprehension strategies shown in this video.

Reading aloud to children has long been supported as the most important means to motivate and demonstrate for children the strategies and motivations for reading (Sharlach, 2008). *"The single most important activity for building the knowledge for eventual success in reading is reading aloud to children. This is especially so in the preschool years. The benefits are the greatest when the child is an active participant, engaging in discussions about stories, learning to identify letters and words, and talking about meanings of words"* (emphasis added; Anderson, Hiebert, Scott, & Wilkinson, 1985, p. 23). More recently, reading books aloud to students has been viewed as an effective vehicle for transporting students into the mindset of learning how to select and apply cognitive reading strategies (Sweeney, 2004; Sharlach, 2008).

START is an instructional framework that can help teachers explicitly teach the selection and use of effective comprehension strategies (see more discussion of cognitive comprehension strategies later in this section) to younger or older children through actively reading by thinking aloud and interacting with them over multiple texts (Campbell, 2001; Martens, 1996; Martin & Reutzel, 1999; Schikendanz, 1990). Using differing grouping structures that encourage greater student involvement and interaction helps motivate students to comprehend what they read (National Institute of Child Health and Human Development, 2000). Most reading aloud in school takes place with an entire class or group of children, but Morrow (2005) reminds us not to overlook the motivational benefits and social importance of reading aloud to smaller groups and individuals. Children whose reading development is lagging behind their peers can be helped a great deal by teachers and parents who take time to read to them in small-group or individual settings and talk through the text with children. During reading aloud (Campbell, 2001), it is expected that teachers and children will stop to ask questions, make comments, or respond to each other and the text. Morrow (2005) suggests that, when possible, individual or small-group readings be recorded and analyzed to provide diagnostic information to inform instruction.

Finally, START interactive reading aloud makes use of simple children's picture books or chapter books, which are a wonderful way to convey complex ideas, topics, and processes. By reading, discussing, and carefully examining the pictures, diagrams, or other visual aids in these books, children who have little background knowledge can improve their reading comprehension (Ebbers, 2002; Giorgis & Johnson, 2002). It is best if you select texts that are of high interest and somewhat familiar to students but contain some challenging new ideas and concepts, as well as texts in which there are multiple opportunities to model the comprehension strategy you have selected to teach to the children.

### Materials

- Books correctly matched to students' interests and strategy learning needs

### Procedure

Graham and Kelly (1997) describe how to get a START interactive read-aloud session started in the classroom. Campbell (2001) suggests that teachers need to (a) prepare for effective interactive read alouds, (b) read the book aloud as a performance, and (c) ensure that children take part. Preparations for an interactive read aloud can be divided into four sequential steps: (1) select, (2) plan, (3) practice, and (4) deliver (Graham & Kelly, 1997). Books selected should match the intellectual, social, and emotional levels of the children to sustain interest and motivation and can be either fiction or nonfiction (Sharlach, 2008; Trelease, 2001).

In planning a START interactive read aloud, review eight strategies to be modeled and scaffolded: predicting/inferring, visualizing, making connections, questioning, determining the main idea, summarizing, checking predictions, and making judgments. Determine which if any resources or props may be needed; decide how much of the book will be read aloud in one sitting; decide how to introduce the book; determine points to be raised for discussion; decide how to end the session if the book is not read in its entirety; and decide how to involve the children in the reading. Campbell (2001) suggests that the book be first presented as a performance; this means that teachers should read the text aloud with enthusiasm and expression. Next, over a course of eight books or lessons explicitly model using "think alouds" the eight START reading comprehension strategies one at a time. With each subsequent book or lesson, scaffold all of the previously taught START strategies along with the new application to be introduced, as shown in Figure 9.15.

By the ninth book session or lesson using START, the teacher should be scaffolding the use of all eight comprehension strategies during every read-aloud session (Figure 9.16). This excellent approach to quickly teaching a "family of strategies" for comprehending texts has been shown to be more effective than dwelling for several weeks on teaching single comprehension strategies (Reutzel, Smith, & Fawson, 2005).

Following each reading, demonstrate for children a quality retelling that contains all of the important elements of the text in the correct order. When you feel that the students are ready to begin producing their own oral retellings, let them know before you read aloud that you will want them to give retelling a try (Morrow, 2005). We have also found that it is best that students be encouraged to try out their retellings with peers prior to sharing with the teacher or the group.

# STRATEGIES TO ACTIVATE AND BUILD STUDENTS' PRIOR OR BACKGROUND KNOWLEDGE

## The Picture Walk

### Purpose

A picture walk is commonly used by teachers to introduce new or unfamiliar **leveled books** to young readers using the pictures. Picture walks were first described by Clay (1991, 1993)

| FIGURE 9.15 | START Instructional Sequence |
|---|---|

| Session | Comprehension strategy | Session | Comprehension strategy |
|---|---|---|---|
| Session 1 | • Predicting/inferring (modeling only) | Session 7 (continued) | • Making connections (scaffolding) |
| Session 2 | • Predicting/inferring (scaffolding)<br>• Visualization (modeling only) | | • Questioning (scaffolding)<br>• Main idea (scaffolding)<br>• Summarizing (scaffolding)<br>• Checking predictions (modeling only) |
| Session 3 | • Predicting/inferring (scaffolding)<br>• Visualization (scaffolding)<br>• Making connections (modeling only) | | |
| | | Session 8 | • Predicting/inferring (scaffolding) |
| Session 4 | • Predicting/inferring (scaffolding)<br>• Visualization (scaffolding)<br>• Making connections (scaffolding)<br>• Questioning (modeling only) | | • Visualization (scaffolding)<br>• Making connections (scaffolding)<br>• Questioning (scaffolding)<br>• Main idea (scaffolding)<br>• Summarizing (scaffolding)<br>• Checking predictions (scaffolding)<br>• Making judgments (modeling only) |
| Session 5 | • Predicting/inferring (scaffolding)<br>• Visualization (scaffolding)<br>• Making connections (scaffolding)<br>• Questioning (scaffolding)<br>• Main idea (modeling only) | Sessions 9 to 40 | • Predicting/inferring (scaffolding)<br>• Visualization (scaffolding)<br>• Making connections (scaffolding)<br>• Questioning (scaffolding)<br>• Main idea (scaffolding)<br>• Summarizing (scaffolding)<br>• Checking predictions (scaffolding)<br>• Making judgments (scaffolding) |
| Session 6 | • Predicting/inferring (scaffolding)<br>• Visualization (scaffolding)<br>• Making connections (scaffolding)<br>• Questioning (scaffolding)<br>• Main idea (scaffolding)<br>• Summarizing (modeling only) | | |
| Session 7 | • Predicting/inferring (scaffolding)<br>• Visualization (scaffolding) | | |

*Source:* From "START Comprehending: Students and Teachers Actively Reading Text," by T. D. Sharlach, 2008, *The Reading Teacher, 61*(1), 26. Copyright © 2008 by the International Reading Association (www.reading.org). Reproduced with permission of the International Reading Association via Copyright Clearance Center.

as one element of an effective book introduction for young readers. More recently, the authors of *Guided Reading* (Fountas and Pinnell, 1996) have also described in some detail how to provide young students effective picture walks for reading leveled books, which are books graded into levels with either numerical (1–20) or alphabetical (A–Z) designations.

During a picture walk, the teacher uses the book illustrations to promote predictions and rich interactions about the book's likely subject matter. The objective of using a picture walk is to help children develop a framework for how the book is organized to improve their reading comprehension and fluency. Until recently, no research was available to suggest that picture walks were effective in promoting students' reading comprehension (Stahl, 2004, 2008). However, Stahl (2008) has demonstrated that picture walks are in fact useful in promoting young students' reading comprehension.

No two picture walks are alike. Each is a unique discussion of the pictures and pages in a new book. The introduction of a book using picture walks can only occur when teachers preread and carefully identify likely challenges that a new book presents for comprehension and reading fluency. These challenges may include particular words to be decoded, unfamiliar word meanings, different text structures or organization, or new text features such as insets,

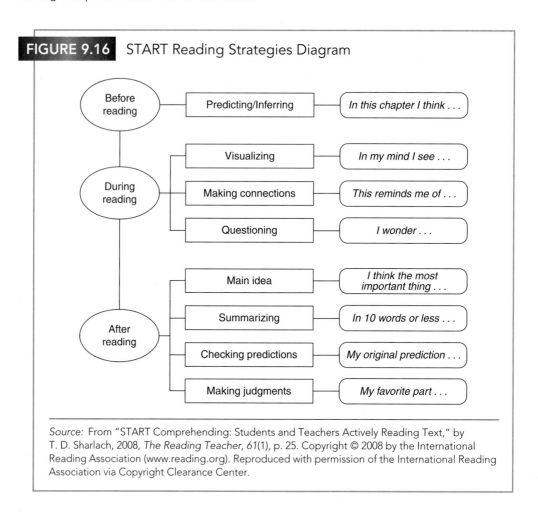

**FIGURE 9.16** START Reading Strategies Diagram

*Source:* From "START Comprehending: Students and Teachers Actively Reading Text," by T. D. Sharlach, 2008, *The Reading Teacher, 61*(1), p. 25. Copyright © 2008 by the International Reading Association (www.reading.org). Reproduced with permission of the International Reading Association via Copyright Clearance Center.

diagrams, and maps. Teachers and children talk their way through the pages of the book, giving students plenty of opportunities to use their word decoding and text comprehension strategies during their initial guided or independent reading. The most ideal setting for picture walks is in a small guided reading group where each child can have their own copy of a leveled book and the teacher can supervise the picture walk through the pages of the book.

### Materials

- A leveled book
- A listing of potentially challenging elements in the book
- Materials for teaching decoding, vocabulary, or text structure in the book

### Procedure

Fountas and Pinnell recommend that teachers provide a brief introduction for books before reading (1996, pp. 137–148). Teachers and students look at the book pages and pictures one-by-one in sequential order as they engage in an interactive discussion about the book. This interaction around the pictures focuses on story or text structure, students' prior knowledge, and making predictions based on the information gleaned from discussing the pictures in sequence. For an information book, topical headings and subheadings are addressed. To engage students in an active interaction around book pages and pictures, a teacher might say,

"What words would you use to describe what you see happening on this page?" or "What do you think the author is telling us on this page?" Teachers should also use picture walks to introduce two to three new vocabulary words before reading. After a picture walk, students are invited to read the text independently at their own rate in a small reading group where the teacher is available to offer support and guidance. When reading is completed, teachers might discuss whether predictions were accurate and allow students to make any necessary corrections to their predictions. Teachers could also guide students to fill in a graphic organizer or work with the small group to collectively summarize the content, organization, and purpose of the text (Fountas & Pinnell, 1996, p. 7).

## Online Reading Comprehension

### Purpose

Online and hard copy print reading comprehension are not the same (Coiro, 2007; Leu et al., 2005). Online reading comprehension is typically focused on reading informational text while adopting an efferent problem-solving stance, often beginning with a topic or question to be researched within a nearly limitless informational space where anyone may publish anything. This of course raises the question of the validity of claims and warrants made in this space and begs for critical reading skills. The new literacies group of the University of Connecticut, found online at www.newliteracies.uconn.edu/iesproject, has shown that online reading comprehension strategies are clustered around five reading processes: (1) reading online to generate a problem or question from one's social context, (2) reading to locate information online, (3) reading to critically evaluate information online, (4) reading to synthesize information online from multiple sources, and (5) reading to communicate and exchange information online with others. The comprehension strategies associated with locating and critically evaluating information are especially important for online reading comprehension.

According to these researchers, online reading comprehension strategies function similarly to phonic and phonemic awareness skills for offline reading comprehension. If one cannot decode words accurately and effortlessly offline, comprehension becomes very difficult. But online, if you cannot read to locate and critically evaluate information, it becomes very difficult to answer the question or solve the problem that initially motivated one's online reading. Online reading comprehension thus can be supported by focusing on helping students evaluate the accuracy and validity of information claims found on the Web (Mokhtari, Kymes, & Edwards, 2008).

### Materials

- Computer access preferably with a fast connection and an updated Web browser such as Explorer or Firefox loaded onto the hard drive

### Procedure

Students will need to access a widely used search engine such as Google to conduct their Internet searches. Most schools also have a server or site-based computer protection program to screen out sites that link to potentially undesirable or inappropriate content. Students may also need to be introduced to how to read and search electronic books with an e-book reader such as the Kindle from Amazon.

Teachers need to focus their online comprehension instruction on the previously mentioned cluster of five strategies: (1) reading online to generate a problem or question from one's social context, (2) reading to locate information online, (3) reading to critically evaluate information online, (4) reading to synthesize information online from multiple sources, and (5) reading to communicate and exchange information online with others. In general, teachers need to begin their lessons by explicitly teaching this cluster of five online reading comprehension strategies one at a time. A first lesson might focus on how to conduct an information search by using an appropriate search engine and reading the outcome of the search. Many students use a subject + dot.com search strategy rather than using a search engine (Mokhtari, Kymes, & Edwards, 2008). After conducting a search for a topic to read about, the teacher might model a question that comes out of browsing or reading on the Internet. This question is then used to recycle the search process by including more specific terms surrounded by quote marks to narrow the search engine's result to information that is highly related to the topic or question of interest.

Teaching students to evaluate the veracity of the information located requires several lessons on how to verify accuracy through multiple sourcing searches of authoritative information sources, including available online encyclopedias from reputable publishers, such as the *World Book Encyclopedia* (available online at www.worldbookonline.com, a subscription is required). Students can access but should conduct multiple source verification searches when consulting Wikipedia because it is open to contributions from anyone and lacks expert verification. Students also need to learn how to look for appropriate citations of sources and how to check sources for validity and authority.

Students need guidance, instruction, and modeling from teachers on how to read and integrate online information from multiple sources without plagiarizing. Many students do not understand that directly copying, cutting, and pasting someone else's ideas constitutes the essence of plagiarism. Helping students develop and write summaries of online information will show them how to integrate and organize ideas they have read in their own way and using their own language constructions.

Finally, students need to learn about the many available online social networks for transmitting information from and to others. Email, chat rooms, blogs, social networking websites such as Facebook and Ning.com, PowerPoint, desktop publishing, and Photoshop and similar programs are all potential candidates for lessons on using the Internet and computer technology to obtain and communicate information learned to a wide virtual social network. Teachers who disregard technology for teaching children reading comprehension are failing to prepare children for a future of increasingly complex technological advances (Coiro, 2007; Leu et al., 2005; Mokhtari, Kymes, & Edwards, 2008).

# COOPERATIVE OR COLLABORATIVE STRATEGIES TO INCREASE STUDENT INTERACTION AND MOTIVATION

## Comprehension Process Motions (CPMs): Engaging Movements to Promote Primary-Grade Comprehension

### Purpose

Block, Parris, and Whitely (2008) describe highly effective comprehension instruction in which students understand significantly more when their lessons include both linguistic and nonlinguistic input systems. In other words, when information is received through a variety of sensory pathways (e.g., auditory, visual, kinesthetic), readers' retention of that information increases significantly (Paivio, 1991; Sadoski, Paivio, & Goetz, 1991). Gardner (1999) also found that action and activity are important for primary students' learning. Kinesthetic movements can be added as a second learning input system as children learn to use comprehension strategies during listening or reading (Block, Parris, & Whiteley, 2008). Comprehension process motions (CPMs) kinesthetically represent the multiple unique mental strategies used by young children to comprehend text such as clarifying, making predictions, inferring, and so on. Recent research shows that the use of CPMs helps young students to learn and spontaneously apply comprehension strategies while listening to text read aloud by the teacher or reading text on their own.

### Materials

- A lesson plan for teaching each CPM
- An appropriate text or story
- A poster showing the CPMs to be taught, displayed during and after lessons (such as shown in Figure 9.17)

### Procedure

Teaching a CPM comprehension strategy lesson begins by selecting one of the four CPM strategies: main ideas, predictions, inferring, or clarifying. Next the teacher should write or be able to state a clear objective—for example, teaching a CPM and its corresponding com-

---

**FIGURE 9.17**    Classroom Poster for Comprehension Process Movements

**Find Main Ideas**
(See Figure 9.18 for instructions.)

**Making Predictions**
When you make a prediction based on the information the author has given you, your mind's eyes (put your forefinger and middle finger [the mind's eyes] on your right temple) must look beyond the obstacle, which is information you have not yet read (put your left hand horizontally in front of your eyes with the palm facing your eyes) to see what is likely to occur (move your right hand's fingertips beneath the left hand and in front of the left hand, facing toward the future, the ending position, as shown in the photo to the left). This is the process the mind follows each time it predicts.

**Inferring**
When you make an inference you think about the things the author didn't write down. When your mind does this, it starts with all it has already read (lift the right arm to side of waist, the starting position) and moves these thoughts forward to a larger idea that these facts are leading toward (move right hand to the left across body to the left side of the waist, as shown in the photo). The mind moves forward like this.

**Clarifying**
Use the clarifying signal anytime you have a question about something you are reading. First, place both hands together, then open them and splay the fingers. At first your mind is closed to meaning (put your hands together with thumbs touching in the center of your chest), then when your mind opens up to see a new meaning it completes a thinking process like this to end the process (move your hands to the splayed position) as shown in photo to the left.

---

prehension strategy to the point that students are able to self-initiate its use during reading. Begin the lesson by reading a section of the selected text or story aloud and model the CPM and thinking involved using a "think-aloud" process. For example, to teach the prediction CPM, you could use the description shown in Figure 9.17. Demonstrate the prediction CPM at certain points in your reading, such as at the ends of pages by making a new prediction. Tell students that as you read a new page your mind moves forward, collecting and adding all the clues together to make a prediction. As you finish each page, demonstrate the prediction CPM again.

On day 2, continue by reading another text aloud. Repeat the process described on day 1 at least five more times to invoke the effects of fast mapping (see Figure 9.18). As you repeat this process over time, you should notice that students begin to voluntarily initiate the CPM with you. Anytime a student signals a CPM (either the one being taught or from a previous lesson), the teacher should stop reading and ask that student to tell what he or she was thinking and why this point in the text was a good time to use the comprehension process signaled.

On day 3, tell students that you are going to read aloud. Anyone who has a prediction to make at the end of each page should signal this knowledge by performing the CPM and you will stop reading and ask that person to describe what he or she was thinking while forming the prediction. Repeat this process at least five more times, asking a different student each time. End day 2 or 3 lessons by asking a student to summarize what he or she has learned about using this thinking process to become a better reader.

During day 4, continue the day 3 lesson until students have mastered the CPM and when it should be used. During days 5 to 11, ask students to read silently and signal a CPM when they use it. Go to students individually and ask them to describe the comprehension they

---

**FIGURE 9.18**  Essentials for Creating a CPM Lesson

**Step 1:** Ensure that the first day of instruction for each CPM includes teacher modeling of that CPM with at least six think-aloud descriptions. During each step in the comprehension process, explain what you see in the text that clues you to use that CPM and comprehension process, and why using it leads to better understanding. The first six or more examples of CPM practice are composed of shared readings, think alouds, and whole-class discussion.

**Step 2:** Gradually begin to assign students to read silently alone or in pairs and to raise their hands when they don't understand. Ask students to signal comprehension processes when they are aware that they are using them. This question can be asked for Step 1 as well. Walk around to help individual students as they read silently.

**Step 3:** Students signal their independent use of the comprehension process as an assessment when they read a new text and implement the comprehension process at an appropriate point to reach a complete understanding.

**Step 4:** On the fourth to sixth days of this lesson plan, assess students' self-initiated use of each comprehension process by marking on a grid or grade sheet each time an individual correctly demonstrates a CPM.

*Note:* Include fast mapping by giving students at least six opportunities a day for six days to learn how to independently initiate the comprehension process without teacher assistance.

*Source:* Adapted from "CPMs: A Kinesthetic Comprehension Strategy," by C. C. Block, S. R. Parris, and C. S. Whitely, 2008, *The Reading Teacher, 61(6),* 460–470. Copyright © 2008 by the International Reading Association (www.reading.org). Reproduced with permission of the International Reading Association via Copyright Clearance Center.

gained by using the prediction CPM signaled and how they knew to use the CPM at that point in the text. Block, Parris, and Whiteley (2008) suggest that these discussions can also be used as individualized comprehension performance assessments to show that students can use the CPM automatically and independently. On day 12, reteach students who have not signaled their independent use of a comprehension process during the silent reading experience described above. This instruction can occur in small groups, peer-paired sessions, or one-to-one student meetings.

## Think-Pair-Share: Readers Collaborate to Comprehend

### Purpose

Teachers often want children to share their ideas and feelings with one another, typically by asking students to voluntarily share ideas one at a time with the group. For teachers who want to increase motivation and collaborative opportunities for their students to respond, share, think, and problem-solve with others around a text, Lyman and McTighe's (1988) think-pair-share strategy provides a successful "across the curriculum" method (Slavin, 1995), especially when reading information texts but also with narrative texts (Wood & Jones, 1994).

### Materials

- A poster that describes the expectations and processes of the think-pair-share strategy, as shown in Figure 9.19

**FIGURE 9.19**   Think-Pair-Share Poster

### Procedure

The process begins with the teacher instructing students to listen to a question or problem and then giving them time to think of a response. Next, students are told to share their responses with a neighboring peer. Finally, students are encouraged to share their responses with the whole group. A time limit is typically set for each segment of the think-pair-share strategy.

## COGNITIVE STRATEGIES TO INCREASE STUDENTS' READING COMPREHENSION

### Explicit Cognitive Comprehension Strategy Instruction

#### Purpose

The primary purpose of explicit cognitive comprehension strategy instruction is twofold: (a) to teach students to clearly understand what is meant by "comprehension monitoring" and (b) to teach students how to self-monitor, evaluate, self-regulate, and otherwise "fix up" their own comprehension problems over time. As quoted before (but worth repeating), "Some students struggle with reading because they lack information about what they are trying to do and how to do it. They look around at their fellow students who are learning to read [fluently and well] and say to themselves, 'How are they doing that?' In short they are mystified about how to do what other students seem to do with ease" (Duffy, 2004, p. 9).

It is typically very difficult for teachers to provide explicit cognitive comprehension strategy explanations for how to monitor one's own construction of meaning from a text. To do so, they must become aware of the processes they use to monitor their own reading comprehension processes. However, because teachers are already readers who comprehend what they read, they do not think deeply or systematically about the processes they use to do so (Duffy, 2004).

#### Materials

- Written lesson plan
- Selections from among several text sources that represent at least the genres of information and story, preferably complete books that can be read and discussed in a single sitting

#### Procedure

To teach an explicit cognitive comprehension strategy lesson, a framework lesson plan template is needed, such as the model developed by Reutzel based on Duffy (2004) called EMS—*E*xplanation, *M*odel, *S*caffold. Explanations include what is to be learned, where and when it is to be used, and why it is important. Modeling requires teachers to demonstrate, often through think alouds with a text, how an aspect of comprehension monitoring, like using fix-ups, is to be done. Finally, teachers gradually release through a series of guided practice experiences the reading of a text to individual application through a process we call *You* (teacher model)—*You and Me* (teacher and student share the monitoring task reading with the whole class or with partners)—*and Me* (student monitors reading comprehension independently). A template lesson on comprehension monitoring is found in Figure 9.20 to demonstrate each of the parts of the EMS explicit cognitive comprehension strategy lesson.

Remember, as unpopular as what we are about to say is with many teachers, to begin the process of becoming an explicit comprehension strategy teacher one must write down a

Go to the Assignments and Activities section of Topic 9: "Reading Comprehension" in the MyEducationLab for your course and complete the activity entitled "Modeling a Think Aloud." As you watch the video and answer the accompanying questions, note why modeling a think aloud is important. "How do you do that?" is a question many students have as they watch good readers. How will modeling a think aloud give students a cognitive or thinking toehold for learning how to think through a text as they read? Explain this to a friend, teacher, or colleague.

| FIGURE 9.20 | Explicit Comprehension Monitoring Strategy Lesson Plan Template |
|---|---|

**Objective:** *Children will monitor their own comprehension processes and use fix-up strategies to repair broken comprehension processes when necessary.*

**Supplies:**
- Excellent story or information text

**Explain:**

**What**
- Today boys and girls, we are going to be learning about how to monitor or check our understanding or comprehension as we read. The first step in learning to monitor our understanding or comprehension as we read is to learn to stop periodically and ask ourselves a few simple questions like: Is this making sense? Am I getting it? or Do I understand what this is about?

**Why**
- We need to monitor our comprehension or understanding when we read because what we read should make sense to us. If it does not make sense, there is no point in continuing to read. Monitoring our comprehension while reading helps us to be aware of whether or not we are understanding or making sense of what we read so we can just keep on reading if we understand or stop and do something to help us understand if the text is not making sense to us.

**When/Where**
- Whenever we read, we should monitor or think about whether or not we are understanding or comprehending what we are reading.

**Model:**
- I am going to read aloud the first two pages of our story, *Thunder Cake* (Polacco, 1990). After reading the first two pages, I am going to stop and monitor my comprehension. I will think out loud about the questions I should ask when I stop to monitor my comprehension: Is this making sense? Am I getting it? or Do I understand what this is about? I have written these monitoring steps (stop and question) on a poster to help me remember. I have also written the three comprehension monitoring questions on the poster to help me remember. After thinking about these questions for a minute, I will answer the question, yes or no. If *yes*, I will continue to read. If my answer is *no*, I will have

to stop for now because I do not yet know what I should do when it does not make sense to me. See, I have also put *yes* and *no* on our poster to help me know what to do when I answer *yes* or *no* to the three comprehension monitoring questions. OK, here I go:

*Thunder Cake*
On sultry summer days at my grandma's farm in Michigan, the air gets damp and heavy. Storm clouds drift low over the fields. Birds fly close to the ground. The clouds glow for an instant with a sharp, crackling light, and then a roaring, low, tumbling sound of thunder makes the windows shudder in their panes. The sound used to scare me when I was little.
*(Stop!)*

Am I getting it? Is it making sense? Do I understand what this is about? *Yes*, I think I do. This story is about going to Grandma's farm and hearing the sound of thunder. So, if it makes sense and I answer *yes*, I just keep on reading. After I read a few more pages, I should *stop* to monitor my comprehension again . . .

(Repeat this cycle with a few more pages and one or two more stopping points for modeling.)

**Scaffolding (Me, You and Me, You):**

**Whole Group (Me and You)**
- Now that I have shown you how I *stop* and monitor my comprehension, I want to share this task with you. So, let us read three more pages. At the end of the page, I want you to call out, *Stop!* After I stop, I want you to ask me the three monitoring questions on our poster: Is this making sense? Am I getting it? and Do I understand what this is about? I will answer *yes* or *no*. If I answer *yes*, tell me what to do. If I answer *no*, then tell me I will have to quit reading until we learn what to do tomorrow. OK, ready.

Grandma looked at the horizon, drew a deep breath and said, "This is Thunder Cake baking weather, all right. Looks like a storm coming to me."
*(Stop!)*

**Small Group/Partners/Teams (Me and You)**
Now that we have shared the process of *stopping* and monitoring our comprehension as a group when we read, I want you to share this monitoring

*(continued)*

---

**FIGURE 9.20** *Continued*

process with a partner. I am going to give you a number 1 or 2. Remember your number. (Count heads by one and two.) We are going to read three more pages in our story. At the end of the three pages, I want the partner with the number 1 to call out, *Stop!* Then, I want partner number 2 to ask partner number 1 the three monitoring questions on our poster: Is this making sense? Am I getting it? and Do I understand what this is about? Then, partner number 1 will answer the questions asked by partner number 2 with a *yes* or *no*. If partner number 1 answers *yes*, partner number 2 tells him or her to keep on reading. If partner number 1 answers *no*, then partner number 2 tells him or her to quit reading until we learn what to do tomorrow. OK, ready.

> Her eyes surveyed the black clouds a way off in the distance. Then she strode into the kitchen. Her worn hands pulled a thick book from the shelf above the woodstove. "Let's find that recipe, child," she crowed as she lovingly fingered the grease-stained pages to a creased spot. "Here it is . . . Thunder Cake!"
> *(Stop!)*

**Individual (You)**
- Finally, today we have learned that when we read we should *stop* every few pages and monitor our comprehension or understanding by asking ourselves three questions. During the day today during small-group reading or in paired reading, I would like for you to practice monitoring comprehension with a friend or by yourself as you read. *Stop* every few pages and ask yourself the three questions on our poster and then decide if you should keep on reading or quit reading and wait until tomorrow when we will learn about what to do when what you read is not making sense.

**Assess:**
- Pass out a bookmark that reminds students to stop every few pages while reading and ask the three questions. Put the three questions on the bookmark to remind students!

**Reflect:**
- What went well in the lesson?
- How would you change the lesson?

---

*Source:* From *Thunder Cake* by Patricia Polacco, 1990. Used by permission of Philomes Books. A Division of Penguin Young Readers Group. A member of Penguin Group (USA) Inc., 345 Hudson Street, New York, NY 10014. All rights reserved.

---

lesson plan. In fact, this is the *only* way for you to become an explicit comprehension strategy teacher! Doing so helps you in at least three different ways. Writing down a lesson plan helps you to (a) think through what to say and how to say it, (b) internalize the lesson template for explicit instruction, and (c) internalize the language necessary for explicit instruction.

## Comprehension Monitoring: Click or Clunk and Fix-Up Strategies

### Purpose

The act of monitoring one's unfolding comprehension of text and taking steps to "fix" defective comprehension is referred to as *metacognition* or, sometimes, as *metacomprehension*. The "click or clunk" strategy was designed to help students recognize when and where their comprehension breaks down during reading. Coupling the click or clunk strategy with instruction on comprehension "fix-up" strategies, students can come to know what to do to detect and correct comprehension breakdowns. If readers fail to detect comprehension breakdowns, they will take no action to correct misinterpretations of the text. If students fail to correct misinterpretations of a text, then their comprehension of texts will likely be both inaccurate and incomplete. Teaching students to actively monitor their own comprehension has been shown to significantly improve reading comprehension (Boulware-Gooden, Carreker, Thornhill, & Joshi, 2007).

### Materials

- One book or story that children have read collectively or individually
- A poster display of the repair strategies shown in Figure 9.21

### Procedure

To help students develop the ability to monitor their own comprehension processes, Carr (1985) suggests a strategy called "click or clunk." This strategy urges readers to reflect at the end of each sentence, paragraph, or section of reading by stopping and asking themselves if the meaning or message "clicks" for them or goes "clunk." If it clunks, what is wrong? What can be done to make sense of it? Once a comprehension breakdown has been detected, it is important to know which strategies to select in repairing broken comprehension, as well as when to use these strategies. In fact, students may know that they need to take steps to repair comprehension but they may not know which steps to take or when to take them. As a consequence, children should be introduced to several well-known options for repairing broken comprehension.

To demonstrate the use of a "fix-up" poster, model for students using a think-aloud process to help them develop a sense for when to select certain repair strategies for failing comprehension. Read part of a text aloud and, as you proceed, comment on your thinking. Reveal to students your thinking, the hypotheses you have formed for the text, and anything that strikes you as difficult or unclear. By doing so, you demonstrate for students the processes that successful readers use to comprehend a text. Next, remind them of the "click or clunk" strategy. Gradually release the responsibility for modeling metacognitive strategies to the children during follow-up lessons on metacognitive monitoring. Display the repair strategies in a prominent place in your classroom. Be sure to draw your students' attention to these strategies throughout the year.

## Elaborative Interrogation

### Purpose

Elaborative interrogation is a questioning intervention that uses student-generated "why" questions to promote active processing of factual reading materials (Wood, Pressley, & Winne,

---

**FIGURE 9.21**   Metacomprehension "Fix-Up" Strategies

**Broken Comprehension Fix-Up Strategies**
- **Read on.**
- **Reread** the sentence.
- **Go back** and reread the paragraph.
- **Seek** information from glossary or reference materials.
- **Ask** someone near you who may be able to help, such as one of your peers.

*Source:* Adapted from Babbs (1994).

1990). Students are encouraged in elaborative interrogation to activate their prior knowledge and experiences and use these to pose their own "why" questions whose answers use statements in the text to link facts together. Facts linked together into a network of relationships improve students' understanding and memory for text information. It is important that the "why" questions generated require students to activate their prior knowledge supporting the facts they need to learn; otherwise, such questions will not enhance comprehension and memory for text. Menke and Pressley (1994) assert, "Answering why questions is as good as constructing images to boost memory for facts, providing the questions are well focused" (p. 644). The elaborative interrogation strategy has been validated to improve readers' comprehension of factual material among students ranging from elementary schoolchildren to adults. It is recommended that teachers use elaborative interrogation when they train struggling students to access relevant prior knowledge in situations in which they typically do not do so spontaneously.

### Materials

- An information or narrative book at the appropriate grade or reading level of your students
- A written lesson plan as shown in Figure 9.22
- A graphic organizer containing the "why" questions generated from the statements found in the book

### Procedure

We describe the elaborative interrogation strategy using a trade book entitled *My Picture Book of the Planets* (Krulik, 1991), in a model lesson shown in Figure 9.22.

- Read each page carefully.
- Stop at the end of each page and pick a statement.
- Write a "why" question for the statement you pick in your reading notebooks.
- Think about an answer to the "why" question using your own knowledge and experiences.
- If you can, write an answer to your "why" question.
- Read the pages again looking for an answer. Read on to another page to look for the answer.
- If you can, write an answer to your "why" question.
- If you can't write an answer to your "why" question save it for our group discussion after reading. (Reutzel, Campbell, & Smith, 2002)

# *E*NGLISH LANGUAGE LEARNERS

## Comprehension Strategy Framework

### Purpose

The comprehension strategy framework (Dowhower, 1999) is designed to teach comprehension using small pieces of text within an instructional framework for teaching cognitive comprehension strategies. The rationale for the comprehension strategy framework (CSF) is found in five important principles of effective comprehension strategy instruction. First, the text is chunked into cycles of instruction either using the parts of a story—setting, problem,

FIGURE 9.22    Example Lesson Using Elaborative Interrogation Question Posing Strategy

**Purpose for Learning the Strategy:** This strategy will help you relate your own experiences and knowledge to the facts you read in books and other texts. By using this strategy, you will improve your understanding of and memory for the text.

**Objective:** Rephrase statements in text as if they were stated as *why* questions.

**Teacher Explanation and Modeling:** This strategy begins by reading a section of text. For example, in the book *My Picture Book of the Planets,* I begin by reading the title. I may ask myself, "Why would someone write a book about the planets?" My answer may include such ideas as the author wanted to teach others and me about planets as compared with stars, or I may wonder if other planets can support life like on Earth, and so on. Next, I read about the first planet, Mercury, in the book. "Mercury is the planet closest to the sun. It is very hot and dry" (Krulik, 1991). I may ask myself the *why* question, "Why is Mercury so hot?" I read on, "Because it is so close to the sun, Mercury takes the shortest amount of time of any of the planets to circle the sun." I ask myself, "Why is closeness to the sun related to a shorter time needed to circle the sun?"

**Guided Application:** Now let us try this strategy together. Mariann, come read this statement aloud for the class. After she has read this statement, I will make a *why* question from the statement. OK, read this statement. Mariann reads, "Mercury is gray and covered with craters." My question is, "Why would Mercury be gray and covered with craters?" Students are invited to use their knowledge and background to answer this *why* question.

Now let us reverse the roles. I will read aloud the next statement and you make this statement into a *why* question. Teacher reads aloud, "Some of Mercury's craters are bigger than the whole state of Texas!" Children raise their hands. Benji is called upon. He asks, "Why are the craters on Mercury so big?" A discussion ensues to potentially answer these *why* questions.

**Individual Application:** Now I want you to read the rest of this book. When you get to the end of each page, pick one statement to write a *why* question in your notebooks. Next, see if you can answer the question from your own knowledge or experiences. If not, try using the book to answer your question. If neither source can answer your question, save it for our discussion of the book when we are all finished reading. Now, go ahead and read. If you forget what I want you to do, look at this poster for step-by-step directions. The teacher displays the following poster at the front of the room on the board.

**Using the Elaborative Interrogation Strategy**

- Read each page carefully.
- Stop at the end of each page and pick a statement.
- Write a "why" question for the statement you pick in your reading notebooks.
- Think about an answer to the "why" question using your own knowledge and experiences.
- If you can, write an answer to your "why" question.
- Read the pages again looking for an answer. Read on to another page to look for the answer.
- If you can, write an answer to your "why" question.
- If you can't write an answer to your "why" question save it for our group discussion after reading.

*(continued)*

**FIGURE 9.22** *Continued*

**Assessment:** After the children read, hold a discussion in which children are asked to share their *why* questions and answers. Ask children to hand in reading notebooks with their *why* questions and answers. Examine these notebooks to determine the success of using this strategy. Unanswered *why* questions can be placed into a *question* web for further reading and research. The web may look something like the one shown here.

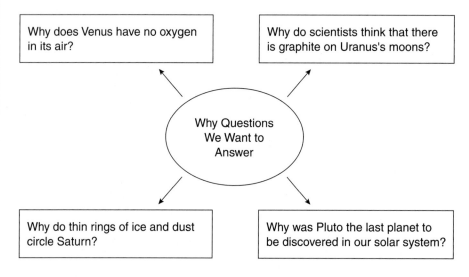

Why does Venus have no oxygen in its air?

Why do scientists think that there is graphite on Uranus's moons?

Why Questions We Want to Answer

Why do thin rings of ice and dust circle Saturn?

Why was Pluto the last planet to be discovered in our solar system?

Other trade books, reference books, and textbooks may be used to answer the questions in this *why* question web.

**Planned Review:** In about one week, plan to review the use of the elaborative interrogation strategy by using trade books or textbooks with other curricular subjects such as health or social studies or with mathematics word problems.

*Sources:* From *My Picture Book of the Planets,* by N. E. Krulik, 1991. Copyright © 1991 by Scholastic, Inc. Reprinted by permission. Elaborative Interrogation Strategy from Reutzel, D. R., Campbell, K., & Smith, J. A., "Hitting the Wall: Helping Struggling Readers Comprehend," in B. Gambrell, C. Collins-Block, and M. Pressley (Eds.), *Improving Comprehension Instruction: Rethinking Research, Theory, and Classroom Practice* (Jossey Bass Education Series). Copyright 2002 by John Wiley & Sons.

events, resolution—or using the subheadings within informational reading to break the text into smaller chunks. Second, a guiding statement is found to provide a purpose for students' reading. Third, students are encouraged to read silently. Silent reading has been shown to be better for facilitating comprehension processes because oral reading diverts attention to an accurate and lively performance of the text rather than to comprehension. Fourth, instruction is embedded in the discussion of a text. Finally, the discussion is focused around a theme or topic because themes or topics help students move beyond literal processes and toward constructing their own interpretations and understandings of texts.

Learning and orchestrating a repertoire of flexible comprehension strategies within a comprehension instructional framework are critically important for all students but especially for ELL students, who need to experience comprehension strategy instruction within a consistent, reliable, and cohesive framework to learn the unique demands of comprehending text in another language.

## Materials

- One well-formed story or storybook
- One copy of the Comprehension Strategy Framework (CSF) Overview (Figure 9.23)
- Lesson plan for using the CSF with the selected story

## Procedure

Select a well-formed story or information text for reading together as a class or small group. Chunk the text into segments to provide several cycles of practice using purpose setting, silent reading, and discussion. Remember to select a large enough text chunk for prereading to allow students to activate and relate the text to their prior knowledge, as well as to provide an example of using a selected comprehension strategy for instruction, such as constructing visual images. At the conclusion of the cycles of practice using text segments from the text, students are encouraged to engage in independent follow-up activities.

**FIGURE 9.23** Comprehension Strategy Framework Overview

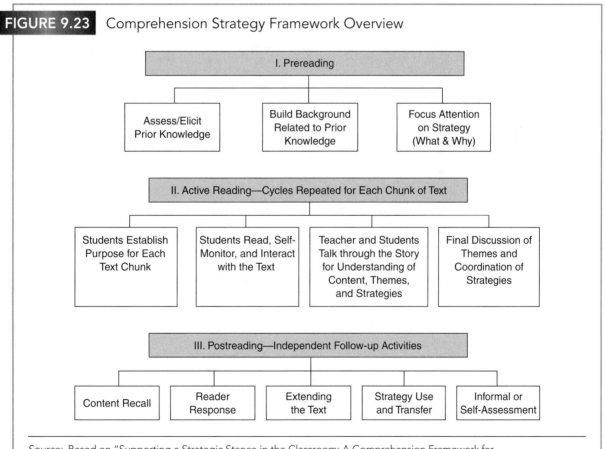

*Source:* Based on "Supporting a Strategic Stance in the Classroom: A Comprehension Framework for Helping Teachers Help Students to Be Strategic," by S. Dowhower, 1999, *The Reading Teacher, 52*(7), 672–683. Copyright © 1999 by the International Reading Association (www.reading.org). Reproduced with permission of the International Reading Association via Copyright Clearance Center.

# ADAPTING STRATEGY INSTRUCTION FOR THOSE WHO STRUGGLE

## Reciprocal Teaching

### Purpose

Palincsar and Brown (1985) designed and evaluated an approach for improving the reading comprehension and comprehension monitoring of students with special needs who scored 2 years below grade level on standardized tests of reading comprehension. Their results suggested a teaching strategy called *reciprocal teaching* that is useful for helping students who have difficulties with comprehension and comprehension monitoring, as well as those who are learning English (Casanave, 1988; Johnson-Glenberg, 2000; Rosenshine & Meister, 1994). Although reciprocal teaching was originally intended for use with expository text, we can see no reason why this intervention strategy cannot be used with narrative texts by focusing discussion and reading on the major elements of stories.

### Materials

- A trade book, basal reader, or textbook selection
- A poster displaying the four comprehension strategies and what they mean: predicting, questioning, summarizing, and clarifying

### Procedure

Essentially, this multiple-strategy lesson requires that teachers and students exchange roles, which is intended to increase student involvement in the lesson. The reciprocal teaching lesson comprises four phases or steps (Meyers, 2005; Oczkus, 2004):

- *Prediction.* Students predict from the title and pictures the possible content of the text. The teacher records the predictions.
- *Question generation.* Students generate purpose questions after reading a predetermined segment of the text, such as a paragraph, page, or section.
- *Summarizing.* Students write a brief summary (see Chapter 11) for the text by starting with "This paragraph was about . . ." Summarizing helps students capture the gist of the text.
- *Clarifying.* Students and teacher discuss various reasons a text may be hard or confusing, such as difficult vocabulary, poor text organization, unfamiliar content, or lack of cohesion. Students are then instructed in a variety of comprehension fix-up or repair strategies.

When teachers have modeled this process with several segments of text, the teacher assigns one of the students (preferably a good student) to assume the role of teacher for the next segment of text. The teacher may also, while acting in the student role, provide appropriate prompts and feedback when necessary. When the next segment of text is completed, the "teacher" assigns another student to assume that role.

Teachers who use reciprocal teaching to help students with comprehension difficulties should follow four simple guidelines suggested by Palincsar and Brown (1985). First, assess student difficulties and provide reading materials appropriate to students' decoding abilities. Second, use reciprocal teaching for at least 30 minutes a day for 15 to 20 consecutive days. Third, model frequently and provide corrective feedback. Finally, monitor student progress regularly and individually to determine whether the instruction is having the intended effect. Palincsar and Brown reported positive results for this intervention procedure by demonstrating dramatic changes in students' ineffective reading behaviors. Other research has demonstrated the effectiveness of reciprocal teaching with a variety of students (Casanave, 1988; Johnson-Glenberg, 2000; Kelly, Moore, & Tuck, 1994; King & Parent-Johnson, 1999; Pressley & Wharton-McDonald, 1997; Rosenshine & Meister, 1994). To add fun to reciprocal teaching (RT) try assigning characters to each RT strategy such as *Clara the Clarifier, Sammy the Summarizer, Paula the Predictor,* or *Quincy the Questioner* (Meyers, 2005; Ockzus, 2004). Ockzus (2004) demonstrates how one can dress up using different costumes to assume the roles of each of the four RT strategy characters in a DVD that accompanies the book cited here. More recently, Ockzus (2004) has made RT strategy character puppets available for teachers who use RT to teach students in engaging ways.

## SELECTED REFERENCES

Anderson, R. C., Hiebert, E. H., Scott, J. A., & Wilkinson, I. A. G. (1985). *Becoming a nation of readers: The report of the Commission on Reading.* Washington, DC: The National Institute of Education.

Asher, S. R. (1980). Topic interest and children's reading comprehension. In R. J. Spiro, B. C. Bruce, & W. F. Brewer (Eds.), *Theoretical issues in reading comprehension* (pp. 525–534). Mahwah, NJ: Lawrence Erlbaum.

Babbs, P. (1994). Monitoring cards help improve comprehension. *The Reading Teacher, 38*(3), 200–204.

Bandura, A. (1986*). Social foundations of thought and action: A social cognitive theory.* Englewood Cliffs, NJ: Prentice Hall.

Block, C. C., & Lacina, J. (2009). Comprehension instruction in kindergarten through grade three. In S. E. Israel & G. G. Duffy (Eds.), *Handbook of research on reading comprehension (*pp. 494–509). New York: Routledge.

Block, C. C., & Parris, S. R. (2008). *Comprehension instruction: Research-based best practices* (2nd ed.). New York: Guilford Press.

Block, C. C., Parris, S. R., & Whiteley, C. S. (2008). CPMs: A kinesthetic comprehension strategy. *The Reading Teacher, 61*(6), 460–470.

Boulware-Gooden, R., Carreker, S., Thornhill, A., & Joshi, R. M. (2007). Instruction of metacognitive strategies enhances reading comprehension and vocabulary achievement of third-grade students. *The Reading Teacher 61*(1), 70–77.

Campbell, R. (2001). *Read-alouds with young children.* Newark, DE: International Reading Association.

Carr, E. (1985). The vocabulary overview guide: A metacognitive strategy to improve vocabulary comprehension and retention. *Journal of Reading, 28*(8), 684–689.

Carr, S., & Thompson, B. (1996). The effects of prior knowledge and schema activation strategies on the inferential reading comprehension of children with and without learning disabilities. *Learning Disabilities Quarterly, 19*(2), 48–61.

Casanave, C. P. (1988). Comprehension monitoring in ESL reading: A neglected essential. *TESOL Quarterly, 22*(2), 283–302.

Clay, M. M. (1991). Introducing a new storybook to young readers. *The Reading Teacher, 45,* 264–273.

Clay, M. M. (1993). *Reading recovery: A guidebook for teachers in training.* Portsmouth, NH: Heinemann.

Coiro, J. (2007). *Exploring changes to reading comprehension on the Internet: Paradoxes and possibilities for diverse adolescent readers.* Unpublished doctoral dissertation, University of Connecticut, Storrs.

Collins, A. M., & Quillian, M. R. (1969). Retrieval time from semantic memory. *Journal of Verbal Learning and Verbal Behavior, 8,* 240–247.

Collins-Block, C., & Lacina, J. (2009). Comprehension instruction in kindergarten through grade three. In S. E. Israel & G. G. Duffy (Eds.), *Handbook of Research on Reading Comprehension* (pp. 494–509). New York: Routledge.

Collins-Block, C., & Parris, S. R. (Eds.). (2008). *Comprehension instruction: Research-based best practices: Solving problems in the teaching of literacy* (2nd ed.). New York: Guilford Press.

Corno, L., & Randi, J. (1997). Motivation, volition, and collaborative innovation in classroom literacy. In J. T. Guthrie & A. Wigfield (Eds.), *Reading engagement: Motivating readers through integrated instruction* (pp. 51–67). Newark, DE: International Reading Association.

Dewitz, P., Jones, J., & Leahy, S. (2009). Comprehension strategy instruction in core reading programs. *Reading Research Quarterly, 44*(2), 102–126.

Dowhower, S. L. (1999). Supporting a strategic stance in the classroom: A comprehension framework for helping teachers help students to be strategic. *The Reading Teacher, 52*(7), 672–688.

Duffy, G. G. (2004). *Explaining reading: A resource for teaching concepts, skills, and strategies.* New York: Guilford Press.

Ebbers, M. (2002). Science text sets: Using various genres to promote literacy and inquiry. *Language Arts, 80*(1), 40–50.

Ellis, S. S., & Whalen, S. F. (1990). *Cooperative learning: Getting started.* New York: Scholastic.

Fountas, I. C., & Pinnell, G. S. (1996). *Guided reading: Good first teaching for all children.* Portsmouth, NH: Heinemann.

Gardiner, J. R. (1980). *Stone fox.* New York: Scholastic.

Gardner, H. (1999). *The disciplined mind: What all students should understand.* New York: Simon & Schuster.

Giorgis, C., & Johnson, N. J. (2002). Text sets. *The Reading Teacher, 56*(2), 200–208.

Graham, J., & Kelly, A. (1997). *Reading under control: Teaching reading in the primary school.* London: David Fulton.

Henk, W. A., & Melnick, S. A. (1995). The Reader Self-Perception Scale (RSPS): A new tool for measuring how children feel about themselves as readers. *The Reading Teacher, 48*(6), 470–482.

Johnson, D. W., & Johnson, R. T. (1999). *Learning together and alone: Cooperative, competitive, and individualistic learning* (5th ed.). Boston: Allyn & Bacon.

Johnson-Glenberg, M. C. (2000). Training reading comprehension in adequate decoders/poor comprehenders: Verbal versus visual strategies. *Journal of Educational Psychology, 92*(4), 772–782.

Kelly, M., Moore, D. W., & Tuck, B. F. (1994). Reciprocal teaching in a regular primary school classroom. *Journal of Educational Research, 88*(1), 53–61.

King, C. M., & Parent-Johnson, L. M. (1999). Constructing meaning via reciprocal teaching. *Reading Research and Instruction, 38*(3), 169–186.

Kintsch, W. (1998). *Comprehension: A paradigm for cognition.* Cambridge, UK: Cambridge University Press.

Krulik, N. E. (1991). *My picture book of the planets.* New York: Scholastic.

Langer, J. A. (1982). Facilitating text processing: The elaboration of prior knowledge. In J. A. Langer & M. Smith-Burke (Eds.), *Reader meets author: Bridging the gap* (pp. 149–162). Newark, DE: International Reading Association.

Leu, D. J., Jr., Castek, J., Hartman, D. K., Coiro, J., Henry, L. A., Kulikowich, J. M., et al. (2005). *Evaluating the development of scientific knowledge and new forms of reading comprehension during online learning.* Final report submitted to the North Central Regional Educational Laboratory/Learning Point Associates. Retrieved May 15, 2006, from www.newliteracies.uconn.edu/ncrel_files/FinalNCRELReport.pdf.

Lindsay, P. H., & Norman, D. A. (1977). *Human information processing: An introduction to psychology.* New York: Academic Press.

Lyman, F. T., & McTighe, J. (1988). Cueing thinking in the classroom: The promise of theory-embedded tools. *Educational Leadership, 45,* 18–24.

Malloy, J. A., & Gambrell, L. B. (2008). New insights on motivation in the literacy classroom. In C. C. Block & S. R. Parris (Eds.), *Comprehension instruction: Research-based best practices* (2nd ed., pp. 226–240). New York: Guilford Press.

Martens, P. (1996). *I already know how to read: A child's view of literacy.* Portsmouth, NH: Heinemann Educational Books.

Martin, L., & Reutzel, D. R. (1999). Sharing books: Examining how and why mothers deviate from the print. *Reading Research and Instruction, 39*(1), 39–70.

Menke, D. J., & Pressley, M. (1994). Elaborative interrogation: Using "why" questions to enhance learning from text. *Journal of Reading, 37*(8), 642–645.

Meyers, P. A. (2005). The Princess Storyteller, Clara Clarifier, Quincy Questioner, and the Wizard: Reciprocal teaching adapted for kindergarten students. *The Reading Teacher, 59*(4), 314–324.

Miller, S. D., & Fairchild, B. S. (2009). Motivation and reading comprehension. In S. E. Israel & G. G. Duffy (Eds.), *Handbook of research comprehension* (pp. 307–322). New York: Routledge.

Mokhtari, K., Kymes, A., & Edwards, P. (2008). Assessing the new literacies of online reading comprehension: An informative interview with W. Ian O'Byrne, Lisa Zawilinski, J. Greg McVerry, and Donald J. Leu at the University of Connecticut. *The Reading Teacher, 62*(4), 354–357.

Morrow, L. M. (2005). *Literacy development in the early years: Helping children read and write* (5th ed.). New York: Allyn & Bacon.

National Institute of Child Health and Human Development. (2000). *Report of the National Reading Panel: Teaching children to read, an evidence-based assessment of the scientific research literature on reading and its implications for reading instruction.* Washington, DC: U.S. Government Printing Office.

National Reading Panel (NRP). (2000). *Report of the National Reading Panel: Teaching children to read.* Washington, DC: National Institute of Child Health and Human Development.

Neuman, S. B. (2001). The role of knowledge in early literacy. *Reading Research Quarterly, 36*(4), 468–475.

Oczkus, L. D. (2004). *Reciprocal teaching at work: Strategies for improving reading comprehension.* Newark, DE: International Reading Association.

Paivio, A. (1991). Dual coding theory: Retrospect and current status. *Canadian Journal of Psychology, 45,* 255–287.

Palincsar, A., & Brown, A. (1985). Reciprocal teaching: A means to a meaningful end. In J. Osborn, P. T. Wilson, & R. C. Anderson (Eds.), *Reading education: Foundations for a literate America* (pp. 299–310). Lexington, MA: D. C. Heath and Company.

Pardo, L. S. (2004). What every teacher needs to know about comprehension. *The Reading Teacher, 58*(3), 272–280.

Paris, S. G., & Jacobs, J. E. (1984). The benefits of informed instruction for children's reading awareness and comprehension skills. *Child Development, 55,* 2083–2093.

Paris, S. G., Wasik, B., & Turner, J. C. (1991). The development of strategic readers. In R. Barr, M. L. Kamil, P. Mosenthal, & P. D. Pearson (Eds.), *Handbook of reading research, Vol. II* (pp. 641–668). New York: Longman.

Paris, S. G., & Winograd, P. (2001). *The role of self-regulated learning in contextual teaching: Principles and practices for teacher preparation.* Ann Arbor, MI: Center for the Improvement of Early Reading Achievement.

Pearson, P. D., & Duke, N. K. (2002). Comprehension instruction in the primary grades. In C. Collins-Block & M. Pressley (Eds.), *Comprehension instruction: Research-based best practices* (pp. 247–258). New York: Guilford Press.

Pearson, P. D., Hansen, J., & Gordon, C. (1979). The effect of background knowledge on children's comprehension of implicit and explicit information. *Journal of Reading Behavior, 11*(3), 201–209.

Pereira-Laird, J. A., & Deane, F. P. (1997). Development and validation of a self-report measure of reading strategy use. *Reading Psychology, 18*(3), 185–235.

Polacco, P. (1990). *Thunder cake.* New York: Philomel Books.

Potter, B. (1987). *The tale of Peter Rabbit.* New York: F. Warne Publishers.

Pressley, M. (2000). What should comprehension instruction be the instruction of? In M. L. Kamil, P. B. Mosenthal, P. D. Pearson, & R. Barr (Eds.), *Handbook of reading research* (Vol. 3, pp. 545–561). Mahwah, NJ: Lawrence Erlbaum.

Pressley, M. (2006, April 29). *What the future of reading research could be.* Paper presented at the International Reading Association Reading Research Conference, Chicago, IL.

Pressley, M., & Wharton-McDonald, R. (1997). Skilled comprehension and its development through instruction. *School Psychology Review, 26*(3), 448–466.

RAND Reading Study Group. (2001). *Reading for understanding: Towards an R & D program in reading comprehension.* Washington, DC: Author/OERI/Department of Education.

RAND Reading Study Group. (2002). *Reading for understanding: Toward an R&D program in reading comprehension.* Santa Monica, CA: Science and Technology Policy Institute, RAND Education.

Reutzel, D. R., Campbell, K., & Smith, J. A. (2002). Hitting the wall: Helping struggling readers comprehend. In C. Collins-Block, B. Gambrell, & M. Pressley (Eds.), *Improving comprehension instruction: Rethinking research, theory, and classroom practice.* New York: John Wiley & Sons.

Reutzel, D. R., Jones, C. D., Fawson, P. C., & Smith, J. A. (2008). Scaffolded silent reading (ScSR): An alternative to guided oral repeated reading that works! *The Reading Teacher, 62*(3), 194–207.

Reutzel, D. R., Smith, J. A., & Fawson, P. C. (2005). An evaluation of two approaches for teaching reading comprehension strategies in the primary years using science information texts. *Early Childhood Research Quarterly, 20*(3), 276–305.

Rosenshine, B., & Meister, C. (1994). Reciprocal teaching: A review of the research. *Review of Educational Research, 64*(4), 479–530.

Rumelhart, D. E. (1981). Schemata: The building blocks of cognition. In J. T. Guthrie (Ed.), *Comprehension and teaching: Research reviews* (pp. 3–26). Newark, DE: International Reading Association.

Sadoski, M., Paivio, A., & Goetz, E. T. (1991). A critique of schema theory in reading and a dual coding alternative. *Reading Research Quarterly, 26,* 463–484.

Schikendanz, J. A. (1990). *Adam's righting revolutions.* Portsmouth, NH: Heinemann Educational Books.

Schmitt, M. C. (1988). The effect of an elaborated directed reading activity on the metacomprehension skills of third graders. In J. E. Readence & R. S. Baldwin (Eds.), *Dialogues in literacy research* (pp. 167–189). Chicago: National Reading Conference.

Schmitt, M. C. (1990). A questionnaire to measure children's awareness of strategic reading processes. *The Reading Teacher, 43,* 454–461.

Schmitt, M. C. (2005). Measuring students' awareness and control of strategic processes. In S. E. Israel, C. C. Block, K. L. Bauserman, & K. Kinnucan-Welsch (Eds.), *Metacognition in literacy learning: Theory, assessment, instruction, and professional development* (pp. 101–119). Mahwah, NJ: Lawrence Erlbaum.

Schunk, D. H. (1996). Goal and self-evaluative influences during children's cognitive skill learning. *American Educational Research Journal, 33,* 359–382.

Schunk, D. H., & Zimmerman, B. J. (1997). Developing self-efficacious readers and writers: The role of social and self-regulatory processes. In J. T. Guthrie & A. Wigfield (Eds.), *Reading engagement: Motivating readers through integrated instruction* (pp. 34–50). Newark, DE: International Reading Association.

Scieszka, J. (1991). *The frog prince continued.* New York: Viking Penguin.

Sharlach, T. D. (2008). START comprehending: Students and teachers actively reading text. *The Reading Teacher, 62*(1), 20–31.

Slavin, R. E. (1995). *Cooperative learning: Theory, research, and practice.* Boston: Allyn & Bacon.

Stahl, K. A. D. (2004). Proof, practice, and promise: Comprehension strategy instruction in the primary grades. *The Reading Teacher, 57*(7), 598–609.

Stahl, K. A. D. (2008). The effects of three instructional methods on the reading comprehension and content acquisition of novice readers. *Journal of Literacy Research, 40*(3), 359–393.

Stahl, K. A. D. (2009). Assessing the comprehension of young children. In S. E. Israel & G. G. Duffy (Eds.), *Handbook of research on reading comprehension* (pp. 428–448). New York: Routledge.

Sweeney, A. (2004). *Teaching the essentials of reading with picture books: 15 lessons that use favorite picture books to teach phonemic awareness, phonics, fluency, comprehension, and vocabulary.* New York: Scholastic.

Sweet, A. P. (1997). Teacher perceptions of student motivation and their relation to literacy learning. In J. T. Guthrie & A. Wigfield (Eds.), *Reading engagement: Motivating readers through integrated instruction* (pp. 86–101). Newark, DE: International Reading Association.

Sweet, A. P., & Snow, C. E. (2003). *Rethinking reading comprehension.* New York: Guilford Press.

Taylor, B. M., Pearson, P. D., Clark, K. F., & Walpole, S. (1999). *Beating the odds in teaching all children to read* (CIERA Report No. 2-006). Ann Arbor, MI: Center for the Improvement of Early Reading Achievement.

Trelease, J. (2001). *The read aloud handbook* (5th ed.). New York: Penguin.

Turner, J., & Paris, S. (1995). How literacy tasks influence children's motivation for literacy. *The Reading Teacher, 48*(8), 662–673.

van Dijk, T. A. (1999). Context models in discourse processing. In H. van Oostendorp & S. R. Goldman (Eds.), *Construction of mental representations during reading* (pp. 123–148). Mahwah, NJ: Lawrence Erlbaum.

Wigfield, A. (1997). Children's motivations for reading and reading engagement. In J. T. Guthrie & A. Wigfield (Eds.), *Reading engagement: Motivating readers through integrated instruction* (pp. 14–33). Newark, DE: International Reading Association.

Wigfield, A., Guthrie, J. T., & McGough, K. (1996). *A questionnaire measure of children's motivations for reading* (Instructional Resource No. 22). Athens, GA: National Reading Research Center.

Wood, E., Pressley, M., & Winne, P. H. (1990). Elaborative interrogation effects on children's learning of factual content. *Journal of Educational Psychology, 82,* 741–748.

Wood, K. D., & Jones, J. P. (1994). Integrating collaborative learning across the curriculum. *Middle School Journal, 20,* 19–23.

Zwann, R. A. (1999). Embodied cognition, perceptual symbols, and situation models. *Discourse Processes, 28*(1), 81–88.

**The Power of Classroom Practice**
www.myeducationlab.com

Now go to Topic 9: "Reading Comprehension" in the MyEducationLab (www.myeducationlab .com) for your course, where you can:

- Find learning outcomes for "Reading Comprehension," along with the national standards that connect to these outcomes.
- Complete the tasks in the Assignments and Activities to help you more deeply understand the chapter content.
- Apply and practice your understanding of the core teaching skills identified in the chapter with the Building Teaching Skills and Dispositions learning units.

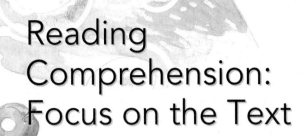

# 10

# Reading Comprehension: Focus on the Text

$M$illie, a student in Ms. Franklin's fourth-grade class, is one of those kids who simply blasted their way through the first several years of school, reading well above grade level. When it came to reading in story and chapter books, poetry, and just about everything else encountered in the core basal reader, Millie was by all accounts through the second grade a very good student in reading.

When Millie reached the last half of third grade and the reading selections and general curriculum took a decided swing toward informational texts and content-area learning, her reading performance began to falter. Especially in science, Millie seemed to be having some serious difficulties with comprehension and vocabulary, and, worse yet, her motivation and excitement about school in general and reading in particular were beginning to fade. At a recent parent–teacher conference, Millie's father expressed some concerns about her not wanting to come to school on Monday mornings—what he called "Mondaynucleosis." It was a humorous but nonetheless disturbing label. Worse yet, Millie's father noted that Millie's voracious reading habits were disappearing and in their place a hardened resistance to reading was developing.

Ms. Franklin had seen this development in children before and knew just what to do. She knew that Millie, like so many other intermediate-grade children, struggled with transferring her previously acquired and well-practiced reading skills in one type of text, like narrative or poetry, into another type of text, like informational or expository text. Knowing that comprehension skills development is genre or text-type specific was critical for Ms. Franklin. She was not panicked at all and set out to peruse the Summary Matrix of Text-Based Comprehension Assessments in this chapter searching for just the right text-based comprehension teaching strategies for Millie and the other children in her class experiencing similar needs. "A piece of cake!" mused Ms. Franklin to herself as she planned lessons that would help her young readers tackle the challenges of differing text types. "They're going to positively love learning how to use these text-based comprehension strategies to read different text structures!" she whispered to herself.

# BACKGROUND BRIEFING FOR TEACHERS

Go to the Assignments and Activities section of Topic 11: "Reading Difficulties and Intervention Strategies" in the MyEducationLab for your course and complete the activity entitled "Intervention Strategies for Nonfiction Reading." As you watch the video and answer the accompanying questions, note how the teacher guides the students in this video to note the specific types of graphic aids in nonfiction texts.

Does this scenario sound familiar? Remember from Chapter 9 the RAND Reading Study Group (2002) and Pardo (2004) asserted that the act of comprehending entails four essential elements: (a) the reader, (b) the text, (c) the activity, and (d) the sociocultural context. The first three essential elements of reading comprehension occur within the fourth essential element of reading comprehension—the sociocultural context of the school classroom, the home, and other social and cultural situations. In this chapter, we discuss the second essential element of reading comprehension—the text or the object to be comprehended. Within the discussion of the **text** as part of the comprehension process, we simultaneously discuss cognitive comprehension strategies and sociocultural contexts that are supported by scientific research evidence for improving children's reading comprehension of texts.

Many elementary, intermediate, and secondary teachers find out sooner or later that their students struggle to read texts that convey information more than those that tell a story (Read, Reutzel, & Fawson, 2008). Some teachers conclude either that some texts are too hard for their students to read or that their students are not putting forth enough effort to read differing text types (Farnan & Dahl, 2003; Graesser, Golding, & Long, 1991; Zabrucky & Ratner, 1992). But the conclusions of many classroom teachers regarding children's text-based reading difficulties are not always the case. For many children in primary-grade elementary classrooms, access to and experience with text that conveys information have been shown to be quite limited (Duke, 2000; Moss & Newton, 2002). Without exposure to and experience with expository texts, elementary children often bring their ideas about stories or narratives to help them process expository texts.

Content classrooms (such as social studies, science, mathematics, and so on) are heavily populated with students for whom reading expository texts is a particular challenge (Romine, McKenna, & Robinson, 1996). These students, who may have been good readers in early grades highly focused on narrative, story, or poetry text, must sometimes think to themselves, "What has happened? Why am I such a lousy reader now when I used to be so good?!"

The answer is relatively simple; differing texts types use very different organizational structures and techniques to convey ideas. One of the most important tasks teachers have is to help students learn to strategically organize and construct new knowledge from differing text types (Alexander & Jetton, 2000; Farnan, 1996; Sanders & Schilperoord, 2006; Simpson, 1996). Even though a number of effective strategies have been identified for use in elementary- and intermediate-grade classrooms to help students succeed (see, for example, Alvermann & Moore, 1991; Guthrie et al., 1996; Hall, Sabey, & McClellan, 2005; Read, Reutzel, & Fawson 2008; Swafford & Bryan, 2000), startlingly few teachers actually use them (Irvin & Connors, 1989; Romine et al., 1996; Stahl, 2004).

When readers approach differing text types—such as narrative or story text, poetry, or informational texts—without the proper frame of reference, they typically experience exertion, frustration, and eventual comprehension failure. Successful comprehension of narrative and expository texts requires that teachers and children understand through substantial experience with both types of texts how these text types differ in the way they are structured or organized.

For nearly three decades, it has been well documented that children are not receiving sustained, explicit, or coherent reading comprehension instruction (Durkin, 1978–1979; Israel & Duffy, 2009; National Institute of Child Health and Human Development, 2000; Pressley,

2002; Sweet & Snow, 2003; Taylor, Pearson, Clark, & Walpole, 1999). Although there is little research that specifically examines the quality and extent of reading comprehension text structure instruction in classrooms, one can safely assume that such instruction would most likely be less commonplace than general classroom reading comprehension instruction. This is truly unfortunate.

Research has consistently shown that increasing children's awareness of differing text structures has positive effects on their comprehension of a variety of text types and structures (Armbruster, Anderson, & Ostertag, 1987; Dickson, Simmons, & Kameenui, 1998b; Donovan & Smolkin, 2002; Williams, Stafford, Lauer, Hall, & Pollini, 2009). Research on text structure can be examined in any number of ways. In what follows, we examine text structure research from two separate perspectives: (a) What are the explicit, physical features of text that affect readers' awareness of text structure? and (b) How does awareness of implicit text structure affect readers' text comprehension?

# *E*XPLICIT TEXT FEATURES: PHYSICAL AND OBSERVABLE TEXT CHARACTERISTICS

How do the physical, observable, explicit, or surface features found in narrative and expository texts help readers understand the importance of ideas as well as the relationship among ideas within a text? Research has consistently shown that placing macro propositions, gist statements, or main ideas in the first sentence of a paragraph helps readers to better identify and remember important text ideas and information (Seidenberg, 1989). A separate body of research shows that explicit main idea statements are better understood by most readers than are poorly stated, hinted, or implicit statements of the main ideas (Dickson et al., 1998b).

Well-crafted topic sentences and appropriately placed signal words positively affect readers' awareness of the structure of a variety of text types. The use of headings and subheadings (including tables of contents), typographic cues, and line and word spacing helps young, adolescent, and adult readers understand main ideas and relate these to other ideas contained within a text (Dickson et al., 1998b). Headings and subheadings are often signaled through the selective use of typographic cues such as font size and font styles, as well as line, letter, and word spacing.

The physical use of spacing cues within lines of text has been shown also to help younger and older readers recognize important information in text leading to improved comprehension of main ideas (Casteel, 1990). When important ideas are signaled by a process known as *chunking,* in which main ideas are separated by four spaces rather than a single space between phrases or clauses in text, struggling readers are significantly helped to recognize and remember main ideas.

The use of insets or adjunct aids in text such as photographs, diagrams, charts, graphs, graphic organizers, captions, questions, or marginal gloss has been shown to help some children, distract or confuse others, or be ignored altogether (Dickson et al., 1998a). The use of insets or adjunct aids tends to be far more pronounced in expository texts than in narratives. These additional layers of information found in expository texts tend to be viewed by many teachers as adding to the complexity of teaching children to comprehend expository texts (Duke, 2000).

In summary, well-presented texts provide several types of layered explicit features that reveal text structure and the interrelationship of ideas within a text. Ideas organized within a text using a predictable pattern of main ideas followed by supporting details also help facilitate identification of text structure and subsequent comprehension of a variety of text types. The use of signal words, headings, typographic features, and spacing, as well as insets and adjunct visual aids, provides additional ways of helping readers discern the structure and flow of text. When readers can determine text organization and structure, they are more apt to comprehend, remember, and use what they read.

# IMPLICIT TEXT FEATURES: TACIT ORGANIZATIONAL PATTERNS AND TEXT STRUCTURE

Go to the Assignments and Activities section of Topic 9: "Reading Comprehension" in the MyEducationLab for your course and complete the activity entitled "Strategies to Use During Reading to Build Comprehension." As you watch the video and answer the accompanying questions, note how either identifying or imposing a structure or organization on a text helps students understand what they read. Also, monitoring their own comprehension should lead students to either continue reading with understanding or take steps to fix broken comprehension. List some fix-up strategies mentioned in this video.

There is convincing empirical evidence that readers' awareness of and use of deep or implicit text structure or organization positively affect reading comprehension (Dickson et al., 1998b). *Implicit text structure* refers to the way in which authors organize text without necessarily telling the reader how they have done so. Research on implicit text structure has generally focused on two types of texts that children encounter in the elementary grades—narrative and expository (Dickson et al., 1998b). As a consequence, we discuss each major text type separately, then together, in the following sections.

## Narrative Text Structure

Narrative texts are most often described as texts that tell a story, such as *Jack and the Beanstalk* or *Summer of the Monkeys*. Some obvious exceptions to story texts are those found in mathematics story problems that are called "stories" but do not follow a traditional story structure or a paragraph structure in which the topic sentence appears first (Reutzel, 1983). Narrative or story structure, the prototypical or traditional way in which authors organize their text to convey a story, is the most common text structure encountered in elementary school classrooms and is the most researched (Graesser et al., 1991; National Institute of Child Health and Human Development, 2000). Narrative or story structure is found in a variety of story genres such as fables, tall tales, folktales, novels, short stories, comedy, fables, epics, mysteries, and myths. Understanding the way in which authors organize and structure their ideas in texts is one key to effective reading comprehension (Pearson & Duke, 2002; Pressley, 2000; Simmons & Kameenui, 1998).

The major elements of story structure have been captured in a system of rules called **story grammars** (Mandler & Johnson, 1977; Stein & Glenn, 1979; Thorndyke, 1977). Story grammars are the rules or descriptions of the necessary elements to make a story and the expected sequence for these elements. Researchers generally agree on the following elements and sequence in a story grammar: setting to include the characters, problem, goal, events, and resolution.

Developing a sense of how stories are written and organized helps readers predict what is coming next with greater proficiency, store information in schemas more efficiently, and recall story elements with increased accuracy and completeness (National Institute of Child Health and Human Development, 2000). Graesser et al. (1991) showed that there is strong research support showing that most students are more sensitive to narrative than to expository text structure. However, at-risk or learning disabled children struggle to remember narrative texts because, as some researchers suggest, they have not completely internalized story structure (McNamara, 2007; Montague, Maddux, & Dereshiwsky, 1990).

## Expository Text Structures

Go to the Assignments and Activities section of Topic 9: "Reading Comprehension" in the MyEducationLab for your course and complete the activity entitled "Content Area Text Structure and Comprehension." As you watch the video and answer the accompanying questions, note how students are helped by their teacher to note differences between stories and nonfiction or expository texts in the content areas. List a few things that you can point out to students that differentiate stories from content area textbooks.

Expository texts (Duke & Bennett-Armistead, 2003) include a range of text types or "genres" that include information texts, reference texts, information texts, biographies, and so on. Nearly 85% of all adult reading has as its purpose to obtain information (Duke, Bennett-Armistead, & Roberts, 2002). Expository texts contain facts, details, descriptions, and procedures that are necessary for understanding concepts and events in the world around us. Children's information books are only one example of many other expository texts, such as biographies, essays, photographic essays, instruction or how-to books, encyclopedias, reference books, activity/experiment books, scientific reports, newspaper articles, and so on.

Authors organize expository texts using several well-known text patterns or structures. Armbruster and Anderson (1981) and Meyer (1975) researched the text structures most used by authors of expository texts. These included time order (putting information into a chronological sequence), cause and effect (showing how something occurs because of another event), problem and solution (presenting a problem along with a solution to the problem), comparison (examining similarities and differences among concepts and events), simple listing (registering in list form a group of facts, concepts, or events), and descriptions.

Readers who understand an author's expository organizational pattern or expository text structure recall more from reading information texts than readers who do not (Bartlett, 1978; Dickson et al., 1998b; Hall, Sabey, & McClellan, 2005; Meyer, Brandt, & Bluth, 1980; Read & Reutzel, 2008; Williams, 2005). Previous research has also shown that poor or struggling readers are less likely to be able to identify and use an author's organization of text to recall information (Dickson et al., 1998b). Thus, teachers need to teach struggling students how to identify the author's implicit organizational patterns or text structures and how to use this knowledge to help them remember, organize, retrieve, and apply what they read.

## Hybrid or Dual-Purpose Texts: Easier to Access or More Confusing?

Researchers have for over a decade been discussing a type of text in which authors combine the explicit and implicit features of narrative story and nonnarrative informational texts (Donovan & Smolkin, 2002; Leal, 1993; Pappas, Kiefer, & Levstik, 1999; Skurzynski, 1992). Donovan and Smolkin (2002) have called these types of texts *dual-purpose texts,* while we have referred to them in our work as *hybrid* texts. Hybrid or dual-purpose texts are intended to present facts about a particular topic or body of content knowledge embedded within the overall implicit text structure of a story or narrative. Very often, the physical format or features of these types of texts combine those features found in both, namely, a predictable story line laying out facts in a temporal order along with graphs, diagrams, photos, and charts. Hybrid or dual-purpose texts ostensibly allow readers to access them either as a story or as a text that contains facts about everyday things. Thus, a reader may enter the book at the beginning and follow the story through to its resolution or a reader may enter the book at any point and find information about the topic on virtually any page.

Research on dual-purpose or hybrid texts and students' comprehension has provided rather mixed results. Leal (1992) found that after a hybrid book was read aloud to elementary-school-age children, the children retained more information and had better story discussions than they did when either a story or an information book was read aloud to them. On the other hand, Jetton (1994) and Maria and Junge (1994) found that embedding information within a story structure actually impeded access to and remembrance of information. Consequently, little is known about how teachers can help students to access dual-purpose or hybrid texts successfully.

In summary, research clearly demonstrates that teachers can help children comprehend text better when they are guided by a knowledgeable teacher to study closely, identify, and use an author's organization or structure across differing text types. Because many books do use a single or "pure" text structure, it is important to begin instruction by using clear examples of single or "pure" text structures (Read & Reutzel, 2008; Williams, 2005). As students develop the ability to identify and use text structure in clear examples, they then can be introduced to books and texts that make use of more than one text structure such as hybrid or dual-purpose texts. However before teaching children to identify and use text structure or text organization to improve reading comprehension, the skilled teacher assesses what children know about text structure in order to determine which of many available instructional interventions will be most effective.

# ASSESSING STUDENTS' KNOWLEDGE OF TEXT FEATURES AND STRUCTURE: NARRATIVE AND EXPOSITORY TEXT

The key to effective text-based comprehension instruction lies in the accurate identification of the types of text structures students are able to read effectively, as well as the genres or text structures that are difficult for them to comprehend. Practically nothing has been done to develop valid and reliable assessments of students' text structure knowledge. We have found several informal text-structure assessments that not only are text-structure specific but also are easily adaptable to differing text types, narrative and expository, and can help teachers plan effective instruction (Stahl, 2009). Offered in this chapter are some examples of each for your consideration.

## Oral Story Retellings: Narrative Text Structure

### Purpose

One of the most effective processes for finding out if a child understands narrative or story text structure is to use oral story retellings (Brown & Cambourne, 1987; Gambrell, Pfeiffer, & Wilson, 1985; Leslie & Caldwell, 2009; Morrow, 1985; Morrow et al., 1986; Stahl, 2009). Asking children to retell a story involves reconstructing the complete story structure including the story sequence, recalling important elements of the plot, making inferences, and noticing relevant details. Thus, oral story retellings assess story comprehension and narrative or story structure knowledge in a holistic, sequenced, and organized way.

### Materials

- Blank audiotape/computer audio file
- Portable audiocassette recorder or computer with an internal or external microphone
- Brief story
- "Parsing" of the story (see "Procedure")
- Scoring sheet

### Procedure

Select a brief story for students to listen to or read. For example, *The Carrot Seed* by Ruth Krauss* (1945) could be selected. Next, type the text of the story onto a separate piece of

*Text copyright 1945 by Ruth Krauss. Used by permission of HarperCollins Publishers.

paper for parsing. Parsing, in this instance, refers to dividing a story into four major and somewhat simplified story grammar categories: setting, problem, events, and resolution, as shown here.

### Story Grammar Parsing of *The Carrot Seed*

#### *Setting*
> *A little boy planted a carrot seed.*

#### *Problem (Getting the Seed to Grow)*
> *His mother said, "I'm afraid it won't come up."*
> *His father said, "I'm afraid it won't come up."*
> *And his big brother said, "It won't come up."*

#### *Events*
> *Every day the little boy pulled up the weeds around the seed and sprinkled the*
>     *ground with water.*
> *But nothing came up.*
> *And nothing came up.*
> *Everyone kept saying it wouldn't come up.*
> *But he still pulled up the weeds around it every day and sprinkled the ground with*
>     *water.*

#### *Resolution*
> *And then, one day, a carrot came up just as the little boy had known it would.*

Oral story retellings may be elicited from children in a number of ways (Stahl, 2009). One way involves the use of pictures or verbal prompts from the story. As pictures in the story are flashed sequentially, the child is asked to retell the story as remembered from listening or reading. Morrow (2005) suggested that teachers prompt children to begin story retellings with a statement such as: "A little while ago, we read a story called [Name the story]. Retell the story as if you were telling it to a friend who has never heard it before." Other prompts during the oral story retelling may be framed as questions:

- "How does the story begin?" or "Once upon a time . . ."
- "What happens next?"
- "What happened to [the main character] when . . . ?"
- "Where did the story take place?"
- "When did the story take place?"
- "How did the main character solve the problem in the story?"
- "How did the story end?"

Morrow (2005) recommends that teachers offer only general prompts such as those listed previously rather than asking about specific details, ideas, or a sequence of events in the story. Remember, when asking questions such as those just listed, you are moving from free recall of text to a form of assisted or prompted recall of text information. Coincidentally, you should know that assisted recall of story text information is especially useful with struggling readers.

A second way to elicit oral story retellings from students is to use unaided recall, in which students retell the story without pictures or verbal prompts. Asking the child to tell the story "as if he or she were telling it to someone who had never heard or read the story before" begins an unaided oral story retelling. To record critical elements of the story structure included in the child's oral story retelling, use an audiotape recording and oral story retelling coding sheet like the one shown in Figure 10.1. The information gleaned from an oral story retelling may be used to help you, the teacher, focus future instruction on enhancing students' understanding of narrative or story text structure.

## Oral Retellings: Expository Structure

### Purpose

McGee (1982) found that children in the elementary grades are aware of expository text structures although good readers in fifth grade are more aware than are poor readers in fifth grade or good readers in third grade. One of the most effective ways to find out if a child understands expository text is to use oral retellings (Duke & Bennett-Armistead, 2003). An oral retelling is an oral recounting of a text that has been read either silently or orally. Asking children to retell an expository text involves reconstructing the contents of the expository text including the major, main, or superordinate ideas; the minor or subordinate details; and the underlying organization of the ideas in the text such as compare/contrast, cause–effect, description, list, enumeration, and so on. Thus, oral expository text retellings assess content comprehension and text structure knowledge in holistic, sequenced, and organized ways.

---

**FIGURE 10.1**  Oral Story Retelling Coding Form

Student's name: _____  Grade: _____

Title of story: _____  Date: _____

**General directions:** Give 1 point for each element included, as well as for "gist." Give 1 point for each character named, as well as for such words as *boy*, *girl*, or *dog*. Credit plurals (*friends*, for instance) with 2 points under characters.

**Setting**
a. Begins with an introduction                                  _____
b. Indicates main character                                     _____
c. Other characters named                                       _____
d. Includes statement about time or place                       _____

**Objective**
a. Refers to main character's goal or problem to be solved      _____

**Events**
a. Number of events recalled                                    _____
b. Number of events in story                                    _____
c. Score for "events" (a/b)                                     _____

**Resolution**
a. Tells how main character resolves the story problem          _____

**Sequence**
Summarizes story in order: setting, objective, episodes, and resolution.   _____
(Score 2 for correct order, 1 for partial order, 0 for no sequence.)

**Possible score:** _____                    **Student's score:** _____

## Materials

- Blank audiotape or computer audio file
- Portable audiocassette recorder or computer with internal or external microphone
- A full or partial expository text such as an information book or textbook chapter
- A main idea/detail "parsing" of the text
- Scoring sheet

## Procedure

Select a brief information tradebook or textbook chapter for students to listen to or read either aloud or silently depending on the grade level and development of the child. We recommend that children listen to the text read aloud in grades K and 1, read the text aloud in grades 2 and 3, and silently read the text in grade 4 and beyond. For example, *Is It a Fish?* by Cutting and Cutting (2002) from the Wright Group Science Collection could be selected. Next, type the text of the book onto a separate piece of paper for parsing. Parsing, in this instance, refers to dividing a text into main ideas or superordinate ideas and details or subordinate ideas as shown in Figure 10.2.

Expository text oral retellings may be elicited from children in a number of ways. One way involves the use of pictures or verbal prompts from the text. As pictures in the text are flashed sequentially, the children are asked to retell what they remember from listening or reading about this picture. This approach is modeled after the work of Beaver (1997) in the *Developmental Reading Assessment* and the work of Leslie and Caldwell (2001, 2009) in the *Qualitative Reading Inventory—3*. Morrow (1985, 2005) suggests that teachers prompt children to begin oral retellings with a statement such as "A little while ago, we read a book or text called [name the text or book]. Retell the text or book as if you were telling it to a friend who has never heard about it before." Other prompts during the recall may include the following:

- "Tell me more about . . ."
- "You said _____. Is there anything else you can tell me about . . ."
- "Tell me about gills."
- "Tell me about fins."
- "Tell me how fish move, look, or breathe."

Asking students to retell what they remember using these types of prompts is a form of assisted recall and may be especially useful with struggling readers.

A second way to elicit expository text oral retellings from students is to use unaided recall, in which students retell the contents and order of the content in a book or text without pictures or verbal prompts. Asking the child to retell the information read "as if he or she were telling it to someone who had never heard or read the content of the book or text before" is used to begin an unaided expository text oral retelling. To record critical elements of the expository text oral retelling included in the child's oral retelling, use an audiotape recording. To make judgments about the quality of an unaided expository text oral retelling, you may use a rating guide sheet like the one shown in Figure 10.3, based on the work of Moss (1997).

As you develop the ability to listen to expository text oral retellings, you may no longer require the use of an audio recording and may just make notes on the scoring sheet as to the features you heard the child include in his or her oral retelling. The information gleaned from

---

**FIGURE 10.2**  Oral Expository Text Retelling Coding Form

**Put a checkmark by everything the child retells from his or her reading of the text.**

_____ **Big Idea: A fish is an animal.**
_____ Detail: It has a backbone (skeleton inside).
_____ Detail: Most fish have scales.
_____ Detail: It is cold-blooded.

_____ **Big Idea: All fish live in water.**
_____ Detail: Some live in saltwater.
_____ Detail: Some live in freshwater.
_____ Detail: Salmon and eels live in saltwater and freshwater.
_____ Detail: Salmon leave the sea to lay eggs in the river.

_____ **Big Idea: All fish breathe with gills.**
_____ Detail: All animals breathe oxygen.
_____ Detail: Some get oxygen from the air.
_____ Detail: Fish get oxygen from the water.
_____ Detail: A shark is a fish.
_____ Detail: Gills look like slits.
_____ Detail: A ray's gills are on the underside of its body.
_____ Detail: A ray breathes through holes on top of its head when it rests.

_____ **Big Idea: Most fish have fins to help them swim.**
_____ Detail: A sailfish has a huge fin that looks like a sail on its back.
_____ Detail: A (sting) ray waves its pectoral fin up and down.

**Scoring:**

**Please tally the marks for the big ideas and details. Place the total number in the blanks shown below.**

Big Ideas _____ /4       Details: _____ /16       Number of Prompts _____

Sequentially Retold (Circle One):              Yes                    No

Other Ideas Recalled Including Inferences: _____

---

an expository text oral retelling may be used to help teachers focus their future instruction on enhancing students' understanding of expository text structures, developing sensitivity to main ideas and details, improving sequencing ability, and summarizing information.

## Scrambled Schema Story Task

### Purpose

A scrambled schema story task assesses how well readers can reconstruct the order of a story based on their innate understanding of story structure. In this task, a story or major portions of a story are divided into its components—such as setting, problem, events, and resolution—and then scrambled. Students are asked to read each element of the story and then organize the story elements in order on a story board. Results from this analysis can be used to help teachers know whether to increase interactions about story parts during teacher interactive reading aloud and/or to provide explicit instruction in story parts to help readers build a better internal sense of story structure.

| FIGURE 10.3 | A Qualitative Assessment of Student Expository Text Oral Retellings |
|---|---|

| Rating Level | Criteria for Establishing a Level |
|:---:|---|
| 5 | Student includes all main ideas and supporting details, sequences properly, infers beyond the text, relates text to own life, understands text organization, summarizes, gives opinion and justifies it, may ask additional questions—very cohesive and complete retelling. |
| 4 | Student includes most main ideas and supporting details, sequences properly, relates text to own life, understands text organization, summarizes, gives opinion—fairly complete retelling. |
| 3 | Student includes some main ideas and details, sequences most material, understands text organization, gives opinion—fairly complete retelling. |
| 2 | Student includes a few main ideas and details, has some difficulty sequencing, may give irrelevant information, gives opinion—fairly incomplete retelling. |
| 1 | Student gives details only, has poor sequencing, gives irrelevant information—very incomplete retelling. |

*Source:* From "A Qualitative Assessment of First Graders' Retelling of Expository Text," by B. Moss, 1997, *Reading Research and Instruction, 37*(1), 1–13. Reprinted by permission of the College Reading Association.

## Materials

- A short story or storybook
- A simple story board made of laminated posterboard
- Parts of the story typed onto regular 8½ × 11-inch white paper and cut into story part strips
- One white legal-size envelope for storing the typed story part strips
- An oral retelling story scoring sheet based on the design of the story board to score each student's response

## Procedure

Choose a simple story for this activity. Parse or divide the story selected into story grammar elements, as shown for the story of *The Carrot Seed* in the "Oral Story Retellings" assessment activity. After parsing the story, transcribe the entire story text if it is a simple story—a story with no more than two lines of text per page. If not, transcribe only a few sentences from the story that provide the reader sufficient clues about where the story parts are in the sequence and structure of the story. Type the transcribed text onto plain white paper and, with scissors, cut the text into the parts of the story. Scramble the pieces and place them into a plain white legal-size envelope. Hand the child the envelope and ask him or her to read each part of the story. You may want to assist the child with any decoding problems. Next, ask the child to put the pieces of the scrambled story in order on the story board. Ask him or her to reread the story strips on the story board to check that his or her ordering of the story makes sense. Record the child's responses to this task on the form shown in Figure 10.1.

Poor performance on this task is typically due to limited exposure to hearing stories read aloud and discussing them with others. As a consequence, daily interactive teacher read alouds along with explicit story structure instruction (National Institute of Child Health and Human Development, 2000) are logical means for helping children who perform poorly on this task to develop an improved sense of story.

## Content-Area Reading Inventory

### Purpose

The content-area reading inventory (Farr, Tulley, & Pritchard, 1989; Readence, Bean, & Baldwin, 1992) is an informal reading inventory assessing whether students have learned sufficient reading and study strategies to succeed with content materials. The CARI can be administered to groups of students and typically includes three major sections (Farr et al., 1989) that assess (a) student knowledge of and ability to use common textbook components (i.e., table of contents, glossary, index) and supplemental research aids (card catalog, reference books, periodicals); (b) student knowledge of important vocabulary and skills, such as context clues; and (c) comprehension skills important to understanding expository texts. For the last two sections of the assessment, students are asked to read a selection from the adopted text.

### Materials

- A text selection from a textbook
- A teacher-constructed content-area reading inventory appropriate for that text

### Procedure

Choose a passage of at least three to four pages from the textbook(s) to be used. The passage selected should represent the typical writing style of the author. Construct about 20 questions related to the text. Readence et al. (1992) suggested that the contents of the assessment should be based on an outline similar to the following:

Part I: Textual Reading and Study Aids
  A. Internal aids
    1. Table of contents
    2. Index
    3. Glossary
    4. Chapter introduction/summaries
    5. Information from pictures
    6. Other aids included in the text

  B. Supplemental research aids
    1. Card catalog
    2. Periodicals
    3. Encyclopedias
    4. Other relevant aids for the content area

Part II: Vocabulary Knowledge
  A. Knowledge and recall of relevant vocabulary
  B. Use of context clues

Part III: Comprehension Skills and Strategies
  A. Text-explicit (literal) information
  B. Text-implicit (inferred) information
  C. Knowledge of text structures and related strategies

Readence et al. (1992) recommended 8 to 10 questions for Part I, 4 to 6 questions for Part II, and 7 to 9 questions for Part III. We urge the use of questions based on writing patterns used in the sample selection; they should reflect the facts, concepts, and generalizations in the selection.

Explain to students that the CARI is not used for grading purposes but is useful for planning teaching activities that will help them succeed. Using a minilesson kind of format, walk students through the different sections of the CARI and model responses. Administer Part I first, then Parts II and III on separate day(s). It may take several sessions to work through the CARI. We recommend devoting only about 20 minutes per day to administering parts of the CARI, so that other class needs are not ignored during the assessment phase.

Readence et al. (1992) suggested the following criteria for assessing the CARI:

| Percentage Correct | Text Difficulty |
| --- | --- |
| 86–100% | Easy reading |
| 64–85% | Adequate for instruction |
| 63% or below | Too difficult |

From careful analysis of this assessment, teachers can plan specific lessons to help students cope with difficult expository readings and internalize important information. Students may be grouped according to need for these lessons while practicing strategies that lead to increased comprehension.

## Story Grammar Questioning

Go to the Assignments and Activities section of Topic 9: "Reading Comprehension" in the MyEducationLab for your course and complete the activity entitled "Guided Comprehension Practice." As you watch the video and answer the accompanying questions, note how the teacher's questions focus on helping students attend to the various parts of typical story structure (i.e., setting, characters, problems, events, and resolution).

### Purpose

Questions are an integral part of life in and out of school. From birth, we learn about our world by asking questions and questioning our answers against the confines of reality. Beck and McKeown (1981) and Sadow (1982) suggest that teachers follow a logical model of questioning to probe those areas of comprehension that may not be freely offered in an oral retelling of a text (Rathvon, 2004; Stahl, 2009). Research (Mandler & Johnson, 1977) indicates that story grammars provide just such a model for asking questions about stories. These same researchers have found that developing questions for stories using a story grammar framework produces improved reading comprehension among children as measured by the ability to correctly and completely answer comprehension questions about stories (Beck, Omanson, & McKeown, 1982). Other evidence from research on story grammar questioning suggests that good readers have well-developed understanding of story structure, whereas poor readers do not (Whaley, 1981). Therefore, using a story grammar to guide teacher questioning and self-questioning can help teachers and students to better assess understanding of story structure.

### Materials

- One simple story to be read aloud or individually and silently
- One copy of an empty or blank story grammar map (see Figure 10.4)
- One set of questions dealing with each element shown in the empty boxes on the story map (see Figure 10.5) (Hint: It is best if questions are sequenced in the order of the story map.)
- One story grammar questioning summary scoring sheet

### Procedure

Select a simple story like *Jack and the Beanstalk*. Construct a story grammar map for the story as shown in Figure 10.4. Next, write one question for selected major elements in the story grammar map, as shown in the example questions in Figure 10.5. Students can be asked, depending on their level of writing development, to answer the questions orally

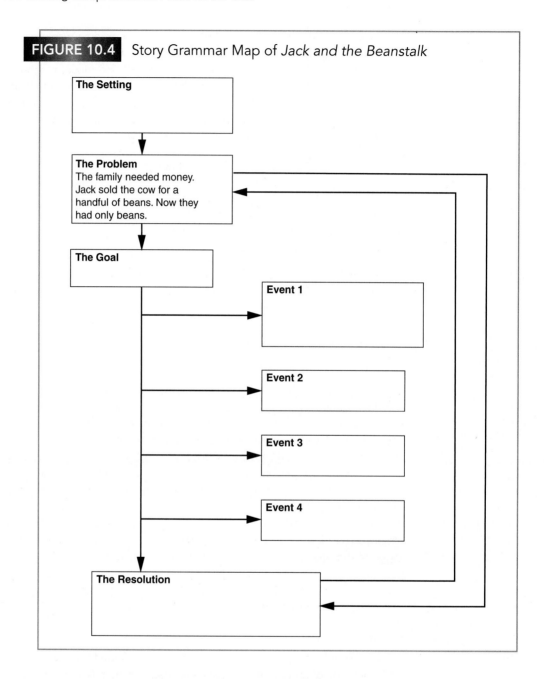

**FIGURE 10.4** Story Grammar Map of *Jack and the Beanstalk*

The Setting

The Problem
The family needed money. Jack sold the cow for a handful of beans. Now they had only beans.

The Goal

Event 1

Event 2

Event 3

Event 4

The Resolution

or in written form. Answers to each question are evaluated for accuracy and completeness. Story elements missed in the story grammar questioning should be stressed in future story discussions and explicit story structure instruction.

## Expository Text Frames

### Purpose

Expository text frames are useful in identifying types of expository text patterns that may be troublesome for students. Based on the "story frames" concept (Fowler, 1982; Nichols, 1980), expository text frames are completed by the student after reading an expository pas-

---

**FIGURE 10.5**   Story Grammar Questioning for *Jack and the Beanstalk*

| | |
|---|---|
| Setting: | In the beginning of the story, why did Jack's mother want him to sell the cow? |
| Problem: | When Jack traded the cow for a handful of beans, what kind of a problem did this decision create for Jack and his mother? |
| Events: | When Jack climbed the beanstalk the first time, relate what happened to him. <br> Why did Jack climb the beanstalk a second time? |
| Resolution: | At the end of the story, what had happened to Jack and his mother to solve the problem of trading the cow for a handful of beans? |

---

sage. Expository text frames can be used to probe students' comprehension of text-based information that is not given in an expository text oral retelling. Abbreviated examples of expository text frames for several of the common expository text patterns are shown in Figures 10.6 through 10.10.

### Materials

- A textbook or information book
- A computer with a word processing program
- Copies of expository text frames for students

### Procedure

Before reading the selection, list the major vocabulary and concepts. Discuss what students already know about the topic and display it on the chalkboard or on chart paper. Next, have students read an expository selection similar to the one you will ask them to read in class. Once the

---

**FIGURE 10.6**   Expository Text Frames: Description

*Decimals* are another way to write fractions when _____
_____
_____
_____

---

**FIGURE 10.7**   Expository Text Frames: Collection

#### Water Habitats

**Freshwater habitats** are found in _____, _____, _____, and rivers. Each freshwater habitat has special kinds of _____ and _____ that live there. Some plants and animals live in waters that are very _____. Others live in waters that are _____. Some plants and animals adapt to waters that flow _____.

---

**FIGURE 10.8** Expository Text Frames: Causation

**America Enters the War**

On Sunday, December 7, 1941, World War II came to the United States. The entry of the United States into World War II was triggered by _____. Roosevelt said that it was a day that would "live in Infamy." *Infamy* (IN · fuh · mee) means remembered for being evil.

---

**FIGURE 10.9** Expository Text Frames: Problem/Solution

**Agreement by Compromise**
**Events that led to the Civil War**

For a while there were an equal number of Southern and Northern states. That meant that there were just as many senators in Congress from slave states as from free states. Neither had more votes in the Senate, so they usually reached agreement on new laws by compromise. One way that the balance of power was maintained in Congress was

_____

---

**FIGURE 10.10** Expository Text Frames: Comparison

**Segregation**

Many people said that the segregation laws were unfair. But in 1896, the Supreme Court ruled segregation legal if _____
_____. "Separate but equal" became the law in many parts of the country.
    But separate was not equal. One of the most serious problems was education. Black parents felt _____
_____. Sometimes the segregated schools had teachers who were not _____ as teachers in the white schools. Textbooks were often _____, if they had any books at all. But in many of the white schools the books were _____
_____. Without a good education, the blacks argued, their children would not be able to get good jobs as adults.

---

passage has been read, model the process for completing expository text frames using mock examples. Now have them read the actual selection for the unit of study. Finally, have students complete the expository text frame(s) you have prepared for this passage. For students who have trouble with any of the frames, conduct a one-on-one reading conference to determine the thinking processes going on as the student completed the expository text frame.

In Figure 10.11, we summarize the procedures and instruments we have discussed previously for assessing factors associated with the text that affect reading comprehension. In this Summary Matrix of Text-Based Comprehension Assessments, we provide information about

**FIGURE 10.11** Summary Matrix of Text-Based Comprehension Assessments

| Name of Assessment Tool | Screening Assessment | Diagnostic Assessment | Progress-Monitoring Assessment | Outcomes Assessment | Norm-Referenced Test | Criterion-Referenced Test | Reliability Evidence | Validity Evidence |
|---|---|---|---|---|---|---|---|---|
| Oral Retellings: Narrative Text Structure | + | – | + | – | – | + | Not Available | Not Available |
| Oral Retellings: Expository Structure | + | – | + | – | – | + | Not Available | Not Available |
| Scrambled Schema Story Task | + | – | + | – | – | + | Not Available | Not Available |
| Content-Area Reading Inventory | + | – | + | – | – | + | Not Available | Not Available |
| Story Grammar Questioning | + | – | + | – | – | + | Not Available | Not Available |
| Expository Text Frames | + | – | + | – | – | + | Not Available | Not Available |

Key: + can be used for
      – not appropriate for

federally related assessment purposes (i.e., screening, diagnostic, progress-monitoring, or outcomes assessment, as well as the type of test or procedure) and any available psychometric evidence of test or procedure scores (reliability and validity evidence). It is noteworthy that there are few classroom-based, informal comprehension assessments that report reliability or validity evidence. To obtain valid and reliable comprehension scores on individual students, one must typically turn to the subtests of norm-referenced reading achievement batteries, for example, the Stanford Reading First or the Iowa Test of Basic Skills.

## Connecting Assessment Findings to Teaching Strategies

Before discussing text-based comprehension teaching strategies, we provide an If-Then guide connecting outcomes on those assessments previously described to intervention and strategy choices for improving students' text-based reading comprehension (see Figure 10.12). It is our intention in creating this matrix to help you, the teacher, select the most appropriate instructional interventions and strategies to meet students' text-based comprehension needs based on text-based comprehension assessment data. In the following section, we offer comprehension teaching strategies that have been shown to be effective in improving students' text-based reading comprehension.

# TEXT COMPREHENSION INSTRUCTIONAL STRATEGIES: A FOCUS ON NARRATIVE TEXT

## Story Grammar Instruction: Learning About Story Structure

### Purpose

Developing a sense of how stories are formed through story grammar instruction helps students who are having reading problems predict with greater facility, store information more efficiently, and recall story elements with increased accuracy and completeness. Without knowledge and understanding of story structure, students cannot be expected to make reasonable predictions, remember important story information, or provide a competent or complete oral retelling. The National Institute of Child Health and Human Development (2000) has recommended the teaching of story structure as a comprehension strategy for which there is abundant scientific evidence of effectiveness.

### Materials

- Well-formed stories
- A visual organizer to guide the introduction of story grammar concepts (such as the blank, poster-sized, laminated story grammar map shown in Figure 10.4, which can be used repeatedly when modeling renderings of complete and properly sequenced oral story retellings)

### Procedure

A number of reading researchers have described instructional procedures for developing readers' story schemata or story grammar awareness. Gordon and Braun (1983) recommended several guidelines for teaching story grammar, which we have adapted as follows:

1. Story grammar instruction should use well-formed stories such as *Jack and the Beanstalk*. A visual organizer can be used to guide the introduction of the concept of story

grammar. For the first story used in story grammar instruction, read the story aloud, stop at key points in the story, and discuss the information needed to fill in the diagram. For stories read after introducing the concept of story grammar, use the visual organizer to introduce the story and make predictions about the story prior to reading. During and after reading, a visual organizer can be used to guide a discussion.

2. Set the purposes for reading by asking questions related to the structure of the story. Questioning developed to follow the structure of the story will focus students' attention on major story elements.

3. After questioning and discussing story structure, specific questions about the story content can be asked.

4. For continued instruction, gradually introduce less well-formed stories so that students will learn that not all stories are "ideal" in organization.

5. Extend instruction by encouraging children to ask their own questions using story structure and to apply this understanding in writing their own stories.

## Graphic Organizers for Stories: Seeing the Structure of Stories

### Purpose

Graphic organizers are visual representations of key story elements and the interrelationships among these parts. Several researchers over the years have demonstrated the efficacy of using graphic organizers to teach children how stories are constructed to improve their comprehension of stories (Beck & McKeown, 1981; Reutzel, 1985, 1986). The National Reading Panel (National Institute of Child Health and Human Development, 2000) has recommended the use of graphic organizers as a comprehension strategy for which there is abundant scientific evidence of effectiveness. Graphic organizers, like story maps or webs, have been used to effectively increase children's comprehension of stories (Boyle, 1996; Bromley, 1993; Reutzel, 1985, 1986).

Reutzel and Fawson (1989, 1991) designed a successful strategy lesson to be used with young readers' predictable storybooks for building children's understanding of story structure. A literature web is constructed from the major story elements in a predictable book by selecting sentences from the book that tell about each major element of the story (i.e., setting, problem, events, and resolution).

To cement or correct comprehension of text after reading, you may want to conduct a class discussion. Most class discussions tend to center around the teacher and a few vocal children, with the rest of the class passively listening, or worse, completely inattentive. A discussion web (Alvermann, 1991) is a practical technique for enhancing student participation and thought during class discussions after reading.

### Materials

- One well-formed story
- Sentence strips
- Hand-drawn or copied pictures from the selected story
- A chalkboard or other display area for posting the literature web
- A felt pen or marker for drawing lines of relationships

### Procedure

Sentences from the story are copied onto strips. The title of the story is copied onto a sentence strip. The sentence strip with the title is placed in the center of the board or display

**FIGURE 10.12**  If-Then Intervention Strategy Guide for Improving Text Comprehension

| "If" the student is ready to learn → "Then" try these teaching strategies | Story Grammar or Structure Instruction | Graphic Organizers for Stories | Schema Stories | Question–Answer Relationships (QARs) | Question the Author (QtA) | Traffic Light Reading | Graphic Organizers for Expository Texts | Summary Writing | I-Charts | Concept Oriented Reading Instruction (CORI) | Collaborative Strategic Reading (CSR) |
|---|---|---|---|---|---|---|---|---|---|---|---|
| Recall main ideas | + | + | + | * | * | + | + | + | * | * | + |
| Recall details | − | + | − | * | * | * | + | − | + | * | * |
| Recall text events in order | + | + | + | * | * | * | + | + | + | * | + |
| Use author's text/story structure(s) | + | + | + | * | * | * | + | + | + | + | * |
| Answering questions correctly | * | * | * | + | * | + | * | − | * | * | * |
| Summarize a test | * | + | * | − | − | * | + | + | + | * | * |

Key:  + Excellent strategy
 * Adaptable strategy
 − Unsuitable strategy

area. The remaining sentence strips are placed in random order on the chalk tray or some other display area (see Figure 10.13 for an example).

Prior to reading the story—whether reading it aloud in a shared-book experience or encouraging students to read it in a guided reading small group, the class or group reads the sentences aloud with the teacher. In the early part of the school year, the sentences selected for the literature web sentence strips are usually heavily augmented with hand-drawn or computer scanned pictures from the book.

**FIGURE 10.13**    Random-Order Literature Web

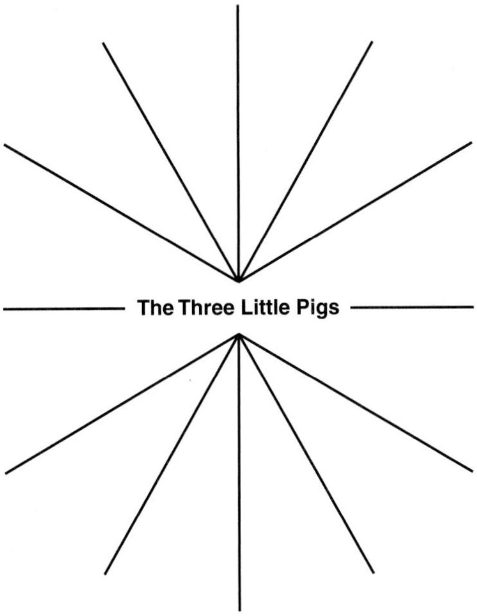

The Three Little Pigs

One pig met a man carrying a bundle of sticks. "May I have those sticks to build myself a house?" asked the pig. "You may," answered the man.

And the three little pigs lived happily ever after in a brick house built for three.

One day the wolf came knocking at the door of the brick house. "Little pig, little pig, let me come in." "Not by the hair of my chinny chin chin," said the pig. "Then I'll huff and I'll puff and I'll blow your house in." But the house would not fall down.

The wolf fell, kersplot, into a kettle of hot water. He jumped out with a start and ran out the door and never came back again.

One day the wolf came knocking at the door of the straw house. "Little pig, little pig, let me come in." "Not by the hair of my chinny chin chin," said the pig. "Then I'll huff and I'll puff and I'll blow your house in." And he blew the house down.

Once upon a time, three little pigs set out to make their fortune.

The wolf got so angry that he climbed to the top of the house and jumped down the chimney.

One pig met a man with a load of bricks. "May I have those bricks to build myself a house?" asked the pig. "You may," answered the man.

One pig met a man carrying a bundle of straw. "May I have that straw to build myself a house?" asked the pig. "You may," answered the man.

One day the wolf came knocking at the door of the stick house. "Little pig, little pig, let me come in." "Not by the hair of my chinny chin chin," said the pig. "Then I'll huff and I'll puff and I'll blow your house in." And he blew the house down.

Organize children into small groups and give each group one of the picture and sentence cards from the board. The children are asked which group thinks it has the first part of the story. After discussion and group agreement is reached, the first sentence and picture card is placed at the one o'clock position on the literature web graphic organizer. The remaining groups are asked which sentence and picture combination comes next, and the sentence strips and pictures are placed around the graphic organizer in clockwise order. Figure 10.14 shows how one group of students arranged a graphic organizer to represent their predictions.

Next, the story is read aloud or silently from a traditional-size trade book or from a big book in a shared reading. Children listen attentively to confirm or correct their graphic organizer predictions. After the reading, predictions are revised in the graphic organizer as necessary (see Figure 10.15).

Children respond to the story, and these responses are recorded near the end of the graphic organizer. Other books similar to the one read may be discussed and comments re-

**FIGURE 10.14** Literature Web Predictions

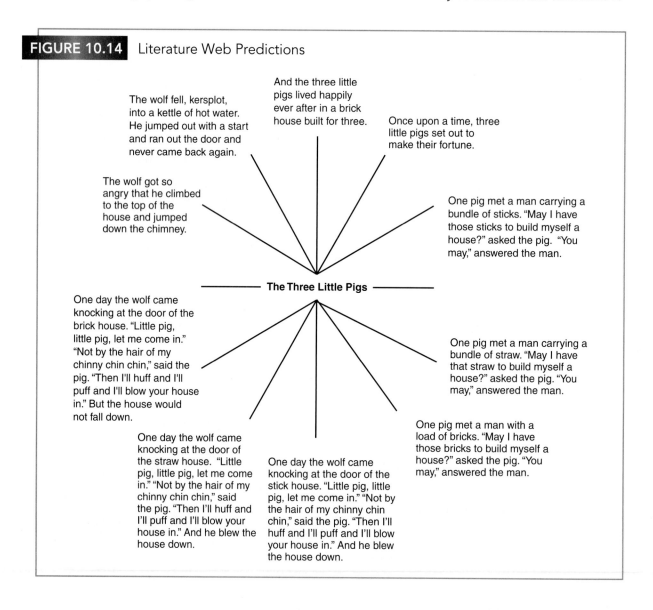

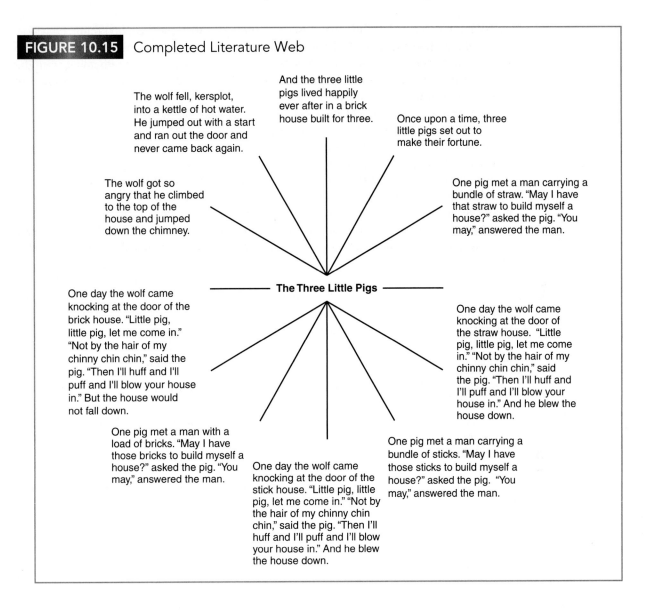

**FIGURE 10.15**   Completed Literature Web

The wolf fell, kersplot, into a kettle of hot water. He jumped out with a start and ran out the door and never came back again.

And the three little pigs lived happily ever after in a brick house built for three.

Once upon a time, three little pigs set out to make their fortune.

The wolf got so angry that he climbed to the top of the house and jumped down the chimney.

One pig met a man carrying a bundle of straw. "May I have that straw to build myself a house?" asked the pig. "You may," answered the man.

**The Three Little Pigs**

One day the wolf came knocking at the door of the brick house. "Little pig, little pig, let me come in." "Not by the hair of my chinny chin chin," said the pig. "Then I'll huff and I'll puff and I'll blow your house in." But the house would not fall down.

One day the wolf came knocking at the door of the straw house. "Little pig, little pig, let me come in." "Not by the hair of my chinny chin chin," said the pig. "Then I'll huff and I'll puff and I'll blow your house in." And he blew the house down.

One pig met a man with a load of bricks. "May I have those bricks to build myself a house?" asked the pig. "You may," answered the man.

One day the wolf came knocking at the door of the stick house. "Little pig, little pig, let me come in." "Not by the hair of my chinny chin chin," said the pig. "Then I'll huff and I'll puff and I'll blow your house in." And he blew the house down.

One pig met a man carrying a bundle of sticks. "May I have those sticks to build myself a house?" asked the pig. "You may," answered the man.

corded on the web. Finally, the children and teacher brainstorm together some ideas about how to extend the reading of the book into the other language arts while recording these ideas on the graphic organizer.

Reutzel and Fawson (1991) have demonstrated that children with reading problems who participate in using a graphic organizer of a predictable storybook learn to read these books with fewer oral reading miscues, fewer miscues that distort comprehension, and greater recall. They attribute this to the fact that children must impose an organization onto their predictions when using graphic organizers rather than simply making random predictions from story titles and pictures.

To use a discussion web graphic organizer after reading a story, begin by preparing students to read a text selection or book as you normally would (see Figure 10.16). Help them think of related background experiences, and invite them to set a purpose for reading the story. You may want to ask an open-ended question about the story. For example, using

*The Widow's Broom* by Chris Van Allsburg (1992), you may ask, "Do you think the widow Minna Shaw should have tricked her neighbors?" Group students in pairs and ask them to answer the question according to their own feelings and the facts they remember from the story. Help them focus on why a certain answer could be true. Ask students to think also of some reasons the opposite answer could be true.

For example, one student may say, "Yes, they were trying to take her magic broom away." A partner may add, "Yes, those rotten Spivey kids were the ones who needed to be taken away." In this example, these students have voiced two *yes* answers. Next, the teacher should ask the students to think of some *no* answers, as well.

After students have discussed their ideas in pairs, you may want to ask them to share their thinking with another pair of students. Ask each pair to choose its best answer to the question, as well as the strongest reason supporting the student's thinking. Then, bring the children together and ask one student from each pair to report the pair's best answer and the reason supporting that answer. As each student speaks, include the reason in the diagram. After each pair reports, invite others to suggest additional ideas for the discussion web. You may want to reach a class conclusion, or you may want to stop just before a conclusion is reached to avoid a "right" or "wrong" feeling for the answers. (*Note:* Some teachers of very young students use the discussion web strategy in a whole-class setting rather than grouping students in pairs. Vary the approach according to your teaching style and class needs.)

Merkley and Jeffries (2001) encourage teachers to use the following guidelines in teaching with graphic organizers to help students improve their comprehension:

- Talk about the links or relationships among the concepts or events expressed in the visual.
- Provide opportunity for student input in shaping the content and order of the visual.
- Connect the new learning to past learning and to other stories to demonstrate relationships.
- Reference an upcoming story that will be read soon.
- Use the text in the visual of a graphic organizer to reinforce decoding and other word study skills.

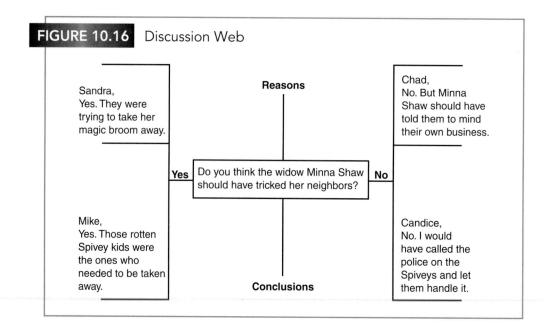

**FIGURE 10.16** Discussion Web

Sandra,
Yes. They were trying to take her magic broom away.

**Reasons**

Chad,
No. But Minna Shaw should have told them to mind their own business.

**Yes** | Do you think the widow Minna Shaw should have tricked her neighbors? | **No**

Mike,
Yes. Those rotten Spivey kids were the ones who needed to be taken away.

**Conclusions**

Candice,
No. I would have called the police on the Spiveys and let them handle it.

- Although the graphic organizer may be distributed as a worksheet, the secret to success is to use graphic organizers to organize discussion, text talk, and thinking.

## Schema Stories: Using Story Structure Knowledge to Guide Text Comprehension

### Purpose

Watson and Crowley (1988), originators of this strategy lesson, describe schema stories as a reading strategy lesson that helps readers "reconstruct the order of a text based on meaning and story grammar" (p. 263). This strategy helps students learn to anticipate such elements as setting, problem to be addressed by the characters, key events in the story, and resolution of the story (Simmons & Kameenui, 1998).

### Materials

- Copy of selected story cut into parts or sections

### Procedure

Start with stories that contain familiar beginning and ending phrases, such as "Once upon a time" and "They lived happily ever after." After choosing an interesting story, prepare the schema story strategy lesson by making a photocopy of the text and physically cutting the photocopy into sections or parts that are long enough to contain at least one main idea. Usually, one or two paragraphs will be a sufficient length to accomplish this purpose.

To begin the lesson, distribute a section or part of the story to each small group of students (four to eight students in each group is about right). Typically, one student is selected in each group to read the text aloud for his or her group. Once each group has read its story part, ask if any group believes it was given the section of the story that comes at the beginning of the story. Students who believe they have the beginning of the story are to raise their hands to respond. Those who raise their hands must state why they believe they have the beginning of the story. After the majority of the students agree as to which section or story part is first, the group proceeds to the next segment of the story. This process continues as described until all of the segments have been placed in a predicted order.

Schema story lessons make excellent small-group or individual activities that can be located at a classroom center or station devoted to developing a sense of story. All of the segments of a text can be placed into an envelope and filed in the center. Small groups of children or individuals can come to the center and select an envelope and then work individually or collectively on reconstructing a story. A "key" for self-checking can be included in the envelope, as well, to reduce the amount of teacher supervision necessary in the center. As children work through a schema story strategy lesson, they talk about how language works, ways authors construct texts, and how meaning can be used to make sense out of the scrambled elements of a text or story.

## Question–Answer Relationships: Answering Questions about Text

### Purpose

The National Reading Panel (National Institute of Child Health and Human Development, 2000) has identified answering and posing questions about texts as comprehension strategies for which there is abundant scientific evidence of effectiveness. Raphael (1982, 1986) identified four question–answer relationships to help children identify the connection between the type of questions asked of them by teachers and textbooks and the information sources necessary and available to them for answering questions: (a) right there, (b) think and search, (c) author and you, and (d) on my own. Research by Raphael and Pearson (1982) provided evidence that training students to recognize question–answer relationships (QARs) results in improved comprehension and question-answering behavior. In addition, using the QARs question-answering training strategy is useful for another purpose: helping teachers examine their own questioning with respect to the types of questions and the information sources that students need to use to answer their questions. By using QARs to monitor their own questioning behaviors, some teachers may find that they are asking only "right there" types of questions. This discovery very often leads teachers to ask other questions that require the use of additional or seldom-used information sources.

## Materials

- A variety of texts for asking and answering questions
- A poster displaying information about the different types of questions and the information sources available for answering them (see Figure 10.17 for examples of each of the four types of question–answer relationships)

---

**FIGURE 10.17**  Illustrations to Explain Question–Answer Relationships to Students

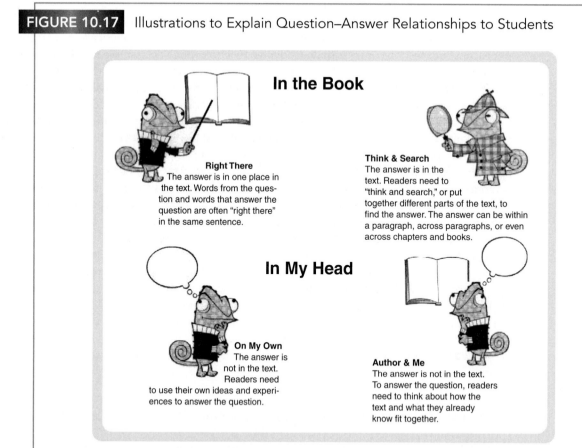

*Source:* From "QAR: Enhancing Comprehension and Test Taking across Grades and Content Areas" by T. E. Raphael and K. H. Au, 2005, *The Reading Teacher, 59*(3), 206–221. Copyright © 2005 by the International Reading Association (www.reading.org). Reproduced with permission from the International Reading Association via Copyright Clearance Center.

### Procedure

Instruction using QARs begins by explaining that when answering questions about reading, there are basically two places a student can look to get information: in the book and in my head. This concept should be practiced with the students by reading aloud a text, asking questions, and having the students explain or show where they found their answers. Once students understand the two-category approach, expand the "in the book" category to include "right there" and "think and search." The distinction between these two categories should be practiced by reading and discussing several texts. For older students, Raphael (1986) suggests that students be shown specific strategies for locating the answers to "right there" questions. These include looking in a single sentence or looking in two sentences connected by a pronoun. For "think and search" questions, students can be asked to focus their attention on the structure of the text, such as cause–effect, problem solution, listing examples, compare/contrast, and explanation.

Next, instruction should be directed toward two subcategories within the "in my head" category: "author and me" and "on my own." Here again, these categories can be practiced as a group by reading a text aloud, answering the questions, and discussing the sources of information. To expand this training, students can be asked to identify the types of questions asked in their basal readers, workbooks, content-area texts, and tests; in addition, they can determine the sources of information needed to answer these questions.

Students may be informed that certain types of questions are asked before and after reading a text. For example, questions asked before reading typically invite students to activate their own knowledge. Therefore, questions asked before reading will usually be "on my own" questions. However, questions asked after reading will make use of information found in the text. Thus, questions asked after reading will typically focus on the "right there," "think and search," and "author and me" types of questions. As a culminating training activity for QARs, children are asked to write their own questions for each of the QAR categories.

### Teacher Self-Evaluation Continuum: Question–Answer Relationships

Teachers, like students, go through zones of proximal development (from novice to expert) in the implementation of new teaching strategies. Cooter (2009) developed a kind of rubric or continuum for implementing QAR to help teachers monitor and improve their use of this method and discover ways to deepen its use in the classroom (see Figure 10.18).

# $\mathcal{T}$EXT COMPREHENSION INSTRUCTIONAL STRATEGIES: A FOCUS ON EXPOSITORY TEXT

## Questioning the Author (QtA)

### Purpose

Research has shown that many students construct very little meaning from the information they read in expository books and textbooks. Several features in expository texts combine to create a number of obstacles for young readers' comprehension of information text. These include (1) incoherence or poorly organized text and placement of main ideas, (2) lack of clear descriptions, headings, signal words, and explanations, (3) an assumption of an unrealistic level of background knowledge, (4) the objective nature of the language used, and (5) the "authority" that places the information in the text above criticism (McKeown, Beck, & Worthy, 1993). These "inconsiderate" features of a textbook's organization and content inhibit

**FIGURE 10.18** QAR Teacher-Self Assessment Continuum

Classroom Implementation of the Question–Answer Relationship Strategy

| | Exemplary A | Above Average B | Acceptable C | Early Implementation D | Traditional Instruction E |
|---|---|---|---|---|---|
| Purpose/Objective | Teacher uses the QAR strategy to help students monitor their understanding of mathematics text and mathematics concepts. | Teacher attempts to use the QAR strategy to help students monitor their understanding of mathematics text and mathematics concepts. | Teacher uses the QAR strategy but not for the purpose of helping students monitor their understanding of mathematics text and mathematics concepts. | Teacher helps students monitor their understanding of mathematics text and mathematics concepts without using the QAR strategy. | Teacher does not use the QAR strategy and does not help students monitor their understanding of mathematics text. |
| Teacher's Knowledge and Preparation | Teacher understands the QAR strategy and is prepared to demonstrate the QAR strategy to help students monitor their understanding of mathematics text and mathematics concepts. | Teacher understands the QAR strategy and is somewhat prepared to demonstrate the QAR strategy to help students monitor their understanding of mathematics text and mathematics concepts. | Teacher partially understands the QAR strategy and is partially prepared to demonstrate the QAR strategy to help students monitor their understanding of mathematics text and mathematics concepts. | Teacher demonstrates a limited understanding of the QAR strategy and is minimally prepared to demonstrate the strategy to help students monitor their understanding of mathematics text and mathematics concepts. | Teacher does not understand the QAR strategy and is not prepared to demonstrate the QAR strategy to help students monitor their understanding of mathematics text and mathematics concepts. |
| Teacher Modeling | Teacher models how to apply the QAR strategy to help students monitor their understanding of mathematics text and mathematics concepts. Teacher thinks aloud while demonstrating. | | Teacher attempts to model the use of the QAR strategy as a means for students to monitor their understanding of mathematics text and mathematics concepts. Engages students in the modeling phase. | | Teacher does not model the QAR strategy as a means for students to monitor their understanding of mathematics text and mathematics concepts. Students were called upon throughout this phase to apply their limited knowledge of the strategy. |

| | | | | | |
|---|---|---|---|---|---|
| **Teacher's Choice of Text** | Teacher chooses appropriate mathematics text for the implementation of the QAR strategy and is connected to the math skill being taught | Teacher chooses appropriate mathematics text for the implementation of the QAR strategy. | Teacher attempts to choose appropriate mathematics text for the implementation of the QAR strategy. | Teacher does not choose appropriate mathematics text for the implementation of the QAR strategy. | Teacher does not choose text in the subject matter of mathematics for the implementation of the QAR strategy. |
| **Gradual Release of Responsibility (Student's Role)** | Students are prepared to use the QAR strategy to monitor their understanding of mathematics text and mathematics concepts in independent practice. | Students are prepared to use the QAR strategy to monitor their understanding of mathematics text and mathematics concepts in a cooperative group (i.e., in pairs or small groups). | Students are prepared to use the QAR strategy to monitor their understanding of mathematics text and mathematics concepts in guided practice. | Students watch the teacher demonstrate/ model the QAR strategy as a means of monitoring their understanding of mathematics text and mathematics concepts. | New strategy to be learned. |
| **Frequency of Use** | Teacher uses the QAR strategy as a means for students to monitor their understanding of mathematics text daily. | Teacher uses the QAR strategy as a means for students to monitor their understanding of mathematics text twice a week. | Teacher uses the QAR strategy as a means for students to monitor their understanding of mathematics text once a week. | Teacher uses the QAR strategy as a means for students to monitor their understanding of mathematics text once a month to every six weeks. | Teacher does not use the QAR strategy as a means for students to monitor their understanding of mathematics text. |

comprehension, and the textbook's authority causes students to attribute their difficulty in understanding text to their own inadequacies. As a result, some students are reluctant to persist in using their natural problem-solving abilities in the face of these perceptions (Anderson, 1991; Schunk & Zimmerman, 1997).

Questioning the author (QtA) lessons provide an instructional framework that focuses on increasing students' understanding of expository texts. QtA lessons are either taught to the whole class as a group or in small reading instructional groups. During QtA lessons, students attempt, in a sense, to "'depose' the authority of the book or textbook through actualizing the presence of an author" (McKeown, Beck, & Worthy, 1993, p. 561). Recent research has shown that questioning the author results in increased length and complexity of recalled ideas from text and answers to comprehension questions as compared with other forms of book discussions (Sandora, Beck, & McKeown, 1999).

### Materials

- An information book or textbook chapter
- A written lesson plan containing questions for students and teacher to discuss prior to and during the reading of the text
- If preferred, questions strategically placed throughout the teacher's copy of the text using sticky notes

### Procedure

To begin, students are shown examples in information books and textbooks where someone's ideas may not be written as well or as clearly as they might be. This should help students conceptualize the text as a fallible product written by less than perfect authors (Laing & Dole, 2006). Next, the teacher prompts students as they read a book or textbook using a series of questions like the following:

- What is the author trying to tell us here?
- Why is the author telling us this?
- Where is the author going with this line of thinking?
- Is it said so that we can understand it?

Asking children to search out answers to these questions encourages them to actively engage collaboratively with the ideas in the text and in discussing the answers. As children encounter difficulties in understanding the text they are encouraged, again through teacher questioning, to recast the author's ideas in clearer language. Questions used for this purpose include:

- How could the author have said the ideas to make them easier to understand?
- What would you say instead?

Asking children to restate the author's ideas causes them to grapple with the ideas and problems in a text. In this way, children engage with text in ways that successful readers use to make sense of complex ideas presented in texts. Once students understand that the text and authors are to be questioned, they are ready to read and engage in discussion about text differently than they have in the past.

Classrooms that use QtA are characterized by lively and extensive teacher–student and student–student discussions about texts. Questions can inquire into an author's ideas or students' ideas within one sentence or longer units of text. Questions can be asked to deepen and broaden students' thinking about a text. The goal in QtA lessons is for teachers and students to assist one another in building a coherent understanding of a text. Initially it will take considerable time to prepare for a QtA lesson but this preparation decreases with time and practice (Laing & Dole, 2006). More information about QtA lessons can be found in the book *Questioning the Author: An Approach for Enhancing Student Engagement with Text* (Beck et al., 1997).

## Traffic Light Reading

### Purpose

Traffic light reading (TLR) introduces students to different reasons to read and different ways to approach differing reading materials (Marcell, 2007). In TLR the reading process is compared to driving a car and a traffic-light visual is used to guide students though what is sometimes called "hard-hat text" (i.e., challenging expository material). The implementation of TLR requires teacher modeling, guided practice, and multiple opportunities for independent usage with varied information texts.

### Materials

- Reading "hats"
- Core content information texts (e.g., social studies, mathematics, science)
- Traffic light bookmarks (Figure 10.19)
- Sticky notes

### Procedure

A traffic light reading lesson begins with the teacher displaying three different hats—a baseball cap labeled "Read for Fun," a plastic construction hat labeled "Read to Learn," and a visor labeled "Read for Information." Next, the teacher picks up an information text like a newspaper. She reads the text until she finds the specific information she is looking for in the text. She then asks, "What is my purpose for reading?" Students respond with "You are reading to locate or find specific information."

To show agreement, the teacher puts on the visor labeled "Read for Information." Marcell (2007) suggests that other examples of reading for specific information be modeled, including following a recipe, looking at a map, or examining the statistics of a sports team. The teacher observes that for this purpose, a reader should proceed carefully while skimming or scanning for specific information using finger-pointing.

Next, the teacher puts on the baseball hat and models the reading of a book for fun or pleasure such as a comic book, Junie B. Jones, or Captain Underpants. The teacher talks with students about how reading for pleasure differs from reading for specific information such as adjustments to reading rate, not skimming or scanning, not using finger-pointing, and imaging pictures of the story in one's head.

Finally, the teacher puts on the construction hat while reading from the science or health textbook. The teacher explains, "A lot of school work involves reading to learn. Someone reading to learn reads more carefully, making sure that the big ideas are understood and remembered." Students generally agree that this kind of reading is typically harder (hence, the "hard" hat). Again Marcell (2007) suggests that teachers model other information text reading, such as passages in a reading test, research books, or an online encyclopedia.

To complete the lesson, the teacher explains: "Reading is a little like driving a car, except *all* of you get to have drivers' licenses no matter how old you are. Before you read, you need to think about your reasons for reading, sort of like planning your trip. And then when you're

---

**FIGURE 10.19** Traffic Light Reading

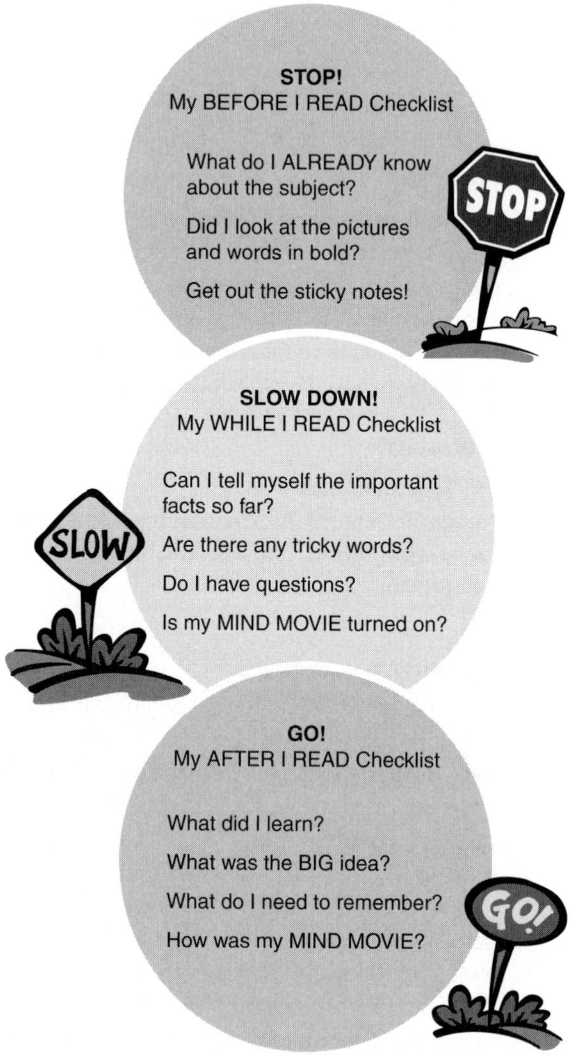

**STOP!**
My BEFORE I READ Checklist

What do I ALREADY know about the subject?

Did I look at the pictures and words in bold?

Get out the sticky notes!

**SLOW DOWN!**
My WHILE I READ Checklist

Can I tell myself the important facts so far?

Are there any tricky words?

Do I have questions?

Is my MIND MOVIE turned on?

**GO!**
My AFTER I READ Checklist

What did I learn?

What was the BIG idea?

What do I need to remember?

How was my MIND MOVIE?

*Source:* From "Traffic Light Reading: Fostering the Independent Usage of Comprehension Strategies with Information Text" by B. Marcell, 2007, *The Reading Teacher, 60*(8), 778–781. Figure 2. Copyright © 2007 by the International Reading Association (www.reading.org). Reproduced with permission of the International Reading Association via Copyright Clearance Center.

---

driving on the Reading Road, you also have to obey the traffic signals. Here's an example of a special kind of signal, a traffic light that can help us become better readers when we have to drive through those hard hat areas, when we have to read to learn" (Marcell, 2007, p. 779). The teacher gives each student an individual traffic light for their use, such as on a bookmark. She also passes out to students some sticky notes. The teacher then models how to use the traffic light with different kinds of texts. Pointing to the red circle at the top of the traffic light, the teacher asks, "What tool should we use for this hard hat kind of reading? How will we keep the information in our brains?" The teacher might also ask students to label some sticky notes with question marks (for what is not understood), others with exclamation points (for cool facts), and others with smiley faces (for the parts already known or with which there are personal connections) during the red light phase of preparing for reading.

The yellow-light components are applied during the actual reading. The teacher discusses the importance of monitoring for understanding as students read. At this point in the lesson, students are divided for partner reading or into small guided reading groups. The teacher then says, "It's time to start your engines! But, be careful. In this yellow-light section, don't forget to switch your Mind Movie to the on position, kind of like activating the navigation screen on your dashboard, and to use your sticky notes to flag certain sections while you read" (Marcell, 2007, p. 780).

When all students have completed the reading assignment, the class reconvenes in order to look at the green-light checklist on the traffic light. The teacher may at this time ask the students to use the margins of a traffic-light handout to write some personal learning log notes. Much as one might record events in a travel journal, students share relevant big ideas or flagged information (connections, questions, and cool facts). At the end of the TLR lesson, all students rate their personal mind movie with a "thumbs up" or a "thumbs down" and discuss with neighbors what their most vivid mind movie images were. TLR lessons help students successfully navigate the reading road of expository texts. Over the course of many reading road trips, students also develop many comprehension strategies such as imagery, predicting, question asking, monitoring, and so on for constructing meaningful representations of text.

## Graphic Organizers for Expository Texts: Visual Representation

### Purpose

Authors of expository texts typically organize their writing using several well-known text patterns or structures. Armbruster and Anderson (1981) and Meyer (1975) researched the text structures most used by authors of expository texts, including *time order* (putting information into a chronological sequence), *cause and effect* (showing how something occurs because of another event), *problem and solution* (presenting a problem along with a solution to the problem), *comparison* (examining similarities and differences among concepts and events), *simple listing* (registering in list form a group of facts, concepts, or events), and *descriptions*.

Readers who understand the organizational pattern(s) or text structure(s) an author has used in producing an expository text recall more from their reading than readers who do not (Bartlett, 1978; Dickson et al., 1998b; Meyer et al., 1980). The National Reading Panel (National Institute of Child Health and Human Development, 2000) has strongly recommended the use of graphic organizers as a comprehension strategy for which there is abundant scientific evidence of effectiveness.

### Materials

- One well-formed expository text using a single organizational pattern or text structure selected from among the common structures previously discussed: time order, cause and effect, problem and solution, comparison, simple listing, and descriptions
- Commercially produced sentence strips
- Hand-drawn or copied pictures from the selected text, especially but not exclusively for working with expository texts with younger children
- A whiteboard or other display area for displaying the graphic organizer
- A felt pen or dry-erase marker for drawing lines of relationships

### Procedure

Begin by selecting an excellent information text that employs a single organizational pattern or text structure. This means finding an expository text that exemplifies the clear and simple use of one of the six expository text structures, such as problem and solution or cause and effect. As we considered these characteristics and you, our reader, we decided to select a simple information text, *Name That Shape!* (Stafford, 2004), as our example. *Name That Shape!* uses a typical expository text structure—problem and solution (formatted in this case as question and answer). Each page begins with a question about a particular shape. Answers are then offered and reinforced by the use of photographs showing an object that exemplifies that particular geometric shape. For younger children, a simple graphic organizer using icons or pictures to accompany the print can be helpful. For older students, a more complex graphic organizer may include student-generated questions for which they will seek and retrieve answers to their questions through reading across a variety of other information texts on the topic of geometric shapes. An example of a question-and-answer graphic organizer for the book *Name That Shape!* is shown in Figure 10.20.

It is very important to scaffold graphic organizer instruction effectively in the classroom. **Scaffolding** refers to gradually releasing the control and responsibility for selecting a graphic organizer design and using it to guide comprehension. Children need to learn to recognize the organizational patterns or text structure the author has used to produce a text. An easy place to begin this process is in the table of contents of the book or textbook. Very often, the way the author titles each section in the table of contents and the order of the sections may give away the structure or organization of the text. Next, children need to be helped to select the appropriate graphic organizer to represent the organization of and information in the text.

In Figure 10.21, we show several different graphic organizers. We have labeled each graphic organizer type with the text structure or organizational pattern that each is intended to

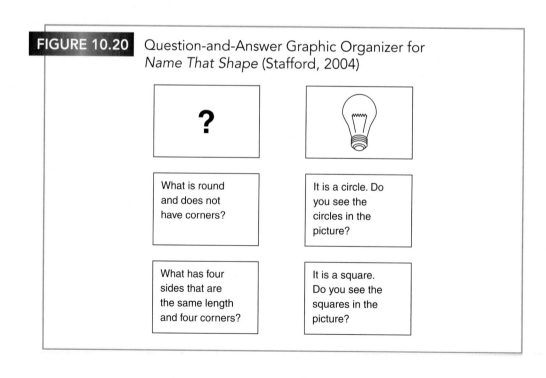

**FIGURE 10.20** Question-and-Answer Graphic Organizer for *Name That Shape* (Stafford, 2004)

What is round and does not have corners?

It is a circle. Do you see the circles in the picture?

What has four sides that are the same length and four corners?

It is a square. Do you see the squares in the picture?

**FIGURE 10.21**   Different Expository Test Structure Graphic Organizers

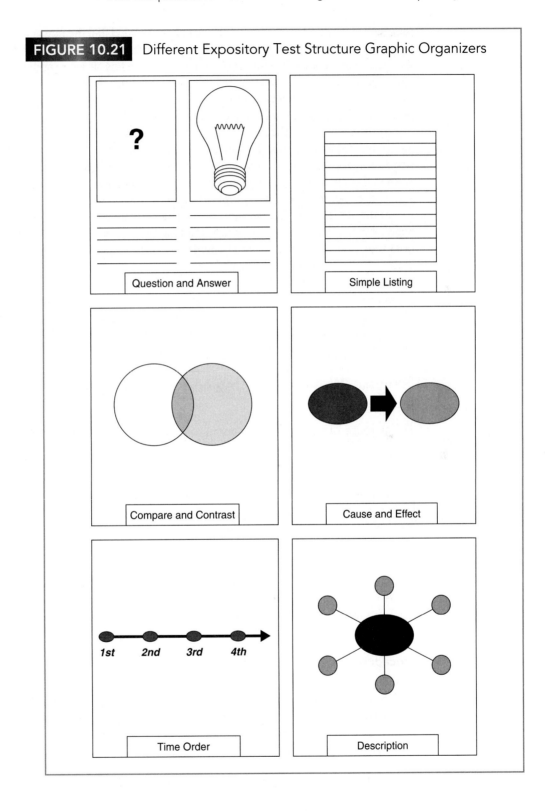

represent. It is important that you, the teacher, understand that the power in using graphic organizers is in selecting the appropriate one to represent the underlying organization or text structure used by the author. Teaching children to recognize text structure and select the appropriate type of graphic organizer will require multiple lessons such as the one just described with *Name That Shape!,* using a variety of expository books with question-and-answer text structures, such as *Bridges* (Ring, 2003) or *How Do Spiders Live?* (Biddulph & Biddulph, 1992).

In the first lesson, the teacher explains and thinks aloud how she figured out that the author was using a question-and-answer structure in the graphic organizer. Next, the teacher selects the appropriate graphic organizer from those in Figure 10.21. Finally, she models reading the text aloud and filling in the question on the one side and the answer on the other side of the question-and-answer graphic organizer until the text reading is complete.

In the second and third lessons, the teacher perhaps shares the explaining of question-and-answer expository text structure, thinking aloud, selecting of the appropriate graphic organizer, and representing the elements of question-and-answer expository text structure in the graphic organizer with the children. Finally, in the fourth lesson, the students do most of the explaining, thinking aloud, selecting, and representing the elements of question-and-answer expository text structure in the graphic organizer. This teaches children the process of determining and using text structure and finding an appropriate graphic organizer to represent the text structure and provides a structure for organizing and remembering important information from reading expository texts.

## Summary Writing: Focusing on the Significant in Text

### Purpose

The purpose of writing a summary is to extract main or important ideas from a reading selection. Good readers are constantly stopping themselves during reading to monitor or think about their comprehension and to take corrective action when necessary. Summaries are important because they help form memory structures that readers can use to select and store relevant main ideas and details from their reading. Some readers do not spontaneously summarize their reading and, as a result, have poor understanding and recall of what they read (Brown, Day, & Jones, 1983).

### Materials

- An expository trade book, basal selection, or content-area textbook selection
- A chart displaying the rules for summary writing (see example, based on the work of Hare and Borchordt, 1984, in Figure 10.22)
- Overhead projector and transparency

### Procedure

Begin by distributing copies of the expository trade book or basal or textbook selections to be read by the group. Have the students silently read the first few passages. Next, on an overhead transparency, model for the children how you would use the five summary rules in Figure 10.22 to write a summary. After modeling how you would write a summary, instruct the children to finish reading the entire chapter or passage. Divide the chalkboard into four sections relating to the topic. For example, if you are learning about an animal (say, alligators), your subcategories may be "Description," "Food," "Home," and "Interesting Facts." As the groups read, students can write facts on the chalkboard under the different category headings.

Next, organize students into cooperative learning groups, or teams of five, to work on writing a summary together. Each student is assigned to take charge of one of the five sum-

their learning in some interesting ways. The direct-instruction components of CORI have also been shown to be effective with low-achieving students in grades 3 and 5 (Guthrie et al., 1996; Swafford & Bryan, 2000). CORI provides a sound basic platform for teaching and learning in the content areas that can be modified to suit your instructional goals.

## Materials

- Subject-linked textbooks
- Materials for the writing process
- Computer with Internet access
- Other research tools usually available in the school library or media center

## Procedure

Because it is a little difficult to generalize a specific list of materials for CORI, as that depends heavily on the subject area, content to be studied, and available texts for instruction, which you will see as we move through our description, the preceding list of materials may have to be adjusted in different cases.

The CORI framework includes the following: real-world observations, conceptual themes, self-directed learning, explicit instruction on strategies, peer collaboration, and self-expression of learning. The instructional model can be described as a four-part process.

- *Part I: Observe and personalize.* Students are led through hands-on experiences designed to activate their prior knowledge relating to the new topic and to motivate them to want to know more. After the hands-on experiences, the teacher leads students through a discussion about what they observed and helps them to form theories and generate questions for further study. The teacher-led discussion can help students move from concrete-only thinking into the more sophisticated forms of abstract thinking.

- *Part II: Search and retrieve.* In this stage, the teacher introduces search strategies for finding answers to students' questions. For each search strategy, the teacher provides a clear description, models using the strategy, and leads practice sessions (guided practice) and collaborative group work. Strategies to be learned include goal setting (what they want to learn), categorizing (learning how information is organized and presented in books and learning how to find information in the library or on the Internet), extracting (taking notes, summarizing, and paraphrasing information), and abstracting (forming generalizations).

- *Part III: Comprehend and integrate.* To help students better understand the new information they have gathered in Part II, the teacher models and the students discuss the strategies of comprehension monitoring (metacognition), developing images or graphics, rereading to clarify, and modifying reading rate to match purpose and varying text types. Identification of central ideas and supporting details is also a priority in this stage of instruction. Guthrie et al. (1996) recommend the use of idea circles (student-led small-group discussions) and group self-monitoring as ways to transfer learning responsibility to students, leading to more productive discussions. This is especially useful when they discover information that is conflicting or that contradicts their earlier hypotheses.

- *Part IV: Communicate.* The communication phase of CORI focuses on students sharing what they have learned. They often communicate their new understandings through debates, discussions, or written reports. Some students prefer more creative expressions such as PowerPoint presentations, poetry, dramas, raps, songs, or graphic illustrations. As with the other phases of CORI, teacher support and modeling are critical in helping

---

**FIGURE 10.24**  Concept-Oriented Reading Instruction

**Part I: Observe and Personalize**

1. Hands-on experiences
2. Relate hands-on experience to prior experiences
3. Teacher-led discussion
4. Form theories
5. Generate questions for further study

**Part II: Search and Retrieve**

*Teacher introduces search strategies for finding answers to their questions . . .*

1. Goal setting (what they want to learn)
2. Categorizing (learning how information is organized and presented in books and how to find information in the library or on the Internet)
3. Extracting (taking notes, summarizing, and paraphrasing information)
4. Abstracting (forming generalizations)

**Part III: Comprehend and Integrate**

*Teacher modeling and students' discussions about . . .*

1. Comprehension monitoring (metacognition)
2. Developing images or graphics

3. Rereading to clarify
4. Modifying reading rate to match purpose and varying text types
5. Identification of central ideas and supporting details

**Part IV: Communication**

*Communication of new knowledge through such media as . . .*

Debates
Discussions
Written reports
Technology (e.g., Microsoft PowerPoint presentations)
Poetry
Dramas
Raps or songs
Graphic illustrations

---

students develop effective communication skills to present their new knowledge and strengthen their social development (Swafford & Bryan, 2000).

The elements of content-oriented reading instruction (CORI) are summarized in Figure 10.24.

# INCLUDING ALL STUDENTS

## Collaborative Strategic Reading (CSR)

### Purpose

CSR is an instructional framework designed to help students who struggle with learning disabilities that place them at risk for failing to understand concepts and information found in content texts and textbooks (Laing & Dole, 2006; Vaughn, Klingner, & Bryant, 2001). In CSR the teacher teaches four specific comprehension strategies students can use with all the informational and expository texts they read. The purpose of a CSR lesson is on developing routines and procedures with struggling students for understanding any expository text they read.

### Materials

- Four comprehension cards with picture icons

- An information text or a textbook chapter in a content area such as science or social studies
- Student CSR Reading Log
- Clunk Card with Fix-Ups

### Procedure

To begin, the teacher introduces CSR by teaching it to the whole class. Through modeling and think alouds, the teacher shows students how each of the four key comprehension strategies is used (Laing & Dole, 2006). Students are then grouped into cooperative learning groups in which they move through the use of four CSR cards, based on four key comprehension strategies: (1) Preview, (2) Monitoring, (3) Get the Gist, and (4) Wrap Up. When using the Preview card, students look for key features of the text such as headings, diagrams and insets, bolded words, and brainstorm what they already know about the topic. As students preview, they predict or ask questions about what they will learn when they read. Students can use learning logs to record their predictions, questions, and answers generated during the preview.

Next, when using the Monitoring card, students read a passage from the text looking for "clicks" and "clunks." They can use prompts or fix-up strategies shown on a "Clunk Card" for figuring out the meaning of the misunderstood word or concept (see Chapter 9). After reading a passage, students use the Get the Gist card to determine and record in their logs the most important ideas in the passage. The entire process is repeated with each passage of a text until the entire information text or content-area textbook chapter is completed.

A Wrap Up card is then used to help them generate a list of questions and answers that show they understand the most important information in the text. Eventually students can be divided into small mixed-ability groups to practice collaboratively using the four comprehension strategies during reading. The teachers will monitor the CSR groups and provide ongoing assistance as needed.

## SELECTED REFERENCES

Alexander, P. A., & Jetton, T. L. (2000). Learning from text: A multidimensional and developmental perspective. In M. L. Kamil, P. B. Mosenthal, P. D. Pearson, & R. Barr (Eds.), *Handbook of reading research* (Vol. III, pp. 285–310). Mahwah, NJ: Lawrence Erlbaum.

Alvermann, D. E. (1991). The discussion web: A graphic aide for learning across the curriculum. *The Reading Teacher, 45,* 92–99.

Alvermann, D. E., & Moore, D. W. (1991). Secondary school reading. In R. Barr, M. L. Kamil, P. B. Mosenthal, & P. D. Pearson (Eds.), *Handbook of reading research, Vol. 2* (pp. 951–983). White Plains, NY: Longman.

Anderson, V. (1991). *A teacher development project in transactional strategy instruction for severely reading disabled adolescents.* Paper presented at the National Reading Conference annual meeting. Palm Springs, CA.

Armbruster, B., & Anderson, T. (1981). *Content area textbooks* (Reading Education Report No. 23). Urbana–Champaign: University of Illinois, Center for the Study of Reading.

Armbruster, B. B., Anderson, T. H., & Ostertag, J. (1987). Does text structure/summarization instruction facilitate learning from expository text? *Reading Research Quarterly, 22*(3), 331–346.

Bartlett, B. J. (1978). *Top-level structure as an organizational strategy for recall of classroom text.* Unpublished doctoral dissertation, Arizona State University, Tempe.

Beaver, J. (1997). *Developmental Reading Assessment (DRA).* New York: Pearson Learning Group.

Beck, I. L., & McKeown, M. G. (1981). Developing questions that promote comprehension: The story map. *Language Arts, 58,* 913–918.

Beck, I. L., McKeown, M. G., Hamilton, R., & Kucan, L. (1997). *Questioning the author: An approach for enhancing student engagement with text.* Newark, DE: International Reading Association.

Beck, I. L., Omanson, R. C., & McKeown, M. G. (1982). An instructional redesign of reading lessons: Effects on comprehension. *Reading Research Quarterly, 17,* 462–481.

Biddulph, F., & Biddulph, J. (1992). *How do spiders live?* Bothell, WA: The Wright Group.

Boyle, J. R. (1996). The effects of cognitive mapping strategy on the literal and inferential comprehension of students with mild disabilities. *Learning Disability Quarterly, 19*(3), 86–98.

Bromley, K. (1993). *Webbing with literature: Creating story maps with children's books* (2nd ed.). Boston: Allyn & Bacon.

Brown, A. L., Day, J. D., & Jones, R. S. (1983). The development of plans for summarzing texts. *Child Development, 54,* 968–979.

Brown, H., & Cambourne, B. (1987). *Read and retell.* Portsmouth, NH: Heinemann Educational Books.

Casteel, C. A. (1990). Effects of chunked text materials on reading comprehension of high and low ability readers. *Reading Improvement, 27,* 269–275.

Chard, S. (1998). *The project approach: Making curriculum come alive.* New York: Scholastic.

Cooter, R. B. (2009). *A fidelity of implementation continuum for Question-Answer Relationships.* Louisville, KY: Memphis Striving Readers Project. Unpublished manuscript.

Cutting, B., & Cutting, J. (2002). *Is it a fish?—Sunshine Science Series.* Bothell, WA: Wright Group/McGraw-Hill.

Dickson, S. V., Simmons, D. C., & Kameenui, E. J. (1998a). Text organization: Instructional and curricular basics and implications. In D. C. Simmons & E. J. Kameenui (Eds.), *What reading research tells us about children with diverse learning needs: Bases and basics.* Mahwah, NJ: Lawrence Erlbaum.

Dickson, S. V., Simmons, D. C., & Kameenui, E. J. (1998b). Text organization: Research bases. In D. C. Simmons & E. J. Kameenui (Eds.), *What reading research tells us about children with diverse learning needs* (pp. 239–278). Mahwah, NJ: Lawrence Erlbaum.

Donovan, C. A., & Smolkin, L. B. (2002). Considering genre, context, and visual features in the selection of trade books for science instruction. *The Reading Teacher, 55*(6), 502–520.

Duke, N. K. (2000). 3.6 minutes per day: The scarcity of informational texts in first grade. *Reading Research Quarterly, 35*(2), 202–224.

Duke, N. K., & Bennett-Armistead, S. (2003). *Reading and writing informational text in the primary grades: Research-based practices.* New York: Scholastic.

Duke, N. K., Bennett-Armistead, S., & Roberts, E. M. (2002). Incorporating informational text in the primary grades. In C. M. Roller (Ed.), *Comprehensive reading instruction across the grade levels: A collection of papers from the 2001 Reading Research Conference* (pp. 41–54). Newark, DE: International Reading Association.

Durkin, D. (1978–1979). What classroom observations reveal about reading comprehension instruction. *Reading Research Quarterly, 12,* 481–538.

Farnan, N. (1996). Connecting adolescents and reading: Goals at the middle level. *Journal of Adolescent & Adult Literacy, 39*(6), 436–445.

Farnan, N., & Dahl, K. (2003). Children's writing: Research and practice. In J. Flood, D. Lapp, J. R. Squire, & J. M. Jensen (Eds.), *Handbook of research on teaching the English language arts* (pp. 993–1007). Mahwah, NJ: Lawrence Erlbaum.

Farr, R., Tulley, M. A., & Pritchard, R. (1989). Assessment instruments and techniques used by the content area teacher. In D. Lapp, J. Flood, & N. Farnan (Eds.), *Content area reading and learning* (pp. 346–356). Englewood Cliffs, NJ: Prentice Hall.

Fowler, G. L. (1982). Developing comprehension skills in primary students through the use of story frames. *The Reading Teacher, 36*(2), 176–179.

Gambrell, L. B., Pfeiffer, W., & Wilson, R. (1985). The effects of retelling upon reading comprehension and recall of text information. *Journal of Educational Research, 78,* 216–220.

Gordon, C. J., & Braun, C. (1983). Using story schema as an aid to reading and writing. *The Reading Teacher, 37*(2), 116–121.

Graesser, A., Golding, J. M., & Long, D. L. (1991). Narrative representation and comprehension. In R. Barr, M. L.

Kamil, P. Mosenthal, & P. D. Pearson (Eds.), *Handbook of reading research, Vol. 2.* (pp. 171–204). White Plains, NY: Longman.

Guthrie, J. T., Van Meter, P., McCann, A. D., Wigfield, A., Bennett, L., Poundstone, C., et al. (1996). Growth of literacy engagement: Changes in motivations and strategies during concept-oriented reading instruction. *Reading Research Quarterly, 31*(3), 306–332.

Hall, K. M., Sabey, B. L., & McClellan, M. (2005). Expository text comprehension: Helping primary-grade teachers use expository texts to full advantage. *Reading Psychology, 26,* 211–234.

Hare, V. C., & Borchordt, K. M. (1984). Direct instruction of summarization skills. *Reading Research Quarterly, 20*(1), 62–78.

Hiede, A., & Stilborne, L. (1999). *The teacher's complete and easy guide to the Internet.* New York: Teacher's College Press.

Hoffman, J. V. (1992). Critical reading/thinking across the curriculum: Using I-charts to support learning. *Language Arts, 69,* 121–127.

Irvin, J. L., & Connors, N. A. (1989). Reading instruction in middle level schools: Results of a U.S. survey. *Journal of Reading, 32,* 306–311.

Israel, S. E., & Duffy, G. G. (2009). *Handbook of research on reading comprehension.* New York: Routledge.

Jetton, T. L. (1994). Information-driven versus storydriven: What children remember when they are read informational stories. *Reading Psychology, 15,* 109–130.

Kletzien, S. B., & Dreher, M. J. (2004). *Informational text in K–3 classrooms: Helping children read and write.* Newark, DE: International Reading Association.

Krauss, R. (1945). *The carrot seed.* New York: HarperCollins Publishers.

Laing, L. A., & Dole, J. A. (2006). Help with teaching reading comprehension: Comprehension instructional frameworks. *The Reading Teacher, 59*(8), 742–753.

Leal, D. J. (1992). The nature of talk about three types of text during peer group discussions. *Journal of Reading Behavior, 24,* 313–338.

Leal, D. J. (1993). Storybooks, information books, and informational storybooks: An explication of the ambiguous grey genre. *The New Advocate, 6,* 61–70.

Leslie, L., & Caldwell, J. (2001). *Qualitative reading inventory—3.* New York: Longman.

Leslie, L., & Caldwell, J. (2009). Formal and informal measures of reading comprehension. In S. E. Israel and G. G. Duffy (Eds.), *Handbook of research on reading comprehension* (pp. 103–127). New York: Routledge.

Mandler, J. M., & Johnson, N. S. (1977). Remembrance of things parsed: Story structure and recall. *Cognitive Psychology, 9,* 111–151.

Marcell, B. (2007). Traffic light reading: Fostering the independent usage of comprehension strategies with information text. *The Reading Teacher, 60*(8), 778–781.

Maria, K., & Junge, K. (1994). A comparison of fifth graders' comprehension and retention of scientific information using a science textbook and an information storybook. In C. K. Kinzer & D. J. Leu (Eds.), *Multidimensional aspects of literacy research, theory, and practice. 43rd Yearbook of the National Reading Conference* (pp. 146–152). Chicago: National Reading Conference.

McGee, L. M. (1982). Awareness of text structure: Effects on children's recall of expository text. *Reading Research Quarterly, 17*(4), 581–590.

McKeown, M. G., Beck, I. L., & Worthy, M. J. (1993). Grappling with text ideas: Questioning the author. *The Reading Teacher, 46,* 560–566.

McNamara, D. S. (2007). *Reading comprehension strategies: Theories, interventions, and technologies.* Mahwah, NJ: Lawrence Erlbaum.

Merkley, D. M., & Jeffries, D. (2001). Guidelines for implementing a graphic organizer. *The Reading Teacher, 54*(4), 350–357.

Meyer, B. J. F. (1975). *The organization of prose and its effects on memory.* Amsterdam: North-Holland.

Meyer, B. J. F., Brandt, D. M., & Bluth, G. J. (1980). Use of top-level structure in text: Key for reading comprehension of ninth-grade students. *Reading Research Quarterly, 16,* 72–103.

Montague, M., Maddux, C. D., & Dereshiwsky, M. I. (1990). Story grammar and comprehension and production of narrative prose by students with learning disabilities. *Journal of Learning Disabilities, 23,* 190–197.

Morrow, L. M. (1985). Retelling stories: A strategy for improving children's comprehension, concept of story structure and oral language complexity. *Elementary School Journal, 85,* 647–661.

Morrow, L. M. (2005). *Literacy development in the early years: Helping children read and write* (5th ed.). Boston: Allyn & Bacon.

Morrow, L. M., Gambrell, L. B., Kapinus, B., Koskinen, P. S., Marshall, N., & Mitchell, J. N. (1986). Retelling: A strategy for reading instruction and assessment. In J. A. Niles & R. V. Lalik (Eds.), *Solving problems in literacy: Learners, teachers and researchers: Thirty-fifth yearbook of the National Reading Conference* (pp. 73–80). Rochester, NY: National Reading Conference.

Moss, B. (1997). A qualitative assessment of first graders' retelling of expository text. *Reading Research and Instruction, 37*(1), 1–13.

Moss, B., & Newton, E. (2002). An examination of the informational text genre in basal readers. *Reading Psychology: An International Quarterly, 23*(1), 1–14.

National Institute of Child Health and Human Development. (2000). *Report of the National Reading Panel: Teaching children to read, an evidence-based assessment of the scientific research literature on reading and its implications for reading instruction.* Washington, DC: U.S. Government Printing Office.

Nichols, J. (1980). Using paragraph frames to help remedial high school students with written assignments. *Journal of Reading, 24,* 228–231.

Noyce, R. M., & Christie, J. F. (1989). *Integrating reading and writing instruction.* Boston: Allyn & Bacon.

Pappas, C. C., Kiefer, B. Z., & Levstik, L. S. (1999). *An integrated language perspective in the elementary school: An action approach* (3rd ed.). White Plains, NY: Longman.

Pardo, L. S. (2004). What every teacher needs to know about comprehension. *The Reading Teacher, 58*(3), 272–280.

Pearson, P. D., & Duke, N. K. (2002). Comprehension instruction in the primary grades. In C. Collins-Block & M. Pressley (Eds.), *Comprehension instruction: Research-based best practices,* (pp. 247–258). New York: Guilford Press.

Pressley, M. (2000). What should comprehension instruction be the instruction of? In M. L. Kamil, P. B. Mosenthal, P. D. Pearson, & R. Barr (Eds.), *Handbook of reading research* (Vol. 3, pp. 545–561). Mahwah, NJ: Lawrence Erlbaum.

Pressley, M. (2002). Comprehension strategies instruction: A turn-of-the-century status report. In C. Collins-Block & M. Pressley (Eds.), *Comprehension instruction: Research-based best practices* (pp. 11–27). New York: Guilford Press.

RAND Reading Study Group. (2002). *Reading for understanding: Toward an R&D program in reading comprehension.* Santa Monica, CA: Science and Technology Policy Institute, RAND Education.

Randall, S. N. (1996). Information charts: A strategy for organizing student research. *Journal of Adolescent & Adult Literacy, 39*(7), 536–542.

Raphael, T. E. (1982). Question-answering strategies for children. *The Reading Teacher, 36,* 186–191.

Raphael, T. E. (1986). Teaching question answer relationships, revisited. *The Reading Teacher, 39*(6), 516–523.

Raphael, T. E., & Pearson, P. D. (1982). *The effect of metacognitive training on children's question answering behaviors.* Urbana, IL: Center for the Study of Reading. (ERIC Document Reproduction Service No. ED215315).

Rathvon, N. (2004). *Early reading assessment: A practitioner's handbook.* New York: Guilford Press.

Read, S., Reutzel, D. R., & Fawson, P. C. (2008). Do you want to know what I learned? Using information trade books as models to teach text structure. *Early Childhood Education Journal, 36,* 213–219.

Readence, J. E., Bean, T. W., & Baldwin, R. S. (1992). *Content area reading: An integrated approach* (4th ed.). Dubuque, IA: Kendall/Hunt.

Reutzel, D. R. (1983). C6: A model for teaching arithmetic story problem solving. *The Reading Teacher, 37*(1), 38–43.

Reutzel, D. R. (1985). Story maps improve comprehension. *The Reading Teacher, 38*(4), 400–405.

Reutzel, D. R. (1986). Clozing in on comprehension: The cloze story map. *The Reading Teacher, 39*(6), 524–529.

Reutzel, D. R., & Cooter, R. B. (2004). *Teaching children to read: Putting the pieces together* (4th ed.). Upper Saddle River, NJ: Merrill/Prentice Hall.

Reutzel, D. R., & Fawson, P. C. (1989). Using a literature webbing strategy lesson with predictable books. *The Reading Teacher, 43,* 208–215.

Reutzel, D. R., & Fawson, P. C. (1991). Literature webbing predictable books: A prediction strategy that helps below-average, first-grade readers. *Reading Research and Instruction, 30*(4), 20–30.

Ring, S. (2003). *Bridges.* Boston: Newbridge.

Romine, B. G., McKenna, M. C., & Robinson, R. D. (1996). Reading coursework requirements for middle and high school content area teachers: A U.S. survey. *Journal of Adolescent & Adult Literacy, 40*(3), 194–198.

Sadow, M. W. (1982). The use of story grammar in the design of questions. *The Reading Teacher, 35,* 518–523.

Sanders, T. J. M., & Schilperoord, J. (2006). Text structure as a window on the cognition of writing: How text analysis provide insights in writing products and writing processes. In C. A. MacArthur, S. Graham, & J. Fitzgerald (Eds.), *Handbook of writing research* (pp. 386–402). New York: Guilford Press.

Sandora, C., Beck, I. L., & McKeown, M. G. (1999). A comparison of two discussion strategies on students' comprehension and interpretation of complex literature. *Reading Psychology, 20*(3), 177–212.

Schunk, D. H., & Zimmerman, B. J. (1997). Developing self-efficacious readers and writers: The role of social and self-regulatory processes. In J. T. Guthrie and A. Wigfield (Eds.), *Reading engagement: Motivating readers through integrated instruction* (pp. 34–50). Newark, DE: International Reading Association.

Seidenberg, P. L. (1989). Relating text-processing research to reading and writing instruction for learning disabled students. *Learning Disabilities Focus, 5*(1), 4–12.

Simmons, D., & Kameenui, E. (1998). *What reading research tells us about children with diverse learning needs* (pp. 239–278). Mahwah, NJ: Lawrence Erlbaum.

Simpson, M. (1996). Conducting reality checks to improve students' strategic learning. *Journal of Adolescent & Adult Literacy, 40*(2), 102–109.

Skurzynski, G. (1992). Up for discussion: Blended books. *School Library Journal, 38*(10), 46–47.

Stafford, J. (2004). *Name that shape!—Reading Power Works series.* Northborough, MA: Sundance.

Stahl, K. A. D. (2004). Proof, practice, and promise: Comprehension strategy instruction in the primary grades. *The Reading Teacher, 57*(7), 598–609.

Stahl, K. A. D. (2009). Assessing the comprehension of young children. In S. E. Israel and G. G. Duffy (Eds.), *Handbook of research on reading comprehension* (pp. 428–448). New York: Routledge.

Stein, N. L., & Glenn, C. G. (1979). An analysis of story comprehension in elementary schoolchildren. In R. O. Freedle (Ed.), *New directions in discourse processing* (pp. 53–120). Mahwah, NJ: Lawrence Erlbaum.

Swafford, J., & Bryan, J. K. (2000). Instructional strategies for promoting conceptual change: Supporting middle school students. *Reading & Writing Quarterly, 16*(2), 139–161.

Sweet, A. P., & Snow, C. E. (2003). *Rethinking reading comprehension.* New York: Guilford Press.

Taylor, B. M., Pearson, P. D., Clark, K. F., & Walpole, S. (1999). *Beating the odds in teaching all children to read* (CIERA Report No. 2-006). Ann Arbor, MI: Center for the Improvement of Early Reading Achievement.

Thorndyke, P. N. (1977). Cognitive structure in comprehension and memory of narrative discourse. *Cognitive Psychology, 9*(1), 77–110.

Van Allsburg, C. (1992). *The widow's broom.* Boston: Houghton Mifflin.

Vaughn, S., Klingner, J. K., & Bryant, D. P. (2001). Collaborative strategic reading as a means to enhance peer-mediated instruction for reading comprehension and content-area learning. *Remedial and Special Education, 22*(2), 66–75.

Watson, D., & Crowley, P. (1988). How can we implement a whole-language approach? In C. Weaver (Ed.), *Reading process and practice* (pp. 232–279). Portsmouth, NH: Heinemann Educational Books.

Wepner, S. B., Valmont, W. J., & Thurlow, R. (2000). *Linking literacy and technology: A guide for K–8 classrooms.* Newark, DE: International Reading Association.

Whaley, J. F. (1981). Readers' expectations for story structures. *Reading Research Quarterly, 17,* 90–114.

Williams, J. P. (2005). Instruction in reading comprehension for primary-grade students: A focus on text structure. *Journal of Special Education, 39*(1), 6–18.

Williams, J. P., Stafford, K. B., Lauer, K. D., Hall, K. M., & Pollini, S. (2009). Embedding reading comprehension training in content-area instruction. *Journal of Educational Psychology, 101*(1), 1–20.

Zabrucky, K., & Ratner, H. H. (1992). Effects of passage type on comprehension monitoring and recall in good and poor readers. *Journal of Reading Behavior, 24,* 373–391.

**The Power of Classroom Practice**
www.myeducationlab.com

Now go to Topic 9: "Reading Comprehension" and Topic 11: "Reading Difficulties and Intervention Strategies" in the MyEducationLab (www.myeducationlab.com) for your course, where you can:

- Find learning outcomes for "Reading Comprehension" and "Reading Difficulties and Intervention Strategies," along with the national standards that connect to these outcomes.
- Complete the tasks in the Assignments and Activities to help you more deeply understand the chapter content.
- Apply and practice your understanding of the core teaching skills identified in the chapter with the Building Teaching Skills and Dispositions learning units.

# 11

# Academic Literacy and New Literacy Studies

*J*ames McLeary, the great-grandfather of Jon McLeary in my sixth-grade class, shared with us his experiences in the early 20th century as an immigrant. He came to the United States an ocean of time ago from his homeland of Ireland at the age of seventeen. Mr. McLeary described his feelings when seeing the Statue of Liberty for the first time with a clarity that made you feel you were there. Later, Mr. McLeary spoke of his journey to Chicago and his first jobs as a roofer, carpenter, and later as a policeman wearing the legendary checkered cap. Tears escaped from his eyes and his voice trembled just a bit when he spoke of meeting Kathleen, his future wife of 53 years. The room was mesmerized.

The next day, I said to my class, "Mr. McLeary's story was a wonderful beginning to our study of world history. His testimony was what is sometimes called a 'primary source' or information that comes to us first-hand. Over the next several weeks we will learn many interesting and important things about Ireland. We'll learn something about Ireland's history, its people today, and its conflicts. We will also take a closer look at the influences Irish Americans have had on the United States. Perhaps the most important things we will learn about Ireland is how the story of Irish immigrants is so much like the stories of immigrants from other countries in the Americas, Africa, Asia, and Europe.

"Folks, we are also going to learn some very cool ways to gather information and write about our world. You will discover along the way some valuable research tools that will save you a lot of time and make learning much easier. In fact, these are tools you can use for the rest of your lives—in high school, college, and in your adult careers. Best of all, these research tools are downright fun! Let's get started."

As students become fluent readers, they apply literacy skills to learn more about the world in which they live. In this chapter, we describe ways students can be helped to read and understand core subject-area texts (social studies, science, mathematics, English/language arts) more effectively, often referred to as *academic literacy*. We will also discuss ideas from the emerging field of new literacy studies.

# $\mathcal{B}$ACKGROUND BRIEFING FOR TEACHERS

## Academic Literacy

Go to the Assignments and Activities section of Topic 9: "Reading Comprehension" in the MyEducationLab for your course and complete the activity entitled "Content Area Literacy." As you watch the video and answer the accompanying questions, list some of the key elements/skills of content area reading that differ from reading a storybook.

**Academic literacy,** sometimes also referred to as **content-area reading,** has to do with applying literacy skills and strategies to acquire content knowledge in core subject areas (i.e., mathematics, science, social studies, English/language arts). A number of specialized academic literacy skills may be used by students to comprehend and interact around texts that are detached from many students' experiences (Lewis, 2007). Research has demonstrated that expanding academic literacy skills, such as in the areas of content vocabulary knowledge and enhanced text comprehension, can lead to improvements in overall student achievement in school (Apthorp & Clark, 2007; Lewis, 2007).

In earlier times, academic literacy was seen as central to becoming an "educated" and "intelligent" person, not to mention as "a significant gateway to economic success and socio-political power" in society (Gee, 2004, p. 91). While one can certainly argue that literacy is the gateway to social justice (Cooter, 2006), any current definition of academic literacy must include skills and strategies applied to each content subject area and which considers the differing demands of each subject's texts—one cannot read a mathematics story problem in the same way or with the same skill set as one uses when reading a novel. This is why Henderson and Hirst (2007) explain that academic literacy must be

> considered in the plural—as academic literacies—and these literacies [should be] viewed as sets of practice . . . in which students learn to participate and make meaning within an academic context. These ways of making meaning are valued by the cultures, traditions or academic disciplines with which they are associated. The more specialised the academic disciplines become, the more specialised the "ways with words" (see Heath, 1986). In this way, academic disciplines are recognised not only by specialised vocabularies, concepts and knowledges, but also by accepted and valued patterns of meaning-making activity, including genres, rhetorical structures, argument formulations and narrative devices (Rex & McEachen, 1999). As students participate in these disciplines, they learn specific ways of making meaning as well as contesting meaning. Thus, there are no singular, unified practices that can be said to count always and only as academic literacy. (p. 26)

Academic literacy strategies generally center on improving students' academic vocabularies (see "Academic Word Walls" in Chapter 8, for example), use of comprehension strategies in content-area texts, expository writing, reading fluency in varied genres of academic texts, and the strategic use of research/study skills. In this chapter we share selected academic literacy strategies found to be particularly useful in science, English/language arts, social studies, and mathematics.

## Research/Study Skills

Readence, Bean, and Baldwin (2000) state that the teaching of study strategies, which includes research and reference skills, is crucial in helping students achieve academic literacy. **Research**

**and reference skills** include such diverse areas as note taking, mapping known and unknown information areas, choosing sources for obtaining information (e.g., Internet search engines, reference materials, expert interviews, etc.), and searching card catalogs electronically and manually. Some of the key strategies offered in this chapter help students to choose areas to research, organize new information, and learn efficient ways to locate facts.

Much of what is contained in this chapter relates ways of helping students read and understand core subject-area materials more effectively, monitor the status of their learning, and strategically select and apply appropriate research and reference skills. Learning in the first part of the 20th century and earlier was basically limited to life experience and books, but with the advent of computers and information technologies the term *literacy* necessarily must be expanded. This is the subject of our next briefing.

## New Literacy Studies

**New literacy studies** (NLS) has been defined as "the skills, strategies, and insights necessary to successfully exploit the rapidly changing information and communication technologies that continuously emerge in our world" (Leu, 2002, p. 310). Thus, NLS has to do with how literacy practices are linked to people's lives, identities, and social affiliations (Compton-Lilly, in press).

A great deal of NLS research focuses on children's interactions with technological texts, viewing these interactions as meaningful and purposeful (Compton-Lilly, in press). Most notable is the ongoing work of the New Literacies Research Team (NLRT) at the University of Connecticut and Clemson University. Their comprehensive website (www.newliteracies.uconn.edu) includes video cases, a team blog, downloadable articles, and many other valuable resources, making it a great starting place for teachers interested in learning more about new literacies.

There is one caveat we feel we must mention. Because NLS is relatively new and in a constant state of flux, valid or reliable assessments are difficult to find and the instructional strategies have yet to yield convergent evidence-based findings as we have tried to use in the rest of the book. Nevertheless, because NLS is an important, timely issue in literacy instruction, we will include assessments and instructional strategies that are currently available as part of our goal of providing comprehensive coverage of the topic of reading assessment and instruction.

# *A*CADEMIC LITERACY ASSESSMENT

Valid and reliable assessments to help teachers determine which research and reference skills students possess are difficult to find and still largely "under development" at this time by teachers and researchers. However, there are some informal assessment strategies available that help teachers survey what students know about a topic of study and the kinds of materials that students may be using in their research. We have included in this next section the assessment strategies found to be useful by many teachers. When explicitly taught, these strategies help students recognize their own needs—an important motivational teaching practice.

## Research Logs

### Purpose

A **research log** is effective for recording and monitoring the kinds of research methods and materials students use. Research logs are a simple listing of materials used over time in the

---

**FIGURE 11.1**   Research Log

Name: _____

Subject: _____ Period: _____ Homeroom: _____

| Date | Assignment/ Topic | Materials Selected | Pages/ Programs Used | Notes |
|------|-------------------|--------------------|----------------------|-------|
|      |                   |                    |                      |       |
|      |                   |                    |                      |       |
|      |                   |                    |                      |       |
|      |                   |                    |                      |       |
|      |                   |                    |                      |       |

---

content classroom to complete research projects. By periodically reviewing research logs, teachers can survey patterns of reading and study behavior in their classrooms and plan instruction to help fill in gaps in students' knowledge about research resources.

### Materials

- Copies of a structured research log form, such as the simple format presented in Figure 11.1

### Procedure

First develop a brief explicit lesson in which you model how to use a research log while completing a class assignment. Using a recent assignment as an example will save time and will help students transfer the instruction to their own use later on. Once you have modeled how to record information on the log form, distribute copies of the research log to the students. If possible, introduce the research log just prior to beginning a new unit of study and provide a folder in which the logs may be kept. Check the logs at the midpoint of the unit of study to determine which research materials are being used and then offer brief follow-up explicit lessons on research skills as needed. Review the logs again at the conclusion of the unit to determine student progress and for future lesson planning.

## Self-Rating Scales

### Purpose

It is often true that no one knows better than the reader how he or she is doing in reading. This is especially true when it comes to the ability to use research and reference materials in the library stacks. A teacher carrying out an assessment agenda should never overlook the obvious—ask what the student is good at doing! Although this may be best achieved in a one-on-one discussion setting, large class sizes frequently make this impractical. A good alternative to one-on-one interviews for older elementary and middle school children is a student **self-rating scale.** In applying this strategy, students complete a questionnaire that is custom-tailored to obtain specific information about the reader's skills with research and reference tools—from the reader's point of view.

### Materials

- A self-constructed rating scale that conforms to the research and reference skills you want each of your students to possess (see Figure 11.2 for an example)

### Procedure

We prefer to use self-rating scales within the context of an actual unit of study about to commence or with a unit just completed. For example, let us assume that you are about to begin a new unit of study pertaining to the evolution of surgery in this country from 1900 to the present. After a brief warm-up conversation with the students about medicine and surgery, distribute the self-rating scale you have developed. Once the students have completed their self-rating scales, collect and analyze the scales to determine in a cursory way the skills the students feel that they possess. (*Note:* This is only a survey of student perceptions. You will also need to collect further observations as the students begin to actually use library resources to complete assignments.)

## Prereading Plan (PreP)

### Purpose

This three-stage strategy by Langer (1981) helps teachers assess and activate the prior knowledge of students about a topic of study. This assessment and instruction activity may be used with a whole class or small groups. The first step uses a question to determine any associations

---

**FIGURE 11.2**    Self-Rating Scale

**Self-Rating Scale: Researching the "Evolution of Surgery"**

Name: _____    Date: _____

**Directions:** Answer the following questions as they pertain to how you will find out more about the ways surgery has improved in the United States in the last 100 years.

The first three things I will do to find out more about how surgery has improved in the United States when I enter the library is:
1.
2.
3.

Three things I know about entries (cards) in the card catalog in the library are:
1.
2.
3.

Three sources of information I can use in this study of surgery are:
1.
2.
3.

I can organize the information and data I find by:

_____

_____

I feel I could use some help in understanding how to use library resources or research skills in these areas (check all that apply):

_____    using the card catalog
_____    taking notes
_____    finding periodicals from a particular time period or topic
_____    finding books that relate to our unit on surgery
_____    using the Internet to find information
_____    organizing information to write a report
_____    interviewing experts
_____    knowing where to begin my research
_____    locating information quickly in a book

students might have with a topic, concept, or term to be studied. The second step asks students to review and interpret their first impressions. The final step has students work with the teacher to identify existing gaps in their knowledge to help guide their research into the topic.

### Materials

- Writing supplies
- Large pictures or other artifacts that relate to the topic of study to help jog students' memories in the first phase

### Procedure

As noted, the first step is to ask students what they know about the topic to be studied. These initial associations provide insights into how much prior knowledge exists in the class and helps students to begin building concept-related associations about the topic (Cooter & Flynt, 1996). For example, in teaching a lesson about the civil rights movement of the 1960s, you might start off by asking your class, "What do you think of when you hear the words 'civil rights'?" Showing pictures from the 1950s and 1960s of lunch counter "sit-ins," the Little Rock, Arkansas, school desegregation incident, or of Rosa Parks and Dr. Martin Luther King Jr. could be quite helpful in stimulating initial discussion. After recording students' first associations, the next step is to have students think about or reflect on their initial associations. During this reflection stage your goal is to have students discuss and explain why the associations they had about the topic came to mind—"What made you think of . . . ?" This interactive stage further taps prior knowledge, builds a common network of ideas about the topic, and facilitates a student-centered discussion.

The last stage of PreP is called reformulation of knowledge, in which your goal is to have students recognize and define what they know about the topic before they begin research to learn more about it. We find that creating an outline or concept web about the topic helps many students see graphically what they already know, create categories for known information, and provoke questions about what must still be learned through the research process.

## Semantic Maps

### Purpose

Another useful strategy to activate students' prior knowledge of a topic and lead them to preview text material via student-centered discussion is the **semantic map.** Based on schema theory, semantic maps are essentially "road maps" of what is known by students, with clusters of related information noted. Semantic maps can help students better understand metacognitively what is known and not known, as well as the research sources that can be employed to help find information. Because semantic maps depict known information in precisely the same way the brain stores information, they are inherently logical for students and can provide valuable insights for teachers.

### Materials

- A large chart or tablet on an easel and colored markers to illustrate the semantic map (alternatively, an overhead projector, blank transparencies, and markers)

### Procedure

The teacher begins by writing the topic on the chart or transparency. Similar to the PreP procedure discussed earlier, students are then asked to volunteer any information they associate with the identified topic. As the students offer their associations the teacher lists them on the chart or transparency. Next the teacher asks students to examine all headings, subheadings, and visuals in a textbook selection to be used as part of the introduction to gather more information. Students may do this work independently or with a partner. The new information is then added to the semantic map, after which students are asked to read the textbook selection carefully to provoke more discussion and to find more relevant information that can be added to the semantic map. A postreading discussion centers on the various questions that remain to be answered more completely and research sources that could be used in answering the questions. In Figure 11.3 we illustrate a typical semantic map created by students with teacher assistance regarding the civil rights movement topic mentioned earlier in the chapter. Note that a product that grew out of the semantic map's construction was a listing of research sources available for locating needed information.

# NEW LITERACY STUDIES ASSESSMENTS

Although new literacy studies (NLS) is somewhat tentative in terms of evidence-based research, some important early work has been done regarding student assessment (e.g., Leu, 2002; Leu et al., 2008; Mokhtari, Kymes & Edwards, 2008). In this section we review NLS assessment strategies that have demonstrated good validity and reliability, particularly on the use of technology to assess online reading comprehension (Leu et al., 2008). The following selected NLS assessment strategies are presented for your consideration. For more information and examples go to the NLS website at www.newliteracies.uconn.edu.

## Student Internet Use Survey and Teacher Checklist

### Purpose

The purpose of the student Internet use survey is to provide teachers with a greater understanding of what students know and can do using the Internet and their comprehension of what they read from online sources. Leu and colleagues (2008, pp. 10–11) have developed computer-based assessment tools that determine "(a) the processes students use (or don't use) and (b) the understandings (or misconceptions) students may have about how best to compose task-related online questions, and use a range of online contexts (e.g., search engines, informational websites, interactive images, email, instant message, and/or blogs) to locate, critically evaluate, synthesize, and communicate their answers to others." In this section we offer as examples excerpts from materials available online.

### Materials

- A student Internet use survey (see example in Figure 11.4)
- A teacher's checklist (such as shown in Figure 11.5 on p. 379)

### Procedure

To produce a student Internet use survey, we recommend you download from the Internet (www.newliteracies.uconn.edu/iesproject/documents.html) the document titled "Final Survey Items." This is a copy of the protocol used by researchers in the Teaching Internet Comprehension Strategies to Adolescents (TICA) project (Leu et al., 2008). You can administer this survey in hard copy form to students in grades 3 to 8 without much difficulty, or one-on-one with younger students or those with learning challenges. In Figure 11.5 we present checklists

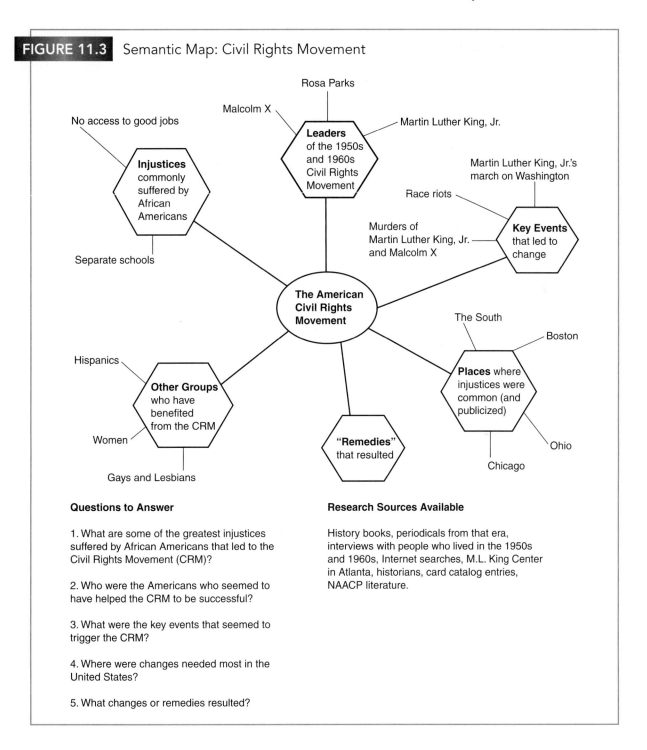

**FIGURE 11.3**    Semantic Map: Civil Rights Movement

**Questions to Answer**

1. What are some of the greatest injustices suffered by African Americans that led to the Civil Rights Movement (CRM)?

2. Who were the Americans who seemed to have helped the CRM to be successful?

3. What were the key events that seemed to trigger the CRM?

4. Where were changes needed most in the United States?

5. What changes or remedies resulted?

**Research Sources Available**

History books, periodicals from that era, interviews with people who lived in the 1950s and 1960s, Internet searches, M.L. King Center in Atlanta, historians, card catalog entries, NAACP literature.

for teachers developed by TICA as formative assessments to aid in future planning for greater student use of technology. The checklists are also available at the new literacies website, in the PDF download of the article by Leu, Coiro, Castek, Hartman, Henry, and Reinking (2008) titled, "Research on instruction and assessment in the new literacies of online reading comprehension."

---

| FIGURE 11.4 | Sample Student Internet Use Survey Items |

**This is how often I have used each of the following on the Internet:**

|  | Never heard of | Heard of but never used | Have used at least once | Have used often |
|---|---|---|---|---|
| Google | O | O | O | O |
| Yahoo! Kids | O | O | O | O |
| Ask Kids | O | O | O | O |
| Dogpile | O | O | O | O |
| Yahoo! | O | O | O | O |
| Altavista | O | O | O | O |

**This is how often I use the Internet to do the following *outside school*:**

|  | Never | Less than 1 time a week | One time a week | A few times a week | One time a day | Several times a day |
|---|---|---|---|---|---|---|
| Surf or browse just for fun | O | O | O | O | O | O |
| Search for specific information | O | O | O | O | O | O |
| Read Web pages | O | O | O | O | O | O |
| Bookmark Web pages | O | O | O | O | O | O |
| Design or publish Web pages | O | O | O | O | O | O |
| Tag objects or Web pages | O | O | O | O | O | O |
| Buy things | O | O | O | O | O | O |
| Play online games | O | O | O | O | O | O |
| Read or post to Wikipedia | O | O | O | O | O | O |

*Source:* The Teaching Internet Comprehension to Adolescents (TICA) Research Project (www.newliteracies.uconn.edu/iesproject). Reprinted with permission.

## Connecting Assessment Findings to Teaching Strategies

Before moving on to specific teaching strategies, we provide an If-Then chart connecting assessment findings to intervention and strategy choices (see Figure 11.6). Teaching strategies described in the next section are listed across the top of the chart, and potential instructional areas are listed vertically in the left-hand column.

# TEACHING ACADEMIC LITERACY SKILLS

Teaching students how to become effective researchers of knowledge is paramount if they are to become independent learners in later years. Thus, we better be good at setting up these kinds of learning experiences! Susan De la Paz (1999; Swanson & De la Paz, 1998) developed an effective process for teaching students the kinds of research and reference skills we

| **FIGURE 11.5** | Teacher Checklists of Student Abilities in Internet Use and Online Comprehension |
| --- | --- |

### TICA Basic Skills (Phase One) Checklist

Most of the students and all of the groups in my class know how to:

**Computer Basics**                                                                  Comment

❐ Turn a computer on/off                                              _____

❐ Use the mouse/track pad                                          _____

❐ Follow classroom and school rules for computer use      _____

❐ Open programs and files using icons and/or the Start Menu (PC)   _____

❐ Log on and log off from individual file space             _____

❐ Create/open a new folder/file                                   _____

❐ Launch a word processor                                         _____

❐ Open a word processing file                                     _____

❐ Type a short entry in a word processing file             _____

❐ Copy text                                                             _____

❐ Cut text                                                              _____

❐ Paste text                                                           _____

❐ Delete text                                                          _____

❐ Name a word processing file and save it                   _____

❐ Open a new window                                                _____

❐ Open a new tab                                                     _____

**Web Searching Basics**

❐ Locate and open a search engine                             _____

❐ Type key words in the correct location of a search engine   _____

❐ Type addresses in the address window                       _____

❐ Use the refresh button                                          _____

❐ Use the "BACK" and "FORWARD" buttons                  _____

❐ Use a search engine for simple key word searches       _____

**General Navigation Basics**

❐ Maximize/minimize windows                                    _____

❐ Open and quit applications                                     _____

❐ Toggle between windows                                        _____

**Email Basics**

❐ Locate and open an email program                          _____

❐ Attach documents to email messages                       _____

❐ Compose, edit and send email messages                   _____

❐ Receive and reply to messages                                _____

*(continued)*

**FIGURE 11.5** *Continued*

## TICA Phase II Checklist

Most of the students and all of the groups in my class know how to:

| UNDERSTAND AND DEVELOP QUESTIONS | LESSON EVIDENCE AND COMMENTS |
| --- | --- |

**Teacher-Generated Questions**

| | |
| --- | --- |
| ❏ Use strategies to ensure initial understanding of the question such as:<br>• rereading the question to make sure they understand it.<br>• paraphrasing the question.<br>• taking notes on the question.<br>• thinking about the needs of the person who asked the question. | |
| ❏ Use strategies to monitor an understanding of the question such as:<br>• knowing when to review the question.<br>• checking an answer in relation to the question to ensure it is complete. | |

**Student-Generated Questions**

| | |
| --- | --- |
| ❏ Determine what a useful initial question is, based on a variety of factors that include interest, audience, purpose, and the nature of the inquiry activity. | |
| ❏ Determine a clear topic and focus for questions to guide the search for information. | |
| ❏ Modify questions, when appropriate, using strategies such as the following:<br>• narrowing the focus of the question.<br>• expanding the focus of the question.<br>• developing a new or revised question that is more appropriate after gathering information. | |

| LOCATE INFORMATION | LESSON EVIDENCE AND COMMENTS |
| --- | --- |

**Locating Information by Using a Search Engine and Its Results Page**

| | |
| --- | --- |
| ❏ Locate at least one search engine. | |
| ❏ Use key words in a search window on a browser that has this or on a separate search engine. | |
| ❏ Use several of the following general search engine strategies during key word entry:<br>• topic and focus<br>• single and multiple key word entries<br>• phrases for key word entry | |
| ❏ Use several of the following more specialized search engine strategies during key word entry:<br>• quotation marks<br>• paraphrases and synonyms<br>• Boolean<br>• advanced search tool use | |
| ❏ Copy and paste keywords and phrases into the search engine window while searching for information. | |
| ❏ Read search engine results effectively to determine the most useful resource for a task using strategies such as: | |

| LOCATE INFORMATION | LESSON EVIDENCE AND COMMENTS |
|---|---|

**Locating Information by Using a Search Engine and Its Results Page** *(continued)*

- knowing which portions of a search results page are sponsored, containing commercially placed links, and which are not.
- skimming the main results before reading more narrowly.
- reading summaries carefully and inferring meaning in the search engine results page to determine the best possible site to visit.
- understanding the meaning of boldface terms in the results.
- understanding the meaning of URLs in search results (.com, .org, .edu, .net).
- knowing when the first item is not the best item for a question.
- monitoring the extent to which a search results page matches the information needs.
- knowing how to use the history pull down menu.

❏ Monitor the multiple aspects of search engine use and make appropriate revisions and changes throughout the process

❏ Select from a variety of search engine strategies to locate useful resources when an initial search is unsuccessful:
- Knows the use and meaning of the "Did you mean . . . ?" feature in Google.
- Adjusts search engine key words according to the results of a search.
  - narrows the search.
  - expands the search.
  - reads search results to discover the correct vocabulary and then use this more appropriate vocabulary in a new search.
- Shifts to another search engine.

❏ Bookmark a site and access it later.

❏ Use specialized search engines for images, videos, and other media sources.

**Locating Information within a Website**

❏ Quickly determine if a site is potentially useful and worth more careful reading.

❏ Read more carefully at a site to determine if the required information is located there.

❏ Predict information behind a link accurately to make efficient choices about where information is located.

❏ Use structural knowledge of a Web page to help locate information, including the use of directories.

❏ Recognize when you have left a site and know how to return back to the original site.

❏ Know how to open a second browser window to locate information without losing the initial Web page.

❏ Know how to use an internal search engine to locate information at a site.

❏ Monitor the reading of a Web page and know when it contains useful information and when it does not.

*(continued)*

**FIGURE 11.5** *Continued*

| CRITICALLY EVALUATE INFORMATION | LESSON EVIDENCE AND COMMENTS |
|---|---|
| **Bias and Stance** | |
| ❏ Identify, evaluate, and recognize that all websites have an agenda, perspective, or bias. | |
| ❏ Identify and evaluate bias, given a website with a clear bias. | |
| ❏ Identify and evaluate the author of a website whenever visiting an important new site. | |
| ❏ Use information about the author of a site to evaluate how information will be biased at that site. | |
| **Reliability** | |
| ❏ Investigate multiple sources to compare and contrast the reliability of information. | |
| ❏ Identify several markers that may affect reliability such as:<br>• Is this a commercial site?<br>• Is the author an authoritative source (e.g., professor, scientist, librarian, etc.)?<br>• Does the website have links that are broken?<br>• Does the information make sense?<br>• Does the author include links to other reliable websites?<br>• Does the website contain numerous typos?<br>• Does the URL provide any clues to reliability?<br>• Do the images or videos appear to be altered? | |
| ❏ Understand that Wikipedia is a reasonable, but imperfect, portal of information. | |
| ❏ Identify the general purpose of a website (entertainment, educational, commercial, persuasive, exchange of information, social, etc.). | |
| ❏ Identify the form of a website (e.g., blog, forum, advertisement, informational website, commercial website, government website, etc.) and use this information when considering reliability. | |

*Source:* Adapted from "Research on Instruction and Assessment in the New Literacies of Online Reading Comprehension" by D. J. Leu et al., 2008, in C. C. Block and S. Parris (Eds.), *Comprehension Instruction: Research-Based Best Practices* (2nd ed., pp. 21–24). Copyright © 2008 by Guilford Publications, Inc. Reproduced with permission of Guilford Publications, Inc. via Copyright Clearance Center.

FIGURE 11.6 If-Then Chart for Academic Literacy and New Literacy Studies

| "If" the student is ready to learn → "Then" try these teaching strategies | Written Academic Learning Summary (WALS) | Graphic Organizers | Note-Taking Strategies | Comprehension Windows Strategy (CWS) | Tech-to-Stretch | Classroom Blogging | Electronic Talking Books | e-Reading/ e-Responding | Wiki Writing | Internet Reciprocal Teaching |
|---|---|---|---|---|---|---|---|---|---|---|
| Academic vocabulary and concepts | + | + | * | + | + | * | + | + | + | + |
| Higher-order comprehension of core subjects | + | + | * | + | + | * | + | + | + | + |
| Organizational skills | + | + | – | + | + | – | – | * | * | + |
| Student-generated questions | + | – | * | * | + | + | * | * | * | + |
| Problem-solving skills | * | * | * | * | + | * | * | * | * | + |
| Research skills | + | * | + | + | + | * | + | * | * | + |
| Computer basics | – | – | – | – | * | – | – | * | * | + |
| Web searching | * | * | * | * | + | * | * | * | * | + |
| Internet navigation | * | – | – | – | * | – | * | + | + | + |
| Email basics | – | – | – | – | * | * | – | * | * | + |
| Locating information: Internet | * | * | + | * | + | * | * | * | * | + |
| Critically evaluating Internet information | + | + | * | + | + | * | * | + | + | + |

Key: + Excellent strategy
 * Adaptable strategy
 – Unsuitable strategy

383

discuss in the remainder of this chapter. We think you will see a familiar Vygotskian thread to the process she calls the **Self-Regulated Strategy Development Model (SRSD),** which we highly recommend as the framework for introducing and practicing research strategies. The following list delineates the gist of her recommendations.

Go to the Assignments and Activities section of Topic 9: "Reading Comprehension" in the MyEducationLab for your course and complete the activity entitled "Promoting Literacy." As you watch the video and answer the accompanying questions, look for ways teachers model new skills and make connections between new concepts and children's experiences.

1. *Describe the strategy.* Explicitly describe the strategy steps and discuss why and when it can be useful and what it accomplishes.
2. *Activate prior knowledge.* Review information the students may have already learned that may be useful in learning the new strategy.
3. *Review students' current level of functioning.* Provide information to students about their current performance levels and how this strategy can help them achieve a higher level of performance.
4. *Model the strategy.* Show the student how to use the strategy using multiple examples. Allow for student input and feedback.
5. *Provide collaborative practice.* Provide numerous opportunities for students to practice the new strategy in the whole group, small groups, pairs, or individually, depending on what you believe will be most effective. Teacher support will be faded out over time.
6. *Include independent practice.* Students should have ample opportunities to practice the strategy alone. They should have teacher or peer support available at first, but ultimately they should demonstrate proficiency in using the strategy alone.
7. *Generalize the strategy.* After learning has taken place, be sure to use the strategy routinely in future teaching and learning experiences. If the strategy is worth teaching, it is worth using and allowing it to become, as they say in the military, "SOP" (standard operating procedures).

## Written Academic Learning Summary (WALS)

### Purpose

A **written academic learning summary** (WALS; Cooter & Cooter, 2008) is an evidence-based activity that helps students write about what they are learning in core subject-area texts (mathematics, science, social studies, English/language arts). Benefits to students include deeper and more permanent learning of important information, increased reading comprehension in informational texts, increased vocabulary learning, and better preparation of students for higher-level coursework in middle and high school. WALS specifically helps students bridge from new vocabulary they have acquired (see "Academic Word Walls" in Chapter 8), to a graphic organizer that features a structure for written retellings (K. S. Cooter, 2002) so as to

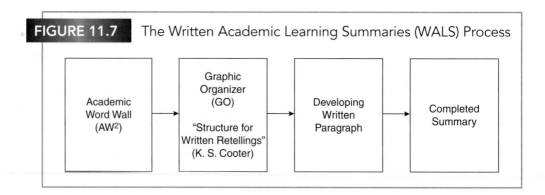

**FIGURE 11.7** The Written Academic Learning Summaries (WALS) Process

Academic Word Wall (AW²) → Graphic Organizer (GO) "Structure for Written Retellings" (K. S. Cooter) → Developing Written Paragraph → Completed Summary

help students connect concepts and see relationships, and finally to create a written summary of three to five paragraphs. Figure 11.7 shows the process used in the WALS strategy.

### Materials

- Academic texts
- Writing materials
- Easy access to your academic word wall or equivalent where new academic terms are displayed and used in interactive activities

### Procedure

Robert and Kathleen Cooter (2008) developed an explicit step-by-step framework for implementing academic word walls ($AW^2$) (Chapter 8). $AW^2$ were then applied to the writing process in the Structure for Written Retellings (Figure 11.8). Following are the recommended

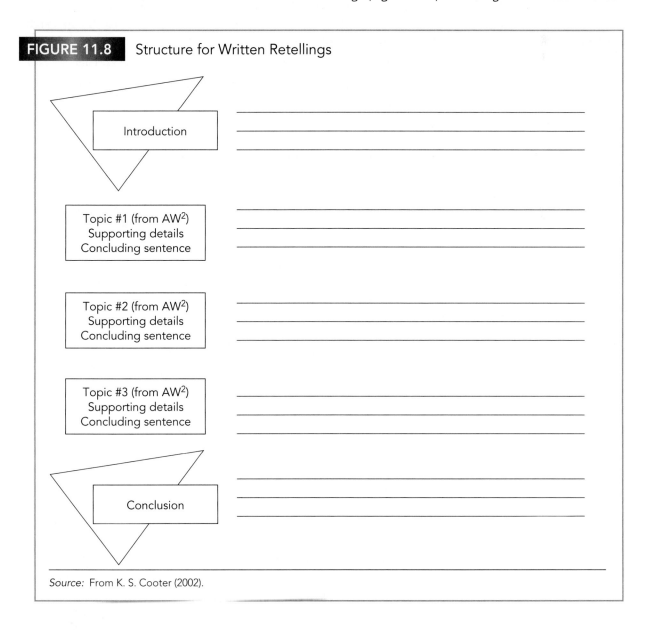

**FIGURE 11.8** Structure for Written Retellings

*Source:* From K. S. Cooter (2002).

steps from the Structure for Written Retellings (K. S. Cooter, 2002) to carry this process to writing summaries. An example of a completed summary for teacher modeling is shown in Figure 11.9.

| Teaching Steps | Teaching Activity |
|---|---|
| **Introduction.** Introducing the Structure for Written Retellings to create a Written Academic Learning Summary (WALS) | Explain the purpose of the strategy and why it is helpful in writing a good summary of what they have learned. Describe (with enthusiasm) what you hope they will learn, and why you feel it is important.<br>**Check** for understanding and **reteach** as needed. |
| **Teacher Modeling.** Using the Structure for Written Retellings to create a Written Academic Learning Summary (WALS) | Modeling is to be teacher-led with little or no student feedback—they are observing you as you "think out loud" how you go about moving information from a thinking map to the structure for written retellings, then expanding the key words and phrases into sentences.<br>Using language students can understand, explain the steps explicitly.<br>Read aloud sections you are creating and how you know when each section is satisfactory, or when sections need further editing and revising.<br>Begin by modeling how you might create a three (3) paragraph summary. After this is done, show how you could expand it to a five (5) paragraph summary using two additional topics and their supporting details.<br>**Check** for understanding and **reteach** as needed. |
| **Guided Practice 1.** Small-group activity (i.e., joint productive activity) with teacher monitoring and feedback | Explicitly **restate** the key steps of the Structure for Written Retellings to create a Written Academic Learning Summary (WALS) that you will want students to do in a small-group activity (or in pairs), also known as a *joint productive activity* (JPA).<br>Have students working in small groups or pairs take a thinking map they have created (or one you provide) to create a written summary using the format we have discussed.<br>Instructional conversation—include conversation about students' experiences so far using the Structure for Written Retellings (K.S. Cooter, 2002) to create a Written Academic Learning Summary (WALS) and your feedback. (See Figure 11.7.)<br>**Assessment: Check** for understanding using key questions (write these out ahead of time). *Hint:* Bloom's taxonomy of questioning is always a good source. |
| **Guided Practice 2.** Individual practice with teacher or peer feedback | Now design an activity whereby students on their own attempt using the Structure for Written Retellings to create a Written Academic Learning Summary (WALS).<br>Students should then share their written summary with the teacher, or a "peer editing group" for feedback.<br>The teacher should now lead an instructional conversation about what has been learned or understood about the process, and ways they can make their written summaries better. |

**FIGURE 11.9**    Teacher Modeling Example Using the Structure
for Written Retellings: *Arachnids*

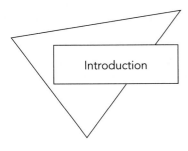

Introduction

Spiders are very interesting creatures, and are even scary to some people. The scientific name for spiders is "arachnids," and they are insects. There are 37,000 kinds of spiders. There are even songs about spiders we learn in school. In this report we will learn facts and misconceptions about this special living thing we learned in our book and on the Internet.

Topic #1 (from AW²)
Supporting details
Concluding sentence

One misconception is that all spiders are poisonous. Some spiders are poisonous, or "venomous," but not all spiders have venom. Spiders use venom to stun or kill creatures they want to eat. Of over 37,000 kinds of spiders, only about 25 have venom that can hurt humans. Two spiders in the U.S. with venom that can hurt humans are the black widow and the brown recluse, but no one has been proven killed in over two decades (20 years).

Topic #2 (from AW²)
Supporting details
Concluding sentence

Another misconception is that some spiders can be larger than a cat. Spiders come in many sizes. The largest is the Goliath birdeater tarantula. It is found in the rain forests of northeastern South America, and can be as big as a dinner plate. It can grab birds from their nests! The smallest spider is from Borneo and is the size of a pinhead. So, there are no spiders larger than a cat, but they can be very large and also very small.

Topic #3 (from AW²)
Supporting details
Concluding sentence

One thing we learned is that different arachnids eat different things. Many spiders eat insects, but not all do. There are spiders that dine on birds, frogs, fish, lizards, and snakes. So it is not true that all spiders eat bugs!

There are other things about arachnids, or spiders, that we still do not now. What is the largest spider in North America? Is it as big as the Goliath birdeater tarantula? We hope not. Also, is the silk spiders make all the same kind? How strong is their silk? Could you make clothes out of spider silk? We wonder where the name "arachnid" came from? And what about water spiders? Do any of them actually live under water? We still have a lot to learn about arachnids.

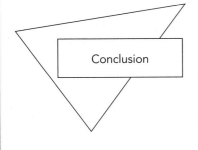

Conclusion

Spiders, or arachnids, are very interesting insects. They come in many sizes, live on different things, and some are poisonous. We want to know more about this special creature.

**Guided Practice 2**
*(continued)*

**Assessment: Check** for understanding using key questions (write these out ahead of time), and decide if you will need to **reteach** all or some of the students how to use the process.

**Student Independent Use & Assessment.**
Student works alone with limited support

Design and implement an independent activity (students working on their own) using the Strategy for Using Thinking Maps to Create a Written Summary.

**Assessment: Check** for understanding using key questions (write these out ahead of time). Decide if you will need to **reteach** all or some of the students how to use the Structure for Written Retllings to create a Written Academic Learning Summary (WALS).

## Graphic Organizers

### Purpose

The purpose of research conducted by students is to gain and understand new knowledge about a topic. Many students struggle with this process and often seem to find disparate bits of information that they are unable to assimilate into what they already know. Without assimilation, no new learning is likely to result. **Graphic organizers** (GOs) can be used to help students comprehend new information, assimilate new information into what they already know, and recall that information later on when needed. Donna Merkley and Debra Jeffries (2001) have developed guidelines for constructing and implementing GOs effectively in the classroom.

### Materials

- Expository text selection (5–15 pages) that is germane to the content curriculum
- Overhead projector and transparencies (or other modeling method)

### Procedure

Merkley and Jeffries (2001) have summarized ways of (1) creating graphic organizers (GOs) and (2) implementing GOs in the classroom. We have adapted and combined these steps so that you can present them as a process tool to students. As always, extensive description and modeling on your part is essential. The goal is to have students internalize these processes so that they begin using GOs as a tool in their research activities. Before beginning, select a simple GO format and construct examples for classroom demonstrations/modeling with the GO in varying degrees of completion.

**Step 1:** Show students ways of analyzing new information for important key words, descriptions, and global concepts. Verbalize relationships between concepts and key words. Provide opportunities for student questions and input.

**Step 2:** Arrange key words and concepts into an illustration to show interrelationships and patterns of organization. As you construct a graphic organizer (GO), verbalize for students how their earlier work in Step 1 flows in a natural way into the selection of an appropriate GO design. Demonstrate how new knowledge can connect to their prior knowledge. Most of the figures in the remainder of this chapter show examples of graphic organizers.

**Step 3:** Review and evaluate the relationships in the GO for clarity, simplicity, and visual effectiveness. Demonstrate how the need for more information in some areas can help them formulate research questions leading to further reading and a search for missing links.

To summarize the key elements to teaching students about GOs (Merkley & Jeffries, 2001):

- Verbalize relationships (links) among concepts in the GO
- Provide opportunities for student input and questioning during your modeling and guided practice experiences
- Connect new knowledge to prior experiences
- Develop "need to know" questions that relate to upcoming readings and further research

## Note-Taking Strategies

### Purpose

There are many different systems for teaching students how to take notes as they listen (Cooter & Flynt, 1996; Lapp, Flood, & Farnan, 2004), such as the Cornell System (Pauk, 2000) and the REST system (Morgan, Meeks, Schollaert, & Paul, 1986). Recommendations about how notes should initially be recorded, the need for subsequent reorganization and expansion of the notes, and a strong recommendation for frequent review exemplify the common threads of these systems.

### Materials

- A notebook students can use exclusively for learning note taking

Go to the Assignments and Activities section of Topic 9: "Reading Comprehension" in the MyEducationLab for your course and complete the activity entitled "Cornell Notes." As you watch the video and answer the accompanying questions, note the key parts of the Cornell note-taking method and then create an example for your own uses in the classroom.

### Procedure

Before discussing each of the components of effective note taking, we would first like to suggest a couple of general guidelines derived from the work of Cooter and Flynt (1996). First, students should be asked to obtain a single notebook specifically for use in learning note-taking skills. Dedicating a notebook for this purpose will help them keep the notes organized and make it easier for you to collect and examine the notes. Second, if note taking is important to you, then some type of credit should be given to students who do a good job of recording and organizing their notes. Finally, adapt the amount and style of lecturing to your students' ability level. If you have an advanced class, more sophisticated lectures might be warranted. On the other hand, if your class has little experience with note taking and effective listening techniques, you might want to begin slowly and use a lot of visuals or perhaps a listening outline to assist students in determining and writing important information.

Two traditional note-taking systems are the Cornell System (Pauk, 2000) and a Notetaking System for Learning (Palmatier, 1973). These systems share several features that we recommend for use in training students how to listen and take notes on lecture information.

1. *Students should divide their notebook paper into two columns.* The left column should be about 2 or 3 inches wide, or one-third of the paper width. The remaining two-thirds of the page is used for recording notes.
2. *Students should write information in a modified outline form on the right side of the page.* Students should indent subtopics and minor ideas using letters and numbers. They should be encouraged to use abbreviations to minimize time spent in writing down information. Heavily emphasized points should be marked with asterisks or stars.
3. *Students should organize and expand their notes as soon as possible.* Early in the school year, considerate teachers provide in-class time for this task. At this time the students literally rewrite their notes on similarly lined paper. The purpose is for the students to

write all abbreviations, expand phrases, and make sure that the information is sequentially organized. This is obviously a form of practice.

4. *Students fill in the left margin for aid in study and review.* As they reread their notes, students identify topics, key terms, and questions that might assist them in remembering the lecture information recorded on the right side of the paper.

5. *Students use their notes for study and review.* Students can now cover up the right-hand side of the paper and use the memory triggers they have recorded on the left-hand side for review. As they move down the left-hand side of the page, students use the headings, key terms, and questions as a means of assessing their ability to remember and paraphrase what they have recorded.

## Comprehension Windows Strategy (CWS)

### Purpose

The **comprehension windows strategy** (CWS; Bass & Woo, 2008, p. 571) was designed as an informational text strategy to enhance students' comprehension during reading and writing and includes an easy-to-create instructional prop. CWS helps students to build content knowledge, organize facts, encourage critical thinking, and use proper documentation and citations. This strategy may be used in small collaborative groups or individual work.

### Materials

- A CWS "prop" prototype (Figure 11.10) as created by Bass and Woo (2008)
- File folders
- Scissors
- Pens
- Sticky notes (2 × 1.5-inch) for headings

### Procedure

Bass and Woo (2008, p. 573) offer the following guide for using the comprehension windows strategy (CWS).*

#### Teacher Preparation

- Begin with a letter-size (recycled) file folder
- Cut along fold to create two equal halves (each folder will make two CWS props)
- Fold each piece in half lengthwise creating a tent
- Provide ample 2" × 1.5" information sticky notes for every student
- CWS prop can be made from recycled file folders (school secretary, parents, and local businesses are good sources)

#### Procedure

- Label each CWS flap with the appropriate headings using sticky notes (e.g., Important People, Events Before, What Happened?)
- Label back section as "References"

*From "Comprehension Window Strategy: A Comprehension Strategy and Prop for Reading and Writing Informal Text" by L. Bass and D. G. Woo, 2008, *The Reading Teacher, 61*(7), 573. Copyright © 2008 by the International Reading Association (www.reading.org). Reproduced with permission of the International Reading Association via Copyright Clearance Center.

Go to the Building Teaching Skills and Dispositions section of Topic 10: "Reading and Writing" in the My-EducationLab for your course and complete the activity entitled "Integrating Reading into the Writing Process." As you work through the learning unit, create a list of examples for each step in the writing process that you could mention during your own teaching.

FIGURE 11.10   Comprehension Window Strategy (CWS) Prop Prototype

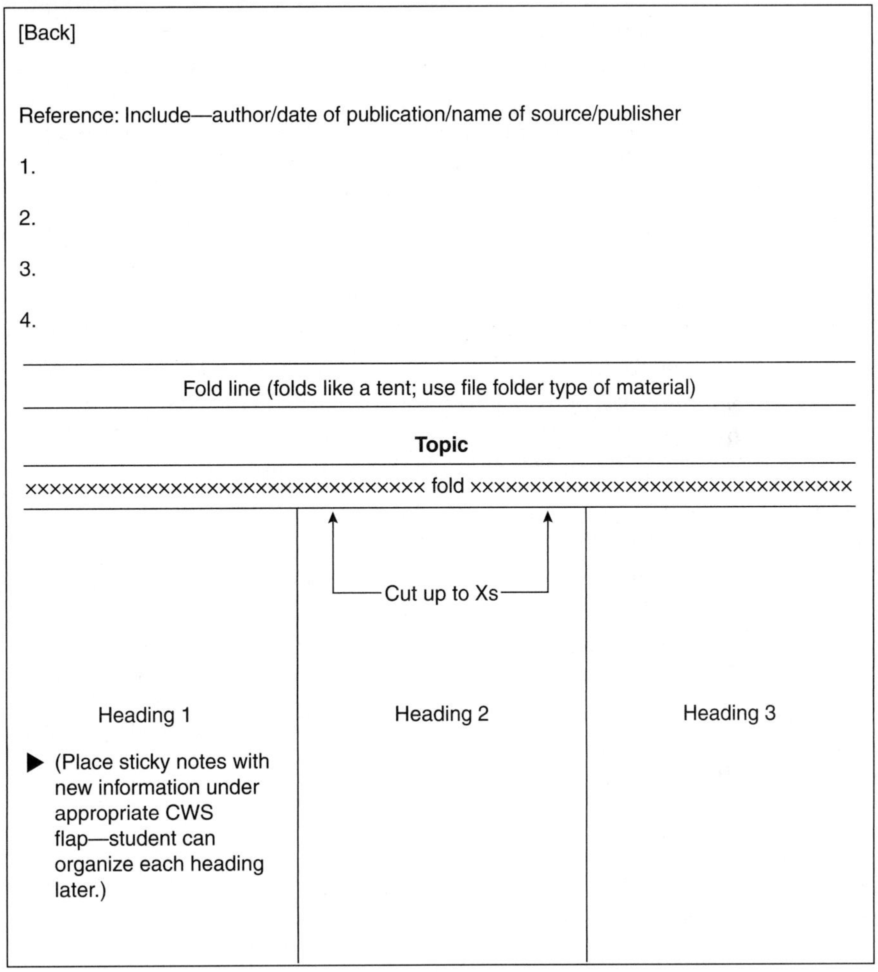

[Back]

Reference: Include—author/date of publication/name of source/publisher

1.

2.

3.

4.

Fold line (folds like a tent; use file folder type of material)

**Topic**

xxxxxxxxxxxxxxxxxxxxxxxxxxxxxxxxxxx fold xxxxxxxxxxxxxxxxxxxxxxxxxxxxxxxxxxx

Cut up to Xs

| Heading 1 | Heading 2 | Heading 3 |
| --- | --- | --- |
| ▶ (Place sticky notes with new information under appropriate CWS flap—student can organize each heading later.) | | |

*Source:* From "Comprehension Window Strategy: A Comprehension Strategy and Prop for Reading and Writing Informal Text" by L. Bass and D. G. Woo, 2008, *The Reading Teacher, 61*(7), 571–575. Copyright © 2008 by the International Reading Association (www.reading.org). Reproduced with permission of the International Reading Association via Copyright Clearance Center.

- As students gather information, they write a complete reference citation for each source on the back section of the tent—number the references (alphabetical order can be done later)
- On each sticky note, students record one idea and its corresponding reference number
- Sticky notes are positioned under the appropriate CWS flaps to help students sort and categorize information

Once information has been gathered, students are ready to engage in writing process activities (prewriting, drafting, revising, editing, publishing). This can be done individually or in small groups. Students begin by organizing information using the information sticky notes from each CWS flap one flap at a time. Information sticky notes can be placed and organized on a flat surface as a preliminary stage leading to a final product. Some possible final products include poster sessions, PowerPoint presentations, reenactments, or Author's Chair (to share compositions).

## Selected Maps and Graphic Organizers for Use with Informational Text

### Purpose

As noted earlier in the chapter, semantic maps and other graphic organizers (GOs) can help teachers assess what students know or don't know about a topic. They can also be used as a research and study tool to help students chart important knowledge they are acquiring, understand steps in a process or sequence, classify or categorize information, compare and contrast two or more features, determine causal patterns, or prepare and defend thesis statements concerning an area of study. In short, maps are a form of outlining that help students determine which areas they must research.

### Materials

- Maps as described in the following table (Figures 11.11 through 11.16 on pp. 393–398)

### Procedure

Sinatra, Gemake, Wielan, and Sinatra (1998) have identified several map forms and their use with informational text. The following abbreviated summary of their research targeting maps highlights points of emphasis.

| Type of Map | Type of Text Structure | Type of Higher-Order Thinking |
|---|---|---|
| Steps-in-a-Process | Time-related events with multiple episodes or a sequence of events, as with many science process steps or social studies events. | Students must be able to select and sequence events, describing processes in order. All are based on the student's ability to locate appropriate information sources. |
| Compare/Contrast Same/Different | Comparison information structures found in many expository texts, particularly in the sciences, literature, social studies, health, and mathematics. | Often inferential or implied in texts, comparison requires students to identify qualities of sameness and differences. Thus, this activity provides a logical framework for identifying and using library/media resources. |
| Cause–Effect | Causal patterns found in the text descriptions, most often the sciences, literature, and social studies. | Identification of causal events that trigger an (often predictable) outcome. |
| Persuasion by Point/Counterpoint | Derived typically from literature, social studies, and studies of the arts. | Identification of problems or issues, location of information to support a thesis/belief/judgment, charting opposing views, and formulating counterarguments in support of the thesis. |
| Turning-Point Map | Useful primarily with literature and history texts. | Students are required to detect important events in sequence that contribute to a final outcome. |

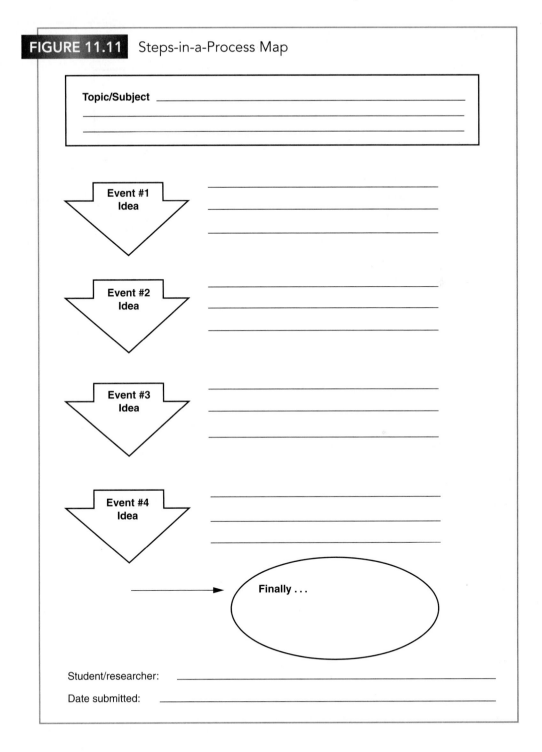

**FIGURE 11.11**   Steps-in-a-Process Map

Topic/Subject _____

Event #1
Idea

Event #2
Idea

Event #3
Idea

Event #4
Idea

Finally . . .

Student/researcher: _____

Date submitted: _____

Note that students may be helped or "coached" by teachers to locate additional research materials or databases to complete the map(s). In the end, it may be concluded that the construction of maps can indeed help students construct their own comprehension of the topic under study. Sinatra and colleagues (1998) urge teachers, as a next step, to challenge students to develop their own maps to represent new units of study and then present them to the class or group.

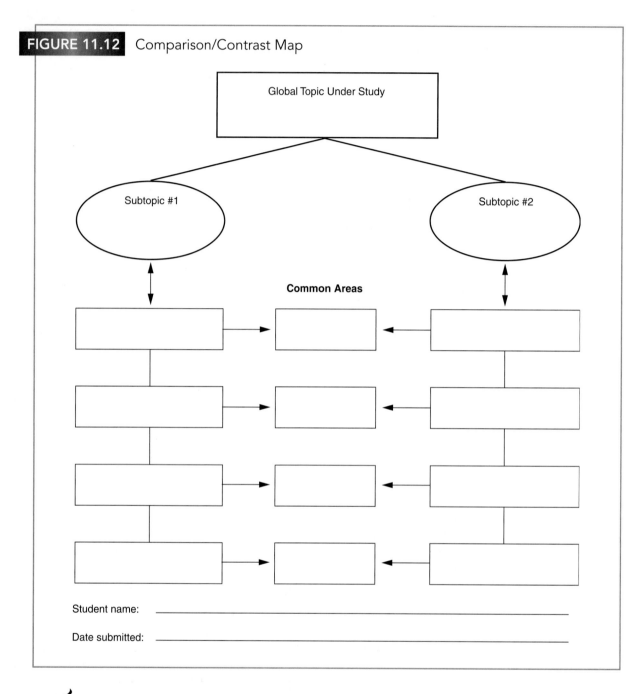

**FIGURE 11.12** Comparison/Contrast Map

# 𝒯EACHING STRATEGIES: NEW LITERACY STUDIES

## Tech-to-Stretch

### Purpose

Phyllis Whitin (2009) finds that teachers can incorporate what she terms "multimodal response strategies" into classroom literacy instruction in such a way as to build comprehension and provide opportunities for children to interpret what they read in a nonfiction literature

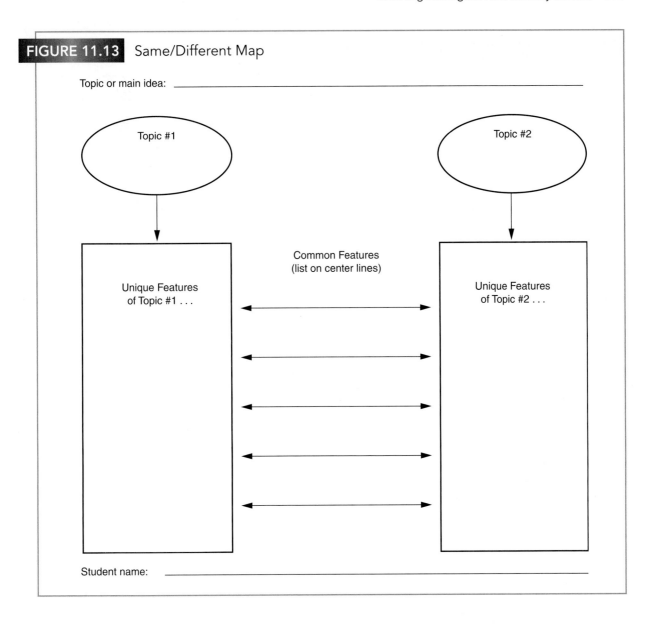

**FIGURE 11.13**  Same/Different Map

Topic or main idea: _____

Topic #1

Topic #2

Unique Features
of Topic #1 . . .

Common Features
(list on center lines)

Unique Features
of Topic #2 . . .

Student name: _____

study. In her **tech-to-stretch** model for instruction, actually an organizational framework or process for teaching and learning, students create a final product (in her research, a digital movie) to showcase their learning (other final products could include a PowerPoint presentation, wiki, or poster). Whitin's work was primarily intended to demonstrate how this tech-to-stretch process may be used with young learners, but we think the tech-to-stretch framework will also work well with students in grade 3 and higher working in small joint productive activity (JPA) groups (*Note:* For more information about how to orchestrate joint productive activities in your classroom, go to the CREDE website at http://crede .berkeley.edu/research/crede/standards.html).

### Materials

- Any of several multimodal possibilities, depending on resources you have available (e.g., computers, Internet access, software, etc.)

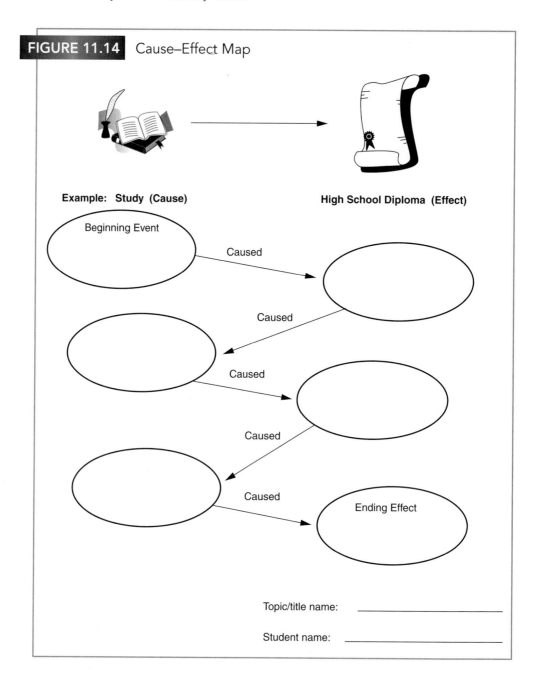

**FIGURE 11.14**    Cause–Effect Map

**Example:  Study  (Cause)**    **High School Diploma  (Effect)**

Beginning Event

Caused

Caused

Caused

Caused

Caused

Ending Effect

Topic/title name:    _____

Student name:    _____

## Procedure

The tech-to-stretch strategy is conducted in three phases. Phase I is intended to help students understand the potential of using multiple modalities to express ideas (Whitin, 2009). In Phase II, students use a range of structured multimodal strategies to respond to text and other information sources. Student artifacts include online responses to prompts, notes from small- and whole-group activities and discussions, written and visual artifacts, and observational notes. In Phase III, digital movies or other products are created to display learning using various modalities (e.g., visual, aural, oral). Figure 11.17 (on p. 399) shows the three phases of the tech-to-stretch strategy.

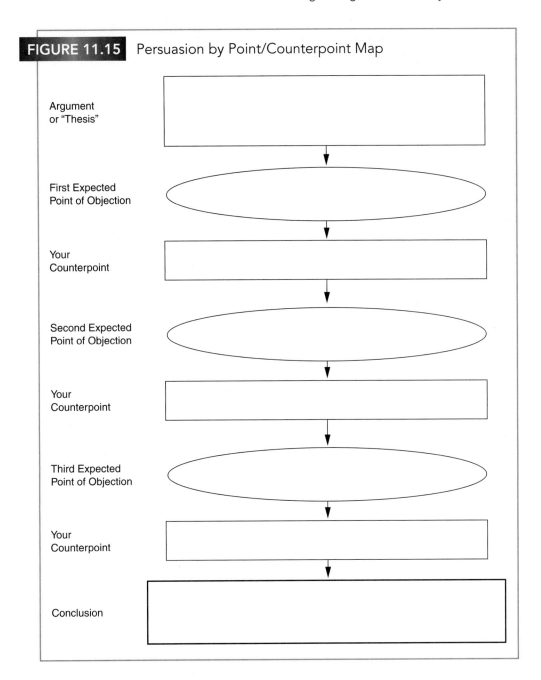

FIGURE 11.15    Persuasion by Point/Counterpoint Map

Argument or "Thesis"

First Expected Point of Objection

Your Counterpoint

Second Expected Point of Objection

Your Counterpoint

Third Expected Point of Objection

Your Counterpoint

Conclusion

## Classroom Blogging

### Purpose

**Blogs** are websites that offer people opportunities to "create personal web pages of text, pictures, graphics, videos, and other multimedia with the same ease as creating a word processing document" (Boling et al., 2008, p. 408). With classroom blogging (Barone & Wright, 2008; Boling et al., 2008), readers are able to post comments and engage in online "chats" with the blog host. For real-world examples, you can see classroom blogging being used in Julia Siporin's third-grade classroom (see her blog online at www.jeffersonbear.motime.com)

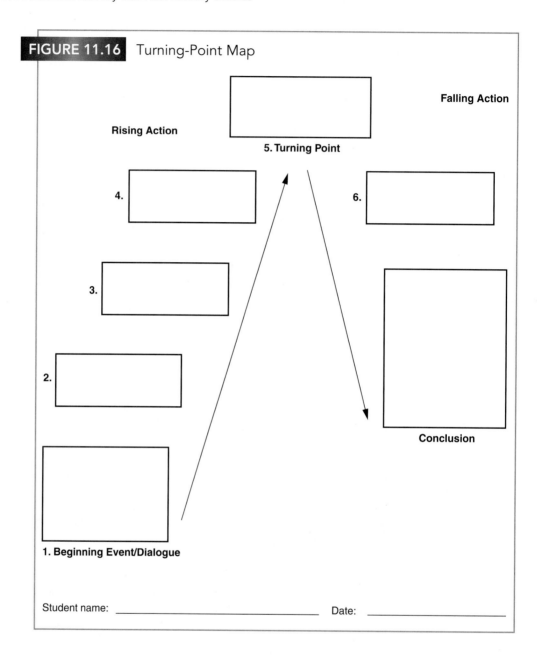

**FIGURE 11.16** Turning-Point Map

and in Todd Wright's fourth grade (see his classroom web page at www.fes.lyon.k12.nv.us) to motivate students to conduct research and write about their learning.

**Materials**

- A blog you have set up
- Computer access for students
- Library resources
- Printer, paper, and possibly other art materials for displaying student responses (optional)

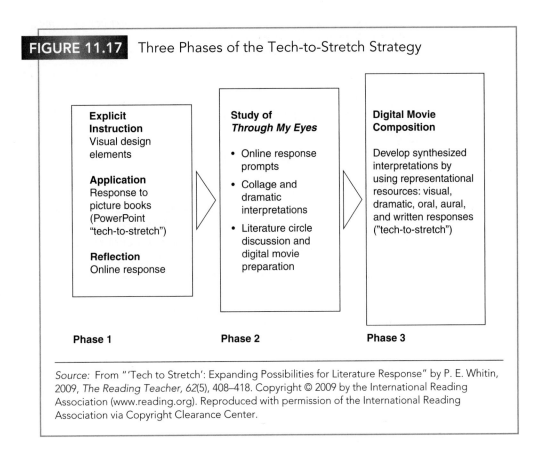

**FIGURE 11.17** Three Phases of the Tech-to-Stretch Strategy

**Explicit Instruction**
Visual design elements

**Application**
Response to picture books (PowerPoint "tech-to-stretch")

**Reflection**
Online response

**Phase 1**

**Study of *Through My Eyes***

• Online response prompts

• Collage and dramatic interpretations

• Literature circle discussion and digital movie preparation

**Phase 2**

**Digital Movie Composition**

Develop synthesized interpretations by using representational resources: visual, dramatic, oral, aural, and written responses ("tech-to-stretch")

**Phase 3**

*Source:* From "'Tech to Stretch': Expanding Possibilities for Literature Response" by P. E. Whitin, 2009, *The Reading Teacher, 62*(5), 408–418. Copyright © 2009 by the International Reading Association (www.reading.org). Reproduced with permission of the International Reading Association via Copyright Clearance Center.

## Procedure

There are a number of online host sites available to teachers, such as edublogs.org, epnweb .org (for podcasts), or the popular blogger.com. The main idea here is to post questions for your students and ask for their written responses. The questions should relate to what is being studied so as to motivate students to dig deeper in their research, think about what they have learned, and write summaries to share with the blog host. In Julia Siporin's third grade she posts blogs from her classroom teddy bear named Jefferson (www.jeffersonbear.motime .com) who asks students to reveal their opinions about various class topics from their studies. For example, here is a question posted by Ms. Siporin . . . er, Jefferson:*

### FRIDAY, FEBRUARY 06

#### *Yo! Tell Me Your Shocking Stories!*

*Yo Dudes & Dudettes,*

    *We loved reading your personal narratives; we laughed, we cried, we ate ice-cream (We always eat ice-cream).*

    *You guys are the best writers my mom has ever had I think. Way AWESOME!*

    *I hear you're learning about electricity; that's one of my favorite subjects. What have you learned about electricity so far? Have you done any cool experiments yet? What did you find out?*

---

*Reprinted by permission of Julia Siporin.

*Gotta go Dudes, I'll come see you for your next party . . . maybe Valentines Day, what are you guys doing then?*
*My bear friends and I will try to write you Valentines.*
*AGAIN, gotta go dudes,*
*Your pal,*
*Jefferson*
*P.S. HI LAUREN and Juhyung ;-)*

## Electronic Talking Books (ETB)

### Purpose

One form of electronic text used with beginning and struggling readers is the electronic talking book (Oakley & Jay, 2008; Pearman, 2008). ETBs, also known as *e-books*, are texts on CD-ROM or available over the Internet featuring not only the written word but also various hypertext options, including spoken narration, animations, music, video, or highlighting of words or sentences with spoken explanations (or pronunciations) of the highlighted content. Some ETBs also include sound effects and "hot spots" for further learning. ETBs can be especially helpful for students with limited decoding ability or motivation to read. Recent research has also shown ETBs to be a valuable tool for reading for home assignments (Oakley & Jay, 2008). Oakley and Jay (2008) recommend online links for ETBs in Figure 11.18.

### Materials

- Traditional print texts leveled according to guidelines offered by Fountas and Pinnell (1999)
- A CD-ROM version of the same text
- Computer access at school (e.g., in a center) and, if possible, at home, for extended practice
- List of prompt questions
- Comprehension assessment tool

### Procedure

The lesson begins with the teacher introducing the text selection, explaining any important key concepts and vocabulary as part of a brief discussion. In Pearman's (2008) study, students

---

**FIGURE 11.18** Links to Online Electronic Talking Books

- Woodlands Junior School:
  www.woodlands-junior.kent.sch.uk/Games/educational/onlinestory.htm#talk
- Read On Audio Stories (audio stories for elementary schoolchildren):
  www.beenleigss.eq.edu.au/requested_sites/audiostories/index.html
- Ziptales (subscription needed):
  www.ziptales.com.au
- CBeebies Stories (for younger children):
  www.bbc.co.uk/cbeebies/stories
- Awesome Talking Library (Awesome Talkster can turn any web page into an ETB, with text highlighting):
  www.awesomelibrary.org/Awesome_Talking_Library.html

were also informed that they would be expected to retell what they remembered from the text selection. Students then read a traditional print text at their appropriate developmental level, either silently or aloud, and then read the CD-ROM book version. Following the readings, students are asked to retell what they remember from the selection following the teacher's prompt questions, such as "Pretend you are telling a friend about what you just read and they have read this selection." If they seem to leave out important information, prompt them again saying "What else do you remember?" or "Can you tell me more?" If you are using a storybook selection (fiction), then you may want to monitor individual retellings using a comprehension assessment tool, such as the one used in Pearman's (2008) study, seen in Figure 11.19.

---

**FIGURE 11.19**  Story Retelling Analysis

**Morrow's 10-Point Scale**

Student's name: _____ Date: _____
Title of story: _____

*General directions:* Place a 1 next to each element if the child includes it in his or her presentation. Credit gist as well as obvious recall.

*Characters and setting*

    **A.** Begins story with an introduction                                        _____
    **B.** Names main character(s)      _____
    **C.** Number of other characters named      _____
    **D.** Actual number of other characters      _____
    **E.** Score for other characters (C/D)      _____
    **F.** Includes statement about time and/or place      _____

*Theme*

Refers to main character's primary goal or problem to be resolved      _____

*Plot episodes*

    **A.** Number of episodes recalled      _____
    **B.** Number of episodes in story      _____
    **C.** Score for plot episodes (A/B)      _____

*Resolution*

    **A.** Names the problem solution/goal attainment      _____
    **B.** Ends story      _____

*Sequence*

    Retells story in structural order: setting, theme, plot episodes, resolutions
    (Score 2 for correct order, 1 for partial, 0 for none)      _____

Highest score possible __(10)__                    Child's score    _____

Comments: _____

## e-Reading and e-Responding

### Purpose

Lotta Larson (2009) recently conducted research in which students, instead of reading traditional texts and writing in student response journals, read e-books on laptop computers and responded to readings in electronic response journals. Use of **e-reading** and **e-responding** was shown to improve student engagement and increase writing to such an extent in the fifth-grade classroom where the research was conducted that the teacher, Mrs. Stitt, decided to move her literacy circles online!

### Materials

- Laptop or other personal computers
- e-books
- A handout for prompt writing, such as Figure 11.20, which was used by the students in Mrs. Stitt's fifth grade and can be easily adapted for your own use with fiction or nonfiction texts
- Projector and screen for modeling laptop activities

---

**FIGURE 11.20**  Instructional Handout for Prompt Writing

Name: _____ Group #: _____

1. Think about the part that you read today in your book.

   What did you like?
   What questions do you have?
   What did this chapter make you feel or think about?
   What would you have done if you were in a similar situation?

2. Write two quality prompts (new threads) that can be used to start a good discussion in your group. Your prompts should relate to the book.

3. You will post your BEST prompt on the Message Board. Your prompt must be approved by Mrs. Stitt BEFORE you post.

Prompt 1: _____
_____
_____

Prompt 2: _____
_____
_____

Check your work:

☐ My prompt relates to the book.
☐ My prompts are open-ended and cannot be answered with a simple "yes" or "no."
☐ My prompts make my group members think about what they have read.

*Source:* From "Reader Response Meets New Literacies: Empowering Readers in Online Learning Communities," by L. C. Larson, 2009, *The Reading Teacher, 62*(8), 638–648. Copyright © 2009 by the International Reading Association. Reproduced with permission of the International Reading Association via Copyright Clearance Center.

## Procedure

In the Larson (2009) study, Mrs. Stitt's fifth-grade students had the choice of reading the e-book version of one of two books. Larson lists some sources for free online e-books (see Table 11.1). In this case, there were 15 reading and responding sessions in which students participated. While reading, students share their reactions, questions, and thoughts about the e-book in an electronic response journal. After reading the e-book, students log onto an online message board to discuss and respond to the reading. Because the e-books, e-journals, and online message boards are acquired through the laptop, the transition to each activity is relatively seamless.

As with all new learning, it is important for the teacher to explicitly explain, model, and allow for student practice of each of the tasks to be performed. If possible, explanations and modeling are best done with the whole class using a laptop, projector, and screen. Some of the most obvious and critical elements to explain include log-in procedures, how to respond to prompts, and vocabulary (e.g., *thread, prompt, post*). It is a good idea to offer a reminder that this is a learning activity and that students are expected to stay on task and use appropriate language. In a typical session, students read and respond in their e-journals before reading and responding to other responses from classmates.

| TABLE 11.1 | Online Resources for e-Book Reading and e-Responding |
|---|---|
| Free e-Books | www.getfreebooks.com |
| | This is a free e-books site where you can access legal, downloadable e-books for free. |
| | Public library websites |
| | Check out your local library website for opportunities to "check out" e-books. (Library card is often required.) |
| e-Books for purchase | www.ebooks.com |
| | This site offers a large selection of children's and young adult e-books in multiple formats. |
| | www.fictionwise.com |
| | Fictionwise.com has a comprehensive collection of fiction and nonfiction books in a variety of popular e-book formats. |
| Online literature response | moodle.org |
| | Moodle is a free course management system that can be used for asynchronous message board discussions. |
| | www.epals.com |
| | ePals.com offers schools and districts safe e-mail solutions, blogging, and opportunities for collaborative projects. |
| | www.pbwiki.com |
| | Using the Peanut Butter Wiki site, students can create a wiki to discuss books online. |

*Source:* From Larson (2009).

Go to the Assignments and Activities section of Topic 9: "Reading Comprehension" in the MyEducationLab for your course and complete the activity entitled "Reading for Information." As you watch the video and answer the accompanying questions, notice how the teacher structures or "scaffolds" her instruction to show children ways of making predictions. Create a step-by-step summary of her actions for your future use.

### Student-Constructed Prompts

Larson (2009) explains that students were shown how to construct five kinds of research-based prompts to deepen the quality of threaded discussions and, we believe, promote higher-order comprehension: experiential prompts, aesthetic prompts, cognitive prompts, interpretative prompts, and clarification prompts.

- *Experiential prompts.* Focuses on what the reader brings to the experience (i.e., prior knowledge and experiences). These threads might begin with the question, "Have you ever . . ."
- *Aesthetic prompts.* These threads, Larson (2009, p. 643) reports, "tend to bring out heartfelt, and sometimes heated, discussions among group members." They promote emotional reactions to the text such as empathy or character identification.
- *Cognitive prompts.* These threads encourage students to make predictions, solve problems, make inferences, and other higher-order responses.
- *Interpretive prompts.* As with cognitive prompts, interpretation prompts involve higher-level reasoning and analysis. Readers are often encouraged to think about morals or values, meaning or message, and make judgments. You can expect students to offer rich replies and express personal thoughts and viewpoints.
- *Clarification prompts.* These prompts are posted when students need more information to find an answer to a specific question related to the text. Entries often offer myriad perspectives. These prompts help students make sense of what they are learning.

## Wiki Writing

### Purpose

A **wiki** is a jointly authored document that is searchable and contains links to other parts of the document or to related information on the Internet. Unlike blogs where readers can only offer comments about the content of an electronic document, wikis allow visitors to the online site to change the content. The online encyclopedia Wikipedia (www.wikipedia.org) is a popular wiki example. Wiki writing (Morgan & Smith, 2008) is a classroom collaboration in which students and teacher use wiki technology to research topics and create online multimedia reports.

### Materials

- A class wiki
- Computers with Internet access

### Procedure

The first order of business is for the teacher to set up the classroom's own wiki site. PBWiki (pbwiki.com) and the Edublogs affiliate Wikispaces (www.wikispaces.com) are examples of resources often used by classroom teachers to set up their own wiki writing projects. Students will then need explicit instruction and modeling about how wikis work, with explanations of usernames and passwords, and how they can create their own composition pages for reports within the classroom wiki site. Students will also need instruction in basic wiki text revising and editing (grammar, thesaurus), as well as due dates.

Students begin by conducting research on the topic in the school library and online. Collaboration is an important aspect of wiki writing (Morgan & Smith, 2008), so students might be assigned to teams with the responsibility of making regular comments as part of the wiki but also making recommendations on team members' comments. Virtual sticky notes and footnotes are wiki tools usually available for this purpose.

Morgan and Smith (2008) offer some helpful hints on using wiki writing for the first time. First, remember that wikis are almost "bulletproof." Any mistake can be easily fixed and original documents are recoverable with a single mouse click. Second, since wikis are set up as a group of linked pages, create a "playground page" where you and your students can experiment without any apprehension. Third, explore other wikis and note the source code of pages you like (there is usually a button on the wiki where the source code is revealed). By copying and pasting, you can borrow these pages. Fourth, create a structure for your wiki writing project. This might include a page for each major category of information, a page for each student, a page for each book to be discussed, a page for each topic in a unit of study, or a page for each collaborative group of students.

# NEW LITERACIES FOR ENGLISH LEARNERS

Go to the Assignments and Activities section of Topic 14: "English Language Learners" in the MyEducationLab for your course and complete the activity entitled "Building on Students' Prior Knowledge." As you watch the video and answer the accompanying questions, look for ways teachers can link student background knowledge to new English vocabulary in content area subjects.

One of our elemental beliefs is that many, if not most, of the high-quality literacy assessment and teaching practices presented in this book are effective for English learners. This belief no doubt grows out of our embrace of a "multilingual perspective of language and literacy development" (Gort, 2003, 2006). This holistic view of bilingual learners values the benefits of students' cultural and linguistic backgrounds as robust storehouses that may be drawn on for learning and also values first languages as a tool for learning new languages. The Internet reciprocal teaching model presented next is a versatile structure that we feel may be used equally well with English learners and monolingual students alike.

## Internet Reciprocal Teaching (IRT)

### Purpose

Based on well-established research on reciprocal teaching (Palincsar, 1986; Palincsar & Brown, 1984), **Internet reciprocal teaching** (IRT; Leu et al., 2008; Reinking & Castek, 2007) was developed around the use of wireless laptops in the classroom to access online informational texts. IRT is a very rich model of instruction that involves the reading, processing, and construction of students' own texts (hypertext links, wikis, and so forth) using varied and unique online texts as sources. It begins with instruction offered by teachers over several sessions with a whole class of heterogeneously grouped students. Students then model online comprehension strategies under instructional supervision, with a focus on questioning, locating, critically evaluating, synthesizing, and communicating strategies. The teacher gradually releases responsibility as students gain competence, leading to increased student collaboration and discussion.

### Materials

- Wireless laptop carts
- Access to the Internet
- Teachers checklist (see Figure 11.5)

### Procedure

Internet reciprocal teaching (IRT) begins with student assessment to identify basic needs relative to Internet and computer usage (i.e., use of Internet tools, online reading materials, Internet-critical evaluations skills, technology self-perception). In the assessment section of this chapter we provided resources to accomplish this part of preteaching.

Leu and colleagues (2008), based on their research, developed a three-phase model of Internet reciprocal teaching revolving around online reading comprehension.

- *Phase 1: Teacher-led instruction.* Students take part in teacher-led sessions to establish basic routines and Internet/computer skills (e.g., handling laptops or desktops, opening and closing programs, managing multiple windows, etc.). The teacher explicitly models online reading strategies, as well as procedures to follow for group discussions. When students are able to perform most of the functions on the teacher checklist (see Figure 11.5), the IRT can move on to Phase 2.

- *Phase 2: Collaborative modeling of online reading comprehension strategies.* Teachers and students begin to share the responsibility of discovering strategies for online reading comprehension. Small groups of students having a common problem often take the lead in sharing strategies they have discovered for finding information. These may relate to key curriculum standards or goals. One example offered by Leu and colleagues (2008) involves student groups trying to solve three problems on the Internet:

  - How high is Mt. Fuji in Japan?
  - Find a different answer to the same question
  - Which answer do you think is most accurate and how did you determine that it was?

Leu and colleagues (2008) explain:

> Students in each group are guided to discuss their solutions, exchanging reading comprehension strategies for locating information and critically evaluating information. Lessons are designed to minimize teacher talk and to maximize the time students are engaged with the task. An essential part of planning is setting aside time at the end of each lesson for students to debrief and to exchange strategies with the entire class after having already done so in their small groups. (p. 9)

Lessons in Phase 2 move from highly structured to less structured over time as student competence and ability to work independently increases. Early lessons focus on the rudiments of locating and critically evaluating online information. Later, the emphasis shifts to using a variety of online tools (e.g., email, wikis, blogs, Google docs, instant messaging).

- *Phase 3: Inquiry.* Students begin to move more into independent online inquiry linked to the curriculum standards. Much of the work is done independently or in small groups. Students also have the opportunity to decide on the most effective ways to share what they have learned. Teachers shift their role to helping individual students and groups find new ways of solving problems. This may involve working with students in other classrooms as well as their own home room.

## SELECTED REFERENCES

Apthorp, H., & Clark, T. (2007). *Using strategy instruction to help struggling high schoolers understand what they read.* Washington, DC: National Center for Educational Evaluation and Regional Assistance (IES). REL 2007-No. 38.

Barone, D., & Wright, T. (2008). Literacy instruction with digital and media technologies. *The Reading Teacher, 62*(4), 292–302.

Bass, L., & Woo, D. G. (2008). Comprehension windows strategy: A comprehension strategy and prop for reading and writing informational text. *The Reading Teacher, 61*(7), 571–575.

Boling, E., Castek, J., Zawilinski, L., Barton, K., & Nierlich, T. (2008). Collaborative literacy: Blogs and Internet projects. *The Reading Teacher, 61*(6), 504–506.

Compton-Lilly, C. (in press). What can new literacy studies offer to the teaching of struggling readers? *The Reading Teacher.*

Cooter, K. S. (2002). *A structure for written retellings.* Dallas, TX: Unpublished manuscript.

Cooter, K. S. (2006). When mama can't read: Counteracting intergenerational illiteracy. *The Reading Teacher, 59*(7), 698–702.

Cooter, R. B., & Cooter, K. S. (2008). *Written academic learning summaries (WALS).* Louisville, KY: Unpublished manuscript.

Cooter, R. B., & Flynt, E. S. (1996). *Teaching reading in the content areas: Developing content literacy for all students.* New York: John Wiley.

De la Paz, S. (1999). Self-regulated strategy instruction in regular education settings: Improving outcomes for students with and without learning disabilities. *Learning Disabilities Research & Practice, 14*(2), 92–106.

Fountas, I. C., & Pinnell, G. S. (1999). *Matching books to readers: Using leveled books in reading, K–3.* Portsmouth, NH: Heinemann Educational Books.

Gee, J. (2004). *Situated language and learning: A critique of traditional school.* New York: Routledge.

Gort, M. (2003). Transdisciplinary approaches in the education of English language learners. In D. Kaufman, D. M. Moss, & T. A. Osborn (Eds.), *Beyond the boundaries: A transdisciplinary approach to learning and teaching* (pp. 117–130). Westport, CT: Bergin & Garvey.

Gort, M. (2006). Strategic codeswitching, interliteracy, and other phenomena of bilingual writing: Lessons learned from classroom-based research. *Journal of Early Childhood Literacy, 6,* 327–358.

Gunning, T. G. (2006). *Assessing and correcting reading and writing difficulties* (3rd ed.). Boston: Allyn & Bacon.

Heath, S. (1986). What no bedtime story means: Narrative skills at home and school. In B. Schiefflin & E. Ochs (Eds.), *Language socialisation across cultures* (pp. 97–124). Cambridge, UK: Cambridge University Press.

Henderson, R., & Hirst, E. (2007). Reframing academic literacy: Re-examining a short-course for "disadvantaged" tertiary students. *English Teaching: Practice and Critique, 6*(2), 25–38.

Langer, J. (1981). From theory to practice: A prereading plan. *Journal of Reading, 25,* 152–156.

Lapp, D., Flood, J., & Farnan, N. (2004). *Content area reading and learning instructional strategies.* Mahwah, NJ: Lawrence Erlbaum.

Larson, L. C. (2009). Reader response meets new literacies: Empowering readers in online learning communities. *The Reading Teacher, 62*(8), 638–648.

Leu, D. J. (2002). The New Literacies: Research on reading instruction with the Internet. In A. E. Farstrup & S. J. Samuels (Eds.), *What research has to say about reading instruction* (pp. 310–336). Newark, DE: International Reading Association.

Leu, D. J., Coiro, J., Castek, J., Hartman, D., Henry, L. A., & Reinking, D. (2008). Research on instruction and assessment in the new literacies of online reading comprehension. In C. C. Block, S. Parris, & P. Afflerbach (Eds.), *Comprehension instruction: Research-based best practices.* New York: Guilford Press.

Lewis, J. (2007). Academic literacy: Principles and learning opportunities for adolescent readers. In J. Lewis & G. Moorman (Eds.), *Adolescent literacy instruction* (pp. 143–166). Newark, DE: International Reading Association.

Martin, B. (1983). *Brown bear, brown bear, what do you see?* New York: Henry Holt.

Maruki, T. (1982). *Hiroshima no pika.* New York: William Morrow.

Merkley, D. M., & Jeffries, D. (2001). Guidelines for implementing graphic organizers. *The Reading Teacher, 54*(4), 350–357.

Mokhtari, K., Kymes, A., & Edwards, P. (2008). Assessing the new literacies of online reading comprehension: An informative interview with W. Ian O'Byrne, Lisa Zawilinski, J. Greg McVerry, and Donald J. Leu at the University of Connecticut. *The Reading Teacher, 62*(4), 354–357.

Morgan, B., & Smith, R. D. (2008). A Wiki for classroom writing. *The Reading Teacher, 62*(1), 80–82.

Morgan, R. F., Meeks, J., Schollaert, A., & Paul, J. (1986). *Critical reading/thinking skills for the college student.* Dubuque, IA: Kendall/Hunt.

Oakley, G., & Jay, J. (2008). "Making time" for reading: Factors that influence the success of multimedia reading in the home. *The Reading Teacher, 62*(3), 246–255.

Palincsar, A. S. (1986). Reciprocal teaching. In *Teaching reading as thinking.* Oak Brook, IL: North Central Regional Educational Laboratory.

Palincsar, A. S., & Brown, A. L. (1984). Reciprocal teaching of comprehension-fostering and comprehension-monitoring activities. *Cognition and Instruction, 1,* 117–175.

Palmatier, R. A. (1973). A notetaking system for learning. *Journal of Reading, 17,* 36–39.

Pauk, W. (2000). *How to study in college.* Boston: Houghton Mifflin.

Pearman, C. J. (2008). Independent reading of CD-ROM storybooks: Measuring comprehension with oral retellings. *The Reading Teacher, 61*(8), 594–602.

Readence, J. E., Bean, T. W., & Baldwin, R. S. (2000). *Content area reading: An integrated approach.* Dubuque, IA: Kendall/Hunt.

Reinking, D., & Castek, J. (2007, November). *Developing Internet comprehension to adolescents who are at risk to become dropouts: A three-year IES research grant.* Paper presented at the National Reading Conference. Austin, TX.

Rex, L., & McEachen, D. (1999). "If anything is odd, inappropriate, confusing, or boring, it's probably important": The emergence of inclusive academic literacy through English classroom discussion practices. *Research in the Teaching of English, 34,* 65–129.

Sinatra, R., Gemake, J., Wielan, O. P., & Sinatra, C. (1998, March 23). Teaching learners to think, read, and write more effectively. The 1998 ASCD Annual Conference. San Antonio, TX.

Smith, C. B., & Elliot, P. G. (1986). *Reading activities for middle and secondary schools.* New York: Teachers College Press.

Swanson, P. N., & De la Paz, S. (1998). Teaching effective comprehension strategies to students. *Intervention in School & Clinic, 33*(4), 209–218.

Whitin, P. E. (2009). "Tech to Stretch": Expanding possibilities for literature response. *The Reading Teacher, 62*(5), 408–418.

**PEARSON**
## myeducationlab
**The Power of Classroom Practice**
www.myeducationlab.com

Now go to Topic 9: "Reading Comprehension," Topic 10: "Reading and Writing," and Topic 14: "English Language Learners" in the MyEducationLab (www.myeducationlab.com) for your course, where you can:

- Find learning outcomes for "Reading Comprehension," "Reading and Writing," and "English Language Learners," along with the national standards that connect to these outcomes.
- Complete the tasks in the Assignments and Activities to help you more deeply understand the chapter content.
- Examine challenging situations and cases presented in the IRIS Center Resources.
- Access video clips of CCSSO National Teachers of the Year award winners responding to the question, "Why Do I Teach?" in the Teacher Talk section.
- Apply and practice your understanding of the core teaching skills identified in the chapter with the Building Teaching Skills and Dispositions learning units.

# 12

# Making School–Family Connections

$\mathcal{M}$. J. has come in for a parent–teacher conference about her daughter. "I want to help Ruth become a better reader, but there's one big problem," said M. J. rather sheepishly. "I don't read so well myself. Y'know, I never finished high school."

"Oh, M. J., that's quite alright. There are lots of things you can do to help Ruth become a better reader and writer," I began. "For one thing, children *love* to read out loud to their mom. All you have to do is be a good listener and ask a few questions. And that's just the beginning. Let's talk about some of the other things you can do for Ruth that will really make a difference!"

M. J.'s face lit up as we talked about three powerful ways she could help Ruth at home. Later, I said, "M. J., we're trying to organize a community reading program and I need some help. Would you be interested?" I could tell by her expression that I had a new "recruit"!

Families, in sending their children to our schools each day, send us the best and most precious gifts they have. When we are able to offer them quality suggestions for ways to help their children succeed, they deeply appreciate the assistance; they are the bedrock of support for their children.

Evidence strongly suggests that when teachers and parents partner to support children's reading and academic achievement, at-risk children exhibit demonstrable gains (Darling, 2005). In summarizing the U.S. Department of Education's (2001) Longitudinal Evaluation of School Change and Performance in Title I Schools, which followed the reading development of third through fifth graders in 71 high-poverty schools, Darling (2005) concluded:

> Growth in reading scores between third and fifth grades was 50% higher for those students whose teachers and schools reported high levels of early parental outreach than for those students whose teachers and schools reported low levels of parent outreach activities for the third grade. (p. 476)

Parent and community involvement is essential for student success in reading (Cooter, 2004). Between birth and age 19, children spend just 9% of their lives in school, and 91% elsewhere. Paul Barton (1992, 1994) of the Educational Testing Service estimated that 90% of the differences among students and their schools across the United States could be explained by five factors: number of days absent from school, number of hours spent watching television, number of pages read for homework, quantity and quality of reading materials in the home, and the presence of two parents in the home. That fifth factor is supremely important because it is apt to decisively influence the other four (Will, 2002). Barton concluded that school success is heavily dependent on the platform of readiness and support of learning created in the home.

If we are to maximize the learning potential of every child, we must enlist the aid of family members. We cannot afford to overlook the needs, strengths, contributions, and perspectives that family members can bring to school programs (Handel, 1999, p. 127). Recognition of adult family members as a valuable resource is evident nowadays in such federal legislation as the 1998 Reading Excellence Act, the Workforce Investment Act, and the No Child Left Behind Act (NCLB).

In this chapter, we share ideas that have been shown to be effective in getting families involved in their children's literacy development. Because this chapter is quite unlike the others (there is no real diagnosis of reading problems to be done), we simply summarize key research briefly and then share some great ideas used by highly effective teachers. We do, however, include an If-Then chart that explains which ideas are appropriate for each age group.

# *B*ACKGROUND BRIEFING FOR TEACHERS

Go to the Building Teaching Skills and Dispositions section of Topic 15: "Parents and Families" in the MyEducationLab for your course and complete the activity entitled "Collaborating with Parents and Families to Improve a Student's Literacy Achievement." As you work through the learning unit, consider ways this school offers parents both voice and choice in terms of ways to be involved with their child's learning.

Sara Williams (2001), a teacher in Texas, conducted an extensive review of the research concerning family involvement in children's education that offers us some valuable insights. First, it is important that we understand that many families are rather passive in their children's education—not necessarily because of a lack of interest in their children's future but often due to a lack of knowing just *what* to do. Sadly, one study (Garshelis & McConnell, 1993) concluded that families having the greatest needs (i.e., poverty issues, children with severe handicaps, etc.) are less likely to feel they have input in their child's education. Williams's second research finding was that "professionals [teachers] should serve a more facilitative and empowering role for families" (p. 10). Given that so many family members lack either the knowledge or financial resources to provide books and reading opportunities in the home, it is incumbent on the teacher to help bring resources and information to the primary caregiver.

Finally, Williams concluded that there is a need for further training and education for teachers in this area. Few teachers are prepared to take charge of family involvement programs, but the need is clear. Therefore, teachers should receive extensive professional development, support, and necessary materials to encourage family involvement.

## Traditional Approaches for Involving Families

Many studies have been published in recent years highlighting successful strategies for increasing family involvement (e.g., DeBruin-Parecki & Krol-Sinclair, 2003; Vopat, 1994;

Wasik, 2004). Findings from works such as these have influenced our selection of strategies presented later in this chapter. Historically speaking, there are also a number of successful in-the-home strategies teachers have suggested to parents for helping their children become literate. Sharon Darling (2005) pulled several of these together in Table 12.1. Later in this chapter we also explore ways to involve illiterate parents, the families of English learners, and recent innovations in family/community involvement.

### TABLE 12.1  Basic Strategies for Involving Parents in Literacy Learning

| Literacy Skill Area | In the Home |
| --- | --- |
| Print concepts | • Point out the title and author's name to their child when reading together<br>• Talk about where reading begins on the page and show how the words flow left to right<br>• Play games to match lowercase and uppercase letters<br>• Talk about how types of texts have similarities and differences<br>• Expose their child to many types of print<br>• Make a book with their child, using large print and illustrations |
| Fluency | • Read aloud often, encouraging their child to read aloud<br>• Let their child choose books to read and reread favorite books<br>• Model reading for fun and pleasure<br>• Act out a book or story<br>• Read aloud a sentence and then invite their child to read the same sentence (i.e., echo reading)<br>• Help their child read new words and talk about the meaning<br>• Talk with their child when they go to the library about how to pick out books of interest at an appropriate reading level |
| Vocabulary | • Read aloud a variety of genres<br>• Talk with their child about daily events and about books they read together<br>• Talk about how the illustrations and text in a book support each other<br>• Use word lists provided by their child's teacher in natural conversation<br>• Search for new words in texts with their child and look them up in the dictionary<br>• Help their child learn new vocabulary based on hobbies or interests |
| Text comprehension | • Ask their child to predict what might happen next in a story<br>• Ask who, what, where, when, and why questions about a book<br>• Ask their child questions about the topic of a book before reading it<br>• Ask their child about books being read at school and be familiar with them in order to extend conversations<br>• Ask their child what the main idea or message of a book might be |
| Writing | • Provide multiple writing materials and tools<br>• Encourage their child to write his or her name and the names of family members<br>• Let their child see them writing for various purposes<br>• Ask their child to say words out loud as he or she writes<br>• Respond to the ideas their child has written<br>• Encourage their child to write the way he or she talks, and then ask the child to read the writing aloud<br>• Plan a time and place for their child to write every day |

Source: From "Strategies for Engaging Parents in Home Support of Reading Acquisition," by S. Darling, 2005, *The Reading Teacher, 58*(5), 476–479. Copyright © 2005 by the International Reading Association (www.reading.org). Reproduced with permission of the International Reading Association via Copyright Clearance Center.

Go to the Assignments and Activities section of Topic 15: "Parents and Families" in the MyEducationLab for your course and complete the activity entitled "Family Literacy Program." As you watch the video and answer the accompanying questions, note the strategies parents with weak literacy skills are offered to assist in their children's literacy development.

## When Mama Can't Read

In our opening vignette, we looked in on a situation that is quite common in many urban and rural classrooms—the parent wants to help her child succeed as a reader but has limited literacy abilities. Kathleen Spencer Cooter (2006) sums up important research into this growing phenomenon in an article titled "When Mama Can't Read: Counteracting Intergenerational Illiteracy." Though many parents may lack even functional literacy skills, this researcher concludes that there is much a proactive teacher can do to help these parents help their children become successful readers. Indeed, in one study done by Miller (1978), when parents were given direct instruction in methods designed to increase their young child's speech and language skills to improve reading achievement, the parents became avid partners and used and maintained the methodologies taught over time to enhance their child's language skills.

Based on her research, Kathleen Spencer Cooter (2006) recommends a number of strategies that can be used by nonreading parents to help their children, including 12 specific suggestions for teachers when working with parents having limited reading ability, as summarized in Figure 12.1.

# INCREASING ORAL LANGUAGE IN EARLY AND EMERGENT READERS

Go to the Assignments and Activities section of Topic 15: "Parents and Families" in the MyEducationLab for your course and complete the activity entitled "Emergent Literacy Development." As you watch the video and answer the accompanying questions, notice how language development early in children's lives is critical for later reading and writing development.

It is widely conceded by researchers that the size of a child's vocabulary is a strong predictor of school success (Harvard Education Letter, 2005). Similarly, when parents set aside time to talk to their children, there can be a long-term positive impact on academic literacy development. Other researchers studying low-income parents at play with their children found that supportive play by both mothers and fathers increased positive language gains in their children (Dickinson & Tabors, 2001; Tamis-Lemonda, Shannon, Cabrera, & Lamb, 2004).

---

**FIGURE 12.1**    When Mama Can't Read: Suggestions for Teachers

1. Value what she knows, how she lives, and the uniqueness of her family.
2. Teach her to use books to make up stories for her children.
3. Urge her to have her own "show and tell" times at home.
4. Teach her to use dialogic reading techniques with her children.
5. Teach her to choose books that engage and can be manipulated with her child.
6. Teach her that speaking in long sentences models strong language for her child.
7. Teach her to be responsive to her child's speech and language—to spend time in language activities.
8. Teach her how to combine language and play.
9. Teach her to use complex or uncommon words when she talks to her child.
10. Urge Mom to tell her child family stories, songs, and rituals.
11. Have Mom point as she talks with her child about objects in the environment.
12. Teach her that just by talking and listening she can help her child to be a reader.

---

*Source:* From "When Mama Can't Read: Counteracting Intergenerational Illiteracy," by K. S. Cooter, 2006, *The Reading Teacher, 59*(7) 698–702. Copyright © 2006 by the International Reading Association (www.reading.org). Reproduced with permission of the International Reading Association via Copyright Clearance Center.

## Mean Length of Utterance

When studying children at an early age, the mother's **mean length of utterance (MLU),** the average number of words spoken together, is predictive of her child's later language development (Cooter, 2006; Murray, 1990). When parents speak in longer word chains—sentences that are longer and more complex, children tend to imitate and create longer sentences as well. Vocabulary becomes more complex and expressive. Sometimes just adding gestures is a valuable hint. Research on increasing a child's mean length of utterance provides some valuable insights for teachers who are coaching semiliterate or illiterate parents (Cooter, 2006).

- Parents who speak or question using complete sentences are more likely to have children who respond in longer word chains and longer utterances (Peterson, Carta, & Greenwood, 2005).
- Parents who read books or talk through books that are both narrative and manipulative—children can touch, pull, or handle the book—can increase their children's questions and length and number of utterances (Kaderavek & Justice, 2005).
- Simply giving children models and opportunities of lengthening and elaborating their sentences significantly increases their oral language ability (Farrar, 1985; Remaly, 1990).

## More Access Leads to More Reading

In *The Literacy Crisis: False Claims, Real Solutions,* Jeff McQuillan (1998) makes a powerful case for increasing student access to books in the home. In summarizing a number of rigorous research studies on the topic of access, McQuillan came to the following conclusions:

- More access to reading materials leads to more reading and, subsequently, higher reading achievement.
- In a study of parental attitudes among a group of African American families in which such variables as speaking to children about certain topics, telling children how to pronounce words correctly, teaching names of countries and states, and so forth were discussed, the *only* behavior that correlated significantly with reading scores was the number of books in the home. Thus, providing reading materials to low-income African American families, concludes this study, may be one of the most important things schools can do.
- In a study of middle school reluctant readers, the primary reason for students' infrequent reading was not a dislike of reading necessarily but because they lacked access at home to the kinds of reading materials that interested them (e.g., comics, magazines, books on relevant topics). In another study, reading performance was improved at elementary and junior high schools when students were given two free subscriptions to magazines of their choice.

## The Need for Community Involvement

Families can be approached either directly or indirectly. For example, an indirect way of getting the attention of adult family members is through community efforts. Cooter, Mills-House, Marrin, Mathews, and Campbell (1999) report success in gaining community involvement in reading through a number of strategies, which we highlight later in this chapter and briefly describe in the following summary:

- *Summer food and reading programs.* Efforts involving community religious organizations provide food to children of poverty and also nourish their minds with books.

Volunteers work with children in motivational read alouds, DEAR (Drop Everything and Read) time, and discussion groups.

- *Public access television.* School districts in metropolitan areas are allotted free public access airtime on television, time that often goes unused. A "Reading Channel" can be put together inexpensively that brings reading ideas into the living rooms of families.
- *Web pages.* The Internet is rapidly becoming a commonplace tool in many homes and businesses. Sponsorship of a community Web page by such groups as the Rotary, chambers of commerce, and local corporations can be quite effective.
- *Citywide DEAR time.* Imagine a day each month when the entire city stops at an appointed time just to pull out a book and read as a sign of solidarity and recognition of the necessity of reading. Citywide Drop Everything and Read (DEAR) accomplishes just that.

# *F*AMILY INVOLVEMENT AND ENGLISH LEARNERS

Go to the Assignments and Activities section of Topic 15: "Parents and Families "in the MyEducationLab for your course and complete the activity entitled "A Welcoming Environment." As you watch the video and answer the accompanying questions, look for ways English learner families are made to feel at home when entering classrooms.

A rapidly growing segment of the school population is composed of English learners (ELs), students who are learning English as their second language. Indeed, in many southwestern school districts in the United States, ELs are the majority. The question then arises, How can we assist the family members of EL children in reading development? This can be quite a challenge for teachers who are not bilingual themselves.

One avenue that shows a great deal of promise relates to adult education as part of family involvement with children. It is a well-known and accepted research finding that the mother's level of education correlates positively with the school achievement of her children (McQuillan, 1998). Many mothers of EL children in urban areas, however, have low levels of education and often cannot speak English themselves. Therefore, there is a double challenge: helping mothers increase their own literacy levels while also teaching them ways to assist their children in reading. Yarosz and Barnett (2001) concluded from their research that parent education programs targeting those with the least education may be especially valuable in trying to improve the literacy levels of children.

A successful research project known as the Harvest America's Family Reading Program (Lanteigne & Schwarzer, 1997) provides us with a splendid prototype that can work in many communities. Adult English classes are held in a local library having an extensive collection of adult education and EL materials. Each week, six children's books are selected that would interest both adults and children. The books are read aloud and discussed as part of the adult class. The focus is on ways of reading aloud to children and strategies for discussing the content, new vocabulary, and reactions to the stories. Test results confirmed that the reading proficiency levels of both children *and* adults in the program (many dads participate as well as moms) improved dramatically.

## Be Proactive

Williams (2001) concluded that teachers must be proactive in seeking family involvement, using an enablement model (quoting Dunst et al., 1994). Teachers, she said, should

1. *Offer supportive assistance.* Contact adult family members rather than wait for a problem in students' reading to emerge.
2. *Help families set reading goals.* Share ideas such as turning off the television at a designated time each night for family reading.

| Reading Backpacks | Classbooks | Write Soon! | Writing Briefcase | Buddy Journals | Family Stories Project | Project FLAME | D.E.A.R. City | Ed Major Pen Pals |
|---|---|---|---|---|---|---|---|---|
| + | + | + | + | + | + | + | + | + |
| + | + | + | + | + | + | − | + | + |
| * | * | * | * | + | + | − | + | + |

language in playful and challenging ways. At the completion of this experience, families leave with at-home kits, which include a book, guidelines for discussion, and suggestions for follow-up activities. The learning centers involve the following:

- Children sort objects by color, size, function, texture, or other shared features. Parents ask children to consider different ways to sort and classify the objects.
- Children select a topic and generate all the words they think relate to that topic. Parents draw or label ideas as their children dictate the list.
- Parents and children sort stuffed animals by location (land, air, or sea), physical attributes (size, color, texture, or body parts), or interest.
- Other centers may include books on themed topics, riddles, and descriptive language.
- Some activities prompt children to describe clothing, food, and photos of families.

The second unit, Opening Windows to the World, has parents learn about the importance of story reading at home. (*Note:* We recommend a good mix of nonfiction materials [e.g., science, social studies] with stories because nonfiction texts offer rich new vocabulary and concepts for language development.) Paratore and Jordan (2007) explain that parents learn in these sessions how stories provide distinctive language, extraordinary words, and inventive ideas for their children. Retelling, dramatic play, and story extensions are often used in these sessions.

At-home books are provided for parents and children to read and discuss. Each book has accompanying activities to help parents prompt children to relate the story experiences to their own lives.

The third unit, Structured for Sound, focuses on concepts of print, phonological awareness, and alphabetical principles. A wide range of hands-on activities is offered that focus attention on identification of letter forms and sounds. As Paratore and Jordan (2007) explain, there is a table set with brightly colored plates where children sort play food items by initial sound. There is another center that has suitcases where clothing can be sorted by initial sound. Other similar themes are possible for inventive teachers.

The last unit, Digging and Discovering, uses math and science nonfiction texts. At-home materials include books about animal life cycles, plants, weather, and other topics that prompt children to think about the world in which they live.

At the conclusion of the program, parents are given materials to maintain and extend previously used activities, and evaluate the program and offer suggestions for improvement. Student outcomes revealed increased vocabularies, improved narrative understanding, more developed phonological abilities, more interest in writing, and better academic preparation.

## Make-Believe Alouds

### Purpose

Reading aloud to children is one of the most common recommendations made by literacy experts and agencies across the nation as a preparation for academic success. But if mama can't read, consider reframing read alouds as simple **make-believe alouds** (Cooter, 2006). This is an alternative to read alouds in which parents use picture books to construct their own stories as a means for interacting with their child and the reverse of dialogic reading in which the child constructs the make-believe story. Either fiction or nonfiction books may be used, but we favor a heavy diet of nonfiction books for improving language and vocabulary. Magazines, comics, and catalogs are also recommended as a low-cost change of pace (Cooter, 2006).

### Materials

- Picture books rich in illustrations that "tell the story"

### Procedure

A parent does not have to know the words on the page to construct a fanciful story about the pictures, nor does storytelling about a picture book story have to be exactly the same for each retelling. A teacher or parent literacy guide can easily demonstrate a variety of ways that any book can be shared without having any knowledge of the words included.

Demonstrate to parents how to move through a book page by page, and create a wildly imaginative tale for fiction selections or rich descriptions and questions that coincide with the pictures and illustrations. Morgan and Goldstein (2004) found that teaching low socioeconomic status (SES) mothers how to use a story book in a fanciful and imaginative manner with their young children increased the type and quality of language in child–parent interactions.

## Using Magazines, Comics, and Catalogs

When books are not readily available in the home, many families have access to magazines, comics, or catalogs. Simply engaging the child in conversations using this variety of texts and pictures can stimulate language, vocabulary, and storytelling. One mother we know plays the "Million Dollars" game with her children using assorted catalogs. "If we win a million dollars, we will buy . . ." A kindergarten teacher borrowed this idea from the family and brought catalogs to create a catalog center in her classroom. She believes it is the most talkative, noisy, and engaging center in her classroom.

## Refrigerator Reading

### Purpose

Whether engaging in a major reading initiative in a large urban center or in a single classroom, communication with families is critical. Many times adults will say to our teachers, "I would love to help my child become a better reader. I just don't know what to do. Can you help me?"

Cooter et al. (1999) found that monthly newsletters for families are a superb vehicle for communicating easy-to-do activities to primary caregivers. Theirs is called *Refrigerator Reading,* a reference to the age-old practice of putting important school papers on the refrigerator for everyone to see.

### Materials

- Computer, printer, and photocopier to produce and distribute newsletters

### Procedure

The idea is to send home tips for parents on ways they can help their child develop in reading and writing in both Spanish and English, if necessary. You may choose to include such areas as helping your child self-select high-interest books using the "rule-of-thumb" method, how to do read alouds, how to encourage recreational writing, being a good listener when your child reads, conducting retellings, questioning after reading, study tips, ways to become involved in your child's classroom as a volunteer, and humorous tales about school life (like one principal's "No whining" rule). Reports from Cooter and colleagues (1999) are that some parents collect *Refrigerator Reading* newsletters and mail copies to grandmas and new moms, confirming the usefulness of this easy-to-do medium.

## Family Projects

### Purpose

Andrea Burkhart (2000), a teacher at a school on the south side of Chicago, asked parents to help her come up with ideas for family–school projects. They responded with many great ideas that she incorporated into her curriculum as family projects that get adults at home actively involved. Sometimes parents are willing to come in with their child to present their product!

### Materials

- Monthly newsletter with descriptions of family project assignments and "deliverables" (products you would like for the students to bring in to school when the project is done)

### Procedure

In Figure 12.3 is an outline of the topics Burkhart (2000) developed for her class. You will want to adapt and expand the descriptions to suit your needs and fit grade-level expectations.

## Voice Mail

### Purpose

Many teachers have access to their school district's voice mail system and usually have their own account or number. Willman (2000), a remedial reading teacher, uses voice mail during the summer break to keep contact with her students. They report back to her verbally about books they have chosen to read, and parents are often involved. We feel this strategy could be used throughout the school, as well as during summers for developing readers (Willman, 2000).

---

| FIGURE 12.3 | Family Projects Curriculum |

**September: Family Tree**
Parents and students work together to trace their family roots. They create a visual display and present an object that reflects their family history, such as an antique picture, clothing, food, music, or literature.

**October: Weather**
Parents and students predict weather patterns for the next month. They watch weather reports to compare their predictions and keep track of their work in a journal.

**November: Family Reading Month**
Parents and students read to or with each other daily. The books read and the amount of time spent reading will be recorded in a daily log and turned in at the end of November.

**December: Biographies**
Students learn about biographies and how they are constructed in class. They then create interview questions and interview a parent or primary caregiver. Students write a biography of that person and share it with their family.

**January: Measurement**
Parents and students predict the measurement (length, width, area, etc.) of an object or distance two or three times each week. After actually measuring each object, a journal entry is completed, showing the predicted measurement and the actual measurement.

**February: Poetry Month**
A book of family poetry is created. Students are responsible for educating their families about poetry, collecting the poems, and compiling them into a book.

**March: Plants**
Each student will take home two plants in milk cartons. The student will care for one, and an adult family member the other. One plant will be given light and the other plant will not. The progress of each plant will be tracked by the child and adult together and their progress recorded in a journal entry regularly.

**April: Decisions**
Two or three times per week students will take home a proposed (hypothetical) question that requires a decision. Topics might include issues related to drugs, gangs, honesty, or others proposed by parents. The parent and child will discuss options together and create a written response.

**May: Simple Machines**
After learning about simple machines in class, students will construct a simple machine with the guidance of a parent.

---

*Source:* From "Breaking the Parental Barrier," by A. L. Burkhart, 1995, *The Reading Teacher, 48*(7), 634–635. Copyright © 1995 by the International Reading Association (www.reading.org). Reproduced with permission of the International Reading Association via Copyright Clearance Center.

### Materials

- Books for self-selection by students (for summer use, three books apiece: two fiction, one nonfiction)
- A phone
- A voice mail account
- Writing materials

### Procedure

Begin by creating a letter to the parents explaining how the assignment will work, how to access the voice mail system, and what your expectations include. If you will be using this activity during the school year (as opposed to summer only), plan on conducting this briefing in person at the first open house.

In Willman's (2000) model, she asked students to call in to the voice mail and read aloud for 3 minutes or summarize a chapter from the book they are reading. It is also recommended that you have specific questions for each book for student response. They can answer these questions when they call in to read. Another adaptation is for students to call in to the school's homework hotline to hear the teacher read aloud portions of the book. This provides a fluent reading model for students. However, a better idea is for parents to read aloud a portion of the book regularly for their child.

Willman (2000) reported that the summer voice mail program succeeded in its inaugural year in preventing all remedial readers from losing ground (26), and one student actually increased his reading level by a half year!

## Reading Backpacks

### Purpose

One of the challenges is getting high-quality books into the hands of children at home. Many families are economically disadvantaged and simply do not have books for their children to read. The **reading backpacks** strategy (Cooter et al., 1999; Reutzel & Fawson, 1990) gets books of appropriate interest and reading levels into each child's home at least once per week.

### Materials

- Five backpacks per classroom (with the school logo or mascot, if possible)
- Leveled books that can be sent home
- Writing materials
- Card stock
- Markers

### Procedure

Based on the Traveling Tales backpacks concept (Reutzel & Cooter, 2000; Reutzel & Fawson, 1990) for promoting writing, reading backpacks contain a supply of trade books on varying topics and readability levels (often in both English and Spanish); easy activities for parents to do with their children on printed card stock adapted from Mooney's (1990) Reading To, With, and By strategies; and materials for written responses (markers, colored paper, scissors, etc.). Also included is a simple Family Report Form for adults to note which books were read by the child and to whom, as well as any reader response activities they were able to do at home. In this way teachers were able to track student interests and, to a degree, outside reading habits. Reading backpacks are regarded as a wonderful success in many schools and are treasured by young readers.

## Classbooks

### Purpose

Laura Lee Scott (2000), a second-grade teacher, recommends the construction of classbooks by students to send home for reading and sharing with parents. Contributions for the classbook are made by each student using the writing process or by the class as a whole using the language experience approach.

## Materials

- Writing materials for individual students
- Easel, markers, and chart paper for a whole-class language experience
- Photocopies of the final classbook for each child

## Procedure

Each student composes a contribution (i.e., story, poem, song, expository passage about a topic of interest, etc.) for the classbook independently, or the class writes together using a language experience approach. After working through the revising and editing process, copies of the classbook are taken home by students to share with adult family members. The book can be read *by* students to adults or *to* students by the adult.

Some classbooks have emphasized academic subjects like science and social studies, as well as other topics of personal interest. Titles of student contributions include "If I Could Be a Dinosaur," "My Mom," and "When I Grow Up." Classbooks constructed by the whole class in a language experience format have included *Halloween Stories* and *Christmas Memories*. Scott (2000) reports a great success using classbooks, including an increase of parent volunteers during her writing workshop period!

# PART II: FAMILY WRITING STRATEGIES

## Write Soon!

Writing, like reading, is learned best when it occurs in authentic situations and for authentic purposes (Rasinski & Padak, 2009, p. 618). At-home writing activities are a part of family life that can easily be coopted in purposeful ways to improve literacy learning. Consider the myriad ways families use writing daily: shopping lists, quick informational notes to other family members, birthday and holiday cards and notes of affection dropped into lunch boxes and hidden underneath pillows on a bed, letters and email correspondence sent to family members, scrapbooking, and many more. As teachers, we can help parents see these regular activities as opportunities for their children to write for real purposes. Rasinski and Padak (2009) list several types of writing teachers might suggest to help parents and children integrate it into family life that we summarize here.

- *Letters, emails, and online chats.* Just as parents sometimes write to family members not living in the same home, children too can be encouraged to write (or email) to family members who may be absent. Children are especially excited and motivated when they receive a letter in reply to one that the child has written. We recommend social networking sites such as Twitter (www.twitter.com) and Facebook (www.facebook.com) as great resources.

- *Making lists.* Lists are often used to help us remember things and reflect on events in our lives. Parents share their own lists with their children and encourage them to make their own lists. Every day children can be asked to make a list of their activities for the day. Later in the evening, the list can be used for reflection—children and parents can go through the list, determine if it was realistic, and make plans for the next day. Examples of lists include to-do lists, shopping lists, invitation lists, birthday wishes, daily chores, or a top-ten list of almost anything of interest to the child.

- *Notes.* Parents, as ever, can lead by example and share different kinds of notes they create and use every day (Rasinski & Padak, 2009). They might also purchase for their child a small spiral notebook that can fit into a back pocket in which notes can be recorded. Examples of notes commonly used include surprise notes hidden away for later discovery (lunch boxes, under pillow, inside the refrigerator, etc.), reminders to self or others to get something done, kitchen bulletin board notes, observations about something encountered in one's life such as the taste of something new, or feelings before or after leaving grandma and grandpa after a summer visit.

- *Journals/Diaries.* More formal than spontaneous notes—journals/diaries are done in an actual book. Journal writers often add to journals regularly, often at a specific time of the day (e.g., near the end of the day, right before bed). Typically, a child will summarize and reflect on the events of a day or period of time. Journaling can lead to a deeper understanding of events in their lives, and can also serve as a keepsake through life. Journals also make excellent gifts to family members. For best results, parents should keep a journal of their own to help their children see how they make entries.

- *Dialogue journals.* Dialogue journals are written conversations between a parent and a child using a notebook to carry on the conversation (Rasinski & Padak, 2009). The parent writes an entry into the dialogue journal (i.e., to ask a question, provide an answer, give or take advice, words of encouragement, apologies, words of affection). The journal is then delivered to the child's room where she or he makes their own entry (i.e., an answer, a new question, etc.) and returns the journal to the parent for the next set of entries. Since this activity is an opportunity for the parent to model fluent writing in the journal entries, the child will improve his or her writing by emulating the words and written conventions used by the parent.

- *Birthday and special event books.* Parents provide and introduce blank books in which family members and other guests at the child's birthday party—or any special event—are invited to share a kind thought, a special wish, or favorite memory of the special person.

- *Parodies.* Families can find great satisfaction in creating and sharing parodies, especially parodies of songs and poems for children. With this activity the text that is being parodied becomes a model or scaffold for the writer to use in creating his or her own version of the text (Rasinski & Padak, 2009). For example, to write a new version "Yankee Doodle," the child needs to change what Yankee rode to town on. If Mr. Doodle comes to town on a llama, the poem might read this way:

  > Yankee Doodle went to town riding on a llama
  > Across the mountains, and over the plains
  > And went to see his mama.

## The Writing Briefcase

### Purpose

The **writing briefcase** (Miller-Rodriguez, 1992) is an inspired idea that helps parents become more involved with their child's literacy learning. In our interpretation of this activity, students periodically take home a briefcase containing materials helpful in the creation of new compositions. We see the writing briefcase as especially useful for emergent writers and readers in the early grades and as a tool for involving parents in their child's literacy learning at home.

## Materials

- An old briefcase (a backpack works just as well), with stickers and other decorations for the outside of the briefcase
- A laminated letter to the family member
- Markers, crayons, magazine pictures, word cards, picture dictionary, index cards, lined and unlined paper, tape, stapler, paper clips, rubber bands, scissors, and any other writing and illustrating materials of your choice
- Easy-to-read books of various kinds that may inspire different text types (e.g., poetry, songs, stories, etc.).

## Procedure

A different child takes home the briefcase each night and writes (or completes, in some cases) a story and illustrates it. He or she also reads his or her story, as well as the other books enclosed, to family members. A letter included in the briefcase is directed to family members explaining the activity and the importance of their involvement. This letter ideally serves as a follow-up refresher course on the writing and other literacy-learning processes previously described by the teacher at the beginning of the school year in a parent meeting expressly held for that purpose. Figure 12.4 is a sample letter to family members.

---

**FIGURE 12.4** Sample Letter for the Writing Briefcase

October 14

Sarah Cannon School
711 Opry Place
Nashville, TN 37211

Dear Family Member:
Children in our class are becoming more and more interested and excited about their abilities as writers and readers. I am interested in helping them realize that writing and reading are not just school activities, but are also skills they can use and enjoy at home and in other places.

This writing briefcase allows your child to experience writing at home using the different tools enclosed. I'd like for you to encourage your child to create a story, poem, song, recipe, rap, or any other composition. You might want to encourage your child to take the briefcase and write outside, perhaps in a favorite hiding place.

Please allow your child to try out the enclosed materials. It would be especially helpful if you would take time to listen to your child's finished products. The product may not look like a story or other composition, but you will find that your child can read and understand it.

I would like for your child to return the written composition, along with the writing briefcase, tomorrow.

Kindest regards,
Mr. Acuff

Finally, students may wish to have their own writing briefcase or backpack that they can use throughout the year in which to take their compositions and writing materials home. Some students like to emulate adults by "taking work home from the office."

## Buddy Journals

### Purpose

**Buddy journals** (Klobukowski, 2000) are a version of reading logs that have students and parents read the same book together, silently or orally (whatever works best), then respond to each other in a journal. Parents often make superb models of fluent reading and respond well to this activity.

### Materials

- Two copies of the book that will be sent home with the child
- Two spiral notebooks to serve as buddy logs

### Procedure

The procedure is simple. The adult family member and the child each read the book or portions of the book, then respond in their journals. Then, the adult and child swap journals, read the entry, and respond to the entry. Here are some further suggestions from Klobukowski (2000):

- Encourage parents to reread portions of the text orally, if they are not already reading the book aloud, so that the child can have a reading role model.
- When parents are making entries in their buddy journal, ask them to relate what happened to book characters, to themselves, and to their family and help their child understand these connections.
- Encourage both parents and students to identify the feelings of the characters and share in their journals what they think the characters should do.
- Ask parents to help their children find information in the text and clarify for them any misunderstandings they detect in the buddy journal entries.
- Urge parents to give their children lots of positive reinforcement and praise for what they can do, and avoid negative criticism.
- Parents should try to include humor in their responses.
- Let parents know that this activity will work best if there is an appointed time to complete the task at home. This avoids last-minute rushes to complete a "homework" assignment.

## Bilingual Connections: Family Stories Project

### Purpose

The **family stories project (FSP)** is a procedure originally developed with fourth-grade Latino students in a bilingual classroom that encourages children's uses of two languages for communicating, reading, and writing in the classroom (Dworin, 2006). Teachers have students write about topics from their homes and communities, including those of relatives living in other countries. This funds-of-knowledge orientation, Dworin explains, draws on students' experiences, what they know and care about, and also lets the children become aware that their lives outside of school have meaning and importance within the classroom. The many benefits of FSP include students working collaboratively while writing, using both languages (home language and English) to promote bilingualism, writing for multiple audiences, and fostering children's desire to write in their classrooms.

## Materials

- Usual writing materials, such as pencils, paper, or a computer (if available)

## Procedure

**Step 1:** *Discussing two stories.* In the original family stories project conducted with Spanish-speaking students learning English, Dworin (2006) began the process using two stories from the bilingual book *Salsa Stories/Cuentos con Sazón* by Lulu Delacre (1999), "The Birthday Party/La Fiesta de Cumpleaños" and "Holy Week/La Semana Santa." This book contains short stories told by family members during a family get-together on New Year's Day and shares experiences of various family members when they were growing up, used to illustrate the kinds of stories children might collect from their own families.

Discuss the two stories—both English and Spanish were used during the workshop sessions, and teachers followed the children's lead in language choice to offer comments and suggestions. After the discussions of the two stories, the following instructions were given: "Ask family members to share a story with you about their lives. Try to listen to several and pick one that you want to write up and bring in for the project. It should be a true story, something that really happened, and not one that you make up."

**Step 2:** *Stories from home.* In the second phase, children collected, wrote down, and brought family stories to school. In Dworin's (2006) research, 15 of 18 stories children brought from home were written in Spanish and included a range of topics including immigrating to the United States to find work, a joke Christmas present, celebrating Easter in Guatemala, and stories about the childhoods of parents and grandparents. Children read the stories aloud while the other children listened and thought about questions. Then, classmates asked questions and offered comments and suggestions about each of the stories, such as, "Where did this take place?" "More details—you need more details!" "How old was your mother when this happened?" "You didn't say why they were afraid!" After going through all of the children's stories in this manner, ask students to use the notes they took to respond to these issues in a second draft. Students may need to ask the family member for more information.

**Step 3:** *Peer conference.* After students have revised their family stories, students again listen to the stories, asking questions, and discussing how to make improvements. Students then return to working on their stories. After revisions have been made, students are asked to have their parents or other family member (whoever told the story to them) sign their name that the story was an accurate retelling of what had happened. The students bring these in, and the process is repeated. Finally, the students write their final drafts of their stories.

**Step 4:** *Translating the stories.* Once a final draft had been written, students are presented with a group lesson on how to translate stories into English. This involves discussing what a translation is—that it is often not a word-by-word process but rather an attempt to capture the sense or spirit of what was written (Dworin, 2006). Some practice with translations is modeled and practiced using, in this case, a paragraph in English and one in Spanish, from the two stories that they had read prior to collecting and writing the family stories.

Next, have students pair up to work on translations. Ask them to exchange their stories with their partner for translation (i.e., none of the students translate their own story; each student translates a piece written by their partner). Students meet three times in groups to discuss and work on the translations. Once completed, ask them to make an illustration (in black and white) for their own stories.

**Step 5:**   *Publishing the stories.* In the family stories project research, Dworin (2006) edited the stories, typed them on a computer, and set them up for layout with the illustrations. Two books were published, one in Spanish and one in English. Students decided on titles for the two books, *El Gran Libro de Bellos Recuerdos de Nuestras Familias* and *The Magnificent Book of Memories.* Two copies of each book were distributed to every student in the class and additional copies were given to family members, asking for a donation for each additional book to defray publishing costs. Dworin (2006) reported that one student ordered eight additional copies of the Spanish book to give copies to his grandparents, uncles, aunts, and cousins!

## Project FLAME

### Purpose

One way to improve the literacy of English learners, as well as children living in poverty circumstances, is to improve the literacy of their parents. There is an outreach program for parents that received a great deal of acclaim in the 1990s called **Project FLAME** (Shanahan, Mulhern, & Rodriguez-Brown, 1995) which stands for Family Literacy: Aprendiendo, Mejorando, Educando (Learning, Bettering, Educating). Though this program does not directly teach children, research results showed that Project FLAME led to improved English proficiency for parents and also improved their children's performance in the knowledge of basic concepts, letter names, and print awareness (Owen & Shanahan, 1993).

### Materials

- Materials vary depending on the sessions offered to parents as described in the next section

### Procedure

FLAME has themes for each session as opposed to a rigidly constructed curriculum. The creators of FLAME state that instruction "should be based on theory and carefully planned, but it also must be responsive to students' needs and concerns. Our curriculum provides a supportive teaching map without blinding us to the realities of our students" (Shanahan, Mulhern, & Rodriguez-Brown, 1995, p. 588). Following are session themes and parent activities commonly used in Project FLAME.

- *Creating home literacy centers.* Creating a literacy activity center in a box, including pencils, crayons, paper, scissors, paste, magazines, pictures, and so on. Emphasis on how to make a home literacy center and how to use it.

- *Book sharing.* The most effective ways to share books with children. How to talk about books and share books when your own literacy is limited (*Note:* See information on "dialogic reading" in Chapter 3).
- *Book selection.* Criteria for selecting books appropriate to children's needs and interests.
- *Library visit.* Public library tour complete with applications for library cards.
- *Book fairs.* Parents buy (with coupons) English- or Spanish-language books for their children.
- *Teaching the ABCs.* Simple ways to teach letters and sounds. Emphasis on language games, songs, and language experience activities.
- *Children's writing.* How children write and ways to encourage writing at home.
- *Community literacy.* How parents can share their own literacy uses with their children during marketing and other daily activities.
- *Classroom observations.* Classroom visitations to gain a sense of how their children are taught in the school.
- *Parent–teacher get-togethers.* Guided discussions about children's education with teachers and principals.
- *Math for your child.* Games and activities for helping children understand numbers and arithmetic. This was a session especially requested by parents.
- *How parents can help with homework.* Ways parents can monitor and help with children's homework even when they cannot do the homework themselves.

# *P*ART III: COMMUNITY INVOLVEMENT

## D.E.A.R. "City"!

### Purpose

Research indicates that young children average reading only about 7 to 8 minutes during the school day (Anderson, Hiebert, Scott, & Wilkinson, 1985, p. 76). Yet we know that the development of fluent reading requires massive amounts of practice in order to satisfy student interest, build fluency, increase vocabulary, and improve comprehension. Clearly, some sort of sustained silent reading on a daily basis is needed. D.E.A.R. [your city's name here] (Cooter et al., 1999) sets up a designated day and time, usually by a mayoral proclamation, in which every business, school, and corporation stop for 5 minutes to pull out a book and read as a sign of their unified commitment to the importance of reading.

### Materials

- Reading materials
- A plan to attract political support, newspaper coverage (an "Op-Ed" piece), media coverage, and a lot of volunteer workers to spread the word

### Procedure

The goal of D.E.A.R. "City"! (modeled after the *Drop Everything And Read* classroom strategy) is to get everyone in the city to join local schools in making a dramatic statement in support of reading. The original vision of the Dallas Public Schools (Cooter et al., 1999) was that citizens would stop whatever they were doing for just 10 minutes at an assigned time (10:00 to 10:10 AM on March 6) and read a book, newspaper, or magazine just for fun.

Publicity was arranged in cooperation with local newspapers, television and radio stations, and with the city buses that would travel about the city brandishing large advertising banners (see Figure 12.5) to help spread the word.

Who joined the original D.E.A.R. Dallas citywide effort? Nearly everyone. The mayor proclaimed March 6 as "D.E.A.R. Dallas Day" and joined in by reading with all teachers and children of Dallas in grades K through 12. The police chief, also a strong supporter of children and education in Dallas, joined in along with downtown businesses and corporate offices as an act of solidarity. Then Governor George W. Bush, told that D.E.A.R. Dallas was consonant with a statewide reading initiative, issued a statement praising the effort and reiterating how we must all encourage our children to read every day for fun and to strengthen their literacy skills for improved life choices.

Getting DEAR time started at the classroom or school level is really quite simple. It begins with an understanding that time set aside for pleasure reading is not a frill but a necessity in a balanced reading program. Teachers should set aside about 20 minutes per day for students to self-select and read books.

We teach students to self-select books using the "rule-of-thumb" method (Reutzel & Cooter, 2000): After choosing a book of interest, open the book to any page with a lot of words and count the number of words you do not know. If you use all five fingers to count unknown words on one page, the book is too difficult; put it back and choose another you like just as well. Schoolwide DEAR time can be achieved with the principal's support. Simply set aside a time daily in which everyone drops everything to read. It is a truly powerful tool that can have magnificent results so long as everyone participates.

**FIGURE 12.5**   D.E.A.R. Dallas Poster

## "Education Major" Pen Pals

### Purpose

Education major pen pals (Flickenger, 1991) is a slight variation on the pen pals theme that has met with great success in many areas. Its only substantive difference is that, instead of pairing students with other students or peers, education major pen pals matches students (usually elementary level) with young adults majoring in education at a local college or university. A final book project based on the elementary student is completed jointly between the youngster and the university student.

In addition to providing an audience and reason for writing, this form of pen pals gives students other motivational reasons for reading: the anticipation and receiving of letters, personalized books, or other compositions from the student teachers. Education students are likewise given opportunities as new professionals to connect with students in a way that offers valuable insights.

### Materials

- A list of education majors interested in working with your students from a local college or university professor (usually specializing in reading, literacy, and/or language arts education) interested in such a project
- Writing center materials for final drafts of letters, such as writing paper, envelopes, pens, and stamps
- Bookmaking materials, such as laminating materials, stiff cardboard for book covers, and art materials for illustrations
- First draft (messy copy) writing materials (paper and pencils) for the elementary students
- Overhead projector, transparencies, and other materials for the construction of examples of each of the writing process stages as they pertain to the composition of letters
- If possible, a computer with word processing software on which students can type letters and other compositions

### Procedure

This activity is essentially the same as with the standard pen pals activity, except that students correspond with student teachers attending education classes at the local college or university. Students in early elementary grades are encouraged to use invented (we prefer the term *temporary*) spellings. Elementary students are encouraged to talk and/or draw about families, interests, friends, and special events taking place in their lives at school and at home.

One expectation, which takes the form of a book project, is that university students write books (text only) for their pen pals using what they have learned about their pen pals' interests. The university students bind the nearly finished books but leave room on each page for illustrations. Then, the elementary students illustrate their personalized books and send them back to the university students. After making one or more copies of the finished books, the university students return the original books to their pen pals. An additional teacher-education benefit is that university students are able to use the letters and other compositions written by their pen pals for analysis of writing development and discovery of children's learning.

## Summer Food and Reading Program

### Purpose

One of the great concerns of urban communities is the welfare of children during the summer months. When schools are out, for example, many children regress in their literacy development. Another worry is that some of the children may not have access to the kind of nutritious meals available to them during the school year. To respond to both of these needs, one community developed a Summer Food and Reading Program (Cooter et al., 1999). Community members discovered that a city with numerous bored 5- to 12-year-olds, comfortable space available at local churches, a pool of enthusiastic volunteers, and thousands of "gently used" donated books can provide all the ingredients needed for a successful summer "reading and feeding" program.

## Materials

- At least five books per child to be served
- A location coordinated by volunteer workers or a local community group

## Procedure

Many have selected the Reading To, With, and By model (Mooney, 1990) to train volunteers and involve the more reluctant readers. Several teachers usually design and deliver interactive training for the volunteers in effective balanced reading instruction. Making reading fun is one of the basic tenets of the training model for the volunteer tutors. Volunteers are taught ways to read aloud favorite poems and stories, encourage buddy reading using big books, make big books, and use supportive strategies for encouraging children's oral reading. Volunteers are also taught how to establish a print-rich environment using primarily children's work.

To start your own summer reading and nutrition program, we suggest contacting local church leaders, social support agencies, and youth organizations (boys and girls clubs, the local Y, etc.). Urban centers have a number of such agencies looking to leverage their resources through partnering. Business-oriented clubs, such as Rotary International and Kiwanis, can also be helpful in recruiting volunteers and securing funding.

## The Reading Channel

### Purpose

The purpose of this project is to use a public access television channel available to a school district as an outreach tool for reading development in the home. This primarily requires official contacts and negotiations between the local PBS network provider and the local school district leadership. At least one full-time equivalent teacher will be needed to organize the Reading Channel and serve as liaison with the television station personnel.

### Materials

- A program developed for communicating with students and their families in their homes on their television sets

### Procedure

One of the tools many large urban school districts have at their disposal is one or more "public access" cable television channels from the local providers. The "Reading Channel" (Cooter et al., 1999) can be organized as a support for families in raising literate children. One way this is accomplished is to air each evening during prime time (6 to 9 PM) alternative television offerings oriented toward positive literacy habits. As part of the Public Broadcasting System (PBS) and cable television charters, school districts having a public access channel can rerun at no charge any PBS program from the prior year. Thus, such programs as "Reading Rainbow," "Mr. Rogers," and "Sesame Street" can be aired on a new Reading Channel. A regular slate of offerings can be planned so that the Reading Channel can become a welcomed friend to families in the region. School districts interested in taking advantage of public access channels should do several key things. First, check with the central office administrator in your school district responsible for communications and distance learning initiatives. This person is a valuable resource who will know the details for public access initiatives in your district and the procedures to get things started. If your district is new to this kind of enterprise, then contact the cable television provider in your area directly and inquire as to the public access provisions in its charter. Finally, if you are interested in rebroadcasting PBS television programs like the ones mentioned, get in touch with your area public broadcasting affiliate to learn about how you can partner with it to make your plan a reality.

### Internet Home Page

#### Purpose

As computers in the home, public libraries, workplace, and schools have become increasingly commonplace, many teachers are establishing an Internet home page. The purpose of the Reading Internet Home Page is to create another tool for your students that is tailor-made to your curriculum. If your school district has a technology department, ask for assistance in setting up a Web page of your own. If not, you may want to consider creating your own Web page on Facebook where you can post various kinds of information. Another way to set up a Web page is by using a software package for creating Web pages sold by most large business equipment retailers.

#### Procedure

We prefer to persuade a talented "Web master" (a techie already on the district payroll) to help us design a new home page as a distance learning tool for parents, teachers, college researchers, foundations, business leaders, and others frequently asking for more information on reading. The Web page enables people from literally around the world to access at any time information on upcoming learning events, how to contact teachers and resource professionals, support materials for assisting children in becoming literate in the home, links to other related Internet websites, and many other options.

The home page is a living document that is constantly under construction and revision (pardon our dust!) and is a terrific tool for serving all stakeholders in the balanced literacy reform effort.

## SELECTED REFERENCES

Anderson, R. C., Hiebert, E. H., Scott, J. A., & Wilkinson, I. A. G. (1985). *Becoming a nation of readers: The report of the Commission on Reading.* Washington, DC: The National Institute of Education.

Barton, P. (1992). *America's smallest school: The family.* Princeton, NJ: Educational Testing Service.

Barton, P. (1994). *Becoming literate about literacy.* Princeton, NJ: Educational Testing Service.

Beals, D. E. (1997). Sources of support for learning words in conversation: Evidence from mealtimes. *Journal of Child Language, 24*(3), 673–694.

Beals, D. E., & De Temple, J. M. (1993). Home contributions to early language and literacy development. In D. J. Leu & C. K. Kinzer (Eds.), *Examining central issues in literacy research, theory, and practice* (42nd yearbook of the National Reading Conference, pp. 207–216). Chicago: The National Reading Conference.

Burkhart, A. L. (2000). Breaking the parental barrier. In T. V. Rasinski, N. D. Padak, et al. (Eds.), *Motivating recreational reading and promoting home-school connections* (pp. 110–113). Newark, DE: International Reading Association.

Cooter, K. S. (2006). When Mama can't read: Counteracting intergenerational illiteracy. *The Reading Teacher, 59*(7), 698–702.

Cooter, R. B. (Ed.). (2004). *Perspectives on rescuing urban literacy education: Spies, saboteurs, and saints.* Mahwah, NJ: Lawrence Erlbaum.

Cooter, R. B., Mills-House, E., Marrin, P., Mathews, B., & Campbell, S. (May, 1999). Family and community involvement: The bedrock of reading success. *The Reading Teacher, 52*(8), 891–896.

Darling, S. (2005). Strategies for engaging parents in home support of reading acquisition. *The Reading Teacher, 58*(5), 476–479.

DeBruin-Parecki, A., & Krol-Sinclair, B. (2003). *Family literacy: From theory to practice.* Newark, DE: International Reading Association.

De Temple, J. M., & Beals, D. E. (1991). Family talk: Sources of support for the development of decontextualized language skills. *Journal of Research in Childhood Education, 6,* 11–19.

Delacre, L. (1999). *Salsa stories/Cuentos con sazón.* New York: Scholastic.

Dickinson, D. K., & Tabors, P. O. (Eds.). (2001). *Beginning literacy with language: Young children learning at home and school.* Baltimore: Brookes.

Dunst, C., Trivette, C. M., & Deal, A. G. (Eds.) (1994). *Supporting and strengthening families: Methods, strategies and practices.* Cambridge, MA: Brookline Books.

Dworin, J. E. (2006, March). The Family Stories Project: Using funds of knowledge for writing. *The Reading Teacher, 59*(6), 510–520.

Farrar, E. B. (1985). *Accelerating the oral language of children of low socio-economic status.* Belle Glade, FL: Unpublished Dissertation. (ERIC Document Reproduction Service No. ED 262 913)

Flickenger, G. (1991). Pen pals and collaborative books. *The Reading Teacher, 45*(1), 72–73.

Garshelis, J., & McConnell, S. (1993). Comparison of family needs assessed by mothers, individual professionals, and interdisciplinary teams. *Journal of Early Intervention, 17,* 36–49.

Handel, R. D. (1999). The multiple meanings of family literacy. *Education & Urban Society, 32*(1), 127–144.

Harvard Education Letter. (2005). Playing with words. *Harvard Education Letter, 21*(6), 7.

Kaderavek, J. N., & Justice, L. M. (2005). The effect of book genre in repeated readings of mothers and their children with language impairment: A pilot investigation. *Child Language Teaching and Therapy, 21*(1), 75–92.

Klobukowski, P. (2000). Parents, buddy journals, and teacher response. In T. V. Rasinski, N. D. Padak, et al. (Eds.), *Mo-tivating recreational reading and promoting home-school connections* (pp. 74–78). Newark, DE: International Reading Association.

Lanteigne, B., & Schwarzer, D. (1997). The progress of Rafael in English and family reading: A case study. *Journal of Adolescent and Adult Literacy, 4*(1), 36–45.

McQuillan, J. (1998). *The literacy crisis: False claims, real solutions.* Portsmouth, NH: Heinemann Educational Books.

Miller, P. (1978). *Direct instruction in language and speaking: A study of mother-child discourse in a working class community.* Rockville, MD: National Institute of Mental Health. (ERIC Document Reproduction Service No. ED 178 203)

Miller-Rodriguez, K. (1992). Home writing activities: The writing briefcase and the traveling suitcase. *The Reading Teacher, 45,* 160–161.

Mooney, M. E. (1990). *Reading to, with, and by children.* Katonah, NY: Richard Owen.

Morgan, L., & Goldstein, H. (2004). Teaching mothers of low socioeconomic status to use decontextualized language during storybook reading. *Journal of Early Intervention, 26*(4), 235–252.

Murray, A. D. (1990). Fine-tuning of utterance length to preverbal infants: Effects on later language development. *Journal of Child Language, 17*(3), 511–525.

Owen, V., & Shanahan, T. (1993). *Validating success: A three-year evaluation of the children's literacy gains.* Paper presented at the annual conference of the American Educational Research Association, Atlanta, GA.

Paratore, J. R., & Jordan, G. (2007). Starting out together: A home–school partnership for preschool and beyond. *The Reading Teacher, 60*(7), 694–696.

Peterson, P., Carta, J, & Greenwood, C. (2005). Teaching milieu language skills to parents in multiple risk families. *Journal of Early Intervention, 27,* 94–109.

Rasinski, T., & Padak, N. (2009, April). Write soon! *The Reading Teacher, 62*(7), 618–620.

Remaly, B. K. (1990). *Strategies for increasing the expressive vocabulary of kindergarten children.* Fort Lauderdale, FL: Nova University. (ERIC Document Reproduction Service No. ED 332 234)

Reutzel, D. R., & Cooter, R. B. (2000). *Teaching children to read: Putting the pieces together.* Upper Saddle River, NJ: Merrill/Prentice Hall.

Reutzel, D. R., & Fawson, P. C. (1990). Traveling tales: Connecting parents and children in writing. *The Reading Teacher, 44,* 222–227.

Scott, L. L. (2000). Classbooks: Linking the classroom to the home. In T. V. Rasinski, N. D. Padak, et al. (Eds.), *Motivating recreational reading and promoting home-school* connections (pp. 93–94). Newark, DE: International Reading Association.

Shanahan, T., Mulhern, M., & Rodriguez-Brown, F. (1995). Project FLAME: Lessons learned from a family literacy program for linguistic minority families. *The Reading Teacher, 48*(7), 586–593.

Tamis-LeMonda, C. S., Shannon, J. D., Cabrera, N. J., & Lamb, M. E. (2004). Fathers and mothers at play with their 2 and 3 year olds: Contributions to language and cognitive development. *Child Development, 75,* 1806–1820.

U.S. Department of Education. (2001). *The longitudinal evaluation of school change and performance in Title I schools, volume 1: Executive summary.* Washington, DC: Author.

Vopat, J. (1994). *The parent project: A workshop approach to parent involvement.* York, ME: Stenhouse Publishers.

Wasik, B. (2004). *Handbook of family literacy.* Mahwah, NJ: Lawrence Erlbaum.

Will, G. (2002, January 6). Mom and dad mean more than Miss Wormwood. *Fort Worth Star-Telegram,* p. 4E.

Williams, S. G. (2001). *Participation of families in interventions.* Unpublished manuscript, George Peabody College of Vanderbilt University, Nashville, TN.

Willman, A. T. (2000). "Hello, Mrs. Willman, it's me!": Keep kids reading over the summer by using voice mail. In T. V. Rasinski, N. D. Padak, et al. (Eds.), *Motivating recreational reading and promoting home-school connections* (pp. 51–52). Newark, DE: International Reading Association.

Wong, H. K., & Wong, R. T. (1998). *The first days of school.* Mountain View, CA: Harry Wong.

Yarosz, D. J., & Barnett, W. S. (2001). Who reads to young children?: Identifying predictors of family reading activities. *Reading Psychology, 22*(1), 67–81.

**The Power of Classroom Practice**
www.myeducationlab.com

Now go to Topic 15: "Parents and Families" in the MyEducationLab (www.myeducationlab
.com) for your course, where you can:

- Find learning outcomes for "Parents and Families," along with the national standards that connect to these outcomes.
- Complete the tasks in the Assignments and Activities to help you more deeply understand the chapter content.
- Examine challenging situations and cases presented in the IRIS Center Resources.
- Access video clips of CCSSO National Teachers of the Year award winners responding to the question, "Why Do I Teach?" in the Teacher Talk section.
- Apply and practice your understanding of the core teaching skills identified in the chapter with the Building Teaching Skills and Dispositions learning units.